ECONOMICS OF HARVARD

iii

WORKS BY SEYMOUR E. HARRIS

Books

1. THE ASSIGNATS, 1930
2. MONETARY PROBLEMS OF THE BRITISH EMPIRE, 1931
3. TWENTY YEARS OF FEDERAL RESERVE POLICY (2 volumes), 1933
4. EXCHANGE DEPRECIATION, 1936
5. ECONOMICS OF SOCIAL SECURITY, 1941
6. THE ECONOMICS OF AMERICAN DEFENSE, 1941
7. THE ECONOMICS OF AMERICA AT WAR, 1942
8. OPA MANUAL ON PRICE CONTROL, 1943 **
9. POSTWAR ECONOMIC PROBLEMS, 1943 **
10. ECONOMICS OF LATIN AMERICA, 1944 **
11. ECONOMICS OF RECONSTRUCTION, 1945 **
12. PRICE AND RELATED CONTROLS IN THE UNITED STATES, 1945
13. INFLATION AND AMERICAN ECONOMY, 1945
14. THE NEW ECONOMICS, 1947 **
15. NATIONAL DEBT AND THE NEW ECONOMICS, 1947
16. ECONOMICS IN GENERAL EDUCATION, 1947 (Z)
17. SAVING AMERICAN CAPITALISM, 1948 **
18. HOW SHALL WE PAY FOR EDUCATION? 1948
19. THE EUROPEAN RECOVERY PROGRAM, 1948
20. FOREIGN ECONOMIC POLICY FOR THE UNITED STATES, 1949 **
21. THE MARKET FOR COLLEGE GRADUATES, 1949
22. ECONOMIC PLANNING, 1949
23. THE ECONOMICS OF MOBILIZATION, 1951
24. SCHUMPETER, SOCIAL SCIENTIST, 1951
25. ECONOMICS OF NEW ENGLAND, 1952
26. TEXTILES AND THE NEW ENGLAND ECONOMY (for New England Governors), 1953
27. JOHN MAYNARD KEYNES: ECONOMIST AND POLICY MAKER, 1955
28. THE AMERICAN BUSINESS CREED, 1956 (Z)
29. INTERNATIONAL AND INTERREGIONAL ECONOMICS, 1957
30. STEVENSON'S NEW AMERICA, 1957 (Y)
31. INVESTIGATION OF THE FINANCIAL CONDITION OF THE UNITED STATES, REPORT FOR MEMBERS OF SENATE FINANCE COMMITTEE, 1959
32. THE INCIDENCE OF INFLATION, STUDY PAPER NO. 6 FOR THE JOINT CONGRESSIONAL ECONOMIC COMMITTEE, 1959
33. HIGHER EDUCATION IN THE UNITED STATES, THE ECONOMIC PROBLEMS 1960**
34. MORE RESOURCES FOR EDUCATION, 1960
35. AMERICAN ECONOMIC HISTORY, 1960 **
36. THE DOLLAR IN CRISIS, 1961 **
37. THE ECONOMICS OF THE POLITICAL PARTIES, 1962
38. PUBLIC POLICY: INTERNATIONAL ECONOMIC PROBLEMS, 1961 **

WORKS BY SEYMOUR E. HARRIS (Continued)

Books

39.   HIGHER EDUCATION: RESOURCES AND FINANCE, 1962
40.   OECD: ECONOMIC ASPECTS OF HIGHER EDUCATION, 1964 **
41.   THE ECONOMICS OF AMERICAN MEDICINE, 1964
42.   ECONOMICS OF THE KENNEDY YEARS, 1964
43.   EDUCATION AND PUBLIC POLICY, 1965 (Y)
44.   CHALLENGE AND CHANGE IN AMERICAN EDUCATION, 1965 (Y)
45.   OECD: EDUCATION AND ECONOMIC GROWTH, 1966 (Z)
46.   THE ECONOMICS OF HARVARD
47.   MY WIFE RUTH

**   Edited with an Introduction
(Y)   Edited with others
(Z)   With others

ECONOMICS OF HARVARD

SEYMOUR E. HARRIS

McGraw-Hill Book Company

New York
St. Louis
San Francisco
Düsseldorf
London
Mexico
Panama
Sydney
Toronto

This book was set in Press Roman by Goodway, Inc., and printed on permanent paper
and bound by Von Hoffmann Press, Inc. Sally Ellyson supervised the production.

ECONOMICS OF HARVARD
SEYMOUR E. HARRIS

Library of Congress Catalog Card Number 72-105422

26832

1234567890 VAVH 79876543210

DEDICATION

To Ruth Harris, my wife, 1923-1965. In these
years, despite serious illnesses, she gave much to this
book and to all my work.

CONTENTS

PREFATORY NOTE: THE WRITING OF THE BOOK

Harvard is the oldest college in the United States, and also the oldest corporation. It has taken about 330 years for Harvard to accumulate its first *billion* dollars. But it required a little more than two centuries to acquire its first *million* dollars. The major growth of endowment as well as enrollment occurred in the twentieth century. But the first large advance occurred under that phenomenal president, Charles Eliot, who over a period of forty years ending in 1909, ruled Harvard in an autocratic but highly productive manner. Eliot was unique.

For many years I have been interested in the economic problems of education. I have published ten volumes on educational problems. I have also been interested in Harvard. The college's generosity made possible a Harvard degree. After receiving my A.B. in 1920, I spent the next forty-four years at Harvard, except for two years at Princeton and a short period in Washington during the war. At Harvard I served on a number of committees that dealt with economic issues and, in the last fifteen years, I have spent much time studying the economics of Harvard.

This has been a difficult and exhausting operation. The material is as fascinating as any; and as voluminous also. In going over the Eliot papers alone, I felt as though I had to cover a physical area equal to the Harvard Stadium. Fortunately, I have had the help of a brilliant and numerous group of Harvard seniors and law school students. Each summer over many years with the indispensable aid of Mrs. Bernice Shoul, we mobilized a dozen or so of these able Harvard and Radcliffe students who sifted tons of documents, reports, letters, accounts and left me with the indispensable residue.

My task was made easier because Professor Samuel Eliot Morison, the brilliant historian of Harvard, through his numerous volumes, dealt definitively with her overall history. The only gap was in the economic area. Perhaps even this is too extreme a statement, for I learned much about economic issues from Morison's five volumes.

In many respects this has been the most difficult of all my books. The vastness of the material; the dependence on script, often difficult to read; and, in the last few years, my residence in California all contributed to my difficulties. President Kirkland (1810-1829), for example, was a great president but a most annoying one to the person who had to read his script. Eliot's letters and memos, fortunately, were legible; and by the middle of his administration he acquired first a secretary and typewriter and then some assistants. I appreciate the typewriter's contribution to civilization as I never had before. In his first twenty years, he meticulously wrote with pen and ink and frequently, a dozen or more letters and/or documents every day. His interest in the university knew no restrictions.

I owe a great deal to Xerox. In the last few years, by Xeroxing tens of thousands of sheets each summer in Cambridge and then reading them at my leisure in California, I could easily cover fifty thousand sheets in a year. My decision had to be, to Xerox or not to

Xerox. In this manner, we achieved a high productivity for the summer's work. But Xeroxing raised problems. First, because the Xeroxed material was difficult to handle; and second, because the Xeroxers often failed to follow instructions and denied the writer an indication of the source of many of these sheets. There is still some material included in this book for which references are not given. It just has been impossible to wade through vast amounts of material again to rediscover *all* these omitted sources. We have sources for the vast majority of items. Yet overall, without Xerox this book could not have been written.

Contents

This book consists of sixty-three chapters divided into ten parts and a brief concluding comment. The kinds of problems I have treated are the resources available to Harvard, the manner in which they were received, the use to which they have been put, the costs to the students and the manner in which these costs were covered, the techniques for choosing the faculty, its size, its pay, both salary and fringe, its work loads, its structure, its history, and the disagreements between faculty and administration on pay and work load.

One whole part is devoted to expenditures and finance. In this part we deal, for example, with a comparison of cost structure in the seventeenth century and 1964; the principle of every tub on its own bottom; the recourse to, and support of, the theory of deficit finance.

Relations with government is the subject matter of Part IV. It was the government that gave birth to Harvard, and the government which contributed greatly to keeping it alive during Harvard's first 150 years. Recent commentators on the relation of Harvard and government, and even Eliot, often have forgotten government's provision of physical plant, the revenue from the ferry and barges assigned to Harvard; support of the president's salary, the bank tax in the early nineteenth century and other largesses by the government.

It is an interesting point that from the early nineteenth century to recent years the tendency has been to belittle the government's contribution. But in 1968, once more the crucial need of government is acknowledged. The prestigious Association of American Universities, with Professor Pusey as a member of the committee, impressed by the recent rising cost of higher education—at least 10 percent a year—and the drying up of sources that might yield additional income, now demands of the Federal government, as the source of most productive funds, substantial aid.[1] The case is especially strong because costs are rising so rapidly, and many of the benefits of higher education accrue to society.

In a special report on Harvard's resources issued by President Pusey in 1968, the case for federal aid could easily be implied. Expenses from 1947 to 1967 increased from $25 to $150 million or a five-fold increase, with the average rate of increase per year put at 11.6 percent in the years 1957 to 1967. In those ten years, the university added a hundred professorships (a rise of 75 percent) and fifty buildings.[2]

The government's help was not limited to grants of money and construction of plant. The college also received large tax privileges.

The subject matter of Part V is gifts. Gifts provide endowment, but also important are buildings and land, and also gifts for current use. Harvard's buildings and land may well be valued at $300 million. Current endowment of $1 billion comes in large part from gifts; but also relevant is the rise of value of equities.

As early as 1643, Harvard under Henry Dunster produced a twenty-six page tract, *New England's First Fruits*, to be used to seek funds abroad. This was, as Professor Morison notes, a promotion pamphlet.

After God had carried us safe to New England, *and wee had builded our houses, provided necessaries for our liveli-hood, reared convenient places for God's*

---

1. The Association of American Universities, *The Federal Financing of Higher Education*, April, 1968.
2. *The University and Its Resources*, 1968.

worship, and fetled the civil government One of the next things we longed for and looked after was to advance Learning *and perpetuate it to Prosperity; dreading to leave an illiterate ministry to the Churches, when our present ministers shall lie in the Dust.*

. . . it pleased God to stir up the heart of one Mr. Harvard (a godly gentleman, and a lover of learning, then living amongst us) to give the one-half of his estate (it being in all about 1700£) towards the erecting of a Colledge; and all his Library; after him another gave 300£. Others after him cast in more, and the publique hand of the State added the rest. The Colledge was, by common consent appointed to be at Cambridge (a place very pleasant and accomodate) and is called (according to the name of the first founder) Harvard Colledge.

Descriptions of the admission requirements, the curriculum, and rules for students and their achievements follow.

With students unable to cover costs with tuition, Harvard from the very beginning had to depend heavily on gifts. Even as late as the nineteenth century endowment income on the average provided half of Harvard's income. Under pressure, Harvard ushered in the modern trend toward begging for college funds. Harvard was fortunate in the loyalty of its alumni, who contributed so much of the gift money. Harvard's gift policies are also deserving of attention because of their innovative aspects. The 1919 drive, for $15 million, for example, was the first of its kind; and the $82,500,000 drive of the late 1950s was not only unique but became a model for other great drives. By the second quarter of the nineteenth century Harvard had introduced the subscription drives—for supporting the observatory, for student aid, etc. But she lagged in introducing annual giving.

Endowments (Part VI) deserve considerable space, if for no other reason, because of their large yield. Their long-term relative decline is discussed fully. There are other important issues. Should income be allocated on the basis of book or market value to the various funds with a stake in endowment? How does a university spend its money when, with the passage of time, it becomes increasingly difficult to abide by the instructions of the donors? To what extent is endowment eroded or cumulated? Is restricted endowment as unproductive for institutes of higher learning as is generally argued?

Harvard, on the whole, has had a favorable investment history (Part VII). The large investments in equities in the last forty years have paid off. But there have been mistakes. Movements into equities might have been more pronounced. Disposition of real estate after the 1929 crash was precipitate and involved costly retrievals later. In the eighteenth century, the college showed much more wisdom in tying investments to a depreciating currency than she has revealed since. The steady and costly decline of the rate of interest in the last decades of the nineteenth century were allowed to erode income without adequate reactions by Harvard's investment managers. Shifts to other investments, e.g. equities and even to real estate, might have helped. Few of the investment managers before the 1930s saw as clearly as Mr. Amos A. Laurence (1857-1862) that with inflation the policy should be a shift away from assets yielding fixed returns.

Part VIII covers numerous subjects. One issue is the productivity of the Harvard operation, thus comparing input and output. Harvard's students turn out very well—an index of high productivity. But also relevant is the high quality of its input.

A special chapter devoted to growth is helpful. We suggest measures of growth, and its extent over long periods of Harvard's history. The great periods of growth are of course the hundred years beginning with Eliot's appointment. It is especially in inflationary periods that Harvard's growth has been stunted.

Our justification for studying briefly Harvard's governing boards and curriculum is that they seriously affect the university's economic strength. The concentration of power and authority on the corporation, with the overseers as watch dogs, has greatly contributed to Harvard's growth. Harvard's economic position is related to the curriculum. Eliot's elective system, for example, was most costly in resources, as is the general proliferation of courses that greatly drains university funds.

The library is a high-cost operation. Harvard has the greatest university library in the world and one of the best libraries of any kind. The library is a national institution; and there is a case for more federal subsidies. The library budget of about 4 percent of the university's does not seem excessive, when one considers what the library means to a great university. Above all, librarians are increasingly aware that their task is not merely acquisition. They have to acquire with consideration of the costs of putting the book on the shelf and in the catalogue, and those of distributing it.

Harvard's accounting procedures have greatly changed since 1636. I believe Harvard accounting could be more helpful. Why not provide estimates of the cost of instruction, of research, of public services (e.g. use of libraries), as well as the less significant variables, e.g. salaries, wages and equipment and supplies? More attention should be given to such problems as the least expensive approach to achieving given objectives—e.g. choose among more professors, more outlays on the library, more teaching fellows, improved living conditions, etc. etc.

In Part IX, I deal with Radcliffe and the professional schools. Actually throughout the book, when relevant, we have discussed the professional schools. But it is well to remember that Harvard was almost 150 years old before the first professional school was opened; and the largest development of professional schools has occurred in the twentieth century. But despite the frequent reference to the professional schools in the years 1783 to 1900, some special treatment of these schools and Radcliffe, which is now virtually a Harvard institution, is required. I pay special attention to growth, comparison of methods of raising money and allocating resources, charges to students as well as help given them, relations with the faculty and the tie-in of the professional schools with the college.

This is a long book. For that reason, I have offered a short version of the book which is essentially a summary, in which I generally do not include references, for they are given in the body of the book.

Obligations

My greatest debt is to my wife, Ruth (now deceased), who urged me to write this book and stiffened my resistance when I was tempted to divert my energies to less costly, easier, and more pleasant work. Her interest in this book could be matched only by her enthusiasm over forty-three years of married life for all my works. Despite a lifelong illness, she not only produced enthusiasm; she also worried over and read manuscripts, galleys, and page proofs. She was a superb editor and proofreader. The fact that she is not around to welcome this book detracts greatly from the pleasure at its birth.

I owe a special thanks to Bernice Shoul who helped greatly in the assembling of material. She allocated responsibilities among twenty-four students at Harvard College and the Harvard Law School over many summers. She chose with mature judgement, an achievement suggested by the fact that many of these research assistants of the 1950s and early 1960s have already become distinguished social scientists. I list these assistants. (I have indicated with an asterisk those who made a special contribution to this book. This in no sense reflects on the value given by the others).

Harvey Belitsky	David Robison
Berdelle Campbell	Gunther Rulier
Paula Cohen	Ann Sheehan
Mona Harrington*	Bernt Steigum
Robert Hendrickson	Zbynek Vancura
Saul Hymans*	Steven Weiss*
Gabriel Kolko*	Edward Charles Witke*
David Laschky	Franklin Fisher
Mary Lefkowitz	Father John Hirschmeier
John Peck	Herbert Levine
Walter Plotz	Egon Neuberger
Daniel Roberts	Roger W. Smith*

I am indebted to many officials of Harvard: President Nathan Pusey; Dean of the Faculty Franklin Ford; William Bentinck-Smith, Assistant to President Pusey; Charles P. Whitlock, Assistant to the President for Civil and Governmental Relations; Eugene

Kraetzer, Assistant Secretary of the Corporation; Carl Janke, Comptroller of the University; Ex-Dean Erwin Griswold of the Harvard Law School; Ex-Dean George Berry of the Medical School; my former student, George F. F. Lombard, now Senior Associate Dean for Educational Affairs of the Business School; Dean Robert H. Ebert of the Medical School; Don Price, Dean of the John Fitzgerald Kennedy School of Government; Dean Peter Elder of the Graduate School of Arts and Science; Douglas Bryant, the University Librarian; and Bayley F. Mason, Assistant Dean of the Medical School.

I have had much indispensable help from that unique enterprise, the Harvard University Archives. Dr. C. K. Shipton, custodian of the university archives, was most co-operative. I dealt especially with Mr. Kimball C. Elkins, senior assistant in the archives. It would be difficult to find a more conscientious, able, and helpful servant of the university.

I should mention especially McGeorge Bundy, the distinguished dean of the Harvard faculty, from whom I learned much over the years; Miss Vern Johnson, the remarkably able assistant to the dean; and Dr. Humphrey Doermann, assistant of the dean of the faculty of arts and science, who generously shared with me many of his findings, and Mrs. Edward Mason, who criticized the chapter on land.

Mrs. John Williams assumed a special protective function for this book. She persevered when losses were immenent; she typed and organized materials with unbelievable loyalty. Without her co-operation, the book would have suffered greatly. Mrs. Hugh Shaw was my first secretary at University of California at San Diego. By assuming all kinds of responsibilities, she saved me much energy for this book. Mrs. Cleo Hoggan helped with the typing along with Mrs. Alita Linsay. My last secretary at Harvard, Miss Mary Watson, helped in many ways, as did the late Mrs. Priscilla White.

In the last year or two Dorothy Harris has helped greatly. She served as a guinea pig for many parts of this book and aided in many other ways. In every possible manner, she relieved me of burdens so that I could concentrate on this study.

I received financial help from Harvard and from the Ford Foundation, and a special grant from the Carnegie Foundation.

Seymour E. Harris
Professor of Economics,
   University of California, San Diego
Professor of Medical Economics,
   University of California, San Diego
   Medical School
Littauer Professor, Political Economy,
   Emeritus, Harvard University

Tables Deposited in the Harvard Archives

Long books are expensive to publish and therefore have to be priced accordingly. I have tried to keep the size of this book down as much as possible. In two final readings, after several earlier attempts at cutting, I experienced the painful process of cutting out about one-third more of my manuscript. In order to save costs further I have deposited in the Harvard University Archives numerous tables which are discussed in the text. These will be bound. (The most important tables are retained in the published book). To anyone who wants one or a few tables that are not reproduced in the book. I shall try to provide them.

A Book Within A Book

Since this is a long book and since I have not generally summarized the contents of each chapter, I have written an overall summary, which follows, with brief conclusions or summaries available for each chapter. This is by no means a substitute for reading the book; but it may be useful to those who can afford but a few hours for this volume and also to all readers who want a quick digest of any particular chapter or part.

Summary

The Major Issues

PART

1
STUDENTS

1. Geographical Representation of Students

Over much of Harvard's history, the college was primarily a Massachusetts or a New England institution. Nevertheless, President Dunster in 1653, seventeen years after Harvard's founding, referred to his students as pupils "coming out of other colonies, lands, and countries, whether England itself or others."

That there was no *national* base in the first 150 years is suggested by the fact that Harvard had not a single New Yorker enrolled from 1737 to 1790. In the years 1735, 1777, 1781, and 1793, a total of 162 students entered Harvard; not one was from outside of Massachusetts. Even as late as 1850, 87 percent of Harvard's college students came from New England and 75 percent from Massachusetts; but the law school, with its great reputation, enrolled only 56 and 39 percent respectively from New England and Massachusetts. Undoubtedly the association of Harvard with Unitarianism in the first half of the nineteenth century cut down the importation of students from outside of New England. Congregational Yale attracted many more students from the Middle Atlantic states and the West than Harvard. Even in the late nineteenth century the Unitarian label seemed to hurt Harvard's position as a national university. In one year in the late 1860s Harvard had two students from Connecticut; but Yale had forty-two students from Massachusetts.

By the 1880s, Harvard began to attract increasing numbers from outside New England. Improved transportation, increased availability of admission examinations in urban communities, and numerous other measures by President Eliot attracted students from outside New England to Harvard. In the years 1900-1940, the gain of these "outsiders" was about 1/3 of 1 percent a year; in the 1940s and 1950s, almost 1 percent a year. By 1964, the percentage of students from New England had dropped by one-half from that for the early twentieth century. Conant's national scholarships contributed to these gains as did improved transportation and Harvard's rising prestige. Closer bonds with Radcliffe also helped. Harvard would have attracted even more from other regions if it did not have to contend with opposition to free movement from the West and South, alerted to the loss of their talented youth to the affluent Northeast.

2. Students' Socio-Economic Background

On the whole Harvard students have come from the upper classes over most of its history, a generalization that holds much more for the first hundred years than for the last hundred years. Thus in the years 1673-1703, ministers and magistrates fathered 123 of the first 300 students. In these years, 27 percent of the students had fathers who were Harvard alumni. In contrast, only 10 to 15 percent had Harvard fathers in the Eliot period.

Predominance of clergy among Harvard alumni gradually dropped after the early years — e.g., 50 percent in 1642-1658 and 40 percent in 1721-1730. By 1950, large shifts in the structure of occupation of Harvard alumni had occurred. The percentage in the professions did not change greatly, for about two-thirds were in the professions in 1642-1658, 1721-1730, and 2949-1950. But medicine, law, and education gained substantially, and mainly at the expense of the church. The contribution of business steadily rose also: 2, 14, and 23 percent in 1642-1658, 1721-1730 and 1949-1950 respectively.

In general, Harvard has been and still is a college for the children of business and professional families, and in recent times with average incomes of more than twice the national average. The Harvard student structure is different than that for the country. Recently, at a time when professional and managerial parents accounted for 81 percent of Harvard students, families with these backgrounds provided but 26 percent of the male students at the University of Indiana.

Professional and managerial groups send a much larger percentage to college than might be suggested from their share of the numbers on the labor market. But Harvard shows a greater concentration on this score than the national sample — e.g.

Sons of Professional and Semi-Professional Parents, Early 1950s

% total labor force	8
% in college	13
% entering Harvard	39

In the classes of 2870-1875, 1903-1904, 1951, and 1958, Harvard consistently showed a representation in the high employments of parents far above what might be expected. With equal representation, the index would show a hundred. In the professions, the Harvard index varies from 466 to 741 in these years.

Incomes of Harvard graduates also indicate the high economic status of Harvard graduates. For example, in 1947 graduates of Harvard, Yale, and Princeton had annual incomes 20 percent in excess of graduates of the other ivy-league colleges and 56 percent in excess of the median income of all college graduates.

Harvard has suffered from its reputation as a rich man's college, and also as an institution that caters to snobbish appeals. There are many reasons for this. Thus, in the years before the Revolution, Harvard classified its students to some extent at least on the basis of social standing. Secondly, Harvard, in the first half of the nineteenth century, tended to become the most expensive college in the country. In the great crisis of the 1820s, and also in the middle of the nineteenth century, the high cost of a Harvard education became a big issue of college administration. At midcentury the complaint of high costs was combined with the charge that nothing of material value was taught. The attacks on Harvard's extravagances continued into the second half of the nineteenth century.

Beginning with the Eliot period, Harvard began to change its image as the home of the rich and pampered. One important contribution came from the rising percentage of students from the public schools, for which Eliot himself was largely responsible. In his inaugural address in 1869, Eliot stressed the point that the poor student with quality will get through. Eliot also insisted that most of the students were neither poor nor rich.

Eliot debated with such snobs as Charles F. Adams and Barrett Wendell: Adams would accept boys of wealth or merit; Eliot insisted on high ability and motivation for incoming students.

A few special episodes deserve comment here. The first is the expulsion for riotous behavior of the son of J. Q. Adams, the former President of the United States. Despite great pressures, President Kirkland refused to budge.

In 1848, Harvard considered the admission of a Negro. Harvard students protested. President Everett declared: "If this boy passes the examination, he will be admitted; and if the white students choose to withdraw, all the income of the college will be devoted to his education."

During most of Harvard's history students and faculty came from its dominant religion. Even as late as 1870, there were but 7 Roman Catholics and 3 Jews out of 563 students. Eliot was outspoken in his demand that Harvard be open to all sects.

In recent years, the opening of the Gold Coast dormitories contributed another undemocratic feature to Harvard's image. The rich, now able to determine their dormitory companions, flocked to Randolph, Westmorely, and other Gold Coast buildings.

3. Student Behavior

A reader may wonder why a long chapter on student behavior is found in a book on economic issues. The point is that student behavior involves the college in substantial costs and also revenues.

Until relatively recent times the faculty, inclusive of the president, devoted a large part of their time to disciplinary problems. The costs of education were greatly increased because students misbehaved.

What student behavior meant to Pres. Edward Everett is revealed in his first report (1846), in which he commented on the numerous severe punishments.

As an example of excessive efforts devoted to disciplinary problems; in the midst of the Civil War, President Hill wrote to President Lincoln to give him the momentous news that "the Faculty last evening voted that Lincoln, Junior be publicly admonished for smoking in Harvard College, after being privately admonished for the same offense. . .I trust, Sir, you will impress upon him the necessity. . .of attention to decorum. . . ."

The college had to provide man power to prevent disorders. Thus in 1733, the college hired seven men to walk and watch at commencement to avoid the commencement disorders. In 1805, the college introduced the proctor system, a costly service to the university ever since. Student disturbances often originated in dissatisfaction with the commons. Property destruction would follow as well as improved food and service. In 1766, a great rebellion followed a protest over rancid butter. A committee of the faculty sampled the butter: of eleven samples, they condemned seven absolutely, and four to be used for sauce only. The college authorities generally tried to maintain decent standards in the commons. Student reactions helped improve standards. The college sought low charges both because of the impact on the price of private commons and also to keep the cost of a Harvard education down. An interesting comment in the middle of the eighteenth century: "that simplicity which makes the fare cheap, wholesome and philosophical, renders it also unsatisfactory to dainty palates."

Destruction of property by students was also costly. On numerous occasions the students wantonly destroyed property. Thus in 1842, the year of the gunpowder plot, a student was dismissed because he was held responsible for some of the damage done. He had purchased 2 1/2 pounds of gunpowder. Within a period of a week, the students had blown up a recitation room, a college dormitory and damaged University Hall with a bombshell which exploded. On another occasion a student throwing bread blinded an eye of one of Harvard's great historians.

Professor Pearson kept a journal of disorders for 1788. He noted intoxication; teacups, and a knife thrown at tutors; stones thrown at Professor Wigglesworth in midst of lectures; pistols fired; excess drink.

On the few occasions when the college called in the police, the damage was multiplied. In 1834, Quincy, disturbed by $300 of damage, a large sum at that time, called in the police. The students reacted by destroying furniture and caused a terrific explosion in the chapel.

As early in 1659, the corporation assessed the contribution that the police might make and the extent to which they might interfere.

Students, misbehavior was costly to Harvard. But they also provided revenue, and especially in the first 160 years, through fines imposed for violation of college rules. A table of student fines in the year 1751 included fifty-three infractions, with the fines running from 1d for tardiness at prayer to 3s for making tumultous noises.

In 1732, the college noted "there has of late been a considerable quantity of lead cut off from he top of ye old college. . .and yt if any scholar be found on ye top of ye said college without leave from ye President or Tutors, he shall be liable to ye penalty of five shillings, and satisfy for all damages. . . ."

In some respects the troublesome problems of to-day seemed to escape Harvard administrators in the first two hundred years. Very little is found in the archives on "relations with dissolute women" though an occasional hint is found. An unusual discovery was the case of a girl who had been impregnated by a Harvard student in 1862. The president commented: ". . .I wrote to his father, urging upon him the importance of furnishing me with the means of settling the unhappy business. . . ."

An early Harvard president was forced to resign, it was learned much later, because he had impregnated a servant.

Harvard students in the past, unlike the current college students, showed little interest in sharing the government of the college. In the midst of President Eliot's administration, the students were asked to participate in some aspects of the government of Harvard. They refused, insisting that running the university was not their business.

In the last hundred years, student behavior at Harvard has greatly improved. Perhaps a few episodes in the 1960s are the exception. More than anything the raising of age of entry at Harvard and the freedom given by the elective system help explain the gains of the last hundred years. Once students could select curriculum on the basis of interests, their behavior greatly improved.

4. The Harvard Product

Over most of Harvard's history, the college was interested not merely in the narrow curriculum but also in the whole man. This broad interest was costly in dollars and in the responsibilities assumed. But the concern over the student's room and board, his spiritual life, his athletics and health, his relations with women, and other aspects of his life were costly in dollars and resulted in much larger budgets than would otherwise have prevailed. To some extent the resources that went into these activities were at the expense of the faculty and the instructional budget. But they were additional as well as alternative outlays. The $40 million or thereabout put into the House Plan would not have been available for more narrow educational objectives. Moreover, these outlays tended to raise the cost of education for the student.

The degree of emphasis on the whole man fluctuated. In the early years the college assumed virtually full responsibilities for the life of the student. In the last hundred years Eliot and Conant stressed more the instructional aspects of education and Lowell and Pusey reverted more to the original concept of Harvard College. Undoubtedly the influence of Lowell and Pusey resulted in larger outlays for buildings and noneducational services, with some relative reduction of expenditures for instruction. But we should emphasize the point that the provisions for living and dining together brought closer relations of students and faculty, with corresponding gains in the educational product. An Oxford don once said that half the education comes from formal instruction and the other half from exchanges among students and students with faculty.

Harvard was not always able to control the lives of its students. Improved transportation loosened the bonds. Even before the horse-drawn cars of the mid-nineteenth century, the students in large numbers walked to town over the West Boston bridge.

What kind of product has Harvard turned out? Much depends on the quality of the input, which on the whole has been very good.

But all were not satisfied with the Harvard student. In the 1860s President Hill complained that the talent produced by this country never attained any high level of culture "without being transplanted to Europe for a few years. . . ."

Harvard's contribution was modest until the Eliot days, in part because the methods of teaching were sterile. What was required of the students was memorizing and recitation, not the capacity to think and use one's imagination. Over many years until the middle of the nineteenth century, examinations were a farce, for the examiners were overseers or their representatives who were generally ignorant of the subjects on which they examined. A few mathematics tutors in midnineteenth century first introduced the written examination.

Although the college began to broaden the curriculum in the 1820s, it was not until Eliot's period that a rich curriculum became available.

5. Costs to Students

A comparison of the structure of costs to students during early Harvard history and currently reveals large changes. In particular, tuition, first, and rents, second, absorb much larger shares of costs today than three hundred years ago. The relative cost of food has greatly declined, a trend prevailing in the economy generally. Charges for instruction accounted for 12 percent of costs in the middle of the seventeenth century and 64 percent in 1966-1967. Whereas commons accounted for about two-thirds of costs in the first seventy-five years of Harvard history, it declined to about 50 percent in 1860, and to 20 percent in 1967. Rents also experienced large relative rises. In part, the explanation of the rising burden of rents is the improved product.

The problem of costs and extravagances troubled the authorities especially in the nineteenth century. In 1823, for example, a standing committee of the faculty intervened. Parents were informed:

. . . one of the greatest evils, to which it [the college] *is exposed is the excessive indulgence of students in the articles of clothing and pocket expenses. Such indulgence is productive among them of a perverted emulation, at once frivolous and pernicious; is a principle source of depraved morals, and is extremely injurious to the wholesome discipline of the University. . .The effect. . .is to deter the less opulent classes in the community from sending their children to our University. . . .*
. . . no student should be permitted to expend on clothing, a greater amount than from $100 to $150 a year. . . .
. . . one dollar a week is the highest amount that should in any instance be allowed [for pocket money] *. . . .*

In 1871-1872 a committee of the overseers noted that some parents allowed students $200 per year and others, $2,000. But the university could take no responsibility for these extravagances. Cambridge was a large city with many temptations.

George Palmer, the famous philosopher, in 1887 observed: ". . . let us not, therefore, shrink from acknowledging the ugly fact; extravagance is here — shameless, coarse extravagance. . . ."

Early in the twentieth century, Eliot observed: "the rise in the scale of living among members of the University continue to excite some apprehension in the minds of friends of higher education. . . ." Eliot added that the dormitory standards of the poorest students exceeded those of the richest fifty years ago. Occasionally a smart commentator tied the rising costs to students to the fact "that the ordinary family of the Community is spending several times as much money as the ordinary family of the Community of two generations ago. . . ."

Concern over costs brought remedial measures. Thus Eliot helped establish co-operatives to assure the availability of books, stationery, clothing, and furniture to students at reasonable prices.

In the eighteenth century, costs were relatively low. But despite this fact and despite the rising population, the increase of enrollment was modest until 1820-1860, when enrollment began to soar. Under Eliot the rise was especially large and, in part, no doubt, because of the rising prestige of Harvard, but also because of the low costs to students. Whereas under Eliot and Conant, costs tended to be relatively low, under Lowell and Pusey they rose more than per capita income. But Harvard's enrollment continued to rise greatly under Lowell. Under Pusey, strong attempts were made to contain the rise of enrollment.

A legislative committee in 1851 accounted for the high cost "by the greater fullness of that education or to the locality of Cambridge, or to the increased luxuriousness of general expenditures and other social habits. . . ."

A committee of overseers in 1845 wanted to know why 394 students at Yale cost $15,201, and the same service for 254 students cost in Cambridge more than $26,500 – ($38 at Yale per student and $104 at Harvard).

Professor Ticknor earlier had dwelt on the same problem. Finding total costs at $300 per student, he suggested "a much greater result should be obtained then sending out into society fifty or sixty young men as imperfectly educated as the graduate from Cambridge certainly is now."

As noted elsewhere, responses of tuition to prices and to changes in per capita income varied under different administrators. From 1900 to 1963, for example, tuition rose about as much as capacity to pay (per capita income); but total expenses rose only half as much. Hence, a Harvard education had become a bargain. But with the college enrollment rising five to six times as much as population, the burden of higher education clearly must have increased beyond what is suggested by a comparison of costs and per capita income. The number of students per family, of course, did not increase five to six times, but there was some increase.

At first Harvard had no competition. But competition increased with time. Over most of the eighteenth and nineteenth centuries, costs at Harvard's competitiors were less than at Harvard. In the years of inflation of the twentieth century, when the tuition especially lagged, Harvard tended to adjust its prices much more tardily than her major competitors.

Costs of £10 to £15 in Harvard's early history seemed to be much more of a burden than $3,500 in the 1960s, a fact supported by the small enrollment in the seventeenth century in relation to population as compared to the 1960s. Harvard's enrollment in relation to the population of Massachusetts, from which virtually all its students came in the first half of its history, declined from 1650 to 1710-1720. Lack of sustained interest in higher education and economic stagnation were relevant. Even in 1870 Harvard's enrollment vis-à-vis Massachusetts' population had fallen greatly as compared with the Puritan period. Harvard's share of the higher education population dropped from 100 percent in 1636 to $\frac{1}{3}$ of 1 percent in 1960.

With rising costs and increased competition, the pressure to reduce tuition increased. In a famous debate with Justice Story in 1834, John Quincy Adams considered a reduction of tuition as "a mere bonus to the merchants of Boston and to a few clergymen throughout the state to send their sons to Cambridge rather than to Amherst or Williamstown." President Quincy supported high tuition on the grounds that the quality of the product was first class; the children of the rich could afford to pay; and others could borrow the excess of Harvard's costs, with no charge of interest.

A visiting committee of the overseers in 1849 pointed to the "extent, the variety, and the completeness of the means of instruction" as justifying Harvard's differential costs. Besides, tuition was low, especially in the face of the fact that "daily expenses of life have increased and continue to increase. . . ."

Costs to students without relation to quality are not very significant. In 150 years costs may have risen 20 times. But these costs should be put against the rise of income to finance them, and the improved quality of the product. We cannot, however, measure the rise of quality which surely has been great.

6. Tuition

A depressant in Harvard's early years was the shortage of money in the colonies. Students paid their tuition only partly in silver. Wheat and malt were acceptable because they were the raw materials out of which the college baked bread and produced beer. Cattle on the hoof and chickens were also acceptable. A bushel and a half of wheat covered tuition for a quarter. In the late 1960s, in contrast, a quarter's tuition would require about 250 bushels of wheat.

As prices of necessaries rose, the college in the first half of the eighteenth century had to raise salaries, and with limited endowment, the increase in salaries had to be financed through rises in tuition.

Tuition charges gradually rose over Harvard's 330 years, and especially in recent years.

Attitudes towards the tuition policy changed from administration to administration. In the seventeenth and eighteenth centuries opposition to rising tuition was vocal. With low incomes of Harvard families and the small endowments and gifts, the proponents of higher tuition often had to yield. Nevertheless, in the first half of the eighteenth century rising prices, and hence pressure for increased faculty salaries, brought increases in tuition as the only way out other than help from government.

In the first quarter of the nineteenth century, the college raised some objections to low tuition. At this early time the college urged repayment of college subsidies — costs in excess of tuition, and suggested "the students may be justly charged for all the expenses of their own education; but whilst many of them find it difficult to maintain themselves, they should not be required to contribute indirectly for the relief of others."

In more recent times, Eliot and Conant tended to support the low-tuition policy while Lowell and Pusey more properly should be classified as belonging to the high-tuition school. From 1870 to 1915, tuition was remarkably stable and here the influence of Eliot was decisive. Once inflation began to advance at a galloping rate, the stability of tuition was jeopardized. Early in the twentieth century a bitter debate on the tuition policy emerged. A select committee of the overseers wanted to raise tuition from $150 to $225, claiming that $225 was equal to $150 in 1869 dollars. Charles F. Adams, pointing to the low salaries, the high costs generally, the capacity of students to pay more, and the deficiency of equipment, suggested raising tuition by 50 percent. In reply to Adams, Eliot in 1904 wrote: "I care for the young men whose families have to little money that it would make a real difference to them whether the Harvard tuition fee were $150 or $225."

Tuition was in many ways tied to salaries. I have constructed a table which gives the relation of a professor's salary to the tuition. In 1712-1713, a professor's salary was equal to 32 times tuition. By 1900, 28 times; 1920, $38\frac{1}{2}$ times; but 1964-1965, 12 times. In general, this table shows that professors suffer impairment of economic status in periods of inflation. They lose not only because salaries lag behind tuition in such periods, but also because tuition lags behind prices in inflationary periods. Of six periods of inflation since early seventeenth century, Harvard professors' pay lagged behind — that is, the salary-

tuition ratios dropped — in all but one period.

A factor tending to keep tuition down at Harvard has been the rising competition. On the whole, Harvard tuition and costs have tended to be high compared to those of its rivals.

Harvard administrations were not unaware of the relation of tuition to costs. Often costs are not easy to reveal. But many Harvard officials dwelt on the low tuition compared to high costs. In some of the Harvard schools, full-cost tuition was held to be the ideal approach. The business school, with graduates expecting high incomes and with non-tuition income available to cover costs rather small, especially favored full-costs tuition. Other schools had varying ratios of tuition to costs.

Anxiety over the impact of rising tuition upon enrollment was a factor that helped keep tuition down. The general view was that enrollment and tuition were inversely related. On a number of occasions, the analysis showed that higher tuition cut enrollment. But precise conclusions are not easily had. Relevant were such factors as the increasing level of income and the rise of demand for higher education. Tuition may rise by $50, but the improved economic situation may increase demand sufficiently to offset losses associated with higher charges.

At Harvard not only tuition but also fees were an important element of the costs imposed on students. When a professorship could not be financed out of available funds, frequently the university would impose fees on the students to finance a professor of mathematics or of science or of medicine or of law. Abbott Lawrence, the founder of the science school, insisted on a professor depending in substantial part on fees, a view earlier held by Adam Smith. Lawrence believed that the fee system improved incentives for good teaching.

7. Room and Board

From the very beginning, room and board were not easily financed. That this was so is revealed by the perpetual problem of indebtedness of students to the college. As early as 1650, the college took strong measures to limit these debts.

Through most of Harvard's history, the college was accused of extravagance and in part because of living expenses. The defense generally was, as Mr. Gray, a member of the corporation, pointed out in 1831, that Harvard turned out a product of quality. The college provided food at $1.75 that cost the college $2.25. "If it can be had in Amherst for less, we may rejoice in their good fortune, but we cannot share it."

Concern over costs to students was related to the high cost of college compared to income available to finance it. As late as 1897, a keen observer noted that annual costs at the better colleges exceeded the average family's annual income. But in 1967, the costs of a year at Harvard were only about half of the average family income and much less in relation to the income of the average Harvard family. A Harvard education is less costly in relation to family incomes than seventy years ago.

One Harvard graduate complained at Harvard's allowing its students to be housed by outside interests at profits while Harvard invested its own funds at low rates. From 1867 to 1900, the number of places in college halls rose by 2 times; in private halls, 71 times.

By reducing maid service and substituting cafeteria service for waitresses, the college kept total costs from rising as much as tuition. Thus from 1939 to 1963, tuition rose by 280 percent; rooms by only 121 percent; and board by only 92 percent.

In this same period, rents in the nation increased only by 61 percent. Harvard's relatively poor record may by explained by the impact of rent control in the nation – and also the large rise of new housing units in the country. In the food area, however, Harvard's record was impressive. Food costs rose only about 57 percent as much as in the nation.

In pricing rooms, Harvard often sought a return on the investment. Massachusetts Hall, for example, yielded income that was used to cover some of the expenses of the college. Even under the House Plan Lowell anticipated a profit of $\frac{1}{4}$ of 1 percent of the investment. When a dormitory was a gift, the policy generally was to subsidize all students by not charging for capital costs. But in 1862 it was announced that when the college provided the capital, it was appropriate to charge the student for capital investment. Harvard has not usually adhered to this policy, however, in the last hundred years.

In 1966, Harvard's buildings were insured at $240 million. The college put aside $2,163,000 to cover repairs and maintenance. These outlays are charged to students and to nonstudent building funds.

Harvard did not have a consistent pricing policy for rooms. In the early years, the college generally listed a few different prices according to the desirability of the rooms. With time the number of rent charges increased. In the nineteenth century there was some sentiment for a one-price system as being most democratic. In the last few years the college has accepted the one-price system. Lowell feared that a one-price system would be costly to the poor students who would lose subsidies derived from the high charges put on the affluent students.

Harvard students were not always pleased with the quality of room services. In the middle of the nineteenth century they complained bitterly of the stench around Holworthy, which was near the place where slaughtering was in vogue. In 1856, Henry Adams complained of winds howling about him in his college room. He could not prevent the water in his kitchen from freezing, he said, and "...my room is the coldest, the dirtiest and the gloomiest in Cambridge." Students in 1854 were "greatly annoyed by the incorrigible want of neatness and general neglect evinced by the female attendents on their rooms. . . ."

Complaints concerning the quality of food were persistent and caused many disturbances. Students were not without support for their low estimates of the quality of the college food. To give one example, in the 1860s, Acting President Peabody allowed that prices were low and quantity adequate. But the food was "so mean in quality, so poorly cooked, and so coarsely served, as to disgust those who had been accustomed to the decencies of the table. . .so that the dining-halls were seats of boisterous misrule, and numerous rebellions. . . ."

Often it was necessary to give permission to eat out because of the crowded conditions. By midnineteenth century the authorities closed down the commons which were by then slightly patronized. But in the seventeenth and eighteenth centuries, the college officials tried to force students to eat at commons. In the seventeenth and eighteenth centuries, the pressure on students stemmed from the interest in the students, and also a determination to achieve a volume of business that would keep costs down. In attempts to reduce the cost of higher education, the college subsidized dining halls in the last hundred years — although at times profits were made — and introduced economical service; that is, a genuine two-price system, low and high.

In response to inflationary pressures the college raised the price of commons. Thus, in 1737, the corporation justified an increase in charges.

In the seventeenth and eighteenth centuries, the college, when short of cash, often priced commons at a level which would yield some profits. In the pre-Revolutionary period the problem was obtaining enough space to accommodate students; but after the Revolution the problem was to get enough business to keep unit costs down.

Complaints were the rule. Under Dunster the government was to investigate the short rations; in 1810, an overseers committee complained of "the great inattention to the cooking. . ."; the coffee badly made, the pudding heavy and indisgestible and the bread not well baked. In 1835, E. E. Hale noted "the bill of fare was as obsolete as if it had been laid down by the Medes and Persians and never changed. . . ."

Prices, in response to inflation and other factors, rose. In more than three hundred years, prices rose from 50 cents a week to $18, or roughly 35 times.

8. Student Aid

From the very beginning, Harvard received funds to aid poor students. T. Hollis financed ten scholarships as early as the 1720s. In 1724, he asked for evidence of the quality of work of his students.

With students impoverished in the early years, the college had to be generous with scholarships. From 1640 to 1652, one-third of all college expenditures were for student aid. In contrast, the university spent but 7 percent of its outlays in 1965-1966 on student aid.

Aid as a percentage of tuition income equalled 7 percent from 1963 to 1712, 3 percent in 1860, and between 23 and 25 percent in selected years from 1860 to 1963.

Harvard was sensitive about its lack of money in relation to the resources of competitors. At one point the concern was so great that seven Harvard graduates subscribed $11,350 to be used for loans to students. From 1838 to 1959 (121 years) this fund had escalated to $2,700,000 and despite many defaults which greatly troubled presidents Eliot and Lowell.

Aid money was not always used in the most effective manner. In the early years, giving excessive grants to relatives of donors and basing stipends on the need of the student rather than his ability, tended to reduce the productivity of these outlays.

As usual, Eliot had some wise remarks on aid: ". . .The community does not owe superior education to all children, but only to the elite — to those who having capacity, prove by hard work that they have also the necessary preserverance, and endurance. The process of preparing to enter college under the difficulties which poverty entails is just such a test of worthiness as is needed. . . ."

Then Eliot in 1869 made a point that has been made many times since: ". . .it is to be expected that the men who in this generation have had the benefit of these funds, and who succeeded in after life, will pay manyfold to their successors in need the debt which they owe. . . ."

Eliot was not inclined to be overly generous in disposing of scholarship money. He would terminate a scholarship upon marriage of the holder or upon evidence of inadequate achievement. In contrast, the tendency now is to offer scholarships for periods of several years, with no cancellation except following serious deterioration in the quality of work.

President Conant did not share Eliot's views. The former would urge students not to work while at college, and in contrast to Eliot, who would pay only part of their expenses, Conant sought generous stipends that would cover all expenses. In the 1940s the excess of costs over stipends rose from $1,082 to $1,709. But the rise of per capita disposable income offset 70 percent of this rise. With expenses now in excess of $3,500 and the average stipend about half that amount, the college still has a long way to go before reaching the Conant goal.

Availability of aid depended on the allocation of resources by the corporation and the condition of the economy. In inflationary periods, the real value of scholarships dropped, and depressions had similar effects. But against the cost of inflation one would have to measure the benefits from rising incomes associated with inflation and increased employment and loans.

Direct aid is one approach to this problem of the impoverished student. Another is to reduce the tuition charge. The latter solution is less welcome than the former, because a cut in tuition benefits not only those in need but all students, and hence is wasteful. Harvard's policies rightly have been to rely on direct aid, not on reductions of tuition.

Crude aid figures may be midleading. From the viewpoint of the college, there is an offset to aid, as Eliot observed, namely, the payment of tuition of students receiving aid. But this is relevant only on the assumption that the effect of aid is to increase enrollment. Aid enables the college to increase tuition without serious changes in the structure of the student body. Thus, over a recent period of about fourteen years, tuition income rose by about $1,500 million and aid by $135 million. The significance of aid is that for every additional dollar of student aid, tuition income increased by eleven dollars; and the rise of tuition was had without a substantial change in the composition of students, i.e., a relative rise of high-income students. The additional aid presumably provides help for the marginal students who otherwise would be excluded by the rise in fees.

In still another way statistics of student aid may be misleading. The recipient of aid is often required to perform services for the college in exchange for aid. Hence, the value of services rendered should be deducted from the aid given.

In the eighteenth century students would keep drains on the houses clean, lock and repair fences, keep pumps and fire engines in good working order, serve as butlers, keep college records, etc.

In the last generation, Deans John Monro, W. Bender, F. Glimp, and others greatly improved the methods of assessing needs and the appropriate amount of aid for each student. On the whole, the college has not tapped the really low-income groups. The cost would have been much more than the average of $1,700 per stipend now made available. In 1952, the median family income in the country was $4,300, for the Harvard scholarship holder, $4,800; in 1960, the respective figures were $5,300 and $7,800. In 1960, the top 5 percent in the nation had family incomes of $13,863; the Harvard scholarship need cutoff point (3 children) was $15,250. Harvard was clearly helping middle-income families much more than low-income families.

Harvard introduced loan programs at a relatively early time. In 1840 the college was depending more on loans than on scholarships. The business school early embraced the loan technique. But there was strong opposition to loans from influential quarters. The main advantages of loans is that they enable students to borrow and, as incomes rise, repay with reduced burdens. Furthermore, if adequately financed, they offer each student of requisite ability an opportunity to matriculate at the college of his choice.

9. Admissions, Enrollment, and Attrition

Harvard's enrollment grew slowly during its first two hundred years. The rise was interlarded with declines, and the governing boards were frequently concerned over an actual loss of students. In 1762, for instance, there was concern that a rise of tuition would discourage enrollment. Even as late as 1772, enrollment was only 172. Thereafter the rate accelerated, and by

1860 the total enrollment had risen to 839. But it was especially in the administrations of Eliot, Lowell, Conant, and Pusey — covering the century from 1869 to 1968 — that enrollment escalated, with rises of roughly 3,000, 4,300, 3,000, and 4,000 respectively. The gains in these four administrations accounted for about 14,000 of the 15,215 enrolled in 1967-1968.

Trends in enrollment are to be explained by numerous factors, the most important of which are: population growth (even in 1790 the population was but four million, a gain in 160 years of but 2 percent of that in the next 170 years); general economics trends; the relationship among price movements, family income, and the cost of higher education to the student; Harvard's standards; its relative prestige; the competition of other institutions of higher learning; the growing national interest in higher education; and such variables as admission standards, the years required for a degree, and the number of professional schools.

On the subject of enrollment Harvard's governing boards were of two views. Many of these men wanted Harvard to grow, for growth was held to be evidence of quality, while others sought high standards and restricted numbers. Early in the twentieth century, Charles Francis Adams spoke for the latter, asserting "Harvard University is not a calico mill nor yet a shoe industry. It will not cheapen its degree in order to hold its share of the degree business."

Under Eliot, the large rises of enrollment were related especially to the growing prestige of the university, the spawning of numerous graduate schools, and Eliot's low-cost policies in a period of rising money and real income of the average family. Higher education has become a bargain.

In Lowell's twenty years (half of Eliot's) the numerical increase actually exceeded that under Eliot, though the relative rise in enrollment was much less. This outcome is surprising to some extent, since Lowell's administration raised costs to the student at a sharper rate than the rise in real income per capita, which must finance these costs. What made possible the climbing enrollment in the Lowell period were the beginnings of the large national enrollment in institutions of higher learning, the continued growth of graduate schools, the large advances of the economy, continued gains in Harvard's prestige, improvements in its admission procedures, and especially admission under the New Plan and under the Top Seventh Plan.

Conant belonged to the Eliot school: he favored low tuition despite the vast rise of the economy. Higher education really became a bargain, with per capita disposable income doubling and tuition stabilized during most of his period, and with economies introduced in the provision of room and board. Conant, like Eliot, also greatly broadened the reservoir from which Harvard students were drawn.

The Pusey administration, on the whole, has pursued policies similar to Lowell's. Costs rose greatly; about two-thirds of the rise could be tied to inflationary pressures and one-third to higher real costs; that is, money costs adjusted for the rise of prices. Lags in the rise of faculty salaries in the World War II period and also in the early postwar years made necessary increases in salaries and consequent rises in tuition. The advance of the House Plan, notably under Lowell and Pusey, also tended to raise costs, though the educational gains were not negligible.

Beginning with Lowell, the pressure of numbers began to trouble the university. Some restrictions had to be put on admissions, and rejections rose greatly relative to applicants. Whereas in 1898 and 1930 rejections were 16 and 20 percent of applications, by 1968 the rejection rate was 79 percent. As the demand for space rose much more than the increase in places, especially since World War II, Harvard emphasized increasingly the quality of the students admitted.

Competition frequently concerned the Harvard management. In the middle of the eighteenth century George Whitefield, a popular preacher, attacked Harvard for its irreligion: "They neglect to pray with and examine the hearts of their pupils," with adverse effects on enrollment. Harvard's protest at the proposal in 1769 to charter a college in the Berkshires put off the opening of Williams College many years.

Harvard's complaint was that Massachusetts could not support two colleges: "The expense of supporting one college well and honorably, would be much less than supporting two meanly and parsimonously."

In the second quarter of the nineteenth century Harvard lost ground to Yale. The Unitarian movement which engulfed Harvard was considered anti-religious and reduced Harvard's enrollment. Yale gained especially in the West, with 915 graduates in the West in one year as against 669 for Harvard. By midcentury Harvard began to gain on Yale. Both Barnard, the able president of Columbia, and Thwing, the head of Western Reserve, associated Harvard's large relative gains thereafter with the elective system. Experts also stressed the availability of rooms and board, an advantage that Columbia especially did not share.

Generally, enrollment rose more than population, but there were exceptions. From 1819 to 1860 enrollment rose by 119 percent, population by 236 percent in the country and 243 percent in the Northeast. (The respective figures for the Eliot period were 269, 132, and 102 percent.) From 1855 to 1869 the population rose five times as rapidly in New England as enrollment in twelve New England colleges. But this time Harvard stood out. Its increase was greater than that of the combined twelve.

In the midst of wars enrollment tended to suffer, but the effects were not serious until World War I. Even in the Civil War enrollment stayed up remarkably well.

Many other factors discussed in the body of this book also influenced enrollments. For example, the dropouts between admission and graduation have tended to fall over the years, contributing to higher enrollments. Again, the tendency toward the three-year degree under Eliot would cut enrollment, whereas the rise of degree requirements in professional schools would have the opposite effect. Higher standards of admission might reduce enrollments, though in recent years the effect is more likely to be improved quality of students admitted. The increased reservoir of students, related to the development of more examination centers and new types of examinations, has tended to increase enrollment and improve quality. And enrollment is obviously dependent on the availability of housing and academic plant.

2
FACULTY

10. Faculty: Growth and Structure

Growth of the faculty was slow in the early years. Even as late as 1801 the faculty consisted only of six professors and tutors. In 1851, the university boasted of sixteen faculty members, "thus ensuring the thoroughness of teaching in as many studies as can be usefully embraced in a course which continues no longer than four years."

In the nineteenth century and especially under Eliot, the numbers in the faculty escalated. Thus whereas up to 1836 (after two hundred years) Harvard appointed 63 to professorships, by 1885 the number had climbed to 279, or 14 times as many per year in the years 1836 to 1885 as to 1836.

Under Eliot the size of the faculty grew in a spectacular manner: 21 in 1869-1870; 123 in 1909-1910. The gain was 81 percent in excess of the rise of enrollment. In Eliot's first ten years, the number of professors increased six times as much as enrollment; but in later years enrollment tended to rise more. Gradually, under Eliot, the appointments of junior faculty became increasingly important, a trend explained by the large increase of enrollment and also the rising demands of professors for help with the teaching and grading.

Growth of the faculty continued after Eliot's day, though in the 1930s the rise was small by past standards. One result was the Walsh-Sweezy crisis in the 1930s when the authorities refused to promote two liberal and popular members of the faculty. The rigid Graustein formula for allocating tenure appointments among departments was then introduced. By various

techniques the authorities managed to avert the restrictive impact of that formula. Despite that formula, from 1940 to 1960, the number of professors and associate professors in the college rose by 122 percent. Just before the Graustein formula was put into effect, there were 161 professors and associate professors. By 1963, the total had risen to 452.

Student-faculty ratios tend to decline as the number of faculty increases. In response to Eliot's elective system, the faculty would have to increase their teaching load or else their numbers, with the latter thus reducing the student-faculty ratio.

The significance of changes in the student-faculty ratio depends partly on modifications in the structure of the faculty. Thus from 1860 to 1960, the percentage of professors and associate professors in the college rose from 54 to 64 percent. Thus, despite great expansion, the college nevertheless retained the maturity of its faculty. *In the university,* however, the student-faculty ratio dropped from $16\frac{1}{2}$ to 1 in 1830 to 4 to 1 in 1950, and the percentage of professors and associate professors dropped from 68 to 16 percent. Obviously the decline in the student-faculty ratio should be considered in the light of the large increase of junior appointments, and the relative decline in professorial appointments.

11. Inbreeding

The quality of a faculty is crucial in institutions of higher learning. Poor methods of choice mean wasted resources and low educational standards.

All institutions of higher learning indulge in inbreeding; that is, appoint and promote their own students. The temptation is to give preference to those known to the faculty. Harvard's appointments from within are surprisingly large. Eliot pointed to the dangers of appointments entrusted exclusively to faculty calling a disproportionate number of appointments from within "...a danger which is very real whenever a faculty has full authority over appointments and promotions."

Over the period 1900 to 1940 Harvard probably accounted for around five hundred Ph.D.s or 10 percent of the total twenty-eight institutions of higher learning offering given by Ph.D.s. In these years Harvard appointments from within were roughly seven times its proportion of Ph.D.s. Yet there has been some improvement.

In the years 1957 to 1967, of 159 appointees of professors and associate professors, Harvard had employed 79 (49.7 percent) immediately prior to first Harvard tenure appointment. Harvard accounted for 44.7 percent of the Ph.D.s of these 159 appointees. These statistics point to some reduction in inbreeding.

In an examination of the problem of choice of faculty Eliot discussed the evidence required to make sound appointments. He was not impressed by the usefulness of recommendations, writing "...Americans are apt to be too charitable and good-natured when writing letters of recommendation."

Eliot was impressed by the potential contributions of associations of scholars. He preferred confrontations with possible faculty members:

...what sort of qualifications shall have most influence...knowledge of subject, capacity to expound it in an interesting manner, published works, success as an investigator, or the total personality, including manners, temper, bearing, and quickness of sympathy. In every case there must be balancing of these different qualities....

12. Rank Structure

By the first quarter of the nineteenth century the faculty had grown to 24, with two-thirds professors; and by 1860, of a faculty of 35, 25 were professors. Eliot greatly changed the structure by extending an elective system which required a large rise of faculty and especially of junior rank. Financial pressures forced Eliot to depend heavily on junior members.

To contend with inflation the college might have increased the salary in each rank. But in the early twentieth century the authorities contended with inflation by concentrating on merit increases; an economical approach, but one that is not likely to improve the relations of the faculty and the administration. Under the crisis conditions of the 1930s, the governing boards had to modify their policies and especially scruntize permanent appointments. Assuming a stable tenure population, the Committee of Eight, however, proved to be excessively pessimistic. Numbers of professors and associate professors increased in the last twenty years from 193 to 330. Moreover, a disguised rise of pay, and notably in recent years, was had as the age of appointment to tenure appointments substantially declined.

13. Salaries

To compare salaries in a significant manner, one should consider not only the dollar income but also the age at which a rank is attained and the proportion of faculty at the higher ranks. In assessing relative salaries, the American Association of University Professors attempts to deal with this problem by considering the salary per full-time student. Where professors are numerous, that figure will be correspondingly high.

A perennial problem in the first 150 years was the president's salary. Neither the colony nor the college was generous. President Benjamin Wadsworth (1725-1737), for example, received some solid support in that the college made available to him the rents of Massachusetts Hall. "...but the unappropriated funds of the College were wholly inadequate to supply the residue, and the precarious favor of the General Court continued to be the sole dependence of the President for an important part of his maintenance...." Continued inflation further cut his real salary.

In the 1770s it was said "the money paid [tuition] would not purchase much more than one-half so much as it would have done when it became due, by which means the College had suffered greatly, and were still liable to suffer." Faculty members suffered and "experienced a painful inability to support their families in a comfortable and decent manner."

In the first half of the nineteenth century, the real pay of the Harvard faculty rose substantially as pay increased and prices dropped. Improved demand for the faculty undoubtedly contributed to this result. The university found the financing of faculty difficult. Substantial rises in enrollment, and hence need for additional faculty, may explain the shortage of salary funds.

Under Eliot, the college achieved its greatest improvement in salaries. Ten years before he became president he complained of low pay and heavy teaching loads. One of his first dramatic moves was to raise the pay of professors from $3,000 to $4,000. He concentrated his favors largely on the high-income faculty.

By increasing tuition from $150 to $175, obtaining $10,000 from dormitory rent and $50,000 from a class subscription fund, Eliot was able to raise salaries and increase the numbers of new professorships by thirteen by 1871.

Eliot, in fact, wanted higher salaries; but he also, with his support of the elective system, sought many more professors. Eliot was frequently criticized for stressing numbers again at higher pay. Henry James wrote "the best salaries that the University paid were modest and there are more instances than it is pleasant to consider of instructors who were kept waiting for full pay until middle age, or until some other institution began to bid against Harvard . . . ."

Eliot strengthened the faculty by increasing salaries, by setting scholars free from drudgery, and by seeking talent everywhere.

In 1967-1968, Harvard professors in comparing outside offers listed the most attractive features of Harvard in relation to competitors offering positions to Harvard faculty. Harvard came off badly in income, housing, workloads, professional or civic appointments, leaves and sabbaticals, and career advancement.[1]

In the thirty years between 1870 and 1899, Harvard was able to raise expenditures per student even though income per student declined – and in part because of the falling yield on investment. Costs per student increased despite the large rise of students, and because of the costliness of the elective system. As prices declined, the status of the faculty improved.

No substantial improvement in economic status occurred after the initial drive of 1869-1870 until early in the twentieth century. The rise of prices and family income and the rising competition of the University of Chicago stimulated the $2,500,000 drive, funds to be used to raise salaries. A 1904 overseers' committee remarked "the expense of student life in Cambridge may have been kept down by an undue sacrifice imposed on those whose lives are professionally devoted to student instruction."

From early nineteenth century to 1919, the faculty experienced a great erosion of economic status as per capita income rose by 115 percent from 1906 to 1919. The increase of prices was of similar magnitude and hence the faculty experienced a decline in real income by about one-half. The solution sought was not raising tuition, with unfortunate effects on the capacity of the poor to enter Harvard, but rather a $15-million endowment drive. President Lowell wanted the faculty "to live comfortably, in a style reasonably appropriate to their position and duties; to lay by enough for illness and old age; and to give their children as good an education as they received themselves. . . ."

At the beginning of the 1930s depression, Harvard announced a substantial rise in salaries—for full professors, an increase from between $6,000 and $9,000 to between $8,000 and $12,000. Since prices were to fall 17 percent more in the 1930s, the improvement was of the order of 60 percent.

Beginning in 1940, the scourge of inflation once more began to reduce the real income of the faculty.

1. *College Books* in Harvard University Archives, vol. IV, p. 119.

In twenty-five years, 1930 to 1955, real income before taxes was down by 20 percent and money income of the faculty had risen but one-seventh as much as for the average worker. Inflation once more proved costly to the faculty. But under the Pusey-Bundy-Ford administration, serious efforts were made to raise the real income of faculty. In one eight-year period, the pay of a full professor rose by 61 percent against a 33 percent increase in per capita disposable personal income in the nation.

Harvard, first on the scene, often watched her competition with concern. But in five periods in the nineteenth century, Harvard's salaries were substantially higher than her rivals in all periods but one. Eliot took a broad view. He wrote President Gilman of Johns Hopkins: "Please don't think I feel in the least annoyed at proposals made by you to Harvard men. On the contrary, I should have thought it very odd if there had been no men here whom you cared to try for. . . ."

Even as late as Eliot's administration Harvard depended on subsidies from faculty to help finance the faculty payroll. Through most of the nineteenth century, Harvard underpaid able faculty members who had large private resources, encouraged some to provide apparatus and equipment, and also urged them to beg for money for the university.

When the university could not obtain the required resources for financing the payroll, they often depended on fees. Thus in the 1820s the college drastically cut salaries but encouraged the use of fees based on enrollment to offset the loss of income.

Another source of faculty pay funds was moonlighting. The governing boards sometimes encouraged and sometimes discouraged this practice.

14. The Structure of Pay

Over the years, the pay of the president and the faculty tended upward. At the outset the tutors or fellows had to be satisfied with pay of £4 a year or about $13. The president's salary was much higher, but payment was often uncertain. The pay of the

professors tended to rise much less than that of those in lower ranks. As economic pressures rose and notably in inflationary periods, the tendency was to offer concessions to the lowest paid faculty, thus assuring them the minimum pay needed to obtain the necessaries of life. From the very beginning the librarians received very little; and treasurers, partly because of the honorary nature of the appointment, also were treated badly. The pay of the tutors and fellows tended to be high, relative to that of the professors in the early Harvard history. In the Eliot period, the high-priced professors were especially favored. The highest increase went to professors now eagerly sought by rivals; the lowest, to instructors. To Eliot, the professors were the most needed and most favored faculty. Thus, from 1869 to 1904 the pay of professors increased by 25 to 40 percent, that of instructors declined by 40 percent.

From 1904 to 1964, the trend was different. The pay of professors, assistant professors, and instructors rose by 6.2, 4.7, and 7.7 times. Here the inflationary trends tended to require special efforts to increase the pay of the low-paid members of the faculty. Competition of emerging institutions of higher learning tended to bring higher salaries, especially for the high-income faculty, for they were the subject of competition among the institution of higher learning.

Yet the rise of faculty pay at Harvard was surprisingly small in the years 1904 to 1964 as compared to the increases of all employees, and especially when one considers the increases of student enrollment in the nation and at Harvard.

15. Fringe Benefits

A substantial part of the salary of the Harvard faculty is in the form of fringe benefits. In providing markets for textbooks written by faculty members, in financing furniture purchases and moving expenses, in bestowing extra pay for married faculty members, in lending funds to presidents and the faculty, the college at relatively early periods supplemented income with fringe benefits.

Early in the nineteenth century, Harvard, unable to draw faculty members from abroad, sent such scholars as Edward Everett and Henry W. Longfellow to Europe for study. Pres. Josiah Quincy was not pleased when Longfellow overstayed his leave. In more recent times, the sabbatical leave and the financing of annuities became two of the most important fringe benefits. But Harvard refused to finance the education of the children of Harvard faculty as most of its rivals do. The attitude seemed to be that Harvard pays its faculty well and if they wish to allocate resources to raising children, then it is the parents' obligation, not Harvard's, to finance their education.

16. Inadequate Salaries

From the very beginning, complaints of inadequate pay concerned the Harvard administration. The reason might be one's pay compared to others who had smaller responsibilities, or the difficulties of supporting a family on the salary allowed by the college. Once Harvard had to face competition from numerous new institutions of higher learning, the university had to make concessions to its faculty. Yet Eliot, in 1891-1892, boasted that seven universities and colleges failed in their offers of improvements in salaries and titles to four professors, four assistant professors, and six instructors at Harvard. They preferred to stay at Harvard for various reasons inclusive of the freedom provided at Harvard.

A troublesome problem was the low yield of endowed chairs. Upon receiving an endowment Harvard would appoint a professor to the chair, although even at the outset the yield of the endowment was inadequate; and with rising prices and incomes it became increasingly inadequate.

17. Dissatisfaction with Salaries

Rising prices and incomes, not accompanied by corresponding increases in faculty pay, have undoubtedly been the major cause of dissatisfaction with faculty salaries. In the first 150 years the government's failure to adhere to commitments also occasioned many complaints. As late as 1781, Pres. Samuel Langdon wrote to the Legislature that the depreciation of the currency reduced his income by one-half and having been dismissed he asked the corporation to "take some peculiar notice of my circumstances and give some token of affection by making a small grant in addition to what was due from my requisitions. . . ."

On one occasion (1829) a corporation committee denied an application of Prof. Henry Ware for an increase of pay saying ". . .To proceed on the assumption that a professor's salary is not sufficient for his support would invite applications from all the other professors, which could not be rejected. . . ."

18. Salaries – Sources

In the first 150 years, salaries were financed in substantial part by the government, though in varying proportions. By the end of the Revolutionary War three professors were paid £450 each though the foundations provided only £150. Hence, heavy assessments were made on students. The college depended on appropriated funds (endowments), the government (e.g., ferry income), and student fees during most of the eighteenth century.

The government's failures were numerous. In 1784, Pres. Joseph Willard complained of the precariousness of his support. He had been reduced to straits and difficulties "by the omissions of the General Court; and the grant made in July [1784] was inadequate to the expectations and necessities. . . ."

For more than a century the university depended heavily on fees of all kinds, and especially for providing funds to cover faculty members' salaries. Thus, in 1809, four professors had to share $1,095, the annual yield of four foundations. Hence, the university relied heavily on fees and nonappropriated (free) funds. The medical school and the law school especially depended on fees in their early history. As the faculty grew in the first quarter of the nineteenth century, the dependence on fees increased. Even as late as midnineteenth century, Mr. Lawrence, the founder of the science school, affirmed that considerable dependence on fees "is the best guarantee to exertion and fidelity – and the permanent prosperity of the institution." But by the middle of the nineteenth century, hostility to fees grew.

In inflationary periods, the college offsets the reduced real income of the faculty to some extent by investing more heavily in equities. In the great inflationary periods of the last hundred years the attack was large endowment drives to yield higher incomes for faculty members, and ultimately raising tuition. Adequate financing of the faculty's salaries depends also on the relation of salaries to other costs of the university.

19. The Rising Costs of Professorial Chairs

Over a period of more than three hundred years the average pay of a Harvard faculty member rose by 78 times in dollars of current value. Of course the product measured, i.e., the faculty member, is a much improved one. The endowment of the first chair amounted to about $4,500. Currently $600,000 is required; and on reasonable assumptions concerning productivity and price rises, about 6 million will be needed to endow a chair fifty years from now. Obviously as incomes rise – say by 10 times in fifty years – the endowment of a professorship becomes increasingly inadequate to cover the professor's salary. Recourse to equity investments helps reduce the losses as does a lag of professor's salary in relation to the rise of pay for the average member of the labor market. The inadequacy of yield of endowed chairs still remains, and is aggravated by the decline of yields of Harvard's investments since the latter part of the nineteenth century

20. Work Loads

Complaints about work loads were numerous, and especially in the nineteenth century. The faculty sought freedom from residence requirements and from excessive hours of teaching, and sought teaching loads that allowed freedom for moonlighting. By the first quarter of the nineteenth century, the practice of assigning tasks to assistants began. Even distinguished faculty members like Supreme Court Justice Story had to insist on freedom from residence requirements. John Quincy Adams in the first decade of the nineteenth century insisted upon concentrating his teaching in one semester since he had outside responsibilities, and he would not allow an assistant to take over part of his work.

Instructional loads were heavy on present-day standards. In the 1820s Professor Ticknor taught $5\frac{1}{2}$ hours a day, Bachi in humanities, taught $7\frac{1}{2}$ hours a day. In midnineteenth century, professors seemed to teach from about twenty-five to almost forty hours a week. In Eliot's day the teaching burdens were reduced as the college made greater use of young faculty members. Thus, from 1889 to 1914, the percentage rise of professors was 114; of other teachers, 543.

The mathematics faculty especially protested heavy teaching loads, and resented burdens beyond those put on their colleagues. In 1830, there were complaints of long hours and of work requiring twice the hours of an instructor in the public schools. The instructor had to spend much time on private instruction, and hear daily recitations for between 160 and 170 students.

Henry Longfellow was a frequent dissenter. He pointed out that his usefulness to the college should not be assessed on the number of classroom hours, for "many days of hard study are often necessary for the preparation of a single lecture. . . ."

Even as late as 1845, a committee of overseers, considering costs of education, urged that faculty teach at least three hours a day during the thirty-nine weeks of the school year.

In the next hundred years conditions improved. Despite the large rise in committee work and the vast increase in courses, and growing demands of research, the Harvard faculty's burdens greatly declined. Increasing availability of assistants for teaching and research, the declining demands for maintaining discipline, the large increase in professorial chairs, and the elimination of residency requirements all tended to relieve the faculty of excessive burdens. The tutorial system of the last fifty years not only increased the burden of teaching for the young, but also relieved older faculty of other responsibilities.

21. Some Problems of Tenure and Retirement

Tenure is of great significance for institutions of higher learning. From an economic viewpoint, its significance is suggested by the commitment to pay out between $1 and $2 million by top universities to a tenure member over the thirty to forty years of tenure begun, say, in 1970. Perhaps even more important is the relationship between tenure and the resultant removal of restraints on freedom of expression. A related problem is the availability of annuities when the faculty member is asked to retire. Eliot, perhaps more than anyone else, put across the idea that the productivity of a college is increased as way is made for younger faculty through retirement accompanied by support.

A genuine tenure system was slow in coming. The removal of Dunster, the first president, because of the unacceptability of his views on baptism would not have occurred if tenure were an accepted principle. In 1721, the first professorship provided for a term of but five years. But in 1726 the appointment was "during good behavior." In 1812, the governing boards dismissed Prof. B. Waterhouse, a great scientist. Not only had he secretly supported the founding of a rival medicine school but "he had repeatedly published in the newspapers without his proper signature suggestions and insinuations injurious to our [as a member of medical faculty] character and highly opposing to our feelings." A case could be made out for dismissal in this case without impairment of proper tenure principles.

Generally, appointments included provision for discharge for good cause such as immoral behavior, incompetence, and the like. But in the middle of the nineteenth century, Prof. Francis Bowen failed to receive approval by the governing boards, apparently because of his lack of sympathy with the Magyar uprising in Hungary. Bowen, himself, believed the crucial issue had been his unpopular views on slavery. In 1870, Bowen, then a professor, was forced to recant his unpopular view on the national debt. He acknowledged the corporation was the final judge whether publication of a college teacher was "likely to be injurious to the interests either of the College or of sound morality." Here was a serious breach of academic freedom.

On the whole, Eliot's record in academic freedom and tenure was good. In 1905, he rejected the idea that the president should have the power of dismissing professors and criticized Stanford for firing a professor because he disapproved of that faculty member's views on Roosevelt's *Winning of the West*.

Under Lowell and Conant, problems of tenure and academic freedom continued to trouble the university. Lowell urged his faculty to confine their discussion to areas of competence. But he supported Harold Laski in the face of strong pressures. Conant was also a victim of the times. The large contributions of Harvard to the New Deal invited fierce criticism of the faculty. An unfortunate administrative appointment contributed to the emergence of the Walsh-Sweezy case, and a re-examination of the tenure system.

22. Faculty Status: Other Aspects

A problem of increasing difficulty troubled the Harvard administrators as other institutions of higher learning with rising resources sought to attract Harvard stars by offering much higher pay. Lowell in 1930 expressed great doubts about this practice. The fixed scale seemed to Lowell the best system for both faculty and institutions.

In earlier years, donors would reserve the right to name the occupant of a chair and even to dictate the terms of the occupany — notably, the influence of Hollis, the donor of the first mathematical chair early in the eighteenth century. By providing $10,000, Mr. Dane reserved the right to pick Justice Story for the legal chair in the early nineteenth century and determine the conditions of work of the Dane professorship.

Only in relatively recent times has Harvard encouraged the use of resources for faculty research. Even in the early 1870s Eliot refused a professor of chemistry a few hundred dollars for research. Even by 1888, Eliot still assumed that Harvard funds were to go primarily for instruction.

3

EXPENDITURES AND FINANCE

23. Costs, Seventeenth Century and 1965

Here I compare prices of higher education, food, books, houses, faculty, and labor. Quality has changed for all these items, though at varying rates. Yet the contrast of cost movements in striking, e.g., from the seventeenth century to 1964, prices of books rose only 8 times, but tuition, 300 times; food at college, 50 times; faculty pay, 133 times; and laborer's wages, 180 times.

24. Income and Expenditures

The available statistics here are not all they might be. I have made brave but not entirely satisfactory attempts to study the long-term trends of income, of categories of income, and also of expenditures.

In general, the rise of Harvard's budget since the early days has been impressive: from about £27 sterling in 1655 to a total of more than $150 million today. From 1840 to a recent year, income had grown by $135 million or 750 times as much as in 204 years from 1636 to 1840; and investment funds, by 1,500 times.

The gains in the eighteenth century greatly exceeded those of the seventeenth century, both in total and on a yearly basis. Of Harvard's 330 years, the major expansion by far has been in the last 100 years.

Eliot (roughly 1870 to 1910) profited especially from the large growth in the economy, the rise of enrollment related to the national economic gains, and Harvard's rising prestige, as well as from the downward trend of prices. But a reduction in yield on investments was an unfavorable factor. Lowell (roughly 1910 to 1930) also could exploit the large gains of the economy. But there were important differences. Lowell administered during a period of rising prices and also of vast gains in capital account. Hence, endowment contributed much more to Lowell's budget than to Eliot's. Moreover, the decline of yield ceased under Lowell.

An interesting contrast was the much greater rise of charges under Lowell than under Eliot. Whereas under Eliot the burdens on students rose about as much as per capita income, under Lowell the student experienced much greater increases of charges in relation to the economic standards (per capita income). Harvard under Lowell was becoming a high-cost experience but it was a bargain under Eliot.

In the body of the chapter, I summarize over the early years, over the first seventy years of the nineteenth century, and also the last hundred years, the structure of income especially, but also expenditures. I assess especially the trend, absolute and relative of tuition, of over-all student costs, of endowment income, of current gifts, and of the government's contribution.

In every period, the net rise of budget is related expecially to the inflationary pressures, the rise of enrollment, and the economic growth of the country. But I should warn the reader that the results are only roughly accurate. In Chapter 52 I consider many of these problems more fully.

25. Patterns of Expenditures

Variations in accounting methods reduce the value of comparisons of the structure of expenditures. A comparison of Harvard's early and recent years reveals a rising importance of wages, and also expenditures on the plant. In inflationary periods, relative outlays on salaries tended to drop, and similarly with student aid. In the nineteenth century, the structure was relatively stable, with wages and salaries accounting for about one-half of expenditures. Outlays on the plant became increasingly important in the twentieth century. In these years wages also contributed increasing shares of expenses.[1]

26. Deficit Finance

Problems of deficit finance were not of great importance in the first half of Harvard's history. The college avoided deficits by transferring potential deficits to the faculty first and students second. The faculty, for example, would accept cuts in pay and often postponement of pay.

Perhaps the most troublesome period was in the 1820s, when the college was confronted with large deficits associated with poor management and the failure of government to continue a $10,000-per-year subsidy. In this period, the college had recourse to the usual methods of treating deficits: reducing expenditures and/or raising revenues were the orthodox approaches, and especially the former.

It is not easy to increase revenues in the midst of deficit periods and especially since deficits often are caused in part by unsatisfactory economic conditions. One approach to increasing revenues was to raise tuition fees. But Harvard often found higher tuition an unpalatable medicine. Eliot preferred, unlike Lowell, to depend on economies and raising more nontuition income. Eliot could be ruthless in dropping junior members of the faculty.

Difference of opinion prevailed on the relationship between tuition adjustments and enrollment. With

costs per student exceeding tuition, the conclusion often was that a reduction of enrollment associated with rising tuition would reduce deficits. But in periods when enrollment declined, e.g., World War I, World War II, and the Great Depression years, deficits soared.

In the last hundred years—though also to some extent in earlier years— deficits were treated to some extent by the consumption of capital. Eliot, as we shall see, believed in deficit finance.

Some of the largest deficits occurred in the late Eliot years, and even in the early Lowell years. Although enrollment rose by 3 times under Eliot in thirty-five years, costs per student relative to tuition rose by 28 percent. (Costs in relation to tuition might have been expected to decline in periods of rapid expansion of enrollment.) This unexpected result was associated with the effects of Eliot's great expansion of the curriculum and the faculty on costs.

Pointing out that deficits have seldom been caused by undue expansion of instruction, but rather by forced expenditures on grounds, buildings, equipment, and maintenance, and also that in the years of surplus, e.g., 1832 to 1857, the trend was not one of great development, Eliot concluded:

... One may also see ... that the period during which deficits have been largest and most frequent is the period where the increase of the invested funds of the University by gift and bequest has been most rapid. There seems to be no connection ... between the occurrence of deficits and University decline. ...

27. Every Tub on Its Own Bottom

During his administration in the first quarter of the nineteenth century, President Kirkland, in criticism of the divinity school, first announced the doctrine that "every tub stands on its own bottom." Even as late as President Conant's regime, the governing boards tried to follow this principle, which had many ramifications. Its most important facet demanded that each unit of the university should finance its own costs; that is to say, the university should not finance the veterinary school, nor the college the law

---

1. Seven pages of tables have been deposited in the Harvard University Archives.

school or vice versa. In practice, however, there were many exceptions which the governing boards did not generally reveal. For example, the board would favor diversions to financially weak schools, e.g., divinity, education, and dentistry.

28. Miscellaneous Issues of Finance

Harvard's growth was slow in the first hundred years. Even as late as 1732, the income not appropriated (i.e., unrestricted) amounted only to £728 (about $2,500). Especially significant was the extent to which faculty salaries absorbed income, a relationship that reflects the uncomplicated nature of Harvard College in its first hundred years.

A problem confronting Harvard over its entire history has been the large proportion of funds that are restricted in use. Even by the first quarter of the nineteenth century, appropriated (restricted) income was $16,149 out of incomes of $19,651. Another problem, namely, the small yield of endowed chairs compared to the pay of professors holding the chairs, troubled Harvard even in the seventeenth century. Thus, endowments of the two Hollis professorships and the Hancock professorship at this time provided $735, but the salaries of the three appointments amounted to $5,100.

By the 1820s, the authorities complained of large sums spent by Harvard "directed to objects foreign to the College, or less immediately connected with the primary instruction required ... others [expenditures] are for chairs of instruction of a kind important and interesting, but not of first necessity in a college, and such as leave the principle departments of teaching for undergraduates still to be supplied. . . ."

President Everett at mid-nineteenth century raised an issue of increasing discussions of late, namely, the relationship "between the public welfare and all elements of national prosperity on one hand, and an englightenment of the population on the other. . . ."

At this time also the authorities attracted attention to the relationship between costs and numbers. "It's often as easy to teach many as to instruct a few;

it makes no difference to the professor whether he lectures to a dozen auditors, or a hundred. . . ."

In the 1830s and 1840,, Harvard experienced a period of stagnation. In discussing high costs, the authorities "would not treat education like merchandise, and knowledge like broadcloth. Cheap bargains could be had at the Group Workshop, when only half the cost of production is charged to the customer, when the Corporation gets no dividends and the Overseers work without pay."

A frequent complaint in the nineteenth century was the high cost of a Harvard education, and a frequent defense, that when Harvard opened Cambridge was a wilderness and Boston a village. The college was later stuck in a high-cost location.

Eliot contended that with rising numbers the financial position improved. He was also prophetic when in 1875 he argued: "any institution which has any real prestige and power will make a money profit by raising its standard, and that either at once or in a very short time." Another problem confronting Eliot was the large rise of costs with the expanding curriculum, higher pay, and growing recognition of research as an indispensable service. Eliot depended especially on gifts and on economies—e.g., on buildings and on dropping faculty members under crisis conditions. He fought rises in tuition. In the last hundred years, the rising importance of wages, associated both with better organization of workers and the increasingly complicated operations of the university, put further strains on Harvard's finances.

An indication of the structure of expenditures and receipts for the early years is given by the account from July, 1693 to July, 1696. The major outlays were salaries of staff and president, first (about one-half); loans, about one-third; and supplies a large part of the remainder. Of the receipts, return of principal of loans and interest accounted for more than half; annuities, rents and interest about 20 percent; and the remainder, largely gifts.[2]

---

2. *College Books,* vol. IV, pp. 414-415. The two tables are deposited in the Harvard University Archives.

4

RELATIONS WITH THE GOVERNMENT

29. Resources for Harvard: Public vs Private

The government has made important contributions to the financing of Harvard, a point of special relevance in Harvard's first two hundred years. Their intervention was not limited to donations. They, for example, allowed exemptions from military service to students and faculty members, approved raising funds through lotteries, and granted exemptions from property taxes. In the first hundred years, the dependence on gifts, both public and private, was substantial, and in part because tuition contributed so little.

The college was disturbed by unfair and capricious treatment by the Colonial government. Inflation damaged the college and yet the government did little to offset its ravages and, in fact, according to some friends of the college, gave nothing in the years of greatest inflation; its support of the faculty and president was intermittent; it diverted college funds to the use of the government, and notably £150 presumably donated to President Dunster for building a house.

A common complaint was that the government had given buildings—six of them—and helped pay the faculty and president, but "the State has never founded a professorship or established a permanent fund for any object whatever in the college . . ."

College supporters underestimated the government's contributions. Thus whereas the spokesman for the university found that before 1780 private gifts had been but one-third of public, an official estimate for 1650 to 1780 put government grants at two-thirds of private.

In 1814-1824, the college had received $100,000, with a resultant burden on the banks, which provided this money out of taxes. S. Eliot in 1849 sought aid for the three Massachusetts colleges, which would reduce costs for the students. The possibilities were a general reduction of costs, a rather wasteful procedure since aid was to be had irrespective of need; a downward adjustment of charges computed on the basis of need; and finally a scholarship program. The colleges needed help. It was urged upon the government to accumulate a $500,000 fund for the use of the three colleges.

At the same time an overseers' committee allowed that education is intended for men as they are on the average "and not for prodigies. . . .It is apparent that the University does not grow rich by parsimony, nor feeble by extravagance." The State had left Harvard "as a rich father does his daughter on her marriage, and has left her, in the maturity of her strength, to the care and kindness of her children." But the government did not yield to the college's ministrations.

After the first quarter of the nineteenth century, government contributions became relatively small though on a few occasions substantial gifts were to be had. After World War II, the large grants and contracts for science once more attracted attention to government aid, with these funds accounting in the middle 1960s to about one-third of total outlays of Harvard.

30. Further Aspects of Government Aid

The government's contributions were indispensable for Harvard's survival in the first two hundred years or so of Harvard's history. As the overseers lost influence in the management of Harvard, governmental contributions declined. Harvard, moreover, discouraged investigations by the government. In 1732, the overseers refused approval to a government investigation; and in reply the court observed that when the college needed money it was wrong for "any branch of the court to be denied or obstructed in their motives covering that college."

The Colonial governments were generous in bestowing land upon the college. But the net gains were not large. One private grant, for example, was marked by "a pine tree at one end and a hemlock at the other."

Harvard's governing boards were also unhappy at the plans for a turnpike which would go through Harvard territory saying, "It deserves seclusion and retirement, and the road will bring much trouble that way and bring Boston too near."

The government was especially generous in financing Harvard's buildings. Thus, in 1730, the governor commented on the "blessing the College at Cambridge has been," and in particular, the favorable effect on land values and noted "while other Plantations were obliged to send their sons abroad for education at Great Expence, and often to their Ruin of Morals, we reap advantage at home."

In 1717, the general court received a memorial to the effect that many students could not be accommodated in college dormitories and "caused them to have uncomfortable views of mischief impending." Massachusetts Hall (1720) was the result. The cost was £3,500. Remodeling costs were $175,000 in 1925 and $70,000 in 1939. These figures suggest rising costs over a period of two hundred years. In 1726, the college completed Wadsworth House for the president; and it was occupied by presidents for 123 years, and was the temporary headquarters of General George Washington. The next important building was Holden Chapel (1744), an all-purpose building. One observer called it "... a solitary English daisy in a field of dandelions." Hollis (1763), Holsworthy (1812) and University (1815) halls followed, all financed by the government.

31. Ferry and Bridges

Over a period of 216 years (1640 to 1856) Harvard received financial support as a result of the grant of right to income from the Charlestown Ferry. Once the Charles River Bridge was built and then the Warren Bridge, Harvard's revenue from the original grant suffered. The college had to accept compensation over a limited time for the permanent rights from the ferry, which losts its business to the two bridges. In all, the college seems to have received about $75,000 from the ferry and bridges, a tidy sum for that period.

Harvard was not always content with this bounty. Fares were originally set at 1 penny, and despite large doses of inflation and rising income, the college was unsuccessful in its attempts to increase fares to a level commensurate with rising prices and income.

32. Taxation

At the outset Harvard was granted a tax exemption of £500. Numerous discussions revolved around the meaning of this exemption. In general, however, tax relief prevailed for all of Harvard's grounds, dormitories, laboratories, commons, and the like.

An interesting source of contention was a piece of property left by Henry Webb to Harvard in 1660. In the latter part of the seventeenth century, it rented for about £12. But in 1961, the property was still tax exempt and was carried on the books of the treasurer at $164,604. Saloons are still on this property on Washington Street, and the exemption still prevails. Street, and the exemption still prevails.

Both Boston and Cambridge differed with Harvard authorities on tax exemptions. Under Lowell, especially bad relations developed, in part because of the large withdrawals, and in part because Lowell policies diverged from those promised by Eliot.

On being threatened with taxes in New York State, the Harvard Governing Board pointed out that Harvard in a year spent $247,500 of its own resources educating students from New York. In 1966, Pusey alluded to the $71 million Harvard payroll, the $15 million spent by students, the 3,250,000 meals served by Harvard. Eliot was in the forefront in urging tax exemption. He noted that gains to the state from tax exemptions exceeded the losses.

33. Harvard and the Government

In 1642 the Colonial government conferred major responsibilities for managing Harvard on a large, cumbersome board of overseers. Its failures resulted in a new charter in 1650, which diverted authority primarily to a self-perpetuating body of seven, the fellows. The transfer of power provided by the 1650 charter resulted in a highly efficient operation, and apparently was especially effective in inducing sound and conservative management of the financial and other trusts of the college.

On numerous occasions the authority of the fellows was challenged. Should all the wealth of Harvard "be at the absolute disposal of men bred to be scholars and teachers and of course nothing but scholars and teachers. . .?" one critic asked. In fact, the scholars would then elect all officers and "fix their own salaries and regulate their own duties. . . ."

The 1780 constitution carried over the provisions of 1650. In 1851, the Legislature fortunately failed in its attempt to increase the number of fellows, reduce their terms to six years, and confer on the people the selection of fellows. Defenders of the system considered the quality of conservatism of the fellows as desirable for a body that administers "faithfully the many and large trust funds, which the hereditary love of learning. . .has accumulated in the custody of the President and Fellows of Harvard College."

By 1865, the Legislature definitely ended state representation and control. By 1921, Harvard had complete control of the selection of fellows and members of the board of overseers. Lay control took over against government and religious control. In this struggle, the overseers lost ground, though the board has contributed much to Harvard's welfare.

PART
5
GIFTS

34. Why Give?

Harvard's major gifts have come in the last 125 years. As late as 1840, Harvard's endowment was only $646,235. About 125 years later, endowments accounting for only part of the gifts had exceeded a billion dollars. In this period the market value of funds rose by more than 700 times and expenditures by about a thousand times. Corrections for inflation would reduce the gains, of course.

All kinds of considerations account for gifts to Harvard: the effective use made of money given to a university with a first-class faculty, plant, and organization; the low pay of professors; the inadequate endowment of chairs; the need for buildings; a desire of alumni to pay back to the university the excess of costs over tuition charged; the importance of the university for our society; help for the able and impecunious students; an offset to the ravages of inflation; honor to relatives and friends through gifts to Harvard.

A great benefactor, H. L. Higginson, commented: "She needs help, and thought and devotion, and gratitude from all of us, for she has given us and our land more than any of us will give back. . . ."

At an earlier period, Samuel Eliot supported gifts on the grounds more for their practical influence upon "the leading minds of the country than for the splendor of its appointments, or the dignity of its offices. . . ."

Higginson on another occasion wrote "Oh! if some dozen men would only put it up high and dry above want! One million dollars to start with and three million more afterwards. . . ."

Charles Eliot said the "endowment of the institutions of education . . . by private persons . . . is a phenomenon without precedent or parallel, and is a legitimate effect of democratic institutions. . . ."

35. Gifts to Harvard

In England, rich men found families; in America, they found universities, or enlarged them.

In the early years, Harvard often encountered difficulties in obtaining delivery of gifts. The Massachusetts court tried to divert Lady Mowlson's gift for scholarships to repairing the college buildings. But the magistrates prevented this diversion.

Harvard's endowment of a billion dollars stemmed from the original gifts—part, of course, not used for endowment—the capitalization of annuities and especially the rise of equity values.

Friends of Harvard in the seventeenth and eighteenth centuries assumed much more authority than modern donors. They would, for example, recommend the incumbent of new chairs, or at least retain veto power, suggest the teaching responsibilities of the relevant faculty, and even insist that the faculty thus financed should do no outside work or receive no fees from students, or not be asked to perform in fields not covered by the terms of the gift, and suggested the conditions of tenure. They assumed these responsibilities even though generally the yield of the gift was much less than the pay of the relevant professorship.

A frequent problem for the college was to meet the conditions of gifts. A $25,000 gift in 1943 to improve the general welfare of Cuba must surely raise problems today. In 1895, a donor (Waterhouse) offered $5,000 on the condition that it be allowed to accumulate to $500,000. The corporation turned down the offer because they wanted to spend all their income. Besides, Harvard did not want to be an investment council. In fact, the growth to $500,000 would be Harvard's, not Waterhouse's accomplishment.

On numerous occasions, donors have given the university discretion in using gift money. In the depression years past donors, several times, gave Harvard the discretion to use up capital, thus easing the financial situation in periods of crisis.

A substantial part of the gifts to Harvard was for scholarships and especially in the first half of Harvard's history. For the most part, much emphasis was put upon need, probably excessively, relative to the weight given to the quality of the student. Hollis, however, would exclude "Dunces or Rakes as persons not fit to partake of my bounty; or persons reasonably judged able to maintain themselves. . . ." A considerable amount of wastage of scholarship funds resulted from the special treatment of descendants of donors.

In the last hundred years, donors in some numbers have tended to provide scholarships on some other criterion than grades. In 1911, ". . . no worthy applicant for the benefit of said fund shall be deprived of it because unsuccessful in obtaining high grade marks. . . ."

These scholarships reflected the unhappiness of those of New England stock at the rising claims of scholarship money of the hard-working students, often of "ordinary" stock. A 1919 grant required "the one so chosen shall be descended from at least two grandparents, or more remote ancestors, who were natives of the United States of America or of what is now known as Great Britain. . . ."

Prizes are of some significance in providing aid for students. It is doubtful that they are as important now as in earlier years. One reason is that the prize of dollars in a year (say 1901) has not increased with the rise of prices and income. Thus, the Wells Prize yielded five hundred dollars in 1901. It still does today, though per capita income is about 12 times as large. Hence, the prize today yields only about one-twelfth as much relatively to sixty-five years ago.

36. Gifts and Their Uses, 1636-1900

Gifts were almost 3 times as great from 1711 to 1805 as from 1636 to 1710, and more than 10 times as large from 1806 to 1900 as from 1711 to 1805. In these first 264 years, gifts to Harvard were only 2 percent of the amount received in the twentieth century.

Governmental contributions were indispensable in the first two hundred years. As F. Rudolph reminded us "on over 100 occasions before 1789, the General Court of Massachusetts appropriated funds for Harvard College, which clearly was not capable of taking care of itself."

In the years 1636 to 1900, nonrestrictive gifts were but 19 percent of the total. In more recent years the unrestricted totals were but 12 percent. But in the first period, 1636 to 1710, the unrestricted gifts exceeded the restrictive. In later years, donors showed less confidence in the college, as they increasingly specified uses of donations.

When resources are small, gifts for current use tend to be much more important than in periods of adequate resources. Thus, we explain gifts for current use 8 times as large as endowment gifts in the years 1636 to 1710, but for the 264 years from 1636, endowment gifts overshadowed gifts for current use by two to one.

37. Methods of Raising Money

Harvard has had a long history of searching for money. As early as 1641, members of an expedition to England were "instructed that they should not seek supply of our wants in any dishonorable way, as by begging or the like. . . ."

By the 1840s the college began to mobilize modern methods. Seeking funds for space for commencement in 1841, the committee "was to organize subdivisions of the alumni in each place upon whom shall devolve the business of exciting their companions in this business. . . ."

It had been a rule that Harvard presidents should not solicit. Under Eliot endowment rose from $2,500,000 to $23,000,000. Yet generally he did not depend on begging. Not solicitation, but approval of his advanced educational views and creation of new schools attracted the funds. But Eliot occasionally begged; and the team of Pusey and Bundy in the late 1950s undertook a twenty-thousand-mile odyssey in furtherance of the campaign to raise $82,500,000.

In seeking funds, Harvard often exploited its faculty. William James, for example, accosted John Rockefeller in an attempt to get money available to finance a professorship of psychology. But James failed. Later, generations of Rockefellers more than made up for this failure.

In its first big campaign—$2,500,000 for faculty salaries in 1904—the effort was concentrated on the Harvard Clubs, with an appeal first to twenty who gave $50,000 each. The cost of publicity was only $500.

In the 1919 drive for $15 million, Lowell advanced the techniques greatly. He relied now on small donors as well as large. A British paper contrasted Oxford and Cambridge, which needed money and did nothing, and Harvard "sturdy beggars in a good cause."

The 1936 tercentenary campaign was unsuccessful: 1,000 contributors compared to 17,278 in the 1919 drive. The failures were the result of Harvard's contribution to the New Deal, the unsatisfactory economic conditions, and the unaggressive methods used.

The program in the late 1950s for Harvard College, $82,500,000, was a great success. Prosperity, the excellent work by Pusey, Bundy, and A. White, the diversified use of the funds, the long period that had

elapsed since the 1919 drive, and the generally excellent organization all helped. Perhaps even more remarkable was the followup campaign of the medical school for $58 million.

Finally, a word about annual giving. Slow to exploit this approach with early opposition of Lowell, Harvard now profits greatly from the $3 million current annual income, an income equal to that of $60 million of endowment, especially because this is unrestricted money for the most part.

38. Sources of Money

Men of affluence have contributed much to Harvard. One of the earliest large gifts was from Governor Stoughton, the unrepentant witch-hanger who financed Stoughton Hall. Eliot and Lowell had their scouts who would apprise them of likely victims — H. Higginson revealed the George Baker potential; and E. H. Wells explored the Philadelphia market, bringing to the attention of Harvard the rich sons of Harvard in this area. August Belmont was a likely catch though the prospects were dimmed when he was given tickets to the Harvard-Yale football game for himself and his young bride right behind the goal posts.

Harvard depended also on small contributions for special occasions: to finance Phillip Brooks House and the library or to purchase chimes.

The faculty helped obtain funds also. J. R. Lowell collected books in Spain "with a view to the college library, whither they will go when I am in Mount Auburn Cemetery. . . ." Professor Shaler contributed to the decision of Mr. McKay to give Harvard his $20 million. Seven medical school professors financed a large part of the cost of the North Grove Street Building.

The Busch beer company gave $50,000 for the Germanic Museum. But a critic pointed out that this was in payment for Professor Münsterberg's article in defense of drink.

The governing boards were not neglected. From the time of Thomas Brattle (1693-1713) to C. Gore (1812-1820) and President Lowell, the governing boards provided much.

Alumni have been sentimental friends of the college; and especially since the midnineteenth century.

Harvard sought help also from foundations and especially since 1900. Ford, the general education board, and Carnegie all gave.

Subscription drives started at the beginning of Harvard's history. In 1654, twenty-six individuals gave £250 for the repair of buildings. In these early years many towns introduced subscription lists to help finance Harvard, and especially on special occasions—e.g., after two large fires, and the memorial to war casualties.

39. Achievements

Until the turn of the century, Harvard depended especially on State Street, Boston, for financial aid. After 1900, New York became an important source of funds.

The campaigns of 1904 ($2,500,000), 1919 ($15 million), 1924 ($10 million), and 1956 to 1960 ($82,500,000), and the recent medical program of $58 million were especially successful, with the tercentenary effort of 1936 unsuccessful.

Clearly the yields were larger in 1956-1960 than in 1904 vis-à-vis the national income and a fortiori vis-à-vis enrollment. But alumni gives; a more meaningful index, rise less relatively than enrollment. The 1956-1960 receipts rose much more than those of 1919-1920 both in relation to income and enrollment. Unusual need, improved organization, rising interest in higher education, and high prosperity help explain the better record from 1956 to 1960.

The major funds came from the affluent despite strong efforts to squeeze the low-income group. A Harvard treasurer discussing the results of the years 1930 to 1950 referred to "the dominant role of larger gifts and bequests . . . nine-tenths of the money received in the last twenty years appears to have come from far less than one per cent of the donors."

In 1919-1920 the top 13 gifts yielded $1,500,000. In 1956-1959, the top 12 provided $22,800,000 and the top 102, $43,100,000. (By late 1959, there were 29,447 contributors.)

Of some interest is an average for gifts of 100, 168, 452 and 2,241 dollars in four drives—in the 1820s, 1830s, 1919-1920 and 1956 to 1958. The ratio of the average gift to per capita income in these four drives was not much out of line except that in 1919-1920 the returns were relatively low.

40. Buildings and Equipment

In the original Harvard Yard buildings had to be concentrated on the 1¼ acres available to the college. By 1814, more than 15 acres were available. By 1869, the university had accumulated 45 acres, with the value of land and buildings estimated at $1,649,826. Late in the nineteenth century, Harvard had 79 buildings (value of $3,380,000), which were not included as investments; 10 buildings ($243,000) were considered investments with no evaluation on the treasurer's books; and buildings occupied by university officers and employees, ($69,000). By 1910, the treasurer estimated land, buildings, and equipment conservatively at $12 million. By the late 1940s, Harvard had 150 buildings. Under Pusey, building advanced even more than under Lowell. In 10 years the university had spent or committed an amount in excess of $70 million, compared with $100 million in the first 312 years.

Inadequate space plagued the college through most of its history. The library, the chapel, dormitories, commons—all lacked space and especially in the eighteenth and nineteenth centuries.

The fire of Harvard Hall in 1764 was a disaster. In it "the most valuable of the halls, which with the best library and philosophical apparatus in America . . . utterly perished."

Harvard's physical expansion often received adverse comment. S. Eliot in 1849 complained of expenditures of $200,000 on four buildings, with three-quarters at the expense of the free funds of the college. He referred to the insane expenditures on buildings, "this taste for architectural abortions."

Maintenance costs indicate the importance of Harvard buildings at different times. Thus, maintenance for the buildings constructed in the years 1915 to 1948 of $1,878,000 roughly equaled those for buildings constructed in the preceding 215 years.

Trollope wrote: "The edifices used for the undergraduate chambers and for the lecture rooms are by no means handsome. They are very ugly brick buildings standing here and there without order. . . .It is almost astonishing that buildings so ugly should have been erected for such a purpose. . . ."

In the late nineteenth century, private interests began to compete with Harvard in the provisioning of Harvard dormitories. Eliot encouraged the building of expensive dormitories by private groups; but he failed to commit Lowell, who embarked on large Harvard enterprises. The private, high-priced buildings finally had to liquidate as Harvard, with no charge for capital, squeezed the private interests out.

A comparison of the cost of construction and insurance coverage is of interest. Thus, for three buildings constructed in the eighteenth century, the insured value in 1957 was 29 times the original costs. Insurance values vis-à-vis construction costs drop as construction moves closer to the present. The farther back we go the greater the windfall.

Some indication of rising costs is given by a comparison of the cost of providing a study in 1644—a little more than $10 compared with outlays of the order of $6,000 today.

Maintenance costs tend to be large in relation to original costs. Thus, for three buildings of the eighteenth century maintenance costs in 1957 were 84 percent of original costs; for buildings of 1916 to 1947 they were only 3 percent. The differences are explained largely by the low original costs of older buildings and their high maintenance costs.

Harvard does not generally include capital costs as part of the cost structure. A rough estimate of costs for land and buildings is about $300 million or an annual charge of $15 million.

41. Land Policy

One of Harvard's most troublesome problems was lack of land. Harvard opened with little more than one acre of land. How much more fortunate have the divisions of the University of California been that started with 1,000 to 2,000 acres. Much of Harvard's scanty resources had to go to the purchase of land. The problem is well reflected by the growth of Harvard's land resources.

Harvard might have been established in a place where more space would have been available. In fact, it was offered a site of 300 acres in Salem. But this was not acceptable. The Oxford-Cambridge precedent suggested a preference for Cambridge to the desolate wilderness and proximity to the ocean of Salem. Moreover, Cambridge offered the advantage of a great public works program needed as outward migrations and large imports brought a depression. Here was perhaps the first public works program in America.

According to a careful study by President Eliot, 106 transactions had yielded Harvard $82\frac{1}{3}$ acres by 1896. By 1910, there were 3,200 acres of which 80 acres were in Cambridge and 63 in Boston. But President Eliot was too optimistic when he said ". . . the University now owns land enough in Cambridge to make it certain that the setting of the University buildings will be an open one for many generations to come. . . ."

Land values varied greatly. Thus in 1858, values of Harvard's Cambridge land (10 parcels) varied from 3 cents a foot for some land near Divinity to 50 cents a corner of Holyoke and Harvard Street. By 1897, the average price of a foot for 70 acres in Cambridge was about $1 a foot. By 1964, the Amoco Station in Brattle Square sold for $28 a square foot and the Baird Atomic Property sold for $33 a square foot in 1967. Harvard has been offered some land in the central business district at $100 per square foot.[1]

---

1. I am indebted to Charles P. Whitlock, assistant to President Pusey, for some help on land values.

6
ENDOWMENTS

42. Why Endowment?

Endowment has been an important source of Harvard's income. In the nineteenth century endowment contributed roughly one-half of total income. Later it became much less important—with drops from about 20 to 4 percent for the nation's institutions of higher learning and from one-half to one-fifth of Harvard's income. Endowment income held up much better at Harvard than in the nation.

The relative decline in the nation is associated with the rise of enrollment—as enrollment increases the relative contribution of endowment falls; with the inflation—each dollar of endowment income yields less in goods and services; and with the reduction of the yield per dollar invested. Harvard's superior record may be explained by the recourse to investment in equities that yield more than fixed-interest assets; and the very large gifts and bequests received. The shift to equities was especially helpful.

With the erosion of investment income, Harvard has depended increasingly on current gifts. In periods of financial inadequacy the temptation is to seek current gifts. Thus, $10 million available for five years yields $2 million per year; but $10 million endowment provides but $500,000 per year.

Administrations tend to exaggerate the gains from endowment. They neglect the erosion associated with the rise of income related not only to inflation but also to rising productivity. On reasonable projections, in ten to fifteen years, the return on investment may be reduced by one-half in relation to per capita income and in fifty years by 90 percent.

43. Cumulation of Endowment Funds

From the very beginning, the financing of endowed chairs was inadequate, in that the yield was less than the salary paid for the chair. In 1721, T. Hollis, who provided funds for the first two chairs, wrote "if I proceed to nominate, as your letter urges me to do, he most be straitened, or he must break in upon the principal, neither of which is agreeable to me at this writing."

Providing adequate capital for salaries and scholarships was a perennial problem. By keeping chairs vacant and accumulating the income of endowed chairs, and in more recent times by diverting gift money to the older chairs, and allocating part of capital gains to these chairs, the governing boards raised the financial support more nearly to the level required to finance each chair. In general, the increases, relative to original gifts, are greater for the older gifts.

Treasurer W. H. Claflin, Jr., commenting on the longevity of the Mowlson bequest, ended by saying "297 years later the fund is still in existence and functioning according to her wishes."

44. The Decline of Endowment

Earlier we discussed the relationship between endowment and total income and its relative decline. That decline is explained by the rising income in the nation, and especially the impact of inflation, rising productivity, and also erosion related to bad management and violation of trust.

A frequent practice has been to finance deficits out of endowment funds in the expectation of raising money to repay later. Often it has proved impossible to raise the necessary funds for repayment. Another issue has been the propriety of using capital gains or income put into endowment funds to cover current expenses.

Harvard's record over-all has been surprisingly good. Capital consumption was also a serious matter in the Kirkland period of the first quarter of the nineteenth century. Inflationary periods, e.g., the first half of the eighteenth century, were of course reflected in much erosion of endowment.

45. Endowment Drives—Objectives

In general, Harvard sought large sums in a drive about once in a generation: 1904, 1919, 1950s. How much for the plant and how much for the faculty is one of the large choices. On numerous occasions, the governing boards received criticism for favoring the plant over men—even as early as the Puritan period. Eliot chose to spend on men rather than on buildings and equipment. Conant belonged to the same school.

46. The Issue of Restricted Endowment

In 1935, President Conant noted that although Harvard had $125 million of endowment the university, once allowance was made for commitments, had but $50,000 annually of free money. Throughout Harvard's history, the complaint has been excessive restrictive, and inadequate free, money. It was seldom that more than 10 to 20 percent of Harvard's endowment income was unrestricted.

The case for more free money was that the university could more easily finance unexpected needs inclusive of aid to programs temporarily in difficulties. Moreover, the more the gift is restricted the less likely it is to perform satisfactorily in a changing world.

In some respects the excessive recourse to restrictions can be treated. For example, it is possible to combine restrictions and some choice to donors, as President Pusey did in the program for Harvard College. Greater recourse to annual giving also increases funds available for unrestricted use, as does greater reliance on tuition.

47. Diversion of Endowment Funds

An impoverished college is tempted to divert income from endowment to uses not intended by the donor. In the first two hundred years of Harvard history in particular, poor administration encouraged misuse of funds. In the nineteenth century, the college appropriated returns on funds earned in excess of 5 percent.

More direct diversions were also in use: Treasurer J. Hancock in the Revolutionary War was guilty of diversions. In 1690, Increase Mather succeeded in obtaining aid for his grandson because Increase had obtained certain funds for Harvard. This was scarcely a proper use of this gift. The Hopkins Trust of the early eighteenth century also raised problems.

Numerous other complaints of misuse are in the records: 1739, 1825, 1870-1871, 1908, 1913, and 1915. For example, Professor Sparks complained of the excessive burden put on the McLain Professorship of History "diminishing instead of increasing a branch of study [history] expressly intended by the Foundation of the professorship to be fostered and enlarged."

48. Endowments: Problems of Evaluation and Growth

A troublesome problem arises from the manner of allocating income among the various claimants of Harvard's endowment. Harvard's approach has been to tie the income of each fund to its book value. In periods when market value has greatly exceeded book value, this approach favors new gifts over old. A gift of $1 million book value of, say, 1850 may be worth a market value of $5 million today. A new gift of $1 million would then receive the same return as the 1850 gift with a book value of $1 million and of market of $5 million.

In 1861-1862 the treasurer noted:

The large percentage of income arises from the fact that the invested funds of the College are much in excess of their valuation upon the books of the Treasurer. The division of all the earnings of these investments gives to funds recently placed, at their full value, upon the books, the benefits of the increase in value of the investments of earlier years and suggests the propriety of new valuation. . . .

Again, in 1875-1876, the treasurer was disturbed by the decline of yield of investments on top of which excessive income was being credited to the new funds at the expense of old funds, now highly inflated in value.

The case for Harvard's tie-in with book value rests largely on the assumption that recent gifts reflect current educational values more than old gifts. Harvard can, of course, neutralize the effects of this system of accounting and notably by distributing realized capital gains, a procedure of great importance in the 1950s and 1960s. Distribution of capital gains reduces the advantage conferred upon newer gifts and increases the share going to older donations. In 1969 Harvard abandoned evaluation at book values.

49. The Structure of Investments

Harvard's investments in its first century were largely in bonds, that is, notes or loans to individuals.

In 1668, Harvard's stock (investments) amounted to £863, or between $2,500 and $3,000. A substantial part of interest was overdue.

In these early years, returns were as high as 9 percent and even as late as the 1860s, as high as 7 percent. Land was not available for investment because there was too much of it and it was, therefore, too cheap. Grants of land yielded small returns and by the first quarter of the nineteenth century the college had begun to dispose of most of its gifts of land. In the years from 1700 up to the Revolution inflation and unsatisfactory economic conditions eroded many of Harvard's investments. The inflationary pressure affected some types of investments more than others. Apparently the college protected itself more effectively through investments in loans than in property. Harvard might well not have survived had not its great treasurer, Ebenezer Storer, speculated by investing in government securities rather than in paper money.

In the nineteenth century, the great advances were in investments in bonds at the expense of notes and mortgages and a strong interest in properties yielding rent. But by 1869, equities accounted for 13 percent of assets and equity income, 22 percent of income, a relationship pointing to the high returns to be had from purchases of common stocks.

The great rise of investments was in the twentieth century – from $10 million in 1900 to an amount in excess of a billion dollars by the middle 1960s. Rises in market values and new money largely account for the gains. The university was slow to exploit rising prices, profits, and productivity in the economy by purchasing equities after 1900. From 1930 to 1940, equities rose from 27 to 44 percent, at the expense of real estate and notes and mortgages. From 1930 to 1937 the yield on common stocks vis-à-vis that on good bonds had risen by about $3\frac{1}{2}$ percent. In the 1940s, policy was cautious. Despite inflation and great improvement in the economic situation, and the large rise of yield on common stocks, investments in equities rose only by four percentage points.

From 1950 to 1965, Harvard's investment policies greatly improved. In this period the price of common stock rose by 380 percent and yield in high quality bonds rose from 2.62 to 4.69 percent. The treasurer did not purchase bonds in large quantities despite the $5\frac{1}{2}$ percent relative gain in yield of bonds. Instead, the university sought equities – they increased in value per year about 3 times as much as the rise in the yield differential in favor of bonds.

Some fears persist that purchase of equities may bring losses if purchase prices are high. But note that Harvard is at an advantage compared to other investors because institutions of higher learning do not have to respond to declines in value by liquidating at low prices.

A problem for institutions of higher learning arises when large investments are made in growth stocks. Current sellers of services, e.g., the faculty, may then be deprived of their appropriate shares of income. The college chooses capital gains rather than rises of current income.

Harvard generally commingles its investments in a general fund. This is an economical approach and besides protects against excessive concentration of investments, with resultant larger risks. Trends of special investments, reflecting increased trust in the university, accounted for $\frac{2}{11}$ of investments at the end of the nineteenth century, $\frac{1}{9}$ in 1915 and $\frac{1}{50}$ by 1965.

50. The Yield on Harvard's Investments

How much Harvard earns on its investments depends on various factors. Much depends on the interest and profits had from the nation's assets generally. The stability of the currency is related to the first. When inflation prevails, the return tends to be larger than otherwise. Creditors seek compensation for the reduction of real value of money used to repay debts. In periods of deflation, such as the latter part of the nineteenth century or in the 1930s, interest rates and profits tend to be low. Intervention by the government to some extent determines the returns. Thus, in 1681, money was invested in loans at 8 percent. The government's later ceiling of 6 percent cut down returns. The structure of investments is important. Large investments in bonds or other fixed-return investments preclude the college from obtaining compensation for rising prices. Again, heavy recourse to equities (common stocks) tends to raise yields in periods when prices, profits, and equities are rising in value. Returns depend on the risks incurred. Excessive investments in equities with uncertain prospects may well reduce returns. Investments in fixed-return assets may assure expected returns in dollars, but compensation for inflation is thereby ruled out.

At times Harvard would accept reduced payments on its investments when adverse conditions prevailed.

Harvard depended heavily in its first 150 years on bonds; that is, loans at a fixed rate of interest. Returns were kept down as many failed to meet their commitments. In the eighteenth century, inflation was the rule. Hence, Harvard's returns were disappointing even though the college tried to protect itself by requiring that loans be repaid not in pounds sterling but in a corresponding weight of silver. In the nineteenth century the big change was the rising interest in bond issues, now becoming available in large amounts, and, secondarily, substantial investments in real estate. In the inflationary period, notably the Civil War and its aftermath, the university responded to some extent by transferring to assets that rise in value with inflation.

The twentieth century was also largely an inflationary century. In the 1930s the treasurer purchased equities in substantial amounts, although this was not an inflationary period. But the yield on common stocks was much above that of bonds, and equities were available at low prices. Financial authorities, however, were slow to extend equity investments in the 1940s. From 1950 on, the university managed to obtain returns 3 times as large by purchasing equities generally rising in value, than by extending investments in bonds, yielding 5 percent more than stocks vis-à-vis in 1950. It is rather surprising that the drop of (over-all) yield was only one percent in the 1930s, a small drop in view of the large decline in output as compared with a 3 percent drop in the years 1870 to 1900, this period being one of relatively satisfactory conditions.

Net returns depend on the relative amounts put into equities, bonds, real estate, and other categories. The more, relatively, in high-yielding assets the higher the over-all return.

8
SPECIAL STUDIES

51. Productivity

The productivity of a college or university can be measured by its output — teaching, research, community service — in relation to the input of teachers, plant, etc. As measured by graduates of quality, Harvard's output has been remarkable. The graduates and faculty have made vast contributions to knowledge inclusive of many of the great discoveries of the last hundred years. But it should be stressed that part of the credit goes to the unusually high quality of its input, that is, the able students and large gifts which have provided so many of the resources needed for teaching and procurement and care of the plant.

Over most of Harvard's history costs have been high. At times—e.g., in the 1820s—the explanation was poor management. But time and again Harvard authorities defended themselves on the grounds that Harvard's location necessarily meant high costs; and, more important, the high costs could be justified by the superior quality of Harvard's output.

In 1845, the charge was made that Yale's costs per student were but $38 per year and Harvard's, $104. But Harvard spokesmen replied that students at both schools got as much as they paid for.

How much an education costs depends in part on the services offered. Harvard insisted upon the collegiate method of instruction with the college assuming responsibilities for teaching, praying, dining, sleeping and provisions for medical services. Hence, the costs were high.

When the college was confronted with crises, as for example in much of the eighteenth century and the first half of the nineteenth, the response was to increase work loads, amalgamate professorial chairs, depend more on young and less costly faculty members, reduce services, and increase prices charged.

The faculty was not always responsive to the demands of the governing boards. The faculty often objected to heavy teaching loads, and often was not impressed by the quality of the product turned out.

Famous professors had many disagreements with the presidents, and particularly on the issue of work loads and the educational practices. In 1837, Henry Longfellow, commenting on his arduous tasks, accused the authorities of giving inadequate weight to "the kind and amount of preparation necessary for an ordinary recitation."

Henry Adams was no more enthusiastic when he said:

The lecture room was futile enough but the faculty-room was worse . . . several score of the best educated, most agreeable, and personally the most sociable people in American united in Cambridge, to make a social desert that would have starved a polar bear. . . .

. . . Four years of Harvard College, if successful, resulted in an autobiographical blank, a mind on which only a water-mark had been stamped.

Another unhappy member of the faculty, William James, in 1894, revealed "When vacation comes, my brain is so tired that I can read nothing serious for a month. . . ."

Harvard's governing boards, however, often rated the faculty high. They pointed to the improved quality of students admitted, the rise of enrollment, the rise of faculty-student ratios, the improving quality of education of both faculty and students, the division of labor for faculty members that was introduced in the eighteenth century, the written examination of the midnineteenth century, the expansion of the curriculum beginning in the first quarter of the nineteenth century and accelerating under Eliot, the departmentalization of the college, the increase of hours of instruction, the improvement of student behavior—all of these suggested the rising quality of the faculty and their important contribution.

Until the last 50 to 75 years, the emphasis of Harvard's contribution was on teaching. Indeed, in 1825, a corporation committee conceded it would be a great honor to the college "if we had professors, who might confine their instruction in each department to such as had mastered its rudiments. . .and extend the boundaries of science of their own." Eliot, in the 1870s, was still not convinced that Harvard had responsibilities for research.

Harvard authorities were aware that productivity would rise with increasing numbers, not only in the classroom but also in commons. Yet there were often objections to increasing numbers. In 1845, for example, President Quincy remarked that increasing numbers "bring increased care, anxiety, and labor in instruction and supervision, greater danger of noisy assemblages, more materials for acquiring of idle, dissipated, rude and ill-regulated habits and manners. . . ."

Harvard's productivity depends on many factors. The method of teaching is germane: the substitution of lectures for recitations, the supplementation of lectures by small classes, and the increasing recourse to assistants who relieve the professors and president of much routine work. All these improve the product. The elective system is very costly also and can be justified only by the additional gains of the educational product; and it requires scrutiny of the resultant proliferation of courses.

Eliot would also have increased productivity by improved admission procedures and requirements of more work and fewer vacations by students. Productivity gains might also be had by consolidation of Harvard schools with those of their competitors. But legal obstacles precluded most of these gains.

52. Growth of Harvard

Harvard's growth can be measured by various indexes: enrollment, graduates, capital funds, size of faculty, the rise of faculty vis-à-vis students; and, finally, the quality of the product.

In assessing growth by periods, one should allow for such items as price movements, the levels of income, and similar variables. For example, from 1910 to 1965, the gross national product rose by 11 times. Hence, any assessment of growth should take into account the reduced significance of a given rise in a period like the 1960s, as compared with the pre-World War I period.

One significant index of growth is the volume of expenditures. But to be highly significant, the rise should be analyzed. What is the expenditure per student? How much at stable prices? To what extent does the rate of growth reflect an improved product, e.g., the Eliot elective system with its accompanying rise of courses and faculty?

Growth was phenomenal under Eliot. But it was also remarkable under Lowell, Conant, and Pusey. The growth from Eliot's days on should be associated in substantial part with the opening and growth of professional or graduate schools. Wars cut enrollment under Lowell and Conant. Under Lowell and Conant, rising prices reduced the rate of growth although the adverse effects of the inflation were felt more by the faculty, with salaries largely frozen, than by the university. Under Eliot and Conant, the emphasis was on growth of the faculty; under Lowell and Pusey, more on the plant.

Most of Harvard's growth has been achieved in the years since the early twentieth century. For example, in the 273 years, 1636 to 1909, endowment per year rose by $83,500; but the gains of investments for the

54 years, 1909 to 1963, was $17,500,000 per year or 210 times as much per year in the later period. Enrollment in the university was but 1,097 in 1870 and 4,046 in 1910; but by 1966, almost 15,000.

The first large rate of growth occurred in the first half of the nineteenth century. In the earlier years stagnating economies, wars, intensive inflation (over much of the eighteenth century), rising competition, and obstacles to profitable investments of the university's funds all conspired to retard the rate of growth. Eliot, discussing the years 1630 to 1810, praised the president and fellows for having "brought the college safely through a series of wars, paper money periods, commercial panic, the Revolution . . . and were naturally proud of their record."

53. Issues of Administration

On the whole, Harvard has had an effective administrative setup provided by the government in 1650 and modified only in detail since. The major responsibilities for receiving gifts, disposing of assets, investing the university funds, and approving appointments rests on a selfperpetuating Board of Seven inclusive of the president and treasurer.

In Harvard's long history, resident fellows, the state government, and the overseers have challenged the corporation's authority. In the 1720s and the 1820s the resident fellows claimed that they alone were eligible for election to the corporation.

The government influence, great at first, gradually was eroded. In 1846, S. Eliot wrote that Harvard would never succeed despite its vast resources until "the preponderance of state influences in its Council is so far reduced that a mere politician shall never set his foot within her walls."

In the 1850s, the commonwealth attempted to reduce the power of the corporation. It would increase the numbers on the corporation, reduce their terms to six years and have them elected by the representatives of the people. This attempt fortunately failed.

In the 1850s, the overseers engaged in an all-out struggle with the corporation, contending that the overseers could exercise important veto powers against the corporation on fundamental fiscal issues. Again the corporation won.

The Harvard system, with the small corporation which retains major authority and is subject to frequent calls, with the overseers prying and retaining some veto powers and even prodding in some important areas, and with the president a full-time officer, with considerable control, has obtained large resources and managed them well.

54. Repercussions of Monetary Instability on Harvard's Economy

In the Puritan period, Harvard was adversely affected by the shortage of money that prevailed in the colony. With metallic money so scarce, the college had to accept much "country pay," that is, commodities like corn and cattle, rather than paper or metallic money. The lack of money depressed the economy and therefore impaired the flow of funds to Harvard.

But the long-run problem was excessive money and inflationary pressures. The New England pound depreciated in relation to the British pound and to silver. By the middle of the eighteenth century, the decline in the value of the New England pound was acknowledged by a conversion of the old tenor to new tenor at a ratio of 7½ old to 1 new.

The substantial and frequent inflations eroded Harvard's capital in the eighteenth century. Loans were repaid in depreciating currency, with resultant capital losses. The losses occurred especially in the Revolutionary War period. And they prevailed even though Harvard protected itself often by demanding repayment in silver equivalent of loans made. That Harvard lost much is attested by the declining contribution of endowment income during inflationary periods as well as by large reductions in asset values, e.g., Treasurer T. Hubbard in April, 1755 "put down the capital sum at only one-fifth of the nominal sums originally given in consequence of the college funds having sunk for a number of years antecedent to 1750, by the depreciation of the paper currency."

It was especially in the Revolutionary War period that Harvard lost money as a result of inflation. The college, by 1786, had received £17,875 in paper. At that time its metal value was £2,570. Hence, the loss was £15,304.

A decision in 1777 to invest all future funds in a Continental Loan Office Certificate or in Massachusetts Treasury notes saved the college. The new government ultimately supported its securities, but not its paper money.

Harvard's tussles with inflation did not end with the Revolutionary period. In three major wars, Harvard later experienced serious inflation. In the Civil War period, the results were not disastrous, in part because the rise of price was large rather than of dangerous proportions and in part because price reductions followed the rise. But in World War I and World War II the costs were great, not so much to the university as to the faculty. The faculty had to accept large reductions in real income, with corrective measures slow to be mobilized.

55. The Economics of the Curriculum

It was especially under Eliot that the costs of instruction escalated. Eliot was not the founder of the elective system, but he was its main accelerator. He was determined to bring languages and science into a respectable position in relation to the old liberal arts subjects.

Eliot was aware that the elective system was costly. Its cost is suggested by a rise in the number of teachers of professorial grade from 45 to 194 in Eliot's forty years and of other teachers from 14 to 416. In fifty years, the number of hours of instruction had risen from ninety to about a thousand.

The rising instructional costs should not be exclusively charged to the elective system. Aside from the demands of the elective system, greater recourse to small-group instruction was on the agenda; and the advance of professional training was a function of many forces. Moreover, the rising popularity of the elective system attracted vast numbers of students, with accompanying falls or rises in per student costs,

and also vast gains in national income that could be associated with the influx into higher education.

56. The Library

Harvard probably has the most outstanding university library in the world. Its ninety libraries inclusive of Widener house almost 8 million volumes and account for about one-twentieth of the university's $150 million of expenditures. These outlays do not seem excessive for a great research library. The costs are roughly one-sixth of the outlays for salaries for faculty members.

Over Harvard's history, purchases of books have often been excessive, because the purchases were greater than could be accommodated by the necessary supplementary services of cataloguing, housing and other services. When a book cannot be catalogued, it is generally unavailable; and when space is not to be had, the book is of little use.

The problem of cataloguing harassed librarians from the very beginning. Thomas Hollis complained in the early eighteenth century that it was difficult to give books to Harvard because, with the primitive cataloguing available, the potential donor was ignorant of the books already acquired.

From the very beginning, acquiring space for Harvard's books was difficult. Books had to be stored in a manner that precluded ready access. Even with the availability of Widener at a cost of $3,500,000 some fifty years ago, the problem of space was not solved.

Another troublesome issue has been the stealing and defacing of books by students. Undoubtedly the college spent too much time on dealing with thefts and damage. Fear of losses reduced the usefulness of the library. Librarians tended to become more interested in acquiring books than in making them available.

Rising costs of libraries are frequently explained by the diseconomics with increasing size; that is, an additional book costs more as the size of the library increases: cataloguing, replacing books on shelves, the rising importance of esoteric items, and other factors, according to Harvard authorities, induce increases in unit costs.

In one respect Harvard libraries experience economical operation. The librarians offer relatively limited services to the consumer of their product.

Financing the library with its rising demands has always been a tough problem. Over most of Harvard's history, endowment for the library has been most inadequate. Under Conant, however, large sums were transferred to the library from university funds.

What concern librarians are the rising costs in the years to come. If the library doubled every twenty years, there would be 32 million volumes at Harvard in forty years. No wonder that Provost Buck urged greater attention to quality than quantity. The toll of inflation also raises costs though the library officials seem to overestimate the likely wage inflation. Rising competition for books and library services raises costs even more. In a recent period of thirteen years, the consumer price index rose by 28 percent as against 62 percent for books. Costs are also destined to rise because the largest increases will be in the size of the faculty; the next largest, graduate students. Their demands on the library are especially large.

57. Books

Until the Civil War Harvard authorities were much interested in the books assigned to students. Thus, in 1735, the corporation approved an agreement with Judah Monis, the Hebrew professor, for the printing of a thousand copies of his Hebrew grammar. The corporation fixed the price (adjusted to rising price of silver) as well as the payment to the treasury for each copy sold by Monis.

Harvard's official interest was related to the high price of books in Harvard's first two hundred years, the need of keeping the cost of a Harvard education down, and also the assumption by the governing boards of some responsibility for the quality of books used by students.

In its anxiety to provide good books at low prices, the college at various times eliminated intermediaries, bargained with competing publishers, sought trade discounts for large sales to the college, and negotiated separately with each segment of the industry.

58. Nonfaculty Wages

In recent years, nonfaculty wages have become increasingly important. Thus, whereas salaries at Harvard were 90 percent of all expenditures in 1832-1833 by 1966-1967 they amounted to about 28 percent. Hence, wages account for an increasing share of expenditures. The plant also absorbs a rising share of outlays. Librarians, stewards, janitors, and unskilled workers were especially vocal in their efforts to improve their economic status. The librarian in 1831 wanted to know how he could get along with ten children on the pay of $1,000 a year. Many of the complaints were related to the rise of prices — even in the 1830s and 1840s, when prices were not rising. The dissatisfied workers pointed rightly to the rising incomes generally which they were not sharing.

9

SCHOOLS

59. The Harvard Medical School

The medical school, Harvard's first professional school, opened in 1783. Its early growth was slow, for its resources were small, and it had to depend at first largely on contributions by the faculty and on fees. Almost every twenty years a space problem emerged, with the school begging from the government, the corporation, the public, or the faculty for the funds to build a new plant.

The largest growth occurred not in the first hundred years but in the last sixty to seventy years. Over the years 1910 to 1965, expenditures rose by 4 percent a year on the average, or, compounded, by 7 times. With an allowance for the rise of prices, the increase of expenditures was 182 percent. Expenditures in the eighteen years ending in 1906 averaged about $1 million a year; but by 1965-1966, in excess of $22 million. This rise in dollars of stable purchasing power was more than 6 times.

At the founding of the school it was decided:

to elect into these professorships gentlemen of public spirit and distinguished ability who would undertake the business for the present for the fees. . . .the utility of the Instruction will soon be so obvious that it will find great encouragement among us, from gentlemen of liberal minds and easy circumstances, who are friends to the University. . . .

Harvard's fees tended to be high just because the faculty had to depend on them, but competition of other schools tended to bring fees down. Even as late as 1888, endowment contributed only one-sixth as much income as fees. But by the 1960s the structure of income had greatly changed. Endowment income yielded twice as much as fees, which in turn now financed one-third of the salaries of the school. Tuition provided only 8 percent of the school's income in 1965-1966 as compared with $18\frac{1}{2}$ percent for the university.

Endowment income was still relatively small as late as the 1880s, but the danger of excessive recourse to fees was becoming increasingly evident. At the hundredth anniversary in 1883, it was said "any institution which is essentially dependent on the number of paying students it can draw, must be tempted to sacrifice its higher aims to popularity. . . ." But even by 1901, endowment was but $1,098,500. Largely as a result of its massive campaign in the 1960s, endowment had escalated to $75,500,000 by June, 1966.

Now the medical school depends heavily on endowment income – 42 percent of relevant expenditures as compared with 30 percent for the university. The school's miraculous $58-million drive in the 1960s was the major factor making this possible.

Because of the limited endowment funds and heavy reliance on fees, the school has had to depend heavily on gifts. But they were slow in coming. Large gifts were scarce.

Under Eliot, the greatest advances in medical education prevailed. Though temporarily enrollment suffered, in the long run quality greatly improved.

60. The Economics of the Law School

The law school faculty from the very beginning spent generously on books. The allocation of funds for the library raises these expenditures away above the relative amounts spent for libraries by the university or other major schools. By 1927, Professor Dicey reported that the Harvard Law School library "constitutes the most perfect collection of the legal records of the English people to be found in any part of the English-speaking world."

Harvard's famous law school is now 150 years old. From the very beginning it depended heavily on student fees to finance not only its faculty but also its library and buildings. Its greatest lack has been endowment income. The school, therefore, has had to depend disproportionately on fees and, in more recent years, on current gifts and particularly on annual giving. Endowment drives have not been spectacularly successful so far.

The contrast between the medical and the law school is striking. The former has 3 times as much endowment income and only one-third as many students. Hence, the medical school has 9 times as much endowment income per student as the law school.

In a recent year the law school obtained 60 percent of relevant income from tuition, 19 percent from endowment, and 20 percent from current gifts. The university figures were 35, 39 and 26 percent, respectively.

Enrollment rose at an uneven pace. Even at the outset of the Eliot period students numbered only 165. The large gains occurred from 1881 to 1891, with 285 students; to 655 in 1901; to 719 in 1908; and to about 1,600 in the middle of the 1960s.

The extent of competition, the prestige of the school, the national market for lawyers, the transportation availability, and general costs all affected enrollment. In the days of Joseph Story (1829 to 1845), the prestige was high and enrollment grew rapidly. With his death, enrollment suffered. In 1828, enrollment was 4; by Story's death in 1845, it had risen to 156; by 1859, it had dropped to 100.

An overseers' committee in 1849 reported that "Story must be regarded as the largest pecuniary benefactor of the Law School, and one of the largest pecuniary benefactors of the University."

Again, under Langdell (and Eliot) in the years 1870 to 1900, the gains were tremendous. The Langdell case system and the Langdell-Eliot raising of standards were decisive. Eliot was surprised at the sound finance of the school despite its rising standards.

Growth was spectacular after 1910. By 1965, enrollment had doubled; the full-time faculty rose from 10 to 62; and the student-faculty ratio dropped from 81 to 1 to 27 to 1. In this period the budget had increased by more than 30 times.

With rising enrollment, finances improved. But the increasing numbers of faculty members and pressure for rising pay absorbed much of the increased funds. Thus, in 1839, Professor Greenleaf asked for a rise of pay from $1,500 to $2,500 at a time when Story was content with $1,000. (Later Story was offered the unprecedented sum of $4,000.)

61. Professional Schools

Except for medicine, law, divinity, and dentistry, the professional schools are of recent origin for the most part. The friends of the college were often hostile to the founding and growth of these schools. Even as late as 1849 an overseers' committee had to defend these schools against those who were primarily interested in the college. The committee acknowledged that these schools were "in some quarters a subject of disquietude and even reproach. . . . Professional schools must exist somewhere in our country. . . ."

It was especially Eliot who was responsible for the growth and improved quality of these schools. He shifted emphasis from rewards for attendance to those for the quality of performance; and he poured resources, in part through the expansion of his elective program, into these schools. His greatest interest was in the graduate school of arts and sciences. But he assumed the chair at faculty meetings in all these schools.

The science school was founded in 1847. Inadequate funds, poor management, excessive recourse to fees, and the tough competition of M.I.T. and Yale all contributed to the early troubles of this school. Eliot tried to achieve an integration of M.I.T. with Harvard at the outset of his regime and on other occasions, but without success.

Eliot pushed for the foundation of a graduate school of business early in the twentieth century. This school depended heavily on fees and loans, and moved close to the policy of full-cost tuition. A gift of $5 million by George Baker in the 1920s and a large successful drive in the 1940s provided some endowment money. But the school on the whole depended primarily on fees and current gifts. The large recourse to fees was especially embarrassing in periods of economic depression.

No school, with the possible exception of dental medicine, has had as much financial difficulty as the divinity school, founded in 1816. Its financial obstacles included the lack of resources of its constituency inclusive of clergy, teachers, and students. Over most of the school's history and despite Eliot's determination to raise tuition for divinity to the university level, the school's tuition has been much below the university level. Its small enrollment meant high unit costs as well as reduced tuition money.

Of some interest in the structure of income and outgo of nine professional schools, and the costs per student in 1965-1966. The costs per student, for example, varied from $13,505 in medicine (and high costs for the other two health schools) to $4,711 for divinity and $4,529 for design. Small-scale operations and high unit costs, because of the nature of the training, explain the high costs in health schools. Education has had almost as serious financial problems as divinity. It also has a low-income constituency and has been troubled by disagreements on methods of instruction. But increased operations (e.g., number of students) should depress unit costs. Arts and sciences unit costs are relatively low — eighth of the ten schools. The rising graduate enrollment tends to raise costs of arts and sciences.

Among Harvard schools, business has depended relatively heavily on tuition and current gifts; dental medicine, on the government and endowment; design, on tutition and endowment income; education, on government grants; law, on tuition; medicine, on the government; public health, on the government; and arts and sciences, on tutition and endowment income.

62. Radcliffe

At present, Radcliffe turns over to Harvard 88 percent of its tuition money and in return the Harvard College of Arts and Science assumes responsibility for Radcliffe's instruction. Harvard's student income in 1966-1967 accounted for 38 percent of its total income, exclusive of government contracts and grants. By excluding room and board, we estimate tuition and fees at 28 percent of the costs of Harvard instruction. On the same basis, Radcliffe's contribution should be 3.6 times its tuition. But since Radcliffe turns over to Harvard only 88 percent of tuition, Radcliffe should give Harvard 4.1 times as much as it actually does.

From this we might draw the conclusion that Radcliffe has obtained a favorable agreement. Note, however, this calculation is based on average costs of a Harvard education in arts and sciences. Should one estimate the marginal costs, that is, the additional cost associated with the joint instruction, then Harvard does not seem nearly so much exploited. It is not clear that Harvard's expenditures for instruction and plant rise by more than $2 million (Radcliffe payments to Harvard), because it assumes the responsibility of Radcliffe's instruction. In most courses, the increase of enrollment by 20 percent — the Radcliffe share of Harvard-Radcliffe enrollment — would not involve the hiring of more professors, although some additional junior faculty members would be needed.

Radcliffe contributes greatly to Harvard's product in the sense that the presence of Radcliffe makes Harvard a much more attractive college. The result is a larger reservoir from which to draw Harvard men, and hence a higher average quality. This is undoubtedly an important offset to any subsidies provided by Harvard. These gains are aside from those that result from the training of 2,600 women of unusually high quality.

Eliot was cautious about not spending Harvard money for Radcliffe. In 1893, he wrote that the corporation would take charge of Radcliffe once its sponsors had added $250,000 to its current endowment.

10
ACCOUNTING

63. Accounting Problems

Harvard's accounting has been and is deficient in some respects. In the early years, the steward would often present net figures for his operations, e.g., receipts minus costs, and thus present less than full accounts. Often items did not appear in the total of disbursements. For example, the Colonial government's payments of salaries were generally not recorded. Another peculiarity was that the president and other officials would at times purchase for the college through their private accounts, and later conclude the transaction with the college. Some individuals would even invest privately on behalf of the college.

This treatment of capital items was unsatisfactory into the nineteenth century. Current operations would be commingled with capital items. Thus, in 1770, different assets, cash, and loans were treated similarly.

Treatment of capital items remained a problem through most of Harvard's history. Even today, the handling of capital gains and the manner of allocation of income from investments are subjects of much discussion. In 1891, the university established a gain and loss account for general investments. By 1909, the account had a balance of $575,499. One might contend that the accumulation of these reserves in a general account involved a perversion of endowment in that these accumulations belonged to individual accounts.

Over much of Harvard's history the authorities paid out less than the earnings on investment. Here again, one might raise some issues concerning allocation of resources. Where donors specified special investments, the returns on these would be credited to the relevant accounts. Other earnings would be credited to the interest account and then be allocated over the accounts under general investments.

Though generally the managers of Harvard's funds were highly competent and faithful to their trust, at times the college used endowment funds to finance construction, or to meet current expenses. The effects on endowment were unfortunate. Often the treasurer failed to collect income due on endowments for many years.

Perhaps the most blatant case of mismanagement came under Kirkland's administration in the first quarter of the nineteenth century. At least the errors of the Kirkland period brought much-improved management, and particularly monthly and annual statements by the treasurer as well as control by the corporation of all disbursements.

Harvard has not really taken much trouble with cost accounting. Institutions of higher learning tend to neglect this kind of accounting, partly because it is difficult, when several products are turned out, to discover the costs of each. Even today, the treasurer's report reveals investments, income, and expenditures of the various departments and little more. The treasurer does not tell us how much instruction of undergraduates, or of graduates, or research, or various other services costs. They only give us the outlays on wages, salaries, plant maintenance, etc., items of considerably less significance than those we would like to have.

PART

1

STUDENTS

1

Geographical Representation

The Issues

Harvard is now much more of a national university than it ever was. But the trend toward national representation has been most uneven. Henry Dunster, who was president of Harvard from 1640 to 1654, considered it much more than a Massachusetts or a New England college. In 1653, he referred to his students as pupils "coming out of other Colonies, Ilands, and countries, whether England itself or others." He affirmed a responsibility to other places. Samuel Eliot Morison lists a number of students at this time from foreign provinces and lands out of the small numbers registered. A current observer (1651) commented on the English residence of some students, "This hath been a place certainly more free from temptations to lewdness than ordinarily England hath been . . . ."

In the years 1673 through 1707, Harvard was more provincial than under Dunster and Chauncy (classes of 1642 through 1671). Of 324 students in 1673 through 1707, 52 came from Connecticut Colony and Valley, 8 from New Hampshire, and 1 from Rhode Island. As small as the numbers coming from outside of Massachusetts were, Harvard at this time was more broadly based than during a good part of the eighteenth century. The lack of a national base is suggested also by the absence of a single New Yorker from the years 1737 to 1790. [1]

Harvard's enrollment outside of Massachusetts was only 15 percent in 1826–1827 whereas Yale's out-side Connecticut was 55 percent. The latter's strong competitive position in the second quarter of the nineteenth century was evident especially in her large enrollment from the South and West. But by the late 1860s, Harvard had gained both absolutely and relatively, for Harvard's outside representation accounted for 67 percent versus 80 percent for Yale. [2]

Of the class of 1964, only Nevada, Hawaii, and Alaska of the fifty states had no students at Harvard. Why has Harvard become so broadly based? One factor clearly has been the improvement of transportation. In the seventeenth century the trip from Salem to Cambridge was much more arduous and relatively costly than the trip from Los Angeles to Cambridge was in 1965. In the discussion of the increasing geographical diversity, this factor is scarcely ever mentioned. For example, the large gains from non-New England areas in the years 1952 to 1960 are generally related to the growing prestige of Harvard, the rise of aid, inclusive of the Conant National Scholarship Program, the improved organization for recruiting, the desire for a broader base, and hence larger numbers from which to recruit. But as important as all of these factors were, surely the broadening of the geographical base would not have been nearly so great if the days or even months of travel in the past had not been converted to hours of travel.

---

1. Samuel Eliot Morison, *Harvard College in the Seventeenth Century*, 1936, pp. 76–77, 448–449 and *Admission to Harvard College*, 1960, pp. 29–30.

2. See especially *Annual Report of the President of Columbia College*, 1870, pp. 58–59, 62–63, 79, 82, (my calculations); cf. C. F. Thwing, *The American College*, 1897, p. 154.

Another factor has received too little attention; namely, the declining relative economic significance of Massachusetts and New England in the economic life of the country. Unless Harvard broadened its base, its contribution was likely to suffer. To give one example: in the fifty years from 1910 to 1960, New England's share of national population declined by almost one-half and Massachusetts' by slightly more than one-half. In addition, her relative per capita income declined. When President Conant first announced his plans for national scholarships, I recall apprising him of the economics of this new program; that is, that as a result of the national scholarships Harvard would be able to tap the centers of great population growth and relatively rising per capita income. In this connection it is of some interest that Harvard students from the central and western states are attracted by larger aid relative to their numbers than other sections.[3]

Eliot was one of the first to understand these issues. In his 1882-1883 report, he stated that the slow increase in New England population, and the influx of foreigners, many of them Roman Catholics, would cause a decline, at least temporarily, in enrollment at New England colleges unless students would come increasingly from other states.[4]

Harvard's rise to a great national university is of relatively recent origin. A famous graduate of the Class of 1852, writing in 1917, apprised Harvard's provincial position even as late as mid-nineteenth century:

Harvard College at the time I entered it was a comparatively small affair, and as provincial and local as could well be imagined, and the idea of its ever becoming the great national university had, I think, never entered into anybody's head. The students in my first year [1848-1849] numbered only 549. ... My own class and all the classes of that time were composed chiefly of New England boys, a very few coming from New York, and about an equal number from the South, whose people of wealth had long been in the habit of sending their boys to Harvard. I call it provincial and local because its scope and outlook hardly extended beyond the boundaries of New England. Besides which it was very denominational, being held exclusively in the hands of Unitarians ....[5]

In analyzing the geographical distribution of Harvard students, we should also consider the effects on the regions sending students to Harvard and those accepting them. In the last generation, congressional leaders and others have indulged in spirited debates on the wisdom of exporting students from talent-deficient areas to talent-surplus areas; that is, from the South and West to the Northeast. Once the student comes to the Northeast, he may well stay in the talent surplus area. The South and West have fought this trend by objecting to generous Federal scholarship programs that would stimulate this movement and by providing increasing capacity in low- or no-tuition institutions of higher learning.

In this connection, a recommendation of the Commissioners of the United Colonies to the General Court of Massachusetts in 1646 is of some interest: "these [students] when finished with learning, remove not into other countries but improve their [ef] forts and abilities in the service of the Colonies."[6]

Some statistics provided by President Conant on the geographical distribution of medical school graduates in the years 1920 to 1929 are of some interest here. New England contributed 473 students; and the number of these graduates in New England in 1936-1937 was 533 or a net importation of talent of 13 percent. From the Middle eastern seaboard 192 came to Harvard; but 243 of the Harvard graduates of these years had settled there; that is to say, the Middle East obtained 26 percent more doctors from Harvard than medical students sent to Harvard. The other regions clearly lost potential doctors.[7]

---

3. *Admission to Harvard College*, p. 31.
4. *Report of the President of Harvard College*, 1882–1883, p. 11.
5. Joseph H. Choate, *The Boyhood and Youth of Joseph Hodges Choate* (Class of 1852), Autobiography privately printed, 1917, pp. 80–81.
6. Josiah Quincy, *The History of Harvard University*, 1840, vol. I, p. 16. (Twelve of twenty graduates prior to 1646 had migrated to Europe.)
7. *Report of the President of Harvard College*, 1936–1937, pp. 218–219.

Geographical Trends

Even in the second half of the eighteenth century, Harvard was still a highly provincial college. Thus in the classes of 1755, 1777, 1781, and 1793 with 44, 49, 31, and 40 entering in these years, respectively, 100 percent came from Massachusetts.

By 1820, of an undergraduate body of 287, New England accounted for 78 percent and the South Atlantic states for 14.6 percent or 42 students.[8]

A table which has been deposited in the Harvard University Archives reveals some broadening of geographical origins in the years 1830 to 1850. But even as late as 1850, 82 percent of all students at the university came from New England and 69 percent from Massachusetts. In the law school, however, students from non-New England regions were already of great importance in these early years of the nineteenth century. But both the divinity school and the medical school continued to be heavily dependent on New England sources.

Widening of the geographical origins did not continue into the years 1860 through 1890. Consult the totals for law and medicine.[9]

In the college a broader appeal was evident during the Eliot regime. Whereas in 1850, the non-New England contingent was only 13 percent, in 1860, 1870, 1880 and 1890, this group increased to 21, 26, 30 and 37 percent.[10]

President Eliot often asked for a broader base for Harvard students. He was pleased in 1872 "to see the multiplication of good preparatory schools in the middle and western states during the past ten years," and the introduction of Harvard admission examina-tions in several populous states outside of Massachusetts which contributed to enrollments from non-New England states.[11]

In the late 1860s, Harvard College's enrollment outside of New England was not large. Of 563 undergraduates, 414 were from New England; 372 from Massachusetts; 51 from New York; 19 from Pennsylvania; 2 from New Jersey; and 75 from elsewhere. Of special significance is the fact that, whereas Harvard had but 2 undergraduates from Connecticut, Yale had 42 students from Massachusetts and Wesleyan had 32. Harvard was much weaker in neighboring states than were the two Connecticut institutions of higher learning in Massachusetts.[12]

Even as late as the 1890s, the charge was made that Harvard was a Massachusetts or a New England, but not a national, university. An observer noted that Yale had 1 1/2 times as many graduates in the middle states and 1 1/3 times as many in the western states as Harvard. Harvard's Unitarianism was blamed.

Pres. C. F. Thwing, in the late nineteenth century, commented:

... Harvard is no longer a Unitarian college but the reputation of Harvard as a Unitarian college still lingers, so hard are sectarian prejudices to remove.... many persons identify Unitarianism with irreligion.... From the conclusion that Harvard is irreligious they draw the further inference that it is immoral.[13]

Harvard continued to suffer as a result of these prejudices, and its enrollment was affected.

In the twentieth century, the non-New England contingent continued to gain. But the rise in the proportion of non-New England students was not impressive until the 1940s and 1950s. The non-New England gain was of the order of less than 1/3 of 1 percent per

---

8. *Students Entering Harvard College*, 1725–1828, vol. III, 15.5.2; in Harvard University Archives; *Harvard University Catalogue*, 1803–1818 (unbound) and *1819–1824;* cf. Samuel Eliot Morison, *Three Centuries of Harvard, 1636–1936*, 1937, p. 198, where Morison puts the non-New England figure at 28 percent. (The catalogue total is 22 percent.)

9. *Report of the President of Harvard College*, 1874–1875, pp. 28–29.

10. Statistics for 1850–1890 from *Harvard University Catalogue*, 1849–1850, 1859–1860, etc.

11. *Report of the President of Harvard College*, 1871–1872, pp. 10–11; 1874–1875, pp. 11–12; 1880–1881, pp. 22–23.

12. Compiled from *Annual Report of the President, Columbia College*, 1870, pp. 82–83.

13. C. F. Thwing, *The American College in American History*, p. 164; cf., *Harvard Graduates Magazine*, 1893, pp. 194–200.

year from 1900 to 1940. But in the 1940s the net improvement was almost 1 percent a year; in the classes of 1950 to 1964 about 7/10 of 1 percent; and in the classes of 1956 to 1964 about 1 1/2 percent per year. These were the years of the largest gains from non-New England sources.

In another table that has been deposited in the Harvard University Archives, I also discover at a few places [1910 and 1940] the percentage of enrollment on the basis of residence as well as schools. Thus, in 1940, the schools in New England provided 65.7 percent of the Harvard students, but New England homes only 49.5 percent, the explanation of the difference being the large numbers in New England schools, both of New Englanders and non-New Englanders, who go to Harvard. The proximity of schools to an institute of higher learning tends to attract students to the colleges in the region.

In the second decade of the twentieth century there was some concern that Harvard was losing its attractiveness as a national university. The 1910 and 1920 figures point in that direction. In response to this view Pres. Abbott L. Lowell announced in 1922 that an investigation had shown that Harvard was drawing increasingly from outside New England. In substantially every department of the university the proportion of students from outside New England was increasing in his view, and especially in the twelve years preceding 1922.[14]

Lowell was rather optimistic. The gains from 1900 to 1920 were small indeed compared to a rise from 2 to 29 percent in the years 1821 to 1884.[15]

Competing institutions of higher learning also tended to draw heavily on local products, and thus reduce migrations to Harvard.

14. *Report of the President of Harvard College*, 1920–1921, p. 30.

15. *Ibid.*, 1882–1883, p. 11.

2

Students' Socio-Economic Backgrounds

Introduction

I am interested in students' backgrounds, or in that of their parents, for various reasons. The first is because it is important to know to what extent Harvard students are a good sample of the nation's youth. The second is because the economic status of Harvard families and students is especially relevant for an understanding of Harvard's finance and quality of education. That Harvard students come from high-income families means (1) that Harvard can provide a high-quality education without being excessively concerned about the student's, or his family's, capacity to finance it; and (2) that a substantial part of the cost can be financed through gifts of Harvard alumni. Surely one reason Harvard can provide a high-quality education is that endowment in the last 150 years has provided as much as 20 to 60 percent of income; and in more recent years current gifts have become of increasing importance. Thirdly, we are very much interested in the extent of democratization of Harvard. Has it always been a rich man's college? Is it today? These are both economic and ideological issues.

Parents' Occupations, Seventeenth and Eighteenth Centuries

Parents' occupations throw a light on students' socio-economic backgrounds. In recent years, investigators have found that the highest correlation of enrollment in institutions of higher learing is with the occupation of the parent.[1]

From the very beginning, Harvard's students were primarily from professional and business backgrounds. In the first years of the college, about one-third of the students came from homes of university alumni, although these groups accounted for but one out of thirty-five in the population. For the years 1673 through 1703, Morison, basing himself on Sibley's fascinating studies, estimated that "Ministers and magistrates together fathered forty-six of the first hundred students, twenty-five of the second, and forty-two of the third; and if we add the sons of merchants, physicians, schoolmasters, and the better farmers (large landowners), militia officers, representatives in the General Court, 64 percent of the student body from 1673 to 1703 came from the gentry and the propertied classes."[2]

In 1700, of 291 living Harvard alumni, 150 were clergymen; 71, other professional men; 30, merchants, planters, etc.; others, 40.[3]

Also of some interest is the extent to which the parents of Harvard students were Harvard graduates. Of the first hundred (1673 to 1689) and the third hundred (1696 to 1703), one-third of the students had Harvard fathers; and one-sixth of the second hundred (1689 to 1696). For these thirty years, 27 percent had

---

1. Lansing, Lorimer, Moriguchi, *How People Pay for College*, 1960, pp. 128-129.

2. Morison, *Harvard College in the Seventeenth Century*, pp. 74-75, 450-451, 562-565.

3. *Ibid.*, p. 565.

Harvard parents. In contrast, in the Eliot period the percentage was only about 10 to 15 percent.[4]

From 1642-1658 to 1721-1730, the proportion of clergymen alumni dropped from a little over one-half to 40 percent; other professionals rose from 17 to 25 percent (teachers from less than 1 to 9 percent), merchants from 2 to 13 percent, planters from 3 to 8 percent. In general, the clergy representation tended to fall relatively as alumni became more interested in other professions, farming, and business.

A study of occupations of 252 alumni in 1949-1950 shows a greatly changed distribution of graduates. Business accounted for 23 percent (13 percent in 1721 to 1730); professional: medicine (18), law (13), science (10), education (10), writing (8), social relations (6), or 65 percent for all professions. Incidentally, the professional representation of alumni greatly exceeds the professional background of parents—as might be expected since the alumni are more highly educated on the average than their parents. The large gains since the early eighteenth century were in the professions, and notably in medicine, law, writing, science (education was relatively unchanged), and business. Of course, the major loss was in the ministry first and agriculture second.[5]

In the first half of the eighteenth century the professional and business classes were not prosperous in the sense that they were in the nineteenth and twentieth centuries. By current standards, many were impoverished. But they were the leaders of society. Shipton's very helpful study of the merchants and business men of the eighteenth century shows the importance of Harvard alumni in the economic advance of the New England colonies.[6]

Table 2-1.
Occupations of Harvard Alumni, Various
Years, Seventeenth and Eighteenth Centuries

	1642-1658	1642-1700	1701-1710	1721-1730
Clergymen	76	266	69	150
Professional men* (exclusive of clergy)	26	119	30	92
Merchants	3	20	10	50
Planters, gentlemen	4	18	2	27
Miscellaneous occupations, unknown, or died young	40	120	14	52
Total	149	543	125	371

*Physicians, public servants, and traders.

Source: 1642-1700 based on Samuel Eliot Morison, *Harvard College in the Seventeenth Century,* 1936, p. 562; 1701-1710 and 1721-1730 compiled from bibliographical sketches in C.K. Shipton, *Shipley's Harvard Graduates,* vols. V-IX.

4. *Ibid.,* p. 451; C.W.Eliot, William Allan Neilson (ed.), *The Man and His Beliefs,* a collection of essays and addresses, 1926, p. 82.

5. *Report of the President of Harvard College,* 1949-1950, p. 430.

6. C. K. Shipton, *Sibley's Harvard Graduates,* vols. VII-IX, various pages, for names.

An indication of the origins of Harvard students is given by the attitude of Harvard alumni toward cheap money. Shipton, for example, shows that among the Harvard graduates in the years 1700 through 1730, 41 were against what was considered inflationary policies and 10 were in favor. In general the property men have been against inflation.

Harvard continued to grow in the eighteenth century, though slowly as the colony expanded; and "a large part of the increase in its undergraduate body came from the well-to-do gentry of the seaport towns who were fattening on land speculation and the triangular trade."[7] But student aid accounted for "a goodly number of sons of plain farmers and artisans."[8]

Classification of Students

One of the troublesome problems concerning Harvard's democratic tradition was the classification of students in the seventeenth and eighteenth centuries, an activity that throws some light on socio-economic problems. The general view has been that students were classified on the basis of social origins, inclusive of the occupation and position of the parent. Where a student was placed was a matter of great concern to him. Morison seems to think that the class stratification theory has been overdone and that a student's position was more largely determined by his school work and promise than had generally been assumed. In the British tradition, whatever the origin, all college graduates were considered gentlemen. Morison himself admits that in the eighteenth century non-scholarly attributes may have played an increasing role in classifications.[9]

Clifford Shipton has recently discussed this issue; and he finds that for catalogue listing, academic procession, and classroom recitals, the college classified students as follows up to the year 1772:

Ten percent were put in group one—the sons of magistrates, e.g. governors, justices of the peace; 20 percent in a second group, the sons of college students (arranged in order of dates of graduation of father); 70 percent in a third group, the sons of farmers, storekeepers, artisans, etc. [10]

Extravagances, Early Nineteenth Century

By the early nineteenth century, there were many complaints of the aristocratic and snobbish aspects of Harvard and also concern over the high costs. In 1813, John Randolph of Roanoke, Virginia, in a letter to John Quincy, complained of the extravagance at Harvard.

Tis said that your principal and professors take a pride in the extravagance of the students and encourage it, whilst Yale zealously inculcates the sublime truths of Poor Richard's Almanack. Be this as it may, some of our southern youths have left a great deal of cash at Cambridge and brought away nothing valuable in return for it. We are so much poorer in this quarter than you wealthy Bostonians that we smart under an expense which you would scarcely feel....[11]

T. W. Higginson had this to say:

... As a rule the Southerners were clearly the favorites in Cambridge Society: they usually had charming manners, social aptitude, imperious ways, abundant leisure, and plenty of money; they were graceful dancers, often musical, and sometimes well taught. ... Contributing sometimes the most brilliant

7. *Ibid., Publications of the Colonial Society of Massachusetts,* vols. V-VIII.

8. R. Hofstadter, and W. P. Metzer, *The Development of Academic Freedom in the United States,* 1955, p. 107, and pp. 102-103. Samuel Eliot Morison, *Three Centuries of Harvard, 1636-1936,* 1937.

9. Morison, *Harvard College in the Seventeenth Century,* pp. 61-64, 451-452.

10. C.K.Shipton, "Ye Mystery of Ye Ages Solved," in *Harvard Alumni Bulletin,* December 11, 1954, pp. 259-263. For further discussion of the classification and its abandonment see Quincy, *op cit.,* vol. II, pp. 157-158 and M.A. DeWolfe, *Classic Studies,* 1928, p. 173.

11. cf. Morison, *Three Centuries of Harvard,* 1636-1936, chapter VI.

young men to the Law School, they furnished also a number who, having been brought up on remote plantations and much indulged, had remained grossly ignorant. . . .[12]

High Costs, 1850 and Later Years

A report to the overseers of 1849 lamented the high cost of a Harvard education as well as the wastage of resources.[13]

A Rich Man's College

By the middle of the nineteenth century, there were frequent complaints that costs were too high at Harvard and that the college appealed especially to high-income groups. Thus a committee of the state Legislature in 1850, to which was referred a request for public money by Harvard, complained that:

there are many young men who would gladly resort to an institution of the higher class, for a limited period of time, if they could thereby obtain instruction which would make them better farmers, or mechanics, or engineers, or merchants. . .instruction now given does not make better farmers, mechanics. . .[14]

The Massachusetts Joint Committee on Education commented in 1849 as follows:

Will legislators . . . avow the doctrine that colleges should of necessity, belong to the rich alone,–that the poor shall not send their children to those institutions at all,–that they have no right to associate with youth reared in luxury . . . . Such a doctrine does not sound very democratic . . . .
Education should be free to the rich and poor. Mass. should open wide its gates, and say aloud "Enter every one who thirsteth."[15]

In 1858, a university committee reported on the high cost of living for students. They were troubled that "the institution may become a place of education for the rich."[16]

In 1881, a Harvard faculty member replied to a statement in the Ohio State Journal to the effect that a student has to spend, and is even required to spend, at least $1,500 per year at Harvard, with the result that poor boys are excluded. "I am convinced that there is no college in the country easier of access to poor men of good parts."[17]

A similar attack was made in the *New York Illustrated American* in 1891.

Harvard is simply a training school for the sons of the rich, a place where wealth is honored and glorified, where the rich man's son is taught his own importance and the dignity of his money bags.

Harvard seemed to have taken notice of these charges, pointing out that one student arrived in Cambridge with but ten cents. The defender of Harvard referred to a commencement address of Professor G. H. Palmer in 1887.

Whenever you encounter a boy of eager, aggressive mind, a youth of energy, one capable of feeling the enjoyments of struggling with a multitude and of making his merit known, say to him that Harvard College is expressly constituted for such as he. Here he will find the largest provision for his needs, and the clearest field for his talents. . . .[18]

12. T. W. Higginson, *Cheerful Yesterdays,* p. 56.

13. *Report of the Visiting Committee of Harvard University Made to the Overseers,* January, 1849, pp. 14-29.

14. Massachusetts Report No. 164, *What Legislation, If Any, Is Necessary to Render Harvard University More Beneficial,* April, 1850, p. 2.

15. Commonwealth of Massachusetts, *Joint Standing Committee on Education, House Report No. 92,* 1849, p. 9. cf. *Reports and Other Papers Relating to Harvard College during the Administration of President Jared Sparks,* Vol. I, pp. 48-49 (Harvard University Archives).

16. Harvard College Library Clipping Sheet, February, 1858, *Evening Transcript,* February 15, 1858.

17. Letter of John Williams White, July 26, 1881, in Harvard University Archives.

18. *The Poor Man at Harvard,* 1891, in Harvard University Archives; also see *The Cost of a Year in Harvard College and The Means of Assistance for Poor Students,* 1886, in Harvard University Archives.

Eliot, in particular, sought to dispel the notion that Harvard was a rich man's college. In his inaugural address in 1869 he said:

Harvard College has always attracted and still attracts students in all conditions of life. From the city trader or professional man, who may be careless how much his son spends at Cambridge, to the farmer or mechanic, who finds it a hard sacrifice to give his boy his time early enough to enable him to prepare for college—all sorts and conditions of men have wishes and still wish to send their sons hither. There are always scores of young men in this University who earn or borrow every dollar they spend here. Every year many young men enter this College without any resources whatever. If they prove themselves men of capacity and character, they never go away for lack of money. . . . They [aids] enable the Corporation to say that no good student need ever stay away from Cambridge, or leave college simply because he is poor. There is one uniform condition, however, on which help is given—the recipient must be of promising ability and the best character. The community does not owe superior education to all children, but only to the elite.[19]

In his 1876-1877 report, however, commenting on the large numbers of withdrawals, Eliot emphasized the economic explanation of the losses. Two years earlier Eliot wrote:

A small proportion only of these families can be called rich; the greater part are neither rich nor poor; and the proportion of the poor, though small, quite equals that of the rich. . . . It is chiefly the people who themselves have trained minds who desire thorough training for their children. . . .[20]

President Lowell continued the campaign. In an address to the associated alumni clubs in 1911, he said ". . . One hears two complaints made about Harvard. . . . Those two complaints are that Harvard is a rich man's college and that it is difficult to enter." He tried to refute these points. In his 1912-1913 report, the president said that Harvard was representative of the nation, and that on the basis of outside work done by students Harvard was more a poor man's than a rich man's college.

Paul Buck, the able provost during the war and early postwar years, continued the debate, saying "Harvard is perhaps more liberal than most colleges in maintaining an equality of opportunity for education to all classes of American youth."[21]

In general, Harvard has been and still is a college for the children of business and professional families and of families with average incomes more than twice the national average. In fact, as H. Doermann showed, the family income cutoff point for scholarships at Harvard for a three-child family in 1960 was substantially higher than the incomes of the top 5 percent of all families. My able research student, G. Kolko, has revealed to me that at a time when professional and managerial parents accounted for 81 percent of the Harvard students, families with these backgrounds contributed only 26.3 percent of Indiana University male students.

From all of this I do not draw the conclusion that Harvard has not tried to democratize the college. Indeed, it has. Moreover, the large scholarship and loan resources and the increasing recourse to employment while at Harvard attest Harvard's efforts. Yet the fact remains that Harvard and Radcliffe children came primarily from high-income groups and even the scholarship students originate in families with incomes substantially above the average of the nation.

19. *Addresses at the Inauguration of Charles William Eliot,* October 19, 1869, pp. 46-47, Harvard University Archives.

20. See *Report of the President of Harvard College, 1874-1875,* pp. 11-12; *1876-1877,* p. 27; *1890-1891,* p. 37, and F. Rudolph, "The Origins of Student Aid in the United States in College Entrance Examination Board", *Student Financial Aid and National Purpose,* 1962, pp. 7-8.

21. *Harvard Graduates Magazine,* vol. V, no. 20, pp. 215-216; *Report of the President of Harvard College, 1912-1913,* p. 13; P. H. Buck, "Who Comes to Harvard," in *Harvard Alumni Bulletin,* January 10, 1948, p. 405.

Parental Occupations, Harvard and Elsewhere, Over a Century

Wolfle has shown that generally those with a more favorable socio-economic background enter college in larger numbers than others, though once in college the rate of survival does not vary greatly. According to Wolfle the proportion of high school graduates who entered college in the early 1950s was 67 percent for children from professional parents, 50 percent from the managerial class and but 26 percent for factory workers, craftsmen, and unskilled workers. These figures suggest that socio-economic origins greatly affect enrollment in the nation as well as at Harvard.

Table 2-2.

National Figures, Students Entering College, by Occupations of Parents, in the Early 1950s

	% of H.S. Graduates Who Enter College (1)	% of Total Labor Force (2)	% in College (3)	% Entering Harvard (4)
Professional and semiprofessional	67	8	13	39
Managerial	50	13	19	36
Sales, clerical, and service	48	11	15	11
Farmers	24	11	8	1.5
Factory, craftsmen, unskilled	26	57	43	11

Sources: D. Wolfle, *America's Resources of Specialized Talent*, pp. 160-62 and other sources given in this chapter. My calculations.

What this table suggests is that, on the basis of entrants to higher education by occupations of parents based on the percent of each occupation in the national labor market, one might expect that college

entrants should equal 13 percent of the professionals labor force, 19, managerial, 15, clerical and services, 8, farmers, and 43, other members of the labor market. But the Harvard entrants from these groups, respectively, are 3, slightly less than 2, 0.70, 0.20, and 0.25 *as numerous,* relatively, as the *national college figures* suggest. Harvard draws much more heavily from the upper occupations than the national college group, and much less from the others.

Generally, incomes of parents with children at college are much higher than those of other parents. In a sample provided by the Department of Health, Education, and Welfare in 1952, those in the $7,000 to $15,000 income class supplied more than 1½ times as many students as its proportion of families, and those in the greater than $15,000 class, 4 to 5 times the number given by the proportion of its families, and those in the less than $3,000 income class contributed only about ¾ as many students as suggested by their proportion of families.[22]

For almost a hundred years, at intervals, we have useful statistics on the occupations of parents of Harvard students. We can compare this parental structure with that of the national labor market. Such a comparison suggests the origins of Harvard students as compared with the whole population. Thus from 1870 to 1875, 21.2 percent of the Harvard students came from professional backgrounds and 43.4 percent from the proprietor, managerial and official class. The corresponding totals in the national sample were 3.9 and 9.1 percent. Harvard in these years attracted 5 times as many students from these high, i.e., professional and managerial and high-paying, occupations as it would have if the student body reflected the occupational structure of the nation. In the laboring classes (exclusive of farmers) Harvard drew but one-ninth as heavily as suggested by the national sample.

In 1958, the same general pattern emerges except that the professional classes have greatly increased their share of Harvard places from 21 percent in the

---

22. S. E. Harris, *Higher Education: Resources and Finance,* 1962, p. 140.

1870s to 39 percent in 1958, and the proprietor, etc., group provided 33½ percent as compared to 43 percent some eighty years before.[23] This gain for the professions reflects the rising educational level of the population.

In his 1921-1922 report, President Lowell observed, on the basis of a Bureau of Education report of 1912, that the choice of occupations by students tended to vary in the same way at Harvard as in the country. Since 1840, the percentage of students entering the ministry had steadily and rapidly diminished—and even more so at Harvard; that of law rose at the end of the eighteenth century and has since been declining; that education and commercial pursuits were attracting increasing numbers; that medicine remained curiously constant; and that engineering did not attract many college graduates.[24]

A summary of the socio-economic background is given by the accompanying table by parents' occupations. Where the value is above a hundred, the inference is that the particular occupational class provides Harvard with more students than its representation in the national picture might suggest; and where the value is less than a hundred, it provides less than might be inferred from the national structure.

A value of 543 (100 = equal representation) for professional parents in the Harvard classes of 1870 to 1875 points to a heavy overrepresentation of students with parents for these Harvard classes. By 1903-1904 the total had jumped to 822, but there was a substantial decline afterwards. The managerial and proprietor class experienced a similar rise, but later a greater decline. In contrast, note that the laboring classes contributed but 7; and sales and clerical, 12, both a small fraction of the 100 reflecting equal representation. Clerical and sales experienced an improvement in the twentieth century, with their contribution finally almost equalling their share of the national sample. The gains for other workers were not nearly so spectacular.

Unfortunately, the values for workers in lower status are difficult to appraise. The classifications vary from census year to census year. But it is clear that all these groups are greatly underrepresented.

Scholarship students come from the top occupational groups to a lesser degree than all Harvard students.

Humphrey Doermann, in a similar study basing himself to some extent on our work, concludes that over eighty years, 1880 to 1960, there has been a spectacular decline in the percentage of sons of professional and managerial parents coming to Harvard relative to the position of these groups in the national picture.[25]

In part the relative decline of parents of Harvard's freshmen in the more desired occupations is related to the gains of the managerial and professional groups in the economy: from 1880 to 1960 their share rose from 12.8 to 18.7 percent.

Another indication of the high economic status of Harvard graduates is given by their incomes. In 1947 graduates of Harvard, Yale, and Princeton had annual incomes 20 percent in excess of graduates of the other ivy-league colleges and 56 percent in excess of

23. The 1870-1875 statistics of Harvard population comes from *Report of the President of Harvard College*, 1874-1875, p. 10; the class of 1958 data is based on materials in *Report of the President of Harvard College*, 1953-1954, pp. 216-217; classification of parents by occupations is based on A. M. Edwards, *Comparative Occupation Statistics for the United States, 1870 to 1940*, Sixteenth Census of the United States, 1943, p. 187.

24. *Report of the President of Harvard College*, 1921-1922, pp. 16-20.

25. The Doermann study is based on a paper in a Harris Seminar, *The Economics of Undergraduates Diversity, Selected Recent Trends*, 1962-1963, table 4. Doermann has also included materials for 1947, 1948 through 1960. These statistics in general confirm the results of our 1951 and 1958 figures.

I am greatly in debt to a young and able research assistant, Gabriel Kolko, who put together much of the material on parental origins of Harvard's entering classes. Since then Kolko has done important work as a mature scholar.

Table 2-3.

Index of Representation of Occupational Classes Among Fathers of Harvard College Students, 1870-1958*. The years are for Entry by Freshmen. (Equal representation = 100.)

	1870-1875	1903-1904			Class of 1951				Class of 1958		
	Total	Total	Harvard	Lawrence Scientific School	Total	Regular	S.S.**	Vet.	Total	Regular	S.S.**
Professional	543	741	822	432	466	507	410	342	533	546	496
Proprietors, Managers, and Officials, excluding Farmers	481	653	611	815	442	477	327	439	313	380	174
Clerical, sales, and kindred workers	7	47	48	40	63	47	109	84	96	69	167
Skilled, foremen, and kindred workers	⎱ 12	26	26	26	32	16	81	38	11		
Semi-skilled workers	⎰ (brace)	6	6	5	14	7	31	20		6	25
Laborers, ex. farm.		3	3	2	5	3	8	13			
Servant classes		2	2	3							
Farm laborers		1		4							
Farmers, tenants, and owners	11	14	13	15	13	10	10	29	13	9	24

*The index represents the disparity in a perfect distribution (100) of the national male occupational distribution with that which actually exists. Occupational distribution for 1870-75 is compared to 1880 data given in U.S. Congress, Senate, *Economic Concentration in World War II*, Report of the Smaller War Plants Corporation to the Special Committee to Study the Problems of American Small Business, 79th Congress, 2nd Session (Washington, D.C., 1946), p. 359. 1903-04 data is compared to 1910 data given in A.M. Edwards, *op. cit*. The classes of 1951 and 1958 are compared to the occupational distribution given in *Statistical Abstract of the United States, 1957* (Washington, D.C.)p. 212.

**Scholarship Students.

Table 2-4.

Percent of Parents of Freshmen from Professional and Managerial Classes

Year	Harvard	U. S.	Ratio (1) to (2)
1880	87.0%	12.8%	7-
1960	73.3%	18.7%	4-

the median income of all college graduates. Again, a study of 221 graduates who obtained employment through the intermediary of the appointment office in 1929-1930 showed an average salary of $2,669, or about 2½ times that of the average member of the labor market, the latter of course averaging a much higher age.[26] Another indication of high attainments is a study of Harvard Ph.D.s from 1872 to 1902. Of 304, 256 were still alive in 1902; and of the latter total, 169 or about two-thirds were in *Who's Who.*[27]

Private-Public School Representation

In so far as entry to Harvard came primarily through private schools the college was likely to depend largely on students from high-income or high-occupation families. Eliot in 1873-1874 was concerned lest the contribution of the public school be inadequate.[28]

By 1884-1885 Eliot was still concerned over the small number of public schools sending students to Harvard regularly, and also that whereas from 1866 to 1869 the public school contribution was 30 percent, by 1882-1885 it was only 26 percent.[29] By

World War I the public school students provided over half and by 1963, 55 percent.[30]

Greater influx of public school students is related to the rise of number of schools preparing for Harvard, the introduction of the policy of admitting the top seventh, and also the rising recourse to aid. The gains of the public schools prevailed even though rejections were larger for public school graduates. Even for those of equal ability, acceptances were relatively higher for private school students.[31]

Schools in the Boston area suffered as Harvard increasingly appealed to the national market. Of 324 students whose homes were known in the period 1673 to 1707, 68 came from Boston Latin. Whereas Boston, Roxbury, and Cambridge in the years 1673 to 1707 provided one-third of Harvard students, today they send a negligible share.[32]

A Broad Survey of the Issues

Undemocratic practices are indeed not unknown in Harvard's history. The early ranking of students, based at least in part on family status, is one example. Concern over excessive spending by the sons of the rich troubled Harvard authorities throughout the eighteenth and nineteenth centuries. Earlier we commented on this issue as it arose in the mid-nineteenth century. In the latter part of the eighteenth century and early in the nineteenth century, the charge was made that Harvard was too expensive and infested with "rakehells and blades . . . wages of profuseness and prodigality in such a Society lay a foundation of a great deal of sorrow. . . ." Many who contributed to the founding of Yale in the early eighteenth century were in fact critics of Harvard students' indulgence in excessive luxuries.

26. Havemann, *They Want to Go to College*, pp. 178-179; *Report of the President of Harvard College*, 1929-1930, p. 353.
27. *Ibid.*, 1921-1922, p. 70.
28. *Report of the President of Harvard College*, 1873-1874, p. 8.
29. *Ibid.*, 1884-1885, pp. 50-51.

30. *Ibid.*, various years; *Admission to Harvard College*, p. 32. *Admission to Harvard College*, p. 32.
31. *Report of the President of Harvard College*, 1889-1890, 1894-1895, 1899-1900, 1904-1905, 1929-1930 and *Admission to Harvard College*, pp. 31-35.
32. Samuel Eliot Morison, *Harvard College in the Seventeenth Century*, 1936, p. 449.

In the early part of the nineteenth century, the stress was on the high costs of a Harvard College education. Declines in enrollments began to reflect the inflated Harvard budgets; and in the crisis of the 1820s, as well as midcentury, competitive institutions began to operate at lower costs—and often at lower standards. In response, Harvard authorities sought to get their costs down to stop losses in enrollment. In the latter part of the nineteenth century, Harvard became increasingly interested in the charges that Harvard was only a rich man's college. In a letter to a correspondent (Mr. Hale), President Eliot, annoyed by the incessant charges of student extravagances, defended the affluent Harvard student:

Doubtless Harvard University contains a larger proportion of children of well-to-do parents than the western universities contain; . . . [but] it remains true that acquiring some property is an evidence of some sort of merit in the parents—that is of intelligence or honesty or health above the average. . . . Free institutions . . . have no tendency to obliterate distinctions founded on such merits. . . .

In the later Eliot period, the expensive and luxurious Gold Coast dormitories, privately sponsored, and the accompanying tendency of the wealthy students to be segregated in these dormitories, invited attention to the division of students between the inhabitants of the Gold Coast and the others. Moreover, the private dormitories tended to operate like clubs, with residents influencing the choice of new occupants. The college, in turn, tried to treat the situation by establishing standards of supervision and conduct in the private dormitories and, ultimately, by improving the quality of the college's dormitories and by building relatively comfortable and modern student quarters, a movement that reached its pinnacle in the days of President Lowell and his successors.[33]

Admission should be available on equal terms, not only to poor and rich, but also to members of different races and religions. During most of Harvard's history, students came from the dominant religion of the area which provided most of the students. Even as late as 1870, there were but 7 Roman Catholics and 3 Jews out of 563 students. Unitarians accounted for 218; Episcopalians, for 129; and Congregationalists, for 96. This is not necessarily evidence that minority groups experienced discrimination; but it may mean that a Unitarian, on grounds of ability, training, or similarity of values and background, might find it easier to enter Harvard than others.[34]

In Eliot's view, no university should be limited to a particular sect. Harvard's students now "belong to every religious communion from the Roman Catholic to the Jew and the Japanese Buddhist. No denomination is represented by more than a small minority among its students; and its officers are selected for their fitness only, without the least regard to their religious affiliation."[35]

Certainly at the time Eliot wrote the above, Harvard was relatively objective in its choice of students and faculty. Yet the above is a strong statement. Even President Eliot, who was far ahead of his contemporaries, as late as 1901, reflecting the prejudices of the time, wrote: "I see no method of dealing with the Hebrew difficulty. It is doubtless true that Jews are better off at Harvard than at any other American college; and they are, therefore, likely to resort to it. As yet they are reasonably distributed through our buildings. . . ."[36]

In contrast, a Harvard alumnus had written to President Walker in 1853 about the son of a New York rabbi, urging the college to accept this promising young man on the grounds that "at Cambridge there would be found less sectarianism, less prejudice, and more freedom to worship God in a form more consistent with his birth and education than at New

---

33. C. W. Eliot to Mr. Hale, November 29, 1904; Jerome P. Greene to Lincoln Hutchinson, September 18, 1909; A. L. Lowell to A. L. P. Dennis, November 29, 1910; S. F. Kimball to A. L. Lowell, August 8, 1912; A. L. Lowell to S. P. Kimball, August 12, 1912. (See especially Harvard University Archives, 1.5.160, 1909-1914.)

34. W. W. Boyd to Professor Gurney, May 19, 1871, in Harvard University Archives, W. A. Neilson.

35. C. W. Eliot, *op. cit.*, pp. 82-83.

36. C. W. Eliot to Professor George A. Bartlett, July 21, 1901, in Harvard University Archives.

Haven. . . ." The alumnus asked for the student the privilege of observing the Jewish Sabbath and of dining with a Jewish family if such could be found.[37]

As the number of Jews seeking entry to Harvard increased, prejudice tended to increase. That many of the liberals, e.g., Brandeis, Laski, and Frankfurter, contributed to the downfall of conservative strongholds tended to strengthen the prejudices. President Lowell, it is well known, seriously considered a quota for Jews. Even under the House Plan introduced in 1931, there were understandings about the equitable distribution of Jewish students among the houses and even some enthusiasm for quotas.

But anyone who examines the Harvard developments, especially since the days of President Conant and Professor Buck, cannot help but be impressed by the great strides made since 1930. The gains are evident in the number of students and faculty from minority groups and also the advances of minority groups in important student activities. It is not surprising that one of my graduate students, a Princeton man who studied the ivy-league treatment of Negroes, found that Harvard had the best record of all. For these great advances, no one deserves more credit than Conant and Provost Buck. But their successors, President Pusey and Deans Bundy and Ford, it may be said to their credit, continued these policies and deserve commendation.

In view of the current situation, President Lowell's concern in 1914 about a Negro's residing in a Harvard dormitory seems to belong to another age.

. . . Opinions would probably be more divided on the question whether it would be wise for a Negro to apply for a room in the dormitories. For myself, I think it would be a mistake for him to do so. It has nothing to do with the education he receives; that, of course, we furnish equally to all men without distinction as to race, color, or previous condition of servitude. It is a different matter from the social commingling in the Freshmen dormitories. . . .[38]

In this connection, a letter of protest by two students at discovering that the college had rented a room to Negroes next door to their room is of some interest. These students protested on the grounds that Harvard is a national not a New England college, and the interests of Southern and Western students are germane, saying ". . .Their wishes, prejudices. . .should get some respect." Apparently President Lowell was unaware of this episode which had occurred four years before his exchange with Hallowell.[39]

On earlier occasions, Harvard seemed away ahead of its contemporaries. I remind the reader of the Everett statement concerning an outstanding Latinist.[40]

There are other evidences of undemocratic tendencies in Harvard's history. As early as 1651, a commentator noted that English parents sent their sons to Harvard because the college was more free from temptations to lewdness than English colleges. But one result has been excesses by these imports followed by expulsions.[41] (In later years the son of John Quincy Adams was expelled for participating in a destructive riot. To the credit of the college, persistent pressure of one of Harvard's greatest sons did not move the Harvard authorities to relax the punishment.) A most critical assessment of the college was the product of Harriet Martineau's visit to Harvard in 1838:

The politics of the managers of Harvard University are opposed to those of the great body of the American people. . .the education she affords is very expensive. . .the sons of the wealthy will therefore flock to her. . .the attainments. . .are inferior to those attained elsewhere. . .new colleges are rising up. . .whose principles and practices are better suited to the wants of the time. In them living is cheaper. . . .

37. A. R. Gardner to President Walker, January 13, 1853, in Harvard University Archives.
38. A. Lawrence Lowell to Colonel N. P. Hallowell, March 25, 1914, in Harvard University Archives.
39. R. E. S. Stifel to Professor S. B. R. Briggs, July 22, 1910, in Harvard University Archives.
40. P. R. Frothingham, E. Everett, *President of Harvard: Orator and Statesman (1925)*, p. 299.
41. Morison, *Harvard College in the Seventeenth Century*, vol. I, pp. 77-78.

When I was in Boston, the state of the University was a subject of great mourning among its friends. . . .[42]

Late in the nineteenth century the attack on luxurious spending continued. The rich sent their sons to college to achieve social distinction. "These students fall into bad habits of extravagance ... they are a hindrance to the progress of the industrious members of the class. . . ."[43] One overseers committee of 1894 revealed a preference for the rich over the poor boys "though many of the poor were splendid fellows."

Many of Harvard's famous professors shared an aristocratic bias. At Harvard's 250th anniversary celebration in 1886, Professor James Russell Lowell said " . . . I do not mean that the courses of study should be adapted to the average level of intelligence, but to the highest; for in these matters it is wiser to grade upward than downward, since the best is the only thing that is good enough." He continued by insisting that the lowest third could at "least have the pleasure of watching the others show their paces."[44]

Professor B. Wendell at the turn of the century also stressed the aristocratic viewpoint. In a comment on a book by Wendell, the president replied that "the sons and daughters of mechanics, farmers, and shepherds have not only the bodily characteristics of persons of 'gentle birth' but their best mental and spiritual qualities . . . ." He regretted Wendell's frequent discourses on the subject of birth, which seemed snobbish to Eliot.

Another supporter of the aristocratic position was Charles Frances Adams, with whom Eliot had many disagreements. Whereas Adams would welcome boys of wealth *or* merit, Eliot would go along only if they were also capable and adequately motivated. He thought the best men were those to whom a $75 difference in tuition was a matter of importance. In a letter to a schoolmaster, Eliot observed that the striking aspects of the son of well-to-do parents "are his undeveloped taste and faculty for intellectual labor, the triviality of his vocabulary, and his lack of judgement and sense of proportion . . . ."

In Eliot's views, Groton, St. Paul's, etc., are the worse for reaching for the rich only. Eliot insisted that a large proportion of the most successful and competent graduates of Harvard come from families of most modest circumstances. Two-thirds of the faculty came from such backgrounds.[45]

From all of this we should not conclude that Harvard has had little interest in the poor boy. From the very beginning the college tried to spare the "scholar" any tuition fees. He was just too poor to finance a large part of the cost of his education. Through provision of dormitories, dining halls with menus for the poor as well as for others, through loans of furniture, and, of course, through financial aid, the university authorities sought to keep total costs down.

In 1826 a committee proposed a reduction of tuition from $55 to $30. A total cut of $100 "would enable the yeomanry of our country and others of not large property to give their sons an education at their college instead of being compelled to send them to other seminaries."[46]

In later years the college tried to increase aid at least as much as tuition rose. But they could not keep up with the rising *total* cost of higher education. An official report of 1960 noted this failure: ". . . We are still to bring to Cambridge only a few students from low income groups, and almost none from the lowest. . . ." The average scholarship in 1958–1959

42. W. Bentinck-Smith, *The Harvard Book* (1953), pp. 338-339.

43. *Four American Universities* (1895), p. 16; Cf., *Report of the Visiting Committee of the Harvard Board of Overseers, January, 1849*, pp. 29-31; *Committee of the Board of Overseers*, January 10, 1894.

44. *Harvard University Commemoration of the 250th Anniversary of the Founding of Harvard College*, 1887, p. 233.

45. Henry James, *Charles W. Eliot: President of Harvard University*, 1930, pp. 148-151; C. W. Eliot to C. F. Adams, May 27, 1904; C. W. Eliot to Barrett Wendell, April 15, 1893; C. F. Adams, *Three φβκ Addresses* (1907), pp. 130-131; C. W. Eliot, *The Aims of the Higher Education*, 1891, pp. 234-235.

46. *The Report of the Committee . . . to Enquire Into the Income and Expenses of the College*, December 26, 1826.

was $1,130; the average cost to a resident student, $2,750.[47]

Eliot was one of the first to see the need of enlarging the reservoir from which Harvard drew its students. President Lowell further extended Eliot's campaign to widen the sources from which Harvard drew its students. President Conant, by introducing the national scholarships, continued the movement initiated by Eliot, and extended by Lowell, and emphasized further merit against birth. It is not surprising that even as early as 1917 Andrew Carnegie, in turning down a request from Lowell for aid, remarked " . . . Let me congratulate you, however, on the great gift that has fallen to Harvard which, under your wise and progressive administration, has become at least a great university, opening its doors to high school scholars upon equal terms . . . ."[48]

The Conant National Scholarship program was democratic in the sense that the large stipends were adequate to attract poor and able students, and incidentally open Harvard to the impecunious in areas formerly sending few men to Harvard. Yet the distribution of these scholars on the basis of occupations of fathers, for students in the classes of 1938 through 1944, though difficult to interpret, does not suggest the scholars predominantly came from low-income families.[49]

Time and again the friends of Harvard insisted that Harvard's students were primarily from middle-income families and only a minority came from the poor or the rich. Help was available to the poor, although throughout a large part of Harvard's history much was made of the need of students' paying at least part of the bill.

A report in the year 1826 commented:

. . . this institution was never designed by the Founders . . . to be an establishment for the rich alone, but rather as one where persons with a moderate property might have their children educated upon equal terms with the rich without being under the necessity of soliciting pecuniary aid in a manner [unacceptable] to their feelings. . . .[50]

In summary, Harvard still is a college for the relatively high-income groups, and for the sons of business managers and especially of professional families. Throughout its history this has been true. Efforts are indeed made to help those who are unable to pay the bill. But the aid is not adequate to attract students from the poverty families, or often from middle-income families. Harvard has also had its share of aristocrats who favored the wealthy and the well-borne and opposed entry of minority origins. No one would claim that Harvard has eliminated prejudice. All that can be said is that a college reflects the attitudes of the population. If prejudices still prevail, there have been great improvements and I doubt that any college has a better record than Harvard. Certainly Harvard is far from being a rich man's college, though there are many rich at Harvard. It is, in fact, a middle-income college primarily, drawing its students from middle- and, to some extent, low-income groups, and increasingly from minority groups. The contribution of the public school steadily increases as does that of outlying parts of the country. For the advance of democracy at Harvard, Presidents Eliot and Conant especially deserve credit.

I cannot refrain from commenting on the issues of democratization of Harvard that arose under President Lowell, who himself came from one of New England's leading families. Believing that consistent with Harvard's oldest tradition students should not only go to classes together but they should also live

47. C. W. Eliot to Colonel Henry Lee, April (?) 21, 1871; C. W. Eliot to Olmstead, January 24, 1902; H. L. Blackwell to E. A. Rowland, June 15, 1909; F. Bowles, *Students' Expenses*, 1893, p. 27; *Admission to Harvard College*, p. 36.

48. Andrew Carnegie to President A. Lawrence Lowell, May 9, 1912, in Harvard University Archives; *Report of the Committee on Admissions on the New Plan of Admission*, 1914, pp. 2-3, 12-17.

49. *The Harvard College Scholarship*, 1941: *A Descriptive Report at the End of Six Years*; Department of Commerce, *Income of Families and Persons in the United States*, 1963.

50. *To President and Fellows: Committee on Income and Expenses of College*, December 26, 1826.

together, Lowell of course sponsored both the freshmen dormitories and the House Plan.

One of the problems that confronted college authorities was the snobbishness of some of the sons of Harvard's leading families. A substantial number of the boys from select private schools sought freedom from house control by moving into the rabbit warrens. They apparently sought especially freedom from parietal regulations and escape from dining with the masses of Harvard students. In 1933, for example, there were 19 students, former house residents, from seven select private schools living in 59 Plympton Street. Their grades at mid-year were 3 unsatisfactory, 2 insufficient, 3 in group VI (average Ds), 11 in group V (all C's, that is, just passing), 1 in group IV (half C's and half B's) and no one in Group I through III. This was scarcely a distinguished group.[51]

51. A. L. Lowell to S. Morison, November 10, 1928; A. L. Lowell to E. Harkness, September 30, 1930; A. L. Lowell to C. A. Coolidge, September 3, 1913; A. L. Lowell to F.W. Taussig, February 13, 1932; A.L. Lowell to Prof. L. P. Dennis, November 29, 1916; in *A. L. Lowell Papers.*

3

Student Behavior

The problem of student behavior may seem of marginal interest in a book on the economics of Harvard. But the problems raised are relevant. Fines, for example, played an important part in the financing of the college during the first 150 years at any rate. The price and quality of commons was an important issue through most of Harvard's history. Students insisted on not getting rancid butter and wanted the privilege of eating out. Through periodic outbursts they fought for decent and adequate food and service.

Another issue relevant for the Harvard economy was the time and energy given to disciplinary problems and especially in the first 200 years. The productivity of the Harvard teacher suffered greatly as a result of the diversion of energy and time to these matters; and the damage done to the plant by the students was costly to the students and to the college, which could scarcely afford the broken windows, the burned buildings, and the destroyed kitchenware. Again, hazing, inclusive of cruel treatment of freshmen, reduced the college's productivity; that is, impaired the quality of its educational product.

An important material loss stemmed from the expulsion of students—even a whole class on occasion—and the effect on enrollment of student excesses, especially in the early nineteenth century, was serious. Enrollments at rival institutions profited at Harvard's expense.[1]

Early Punishment

Harvard's first president, Nathaniel Eaton, caused "two men to hold a young gentleman, while he so unmercifully beat him with a cudgel that upon complaint of it in Court in 1639, he was fined a hundred marks . . ."[2]

Under Henry Dunster, "if any student shall violate the law of God or of this College, either from perverseness or from gross negligence, after he shall have been twice admonished, he may *be whipped* (virgis coerceatur), if not an adult [eighteen]; but if an adult his case shall be laid before the Overseers, that notice may be publicly taken of him according to his deserts . . ."[3]

In an instance when a student spoke blasphemous words, the offender was sentenced to be whipped before all the scholars and, besides, had his degree suspended and had to sit alone in the hall at meal time.[4]

From the very beginning the conduct of students was meticulously regulated. Thus in 1650:

During their Residence, they shall studiously redeeme their time, observe ye generall houres . . . diligently attend ye lectures . . . .

No Scholar shall buy, sell, or exchange anything to ye value of six-pence without ye allowance of his parents, guardians, or tutours . . . .

---

1. Morison, *Three Centuries of Harvard, 1636-1936*, p. 253.
2. J. Chaplin, *Life of Henry Dunster*, 1872, pp. 60-61.
3. *Ibid*, p. 67, italics in original.
4. *Ibid.*

*The Scholars shall never use their Mother-tougue . . . .
All students shall be slow to speak and eschew (as
much as in them lies), shall take care that others may
avoid all swearing, lying, cursing, needless asservations, foolish talking, scurrility, battling, filthy speaking, chiding, strife, railing, reproaching, abusive jesting, uncomely noise, uncertain rumors . . . .*

The General Court, in 1649, ordered:

*Forasmuch as the wearing of long hair after the
manner of ruffians and barbarous Indians, hath begun
to invade New England contrary to the rule of God's
word which sayeth it is a shame for a man to wear
long hair . . . doe declare and manifest our dislike and
destestation against the wearing of such long haire . . .
whereby men doe deforme themselves, and offend
sober and modest men, and doe corrupt good
manners . . . .*

In the 1760s the following offenses were listed
among others:

*Sometimes the evils to be remedied were "the breach
of the Sabbath, more especially in time of public
worship," the remedy for which was "the Tutors sitting in the meetinghouse so as more conveniently to
oversee the scholars;" "combinations among the undergraduates for the perpetration of unlawful acts;"
the "disorders of which they were guilty by being
absent from their chambers, contrary to law, at unseasonable times of night;" "the crime of taking cuts
out of books" belonging to the public Library; the
loose practice of "going and staying out of town
without leave;" "the costly habits of many of the
scholars, their wearing gold or silver lace, or brocades,
silk night-gowns, etc., as tending to discourage persons from giving their children a college education."[5]*

Commons

I recall as a senior tutor of one of Harvard's houses
that the food in Dunster House in the 1930s was
excellent. Yet complaints of institutional food were
persistent despite the high quality.

In 1807 discontent with commons led to a serious
rebellion, when a student did "publicly in the Hall
insult the authority of the College by hitting one of
the officers with a potatoe." A freshman and sophomore row in commons brought about the suspension
of many students. In 1828 the faculty announced its
interest in barring disorderly students from commons;
but considered effects on finance. In 1842 the college
abandoned commons, with a resultant improvement
of student behavior. But in the latter part of the nineteenth century the college again made commons available, the occasion being a wish to reduce costs of a
college education.[6]

*Before the Revolutionary War, the college had already expressed a large interest in the effect of
commons on student costs. They not only furnish a
salutary diet, but they also contract the price of a
college education. The Commons . . . regulate the
price and quality of board even in private families;
and thus secure in the town a general style of living,
at once economical and favorable to health and to
study . . . that simplicity, which makes the fare cheap
and wholesome and philosophical, renders it also unsatisfactory to dainty palates . . . .[7]*

Dissatisfaction with commons was, as noted above,
a frequent cause of trouble. In 1766 a great rebellion
occurred at Harvard following a protest at the serving
of rancid butter.[8]

The rules of 1765 provided for compulsory attendance at the commons, with some exceptions.

5. *College Books* in Harvard University Archives, vol. I,
   1650, p. 26; Samuel Eliot Morison, *Harvard College in the
   Seventeenth Century*, 1936, vol. I, p. 88; *The Laws of
   Harvard College*, 1796; *The Harvard Book*, 1953, pp.
   141-143; *History of Harvard University,* pp. 216-216.
6. *History of Harvard College*, p. 70; *An Historical Sketch of
   Harvard University*; *Four American Universities.* p. 42;

and H. Ware to Mr. Gray, November 17, 1828, in Harvard
University Archives.
7. *History of Harvard University*, pp. 218-220.
8. Especially, W. C. Lane, "The Rebellion of 1766 in Harvard College," in *Publications of the Colonial Society of
   Massachusetts*, vol. I, (1906), pp. 34-59.

Vote 1. All the Tut^rs. & Professors, Graduates & Undergraduates Who have Studies in College, shall constantly be in Cŏmons, while actually residing at the College, Vacation Times excepted, & shall breakfast dine and sup in the Hall, @ the stated Meal Times except Waiters . . . .

Among other matters dealt with were availability of clean cloth, conduct at meal time, provisions to be made available, prices to be charged, and menu plans of the scholars

The Tables shall be cover'd with Clean Cloths twice a Week or oftner if judg'd necessary by the Pres^dt. & Tut^rs & properly furnish'd for the respective Meals, @ the Charge of the College; And that a just & equal Assessment of any Damage may be made, all the Tables shall be mark'd & Number'd, & the Waiter for that Table where such Damage may be done, shall return to the Stew^d. or Butler respectively, and Acc^o. therof . . . .

And all the Scholars while @ their Meals shall sit in their Places & behave with Decency; & whosoever shall be rude or Clamorous @ such Time, or shall go out of the Hall without leave, before Thanks be return'd, shall be punished by one of the Tut^rs. not exceeding five Shillings.

The Provision for the Comons shall be purchas'd by the Steward with the College Stock, wth. Provision spent @ the College.

On one occasion, a complaint on butter was followed by a rebellion of the students. The following gives the part of the students version of the developments. (Asa is Asa Dunbar of class of 1767.)

1. *And it came to pass in the ninth Month, on the 23^d Day of the Month, the Sons of Harvard murmured and said,*
2. *Behold! bad and unwholesome Butter is served out unto us daily; now therefore let us depute Asa, the Scribe, to go unto our Rulers, & seek Redress.*
3. *Then arose Asa, the Scribe, and went unto Belcher, the Ruler, & said, behold our Butter*

stinketh, and we cannot eat thereof; now give us, we pray thee Butter that stinketh not.
4. *And Belcher the Ruler said, trouble me not, but begone unto thine own Place; but Asa obeyed him not.*
5. *So when Belcher and others of the Rulers departed, the Sons of Harvard clapped their Hands, & hissed & cried, aha! aha!*
6. *Now therefore let us punish Asa the Scribe, & make him confess before all Harvard; and Belcher the Ruler (sirnamed Bowl, alias Beelzebub) said, let him also be placed below his Fellows, & they agreed to that also.*
7. *And all, even all, the Sons of Harvard met and agreed also . . . .*
8. *So on the Morrow, bad and unwholesome Butter was served out unto them, and they rose up and departed every one unto his own Place.*
9. *But the Rulers were greatly affrighted; and Edward the Chief Ruler (Sirnamed Gutts) rose up and said, Men and Brethren, what shall we do? Behold our Pupils have risen up in Rebellion against us, & have hissed & clapped their Hands, & have committed diverse Offences against us. . . .*

The sons of Harvard rebelled when classmates were threatened with expulsion. They announced their withdrawal from college should the leaders be expelled.

A committee of the faculty sampled the butter: of eleven samples, they condemned seven absolutely and four could be used for sauce only. The committee criticized the steward severely.

Disciplinary Action: Examples

A few instances of early disciplinary action are worthy of recording. In 1682:

W^n for his abusive Carriages in requiring some freshmen to go upon his private Errands, in striking them; and in scandalous negligence of these Dutyes he is *bound to attend by Colledge Law; and having persisted in his evills, notwithstanding means used to reclaime him; and not attending the Corporation this day, w^n required; he is sentenced first to be deprived of the pension formerly allowed him, and also to be expelled the Colledge; and in case he p^{r}sume after the space of 24 hours to appear within the Colledge walls, there the fellows are to cause him to be carried before Civil authority.*[9]

Even faculty members were not immune. Mr. Nathan Price, a fellow and tutor came under the surveillance of the corporation in 1742. The corporation ordered Price removed from his rooms and his relations with the college severed for various wrong doings. But Price was recalcitrant. " . . . That then the Pres^{at}, Tut^{rs} and Professors be and hereby are impowered and directed to break open or cause to be broken open, the Doors of the said Chambers and Studies, and to remove out of them the s^d Price's goods. . . ."[10]

Behavior in the First Half of the Nineteenth Century

In 1805 the college experienced a bread and butter rebellion. When the college suspended half the college, students would not submit to unconditional surrender. A committee of the overseers led by a Republican urged reform of the commons; the Democrats insisted on support of authority.[11]

In March, 1807, the three lower classes complained to President Webber of the unsatisfactory state of the commons. The usual sequence of events followed. Students left the commons in a disorderly manner. Apparently the three classes held a meeting to discuss their common interests. Students insulted members of the faculty, for which they received admonitions and then suspension. What especially aroused the government of the college was the assembly of the classes without approval of the president. "The first question that engaged the attention of the Corporation was, whether this extraordinary combination, publicly entered into and deliberately executed, should pass over into silence."

To pass this unnoticed "would make the Seminary worse than useless; it would be a public nuisance." [12]

The administration was puzzled nevertheless at what remedial measures should be taken. They were not anxious to rusticate or expel all the students. The ringleaders and offenders were not generally known. Hence the suggestion was made of sending them home in the custody of their parents. The corporation would suspend the law on combination and give the students an opportunity to sign a certificate which admitted their excesses. Several did not sign statements.

In 1818 a prolonged fight in the commons broke out with most of the crockery and many heads broken. As usual the college made an example of several students, whereupon the students, rallied around the Rebellion Tree. The venerable John Adams supported a return to flogging but after some more punishment, one victim being R. W. Emerson, the clash petered out.

In 1821 a corporation committee raised some questions concerning student behavior.

Do the students . . . habitually or frequently indulge in excessive drinking. If so, what number or proportion of them, and how frequently . . . ? What facts do you know with respect to improper connections with abandoned or other females? Is this species of vice more frequent than in other times . . . ?[13]

Prof. John Popkin replied on January 1, 1822. His reply reminds one of abuses of parietal regulations in the Harvard of the 1960s.

---

9. Morison, *Harvard College in the Seventeenth Century,* p. 451 and ch. 2.

10. *Ibid.*

11. *Harvard Graduates Magazine,* vol. XVI, no. 62, p. 291, December, 1807.

12. Narrative of the Proceedings of the Corporation of Harvard College Relative to the Late Disorders in That Seminary, April, 1807, in Harvard University Archives, pp. 4-19.

13. Copy of circular from corporation sent to the Reverend Wm. Popkin, September 12, 1821; *College Books.*

. . . Some who have rooms assigned them go out and leave the other occupant alone by agreement. This practice has sometimes [been] opposed and sometimes allowed, and sometimes carried on by collusion. But it is an evil, for the present and other obvious reasons.

Professor Popkin was not greatly concerned over increases in vice. Drinking of strong liquor was not on the increase nor, for that matter, was gambling. He was aware of vices in Boston that were not easily controlled. One of the first attacks would be control of expenditures.[14]

Another rebellion broke out in 1823, an event well described by Samuel Morison in his *Three Centuries of Harvard, 1636-1936*. The class was unruly, dropping cannon balls from upper windows, battling in the commons, and drenching bypassers with pails of mixtures of water and ink. A climax occurred when a "black" (not a participant) informed against a "high fellow" who was then expelled. Then hell broke loose, with the result that although John Quincy Adams, the father of a rebel, protested, 43 out of a class of 70 were expelled on commencement eve.[15]

Apparently the net effect of the troubles of 1821 and 1823 and the questionnaire on student behavior that followed was not startling. In 1824 the college published a revised code.[16] This code included the usual rules. Of special interest is the appointment of patrons for students living a hundred miles or more from Cambridge who were to supervise expenditures of the students.

In 1824, a committee with Justice Story as chairman considered the techniques for maintaining discipline.[17] The committee recommended various changes, the principle:

---

14. John Popkin to Messrs. Porter, Prescott, and Lowell, January 1, 1822, in *College Books.*
15. Morison, *Three Centuries of Harvard, 1636-1936*, pp. 251-252.
16. *Revised Code of College Laws, Reported to the Corporation by the Immediate Government, Harvard College,* December 27, 1824.
17. *Report of the Committee of the Overseers of Harvard College, January 6, 1825,* Harvard University Archives.

---

being that the President should be accorded larger authority and should be relieved, as far as possible, from merely ministerial duties; . . . *that fines should be abolished, and records of conduct kept and sent quarterly to students' parents; that some officer should visit every evening the room of every student. . . and a scheme of punishment—the various penalties of which were caution, warning, solemn admonition, official notice to parents, rustication and expulsion—were adopted.* [18]

At this time an overseers committee also urged the nonadmission of students aged less than sixteen "as the most effectual check upon gross irregularities." In order to encourage students of moderate means the committee would also introduce sumptuary laws as an instrument for keeping expenditures of rich students down.[19]

With time disciplinary problems seemed to require less attention. At least the rules became less comprehensive. Yet as late as 1839 to 1842, the Parietal Committee, which included professors, tutors, and proctors living within the walls of the college, had plenty to do.[20]

The case involving John Quincy Adams, whose son along with the largest part of his class was dismissed in 1823 for violation of college rules is of special interest. Although Adams would not "justify the disobediance and much less the violences of the young men who have incurred the censure of their institutions," he nevertheless argued that the punishments were too severe, and that dismissal without a commitment to take back the students and grant a degree was so severe a punishment that no greater punishment would be found for more serious transgressions. Such administration of the laws of the college would injure the college even more than the students who at least would be relieved by death, he argued, " . . . but the *degraded class!*—would it not necessarily shed some of its dishonor upon the University itself?"

---

18. *Four American Universities*, p. 21.
19. *Board of Overseers Report*, May 4, 1824, pp. 8-9.
20. *Records of the Parietal Committee, 1839-1842*, vol. II.

In a second letter Adams appealed to the overseers and corporation. He would relieve the college authorities, he said, "from the appearance of a vindictive exercise of authority against young men to whom character is everything, and towards whom I could not but hope that some feeling of tenderness would mingle even with the obligation of passing censure upon them...." [21] But the college authorities did not yield, despite a $1,000 gift from John Quincy Adams late in the year.

President Edward Everett, a very able scholar and government official, could only endure the presidency of Harvard for four years in the middle of the nineteenth century. He had no time for scholarship or the important duties of a president. His time went mainly to dealing with petty disciplinary problems Everett's unhappiness is revealed in the passages below.

I saw but a few weeks ago, and while I was thinking most favorable of this proposal, that a row of buildings, including that in which the beautiful panorama of Athens was preserved (bought at my instance by General Lyman), had been set on fire by an incendiary. Cambridge incendiaries, in my day, were generally students.

Mr. Francis, the superintendent of public buildings, brought me a small vial of gunpowder found in one of the privies with twine and cord wound about it; to increase the exploding, a small roll of paper was stuck in the cork by the way of match.... I instantly perceived the writing on this paper to be that of one of the parts for the exhibition of Tuesday next that then lay in my drawer, written, however, by a young gentleman hardly capable of this gunpowder plot.

Hateful duties in the morning to question three students about beckoning to loose women in the College Yard on Sunday afternoon; to two others about whistling in the passage; to another about smoking in the College Yard. Is this all I am fit for...? The life I am now leading must end, or it will end me.... It is necessary I understand to send in a proctor to protect the Professor from being pelted with chestnuts.... At Prayers in the evening, owing to the jostling and crowding of the Sophomore class in going out, the stove was thrown over with a crash.... In the evening, at about twenty before nine, I was told by my servant that University Hall was on fire. Found the south door burned through at the bottom and cotton and spirits of turpentine. My time taken up all day with the most disgusting details of discipline, such as make the heart perfectly sick—fraud, deception, falsehood, unhandsome conduct, parents and friends harassing me all the time and foolishly believe the lies their children tell them.... When Professor Peirce's house was building, he was obliged to keep the roof wet at night to prevent its destruction.

But the pressure of my duties here—great and severe beyond my expectation—makes it impossible for me to think even of anything else. Instead of two or three hours daily, in which I was told the routine of the work could be gone through, I find the whole day, from five in the morning till ten at night too short for it.... [22]

With the passage of time, the college continued to issue rules and regulations. By the 1860s the government of Harvard had become much more precise, [23] each student received ranking based on tests of various kinds and with deductions for misbehavior. The granting of scholarships was related to the annual scale.

Perhaps the most serious disturbances of all occurred in 1834. Of special interest is the fact that John Quincy Adams was chairman of the overseers' committee which supported the president in the actions taken by the administration inclusive of the calling in of the civil authorities to contend with the

21. John Quincy Adams to President Kirkland, May 19, 1823 and July 15, 1823, and from President Kirkland to J. Q. Adams, August 12, 1823, in Harvard University Archives.

22. P. R. Frothingham, *Edward Everett, Orator and Statesman*, 1925, pp. 268, 277-278, 281.

23. *Orders and Regulations of the Faculty of Harvard College*, July, 1863, in Harvard University Archives.

excesses perpetrated by the students. [24] The committee vigorously criticized student behavior and supported the punishment meted out.

In 1834, the college authorities were confronted with the most violent rebellion of Harvard's history. The occasion is not clear, but the college greatly damaged itself by dismissing the whole sophomore class and, worse, calling in civil authorities.

Upon the withdrawal of the student involved in the 1834 disturbances his classmates broke every window and destroyed every piece of furniture in the recitation room of the tutor. The students groaned and whistled at prayers and exploded firecrackers.

At a meeting of the board of overseers of August 25, the board held that the students had no just claim for exemption before the civil and criminal tribunals of the Commonwealth "for trespass upon property or against persons, whether belonging to the University or otherwise." Ultimately the college expelled seven members of the senior class who had contributed greatly to the disorders.

These were not the only problems. Bad behavior continued through most of the first half of the nineteenth century. Overseers in 1812 complained then of students at worship "sleeping, yawning, laying down their heads, noise in moving their feet, and at times laughing and grimace. . . ." In 1829, the president reported "trespasses of a grave nature were committed on the property of the College . . ."; and, he added, the guilty ones were expelled. [25] In reference to the gunpowder episode of 1842, the president reported:

"... in a time of great apparent tranquility . . . several attempts were made in the night time, to injure the college buildings and rooms by means of gunpowder, and which finally effected in the Northeast recitation room, in the second story of University Hall,

by placing and discharging in it, after midnight a bombshell of great fire and power, whereby the whole recitation room was destroyed, and every window blown out, the adjoining room, the room above and below, and the adjoining entry, greatly injured . . ." [26]

Fines

From the very beginning, Harvard College disciplined students by imposing fines. For more serious offenses the student might be punished by private or public admonitions and even by dismissal.

Students were subject to the fines for all kinds of offenses or failures: for being absent from classes or from the college, or being late at chapel, for purchasing distilled liquors, for damaging furniture, for staying at the college after commencement, for attending unauthorized lectures or entertainment, for sending Negroes to town to purchase liquor, for not wearing college dress at college, for not paying bills on time, for cutting pages out of library books. On the last the college in 1748 ordered that prior to lending a book, the librarian was to count the number of cuts in it. [27]

Students on occasion would steal lead from the roof of college buildings. Hence, a 1732 vote of the corporation:

Whereas there has of late been a considerable Quantity of Lead cut off from ye top of ye old College, to ye great Detriment of the said House; therefore voted yt ye Door leading up to ye top of said College, be locked, and yt there be two Keys to said Lock, one with ye President and ye other with ye Butler, and yt if any scholar be found on ye top of ye said College without leave from ye President or Tutors, he shall be liable to ye penality of five shillings, and satisfy for all Damages. Amd whosoever shall be privy to any

24. *Proceedings of the Overseers of Harvard University Relative to the Late Disturbances in that Seminary,* August, 1834, in Harvard University Archives, especially pp. 2-7, 22-27, 32-33, 46-47.

25. *Overseers Book,* October 27, 1812; *Report of the President to His Excellency the Governor and Board of Overseers of Harvard University,* October 20, 1829.

26. The President to the Committee of the Board of Overseers Appointed to Visit the Seminary on the 18th Day of October, 1842.

27. *Corporation Records,* 1748, vol. I, pp. 471-472, in Harvard University Archives; cf., *Sessions,* pp. 130-131.

person's transgressing ys Law in any part of it, without making Complaint to ye President or Tutors, shall suffer ye like penality of five or ten shillings at ye Discretion of ye President & Tutors. [28]

Even as late as 1860, the records of the parietal committee listed recurrent activities of the students requiring discipline.

Behavior at Commencement

In the early eighteenth century the college authorities were especially concerned over the students' exuberance during the commencement festivities. At the corporation meeting of June 11, 1722, it was observed that the college has "bin under such circumstances as to call aloud for humiliation and all due manifestation of it." The corporation continued to discuss that the preparation and provisions had been "the occasion of no small disorder." It was voted that "no plum cake, roasted, boiled or baked meat, no pies of any kind shall be made by any commencer, nor any distilled liquors." Violations were punishable by confiscation of illegal provisions and a 20-shilling fine. [29]

In the middle of the eighteenth century, commencement was still a source of trouble. At that time during commencement week, the commons in Cambridge "was covered with booths, erected in lines like streets, intended to accommodate the populace of Boston and the neighborhood with the amusements and refreshments of a fair, in which gambling, rioting, and dissipation of all kinds prevailed . . ." [30]

Termination of Fines

Fines continued to be imposed on a substantial scale until the middle of the nineteenth century. But the results were not good. As early as 1735, the corporation had expressed dissatisfaction with the deterrent effect of fines and hence would also admonish, degrade and expel. [31] Almost ninety years later a committee of the overseers reported that "it is designed to abandon the practice of imposing fines as an ordinary punishment: They are still enumerated however among the punishments which may be inflicted, but are to be applied only in such cases as may seem peculiarly to require them." [32]

In 1825, George Ticknor, the Humanist, expressed grave doubts of the efficacy of the fine system. In seventeen years, 354 students had been suspended, dismissed, expelled, and rusticated and less than 1400 had been admitted. He continued:

. . . it appears, that the fines received during the last seventeen years, have amounted to $11,392, and consequently that the annual average of fines has been about $670. This is a large sum, certainly, but the most unpleasant circumstance about it is, that such fines do little or no good at any College and by far the greater part of this ungracious branch of revenue was derived from the assessment of thirty-three cents for absence from a lecture or recitation, three cents for tardiness; three cents for absence from prayers, two cents for tardiness, and similar petty expedients. . . . [33]

Deterioration of Student Behavior

In his history, Quincy commented on the changes in morals and manners that had occurred in the middle of the eighteenth century. Students increasingly consumed beer and spirits, visited taverns and alehouses, and used bad language. In one disturbance in 1768, during which students broke tutors' windows and endangered their lives, the authorities expelled three

28. *College Books,* vol. IV, 1732, p. 155; *Publications of the Colonial Society of Massachusetts,* no. 16, p. 598.
29. *Corporation Records,* vol. I, 1722, pp. 140-141; *College Books,* vol. IV, p. 78; and *Publications of the Colonial Society of Massachusetts,* vol. V, no. 16, pp. 470-471.
30. J. Quincy, *op. cit.,* vol. II, pp. 92-93.

31. *Corporation Records,* vol. I, 1735, p. 316.
32. *Report of the Committee of Overseers of Harvard College,* January 6, 1825, in Harvard University Archives.
33. G. Ticknor, *Remarks and Changes Lately Proposed or Adopted in Harvard University,* 1825, p. 9.

students and rusticated others; and others withdrew from the college. But pressure from friends and families of students from leading families brought pardons for three of the culprits. President Holyoke protested the reversal:

He saw and lamented the weakness and injustice of thus allowing ringleaders in a rebellion to escape, because they were the sons of men of influence or wealth, at the same time that others, in truth less guilty, who were destitute of such external connections, were subjected to the penalties, and made to suffer the highest severities the laws of the College could inflict. . . .[34]

But even as late as 1823, there remained much dissatisfaction with the conduct of students, with the result that the university issued a new code of statutes and laws. The authorities rearranged the holidays on the theory that warm weather induced rioting; proposed stricter supervision of students, and introduced a revolutionary division of classes according to proficiency and ability of students.

It is of some interest that despite the numerous violations for which students might be punished, President Quincy in 1831 had to affirm support of the faculty's right to expel students for neglect of studies. [35]

In the last hundred years fines and other punishments have been of much less importance than in the first hundred to two hundred years. Fines imposed on students are largely a thing of the past. The reason is that students behave better than they did in Harvard's first two hundred years. Another relevant point is that the college increasingly takes precautionary measures, though the college took many preventive measures even in the first two hundred years. Thus in 1733, the college hired seven men to walk and watch commencement eve and day, for commencement disorders were troublesome. In 1805, the college introduced its proctor system. They were to "reside constantly and preserve order within the walls, and to exercise the same

inspection and authority in their particular district and throughout College which it is the duty of a parietal tutor to exercise . . . ." [36]

It remained for President Quincy, a brave but tactless man, to experience the most serious problem. In his 1831-1832 report, the president commented on some problems.

Trespasses having been committed on the College buildings which could not be permitted to pass without punishment, and the laws of the University not being sufficient for the detection of the offenders, the Faculty, with the approbation of the Corporation, directed the evidence in their possession to be laid before the Grand Jury. In consequence of which, disorders having occurred in the Chapel, chiefly in the Freshmen class, the matriculation of all concerned in them was revoked and the whole Class put under probation . . . . [37]

In 1834, a bonfire occasioned a crisis. Several students were punished whereupon the students rebelled. Since the students had broken furniture and windows, and caused $300 of damage, a large sum at that time, and no one would confess, Quincy laid his problems before the Grand Jury. The President had broken an unwritten law that no police are ever called in unless outsiders are threatened. Then the students destroyed furniture and glass in the recitation rooms, hanged the President's effigy to the Rebellion Tree and caused a terrific explosion in the chapel. On May 29, 1834, the college dismissed virtually all sophomores.[38]

Quincy continued to have problems. In his 1841-1842 report, he discussed further rebellions and wanton destruction of property.[39]

On July 18, 1842, another serious disturbance occurred which has been labeled the Gunpowder Plot.

34. Quincy, *op. cit.,* vol. II, pp. 116-119.

35. *Report of the President of Harvard College,* 1830-1831, p. 4.

36. Quincy, *op. cit.,* vol. II, p. 292.

37. *Report of the President of Harvard College,* 1831-1832, p. 19; cf., 1833-1834, pp. 1, 17-18.

38. See especially Morison, *Three Centuries of Harvard, 1636-1936,* pp. 251-253, and *Report of the President of Harvard College,* 1833-1834, pp. 1, 17-18.

39. *Report of the President of Harvard College,* 1841-1842, p. 1 and pp. 9-11 of the appendix.

This was the title given to the July 18, 1842, disturbance. In the Corporation Papers was found the original hand written letter [and 2 printed copies of same] from Pres. Quincy to one William P. Hallett [with red Postal Cancellation] regarding Hallett's son, J. R. Hallett. The latter was dismissed by vote of the Faculty for violation of the rule forbidding the possession and/or use of gunpowder. On June 29, a College House had been blown up, on June 30, a recitation room had been blown up and on July 4, [there is some disagreement as to whether it was July 4th or 5th] a bombshell was exploded in University Hall doing much damage.

It was ascertained that Hallett had puchased 2 lbs. of gunpowder on June 29 and ½ lb. on the preceding May 23. Hallett produced 2 lbs. when questioned by the faculty but was dismissed anyhow. [40]

In the 1840s students set a bonfire in University Hall and while the faculty was investigating they set fire to the doors of University Hall. Of a total enrollment of 269, the college in 1845-1846 dismissed 25, and 42 were publicly admonished. Obviously such attrition increased the costs of higher education relative to the investment, and in absorbing so much time of the faculty and the administration greatly reduced the effectiveness of higher education.[41]

Improvement of Behavior

But beginning with the Sparks regime (1849 to 1853), students began to behave better. Spark's policy of salutary neglect seemed to work.[42]

At the very beginning of his administration President Eliot was confronted with a gunpowder explosion that almost wrecked Stoughton Hall. The college failed to find the perpetrators.

In general, conditions improved greatly under Eliot. The increased responsibilities on the student

under the elective system and the higher requirements for admission inclusive of admission at more advanced age seemed to Eliot the explanation of the greater maturity and sobriety of Harvard undergraduates during his regime. Even at the beginning of his administration, he commented on the harmonious, not conflicting, relationship between the faculty and students.[43]

Persistent Problems

In the last generation, a good part of the time of college administrators and even faculty members has been spent on revising parietal regulations and enforcing them. One of the surprising aspects of Harvard history is that little space is given these problems in the Harvard documents until relatively recent times. Indeed, vague hints appear about dissolute women. For example, the 1734 College Laws announced fines for any student "who would familiarly associate with any person of a loose or ill character . . . ." [44] But in the college rules there is scarcely a specific reference in the first two hundred years of Harvard to relations of students with women. Only an occasional hint appears that students go to town for immoral reasons. Indeed, one of Harvard's early presidents, it was discovered later, had resigned because he had impregnated a servant in his home. But the college remained discreetly silent.

A rare document is the following. A student had apparently had relations with a young lady. The student's family, it was expected, would reimburse the expectant mother. The acting president of Harvard was interested in settling the matter.

From what was said to me by Young Coleman a few days since, I am not surprised at the woman's communication to you. In consequences of that interview I wrote to his father, urging upon him the importance of furnishing me with the means of settling the

---

40. *Corporation Papers*, July 12, 1842.

41. *Report of the President of Harvard College*, 1845-1846, p. 14; 1846-1847, pp. 16-22.

42. *Ibid.* 1849-1850, p. 15.

43. *Report of the Board of Overseers of Committee to Visit the College*, 1871-1872, pp. 30-31; C. W. Eliot to Albert Stickney, February 5, 1889 and April 11, 1891.

44. *College Books*, vol. I, p. 141.

unhappy business if possible, and promising, in that event, to see the woman. I am awaiting an answer to that communcation. [45]

Among the troublesome problems confronting college authorities is the appearance of the student. The laws of 1734 required that "no scholar shall go beyond ye college yar[d] or fences without coat, cloak or gown . . . ." If he should the fine would be 2 shillings or less.[46]

Harvard assumed much greater responsibilities in these areas in her first two hundred years than is assumed in more recent times. Strong views on long hair prevailed in the seventeenth century, as noted earlier, and there has been a renewed interest in this problem in recent times. But clearly the student has much more freedom in mid twentieth century than in the first two hundred years.

Relations with the police have been a difficult problem in the early years of higher education abroad and as early as the seventeenth century at Harvard. Students have always resented the "interference" of civil authorities, as they clearly showed in the Quincy period at Harvard and in the 1960s at Berkeley, California. Quincy, in calling upon the civilian authorities in the 1830s, earned the unending hostility of the students.[47]

In 1659, the corporation, impressed by "exorbitant practises" of some students, gave the town watch power of inspection into the manner and orders of all persons related to the college, whether within or without the precincts of the said college house and lands.

Whereas there are great complayntes of the exorbitant practises of Some stud^ts of this Coff. by their abusive wordes and acc̄ons to the Watch of this Towne. The Corporacc̄on accounting it their duty by all lawfull, meanes to seeke the redress thereof for the future, do hereby declare to all persons whom it may conc^rne, That the Watch of this Town from time to time, and at all times shall have full pow^r of inspec̄c̄on ino the mann^rs & orders of all persons related to the Coff. whether wth in or wth out the p^rcincts of the said Coff. houses & lands, as by law they are impowred to act in cases they within the lim̄itts of their Towne, any law, vsage, or costome to the contrary not withstanding. Provided always we Judge it not convenient, neither do we allow that any the said Watchmen should lay violent hands on any of the stud^ts being found with in ye p^rcincts of the Coff. yard, otherwise then so as they may secure them vntill they may informe the Presid^t or some of the fellowes, neithe[r] shall they in any case break into their Chambers or studjes, without speciall order from Presid^t or fellowes . . . . [48]

Student participation in the government of a college is a perennial problem, one that has emerged as a very important one in the 1960s. In this connection, the lack of interest of Harvard students in such matters until the 1960s is of some significance. President Eliot related an experience in the early twentieth century when a proposal was made that undergraduates would accept some of the responsibilities for governing the college now exercised elsewhere. Their reply was "they would have nothing to do with such an enterprise; that the government of the College was not their affair . . . ."[49]

The hazing of freshmen, interclass roughhousing and the like are in part an economic issue. They tend to reduce the value of the education product. The costs of this kind of behavior were high through most of Harvard's history. Such costs to higher education continue. But they are of declining importance.

In 1860, President Felton complained of the brutal tussles between freshmen and sophomores: " . . . the meeting has degenerated into a match at boxing and fighting . . . and the scenes have been

45. The Reverend Dr. Peabody to J. S. Hillard, May 12, 1862.
46. *College Books*, vol. I, p. 141.
47. *President to Visiting Committee of the Board of Overseers*, May 1, 1832; *Committee of Overseers . . . to Visit Harvard University*, October 19, 1841, p. 124.

48. Quincy, *op. cit.*, vol. II, p. 514; *Meeting of Corporation*, June 10, 1659; *College Books*, vol. I, p. 44.
49. C. W. Eliot to Professor W. M. Wilson, October 29, 1907.

described as not only not suitable to a literary institution, but as coarse and violent in character and dangerous to the persons engaged in them . . . ."[50]

To the overseers in Eliot's days the whole business seemed deplorable. The overseers cried out against practices that blurred the fair fame of the college. Thus they reported that although reduced or abolished elsewhere, hazing "maintains its hold here, and will probably continue to do so . . . until the student body improves!!"[51]

Harvard authorities often were inadequate to the task of keeping order. A rather elderly tutor, Joseph Mayhew, in the eighteenth century, became a target for undergraduate attacks. The student soon discovers the incompetent. Students rolled logs down the stairs by his door, broke his door knob, and stole his liquor. When his window was broken, however, he detected the culprit by calculating the arc of the missile.

Professor Pearson, in 1788, kept a journal of disorders. His journal revealed intoxication, noisy conduct, snowballs, biscuits, teacups, and a knife thrown at tutors, lights extinguished at evening prayers, all but one sophomore assembled, all tutors' windows broken, stones thrown at Professor Wigglesworth in midst of a lecture, pistols fired, excess drink and boisterous behavior, and concealed Bibles at prayer time.[52]

Thomas Hill, later president of Harvard, entered Harvard in 1839. He was religious and studious—traits that encouraged other students to persecute him. He experienced gravel stones thrown at his window as well as rifle shots, mattresses removed and pails of water emptied on him, and windows broken every night.[53]

As president of Harvard during the Civil War, Hill sent the following letter to President Lincoln. One may question the wisdom of this action.

Dear Sir,

The Faculty last evening voted that Lincoln Junior, be publicly admonished for smoking in Harvard Square, after being privately admonished for the same offense. The word "publicly" simply means that it is my duty to inform you of the admonition, and I trust, Sir, that you will impress upon him the necessity not only of attention to matters of decorum, but of giving heed to private admonitions of his instructors . . . .

50. C. C. Felton to Anonymous Recipient, August 20, 1860.
51. *Report of the Board of Overseers of the Committee to Visit the College,* 1871-1872, p. 31.
52. *The Harvard Book,* pp. 49-50, 111-113.
53. *Ibid.,* 155-158.

4

The Harvard Product

The Harvard Product

I am interested in this subject primarily because the activities of the students suggest the kind of product the college turns out. Harvard, not content to give the student merely a series of lectures and recitations, has provided much more. That it has taken responsibility for his physical comforts, e.g., food and lodgings, his conduct throughout the day, his spiritual life, and, later, athletics, social activities, and medical care, meant that the college was providing an increasingly complex and costly product.

A substantial part of the cost of a Harvard education is related to the services that are not strictly educational.

Moreover, the ingredients offered by the college varied over the years. Under the stress of modern conditions and especially with increasing mobility, and the impact of Darwinism and Spencerism, the college has tended to reduce the content of its non-educational services, and particularly during the second half of the nineteenth century. But Lowell, and also Pusey, returned at least part of the way to the service-mix of the seventeenth and eighteenth centuries, whereas Conant showed a much greater interest in the pure, narrow educational product of the university.

In this chapter and elsewhere, we also discuss some aspects of a Harvard education. Until relatively recent years, the emphasis was not on teaching young men how to think, communicate, make mature judgments, etc.; rather, the emphasis was on memorizing and reciting on parrot fashion. Hence the product was not as valuable as it might have been. Also, examinations were primitive and there was strong opposition to attempts to classify students on the basis of tests of any kind.

Education at Harvard

Anyone who is at all conversant with modern theories of education and the practice of higher education in the seventeenth and eighteenth centuries and the first half of the nineteenth century at Harvard is not likely to be overly enthusiastic about the kind of training that was received by the Harvard student.

Even up to Eliot's day the education in some of the professional schools, e.g., medicine, was shockingly low. In the college, in the first two hundred years the student devoted most of his time to memorizing and reciting. The authorities did not encourage independent work or the application of intelligence or imagination to the problems treated, and the curriculum was narrow by present-day standards.

Even as late as 1868-1869, Acting President Peabody complained, not of the cramming practice of private tutors, but rather of their unavailability and high charges. Finally, in 1894, the college authorities, impressed by the steady rise of cramming and last-minute seminars, voted discontinuance of cram sessions.[1]

---

1. *Report of the President of Harvard College,* 1868-1869, p. 5; *Harvard Graduates Magazine,* vol. 3, p. 79, 1894.

Gradually the student escaped from the confining pressures of college rules. In the early nineteenth century, Morison tells us that students increasingly found ways to avert excessive confinement in the college yard. Even in the prehorsecar days in the early nineteenth century, students in large numbers walked to town over the West Boston Bridge. With the help of the horsecar in the middle of the nineteenth century, students more easily could avoid excessive restraint imposed by the college. In 1862-1863, the president blamed the horsecars for the college's inability to save students from temptations of the city.[2]

Examinations and Standards

Over most of Harvard's history, examinations were oral rather than written and, on the whole, not very satisfactory. Students rebelled against attempts to classify them on the basis of tests of any kind. In 1791, the students petitioned the college for exemptions from examinations, objecting especially to the reports and records of merit. Even the visiting committee of the overseers, responsible for the examinations, complained of the "labor, tediousness and consumption of their time occasioned by these examinations..." In 1826, the classification of students in divisions according to their proficiency, a practice introduced against the wishes of faculty and students, brought disturbances; and finally the overseers yielded.[3]

It was not until the middle 1850s that written examinations were introduced. After a year of experience the president wrote: "This mode of examination, from its greater thoroughness and its entire fairness, is found to be of great service, whether regarded as a motive to study or as a test of scholarship."[4]

Joseph Choate, of the class of 1852, described well the earlier oral examinations:

Our examinations did not amount to much, and I think never did until long after we left college. We were pretty carefully examined on entering to test our qualifications for admission, but never after that, that I can recall, were we subjected to any serious examination or to any written examinations at all. Every year the corporation appointed a board of examiners in each of the subjects into which our curriculum was divided. They were gentlemen of distinction from various parts of the State of Massachusetts, and I think none from any other part of the country. They were not especially versed, as a rule, in the subjects on which they were appointed examiners. ...[5]

The School Year

In view of the paternal attitude of the college authorities, it is not surprising to find the school year much longer in Harvard's early than in its later history. In this sense the college was then more productive, for the plant was in operation and the faculty available most of the year. Theoretically the student was in residence the whole year in the early Harvard period. This does not mean that in fact he always was in residence. He found many excuses to go home, the explanation being a tooth to be pulled, a grandmother's death, escorting a young man to school, etc., etc.[6]

The 1734 laws of the college provided:

Those Scholars, who live within ten miles of the College, may have leave four days in a Month, to visit their friends; those who live from ten to fifty miles, may have leave for ye Purpose Aforesaid, once a quarter, not to exceed ten days each time; those who live fifty miles & upwards, may have leave, for the like purpose, twice in a year, not to exceed Twenty one days each time. ...

2. *Report of the President of Harvard College, 1855-1856*, pp. 4-5; *1862-1863*, pp. 13-14; Morison, *Three Centuries of Harvard, 1636-1936*, p.296.
3. Quincy, *op. cit.,* vol. II, pp. 280-281, 369.
4. *Report of the President of Harvard College, 1857-1858*, p. 4; cf. *1856-1857*, p. 4.

5. Choate, *op. cit.,* pp. 88-89.
6. Cf., Morison, *Harvard College in the Seventeenth Century*, pp. 110-111.

Between 1713 and 1749, there was a summer vacation of several weeks duration following commencement. In 1749, the college introduced a 5-week winter vacation and shortened the summer vacation to 5 weeks. In 1766, the students were allowed four vacations, 13 weeks in all, a calendar which continued until 1802 with slight modifications. Confronted with fuel problems, the authorities in 1802 provided for a 7-week vacation in the winter, with additional vacations of 4 weeks after commencement and 2 weeks in May. By 1825-1826, term time consisted of three terms covering 38 weeks and vacations at four intervals of 14 weeks. More frequent vacations might, it was hoped, reduce absences. In 1826, the college announced 42 weeks of college attendance in the future and in 1850, 40 weeks of school and two 6-week vacations. Clearly, in the first two hundred years, term time was much longer than in recent years, e.g., 34 weeks in the 1960s. The long summer vacation was still not the practice.[7] But pressures for vacations seemed to intensify, the explanation in part being economic pressures.

Under crisis conditions, the college modified the calendars. Thus, the college deprived the students of a vacation in 1730 following loss of time during a smallpox epidemic, and also in 1764 following another epidemic and the burning of Harvard Hall. In the Revolutionary War period, the college modified the winter vacation and cut the spring vacation in response to the unavailability or high prices of wood.[8]

How productive the college is depends in no small part on the quality of the entering student. This is especially important since psychologists (e.g., Bloom) estimate that 90 percent of a student's intelligence is determined by age seventeen. In Harvard's first hundred years, the students came largely from the upper classes.[9] It may be assumed that the students with these origins were also highly intelligent and cultured. But the evidence is not all on that side.

Even as late as 1863, President Hill wrote: "Our country produces men of as fine natural talent as can be found among any people. But the talent almost never attains any high degree of culture without being transplanted to Europe for a few years."[10]

Assessing the students of the 1880s and 1890s, George Santayana, the Harvard philosopher, wrote as follows:

About high questions of politics and religion their minds were open but vague; they seemed not to think them of practical importance; they acquiesced in people having any views they like on such subjects; the fluent and fervid enthusiasms so common among European students, prophesying about politics, philosophy and art, were entirely unknown among them.[11]

It will be recalled that in the Eliot period, there was much discussion of the greater interest of scholarship students and public school students in their studies than among the sons of affluent parents. Bishop William Lawrence thus commented on this matter as it appeared in 1871.

Of the one hundred and fifty-nine members of my class who graduated, I recall only three or four who took high rank because they loved literature, the classics, or mathematics for their own sake. The very large proportion of those who took excellent or high rank were impelled by the necessity of earning scholarships. The rank and file of men, some of whom had excellent ability and latent intellectual ambitions, either loafed away much of their time, or read and studied in lines outside the college curriculum.[12]

7. *Report of the President of Harvard College,* 1825-1826, p. 10, and *Harvard University Catalogues;* cf., *Corporation Records,* vol. I, pp. 139, 488; vol. II, pp. 253, 257; *Treasurers' Journals* in Harvard University Archives, vol. III, pp. 174-176; vol. IV, pp. 616, 620; and *Williard's Mss. Account of the College* in Ebeling's copy of the 1794 Triennial.

8. *Corporation Records,* vol. I, p. 255; vol. II, pp. 188-191, 205, 207, 430, 475, 483.

9. Morison, *Harvard College in the Seventeenth Century,* p. 451 and ch. 2.

10. *Report of the President of Harvard College,* 1862-1863, p. 7.

11. G. Santayana, *Characters and Opinions in the United States, passim.*

12. W. Lawrence, *Memories of a Happy Life,* 1926, p. 21.

Undoubtedly in some respects the Harvard students have been disappointing, in part the explanation being the primitive methods of instruction until Eliot's day; and all the more disappointing in view of their origins. Both from the occupations of their parents and, later, from aptitude tests, it is clear that the Harvard students should achieve much.

By 1960 the college authorities could boast of the high quality of its students.

... the upper half of the entering class, in terms of these mathematical and verbal aptitude scores, falls in the top 2-4% of the total national group tested by the College Board and in the top 1-2% of their contemporaries in secondary school last year. On the basis of verbal aptitude, the upper 90% of this entering class falls within the top 5% of last year's secondary school seniors in the country; on the basis of mathematical aptitude, within the top 9% of the same group. [13]

Clearly, Harvard students are of unusually high quality, and seem to be improving; but once we take the high quality of the input into account, we have to discount to some extent the Harvard contribution as suggested by numbers of Woodrow Wilson scholars, numbers in *Who's Who*, and similar compilations as well as the high incomes of Harvard graduates.

Emphasis on the Whole Man

From the beginning Harvard's approach to education was to consider the whole man. Harvard's problems might have been less troublesome if the college had put upon the town the responsibility to feed and board its students. But it took the more difficult approach of seeking resources to provide these services. (Once the college abandoned its commons in the 1840s, much of the trouble with students evaporated.) Undoubtedly the concern for the students' material well-being improved the Harvard educational product.

---

13. *Admission to Harvard College*, p. 24.

Release from College Bonds

As means of transportation improved, the college found it increasingly difficult to be responsible for the student's well-being. A greater degree of freedom was reflected in riots and rebellions of the first third of the nineteenth century. The college, however, tried to watch over its wards. Thus, late in 1813, the corporation voted that each student coming from a greater distance than three hundred miles would have a patron who would supervise and, to some extent, control the financial transactions of the student. [14]

Again, Concern for the Whole Man

Under Lowell, in contrast with the Eliot period, a rising concern was expressed for the whole man. Lowell assumed large responsibilities for the students' room, board, recreation, social intercourse, and health. The freshman dormitories, the Harvard union, the Harvard houses, dormitory facilities in some of the professional schools, and the recourse to advisors and tutors, all reflected Lowell's interest.

With the rise in the size of classes, the unusually close relations of classmates that had prevailed until Eliot's day suffered. A substitute had to be found. Joseph H. Choate in 1917 could suggest the great changes that had occurred in sixty years or so.

There was one immense advantage which the boys of our time at Harvard enjoyed over those of recent years, the classes were so small in number that we became intimately acquainted with each other, much more intimately than at any subsequent period of life with any similar number of acquaintances, understood one another's character perfectly, and formed the closest ties of friendship and a strong class-feeling that continued unbroken through life. [15]

In his 1910-1911 report, the president said that the "efforts of the students, encouraged in every

---

14. *Corporation Papers*, 1813 (unpublished); *Records of Overseers*, vol. VI, pp. 423-24, October 1812 to 1823.

15. Choate, *op. cit.*, p. 84.

possible way by the College authorities to promote solidarity among themselves, to prevent the student body from being divided into exclusive groups, to make the College, in the common use of the term, more democratic, have had a notable growth. . . ."[16]

Rudolph well observed the objectives of President Lowell to recover the ancient collegiate values:

The great monuments to the return to Aristotle, the great monuments that symbolized the revolt against the university idea, were the benefactions of Edward S. Harkness which provided Harvard in 1928 with its house system and Yale in 1930 with its system of colleges.[17]

In the House Plan Lowell saw the way to more attention to each student, and opportunities for increased association with faculty members, and a means towards democratizing the college.[18]

President Conant accepted Lowell's House Plan and tutorial system; but not with the enthusiasm of his predecessor. President Pusey, and notably in his Harvard program to raise more than $80 million, revived the Lowell enthusiasm for the House Plan which, under the pressure of rising numbers and financial stress, had experienced some deterioration in the later 1930s and 1940s. The program for Harvard College included provisions for protecting the House Plan against excessive numbers.[19]

Lowell was also interested in easing the transition from high schools to the freshman year. Here again his policies reminded one of Harvard's earlier history. Early in the twentieth century, C. F. Adams, a critic of Eliot's policies, expressed views that were not unlike those of Lowell in his later years. Like Lowell, he expressed admiration for the Oxford-Cambridge colleges. In fact, he proposed a House Plan.

. . . Released from the preparatory school the boy is turned out, and left, so to speak, to browse around at his own sweet will; and this too at a period when his judgment is most immature, when he least understands himself or knows the world, when all the hard lessons of life are yet to be learned.[20]

Harvard has also assumed some responsibility for the health of its students. Morison points to the fine health record of students in the middle of the seventeenth century. Over a period of ten years, Morison found that of the 260 seventeenth century alumni, only 10 died as undergraduates; "and of these at least half met their death by accident." [21] By modern standards, this is not a good record.

The college could boast of but 15 deaths out of 7,196 students in four years, 1895-1896 to 1898-1899, or 1/5th of 1 percent as compared to the 4 percent in the seventeenth century.[22]

In the early part of the twentieth century, the corporation actually appointed a medical advisor, Dr. Alfred Worcester. In 1913-1914, the college received funds for a professorship of hygiene. Under Dr. Worcester and later under Dr. Arlie Bock and Dr. Dana Farnsworth, the university took increasing responsibility for the health of the student. In 1902-1903, Stillman Infirmary's budget was only $11,898. Beginning with 1904-1905, the university charged each student $4 for the maintenance of the infirmary. By 1956, Dr. Dana Farnsworth, the best man in medicine

16. *Report of the President of Harvard College*, 1910-1911, p. 13; cf., 1912-1913, pp. 12-13.

17. F. Rudolph, *The American College and University: A History*, 1962, pp. 460-461.

18. *Report of the President of Harvard College*, 1929-1930, pp. 7-8; 1931-1932, pp. 89-90.

19. *Program for Harvard College*, pp. 13, 17; *Report of the President of Harvard College*, 1956, p. 7.

20. C. F. Adams, *op. cit.*, pp. 112-114; cf., *Report of the President of Harvard College*, 1927-1928, pp. 90-91, and 1930-1931, pp. 94-96.

21. Morison, *Harvard College in the Seventeenth Century*, p. 102.

22. "The President's Report," in *The Harvard Bulletin*, vol. II, no. 21, p. 1, 1900.

for students, achieved a multimillion-dollar program and medical center.[23]

Relevant Economic Issues

Undoubtedly the rising interest in the students' health, housing, rooms, extracurricular activities, and religion affects the economic status of the college and university. As more resources are put into those areas, less are available for education in the narrow sense. Undoubtedly to some extent the funds made available for, say the houses would not be available for other purposes. Yet, even the house system, with a capital outlay of, say, $40 million, comes in part at the expense of other categories of expenditures. Moreover, the cost of operation, even with free capital, puts additional burdens on students, and especially in the 1930s. The houses were a bargain that many could not afford.

In still another aspect, the noneducational outlays are significant. These may well improve the health of students, and good health means a better student. It may well be that the additional few hundred dollars of costs per student per year involved in these auxiliary programs yields an improved education worth as much or more.

23. *Report of the President of Harvard College,* 1902-1903, p. 43; 1903-1904, p. 45; 1905-1906, pp. 112-113, 1913-1914, p. 12; 1954-1955, pp. 554-555; Dr. A. Worcester, *The Henry K. Oliver Professorship, 1925-1935, Reminis-* cences, unpublished typescript in Harvard University Archives, ch. 10, pp. 44-45; also see A. B. Hart, "Ten Years of Harvard," in *Harvard Graduates Magazine,* vol. II, p. 61, 1902.

5

Costs to Students

An examination of the table on the structure of student costs reveals the changing composition of costs over a period of 330 years. The relative burden of tuition or instructional charges to total costs tended upward, and especially since 1940. (Cf., the 12 percent in the middle of the seventeenth century and 64 percent in the year 1966–1967). But in the century preceding 1860, the relative burden of tuition varied only moderately. An explanation of these trends lies in the growing affluence of the nation. In the seventeenth century, the college could not depend largely on *tuition,* for few could afford to pay even a few dollars, the average charge in the years 1650 to 1712. As real incomes rose, tuition could gradually be increased, and the number who were capable of paying would rise.

Tuition in the first two hundred years gives an inadequate view of the full instructional costs. The college imposed charges of all kinds on top of tuition. Among the relevant items were detriment, a charge on the student absent for a considerable period; the payment to cover a fair share of overhead expenses; fines; charges (I discuss in Chapter 3); and commencement fees, an item of much importance in the early history of Harvard. Thus during a good part of the seventeenth century, commencement fees accounted for almost 10 percent of the total student costs. In this presentation of the total instructional charges I have included commencement fees, fines, special charges to cover chapel service, library assessments,

and fees to cover special lectures or the pay of some professors.

Among the fees paid by students was a charge in the early nineteenth century adequate to cover the pay of the steward. The cost was $6.40 annually for two hundred students.[1] Again, professors frequently were allowed to charge students special fees for attendance at lectures. On one occasion, President Webber questioned one of the more troublesome professors, B. Waterhouse, concerning such charges.[2]

As the relative burden of instructional costs tends to rise that of food tends to decline, a trend explained perhaps by the same factors that account for declining weight of food in the average consumer's budget as per capita income rises. The decline has been uneven, and is especially marked by the fall from 51 percent of student costs a hundred years ago to 22 percent in 1960. A spectacular drop from 67 percent between 1713 and 1722 to 22 percent between 1743 and 1752 is explained largely by closing of the Harvard commons from 1745-1746 to 1749-1750. In response to the frequent complaints about the food, the students in 1821 and in some later years were allowed to eat outside if they paid a

---

1. Letter from President Webber to B. Waterhouse, October 23, 1806, in Harvard University Archives.
2. Letter of January 25, 1803, in Harvard University Archives. This is a letter from a high administrator, either the president or the treasurer.

Table 5-1.

Structure of Student Costs, Harvard 1650-1652 to 1967, Various Years, by Percents and Total Costs to Students

| Year | Instruction | Percent of Total | | Commencement | Total £s and $s |
		Commons	Rents		
1650-1652	12	71	8	9	£ 11.7s
1687-1712	17	64	9	8	16.3s
				Fines, fees, misc.	
1712-1713 to 1721-1722	19	67	9	5	14.2s
1742-1743 to 1751-1752	48	22*	17	13	21.355
1752-1753 to 1761-1762	32	48	9	11	11.712†
1762-1763 to 1771-1772	22	61	6	11	22.821
1806-1807 to 1809-1810	23	48	12	16	$ 175.08
1827	23	48	5	24	206.00
1859-1860	27	51	7	15	273.00
1889-1890	32	32	14	20	372.00
1899-1900	29	31	20	20	510.00
1929-1930	33	29	20	17	1,200.00
1939-1940	30	29	17	24	1,350.00
1949-1950	39	26	16	19	1,620.00
1959-1960	48	22	16	14	2,768.00
1966-1967	64	20	16	—	3,600.00‡

* Commons suspended, 1745-1750.
† A substantial devaluation occurred in 1750 and the decline reflects costs in a higher-valued new currency.
‡ All expenditures not included. Tuition, rooms, board and fees - 100 percent. Thus in 1966-1967, $470 for books, clothing, personal, etc. excluded.

Sources: 1650-1652, 1687-1712, Margery Somers Foster, *Out of Small Beginnings . . . An Economic History of Harvard College in the Puritan Period (1636-1712),* 1962, pp. 66, 77; 1712-1772, *Stewards' Quarter Bill Books,* in Harvard University Archives; 1806-1810, A. H. Cole in *Harvard Business School Alumni Bulletin,* vol. XXXVIII, pp. 537-543; 1827, *Stewards' Quarter Bill Books* in Harvard University Archives, UAL 70.15.100; 1859-1860, 1889-1890, 1899-1900, 1929-1930, *Harvard Alumni Bulletin,* vol. XXXIII, pp. 965-970; 1940-1950, *Expenses and Financial Aids in Harvard College,* November, 1949, p. 7; 1959-1960, *Report of Admission and Scholarship Committee,* 1966-1967, p. 23, Letter from Dean F. Glimp, March 15, 1967. My calculations throughout.

$2.50 fee each quarter and $1.50 per quarter for the privilege of eating out.[3]

Rents also tended to become increasingly important on a relative scale, and particularly since 1860, with the rent category inclusive of fuel and other utilities, sweepers' pay, and the like rising from 7 percent in 1860 to 20 percent in 1900 and 1930 and 16 percent in 1967. The Eliot period witnessed large improvements in housing conditions; but the heavy increase of tuition in the last generation has induced some economizing on rooms and also on food. The rising percentage of rents to total costs in the last hundred years or so reflects also substantial gains in the quality of the service, and hence should not be considered merely a rise in prices. Among the increased services are central heating, improved bathing facilities, maid services, and recreational services.

Some Details on Costs

In 1796 George Wingate spent $36.27 in one quarter. Food accounted for $23.71 or almost two-thirds; instruction, $5.60 or one-sixth; rents $2.50 or 7 percent. Food accounted for a much larger part of expenditures and instruction, much less than is suggested by the overall figures of the college during this period.[4]

John Farrar's bill for the quarter ending August 29, 1799 gives an entirely different impression. The total is only $13.48. Outlays on commons match well the over-all structure; and instruction, about 30 percent is not much out of line; nor is the rent.[5]

A summary for the college for 1803 (fourth quarter) is of some interest. The breakdown reveals that between one-fourth and one-third of the instruction bill is included as extras, e.g., librarian, medical instruction. Among the other interesting items are the catalogue and dinner (2 percent); repairs (2 percent); sweepers and sand (1 percent), wood (4 percent), books (2 percent), fines (3 percent), assessments for delinquency (1/2 of 1 percent), seats at the Episcopal Church (1/4 of 1 percent).[6]

Of unusual interest is the account of Christopher Gore for the years 1806-1807 through 1809-1810. Especially worth noting are the large outlays not accounted for by the college. Of the total only $700 stems from the College Steward's Account. The shares going to instruction, commons, and rent are roughly in line. But note the $889 spent for clothes, $95 for expenses to New York, and $1050.74 for pocket money and miscellaneous. In relation to total expenditures, steward charges were only 11 percent, and instruction only 5 percent.[7]

An official estimate of expenditures in 1820 shows the lower limit of annual expenditures at $228 charged by the university.[8] Of this sum, commons accounted for $105; instruction and library, $61.50; and rent, $12. These check well with the college survey for 1827.

But other costs fall between $161 and $223, or 72 to 98 percent of the quarterly bills. Clothing and laundry are especially costly, for they account for almost 30 percent of all expenditures at the lower level and 38 percent at the higher level—the current figure is between 5 and 6 percent.

By 1844, the pattern of spending was approaching a more modern one. Instruction was roughly half the bill for the second term; rent, 20 percent; books, 12 percent; and fuel, 11 percent. But the large share going to instruction and rooms is explicable by the nonexpenditures on commons.[9] A similar pattern is

3. *Corporation Records,* vol. VI, 1819–1827, Harvard University Archives, UAI 1.5.30.

4. George Wingate to the President and Fellows of Harvard College, Quarter Bill Ending May 26, 1796, in Harvard University Archives.

5. John Farrer to the President and Fellows of Harvard College, First Quarter ending August 29, 1799, in Harvard University Archives.

6. *Stewards' Accounts,* fourth quarter, 1803, in Harvard University Archives; cf., Abraham Haskell to the President and Fellows of Harvard College, quarter ending November 27, 1899, in Harvard University Archives.

7. A. H. Cole, "College Expenses of 1806–1810", in *Harvard Alumni Bulletin,* date unknown, p. 541.

8. Harvard University, Letter to Parents, 1820, among Harvard University documents.

9. Mr. Hale, To Bill for Second Term, Ending July 12, 1844, among Harvard University documents.

to be found for 1858, with instruction rising to 63 percent.[10]

In 1870, with college board once more available, instruction accounted for 44 percent; board for 43 percent; rooms, 6 percent; fuel, 6 percent. In comparison with the 1960s, instruction was low, commons high, and rent low.[11]

Miscellaneous items vary in importance, but they tend to become more important. Where possible they have been included in the major categories, but to some extent they fall outside. As incomes rose, larger expenditures for transportation, clothing, laundry, recreation, and club dues emerged. In the early part of the nineteenth century, miscellaneous charges included librarian fees, books, catalogues, repairs, fines, gallery of the Episcopal Church, natural history fee, assessment for delinquency, sweepers, lecture room fees, boarding out costs (1823 to 1825), and degree and diploma fees. Most of these items could be included in instruction costs or commons or rent.[12]

Jared Sparks (A.B. 1815), a later president, estimated costs including clothing at $250 a year. Economical management accounted for this low estimate. Some spent as much as $500, and Sparks had to work to meet his $250 budget.[13]

In 1825-1826, the president estimated total necessary expenses at $172, with other charges varying with the student. The college provided wood at $7 a cord; rooms in a private house cost from $30 to $45 a year; washing, $3 to $5 a quarter; board in town, $1.75 to $3 a week ($1.75 in the Harvard Commons).[14]

Books were a relatively expensive item in the first two hundred years of Harvard's history. Thus, in the years 1806-1807 to 1809-1810, they accounted for 7 to 8 percent of *instructional* costs or the equivalent of about $120 at current tuition charges. Again in 1812, the text book cost was between $12 and $17 or 7 percent of *total* costs.[15]

Extravagances

Accounts for James Gore King for 1806-1807 to 1809-1810 reveal the large outlays of some students from prominent families. King spent $2,963.61 in four years. What is striking is that instruction cost but $160, whereas boots and shoes required $279 and other wearing apparel, $710. In general, clothing was a large item in the nineteenth century and especially for wealthy students. Even the president's advice to parents allowed from one-third to one-fourth of the budget for clothing. The current cost of clothing surely is no more than between 2 and 3 percent.[16]

In 1823 President Kirkland warned parents against extravagances:

It is the united opinion of those intrusted with the care of this Institution, that one of the greatest evils, to which it is exposed, is the excessive indulgence of Students in the articles of clothing and pocket expenses. Such indulgence is productive among them of a perverted emulation, at once frivolous and pernicious; is a principal source of depraved morals, and is extremely injurious to the wholesome discipline of the University. The example of the more affluent is contagious, and extends to those whose limited means forbid such indulgence. The effect of this course is to deter the less opulent classes in the community from sending their children to our University, and thus to weaken the interest, which it is desirable the public at large should continue to feel in this oldest and best founded seminary.

10. B. L. Cilley, Bill for Second Term, Ending July 21, 1858, among Harvard University documents.
11. Bill First Term, Ending January 19, 1870, among Harvard University documents.
12. *Stewards' Quarterly Bill Books,* 1812–1827, in Widener Archives, UAI, 70.15–100.
13. H. Adams, *The Life and Writings of Jared Sparks,* 1893 vol. I, p. 55.
14. *Report of the President of Harvard College,* 1825–1826, pp. 33–34.

15. A. H. Cole, *op.cit.,* pp. 537–543.
16. *Ibid.* p. 541; and Letter of President Kirkland of 1823 to Parents, in Harvard University Archives; also see *Report of a Committee of the Overseers of Harvard College,* January 6, 1825, in Harvard University Archives.

Under these regulations the following is the estimate of Expenses for a Year, exclusive of chamber furniture, stationary, and personal service beyond what is provided by the College.

Steward and Commons,	
including $2 50 a quarter	
and board for 38 weeks at	
$2 50 a week	*105 00*
Instruction two first	
years $46, third year $64,	
fourth $74–average	*57 50*
Room rent.	*12 00*
Library	*4 00*
Text books	*15 00*
Wood	*20 00*
Expenses of public rooms,	
repairs, catalogue, &c	*15 00*

Amount of charges in the	
Quarter Bills.	*$228 00 – 228 00*
Clothes	*100 00 to 150 00*
Laundress	*12 00 to 24 00*
Candles or Oil.	*10 00 to 10 00*
Pocket expenses	*39 00 to 39 00*

$389 00 to 451 00

By a law of the State made in 1819, "in furtherance of good discipline in the Colleges of this Commonwealth," it is enacted, "that no innholder, tavernkeeper, retailer, confectioner, or keeper of any shop or boardinghouse for the sale of drink or food, or any livery stable keeper, shall give credit to any undergraduate of either of the Colleges within this Commonwealth, without the consent of such officer or officers of the said Colleges respectively.

In his reply to a committee of the corporation of 1822, Prof. John S. Popkin, representing the immediate government, dwelt especially on the extravagance of students; on the tendency of students living near Cambridge to emulate the southern gentlemen at Harvard who were free of parental restraint; of the unfortunate recourse to deficit financing; and on the large outlays on clothing, an excess which could be treated only by imposing uniform college dress.[17]

By 1939-1940, the costs for basic expenses (tuition, lodging, board and medical fees) were $890 (low) and $1,030 (average). But personal expenditures, exclusive of travel, were estimated at $160 (low) and $295 (average). In 1949-1950, the low figure was $1,430 and the high, $1,620.[18]

One of the most expensive items in the miscellaneous group (included in rent when information is available) was fuel. To give one example. In 1827-1828, wood (6 cords to a room) cost $22.50, or more than 10 percent of total costs. The high cost of fuel reflected the limited supplies in the economy prior to the days of modern mobilization of fuel resources. Fuel and books in this year accounted for more than 20 percent of total costs, or about $720 at 1967 budgets.[19]

Criticism of Extravagance

Criticism of the college for tolerating excessive expenditures by students prevailed through most of the nineteenth century. In response, a committee of the overseers in 1824 proposed that all students dine simply in the commons, that dress be uniform and simple, and that the habit of hiring servants be discontinued. " . . . Parents of moderate property and in the middle rank of life [should] not be deterred from sending their children to Cambridge, nor obliged to seek a cheaper, or more defective education elsewhere . . . ." [20]

The college in 1828 took strong measures to control student outlays:

The parent or guardian of such student shall be informed what are the necessary annual expenses of College, and also what is the most liberal allowance

17. Harvard University Archives.
18. *Expenses and Financial Aids in Harvard College, 1939,* p. 7; 1949–1950, p. 7.
19. *Report of the Treasurer of Harvard College, 1827–1828,* p. 58.
20. *Board of Overseers Report,* May 4, 1824, p. 9.

that is permitted for other expenses; and shall also be informed that the regulations of the College require that all funds for the support and use of his son or ward must be remitted to the patron only, who is to have the whole control of the same under the direction of the Instructers of the College.

Harriet Mortineau visited the university in 1838. She observed that Harvard had a great name. In her view Harvard was the aristocratic college of the country, though in a state of decline. Harvard's education was in her view very expensive. Despite her relative decline as an educational institution, "she will probably receive a sufficient patronage from the aristocracy, for a considerable time to come, to encourage her in all her faults . . ."[21]

Anthony Trollope visited Harvard in 1861. He also found much extravagance there, though in England extravagances exceeded those at Harvard. He also found deficiencies at Harvard:

". . . there is . . . none of that old fashioned, time honoured, delicious, mediaeval life which lends so much grace and beauty to our colleges. There are no gates, no porters' lodge, no butteries, no balls, no battels, and no common rooms . . . no proctors, no bulldogs, no bursers, no deans, . . . no quads, no surplices, no caps and gowns. . . ." [22]

An interesting example of extravagant living is found in a letter from a Saltonstall to President Eliot in 1875. The total expenditures for a year were $2,448.80, a sum that would correspond to considerably more than $10,000 today. Among the luxuries were clothing, $448; furniture, $387; rent, $247; vacation, $200; housekeeping and miscellaneous, $257; riding clothes, $66; private tutor, $49.[23]

One of the most useful appraisals of the degree of extravagance was the work of the famous philosopher, George Palmer in 1887.

. . . Probably nowhere on this planet can a thousand young men be found, between the ages of eighteen and twenty-four, who will not show example of the heedless, the temptable, and the depraved. Let us not, therefore, shrink from acknowledging the ugly fact; extravagance is here—shameless, coarse extravagance. . . .[24]

To parents, Palmer warned: "If, in a haphazard way you pour $2,000 into his pocket then, in an equally haphazard way, $2,000 will come out. . . ."

In his study Palmer solicited budgets from many students. Most did not seem extravagant. Thus, one student spent $2,860 in four years. He earned $500 in college and $1,500 during vacations, obtained $860 from parents and other sources, borrowed $200, and earned the $450 for summer expenditures.[25]

F. Bowles, a college official, presented the following for the class of 1891.

Student Expenses in 1893

Amount of Expenses	No. of Students
1. Below $ 500	25
Boarded at home	14
2. $ 500 to $ 700	49
3. $ 700 to $1,000	58
4. Above $1,000	83
5. $2,000	11
6. $3,000 ;	3

Source: F. Bowles, *Student Expenses, 1893.*

President Eliot, early in the twentieth century, feared that "the rise in the scale of living among members of the University continue to excite some apprehension in the minds of friends of higher education. . . ." He found the rise pervasive. Board at Memorial Hall was higher priced than the highest rates in private homes fifty years before; the poorest

---

21. *The Harvard Book*, p. 339; and *Announcement of Harvard University*, September 3 (?), 1828.
22. *The Harvard Book*, pp. 346–347.
23. H. Saltonstall to Charles Eliot, October 11, 1875.

24. *College Expenses at Harvard, Memorial Hall, Cambridge,* June 29, 1887.
25. *Ibid*, p. 11.

student in 1903 living in the cheapest college dormitories "is better provided with light, heat, books, and apparatus than the richest student fifty years ago...."

The Average Rise of Costs

Costs, with some exceptions, have steadily risen (see table). The rise may be explained by an improvement in the product, inflationary trends, and the rising productivity of the economy. Higher education would have to meet the competition of other employers who, with rising productivity, could afford to pay higher prices for services and supplies.

Limited information is available for the Puritan period. Thus, Miss Foster finds that the *annual* cost was as follows:

Annual Costs During the Puritan Period

1650 to 1652	11£ 7s
1655 to 1659 (Probably until 1686)	14 3
1687 to 1712	16 3

Source: Foster, *op. cit.,* p. 66.

For almost a century and a half (to 1771-1772) total costs did not at any time substantially exceed $75 and generally the costs were less. The large rise to £56 18s or about $190 in 1778 reflected the Revolutionary War inflation. In the eighteenth century, shortage of money tended to depress costs though at times inflationary policies had the opposite effect. Shortages of cash, frequent wars, and rather stagnant economic conditions help explain the trends.

It is not easy to estimate costs over the years, for costs do not always include the same items.

Occasionally a commentator analyzed the rise of costs in a sophisticated manner. For one the rise of costs to a student was explained by developments in the community. "The ordinary family of the community is spending several times as much money as the ordinary family of the community of two generations ago. The college man does as the family does of which he is a member...."[26]

President Eliot well expressed the interests of the university in keeping prices down for its students, even if the private markets suffered thereby.

Since, however, it is the duty of university trustees to see to it that safe and convenient lodgings are accessible to their students, and that wholesome food can be obtained at low prices, it is possible for trustees, who attend to their duties in these respects, to interfere somewhat with the business of those residents of the municipality who let rooms to students, or feed them. University trustees may reasonably regard it as their duty also to see to it that all the supplies which students need, such as books, stationery, clothing, and furniture, are brought within the reach of students at moderate prices through the agency of a cooperative society. Unless a university be willing to take its students only from well-to-do families, it must see to it that lodgings, food, fuel, and indispensable supplies are accessible to students at moderate prices.[27]

In contrast to Lowell's policies and remindful of Eliot's, student costs under Conant rose but 30 percent, a small rise indeed compared to the increase of prices, and even smaller when compared with the increase of per capita income. Under Pusey the pressure to increase salaries, and unusual demands by students for enrollment allowed a very large rise of charges, one exceeding the gain of per capita income and accompanied by an improvement in the quality of students. Enrollment was virtually stabilized, though, since in 1950 there were still some overage veterans, the net change of enrollment since 1950 measured by excluding the overage enrollment in 1950, may be considered substantial.

Appearing before the Legislature in 1851, the president and fellows pointed out that fifty years earlier there were 25 colleges in existence, some really

---

26. Thwing, *op. cit., p. 248.*
27. C. W. Eliot, *op. cit.,* pp. 20–21.

inoperative, and Yale, the only substantial competitor. But in 1851, there were 120 in full operation. No wonder enrollment at Harvard had suffered. [28]

A frequent complaint was the high cost of living, leading in turn to increased costs of higher education: " ... Again the expenses of living at Cambridge are unavoidably greater than at any other place in the United States where a college is established, except in one or two of the large cities." [29]

A joint committee of the Legislature related the high costs to the "greater fullness of that education or to the locality of Cambridge, or to the increased luxuriousness of general expenditures and other social habits in the more wealthy and populous parts of the Commonwealth." [30]

A committee of overseers wanted to know why 394 students at Yale cost $15,201, and the same service for 254 students cost in Cambridge more than $26,500. (Note that unit costs were $38 and $104 respectively.) [31]

In a comprehensive report on the effectiveness of the Harvard system, Prof. George Ticknor, in 1827, emphasized high cost and loss of competitive position by Harvard. Finding that unit costs were $200 exclusive of $100 to be charged against an unproductive plant, Ticknor wanted to know if adequate returns were being obtained. " ... a much greater result should be obtained than sending out into society fifty or sixty young men as imperfectly educated as the graduate from Cambridge certainly is now." [32]

In the nineteenth century there was persistent criticism of Harvard's high-cost policies. An examination of the costs to students at Harvard and its competitors does not show consistently higher costs at Harvard. But often the low estimates of over-all costs were less than the costs at Harvard. In the late 1830s, for example, the low estimates of costs were consistently lower than the $188 estimate for Harvard. For William and Mary, Yale, Princeton, Dartmouth, and Williams the student could get by with outlays of $205, $140, $163, $96 and less than $100 respectively. Harvard was not always the most costly institution. In the twentieth century with the strengthening of inflationary forces, as we shall see in a later section, Harvard tended to lag more than its rivals in adjusting costs to rising prices. [33]

Costs and Capacity to Pay

A chart covering the years since Eliot's inauguration (93 years in all) shows at a glance the trends of tuition; tuition, board, room and medical fees; per capita gross national product; and, sporadically, per capita personal income.

In the Eliot years, it is clear that costs at college dropped relative to the index for gross national product per capita; that is, going to college became a bargain. The reverse is true for tuition during the Lowell administration, with the rise of tuition greatly exceeding that in per capita income, though total student costs rose somewhat less than income. But the

28. *Memorial Concerning the Recent History and the Constitutional Rights and Privileges of Harvard College Presented to the Legislature,* January 17, 1851, p. 7, in Harvard University Archives.

29. *Ibid.,* p. 8.

30. Commonwealth of Massachusetts, *Joint Select Committee, . . . as Related to Harvard College,* May 5, 1851, p. 3.

31. G. Bancroft, Linus Child, *Report on Diminishing the Cost of Instruction in Harvard College, Together with a Minority Report on the Same Subject,* February 27, 1845.

32. George Ticknor, *Paper dated April 11, 1827,* in Harvard University Archives.

33. The years compared are not identical. See especially *History of the College of William and Mary,* p. 172; *Yale College, Society of the Alumni,* 1879, p. 6; C. F. Thwing, *op. cit.,* p. 245; G. W. Pierson, *Yale College, 1871–1921,* pp. 411–414; J. MacLean, *History of the College of New Jersey,* vol. I, pp. 163, 250, 312–330; vol. II, pp. 182, 188, 303–308; T. J. Wertenbaker, *Princeton, 1746–1896,* pp. 64, 177, 193, 1946; W. L. Collins, *Princeton,* 1914, pp. 134–148; *Princeton Annual Catalogues,* various issues; L. B. Richardson, *History of Dartmouth College,* 1932, vol. I, pp. 119, 177; vol. II, pp. 480, 712; *Dartmouth Catalogues;* D. A. Wells and S. H. Davis, *Sketch of Williams College,* 1847, pp. 17–36; and *Annual Catalogues.*

Table 5-2.

Harvard College Charges vs National Ability to Pay (Rough)

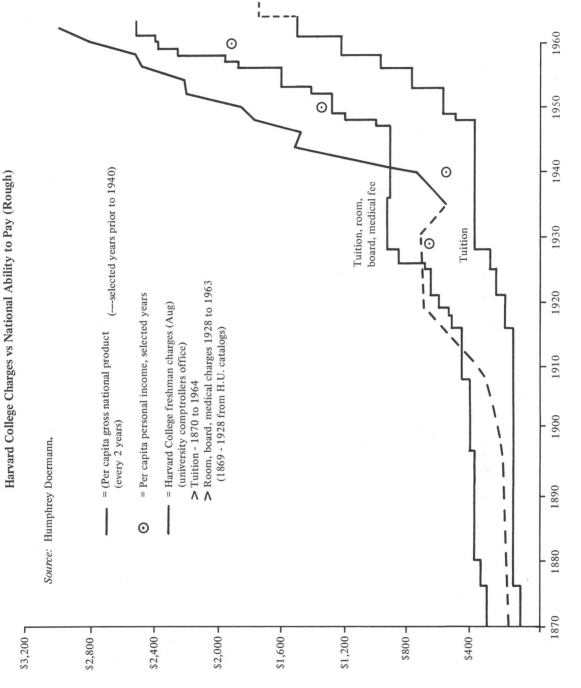

Source: Humphrey Doermann.

————— = (Per capita gross national product   (---selected years prior to 1940)
(every 2 years)

⊙ = Per capita personal income, selected years

————— = Harvard College freshman charges (Aug)
(university comptrollers office)
❯ Tuition - 1870 to 1964
❯ Room, board, medical charges 1928 to 1963
(1869 - 1928 from H.U. catalogs)

47

gains thus measured did not nearly equal those of the Eliot period. In the 1930s as per capita income declined and college expenses were stabilized, support at college became a more formidable problem. In the 1940s, however, the rise of costs lagged far behind the increased capacity to pay.

In a general way charges follow movements in per capita income, but the exceptions are important, and particularly in periods of price and income instability —e.g., World War I, World War II, and the Great Depression. The per capita gross national product is not a perfect measure of ability to pay; firstly, because it diverges to some extent from personal income; secondly, because the tax take varies; and thirdly, because the burdens may vary from time to time, for example, as the number of children per family to be educated rises.

Here are some other statistics for recent Harvard history.

Table 5-3.

Tuition, Total Student Costs, Per Capita Income, 1900-1963, Various Years (Year 1900 = 100)

Year	Tuition	Total Student Costs, Tuition, Room, Board, Medical Fee	Per Capita Disposable Income
1900	100	100	100
1910	100	115	157
1920	133	147	315
1930	267	223	386
1940	267	217	290
1950	400	307	690
1963	1,013	616	1,113

Source: Humphrey Doermann, *Paper written in Economics 351* (Seminar of S. E. Harris); my calculations.

This table generally supports earlier conclusions, but also modifies them to some extent.

Under Eliot (1901-1910) the lag in costs in relation to ability to pay is clear.

Under Lowell, the response of tuition to rising capacity to pay lagged from 1910 to 1920, but exceeded the gains of capacity to pay from 1910 to 1930. But total charges lagged—a rise of less than 100 percent as compared with an increase of per capita disposable income of about 150 percent.

Under Conant (1930 to 1950) and notably from 1940 to 1950, tuition and all charges lagged greatly. The increase of capacity to pay was about 80 percent in these twenty years, of tuition only 50 percent (and the rise coming near the end of the period) and of all charges about 40 percent.

In the Pusey years (1952-1953 through 1962-1963) the results are suggested by comparing 1950 with 1963 (capacity to pay rose by 60 percent, tuition by roughly 150 percent and all college charges by 100 percent). In the actual Pusey years (1953-1963) capacity to pay rose by one-third, tuition almost 5 times as much, and all charges by 83 percent (or close to 3 times as much as capacity). But it should be noted that in part the large rises under Pusey reflect slow adjustments under Conant. Cost rose somewhat more than is here suggested when allowance is made for some deterioration in quality of room and board since the 1930s.

The entire period of 63 years (1900 to 1963) reveals indices of 1,013 for tuition (1900 = 100), 616 for total charges and 1,113 for capacity to pay, that is to say, the burden of tuition, i.e., the relation of tuition to capacity to pay, is roughly what it had been at the beginning of the century; but total charges rose about 50 percent as much as capacity to pay—hence a college education had become a relatively less expensive product. In so far as the numbers to be educated in relation to population rose, these conclusions overstate the reduction of burdens. *In fact, from 1900 to 1960, the enrollment in institutions of higher learning vis-à-vis population rose between 5 and 6 times.*[34] With such increases of enrollment, the sacrifices involved in sending children to college increases on this account to some extent.

34. Based on *Economic Report of the President,* January 1964, *Statistics of Higher Education, 1957–1958,* and *Historical Statistics of the U.S.*

The Impact of Competition

Earlier in this chapter we pointed out the adverse effects on Harvard of the rise of competitors. Here we go into some detail in considering the manner in which tuition charges are determined by the policies of competitors.

College authorities in determining charges and the level of services consider policies of competitors. In the early part of the nineteenth century, there was much concern in Cambridge with the high costs of a Harvard education. Morison reminds us of the high costs in the Kirkland and Quincy administrations, that is, in the years 1810 to 1845. According to Morison, Harvard was then the most expensive college in the country, with the possible exception of Virginia.[35]

In 1875, Harvard's tuition was $150, exceeded only by Columbia ($200), with nine other competitors charging from $60 to $140 (Yale), the average for all being $100.[36]

College officials watch with care the pricing policies of their competitors. No college wants to be much out of line. Even in these days of excess demand, they are concerned lest high relative prices exclude the able but impecunious students, and attract excessively the sons and daughters of high-income parents. In my interviewing for a study of the economics of higher education,[37] presidents of institutions of higher learning competing with Harvard expressed the hope that Harvard would increase its fees so that they in turn might. And Harvard's delayed rises contributed to the general lag of charges in the inflationary years of the 1940s and the 1950s.

In general Harvard tended to lag in the inflationary years, and except for the Great Depression the first sixty years of the century were years of price rises. The whole experience suggests not only that the colleges should watch prices and per capita income and

adjust to these quickly if not automatically, but also that the major competitors operate like any other oligopolist, i.e., a seller in competition with only a few other sellers. Since institutions of higher learning are not profit-making they are not subject to antitrust proceedings. This failure to adjust has cost the university and the faculty of Harvard millions of dollars. In this period of sixty years, Yale and Princeton adjusted to price and income movements more effectively than Harvard.

Costs and Enrollment

Throughout Harvard's history the issue of keeping down costs to students was a serious subject of debate. Even when costs were of the order of £10 to £15 in the first eighty years of Harvard history, students found the charges beyond their means. Undoubtedly they were more oppressive than in 1967, when costs had risen to about $3,500. The greater burden per student in the early years is suggested also by the small *national* enrollment relative to population in Harvard's first century compared to that in the 1960s, when costs per student in the country averaged at least $1,500.

A few words on Harvard's enrollment in relation to population are in order. Harvard's relative enrollment was of course related to costs; but to other factors as well, e.g., the quality of its education. Until 1820 and largely until 1870, since Harvard students came primarily from Massachusetts, the significant comparison of enrollment is with Massachusetts' population. From 1650 to 1710 through 1720 the ratio of Harvard students to Massachusetts population declined, suggesting Massachusetts' lack of sustained interest in higher education, and also its unsatisfactory economic conditions. Competition was not relevant during most of this period, for Yale was only founded in 1701. Even as late as 1870, the ratio of Harvard's enrollment to Massachusetts' population was one-half to one-fourth as large as in 1650 and about one-half as large relatively to 1710 through

---

35. Morison, *Three Centuries of Harvard, 1636–1936,* pp. 200–201.
36. C. F. Thwing, *op. cit.,* p. 38.
37. Seymour E. Harris, *Higher Education: Resources and Finance,* 1962.

1720. After 1870, Harvard's enrollment rose much more rapidly than the population of Massachusetts and New England and even of the nation, although not vis-à-vis the nation's from 1930 to 1960. In relation to enrollment in institutions of higher learning, Harvard's share dropped steadily from 2.1 percent in 1870 to 1/3 of 1 percent by 1960. The decline in the index was from 100 percent at the beginning of Harvard's history to but one-three hundredth by 1960.[38]

As costs rose and competition became more serious, the debates became more tense. As early as 1834, John Quincy Adams and Judge Joseph Story of the United States Supreme Court and Dane Professor of Law vigorously debated the merits of high and low tuition. They were both prepared to seek additional funds for the college's two hundredth anniversary, but the former could not see why the funds should be used "indiscriminately for the wealthy and the indigent. . . ." Adams considered the use of funds to reduce tuition as "a mere bonus to the merchants of Boston and to a few clergymen throughout the State to send their sons to Cambridge rather than to Amherst or Williamstown, or New Haven or Providence for education; and I [Adams] likened it to a stage or steamboat competition in which the parties underbid each other, for custom, till one offers to convey passengers for nothing, and the other to pay them, instead of receiving pay from them for their passage."[39]

President Quincy in 1834 urged the corporation to provide more generous beneficiary aid, both in the size of stipends and the number aided. The result would be an increased enrollment and a net gain of income for the college, and in part because unoccupied rooms would now yield income. His general position was that a reduction of x in net costs per student (through aid) would bring a rise of enrollment and of

rents that would provide additional revenue much in excess of the additional costs of beneficiary aid.[40]

In 1845, George Bancroft and Linus Child, two overseers, wrote a pamphlet in which they demanded much lower tuition. "Access to the college should be as free as possible," they said. They resented especially a charge of $45 per year even when the student was not in residence. Such a charge in their view, taxes "the sons of our citizens for the privilege of resorting to an institution which belongs to the public." But President Quincy disagreed. He did not like the practice of parents educating their sons for one to three years elsewhere and then sending them to Harvard for their degrees. In his view the finances of Harvard were based on a four-year stay, and the advanced standing students must pay a fair share of the costs. On the supposed rise of costs, Quincy showed that costs had not risen from 1817 to 1845. Against the charge of higher costs at Harvard than elsewhere Quincy replied that the Harvard product was better, the sons of rich could afford to pay, and the children of parents with moderate income could borrow more than the difference of costs, and at no interest. Quincy was not sure that lower prices and more students were desirable. In his opinion, numbers bring not merely honours, reputation and equivalent income . . . They bring increased care, anxiety, labor in instruction. . . ."[41]

A visiting committee of Harvard University in 1849 also discussed the high costs of a Harvard education. In fact, this committee considered the rising price of an education at Harvard as an important part of the explanation of loss of state aid. But the committee defended Harvard's financial policies.

If there are any advantages at Harvard College beyond those offered elsewhere, they are found in the extent, the variety, and the completeness of the means of

---

38. The relevant table is deposited in the Harvard University Archives.

39. Extracts from the *Diary of John Quincy Adams and His Son, Charles Francis Adams,* Relating to Harvard College from 1786 to 1825, selected and transcribed by Henry Adams (1898) and William C. Roelker (1909), typed, in Harvard University Archives.

40. J. Quincy to Francis Gray, April, 1834; *President's Recommendation of a Reduction in the Charge of Instruction to beneficiaries,* April 4, 1834; F. C. Gray to T. W. Ward, April, 1834.

41. G. Bancroft and L. Child, *Report on Diminishing the Costs of Instruction in Harvard College,* 1845; Josiah Quincy, *Speech to the Overseers,* 1845.

instruction. They are seen in Professorships with whose foundation the State has had very little [to do] . . . .

In the view of the committee, tuition expense is small and may well fall—but other costs continue to rise as the daily expenses of life have increased and continue to increase. . . .[42]

Another Adams, Charles Francis Adams, in 1904, presented a view very similar to that of his ancestor.[43] Adams's general line was that tuition should rise by 50 percent (from $150 to $225), an increase which would offset the rise of prices in the last thirty-five years. He would use half the proceeds for scholarships and thus charge the wealthy something like full costs and improve the prospects of entry for the able but poor. In contrast to Eliot's views, the way out to him was higher charges, not economies. Every dollar received from gifts and bequests was in his view mortgaged for professors and the plant. Tuition has to finance other costs. A rise of tuition by 50 percent would only increase total costs by 15 to 30 percent. Harvard, the most expensive and the leading institution of higher learning, may well increase enrollment despite rising tuition. Adams would not compete with others for numbers.[44]

In the last quarter of the nineteenth century, the faculty and administrators sought ways of reducing costs of board and room. President Eliot showed a special interest in special measures directed to this end.[45]

Costs and Quality

Against the rising cost of a college education, the critic has to consider the improved product. It is not, however, easy to put a rise of, say, 20 times in costs over a period of 150 years against a measurable improvement in the product. About all we can say is that the product is greatly improved through the quality and education of teachers, improved libraries and laboratories and curriculum, and vast advances in the quality of room and board. In relation to income available for higher education, the burden is much easier to bear today. In some respects, e.g., medicine, there has been almost infinite improvement. In 1790 a student went to a hospital or infirmary and paid 18 shillings for board and 18 shillings for a doctor. These are very costly services when compared to the $82 for first-class medical service at Harvard today.[46]

Cutting Costs

In discussions of the high cost to students, there was a disposition to concentrate on the pay and the work-load of the faculty. More than once when the college was in financial difficulties and appealed to the government for help, the response was to reduce the size of the faculty and increase the work-load. The Legislature wanted to know, for example, why the president should be a nonteaching member of the faculty.

Costs to student are related to, though not determined by, costs of educating the student. In my higher education book, I showed that tuition was not unrelated in the various parts of the university to the costs of providing the required training.[47] On various occasions the Harvard authorities revealed their interest in the costs to the institution as a factor affecting tuition charges. Thus, in 1900, the president revealed that freshmen pay $75,000; but the cost of their instruction was considerably less. Seniors, however, pay $50,000, and costs for their studies are much more. At about the same time Dean LeBaron Russell Briggs, dean of the faculty of arts and sciences, also commented on the high costs of the elective

42. *Report of the Visiting Committee of Harvard University Made to the Overseers,* Boston, January 1849, pp. 14–29.
43. C. F. Adams, "The Harvard Tuition Fee: Its Proposed Increase," reprinted from the Harvard Graduates Magazine, September 1904.
44. *Ibid.,* p. 18.
45. *C. W. Eliot Papers,* January 19, 1874; and March 29, 1889.

46. *Sessions,* p. 140.
47. Harris, *op. cit.,* pp. 50–56.

system with many courses enrolling but a few students. " . . . I suspect that if the receipts and expenditures of Harvard College could be disentangled once more from those of Graduate School and the Scientific School, the process would reveal some of the sacrifices of the College to its neighbors." At an earlier period, the board of overseers commented on the small number of teachers, low costs, and relatively small demands on the general unappropriated funds of the College of the Moral Sciences against the language and literature and physical science departments.[48]

48. *Report of the President of Harvard College, 1901–1902,* p. 103; *Report of the Board of Overseers of Harvard College on the Condition, Needs and Prospects of the University,* 1869, p. 58.

6

Tuition

Trend

The trend of tuition has been upward, and especially in recent years. When tuition was inadequate to cover the financial gap, the college and professional schools resorted to additional fees, fines, and the like. The fees were payments for special services, often not wanted by the student and at times unjustly imposed. Thus if the college could not pay a professor of mathematics an adequate salary in the eighteenth century, students might be assessed $5 or $10 to cover the deficiency.

In the seventeenth century, a shortage of hard money complicated matters. Thus silver provided only a small part of the students' payments in the 1650s. Wheat and malt were popular forms of payment since they provided the raw material for bread and beer. Cattle on the hoof could also be used advantageously by the college. Even poultry was acceptable. Among other items used as the equivalent of money were sugar, sack (for commencement), spice, nutmeg, hardware, glass, and textiles.

Tuition was a low-priced commodity. A bushel and a half of wheat would cover a quarter's tuition under Dunster. In the late 1960s, a quarter's tuition would be the equivalent of about 250 bushels of wheat.[1]

A brief survey of tuition escalation in the first half of the eighteenth century, a highly inflationary period, is of some interest. Thus in 1727, the corporation supported a rise of tuition.

... Whereas there is thro ye favour of God to ye college an increase of Jnstructors in it; and whereas ye expensiveness of ye times calls for an addition of ye Salaries of those that are Jmployed in ye Tuition and Junstruction of ye Students, therefore ye Tuition money be advanced from ten to fifteen shillings Per Quarter for ye five years ensuing.[2]

Admitting that tuition had continued at 15 shillings in 1732 for only three years, the corporation nevertheless announced a rise in tuition in 1734 to 20 shillings:

Whereas ye Act of ye Corporation for continuing ye Tuition money at fifteen shillings per Quarter, confirm'd by ye Overseers Sept. 21. 1732. will expire on ye 22. of May next; and forasmuch as there is an extraordinary Depression of ye value of ye Bills of Credit, which hath rais'd ye price of many commodities & necessaries of life, therefore voted, yt at ye Expiration of this Quarter, ye Tuition money be advanced from fifteen to twenty shillings per Quarter, to enable ye Corporation to make Additions to ye Salaries of such officers of ye College as they shall think proper, and this Act to continue not exceeding three years.[3]

Again in 1738, the corporation announced an increase to 30 shillings old tenor and 10 shillings new tenor for the next four years. Anticipating protest,

1. *Founding of Harvard College,* p. 231; Morison, *Harvard College in the Seventeenth Century,* pp. 102-106.

2. *College Books,* vol. IV, pp. 547, 552, May 22, 1727.
3. *Ibid.,* pp. 628, 633.

the authorities noted: " ... Which Sum is not equal to the Settleme[t] of the S[d] Tuition money more than fifty years agoe. . . ."[4]

At this point the corporation explained why the added burden had to be put on tuition. " ... And Janasmuch as we are Assur'd by the Treasurer, that the Treasury is not able to answer any suitable Addition . . . ."[5]

A table follows which gives tuition charges over a period of more than three hundred years.

It will be recalled that tuition at Harvard has become an increasing part of costs to students over the years, with largest rises, of course, occurring in recent history. Even after a century Harvard tuition was only £1 a quarter or about $13 a year. By 1827, after nearly two centuries, the charge was only $55 a year. But in the next 140 years or so tuition had climbed to $2,000, with two-thirds of this rise since 1950. In the middle of the seventeenth century tuition accounted for little more than 10 percent of the college receipts from students; by the late 1960s, tuition was about 65 percent of college charges for instruction, rooms and board and medical fees and about 55 percent of total student costs.

The Relation of Tuition to Price Movements and Income

As prices rise, college authorities are inclined to increase their tuition. This follows because rising prices mean increased costs for the college, and if other resources are not available an increase of tuition becomes imperative. Another relevant consideration is that by relating tuition to price movements the fee asked is unchanged in purchasing power, a pricing policy that suggests fairness. It is not surprising that even today the average college administrator relates tuition to price movements.

But there is much more to be said for tying tuition to per capita income. Since per capita income has risen about 3 percent a year in recent years, the ad-

justment of tuition to movements in per capita income may well mean a rise of tuition in recent years of perhaps 2 to 3 times as much as if the tie-in were with prices only. The case for relating tuition to per capita income is that income movements reflect capacity to pay more than prices. The rise of per capita income reflects both rising prices and increases in productivity.[6]

Tuition Trends and Their Explanation

In early Harvard history tuition generally responded to inflationary pressures. Other income sources were not elastic and as costs rose, tuition increases were likely to follow. Fairly consistent inflation brought steady rises of tuition in the inflationary first fifty years of the eighteenth century. In fact, the Harvard authorities were far ahead of modern reformers in that they increasingly tied repayments of their loans to the price of silver. In this manner they, to some extent, protected their investments against the ravages of inflation. They were not likely, then, to be unresponsive to inflation when fixing tuition rates. In the Revolutionary War period, a highly inflationary era, tuition charges rose from 18 shillings to £75 a quarter in a period of less than four years. But this was not enough to preclude erosion of capital.

In the second quarter of the nineteenth century Harvard was severely criticized for its high tuition. But the defense often was that a high-quality education was costly. "There may be less money paid for it by students elsewhere than in Cambridge, but they do not get so much out of it in proportion to cost, and therefore it is not so cheap . . . ."[7]

On a number of occasions, the college begged help from the state government as a means of reducing

4. *Ibid.*, pp. 676, 737, December 28, 1742.

5. "College Laws, 1734," in *College Books,* vol. I, pp. 134-135.
6. Harris, *op. cit.,* pp. 137-143.
7. Mr. Gray's Letter to Governor Lincoln, 1831, p. 11; also see *Harvard College and Early Education in Massachusetts,* Section no. 21, p. 98.

Table 6-1

Tuition, 1650 to 1967, Various Years. (1650-1651 to 1810-1811 Quarterly; 1827 and Later Years Annually)*

Year	Tuition Per Quarter	Reasons Given for Increase	Source
1650-1652	6s 8d		Foster, *op. cit.* p. 66
1655-1659	8s		*Corporation Records*, vol. I, p. 216
1687-1712	10s		
1727	15s		
1735	20s	High cost of living.	*Ibid.*, pp. 306-308
1750	10s (new currency)[1]		*Ibid.*, p. 503
Sept. 1777	18s		*Corporation Records*, vol. II, p. 472
May 1781	£75		*Corporation Records*, vol. III, p. 113
Sept. 1788	24s (Fresh. & soph.) 30s (Seniors)		*Ibid.*, pp. 321-322
Sept. 1806	$ 9.00 (Fresh. & soph.) 11.00 (Jun. & sen.)[2]		*Corporation Records*, vol. IV, p. 111
Sept. 1810-1811	12.00 (Fresh. & soph.) 14.67 (Jun. & sen.)	To meet expenses of increasing numbers and salaries of tutors.	*Ibid.*, p. 40
	per year		
1827	$ 55.00[3]		*Corporation Records*, vol. VI, p. 20
1844-1845	75.00[4]		*Report of the Treasurer of Harvard College*, 1844-1845, p. 10
1860	104.00	Rising prices.	*Report of the President of Harvard College*, 1914-1915, pp. 24-25
1869-1870	150.00		C. F. Adams, *op. cit.* p. 16
1916-1917	200.00[5]	Deficits; choice of reduced quality or rise of tuition; prepare for rise of expenditures.	*Report of the President of Harvard College*, 1913-1914, pp. 12-14; *Report of the President of Harvard College*, 1915-1916; *Report of the Treasurer of Harvard College*, 1915-1916, pp. 5-6; *Report of the Committee to consider an Increase in the Tuition Fee*, 1914-1915, C. H. Moore, chairman.
1921-1922	250.00[6]	To meet growth of other expenses. Endowment drive would finance faculty.	*Report of the President of Harvard College*, 1920-1921; *Report of the Treasurer of Harvard College*, 1920-1921, pp. 5-6.
1925-1926	300.00[7]	Salary increases. Follow lead of others. Harvard embarrassed by lack of funds.	*Report of the President of Harvard College*, 1924-1925, p. 7.

Table 6-1 cont'd.

Year	Tuition Per Year	Official Explanation	Source
1928-1929	$400.00		
1948-1949	525.00	Decline in numbers and higher unit costs; lower return on capital and inflation.	*Report of the President of Harvard College*, 1946-1947, pp. 34-35; 1937-1938, p. 15; 1948-1949, p. 41; Doermann, *op. cit.*, table 5.
1949-1950	600.00		
1953-1954	800.00	New programs, higher faculty salaries; rise of other costs.	*Report of the President of Harvard College*, 1952-1953, pp. 36-37.
1956-1957	1,000.00	We should not meet rising costs by gradually squeezing professors' pay.	*Report of the President of Harvard College*, 1955-1956, p. 40.
1958-1959	1,250.00	Alternative is to make college teaching a depressed profession.	*Report of the President of Harvard College*, 1957-1958, p. 15.
1962-1963	1,520.00		
1964-1965	1,760.00		
1966-1967	2,000.00		

* Tuition varies to some extent according to the sources used, and the exact year indicated. Thus a committee of the faculty gave the following figures. They vary some from the material in the table. Before 1807 - $20; 1807 - $40; 1814 - $50; 1815 - $52; 1816 - $57. *Report of a Committee of the Board of Overseers of Harvard College,* January 6, 1825.

(1) Following a devaluation: 7½ old = 1 of new currency.

(2) Includes tuition fees to Harvard profs., monitors and gallery for freshmen and sophomores; these plus library for juniors and seniors.

(3) Corporation committee recommended reduction from $55 to $30; but no evidence of change. The receipts divided by the number of students gave a charge per student of $55 in 1826 and $47 in 1827. But nonpayment may be relevant here. *Corporation Records*, vol. VI, p. 20.

(4) The college points out that $75 is not really tuition; for $20 covers use of library and lecture rooms.

(5) To apply only to new students and hence though voted in 1914-1915 was introduced only in 1916-1917. Moreover, those paying the $200 were to be freed of paying various fees.

(6) Applies to old and new students. Additional courses now $65 instead of $25.00.

(7) All new students.

tuition, covering deficits, and/or paying adequate salaries to the staff. In 1791, on making such a plea, the college authorities pointed out that unless help were made available, the college would have to call in its loans in order to pay its bills and thus impose severe hardships upon its debtors.[8]

An extreme statement against subsidies to students is the following. Having pointed out that tuition covers only two-thirds of the pay of instructors and only one-third of total costs, a committee of overseers in 1827 then made an extreme statement against favoring the indigent:

. . . The Committee believes that it will better answer the purposes of the founders and benefactors of the University, to furnish the best possible means of education at a cheap rate to those who are in moderate circumstances rather than to exhaust its resources for the support of a large number of indigent persons, who if they were not thus invited to the University, might become useful and respectable in some other course of life . . . ."[9]

In the 1840s another crises emerged. One committee of the overseers would cut tuition from $75 to $33 per annum: " . . . any person should be admitted to the standing for which he is qualified, without any pecuniary consideration." The committee contrasted the 5 to 6 hours of teaching at Boston Latin and Harvard's small burden.

This committee envisaged reductions in expenditures and increased teaching loads.

But another committee would not reduce tuition, and in their view the charge was moderate in view of the unusual Harvard product.

Economies can only be achieved through a reduction of staff and a rise of the work load. On the first, this committee emphasized the lack of freedom in dealing with holders of endowed chairs, and also limitations set by salary contracts. On work load, the committee noted that hours in classroom are a most inadequate measure of hours of work.

But if the question be whether education be dearer at Harvard University than at other New England Colleges; due regard being had to the equivalent received, by the student in the intellectual advantages offered to him, *the undersigned is firmly convinced that the very opposite answer must be given . . . .*[10]

One of the surprises of Harvard tuition policy was the stability of tuition rates from 1870 until 1915-1916, a period of almost fifty years, in which prices rose more than 20 percent. This alone would have supported a substantial tuition increase. But with per capita incomes rising considerably more than 100 percent, one might have expected rising tuition, supported by the ability-to-pay argument. In fact, back in the early part of the twentieth century, the possibility of a rise of tuition was seriously considered.

In 1903, a special committee of the board of overseers urged a rise of tuition from $150 to $225, contending that $225 in 1903 was worth no more than $150 in 1869. In its view an improvement of standards would generally be welcome; and half the added income could be used for scholarships.[11]

Charles Francis Adams, as noted earlier, strongly espoused a rise of tuition of 50 percent in 1904.[12] He argued that " . . . it would, on the whole, seem to be less difficult and far more in consonance with the true interests of the University, to increase its income than to decrease its outgo . . . ."[13]

But Eliot was not convinced. He was a low-tuition advocate and feared the loss of able and poor

---

8. *Memorial of January, 1791; Statement of Treasurer Davis of February, 1824; S. A. Eliot, Harvard College and its Benefactions, 1846, p. 17.*

9. *Report to the President and Fellows of Harvard College of November 15, 1827, of the Committee of the Board . . . to Consider the Subject of Appointment and Compensation . . . and what Services may be Required from the Beneficiaries . . . .*

10. *Report on Diminishing the Cost of Instruction in Harvard College To-gether with a Minority Report on the Same Subject,* 1845, italics in original.

11. *Report of the Special Committee of the Board of Overseers on the Financial Requirements of the University and the Deficit Incurred . . .* in Harvard University Archives, UA, II 10.30.104.

12. C. F. Adams, *op. cit.*

13. *Ibid.,* p. 12.

students should tuition rise.[14] He also received support from the *Harvard Bulletin* editors, who preferred cuts in courses to rises of tuition; and was fearful that higher tuition would make Harvard a college for the rich. [15]

On June 9, 1904, Eliot wrote to Charles Francis Adams:

You said at the start of this discussion about raising the College fee that you wanted the College open to young men who had either money or brains. The gist of our difference lies, I think, in this restricted alternative. I want to have the College open equally to men with much money, little money, or no money, provided they all have brains . . . .

Lowell was disposed to adjust tuition to rising prices and incomes. It will be recalled that under Lowell, tuition rose more than prices or per capita income. In the Lowell years, tuition doubled. Conant proved to be an Eliot disciple. Tuition was $400 in 1928-1929, and it was not until 1948-1949 that tuition was raised and then only to $525. In a period of twenty years when per capita disposable income roughly doubled and prices increased by 40 percent, tuition had not risen. It is not surprising then that faculties continued to be squeezed and that even as late as the mid 1950s, the real pay of a full professor at Harvard had declined by 20 percent while the average per capita real disposable income of the nation had risen by 50 percent. Pusey helped correct the situation by fairly drastic increases of tuition—a rise from roughly $600 to $2,000 in less than fifteen years, an increase greatly exceeding the roughly 75 percent rise of per capita disposable income during this period. But the rise could be supported by the failure of tuition to rise as much as per capita income after 1929 or 1939.

Enrollment and Tuition

In Chapter 9 we shall discuss the relationship of costs to students and enrollment. Many factors in addition to costs determine enrollment. When, for example, family or per capita incomes rise more than costs, an increase of costs should be consistent with rising enrollment. Again, the extent of competition and Harvard's rising prestige are relevant.

Over the many years when increases of tuition were under consideration, one strong argument directed against rises in tuition has been the presumed adverse effect on enrollment. Moreover, as tuition became an increasing share of costs, the argument carried increasing weight. Under Eliot tuition and costs were stabilized. The large rise of enrollment was associated with the stability of costs, with the increased prestige of Harvard, and with the large gains of endowment income and gifts. With rising personal incomes and a growing interest in higher education, the total demand for higher education rose, with favorable effects on all competitors. In the years 1870 to 1910, the Eliot years, national enrollment rose from 52,000 to 355,000, or a rise of 6 times. Under Lowell the increase of enrollment was at a slower rate, and tuition rose beyond a level justified by the increase of capacity to pay. But this was a period of rising demand—national enrollment increased from 355,000 in 1910 to 1,100,000 in 1930, a much larger absolute rise per year, but a smaller relative rise per year than under Eliot. Undoubtedly the general rise of tuition and costs under Lowell reduced demand, if not enrollment. The president was concerned over the possible change in the type of student following tuition rises, though this was a consideration that seemed to carry much more weight with Eliot and Conant than with Lowell. Even at the new high tuition rates, Lowell found it necessary to restrict enrollment. National enrollment rose from 1,100,000 in 1930 to 2,700,000 in 1950 (roughly the Conant years), a smaller relative rise per year than in the Eliot and Lowell years but a much larger absolute rise per year.[16]

---

14. James, *op. cit.,* vol. II, pp. 150-151.

15. *Harvard Bulletin,* vol. II, no. 19, p. 2, February 1900; and vol. VI, no. 24, p. 2, March, 1904.

16. Enrollment figures from *Statistics of Higher Education, 1957-1958, Faculty, Students, Degrees,* U.S. Department of Health, Education, and Welfare, 1962, p. 6.

In the Conant period, stable tuition did not result in rising enrollment so much as in increased capacity to accept students more on the basis of ability than on that of economic status. Inadequate physical facilities tended to put a limit on enrollments as did a growing fear of the octopus university.

On a number of occasions the college authorities commented on the relationship between tuition increases and enrollment. But the relationship is not so close as they seemed to assume. Thus in 1915-1916, tuition rose from $150 to $200. The entering freshmen numbered 647 in 1915 and 645 in 1916. "Taken all together, it seems clear that the increase in tuition fee—which was the result of dire necessity—has not deprived us of a very large number of students." In 1921-1922, a rise of tuition in the business school seemed to reduce the number of students. But the authorities should also have considered the worsening economic situation.[17]

The case for the great 1919 endowment drive rested in part on the theory that higher tuition would lay Harvard open to the charge of being a rich man's university.

Among Harvard authorities there were different views on the effects on enrollment of increases or decreases in tuition. But the majority found an inverse relationship. Thus, in the first quarter of the nineteenth century, losses of enrollment were associated with high tuition, and with a reduction of tuition, it was expected that enrollment would rise substantially. In the 1850s, a rise of tuition from $75 to $100 was proposed, but only if enrollment would not be adverse. Again later in the 1860s, the college would provide economical board so that tuition could be raised without adverse effects through rising total costs on enrollment. Eliot, on numerous occasions,

insisted that a rise of tuition would result in reduced enrollment and/or deterioration of quality of applicant. Overseers expressed similar views in 1894. But another group of overseers noted that with a rise of tuition of one-third in 1864-1865, enrollment had risen by one-sixth between 1868 and 1872; and with a rise in 1869-1870 of tuition of one-half, enrollment rose by 51 percent between 1873 and 1877. An increase in costs by 50 percent in the medical school—a change from a two- to a three-year curriculum—seemed to have no adverse effect on enrollment. These examples, however, are not convincing. Economic conditions were improving, and interest in higher education was increasing. Had enrollment not been stimulated by such factors, higher tuition would have brought reduced enrollment.[18]

A minority of an overseers committee in 1894 summarized the issues as follows:

There are some students who could easily pay the entire cost of their tuition; there are others by whom the charge of any tuition fee is seriously felt, and for them the addition of $50 per year would be a still more difficult burden to bear . . . .[19]

Costs and Tuition

In the private economy, the seller seeks a price equal to costs (inclusive of a normal profit) and if monopolistic conditions prevail he may well get more. It is not easy for those who run our institutions of higher learning to discard cost pricing. Thus in the 1840s, President Everett wrote:

. . . I cannot think even now, that college education is unreasonably high. The charge for tuition at Cambridge, where it is somewhat higher than at the other

17. *Report of the President of Harvard College,* 1915-1916, pp. 5-6; 1921-1922, p. 21; cf. 1923-1924, pp. 123-124; Harvard University Archives, UAV, 136.124.173.

18. *Report of the Board of Overseers,* January 10, 1894, p. 5; *Report of the Committee . . . to Inquire into the Income and Expenses of the College,* December 26, 1826; *Report of the Committee of the Corporation,* C. Jackson, chairman, November 15, 1827, p. 145; C. W. Eliot,

University Trustees, p. 16; C. W. Eliot to the President and Fellows of Harvard College, November 14, 1862; *Committee Respecting the Expenses and Emoluments of the Department . . . ,* September 25, 1858; *Memorandum for a Petition from the Finance Committee of Memorial Hall, Committee of 50,* May 22, 1869.

19. *Minority Report, Board of Overseers,* January 10, 1894.

colleges, is seventy-five dollars a year. This pays for thorough and accurate instruction given by fifteen or sixteen able and accomplished men in the ancient and modern languages, in the exact, the critical, the applied, and moral sciences, in addition to general supervision three fourths of the year. For the instruction of a day school in Boston, five hours in the day, one hundred dollars per annum are paid. Gentlemen in practical life can say where else, for seventy-five dollars per annum, they can procure such an amount of intellectual labor to be done, requiring equal talent and preparation, and involving equal responsibility. The sum of seventy-five dollars per annum is, moreover, not quite half what the service costs the university. . . .[20]

Again in the debates of the early twentieth century, the overseers' committee and C. F. Adams both stressed the point that the high tuition was related to the high costs of instruction. Adams went further. He noted all were being subsidized, but he would subsidize at varying rates according to need.[21]

A frequent argument used on behalf of the Harvard pricing system and presented as early as the middle of the nineteenth century was that Harvard could not compete with the low-cost public institutions of higher learning. Harvard had to offer a high-quality education and charge accordingly. The alternatives were increased tuition or reduced quality.

Lowell stressed rising costs and the need of matching them with higher tuition. He affirmed that with higher prices students could afford to pay more. Incidentally, whereas Lowell tended to tie tuition to prices, the 1903 overseers committee more appropriately compared the *burden* of a $150 tuition in 1869 with a $225 one in 1903. Incomes, not prices, are the relevant factors.

In the postwar period the Conant administration boasted of the general stability of tuition and costs in the face of large rises of prices. This stability, in the view of the administration, was made possible by the large number of students, and hence low unit costs, and by the large economies in that period. Once student enrollment was to decline from postwar peaks, the administration would have to increase tuition. Pusey, as noted earlier, was more disposed to contend with rising costs by raising tuition.

Even as early as 1805, the corporation charged students admitted to advanced standing $60 to $100, a substantial burden at that time. Yet as wedded as Mr. Lowell was to the cost theory he nevertheless would not charge tuition on the basis of cost of instruction, school by school.[22]

It is not easy to estimate costs of higher education, and especially when the institution provides services of different kinds on what economists call output under joint costs. But before the twentieth century the product was less complicated than today. For academic services, the college provided a teaching service for the undergraduate and little beyond that. Graduate study was just beginning, and few college administrators were prepared to accept any responsibility for research. Hence one could divide total costs inclusive of capital by the number of students and thus obtain costs per student. Thus in 1894 tuition fees were $150 and costs $450. The overseers were not pleased that the rich students could thus obtain their training at one-third of costs. In 1901, Eliot estimated costs exclusive of interest on plant at $300 and tuition $150. By 1914, cost had risen to $600; tuition was still $150.

In view of the large endowment income, critics of Harvard were inclined to be critical of tuition charges.

20. E. Everett, *Harvard's Need for State Funds, 1848-1849,* p. 385.
21. C. F. Adams, *op. cit.,* pp. 16-19; *Report of Special Committee of Board of Overseers, 1904,* in Harvard University Archives, UA II, 10.30-104.
22. For material in this section, in addition to earlier references, see: "Why Harvard Needs Money," in *Harvard Alumni Bulletin,* vol. XIX, pp. 304-304, January 18, 1917; *Harvard and the Future,* 1919, p. 7, in Harvard University Archives, UAV 136.124.273; *Report of the President of Harvard College,* 1914-1915, pp 24-25; 1919-1920, pp. 7-9; 1920-1921, pp. 5-7; 1924-1925, p. 7; 1946-1947, pp. 34-36; 1947-1948, pp. 15, 41; 1957-1958, p. 10; *Corporation Records,* vol. IV, p. 74; G. Bancroft and L. Child, *Overseers Report on Diminishing Cost of Instruction in Harvard College,* 1845.

But Harvard's position was that the income on endowment was well used on behalf of the students, but was inadequate to cover all costs. Hence, tuition had to be charged. The only other alternative was to reduce expenditures through curtailment of personnel and courses.[23]

Another aspect of this problem is the relationship of education to income. In the post World War II period, economists increasingly studied the relationship of education to income; that is, how much does income respond to additional years of education. These large gains are held to justify students paying a large part of costs of their education. In 1901, President Eliot recommended to a friend that he examine class reports and he would "get abundant evidence that college and scientific school training nowadays is profitable, indeed indispensable to young men going into the higher walks of life."[24]

The Scourge of Inflation and the Salary/Tuition Ratio

An interesting exercise is to compare the pay of a full professor and the tuition charged the student. The accompanying table gives the ratio of a full professor's salary and tuition charges. The ups and downs of this ratio reflect largely the instability of prices, and, to some extent, incomes. The most important conclusion is that professors tend to lose economic status in periods of inflation; that is, incomes lag behind the rise of prices and even behind the rise of tuition. Since tuition also lags behind the increase in prices, the salary of teachers experiences a double lag. It is not surprising then that whereas the ratio of the salary of a full professor in 1712-1713 relative to tuition (before this the college relied primarily on tutors) was 32 times one student's tuition fee, it was only 12 times as much in 1964-1965. Apparently, the professor's salary had experienced a secular decline relative to tuition.

In Harvard history since the early eighteenth century, there have been six periods of substantial inflation—1722-1756, 1771-1778; 1860-1870; 1910-1920; 1940-1950 and 1950-1964. In all of these periods but one (1910-1920), the rise of tuition exceeded that of professorial salaries. With these relative movements the ratios of the modal salary for a full professor to tuition fell in these periods from 43 times tuition costs to 22; 35 to 31; 42 to 26; 26 to 19; and 19 to 12. Between 1910 and 1920, however, the ratio rose from 26 to 38 times tuition costs as salaries rose more than tuition. Again I emphasize the point that the full weight of the lag of salaries is not given here because tuition also lagged behind the rise of prices.

It might be expected that the ratio would rebound; that is, salaries rise relative to tuition in the stable periods following inflationary episodes, but not consistently. From 1756 to 1772, relatively stable years, the ratio did rise from 22 times tuition costs to 35 times costs but from 1920 to 1930, the ratio actually fell from 38 times costs to 25 times costs, with tuition rising greatly relative to salaries.

In the years of relatively stable prices (net) but of rising per capita income—e.g., 1809 to 1840 and 1870 to 1910, there was a remarkable stability of both tuition and salaries. In these years, clearly, the college had failed to match the growth of the economy with increases of tuition and salaries. But 1840 to 1860, years of growth, witnessed a substantial rise of salaries and stable prices, and, therefore, large gains in the ratio of salary to tuition. Especially in the years since 1920 has the professor experienced losses as reflected in this ratio: in 1920 a professor's pay equaled 38.5 times one student's tuition costs; 1964 it equaled 12.2 times a student's tuition costs.

23. *Minority Report of Board of Overseers*, January 10, 1894; *Report of the Visting Committee of the Harvard University Overseers*, January, 1849, pp.4,20,27;L.E. Sexton to F.W. Hunnewell, March 26, 1914 in *Letters of A.L. Lowell;* F.W. Blackmer, *The History of Federal and State Aid to Higher Education,* U.S. Bueau of Education, 1890, pp. 9, 18-19; C.W. Eliot ot R.T. Crane, September 12, 1901.

24. *C. W. Eliot to R. T. Crane*, September 12, 1901; S. E. Harris, *op. cit.*, pp. 150-154; S. E. Harris (ed.), *Economic Aspects of Higher Education*, Organization for Economic Cooperation and Development, 1964, pp. 47-59.

Table 6-2.

Salary-Tuition Ratios, 1713 to 1964, Various Years

Year	Modal Salary Full Professor*	Tuition[+]	Ratio of Salary/Tuition ¶
1712-1713	£66 13s4d (A)	£22s5d	32
1715	66.13.4	1.15.0	38
1722-1723	75.0.0	1.17.2	43
1755-1756	64.8.7	2.18.10	22
1771-1772	100.0.0	2.17.0	35
1777-1778	200.0.0	6.9.11	31
1809	$ 1,500	$ 51.90	29
1818	1,700	56.80 §	30
1829-1830	1,500	55.00	27
1839-1840	1,500	55.00	27
1849-1850	1,800	55.00	33
1859-1860	2,300	55.00	42
1869-1870	4,000	150.00	26
1879-1880	4,000	150.00	26
1889-1890	4,000	150.00	26
1899-1900	4,160	150.00	28
1909-1910	4,000	150.00	26
1919-1920	7,700	200.00	38
1929-1930	10,000‡	400.00	25
1939-1940	10,517	400.00	26
1949-1950	11,350	600.00	19
1963-1964	20,970‡	1,500.00	14
1964-1965	21,500 (est)	1,760.00	12

* Average salary used through 1755-1756. Thereafter modal to 1889-1890, where it is the average of 3 modals; 1919-1920 is average, as are 1939-1940 and 1949-1950, as stated in *The Economic Status of the Faculty of Arts and Sciences,* Harvard University, 1950, p. 28.

† Tuition is average instruction charge per student through 1755-1756; thereafter through 1859-1860 it represents the standard tuition fee. After 1859-1860, because of the catalogue and term bill formats, which show instructional fees plus library, laboratory, and other fees, the fee for instruction per se cannot be filtered out.

‡ Total for 1963-1964 includes fringe benefits. The average for all full-time faculty equals $16,600. *Bulletin of Association of University Professors,* June, 1964, p. 166. For the 1930 estimate see S.E. Harris, "Salaries of Full Professors," in *Harvard Alumni Bulletin,* April 9, 1955, p. 513.

§ Represents data for 1819.

¶ Through 1777-1778 it is computed to the nearest shilling (20 shillings equal £1.

Sources: salary: *Treasurers' Ledgers,* in Harvard University Archives; *Treasurers' Journals,* in Harvard University Archives; *Treasury Cash Books; Corporation Records;* tuition: *Official Registers; Stewards' Quarter Bill Books.*

equalled 38.5 times one student's tuition costs; 1964 it equalled 12.2 times a student's tuition costs.

In general there has been a tie between tuition and salaries. This is to be expected since tuition has covered a substantial though varying, part of the educational costs. In the middle of the twentieth century, tuition covered more than half the educational costs, although the exact proportion is not easily calculated. The tough problem is to determine—especially when costs are joint, e.g., undergraduate instruction, graduate instruction and research—what are the relevant costs.

In the eighteenth century, the relation of tuition and faculty salaries was often more direct than is customary today. Thus, the students were asked to pay special fees to support the professors of Hebrew or the professor of mathematics. In 1778, when the condition of the faculty was especially precarious, the corporation asked "for a rise of salaries in a way that will not lessen the College funds, nor increase the quarterly payment of the students to such a degree as to prevent the growth and increase of the College." The corporation proposed a moderate assessment on the students, but the overseers did not concur.[25] Similar proposals were made, but not put into effect, in 1782.

Salaries have been a persistent concern of the college. In 1796, the corporation petitioned the commonwealth, with success, to use its subsidies for instruction, rather than to reduce tuition.[26]

More recently, Dean McGeorge Bundy put well the relation of tuition and salaries. This was a period in which the faculty was being squeezed hard. The following year President Pusey also stressed a similar point.

Dean Bundy: . . . It seems wrong that the rising costs of private education, at any level, should be met by gradually squeezing down the real income of the teacher—yet this is in fact what has been happening in American schools and colleges, Harvard among them. I believe this trend should be stopped, and reversed. [27]

25. *Corporation Records*, vol. III, pp. 19-20, 141-142.
26. *Ibid.*, vol. IV, pp. 483, 487.

Variations Among Schools

Tuition has tended to be low in the divinity school and high in the health schools, and especially in the business school.

The structure of tuition fees is explained by various factors. Where the costs are high, the tendency is to set high tuition rates. This, for example, may explain the high charges in the business, medical, and public health schools. Law school charges are low compared to arts and sciences and medicine, a fact explained in part by the low unit cost of instruction: large classes and a low teacher-student ratio. Perhaps competitive rates are also relevant here. Capacity to pay and material benefits expected by students are also relevant considerations. Here the large incomes available to business and medical school graduates are relevant. The high costs of medical education result in a disproportionate number of medical students coming from families with incomes of $10,000 a year or more. Divinity school students, and to a lesser degree education students, pay little, in part because the expected material gains of the Harvard education are small, and because they frequently come from low-income families. The relevant table is deposited in the Harvard Archives.

Another factor of some importance is the availability of endowment and gift income. Since the Harvard theory is that each department finances its own needs, those that have large endowments relative to total budgets can get by with lower tuition. Here the college especially benefits. Where costs are high—e.g., medicine—the tuition is likely to be high. The medical school operates on an interesting principle. Tuition is high in part because a very large part of tuition income is used to finance aid.[28]

Expenditures tend to be high per student when the number of students is small. Thus, expenditures per student are especially high in the schools of medicine, public health, dental medicine and education. In some of these schools, e.g., medicine and public

27. *Report of the President of Harvard College*, 1955-1956, p. 40; 1957-1958.
28. *Harvard Crimson*, November 28, 1959.

large enrollment, also has a high expenditure per student. Here the explanation is expensive curriculum as it surely is in part for the medical school. The expenditures for the School of Public Administration (now the J. F. Kennedy School) are small, despite low enrollment. Relevant here is the availability of faculty from the school of arts and sciences, who are mainly financed by arts and sciences. Divinity has a small enrollment and moderate expenditures. Again, low-cost curriculum and inadequate funds are relevant.[29]

For the year 1962-1963, I have compared tuition and income minus government contracts and grants for the various schools (I deduct government grants on the assumption, not wholly justified, that these outlays are not relevant for teaching.) The contribution of student income to the total (minus grants) is especially high for the law school (60 percent). Here the low endowment is relevant. The other schools that are substantially out of line are largely the small schools, where, obviously, costs are high and tuition income tends to be low: public health (8 percent), dentistry (16 percent), public administration (16 percent), divinity and medicine (20 percent) and education (28 percent). The relevant table is deposited in the Harvard Archives.

Dependence on Special Fees

Throughout its history, Harvard relied heavily on special fees. But this method of financing pleased neither students nor faculty. Thus, Professor Eliot (later president) refused to accept payments through the recourse to fees:

. . . the proposed tenure is extremely repugnant to my feelings as a teacher and as a student of science. A constant reference to the money relation between master and pupil is demoralizing to both, and nothing could be more distasteful to me than such a necessity. . . .[30]

Excessive dependence on fees militated against high standards in the medical school. In 1849, a visiting committee of the overseers complained that, despite the high quality of its faculty, compensation was most inadequate in relation to salaries paid in competing institutions. "The principal compensation is derived from the pupils, and must vary with their number, they reported.[31]

In the nineteenth century the issue of fees charged by one school to students of another part of the university received much attention. The law school in its early days relied heavily on fees. At the outset the university professor was to rely on student fees "like a kind of legal Elijah fed by ravens, the size of his meal depending upon the number of ravens he could attract. . . ." But its students had the privilege of attending lectures in other departments of the university without payment of fees. In 1847, the law school faculty protested the imposition of a $5 fee for lecture courses attended elsewhere in the university. In Law Prof. Simon Greenleaf's view, legal education was already too expensive. In other instances the university carefully regulated the fees to be charged for attending lectures in other departments of the university. Thus, those attending a course of lectures of professors Alexander Agassiz and Eben Horsford had to pay $5. When Prof. of Music John K. Paine wanted to charge law school students $5 for music instruction, the steward objected, one reason being that he did not want any such charges to be put on the term bill.[32]

Mr. Abbott Lawrence, the angel of the Lawrence Scientific School, believed in the fee system: he

29. S. E. Harris, "Economics of Harvard," in *Harvard Alumni Bulletin*, February 20, 1960, p. 382.

30. C. W. Eliot to President Hill, January 31, 1863, In Harvard University Archives.

31. *Report of the Committee of the Overseers of Harvard College Appointed to Visit the Medical School, 1849.*

32. *Committee on Fees . . . by Students of Other Departments of the University, for Attending Courses of Lectures . . . to Undergraduates,* October 9, 1847, in Harvard University Archives; *Committee on Fees on Members of the Professional Schools and Undergraduates for Attending the Scientific Lectures, March 13, 1848,* in Harvard University Arvhices; Batchelder, *Bits of Harvard History,* p. 204; Steward to President Hill, January 9, 1863, in Harvard University Archives.

would have the professor of engineering obtain half his income from fees. In 1862, a committee headed by J. R. Lowell approved the corporation's vote to abolish the system under which professors depended on fees for their salaries in the science school. Yet Eliot, in 1871, would depend on fees of fourteen students to bring the engineering professor's income up to $4,000.

As noted earlier, Harvard College depended heavily on fees from the very beginning. Fines were a form of fee, though payable only for violation of rules; and we observed earlier the significance of fines.

Competition

Harvard has been criticized as a high-cost college in various periods in the eighteenth century and also in the first quarter of the nineteenth century. I have put together in a table tuition charges for Harvard and its competitors. This table is deposited in the Harvard Archives. Against the Harvard charge I have put the competitors' charge for the nearest year during which tuition charge is available. In general, Harvard was clearly a high-cost college *for tuition* during most of the nineteenth century. For example, in 1827 Harvard's tuition was $55 against $33, $40, $27, and $24 among its most serious rivals. By 1895, however, Yale's and Princeton's tuition matched Harvard's. But not so Dartmouth, Cornell, and Williams.

During periods when the university was especially concerned over its financial position, the issue of increases in tuition was vigorously debated. The years 1849 and 1894 were two such years. In the earlier year, the commonwealth was critical of the college for considering a rise in tuition, and also for its current high rates. Whereas Harvard's tuition was $90, Amherst and Williams charged only $42 and $40 respectively. The Harvard authorities defended their financial policy on the grounds that they turned out a better product. "The Committee disclaim all comparisons with other colleges, which are doubtless doing all they can honorably to advance and extend the benefits of a liberal education. . . ."[33]

The minority committee objected to a rise. This committee listed the tuition of fifteen institutions inclusive of two public ones. All but three had lower tuition than Harvard, with two of the three charging $150, the tuition at Harvard.[34]

Higher Tuition and Student Aid

We discuss aid in a later chapter. But here we should briefly comment on the relation of rises in tuition and provision of additional scholarships or other aids to offset the additional costs for those unable to pay the increased tuition.

In recent years, college officials have universally increased financial aid *pari passu* with rises in tuition. But in earlier years there was some opposition to scholarships. A minority report of the overseers in 1894 stated, ". . . It is unwise to compel the entire number of undergraduate and graduate students to pay largely increased charges, out of which prizes in money for superiority in scholarship shall be awarded. . . ."[35] But the majority would have used $40,000 of $100,000 to be obtained through a $50 increase of tuition to finance free scholarships. These would have been available to all, irrespective of income. The committee called this plan a "blessed emulation of rich and poor lovers of learning, of whom in either event you reward and retain the best. . . ."[36]

C. F. Adams also had some doubts about scholarships:

. . . In fact, poor scholarship, if combined with lack of means, has figured somewhat sentimentally perhaps, as indicative of our most precious educational material . . . for, while the dull, lumpish, and mentally

33. *Report of the Visiting Committee of the Harvard University Board of Overseers*, January, 1849, pp. 20-21, 26-27.
34. *Board of Overseers, Majority and Minority Reports*, January 10, 1894, pp. 6-7, 11.
35. *Minority Report of the Board of Overseers*, January 10, 1894, p. 11.
36. *Majority Report of the Board of Overseers*, January 10, 1894, pp. 6, 10.

inert, provided only they are also poor, have been almost passionately adhered to as the possible flowers of the flock, others of the same general type, but more fortunate in their worldly belongings, have been roundly denounced, and characterized as college barnacles. . . .[37]

As usual, Eliot was most sensible in his proposals. He maintained a well-conducted university, offering a moderate number of scholarships and a variety of remunerative employment and charging substantial tuition fees, thereby meeting the competition of institutions with low tuition.[38]

---

37. C. F. Adams, *op. cit.* pp. 180, 182.

38. C. W. Eliot, *op. cit.*, p. 16.

7

Room and Board

Introductory

Earlier I noted that rents were much less important relatively and board much more important in Harvard's early than in her later history. Over the Puritan period, for example, food cost from 4 to 5 times as much as tuition. In contrast, food costs only about one-third as much as tuition in the late 1960s, or a relative rise of tuition of about 12 to 15 times.[1] The proportion of rents (inclusive of detriments, a penalty payment for not being in residence) to student costs was 11 percent in these early years and about 15 to 20 percent of corresponding outlays in recent years. The largest net changes were in board (inclusive of commencement dinner charges), a decline from more than 70 percent to about 20 percent. I scarcely need add that the quality of products and services has greatly improved. Morison has well described the menus and the shortages in the seventeenth century. Rooms were small, with students frequently rooming two in a bed; and the furniture, sparse and inadequate.[2] In 1777 one student, Silvannus Bourne, wrote to his father that he expected to be home in a few days since, with nothing to eat, he expected the president to close the college.[3]

In general, the college was persistently confronted with the problem of keeping down costs to students. As tuition became of increasing importance, the college had some control over costs, but the usual defense of the college, when charged with extravagances, was that a high-quality product was costly. Thus, in a letter to the governor in 1831, Mr. F. C. Gray, a member of the corporation, defended the college against charges of excessive costs. Indeed, Gray conceded that in some places room and board and fuel were likely to be cheaper. In his view this was a good thing for it enabled students with meager resources to go to college. But the college provided food here at $1.75 per week at a cost to the college of $2.25. "If it can be had in Amherst for less, we may rejoice in their good fortune, but we cannot share it," he wrote.[4]

In 1959, the *Harvard Crimson* complained of the inadequacies of the food served by Harvard and inquired whether an endowment should not be procured in order to improve the quality and keep costs down. Unknown to the *Crimson*, Captain Robert Keayne, of Boston, in 1653 suggested that the income of his gift might be used "for an addition or an enlargement to the Commons of the poorer set of scholars, which I have often heard is too short and bare for them."[5]

Impressed by the competition of tuition-free public institutions of higher learning and of small colleges with relatively low costs for room and board,

---

1. Foster, *op. cit.*, pp. 67, 77, 151.
2. Morison, *Harvard College in the Seventeenth Century*, pp. 85-86, 96-99.
3. *Bourne Papers,* in Harvard College Library, (from Professor Morison's files).

---

4. Mr. Gray's Letter to His Excellency Levi Lincoln, Governor of Massachusetts, 1833, pp. 9, 14.
5. Morison, *Harvard College in the Seventeenth Century*, vol. I, p. 101.

President Eliot said that "cheap board and cheap rooms in Cambridge are a necessary means for building up here a great, popular institution."[6]

Harvard authorities also had another objective in mind when one wrote " . . . there is a larger proportional amount of vice among those who live out of college walls than among those who live within them." Hence, the need of more college dormitory space.

In an acting president's view, there would be no problem of filling a new dormitory. In fact, a lottery would have to be used to reduce assignments to the space to be made available. Since the dormitory now involved subsidies to the students, all would be entitled to apply. If the university invested its own money, however, students would have no such rights and the college might seek a reasonable return on its money.[7]

Eliot was indeed pleased when Nathaniel Thayer in 1870 gave the college the funds to construct Thayer Hall. No such unrestricted gift had been received before, according to Eliot. Since the college could house only three-fifths of its students, the gift was especially welcome. "Fathers will want to have their sons live where they did in Thayer and so down to children's children. I have seen all sorts of monuments but never one which seemed better worth having than a college hall. . . ."[8]

Perhaps one reason for the concern over costs to students was the relationship of these costs to family income. Even as late as 1897, a keen observer noted "that the average cost to the student per year at the better college is larger than the total income of the average American family . . . ." In 1967, the relative burden is much less. Harvard's $3,500 cost in 1967 is but one-half the average family's income and perhaps not more than one quarter of the average Harvard family's income. That is to say, incomes have risen more than costs to students.[9]

Actually, through most of its history, Harvard tried to provide rooms and commons for the poor students at costs or even below. When the pressure was really great, the college did not hesitate to charge commons sums in excess of costs, but in the last hundred years the problem more often has been to cover noncapital costs. Capital costs were not charged to the students.

Harvard did, however, obtain profits on some of its dormitory enterprises. President Lowell in 1931 conceded that profits of 1/4 of 1 percent on the capital invested in the two new houses were expected. He considered this a small return in view of the fact that the estimated allowance for repairs and depreciation was only $90,000.[10]

Competition of Private Dormitories

One of the most troublesome issues arose in the Eliot period when private interests began constructing dormitories to attract the high-income students. The college in 1890 had but twenty-five rooms, with rents of less than $50, but rooms in Cambridge generally cost $100 or more. In 1895 the president complained of the elegant dormitories with private rooms at $300 and doubles at $500, on which Eliot noted large profits could be made.[11]

A Harvard graduate, A. P. Loring (1878), wondered why:

the College should allow its best paying class of students to be housed at a large profit by outside investors while it has invested its funds in property elsewhere, or in securities at low rates, and when the increase in values has been much less than those inevitably brought about in the neighborhood of Harvard Square by the regular and normal growth of the University.[12]

6. *Report of the President of Harvard College*, 1890-1891, p. 37.
7. A. P. Peabody to F. B. Crownsfield, November 27, 1862.
8. C. W. Eliot to N. Thayer, January 31, 1870.
9. C. F. Thwing, *op. cit.*, p. 244.

10. A. L. Lowell to Rt. Rev. William Laurence, January 17, 1931 in *A. L. Lowell Papers*, Folders 196 and 459.
11. *Report of the President of Harvard College*, 1889-1890, p. 19; 1894-1895, pp. 41-42.
12. *Harvard Graduates Magazine*, vol. XIII, p. 209, 1904.

In this period of rapid growth, there were not enough dormitories for the students. From 1867 to 1900 the number of students in college halls increased from 330 to 956; in private halls from 15 to 1,076 and of all students from 660 to 3,599.[13] Clearly the college was losing to private halls and private housing.

This large relative gain for noncollege housing persisted despite efforts of the college to meet the competition by incurring deficits in the early twentieth century, in part through installing hot water and steam heat in some of the dormitories. But the university was not disposed to counter private competition by building dormitories with its own funds. Improved transportation also weakened the competitive position of the university, for students increasingly were disposed to remain at home. In 1885, there was only one private dormitory in Cambridge; in 1905, there were twenty. Ultimately, and in part because of Lowell's success in mobilizing funds for college dormitories and the houses, the university won the competition. One reason was that private dormitories had to charge for capital costs while Harvard did not.[14]

In 1898 Prof. Archibald Coolidge finished Randolph Hall, the first of the Gold Coast dormitories. He saw in it a rent-free suite for himself and architectural and legal fees for members of his family. President Eliot assured him that the college would not build tax-free dormitories in competition with private dormitories. But Eliot could not bind his successors. President Lowell forced students into his freshman dormitories, thus reducing the revenues of the private dormitories and inducing the owners to sell to the college at about half of cost.[15]

An investor in the private dormitories protested against the practice "of the Harvard authorities in advising students not to rent rooms in buildings not now owned by the college. This practise is causing us serious inconvenience and loss of rent." The writer was especially annoyed since he was co-operating in a program for developing Harvard properties. By March, 1912, the owners of the private dormitories were prepared to enter negotiations of sale to the college.[16]

In the 1880s Santayana was fortunate enough to get a cheap room in Hollis–$44 a year. The reason was that it had no bedroom, no water, no heat, and it was on the first floor, the least desired location.[17] Today I understand the same room with water and heat rents for $450. Incidentally this may not be an out-of-line increase if allowance is made for inflation and the rise of costs of services.

Relative Cost Movements of Room and Board

I have already noted the relative downward movement of costs of board and room vis-à-vis tuition and total costs. Here is the trend in sixty recent years.

Table 7-1.

Room and Board Costs 1901 to 1963

	Room	% Total Cost	Board	% Total Cost
1900-1901	$115	27	$160	38
1929-1930	215	23	323	34
1939-1940	215	23	289	31
1962-1963	475	18	620	24

Source: I owe the raw materials to Humphrey Doermann's unpublished manuscript. My calculations.

It is clear from these figures that by economizing on rooms, e.g., doubling up; and on board, e.g., self-service, the college was able to raise tuition in the last generation without corresponding rises of cost. For

13. *Report of the President of Harvard College*, 1905-1906, p. 50.
14. *Ibid.*, 1890-1891, p. 94; 1893-1894, pp. 39, 42; 1894-1895, pp. 41-42; 1903-1904, pp. 14-15; 1905-1906, pp. 49-51; 1910-1911, p. 13; 1912-1913, pp. 12-13; M. Prince to A. L. Lowell, June 5, 1911.

15. A. J. Coolidge, *Archibald Cory Coolidge*, pp. 64-65; To The Trustees of the Harvard Riverside Trust, November 17, 1915, in Harvard University Archives.
16. J. L. Stackpole to A. L. Lowell, October 6, 1911. A. L. Lowell; *Memorandum for Corporation Meeting March 25, 1912.*
17. G. Santayana, *Persons and Places*, 1944, p. 1186.

example, from 1939 to 1963 tuition rose by 280 percent; but rooms by only 121 percent and board by only 92 percent.

To some extent these are puzzling figures. In the nation, rents from 1939 to 1963 increased only by 61 percent against 121 percent in the college, and despite doubling up and similar deterioration of product at Harvard. Rent controls outside undoubtedly contributed to this result, and possibly also the large increase of new housing units in the country not matched by Harvard from 1939 to 1963. But all in all the Harvard record here is not impressive.

On food, we can draw exactly the opposite conclusion—a rise of 162 percent in the economy and only 92 percent (with some deterioration of services) in the college. But this was exceptional. Usually prices at commons rose more than national food prices.

Rooms

From the beginning the college assumed responsibility for housing the students and keeping them together in the college. The governing board in 1671 commented on the advantages accruing to learning "by the multitude of persons cohabiting for Scholasticall communion, whereby to actuate the minds of one another and other ways to promote the ends of a Colledge Society. . . ." [18]

But even in the early seventeenth century college rooms were not always available. Thus, on September 6, 1717, the college decreed that "students who are obliged to board in the town for want of room in the college to entertain them be exempt from paying detriment during this year." [19]

In so far as rooms were available, the college was disposed to require students to live in. Thus in 1735 it was decreed "That no Detriment may accrue to Ye

College by Ye Chambers lying vacant, it is ordered yt no Undergraduate have leave to live out of College (unless for very weithty reasons) untill all Ye Chambers in Ye College be occupied." [20]

In 1760, the corporation petitioned the general court to finance a new dormitory since ninety undergraduates could not be accommodated in college halls. They wanted a new dormitory in part because "such inspection cannot be had of those who live in families in the town, as might be had if they resided within the walls of the College." [21]

Compulsion in the early years stemmed in part from the educational values involved as well as the paternalistic attitude of the college authorities. In later years financial considerations were also relevant. Once the number of students tended to rise much more rapidly than the increase of college dormitory capacity, the problem became one of excess demand. With inadequate space, the college insisted on students' doubling up. [22]

The problem became one of increasing difficulty in the last hundred years of Harvard history. Eliot had made little progress in finding additional accommodations; and, in spite of expressions of interest, he was not disposed to concentrate much effort in this direction. Lowell, however, being interested in assembling students of different social and regional backgrounds, made a genuine breakthrough with his freshmen dormitories and the House Plan.

Undoubtedly Lowell's success was the result in part of the high standards made available under both enterprises as a result of large gifts by friends of Harvard and particularly of Mr. Harkness. Robert Grant of the class of 1873 described well the primitive furnishings and lack of taste in the dormitories of his day. ". . . It was a Boston axiom then that nothing

18. Morison, *Harvard College in the Seventeenth Century*, p. 49.
19. *College Books*, vol. IV, p. 60; *Corporation Records*, vol. I, p. 108; *Publications of the Colonial Society of Massachusetts*, vol. XVI, p. 437.

20. *College Books*, vol. IV, pp. 18, 51; *Publications of the Colonial Society of Massachusetts*, vol. XVI, pp. 641-642; *Corporation Records*, vol. I, p. 317.
21. Vote of Corporation for "Some Enlargement of the College Buildings." 1759; B. Peirce, *A History of Harvard University*, pp. 266-267.
22. Committee on Rooms, *Report of April 1, 1822*, in Harvard University Archives.

need match in a college room, but fond mothers exerted themselves to make their sons comfortable...." [23]

The freshmen who did not live within commuting distance were required to live in college dormitories. Aside from compulsory living in houses for non-commuting upperclassmen during part of the years since 1930, the element of compulsion in the House Plan was involved in that a student who stayed out would give up rather luxurious living inclusive of room, board, recreation, library, and also the companionship of many friends. Students, and particularly Final Club men, at times preferred less attractive and less comfortable and perhaps dirtier quarters in rabbit warrens to the houses. Rents were often lower in the rabbit warrens. Also they gave the students more freedom and appealed to snobbish tendencies. I recall that as a senior tutor in Dunster House in the 1930s, five sons of the richest and most prominent families in the country asked by permission to move out of Dunster House. Their case rested in large part on the need for economy. I reminded them that they particularly might gain from meeting with young men of varying backgrounds.

Pricing of Rooms

Pricing policy varied over the years, though in a rough way the policy seemed to be to cover operating costs. This was not always possible. The college throughout depended primarily on gifts of dormitories, and hence did not *ordinarily* seek a return on capital, and did not provide a depreciation fund. In the early history of Harvard, the college appropriated part of the rents to help pay the president's salary; and for some years the corporation fixed rents in a manner to yield a profit of $100,000 to be made available to the faculty of arts and sciences. But this was not always possible. [24] In general the college sought coverage of

operating costs only, but there were exceptions when rents included an allowance for a return on capital.

In 1765, the authorities proposed a rent that would yield a net revenue of £100 on a new dormitory, the money being used to pay part of the salary of two tutors, to purchase £25 worth of books per year for six years, and to pay part of the president's salary.

A document discovered in the archives also revealed some aspects of the pricing policy. This document showed that the yield greatly exceeded costs. (The exact date is not given, but it seems to be around the end of the nineteenth century.) For three college dormitories, the average rent per student was $131.29, the cost of running and repairs per student was $51.38; the net return for 233 students was $22,694. This same table reveals that the average rent for the three Harvard dormitories was $131; for three private dormitories, more than twice as high, or $282. [25]

On occasion the college would insist that charges were related to costs. In reply to the claim that since dormitories were gifts and hence costs did not have to be recovered and rents charged, the college stated that the $15 rent in 1849 "exceeds very little the actual cost of repairs and the general supervision of the buildings and grounds...." [26]

An interesting development was the practice of students' applying for rooms and then renting them at a higher price to others and pocketing the difference. The corporation voted to reduce or eliminate the activities of these intermediaries by requiring them to pay a substantial fee on rerenting. In this manner the college would appropriate the excess of rent over the charge to the students. [27]

23. R. Grant, *Harvard College in the Seventies,* in Harvard University Archives.
24. *Harvard Alumni Bulletin,* 1951-1952, pp. 204-205; *Treasurer's Statement,* 1866-1867, p. 7.
25. Table (year not revealed) giving rooms, rents, various costs, receipts, and revenue of three private and three public dormitories, in Harvard University Archives; B. Peirce, *A History of Harvard University,* pp. 148-149, 270-271.
26. *Report of the Visiting Committee of the Harvard University Board of Overseers, January, 1849,* pp. 19-20.
27. *Report of Committee on Assignment of Rooms, March 24, 1862.*

I am indebted to Mr. Carl Janke, the comptroller of the university, for the following:

Maintenance and repairs of buildings are charged on a reserve provision plan. The reserve provision is determined periodically by engineering surveys. The 1965-1966 charge to expenses and credit to reserves was $2,163,000; actual expenditures from reserves was $1,885,000.

(The insured value for all buildings in 1966 was $240,000,000.)[28]

One of the tough problems confronting the financial officers of the college has been the placing of price tags on rooms of varying attractiveness.

A simple approach is to charge all students the same rent, irrespective of differences of quality. On occasion this has been done—for example, freshmen in recent years have paid identical rents. When the product varies and rents are the same, the college in fact discriminates in favor of those who obtain the more desired rooms. When pricing of Quincy House was under consideration the authorities seriously considered uniform pricing, and especially since the rooms were more nearly of the same quality and appeal than in earlier dormitories and houses. Apparently, the authorities introduced uniform pricing for all houses in the middle 1960s.

But over most of Harvard's history the policy has been price differentials, with prices to some extent reflecting variations in the quality of the product: higher rents per student were generally obtainable for the lower floors (not so first and cellar), for the newer dormitories, for singles against doubles, for the dormitories that had greater social appeal, e.g., Holworthy, and those that had greater comforts; e.g., private bathrooms, heat, and hot water.

On the whole, the recourse to price differentials in excess of what might be justified by variations in quality is explained by the objective of subsidizing the poor at the expense of the rich. For example, the range of rents in 1930 was $100 to $600 (average $240) in comparison with $30 to $200 (average $100) in 1900. It is difficult to justify a range of $100 to $600 on the basis of costs.[29] All students profit from janitorial service, heat, maid service, use of the library, squash courts, services of the masters and tutors, and care of grounds. Surely all these services account for much more than $100 of costs. On the basis of costs the defensible extremes might well be, say, $200 to $400. Hence, the occupant of the cheapest rooms receives a subsidy of $100 and of the most expensive room pays, say, $200 in excess of costs. As noted earlier the range was narrowed in the depression years.

In Lowell's day, much difference of opinion prevailed. Critics argued that the same rent should be charged all as an expression of democratic principles. But Lowell feared that poor boys would then be excluded by the resultant higher rents charged to students from low-income levels; and we would be making charity students out of men who are not at all poor. He did not believe that price differentials would lead to stratification.[30]

The authorities are likely to react to rising demand by increasing the degree of differentiation, raising the prices of rooms with high demand at current prices and reducing those on the less desired, and perhaps rooms not sought by students. As a result of this kind of pressure the college under the House Plan had set twenty-seven different prices. Serious support for a single price emerged, but at first the compromise was to reduce the number of price brackets.[31]

Over the years, variations in rents charged prevailed. Differentials in rents seem to have been much greater in the last fifty to a hundred years than in earlier years. The explanation may be the higher incomes and higher rents in recent years.

Over the years the room prices increased. Thus, in 1720, the college imposed a one-rent system; in 1739,

28. Carl W. Janke to S. E. Harris, June 23, 1967.
29. *Harvard Alumni Bulletin,* vol. V, no. 33, pp. 965-970, 1931.
30. S. Kimball to A. L. Lowell, August 8, 1912; A. L. Lowell to S. Kimball, August 12, 1912.
31. *Harvard Crimson,* December 2, 1958; December 12, 1958; January 28, 1959; February 4, 1959; February 13, 1959.

two rents; by 1780, no less than sixteen rents; in the 1850s, rents varied from $30 to $80, with a hundred rooms priced from $30 to $80. In 1892, the university accommodated 973 students with rents varying from $25 to $350 a year.[32]

In 1930, Harvard introduced its House Plan, which provided rooms and other services to most upperclassmen. The net effect of the House Plan was a substantial rise of room rents. In contrast to an average rent of $240 in 1930, the average price of a house room was $300. Such a rise could not have come at a more inopportune time, for the students were now to be confronted with family incomes drastically reduced with the onset of the Great Depression. Indeed, the students were getting a bargain at $300, for Edward Harkness had sunk about $15 million in capital costs. In 1933, the president had to take cognizance of the situation. He not only modified the rent structure and thus provided a more equitable system, but he also reduced average rents from $300 to $264.[33]

In the later years dormitory rents continued to rise as inflation progressed and costs of services increased greatly. By increasing the number of students in relation to space and by reducing services, e.g., maids, the authorities were able to reduce substantially the ratio of rent to total costs in the last 25 years.

The Rising Trend of Rents and Services

Most observers are likely to be appalled by the rise of room rents, from 20 shillings in the early eighteenth century to $500 today. But there are offsets. In relation to current family incomes or, better, surpluses above absolute necessities, the burden is probably less than two hundred to three hundred years ago. Moreover the product has greatly improved.

Sessions describes housing facilities in 1787 as follows:

In 1787 the Yard, despite a lack of finish in limits and landscaping, was as academic and unpretentiously dignified.... Massachusetts Hall was there, built nearly seventy years before, and Stoughton and Hollis; Harvard Hall had risen from the ashes of its previous destruction by fire. The dormitories were cheerless contrasts to present-day standards, but built for hardy youth. No plumbing, no central heating, no lighting save that of candles or sperm-oil lamps; for warmth there were open fireplaces and a college wood-yard filled with logs from which a man might chop his own firewood or pay to have it chopped for him and carried up many flights of stairs perhaps or assigned to some place of storage. Very little furniture was provided in rooms....[34]

Even as late as the 1840s a distinguished Harvard alumnus noted that "the rooms were furnished very simply almost always without carpets, though in rare instances the floors would be covered with a cheap carpet which did not last very well under the wear and tear of boyish occupation."[35]

By the middle of the nineteenth century the quality of the product had improved. Joseph Choate, a famous alumnus, seemed to be more than satisfied.

... The first year we [the two Choates] *roomed in Holworthy, and our apartment seemed to us to be royal, for there was a parlor, very simply but comfortably furnished, of course at our own expense, and two bedrooms, and the only service we had or thought of was that of the "goody" so-called, who*

32. *Publications of the Colonial Society of Massachusetts*, vol. XXIV, p. 86; *Corporation Records*, vol. I, p. 363; *Regulations for the Assignment of Rooms*, 1853-1854, in Harvard University Archives; *Memorandum to the President and Government of Harvard from Peters and Worland and* others (date missing, but probably late nineteenth century), in Harvard University Archives; F. Bolles, *Harvard University*, 2d ed., 1892; and numerous issues of *Corporation Records*.

33. *Report of the President of Harvard College*, 1931-1932, pp. 15-18; 1932-1933, pp. 92-95; "Student Council Report, June 19, 1933," in *A. L. Lowell Papers*, folder 755.
34. *Sessions*, pp. 128-129.
35. G. F. Hoar, *Autobiography of Seventy Years*, 1903, vol. I, p. 119.

came every day to make the beds and clear up the rooms. . . .

The third year in Stoughton, where we were similarly accommodated, and the fourth year as seniors again we got into the third story of Holworthy in the east entry, and paid for each of these years the same rent of thirty dollars, fifteen dollars apiece, rooms that I think now rent for many times that amount. But the college then was not so much in need of money, and treated the rooms in the various dormitories, as they had been intended to be treated by their munificent donors fifty or one hundred years before, as the practically free homes of the students whom they housed.[36]

In 1856, Henry Adams complained of winds howling about him in his college room. No heat attainable could prevent the water in his pitcher from freezing inches deep in cold weather, he said, continuing ". . . my room is the coldest, the dirtiest and the gloomiest in Cambridge." [37]

Students were not entirely pleased with their service. One day a "goody" left the only bathtub full of slops. At that time few students took baths, though those who participated in sports increasingly did. Beck was the only dormitory that provided private bathrooms. Holworthy had the charm of tradition but not central heating; and the removal of the fireplaces was unforgivable in Santayana's view.[38]

Students were not always pleased with the service of the maids, as shown by the following petition:

We the undersigned . . . greatly annoyed by the incorrigible want of neatness and general neglect evinced by the female attendants on their rooms, we respectfully petition the Faculty to take measures to insure their greater comfort. . . .[39]

In the 1850s a spirited debate prevailed on the question of gas versus oil as the most economical fuel for providing light. The authorities introduced gas in the public rooms of Harvard and, despite concern over the possibility of abuse by students, it had proved workable and free of misuse. The college also installed gaslight in the students' rooms, with each room separately metered to prevent uneconomical use.[40]

As late as 1898 (January 31), students petitioned the college:

We, the undersigned, members of Harvard University, rooming in Holworthy Hall, do hereby respectfully petition your honorable body that baths be put into Holworthy Hall, for the reasons herein set forth.

1. The inconvenience of moveable tubs of rubber, tin and like materials, which can at present be used in the rooms, is considerable, and except from the point of cleanliness alone, the results to be obtained from the use thereof are very unsatisfactory.

2. The distance to Hemenway Gymnasium is sufficiently great to render daily baths on rising a practicable impossibility; and we, your petitioners, think we are justified in saying that such daily baths are of great benefit to the health, as well as a great physical comfort.

3. Likewise the trouble of going to Hemenway Gymnasium for one's baths is so great that we believe that many of the inmates of Holworthy Hall are prevented thereby from bathing as often as strict rules of hygiene and cleanliness require.

4. We, your petitioners, believing that the advantage of having baths in Holworthy Hall would be great, respectfully submit the following suggestions as means of meeting the undoubted expense and inconvenience of putting such baths in the building.

We suggest that a shower bath (and nothing more), might be installed between the first and second and between the third and fourth floors in each entry of the building. . . .

We suggest, that as a method of meeting the expense entailed, the rent of each room be increased not more

---

36. Choate, *op. cit.*, pp. 70-72.
37. *The Harvard Book*, p. 223.
38. *The Harvard Book*, pp. 74-78.
39. June, 1854, in Harvard University Archives.

40. B. Silliman (?), Jr. of Yale University to Professor C?, June 21, 1856; *Committee Appointed by the Faculty to Report a Plan for Introducing Gas Into Holworthy Hall to the Corporation of Harvard College*, September, 1856.

than $20 per year, this increased rent to be continued until the baths are paid for, or till the corporation sees fit to reduce the rent again to the present amount. . . .[41]

Board: Provision of Commons

From the very beginning the college provided commons and penalized students who would eat out. The frequent statements of the corporation concerning losses of utensils and the numerous inventories of kitchenware suggested that the students in the seventeenth and eighteenth centuries frequently borrowed or stole silverware and other kitchen ware. Though the authorities were anxious to provide commons, there were times when because of great inflation or war they were unable to offer commons and at such time would allow students to stay out of commons.

Some of the problems of the college are well revealed by announcements in the middle of the seventeenth century:

The Butler and Cook shall see that all the Roomes. . . bee daily set and kept in order, clean and sweet from all manner of noysommes and nastines. . . neither shall the Butler or Cook suffer any Schollar or Schollars whatever except the ffellows, Masters of Art, ffellow Commoners or officers of the House to come into the Butleryes or Kitchen save with their parents or guardians or with some grave and sober strangers, and if they shall presume to thrust in they shall have three pence on their heads. But if praesumptuously and continually they shall dare so to offend, they shall be lyable to an admonition and to other proceedings of the Colledge Discipline. . . .
The Butler upon every Sixt day of the week at noon is to give an account of every Schollar demanding his weeks sizings in the Butlery after the Tolling of the Bell. . . .
The Butler and Cook may not deliver at meal-times save in case of Sicknesse or just causes to the Praesident (if it may bee). . . by him allowed. . . .

41. Harvard University Archives.

In damage to College vessels and utensils the Cook and Stewart was to discover whether the damage was the result of wearth in their just usage. . . or by any abuse of any person or persons whatsoever.
. . . fforasmuch as the students whose freinds are most careful to discharge their due expences, have sundry times sorely & unjustly suffered by such as neglect to pay their debts; therefore the steward shal not pmit but upon his owne peril, any students to bee above Two pounds indebted, but acquainting the Praesident, w[th] *his leave send them to their freinds, if not above a dayes journey distant. If otherwise then shall the steward at the Admission of such Schollars, enforme himself from whom hee shall bee supplied or to whom they shal have recourse in the aforesaid Case of Debt; Neither is the Steward at any time to take any pay that is uselesse, hazardful, or importing detriment to the Colledge, as lean Cattle to feed turning over of Bills to shops &c but at his owne discretion & perill. . . .*[42]

Dissatisfaction prevailed despite heroic efforts by President Quincy in the 1830s to please the students.

Throughout Harvard's history commons was a problem. Students consistently complained of the inadequacy and the poor quality of the food. Finally, following gradual withdrawals of students and increased private competition, the commons shut down in 1849, and for a number of years the college provided no commons.[43]

In the 1860s the students tried running a commons and in the latter part of the nineteenth century, the university again attempted to provide one and to some extent through mixed control of the college and students; but in the middle 1920s the authorities gave up as both Randolph and Memorial halls had failed to satisfy the students. With the introduction of the freshmen dormitories and especially the House Plan the students once more largely abandoned the practice of eating out and returned to civilized living under the college's aegis.

42. *College Books,* vol. I, pp. 32-35; vol. IV, p. 792.
43. *Report of the President of Harvard College,* 1848-1849, pp. 8, 9.

But complaints continued. In the economy drive of the 1940s and 1950s, the college abandoned the practice of hiring attractive waitresses, substituted self-service, and introduced other economies. In response to complaints of students, the college improved the quality and reduced the quantity of food. The *Harvard Crimson* commented: "The food may be better but our boys are starving; they could feast royally around the Square for the amount they spend in discouraging meals in the Houses and Union. . . .[44]

That the students were generally dissatisfied is suggested by the pressure of the authorities to force students to dine at the commons. At a corporation meeting of September 13, 1725, the corporation commented on the disorders arising from students' not attending the commons and ordered that all students in the college must attend unless they were preaching or waiting on tables, or because of bodily infirmity.[45]

In 1734, in response to complaints, a new Harvard code required the steward to substitute pewter plates for the greasy old wooden trenchers, to sweep the hall daily, to wash it down four or more times a year, and to supply clean linen cloths.[46] Again in 1747-1748 most students avoided commons and were ordered to return.

The cost of commons over most of Harvard's history is given in the following table.

In the middle of the eighteenth century, dissatisfaction with commons erupted into a number of crises. Before 1747, the college had given general permission to board in private families. But in October, 1747, the overseers announced it would be beneficial for all students to dine in commons.

The construction of Hollis Hall in 1765 facilitated eating in, though those living out found it inconvenient to dine in. The college now compelled faculty and students having studies in college to board in commons. But trouble continued.[47]

Utensils continued to be a problem for those who managed commons. Over long periods students brought their own forks and when the meal was over the students (wearing hats in the dining hall) would wipe their forks on the tablecloths. In 1650 the students were warned not to take out any "vessel of the College's, great or small" and the butler and cook were to see to it that "they be kept clean and sweet and fit for use. . . ."[48]

In 1765, the corporation ordered tablecloths changed twice a week or more often if necessary. The regulations then provided for grace and behavior with decency.[49]

But there was still room for improvement as evidenced in purchases of 1817. For the first time dessert plates, knives and forks, carving knives, and bread plates were provided. Tablecloths were smaller than the table. The college corrected this. In all, the college expended $893 for kitchenware in 1817, a substantial item at that time.

In 1821, following persistent complaints, the overseers abandoned compulsory commons. All students, however, were required to pay a flat fee of $2.50 per quarter to the stewards and commons in order to help support the commons, and for a few years the students eating out had to pay $1.50 per quarter for this privilege.[50] In this manner the college could finance much overhead.

Once the university became interested in the students' food again after the establishment in the 1870s of the Memorial Hall Dining Hall with an outlay by the College of $40,000 on behalf of the student association, the old problems emerged once more. By 1876, the students were complaining of poor food and high prices. To appease them the corporation guaranteed a price not to exceed $5 per week. But the college in turn reduced the freedom of the student to withdraw, for unit costs depended on numbers.[51]

44. *Harvard Crimson*, October 16, 1957.
45. *Corporation Records*, vol. I, p. 195.
46. Morison, *Three Centuries of Harvard, 1636-1936*, p. 116; *Corporation Records*, vol. I, pp. 460, 473, 488; Quincy, *op. cit.*, vol. I, p. 442.
47. Quincy, *op. cit.*, vol. II, pp. 90-100.
48. Blackmer, *op. cit.*, p. 11.
49. *Corporation Records*, vol. II, pp. 227-228.
50. *Ibid.*, vol. VI, p. 20, April 1820.
51. *Report of the President of Harvard College*, 1873-1874, pp. 16-20; 1876-1877, pp. 13-18; 1894-1895, pp. 42-44.

Table 7-2.

Weekly Board Charges, 1654 to 1963, Various Years

Year		Weekly Charge	Source
1654		3s 1½d	Morison, *Harvard College in the Seventeenth Century*, p. 99.
1687-1712		4 1	Foster, *op. cit.*, p. 66.
1765		7 4	*Corporation Records*, vol. II, pp. 229-230.
1780		11 5	*Ibid.*, vol. III, p. 94.
1799-1800		$ 1.91	*Ibid.*, pp. 559, 564, 570.
1812		2.11	*Stewards' Quarter Bill Books*, 1812-1827.
1829-1830		1.75	*Harvard University Catalogue*, 1829-1830, p. 32.
1848		2.50	*Corporation Papers*, vol. I, February 12, 1848; *Report of the President of Harvard College*, 1848-1849, pp. 8-9.
1859-1860		3.50	*Harvard University Catalogue*, 1859-1860, p. 38.
1876	Memorial Hall	5.00	*Report of the President of Harvard College*, 1876-1877, pp. 13-18.
1874-1891	Memorial Hall	$4.00–$4.10	*Ibid.*, 1890-1891, p. 35.
1890-1900	Memorial Hall Foxcroft	4.00– 4.10* 2.50	*Ibid.*, 1898-1899, pp. 14-15, 310-311.
1902	Memorial Hall	4.69	*Ibid.*, 1902-1903, p. 328.
1905	Memorial Hall	4.80	"Charges at Memorial Hall," in *The Harvard Bulletin*, vol. VII, no. 22, p. 5.
1907-1908	Memorial Hall	5.00†	*Report of the President of Harvard College*, 1907-1908, p. 45.
1913-1914		6.20	Doerrman, *op. cit.*, (calculations)
1929-1930		9.50	
1939-1940		8.50	
1949-1950		12.50	
1959-1960		18.00	*Report of Admissions and Scholarship Committee*, 1959-1960, p. 23.
1962-1963		18.20	*Ibid.* 1962-1963.
1966-1967		17.82	Letter, Dean Glimp.

* The authorities complained of much waste, for provisions cost only $2.65 per week. *Report of the President of Harvard College*, 1893-1894.

† Fixed charge; order list subject to additional charges.

In 1891, President Eliot boasted of the experience of the past seventeen years. Now food could be provided for $4 a week.[52] Not only had the college provided adequate food at $4, but in order to take care of the impoverished student, the college provided Foxcroft (later Randolph) where in 1893-1894, students could obtain 21 meals at $2.50 maximum a la carte. The student could procure luncheon at 10 cents, and food for the whole day at 35 cents. The seriousness of the food problem was suggested by the space given to it in the president's reports in the years after the Civil War. President Eliot commented:

The articles of food are tolerably well selected; but stews and leguminous soups are not in favor with the students, the admirable dietetic qualities of these articles being for the most part unknown in American households.

The president continued that the cost of living in Cambridge was then (1888-1889) lower than at any time since 1861—provided one consumed leguminous soups.[53] He did not note that prices had generally been falling during most of this period. By early 1900, the president could claim 1,150 paying customers in Memorial Hall at an average price of $4 a week and at the new Randall Hall, 800 frugal students at around $2.50 a week. He might have a combination meal at 14 cents for breakfast, 14 cents for lunch, and 16 cents for dinner. Outside the cost was between $5 and $8 a week.[54]

Early in the twentieth century the authorities, in an attempt to reduce costs and provide a more equitable system, divided the menu into two parts:

The first part is for meat, fish, and eggs ordered and paid for by the plate; the second is for all other provisions, such as tea, coffee, cocoa, milk, vegetables, bread, butter, cereals, desserts and fruits. These and the service, coal, light and all other running expenses are shared alike by all. . . .[55]

Even these measures were inadequate. With the life of the Memorial Hall Association threatened in the early part of the twentieth century, the corporation offered the association an extinction of the annual charge for the debt incurred in providing plant and equipment and a $5 charge for board, with supplementary charges for additional dishes.[56]

By the middle of the 1920s, the desertion of college dining halls, much to the annoyance of college authorities, resulted in the closing of Memorial Hall.

It is clear from what has gone before that the college found running the restaurant business anything but profitable. Not only were deficits involved, but the problems assumed too much of the valuable time and effort of the administration inclusive of the president. Even President Dunster, when the students moved into the old college in 1642, had to "bee their Steward, and to Direct their brewer, baker, buttler, cook, how to proportion their commons."[57]

In the early years, the college was not averse to making a profit from the commons. When the steward's income exceeded costs the college would at times share the profits. In the years 1713-1765 the steward was allowed compensation on the basis of the excess of receipts over costs. But, being subject to abuse, this was soon changed to a fixed salary, and student markups were also controlled. The college obtained substantial revenues, at least in the Puritan period, from the difference between receipts and costs. Thus from 1687 to 1712 the receipts from the commencement dinner alone were 8 percent of all gross receipts and 12 percent of net receipts.[58]

As early as 1650, the problems of providing a satisfactory commons were beginning to emerge. What part of the payments of the students were to be divided between the steward and the college was a troublesome issue. Students often failed to pay their bills, and utensils disappeared.

The college also noted the hours for serving the students and measures to preclude getting sizings

52. *Ibid.*, 1890-1891, p. 35.
53. *Report of the President of Harvard College*, 1888-1889, pp. 14-15, 1893-1894, p. 41.
54. *Ibid.*, 1898-1899, pp. 14-15, 310-311.
55. *Report of the President of Harvard College*, 1902-1903, p. 38.

56. *Ibid.*, 1907-1908, p. 45.
57. Morison, *Harvard College in the Seventeenth Century*, p. 98.
58. Foster, *op. cit.*, p. 77.

(beer and bread) outside the commons ". . . whereas young scholars, to the dishonor of God, hindrance of their studies, and damage of their friends' estate, inconsiderately and intemperately are ready to abuse their liberty of sizings beyond their commons. . . ."[59]

The introduction of Randall in 1899, where a poor student could be fed at reduced prices as against the relatively high costs in Memorial, was also an attempt to keep costs down. The college was also impressed by the relation of costs and number eating in commons. Hence, it would seek more students for commons as a means of getting costs and prices down.

By 1828, the college had already imposed for many years a charge of $10 to help finance the steward and commons. Half was to pay the steward's salary; the other half was needed to compensate for the use of kitchens, utensils, dining room, and furniture, all belonging to the college and requiring repairs.

As this provision is made for the equal benefit of all the scholars, it is proper that the expense should be borne by all. . . . To exempt those students who choose to board out of commons from any part of it would increase the expenses of those, who, from economy or other motives, board in commons. . . .[60]

Whereas in the first century the problem was to find adequate space to house the diners, in the years after the Revolution the problem increasingly became one of obtaining enough business to wipe out excess capacity and keep unit costs down. Thus, in 1760 the corporation proposed severe penalties for those who dined out.

The college was interested in commons not only because of the assumed advantage of close supervision of students outside the classroom, but also because the college presumably kept the price of board down. In 1840, the steward complained that the price structure was unfortunate. He would introduce a two-price system, the high price to exploit the well-to-do and the low price to hold the poor.

Of course, with one-fifth to one-sixth of the students in commons, the service seemed altogether too costly in dollars and time to merit continued operation. Yale had already shown that dropping of commons was not likely to be disastrous. When the college abandoned it in the first quarter of the twentieth century, again the dissatisfaction of the students was decisive. Attempts to reduce prices, improve service, introduce economies, and provide higher quality utensils and better light all proved to be inadequate. The students preferred to dine outside. Only the freshman dormitories and the House Plan once more made commons a reality. Here elements of compulsion and other advantages of living in the freshman dormitories and the houses were decisive.[61]

Even in the eighteenth and nineteenth centuries the appeal of commons was weak. Students with adequate funds would pay and dine out. Other students might feast on stolen poultry. In some instances they would introduce spreads in their dormitories. Even in 1761 more than half the students were dining in private families. When this privilege was denied them, students patronized different places offering luxury, intemperance, and ruin. One student in 1793 provided a perpetual spread in his room at Hollis Hall, which was referred to as the tavern.[62]

Soon after the Civil War students had to pay $5 a week for commons, but could board out at $2.50 to $3. The milkmen and peddlers tramped through the halls. Smells of cabbage, fried onions, and beefsteak in the halls was too much for some of the students.[63]

Dissatisfaction with Menus and Service

Complaints of inadequacy persisted. In the Dunster years the general court appointed a committee "to

59. Quincy, *op cit.*, vol. I, pp. 582-585; *College Orders,* March 28, 1650, 1657; *College Books,* vol. I, pp. 32-33, 44-47.
60. "Pecuniary Affairs of the College in January, 1828," in Quincy, *op. cit.,* vol. I, p. 566.

61. *Meeting of Corporation,* May 6, 1760; J. Whitney to the President and Fellows of Harvard College, July, 1840, and J. Whitney to the President, June 29, 1840; *Report of Committee on the Subject of Discontinuing Commons,* May 28, 1842; S. A. Eliot to Corporation of Harvard College, June 20, 1849.
62. Batchelder, *op. cit.,* pp. 102-105.
63. G. H. Williams (ed.), *The Divinity School,* p. 153.

examine the state of the college, one of their specific objects being to 'direct some way how the necessary officers, as steward, buttler and cooke, may be provided for, so that the schoolers commons may not be so short as now they are occasioned thereby. . . .' "[64]

In 1810, a serious disturbance occurred as a result of dissatisfaction with the food. A committee of the overseers reported that the provisions were good "but that there was great inattention to the cookery, which required correction; that the coffee was often badly made and the pudding heavy and indigestible; and that the baker's bread was not well baked and bad . . . it should be made the duty of some person, to inspect frequently and without previous notice, the commons, and to make at stated times reports to the Government. . . ."[65]

Edward Everett Hale described well the attitude of students towards the commons in the years 1835-1839.

Eighty minutes after the morning prayer bell stopped we were rung in to breakfast. The breakfast was coffee or milk ad libitum, hot and cold bread, and butter. I think no meat was served at breakfast. We knew what would be the variety of the hot bread; it was made in different rolls or biscuits for different days, and the order was never changed. Dinner was at one, and always consisted of one sort of meat, potatoes, and something called pudding. Here, again, the bill of fare was as absolute as if it had been laid down by the Medes and Persians, and never changed. I think it is burned on my memory so that, to this day, when certain provisions appear on certain days of the week, I take it as something preordained. For meats, Sunday was roast beef, Monday was corned beef, Tuesday was roast veal, Wednesday was beefsteak, Thursday was roast lamb or mutton, Friday meatpie with fish, Saturday was salt fish. I think we never had pork in any form, either fresh or in the shape of ham. To make Friday dinner more substantial meatpie was added; I suppose a housekeeper would tell us that it was made out of such meat as had not been eaten in the preceding days. We remember it because after eating this solid meatpie we went to our rooms to write our Friday themes. The puddings were boiled rice, baked rice, hasty pudding, baked Indian pudding, apple pudding, and, on one day, some sort of pie took the place of pudding. Every now and then there would be a complaint that the butter was bad; in that case we did not stand it. Somebody went right round to the president and told him, and he sent for the contractor and gave him a blowing up. We always pretended at home and elsewhere that the fare was not good, but it was good.[66]

A constant source of friction between students and the college was kitchen utensils. In 1736, the college reminded the students:

Agreeable to a Law of Ye College relating to Ye Scholars maintaining Ye plates in Ye Kitchen, it is ordered for ys year, yt when the Steward shall give in an account of ye number of plates yt have been lost out of ye kitchen this year, according to ye best of his Judgement, yt three quarters of yt number shall be equally charged upon ye scholars graduates and undergraduates (yt have studies in the College) in their quarter bill.[67]

President Quincy (1829-1845) reformed the college commons by requiring that the tables be "properly served, simply, but plentifully, and neatly." He ordered a set of china from Liverpool with college buildings on each piece and replaced the dubious metal with genuine articles, each authenticated by the college arms. These changes removed all complaints. . . ."

When the students complained that they had no toast, the contractor replied that he could not afford to toast bread at present remuneration." 'Very good,' the President replied, 'toast the bread, and charge the

---

64. Morison, *Harvard College in the Seventeenth Century*, p. 101.

65. *Committee of Overseers of Harvard College Appointed . . . To Visit The College, October 10, 1810.*

66. E. E. Hale, *A New England Boyhood and Other Bits of Autobiography*, 1900, pp. 198-200.

67. *College Books*, vol. IV, pp. 189-190; *Publications of the Colonial Society of Massachusetts*, vol. 16, p. 548.

additional expense on your bill.' And so the great toast question was settled forever."[68]

Menus were always a problem. Quality and quantity varied over the years and hence price movements should be considered in the light of these variations.

In the seventeenth century, Morison tells us that the eleven o'clock dinner consisted of meat, bread and beer. Beef would be varied with veal, mutton, and pork. The dinner also included hasty pudding, a dumpling, or a dish of pease.[69]

At a corporation meeting of August 15, 1750, the corporation announced that as usual dinner would consist of two portions of bread in the morning, one pound of beef at dinner, with sufficient sauce, and half a pint of beer; and at night, "that a part pye, be of the same quantity, as usual, and also half a pint of beer."[70]

The corporation announced in October, 1754, that students might have milk and two portions of bread at supper instead of beer.[71]

The ruling on May 9, 1763, was that students who wanted puddings may have 3/4 pound of meat; others might have 1 1/4 pounds of meat. But on September 5, 1763, the commons was fixed at 3/4 pound of meat and pudding.[72]

In 1765, there is evidence of the broadening of the menu and attempts to vary meals day by day.

Supply in Buttery to include Wines and other Liquors, Tea, Coffee, Chocolate, Sugar, Bisket, Pens, Ink and Paper and other suitable articles for the Scholars. . . .
There shall alwaies be two dishes for dinner, a pudding of some sort to be one of them, except on Saturdays, salt fish alone; and the same dish shall not be ordinarily provided, above twice in a week, puddings excepted: And there shall alwaies bee Coffe and Tea. Chocolate and Milk for breakfast, with bread or bisket and butter; and bread and milk, rice, applepye or something equivalent for supper.
Each scholar to notify Steward what he wants for breakfast and supper, on the first Friday of each month.
Cost per week to each scholar, 7s 4d.
No scholar allowed to be in debt to the Butler more than 5 dollars.[73]

Shortages and inflation account for a reduction of the butter ration to one ounce in 1776,[74] and also a denial to students of tea, coffee, chocolate, butter, and sugar for breakfast, which they were then invited to procure for themselves.

In 1807, students were dissatisfied with the commons and rioted. In spite of the riots, the corporation deemed no change necessary—simplicity of diet was better morally than variety. Actually breakfast was more varied than it had been and supper more simple.[75]

Over a period of more than three hundred years, the price of board per week at Harvard rose from about 50 cents to $18, or roughly 35 times. The major rises occurred in the last century. A table concerning this is deposited in the Harvard Archives. Even by 1848, just as the commons was to be shut down permanently, the cost was only $2.50, 5 times the early cost, but only $2 in excess of that cost. In dollars the major rise occurred in the twentieth century, with costs increasing by $14 or 350 percent (an average of less than 6 percent a year as compared to 2 percent in the years 1654 to 1848. On a compounded basis, the differences are much greater).

The college at first was interested in the students' commons in no small part because it increased the capacity of the authorities to watch over their wards. But in the early Harvard history and later on, the unavailability of private facilities was relevant. In the last hundred years, the objective of food at reasonable prices in order to ease the financial and health problems of the students was dominant. The college

68. Quincy, *Life of Josiah Quincy*, 1874, pp. 439-490; A. P. Peabody, *Harvard Reminiscences*, 1888, p. 29.
69. Morison, *Harvard College in the Seventeenth Century*, pp. 90-97.
70. *Corporation Records*, vol. I, p. 502.
71. *Ibid.*, vol. II, p. 57.
72. *Corporation Records*, vol. II, pp. 170, 177.

73. *Ibid.*, vol. II, pp. 229-230.
74. *Ibid.*, vol. II, p. 452; *College Records*, vol. V, p. 2, August 11, 1777.
75. *Ibid.*, vol. IV, pp. 137 et seq.

at various times sought to keep costs down by providing special facilities for the poor by charging extra for items not included in a minimum menu, and also by offering jobs in the dining halls to the impecunious. From Dunster to Eliot, the concern for an adequate and low-priced commons was a crucial and demanding problem. Almost every year, pages in the Eliot annual reports were devoted to this problem. It is difficult to envisage Conant or Pusey devoting much of their space to such problems, an indication of the declining burden of the cost of food.

A table here throws light on trends. Generally, the price of Harvard commons rose less than food prices in the nation or declined less.

The Issue of Quality and Choice

One may be surprised that Harvard students in 1848 rebelled at a $2.50 board charge. But these were not modest prices. Good wages were about $6. One could dine in 1849 at the famous Delmonico's for 14 cents or $1 a week. For the other two meals the cost would be between $1 and $1.50 or really less than the Harvard charge. Surely there was no comparison in quality. At Delmonico's, one could purchase coffee at 1 cent; corned beef and cabbage at 4 cents and roast chicken at 10 cents.[76]

Again and again we must stress the difference of the product. Clearly the quality and quantity tended to improve. There is no comparison of the qualities and limited choice of the seventeenth century and that of the early twentieth century. In 1908, the president stressed the difference in standards with earlier times. In recent years even the poor student could choose from twenty varieties of steaks and chops, six different types of oysters, and generally in comparison with the average diets the standard for

76. *New York Times*, March 5, 1849.

Table 7-2.

Food Prices, U.S.A. and Charge for Harvard Commons, 1812-1963

| | U.S.A. | |
	Percent Increase(+) or Decrease(-) of Food Prices, 1812-1963, Various Years	Increase(+) or Decrease(-) of the Price of Harvard Commons
1812-Late 1820s	−40	−17
1830-1860	No change	+100
1860-1900	−20	+14
1890-1913	+49 (prewar)	+50
	(But Foxcroft available at lower prices)	
1913-1929	Price of Food = +60	+52
1929-1939	Price of Food = −26	−11
1939-1949	Price of Food = +112	+47
1949-1963	Price of Food = +22	+46

Harvard College students was clearly that of the very rich.[77]

Charges and Costs

Generally the college would justify any increase in the cost of commons by pointing to the rise in the cost of the relevant products. The three crucial items in the seventeenth and eighteenth centuries were meat, wheat (bread), and malt (beer).

Especially in the first quarter of the eighteenth century, a highly inflationary period, the authorities repeatedly announced the prices of the basic commodities and the resultant increase in the charge for parts.[78]

From 1715 to 1749 we have a comparison of the price of silver, wheat, tuition, molasses, and cider. In general the trend is upward for all items, but there are substantial variations. Thus, the price of wheat rose by 8 times; silver, 5 2/3 times; tuition fees, more than 7 times (10 shillings old to 10 shillings new tenor).[79] At times the presentation was more sophisticated. Thus, in the second quarter of 1776-1777 the outlays for provisions were given at £498 9s 3 3/4d, which together with a quarter year's interest, gives the cost of commons at 9s 3d per person per quarter.[80] In the nineteenth and twentieth centuries, though there were occasional surpluses and frequent deficits, the general guide was a charge based on total costs, that is, total exclusive of capital.

Costs of commons had some relation to costs of provisions and services, though the relationship was not always very close. In a general way commons rose with the upward trend of the price level. Thus costs per *week* were estimated as follows:

Weekly Costs of Commons, Various Years	
1664	$ .75
1765	1.22
1805	2.24
1806	1.89
1808	1.75
1833	1.90
1836	2.25
1840	$1.75 - $2.25
1864-1890 (Memorial Hall)	3.75 - 4.25
(Foxcroft lowest)	2.00
Private board was higher in 1890s	5.00 - $8.00

Sources: Four American Universities, 1894, p. 43; Batchelder, *op. cit.,* pp. 110-111.

After the Revolution, the buttery sold wines and stronger drinks in order to keep students from leaving the college precincts. This was convenient for the young men, since the charges were put on the term bill. Large profits were made on these sales.

A board responsible for charges was critical in 1881 of a system which provided a fixed and a contingent return for the steward. In two preceding years the steward had received $3,500, but now because of the improvement in quality and higher costs his compensation was reduced to $2,500.[81]

The steward played an important role in Harvard's history. It was his task to buy cheaply the provisions needed for commons. He had to adjust the price of board quickly to the rising prices which generally prevailed. The government of the college vacillated between allowing the steward to fix prices to students, and controlling prices and markups. The markup on inventories varied generally between 15 and 20 percent. But when the amount of traffic declined the steward sought higher prices and markups. Compensation to the steward might be set at a fixed sum or be

77. *Report of the President of Harvard College,* 1907, pp. 44-45.

78. *Corporation Records,* vol. I, pp. 331, 502.

79. A. H. Cole, *Wholesale Prices in the United States 1700-1861,* 1938, pp. 117, 119; *College Books; Publications of the Colonial Society of Massachusetts,* vol. XVI, ch. 6.

80. *Corporation Records,* vol. II, pp. 446, 453.

81. Morison, *Harvard College in the Seventeenth Century,* vol. I, p. 478; Batchelder, *op. cit.,* pp. 88, 110; *Four American Universities,* pp. 40-41; *W. B. Lawrence for the Board to the President and Fellows of Harvard College,* June 2, 1881.

tied to the difference between costs and revenue received from the students.

The Current Situation

In some respects the life of the student at Harvard is much closer to that of the pre Revolutionary period than to that of the nineteenth century. The college provides housing and board for most students. With the House Plan in operation for almost forty years and with no major withdrawals, riots, or more than the usual complaints that come with the boredom of living in the same place day after day, it may be said that the college's interest in the whole man is remindful of the early concern of the college. By sponsoring the freshmen dormitories, the House Plan, and comprehensive athletic and medical programs, the college program has introduced a democratizing influence and yielded an improved educational product.[82]

---

82. *Report of the President of Harvard College,* 1927-1928, pp. 10-16; 1930-1931, pp. 94-96; 1931-1932, pp. 89-96.

8

Student Aid

The Beginnings

As early as 1643, Lady Anne (Radcliffe) Mowlson donated £100 sterling for scholarships at Harvard. The danger of diversion of funds is clearly revealed in the history of this gift. It is of some interest also that this fund has escalated to $9,982.

According to Morison scholarships existed as early as 1643: scholars of the house were the most important recipients of aid. The scholar had strictly to account for all the buildings, "Cambers Studyes, and fences, belonging to the Cooledge," and give a quarterly account of damage to the treasurer.

In these early years scholarships were surprisingly important. For example, from 1640 to 1652, the college collected £426 from tuition, scholarship funds, gifts, rents, and contributions of corn. Scholarships cost £168 or more than one-third of receipts. In 1965-1966, they accounted only for 7 percent of expenditures of the university.[1]

History

Here is some history of the scholarships.

Among the early transatlantic benefactors of Harvard College was Lady Mowlson. . . . Fortunately for the College, Lady Mowlson had taken a bond of Welde,

that the money should not be diverted from the charitable objects to which she had devoted it. For in 1655, on a petition of the College for relief, in a state of great distress on account of the insufficiency of their buildings, the House of Deputies ordered the amount due on account of her gift to be "improved for" the repairs of those edifices. [2]

The terms of this gift were as follows:

Know all men by these presents That I Thomas Wells alls Weld Pastor of Roxbury in the plantacion of New England doe by these presents acknowledge that I haue receiued of the Lady Ann Mowlson of London, widdow the full and intire somme of (one) hundred pownds current English mony the which she hath freely giuen to Harvards Colledge in New England to be imp(roved) by the feofees of the said colledge for the time being to the best yearly revenew that may be thought fitt in theire wisdomes, which yearly revenew according to her good and pious intention is to be and remaine as a perpetuall stipend for and toward the year(rly) maintenance of some poor schollar. . . .

In 1659, Robert Keayne also provided funds to help poor scholars. Of interest is the point that he did not want the money to be used for buildings though he was not adverse to its use for subsidizing of the commons for the poorer students who apparently were not well provisioned.

---

1. *Scholarship, Beneficiary Aid and Loan Funds of Harvard College,* 1963, pp. 7-8, in Harvard University Archives; Morison, *Harvard College in the Seventeenth Century,* vol. I, pp. 37, 60, 107-109; *Financial Report to the Board of Overseers of Harvard College,* published by the university, 1965-1966, pp. 14-15.

2. Quincy, *The History of Harvard College; Endowment Funds of Harvard University,* 1947, p. 135.

Bequest of Robert Keayne of £230 and half a house, later sold for £150. *My desire is that it shall be improved, (not about the buildings or repairs of the College for that I think the Country should do and look after) but for the use and help of such poor and hopeful Scholars, whose parents are not able to maintain them comfortably there for their diet and learning or for some addition yearly to the poorer sort of Fellows or Tutors, whose parents are not able, nor themselves have not ability nor supplies, otherwise to defray their charge and make their studies comfortable . . . .*[3]

In 1667, scholars were to "take a strict account of all the buildings, chambers, studyes, and fences belonging to the College and shall give an account quarterly to the Treasurer what dammage the College had susteyned in any of the aforementioned particulars and by whom."

Even as late as the first quarter of the nineteenth century, President Kirkland set up numerous jobs for the poor students, e.g., as monitors and bell-ringers. The college also extended vacations so that students could teach in the winter.[4]

According to Miss Foster, scholarships accounted for £53 or 6 percent of the £912 of the college costs from 1693 to 1712, and they financed from one-third to one-half of student costs. In the early eighteenth century, sixteen of forty-nine students were receiving scholarships.[5]

An indication of the scholarship money available is to be had from the following:

a. 1650-1771

Exhibitions—Funds for Poor Scholars: The total value of funds made available in this period was $5,016.67 (capital sum, not income.)[6]

b. 1814-1824

In response to the $10,000 a year subsidy of the commonwealth, the college revealed that $24,381 of the $100,000 donated by the state went to scholarships, the grants ranging from $215.92 to $4, the beneficiaries numbering 297.[7]

c. 1891

Sums available (income) in 1890-1891 in Harvard University as money aids to students equaled $85,003. But note that only $46,000 was available to the college.[8]

d. Aid, 1910

The amount available was $130,000. Fellowships number 49 with an average stipend of $326; scholarships yielded $67,546 or an average of $157 to 430 scholarship holders; and $47,830 was paid for loans and prizes. In all, about $130,000 was had for student aid.[9]

e. Aid, 1964-1965

By 1964-1965, more than $2,388,553 were estimated to be available. Of this total, scholarships accounted for $1,543,646; college controlled beneficiary aid, $646,890; and other beneficiary aid, $152,772.[10]

The Theory of Scholarships

Perhaps as good a statement as any of the theory of scholarships is that given by Charles Eliot in his inaugural address in 1869.

There are always scores of young men in this University who earn or borrow every dollar they spend here.

3. *Ibid.*
4. Morison, *Three Centuries of Harvard, 1636-1936*, p. 201; *Report of the President of Harvard College*, 1888-1889, p. 91; Morison, *Harvard College in the Seventeenth Century*, pp. 60, 107-109.
5. Foster, *op. cit.*, pp. 138-141, 155.
6. Exhibition, *Funds for Poor Scholars*, date not given, in Harvard University Archives.
7. *An Act to Continue for the same Term of 5 years the Grant to the University in Cambridge*, statement of Treasurer Davis to the Joint Committe of the Legislature of the Commonwealth of Massachusetts, February 10, 1824.
8. Bolles, *op. cit.*, p. 7.
9. C. C. Little to S. A. D. Cox, September 21, 1910 in *A. L. Lowell Papers*, F. 1428.
10. *Report of Admission and Scholarship Committee*, 1963-1964, p. 11.

Every year many young men enter this College without any resources whatever. If they prove themselves men of capacity and character, they never go away for lack of money. More than twenty thousand dollars a year is now devoted to aiding students of narrow means to compass their education, besides all the remitted fees and the numerous private benefactions. These latter are unfailing. Taken in connection with the proceeds of the funds applicable to the aid of poor students, they enable the Corporation to say that no good student need ever stay away from Cambridge or leave college simply because he is poor. There is one uniform condition, however, on which help is given: the recipient must be of promising ability and the best character. The community does not owe superior education to all children, but only to the elite—to those who, having the capacity, prove by hard work that they have also the necessary perserverance and endurance. The process of preparing to enter college under the difficulties which poverty entails is just such a test of worthiness as is needed. At this moment there is no college in the country more eligible for a poor student than Harvard on the mere ground of economy. The scholarship funds are mainly the fruit of the last fifteen years. The future will take care of itself; for it is to be expected that the men who in this generation have had the benefit of these funds, and who succeed in after life, will pay manyfold to their successors in need the debt which they owe, not to the College, but to benefactors whom they cannot even thank, save in heaven. No wonder that scholarships are founded. What greater privilege than this of giving young men of promise the coveted means of intellectual growth and freedom? The angels of heaven might envy mortals so fine a luxury. The happiness which the winning of a scholarship gives is not the recipient's alone: it flashes back to the home whence he came, and gladdens anxious hearts there. The good which it does is not his alone, but descends, multiplying at every step, through generations.[11]

Later I shall discuss the case for scholarships. In the early years the emphasis generally was one on need. Without aid, the poor students could not survive. In more recent years, this argument is still crucial. But other points are also relevant. One is suggested by a comment made by Eliot, namely that the bright but poor boy who is helped will repay the college many times later when he has become prosperous.[12] A more subtle point which has generally been missed by college administrators is that the availability of scholarships enables the college to increase tuition without experiencing an unfortunate shift of the student body from the poor and able to the rich and incompetent. Thus, we can explain a rise of tuition payments nationally of about $1,500 million in the last generation as being made practical by an increase of scholarships of between $100 and $150 million.

Even in the Eliot days, the emphasis was put on both the quality of the student and his need. The relevance of need is suggested by the high proportion of scholarship holders coming from the public schools. Thus in 1906-1907 public school boys with the best grades obtained 40 of 48 scholarships while those with lower grades received 89 of 151 scholarships.

At that time President Eliot commented:

. . . the public schools deliver to Harvard College a large majority of the men who, during their college `life, attain high standing as scholars . . . . In all probability, the boys who come from public schools have a more vivid sense than the others that they must acquire in college the capacity to earn a good living in some intellectual calling.[13]

In the early years, the emphasis was on need. This is especially evident in the deeds of gifts.

At a meeting, presumably in 1826, the trustees of the Hopkins fund admitted "they had not been sufficiently careful to ascertain that the beneficiaries of

11. President Eliot's Inaugural Address, October 19, 1869, Samuel Eliot Morison (ed.), *The Development of Harvard University, 1869-1929*, 1930, pp. 68-69.

12. *Report of the President of Harvard College*, 1887-1888, pp. 13-14.
13. *Ibid.*, 1906-1907, p. 16.

this charity are always such 'whose circumstances may require such charitable assistant. . . .' "[14]

Letters addressed to the president in which the writers seek aid for students are of some interest. The emphasis is on need first and moral character second. Limited attention is given to intelligence and likelihood to profit from a college education, as shown by a letter written in 1824:

. . . subscribers inhabitants of Pepperell are acquainted with the pecuniary circumstances of Horatio Shipley . . . he has no property and his father has a large family and is unable to assist him through college . . . he sustains an unblemished moral character. . . .[15]

One way of helping students is to provide aid directly to those in need; another is to reduce the charge for all students. It is obviously wasteful to reduce the tuition by $50 for all students, both rich and poor. For that reason, the college has generally preferred direct aid. It is less costly. This issue was hotly debated in the nineteenth century. But in the long run, the direct-aid school attracted increasing support.

Thus, in 1834, there was much discussion of a plan to reduce total student costs from $180 to $140, a program which President Quincy was pushing. But he would limit these reductions to students who could show need. His main objective seemed to be to improve the financial position of the college. This would follow as enrollment responded to increased aid and fuller occupancy of rooms.

The direct approach (i.e., scholarships) was not always the recommendation. In 1827 a corporation committee held:

. . . it will better answer the purposes of the founders and benefactors of the University to furnish the best possible means of education at a cheap rate to those who are in moderate circumstances rather than to exhaust the resources for the support of a large number of indigent persons, who if they were not thus invited to the University might become useful and respectful in some other course of life . . . .[16]

On what tests should aid be given? The Eliot inaugural address quoted above insists on the relevance of hard work, moral character, and ability. He would also pay some attention to need. Elsewhere Eliot stressed hard work, moral character, and ability. If a student should not maintain a high level of performance after a half-year or a year's appointment, he would lose his scholarship. In recent years the dispensers of scholarships have been more generous. They seek to free the student from any pressures associated with possible loss of scholarship following a deterioration in the quality of work.

Eliot also would have disqualified a student on other grounds:

Marriage should cause the forfeiture of a scholarship or fellowship. During the past thirty years I have seen many cases in which holders of scholarships or fellowships actually married on the strength of them, alleging either that two could live on the fellowship, or that it was cheaper for the man to have a wife to work for him.[17]

As a rule, the emphasis was on need. But many were not pleased with the importance attached to the need criterion. It will be recalled that early in the twentieth century C. T. Adams complained of the policy of giving help to needy but sluggish students. That those of modest origin captured most of the scholarships and fellowships annoyed many persons

---

14. *To the Reverend and Honorable President and Fellows of Harvard College . . .*, Committee of Trustees for Perpetuating the Charity of Edward Hopkins, 1826, in Harvard University Archives.

15. A. Jewett and others to President Kirkland, August 28, 1824, in Harvard University Archives.

16. *Report of Corporation Committee*, Charles Jackson, Chairman, November 15, 1827. S.A.Eliot to President Everett, January 30, 1849; *to the Corporation of Harvard University, the President . . . submits for their consideration . . . the following Proposition*, April 22, 1834; President Quincy to Francis C. Gray, April 22, 1834; Francis Gray to T. W. Ward, Esq. (Treasurer), April, 1834.

17. C. W. Eliot to E. W. Blatchford, April 22, 1899.

from leading families.[18] Hence, when a scholarship was established to honor Wendell, it was specifically stated that need was not to be considered.

How effectively is aid money used? This is an important question. One has to measure ability and need. More than once officials complained of the difficulties of assessing need. Thus, in 1828, the steward wrote to the treasurer:

The fact is, it cannot be ascertained what real wants of the students are, without going into a great deal of minute inquiries not only here, but in the places where they belong—I still believe, what I suggested to you some time since, is the best method; to require of them written statements, under their signatures, of their reason for requesting assistance, and for this purpose all the students should receive notice that anyone who neglected to make a statement should not receive aid....[19]

As student aid became a larger enterprise, the relevant officials improved their methods of assessing students. In 1886, a committee of the faculty criticized methods of selecting scholarship winners. Beyond scholarly aptitude and need, the committee would stress recommendations of the schools.[20] Even as late as 1910, J. D. Greene suggested that the current system favored mendicants. What was needed was a centralized system with all scholarships widely advertised, he said.[21]

By the middle 1960s, with direct aid around $1,500,000, and all aid inclusive of loans and employment another $1,500,000, the dispensation of aid had reached a sophisticated level. In allocating aid, authorities relied on aptitude and achievement tests, grades in schools, and also letters of recommendation. Assessment of need had become a highly technical process. The parent had to provide information on income, assests, expenditures, size of family, etc. In order to preclude excessive scholarship payments, through competition bidding, major institutions of higher learning organized in a cartel fashion. Any institution that offered a scholarship in excess of that justified by the student's need could be challenged by a rival institution.

Anxious to make limited scholarship funds as productive as possible, the colleges depend increasingly on loans. Interest and repayment of loans provide cash for additional aid. As early as 1893, Prof. N. S. Shaler wrote of the greater effectiveness of loans "... for more than half the money thus disbursed [scholarships] could have been obtained by the recipient from other sources...."

It is not surprising to find that monetary assistance at Harvard rose from $333,000 in 1940-1941 to $2,235,776 in 1963-1964. This increase of 6 times was much less relatively than the rise by 11 times of loans ($55,000 to $664,000). By 1963-1964 term time earnings provided no less than $766,000 additional.[22]

By mixing scholarships with beneficiary aid—less attention being paid to ability in giving beneficiary aid than in offering ordinary scholarships—and with loans and employment income becoming more important, the college increased the potency of the aid dollar. But though the system is much more effective than in the past, wastage is still prevalent. To some extent the waste is a product of the terms of gifts. Giving priorities to descendants of donors is a frequent practice which means a less than optimum use of scholarship money. Thus, as late as 1927, the Downer Fund was established for "Descendants of Joseph and Robert Downer of Wiltshire, England (1650) bearing the surname of Downer, or to those of English or Anglo stock, bearing the surname of Downer by right of birth or inheritance...."

These are not the only elements of wastage. Excessive use of scholarships to direct students into particular colleges or areas of study and provision of

18. L. B. Briggs to C. W. Eliot, January 6, 1900.
19. C. Saunders to Ebenezer Francis, February 19, 1828.
20. "Report of E.Pickering," December 24, 1886, in C.Eliot *Papers, 1869-1886.*
21. J. D. Greene to A. L. Lowell, February 15, 1910.

22. N. S. Shaler to the President and Fellows of Harvard College, October 31, 1893; *Report of Admissions and Scholarship Committee,* 1963-1964, p. 10.

scholarships that pay more than the student needs are also relevant.[23]

Eliot raised some interesting problems concerning the amount of resources required for aid. He was inclined to moderate the demand:

. . . Nevertheless, the chances always are that the most promising and valuable young men will come of families who are able to pay for their education. . . . The fact is that the ability of parents which enables them to lay up resources for the education of their children is ground for hope for the future of their children. . . .

A board of overseers' committee in 1849 had anticipated the Eliot position. Pointing to the very rich who would get their education irrespective of costs and the indigent who would receive the necessary help, the committee then referred to "a class larger than either one which had furnished a majority in all the professions and useful avocations of society; a class able to pay moderate charges, but too restricted to meet high expenses. . . ."[24]

Eliot would not finance the full expenses of a student out of a scholarship on the grounds that the moral effects would be harmful. Eliot and Conant differed on this subject. On the whole, the trends in recent years have conformed more to Eliot's than Conant's position. The pressure increasingly is on the student to supplement his scholarship with loans, employment, or his parents' income. With costs averaging at least $3,500 in 1967 and scholarships averaging $1,750 (class of 1968), it is clear that poor students do not depend exclusively on scholarships.[25]

How much goes into scholarships depends on the amount of the average stipend. The trend has been toward higher average scholarships rather than relative increase in number of scholarships. The upward movement of the average stipend is explained not merely by rising cost of living or per capita income. It follows also from a growing realization that small scholarships or fellowships are wasteful. They do not substantially increase enrollment. It is today more effective to offer one scholarship of $1,500 than five of $300. The college, in 1885, reduced the number of scholarships from 118 to 108 and announced that it was inexpedient to reduce stipends below $150. In 1910, the dean of the graduate school wanted to substitute fellowships of $400 to $600 for the numerous $200 to $300 fellowships. But he would not object to $150 scholarships that were needed to offset the high relative cost of living in Cambridge.[26]

How much a scholarship is worth to the college is not clearly given by the payment made by the college. Eliot, for example, insisted that the student should continue to pay tuition. ". . . We pay out perhaps sixty thousand a year in scholarships and other aid but we take in thirty thousand dollars of that sum as tuition fees. Aid funds thus yield half their income for instruction. . . ."[27]

Again, the student's aid may be increased through special advances for purchases of books or remission of rents; and it may be reduced as the college finances the scholarship program out of increased rents charged for rooms. Moreover, when the student is forced to contribute services for scholarships he is in fact receiving smaller amounts of aid than appeared on the surface.

How much he gets depends also on the charge for tuition. If instruction early in the nineteenth century cost $150, the college might charge $125. Then a scholarship of $100 might in fact involve a subsidy of $125. Ordinarily the college has charged less than costs to all students.

23. For further discussion of these issues, see S.E.Harris, *Higher Education: Resources and Finance,* Part III, especially ch. 15.

24. C. W. Eliot to F. L. Olmstead, Esq., January 24, 1902; *Report of the Visiting Committee of Harvard University Overseers,* January, 1849, p. 30.

25. *Admissions and Scholarship Committee,* 1963-1964, b4; C.W.Eliot to Professor Gross, July 25, 1908; C.W.Eliot to J. M. Peirce, June 10, 1889; and Letter from Dean Glimp, March 15, 1967.

26. Dean Charles Haskins to A. L. Lowell, March 8, 1910; *Committee of College Faculty on Scholarships,* October 26, 1885.

27. C. W. Eliot to J. M. Pierce, June 10, 1889.

Through most of Harvard's history, the major subsidies to students have come from the excess of costs over tuition, a contribution many times that provided by scholarships.[28]

Scholarships, Seventeenth and Eighteenth Centuries

At the beginning of the eighteenth century the college provided £4 to each of five students, and by 1710-1711 the stipend was £4 9s for sixteen students, about one-third of the student body. Following a period of inflation the college raised the stipend in 1742-1743 to £6 and in 1747-1748 to £8, rises which were relatively much less than the increase of prices. But in 1754-1755, the authorities increased the payments again, this time by 50 percent, a rise made possible by the letting of bonds (loans) on the basis of the price of silver. Apparently until 1717 the numbers thus helped were less than twenty, and from 1720 to 1777, forty per year.[29]

Samuel Ward in 1681 left Bumkin Island to the college and asked that the income "should be applied for the 'easement of the charges of the dyet of the students that are in Commons . . . .'"

A bequest of £112 10s (old tenor) by Henry Flynt was to take care of "one or more needy scholars who are diligent and virtuous at the discretion of the Corporation . . . ."[30]

In the early years, as mentioned, the college generally demanded services in exchange for aid to the scholars. Thus, in 1724, scholars of the house were "to take care of the doors upon the roofs of the several colleges be kept locked and the gutters, troughs and trunks be cleansed as there be occasion."

One student wrote to his father on October 14, 1787:

. . . Obtained the Butler's Freshmanship; which exempts me from all expences this year except tuition and washing—I think myself highly favoured, and happily accommodated, as the Butler is very kind to me, and in all respects, appears to be a Gentleman— and on the whole, I am encouraged to hope that I shall secure an Education with a moderate expense, which will depend principally on my conduct this year. . . ."[31]

Funds made available by these early friends of Harvard were substantial. They accounted for a significant part of the college's expenditures or income. But the income was irregular. Not only would the income stop but at times the college would divert these funds to unintended uses. Under great pressure for funds, the temptation to divert scholarship funds was at times irresistible. One official list included additional funds which were given for scholarships but which had fallen into disuse and probably were consumed during periods of financial crises.

The fact is that the college was not always sympathetic when scholarship help was given. In 1796, the college induced the commonwealth to divert £200 of Harvard's income from the West Boston Bridge from scholarships for the support of two new tutorships.[32]

That the college did not always use gift money in the manner requested by the donor, and that students were to some extent denied the help that was intended for them is suggested by a study in 1803. In some instances, money was received but not appropriated and its ultimate use is not at all clear.

The committee appointed to consider the subject of appropriations made for the relief of indigent students, have attended to the business and find:

That in 1690 Robert Thorner bequeathed £500 sterling "for the propagating of learning and piety."

28. *Report of Committee on Assignment of Rooms,* J. Lovering, chairman, January 8, 1827; *Committee of the Corporation,* C. Jackson, chairman, November 15, 1827; *Report of the Committee on Textbooks and Rents for the Divinity Students,* May 19, 1831.

29. *Corporation Records,* various years, especially vol. I, pp. 40, 109; vol. II, pp. 32-49, 116; and Foster, *op. cit.,* pp. 66, 141.

30. *The Exhibitions of Harvard College Prior to 1800; The First Scholarship at Harvard College* (£100) in Harvard University Archives.

31. *Corporation Records,* vol. I, p. 182; vol. II, p. 231; I owe this to the kindness of Professor Samuel Morison.

32. *Ibid.,* vol. IV, pp. 483, 487.

N.°B.° £300 were received in 1772, and the residue soon expected; but no appropriation has yet been made.

That in 1678 Sir Mathew Holworthy bequeathed £1,000 sterling "for promoting of learning and promulgation of the gospel in these parts," and that the said legacy was paid to the treasurer Richards; but have found no appropriation of it.

That in 1680 Samuel Ward bequeathed Bumpkin's Island, "the rent of it to be for the easement of the charges of the students that are in commons:" but do not find that it has ever been so applied. [33]

Scholarships, Nineteenth Century

In 1814, the commonwealth imposed a bank tax which provided $10,000 yearly for ten years to Harvard College, a subsidy of considerable value at that time:

It is further enacted, that at least one-fourth part of the sums to be received by the said colleges, shall be appropriated for, and towards the partial or total reduction of tuition fees of such to students, not exceeding one-half the number of any class, who may apply therefore according to the judgment of the respective corporations of such colleges.

Aside from this state subsidy, the amounts available for scholarships in the first quarter of the nineteenth century were not large:

The amount of income appropriated for the support of indigent scholars has been estimated at thirteen hundred dollars, which is annually paid and allowed by the government of the University to such as they think entitled according to the will of the several donors . . . . [34]

In addition, the college provided $750 to $1,000 annually instead of waiterships, which had been discontinued. But the college would now discontinue these subsidies. [35]

Scholarship money became more plentiful in the nineteenth century. But all problems were not solved. The following from the John Quincy Adams Diary, August 19, 1837, suggests a problem. Harvard's competitive position with Yale seemed to trouble Mr. Adams.

President Quincy paid me a morning visit. The university is now in vacation. Commencement next Wednesday week, the day after that on which I propose to depart for Washington. Mr. Quincy was evidently anxious on account of the small numbers of the students and said they wanted beneficiary funds. He said that twenty thousand dollars a year were expended by individuals for the education of children at Yale College for the sake of orthodoxy, and he had received only two days since Letters from two clergymen desirous of placing their sons at Cambridge, by enquiring how much assistance they could receive from the beneficiary funds. [36]

Quincy had complained of the loss between twenty and thirty first-class men deterred by the lack of assistance. The result was the creation by seven Harvard graduates in 1838 of a trust of $11,350 to be used to lend funds to impoverished students. As a result of smart investment policies and compounding of investment income, by 1959 the college had available $2,700,000 in two funds, the income of which could be used for loans to students. In 121 years $11,350 had escalated to $2,700,000. [37]

In 1849 an anonymous review of *Eliot's Sketch of Harvard College* dwelt upon the problems of the poor students who had been helped under the grants of 1814-1824.

---

33. *Gifts, 1803*, vol. I.
34. *Act for the Encouragement of Literature, February 24, 1814 and February 16, 1816.* Book V, pp. 267, 304.

35. *Report to the President and Fellows of the Committee on Appointments and Compensation of Proctors . . . Exhibitions . . . Services . . . Required from Beneficiaries,* November 15, 1827.
36. John Quincy Adams and Charles Francis Adams, *op. cit.*
37. *Scholarship, Beneficiary Aid and Loan Funds, Harvard College,* 1963, pp. 182-185, *Report of the President of Harvard College,* 1875-1876.

Moreover, as the poorer class of students, who were primarily encouraged to come to Harvard by the aid they received from the State grant, have ceased to enter its classes, these are filled in a larger proportion by the sons of wealthy persons, and a different standard of expense, in regard to dress, pocket money, furniture, etc., has been established, which renders it almost a hopeless matter for a young man of slender means to obtain an education there. [38]

Taking a most advanced position, the reviewer then proposed on the Oxford-Cambridge model scholarships which would cover the total expense of the student, perhaps $300 at Harvard. The scholarship holders would be judged on ability, need, character, and proficiency of study.

The writer continued:

Every boy in Massachusetts, however indigent and obscure his position, if he distinguished himself at school, and felt the promptings of noble ambition, would know that a university education was open to him, a full course of liberal studies, obtained with high honor, and a full support secured to him while prosecuting them. At the same time, the openness of the competition and the severity of the trial would effectually separate the bran from the wheat, and those who had mistaken a mere dislike of manual labor for a call to higher and more intellectual pursuits would find it necessary to fall back upon the avocations for which alone nature had qualified them.

An indication of the paucity of scholarship money in 1830 is well expressed by a graduate of that time sixty years later:

Scholarships in the present sense of the word were very few; but there were certain funds in the hands of the College from which poor students, who enrolled themselves as "beneficiaries," received moderate sums of money in proportion to their standing as scholars. There were also various minor offices filled by those who desired to earn something by doing duty as fire-makers, bell-ringers, monitors at church and prayers, *special messengers, theme-bearers, etc. The office of sizar, or waiter at the tables, had been abolished some years before, though tradition still told how it had been filled by a young man who afterwards became an eminent clergyman, historian, and president of the College. By these various helps the capable and ambitious student could usually make his way through college, sometimes adding to his savings by "boarding himself" in his room on sums so small that I do not dare to mention them. Bread and milk were largely his diet, which served to keep in good condition some stalwart specimens of youthful vigor.* [39]

Even in the late 1840s the presidential reports had little to say about scholarships. But Harvard catalogues under *Pecuniary Assistance to Meritorious Students* listed *Beneficiary Funds.* The college distributed about $1,400 from these funds in sums ranging from $20 to $60. (The $60 was about one-fifth the cost of a Harvard education at that time.) Also available was a loan fund of $1,000 and monitorships yielding about $350 per year. In 1849-1850, twenty-four seniors received an average amount of between $24 and $60 and twenty-four juniors, $16. [40]

By the second half of the nineteenth century, the interest in scholarships greatly increased. Some of the old aids also continued. For more than two hundred years the president's freshmen, i.e., errant boys, continued to function. Among the president's freshmen were Ralph Waldo Emerson (1821) and Horatio Alger, Jr. (1852).

That conditions improved in the third quarter of the nineteenth century is attested by a comparison of scholarship funds available in 1875 with those available in the early 1850s. Harvard, with 112 scholarships averaging $235 or $26,320 in all, was far in the lead among ten colleges inclusive of seven ivy-league colleges, Boston University, Williams, and Bowdoin. Harvard's advantage was especially in the size of the

---

38. *Eliot's Sketch of Harvard College*, 1849, p. 118.

39. T. Cushing, "Undergraduate Life Sixty Years Ago," in *Harvard Graduates Magazine*, vol. I, pp. 555-556, 1893.

40. *Harvard University Catalogue*, 1849-1850, pp. 76-77; *Report of the Treasurer of Harvard College*, 1849-1850, pp. 2, 10; *Report of the President of Harvard College*, 1849-1850, pp. 33, 34.

stipends. No rival seemed to have an average as high as $100. But all in all Harvard was a more expensive place even if allowance is made for scholarship differentials.[41]

The Spectacular Rise in the Second Half of the Nineteenth Century

That the aid funds increased in so spectacular a manner in the 1860s, a period of economic stagnation, is rather unexpected. As early as 1852, the Harvard Alumni Association urged, and with some success, each class to give the college a capital fund of $2,000, which at the going rate of return would yield about $120 a year. In 1852, the college embarked on a scholarship program. Previous funds for helping students were not considered scholarships but rather beneficiary aid. In 1853, the commonwealth established scholarships to aid in educating and training young men for the office of teacher in the schools of the commonwealth, the students chosen were to matriculate at Harvard or Williams. Within four years, forty-eight scholars had been appointed with a generous stipend for that time of $100 a year. In January 1864, Mr. Bowditch donated $70,000 for scholarships, a vast sum for this period, the income to yield sixteen scholarships at $250 each. These various items help explain the great advance in the 1860s.[42]

That scholarships were not easy to obtain and hold is revealed by much evidence. John Fiske, class of 1863, and later a Harvard librarian and lecturer and noted positive philosopher and historian, wrote his mother as follows:

You do not understand about the scholarships. You ask if I am "working for one." They are given on the general rank so that all I have to do is get my lessons well, which I do. I asked President Felton for my September marks and he said he would give them to me, "I assure you, however," said he, "they are very good."

A year later in 1861, Fiske learned (the hard way) that he had to do a little more than get his lessons well in order to keep his scholarship. After attacking the college religious regulations as "fitted only for the dark ages," he wrote to his mother again: "Then, too, in the 'scale of merit,' attendance at prayers and church services plays an important part. You know I lost my scholarship by cutting too many prayers."[43]

That great observer of the American scene, James Bryce, wrote as follows:

It is the glory of American universities . . . to be freely accessible to all classes of the people. In the Eastern states comparitively few are the sons of working men, because parents can rarely bare the expense of a university course, or dispense with a boy's earnings after he reaches thirteen. But even in the East a good many come from straitened homes, receiving assistance from some richer neighbor or some charitable funds belonging to the college at which they may present themselves. . . .[44]

By 1877-1878, Eliot could boast that since the first scholarship had been established in 1852, there were 112, of which 107 were available in 1877-1878. In these twenty-six years $275,634 had been paid out and the current outlays were $25,000 per year.[45] By 1880-1881, the annual total had risen to $40,000 inclusive of loans. According to Eliot, one-eighth went to theology, one-seventh to B.A.s or B.S.s pursuing nonprofessional studies and about five-sevenths

41. Thwing, *op. cit.,* pp. 36, 38.
42. *Report of the President of Harvard College,* 1849-1850 to 1854-1855; *Report of the Treasurer of Harvard College,* 1849-1850 to 1854-1855; *Treasurers' Ledgers,* 1836-1865, pp. 7, 528; *Treasurer's Journals,* 1861-1865, p. 251; *Acts and Resolves passed by the General Court of Massachusetts,* 1864, p. 149; 1866, p. 164; Morison, *Three Centuries of Harvard, 1636-1936,* pp. 295-296. For later substantial bequests used for scholarships and fellowships, see *Report of the President of Harvard College,* 1872-1873, pp. 11, 23-24; *Plan for Scholarships,* July 12, 1852, in Harvard University Archives.

43. E. Fiske (ed.), *The Letters of John Fiske,* 1940, pp. 56, 74.
44. J. Bryce, *The American Commonwealth,* 1891, vol. II, p. 550.
45. *Report of the President of Harvard College,* 1877-1878, p. 8.

to *candidates* for the B.A. Two-thirds of the funds paid out to undergraduates in arts came back as tuition, a fact suggesting that the scholarship funds were gross, not net, costs.

By the early twentieth century there were increasing complaints of the inadequacy of scholarship funds. In 1844-1845, 12.1 percent of the students had received scholarships or other aid; by 1902-1903, but 6.1 percent received help. Scholarships had not increased as rapidly as enrollment.[46] It is not surprising then, as noted elsewhere, that a committee of the board of overseers, along with C. F. Adams, early in the twentieth century pressed for additional scholarship funds to be financed out of a rise of tuition, and this despite the availability of 213 scholarships and 30 endowed fellowships, the annual income of which was $62,730.[47]

At this time the proportion of scholarships to the number of applicants was 22 percent (1899-1900) and 21 percent (1901-1902). Clearly the numbers seeking aid greatly exceeded those helped. But of course requests do not measure need accurately.[48]

The availability of scholarships apparently raised questions in the minds of critics who seemed to believe that the monetary incentive was needed to induce scholarly work. But the president assured critics "that a decided majority of the highest scholars in Harvard College are young men who stand in no need of pecuniary assistance." And the dean later said "by far the greater part of work done in the College is done by men who are absolutely independent...."[49]

Even in the early part of the twentieth century, there was much concern over the inadequacy of aid money. An interesting episode is revealed in a letter of 1908 from President Eliot to Professor Kittredge, the great Shakespearian scholar.

Asticou, Mo., August 24, 1908

Dear Mr. Kittredge:

The case of John James Munro is certainly an interesting one, and I am sure that the Corporation would desire ... to excuse Munro from payment of the tuition fee. With this assurance as a starting point, I should advise you to write to J. G. Hart about the terms of Munro's admission as a special student, and to Dean Hurlbut about some aid for him from some funds, the income of which is applicable to special students. If you will also write to Edgar Wells on behalf of Munro, I think he may be able to secure an appropriate employment for him for three or four hours a day—best as an operator in a foreign cable office.

Are you in position to ask Dr. Horace Furness to aid this particular man to a small—say, $250— privately during his first year at Cambridge? Do you think of any well-to-do young graduate who has studied with you while in Cambridge who might be willing on your request to provide $250 per year for three years?[50]

Aid in the Twentieth Century

Under Eliot (1870-1910) scholarships became an important factor in the financing of the students' costs. Growth of scholarship funds was especially large in the twentieth century. From 1902 to 1962-1963, tuition income rose by $6,380,000 and gift aid by $1,519,000, or roughly a rise of 24 percent of the increase of tuition income. Similar ratios prevailed for the years 1933 to 1963 and 1953 to 1963.[51]

46. *Ibid.*, 1898-1899, p. 122; 1902-1903, pp. 109-110.47.
47. *Report of a Special Committee of the Board of Overseers on the Financial Requirements ...*, 1904, in Harvard University Archives; *Harvard Bulletin*, vol. 3, no. 6, p. 2, 1900.
48. *Report of the President of Harvard College*, 1900-1901, p. 20.
49. *Report of the President of Harvard College*, 1896-1897, pp. 7-8; "The President's Report," *The Harvard Bulletin*, 1896-1897, vol. II, no. 21, p. 1.

50. C. W. Eliot to Professor George L. Kittredge, August 24, 1908.
51. *Report of the President of Harvard College*, 1959-1960. I owe these statistics to H. Doermann.

From 1941 to 1960, total undergraduate aid rose from $333,000 to $1,776,000, with 32 percent receiving help in 1941 and 34 percent in 1960. By the middle 1960s, as noted earlier, aid inclusive of income from employment exceeded $3 million.

The percent of categories of aid in the two years was as follows:

Divisions of aid in percentages	1940-1941	1959-1960
Undergraduate Scholarships	80	57
Beneficiary Aid	4	14
Loans	17	29

Source: Calculated from *Admission and Scholarship Committees,* 1960 (Reprint from *Report of the President of Harvard College,* 1959-1960, p. 11.)

These statistics point to the declining *relative* importance of scholarships, the rising significance of beneficiary aid (suggesting a reduced emphasis on scholarly attainments of students and more emphasis on need) and the steadily rising importance of loans. Another factor of increasing significance has been employment income. Unfortunately, statistics on this kind of income are not available except for recent years. But the dean in 1908-1909 suggested that one man in three in Harvard College is working to pay his way wholly or in part."[52] It is clear that in recent years the college authorities have mobilized jobs for undergraduates in an unprecedented manner and that the income provided has been a significant part of total aid. Thus in 1962-1963, 1,898 students (approximately 40 percent of enrollment during term time) earned $820,854 or about $420 per student employed.[53] Should summer employment be added then employment may well account for about 40 percent of the costs for students employed in term time

and summer. The term-time jobs are largely university sponsored.

Not only the greater use of beneficiary aid, but also the introduction in 1958-1959 as a quasi-guarantee of scholarship aid over four years, and also extension of aid to students in the fourth grade-rank list, that is, with half C's and half B's, reflected a shifting of criteria for aid from the ability of the student to his need.[54]

In the 1950s, loan financing attracted increasing attention and received a stimulus from the National Defense Education Act. As early as 1846-1847, a substantial part of the beneficiary fund was diverted to a loan fund. And even before the turn of the century, the Lawrence Scientific School introduced a loan program in response to the excess of needs beyond available scholarship funds; and by 1904-1905 the program was considered a success.

The percentage of tuition financed by loans was 10.25 and 5.64 percent in the college in 1909-1910 and 1919-1920 respectively, 1.37 and 4.52 in the business school, and 9.7 and 22.0 percent in the divinity school in these years.[55]

As tuition and/or costs rise, there is a disposition for the college to raise the scholarship stipend. But also relevant is the changing capacity of the student to finance his education. A relevant comparison is the relation of per capita disposable personal income and tuition. But much depends on the base year chosen for comparison. Thus, Doermann shows that tuition should have been as follows in 1962 if the ratio of tuition to disposable per capita income equal to that of the years 1900, 1927 and 1932 held: (Actual tuition was $1520).

Relations of Tuition to Per Capita Income

1900 Base	$1,670
1927 Base	961
1932 Base	2,113

52. *Report of the President of Harvard College,* 1908-1909, p. 115.
53. Statistics from H. Doermann.

54. Cf., *Harvard Crimson,* April 11, 1958.
55. *Report of the President of Harvard College,* 1846-1847, pp. 10-11; 1904-1905, pp. 125-127; 1905-1906, pp. 48-49; and various other sources.

Thus, tuition in 1962 would have been much higher than it actually was on the base of 1932 because in that year tuition was very high vis-à-vis the low per capita income; and on the base of 1927, very low because tuition was low compared to the high per capita income.

In the 1950s the college contributed substantial sums to finance scholarships out of unrestricted income. But Dean Wilbur Bender wrote in 1960:

... The general assumption that a significant proportion of the increased tuition income from higher tuition charges would be used for financial aid to students so that the net return from a tuition increase would be only about 75 percent of the increase has proved false in Harvard's case. After a decade of tuition boosts of unprecedented size and rapidity, all of the 1960-1961 financial aid budget of the College is being financed from designated College scholarships and loan funds.[56]

Bender also complained that whereas the self-help gap in 1950 was only $450, by 1960 it was $800. The difference between the average scholarship stipend and costs to students in these years had increased from $1,082 to $1,709.

As prices rose in the period 1940-1962, the value of scholarships declined. In his 1948-1949 report, President Conant said:

... at the very time when the independent colleges and universities need more money for scholarships to provide in some degree opportunities similar to those open to veterans from low income families, the value of our scholarship funds has drastically diminished. This is a consequence, of course, of the change in price levels without any appreciable offsetting factor in the way of increased endowment or high return on investments.[57]

Indeed inflation is a serious matter, as noted by Conant, but it is well to recognize the fact that the large rise of equity values in the 1950s and early 1960s brought a rise of income (e.g., capital gains) from endowment funds that largely offset the losses due to the rising cost of living. In this connection, the rise of endowment scholarship, beneficiary aid, and loan *funds* from $9.9 million to $26.7 million between 1950 and 1960 is not without significance.

Bender also notes the increased availability of outside scholarships and the increased significance of loans and employment as indications that the deprivations were not so large as they seemed. Moreover, per capita disposable income rose by 42 percent in the 1950s, a rise that accounts for more than 70 percent of the difference between $1,082 and $1,709.

As costs of a Harvard education rise, there is much concern lest the college increasingly become a haven of the rich and second rate. Both Bender and Doermann have discussed this issue well. The median family income of scholarship holders has risen more than median family income in the nation:

Harvard Scholarship Holders Family Income Compared with U.S. Median

	1952	1960
1. U.S. median family income	$ 4,300	$ 5,300
2. Family income, Harvard scholarship holders	4,900	7,800
3. Percentile equivalent of (2) in national sample	58	75

These statistics reveal that in eight years, family incomes of Harvard scholarship holders rose by 59 percent, but the median income for the nation by only 23 percent.[58] Hence, scholarships tend to go to Harvard students who come from families with high relative incomes and with incomes rising relative to the national level.

Concern is expressed for the rise of incomes of families of all Harvard Students in relation to national levels. To finance a Harvard education, the appeal increasingly has to be to higher income groups. At a

56. *Admission and Scholarship Committee*, 1959-1960, p. 28.
57. *Report of the President of Harvard College*, 1948-1949, pp. 18-19.
58. *Admission and Scholarship Committee*, 1960, pp. 28-29.

cost of $3,000 per year, Bender finds that a Harvard education without aid is open to the top 5 to 10 percent of families with the highest incomes. For the class of 1951 (entering in 1948) Stouffer found average family incomes of the nonscholarship students were $12,250. For the class of 1964, the corresponding average family income was between $13,000 and $14,000.

Doermann compares the base income level for the top 5 percent of United States families and the scholarship cut-off level at Harvard for a three-child family.

Income Levels, Harvard Scholarship and all U.S. Families

Year	Family income top 5 percent, U.S.	Harvard, scholarship need cut-off, 3-child family
1951	$ 9,069	$ 111,000
1960	13,863	15,250

He also estimates the number of prosperous families (top 5 percent income group) in any one year and the number of nonscholarship applicants (classes of 1955 and 1965).

Comparison of Number of Wealthy Families with Number of Harvard Applicants

	1950	1960
Top 5 percent income families, U.S.*	154,000	183,000
Harvard nonscholarship applicants	1,467	3,050

* This figure is adjusted for the appropriate age of family head and the numbers in any one year.

It is clear that Harvard attracts an increasing proportion of paying students from the top 5 percent families.[59]

59. H. Doermann, *op. cit.;* and *Harvard Alumni Bulletin,* January 10, 1948.

University Aid

Most of the discussion of aid so far has been related primarily to the college. But the other departments of the university contribute increasing amounts of aid. Even by 1912-1913, Harvard College's scholarships and fellowships amounted to $57,155 or a little more than one-half of the total for the university of $111,438. Whereas the college provided this aid to 265 students, the whole university helped 478. Outside of the college, the Graduate School of Arts and Sciences spent almost $33,000 and five other professional schools around $20,000 in all.[60] At his inauguration, Eliot estimated aid at $20,000 and by 1893-1894, the estimate was $50,000. This aid was primarily for the college.

By 1965-1966, scholarships and other student awards amounted to $11,568,000, of which total the faculty of arts and sciences accounted for $6,988,000, or about 60 percent. But the 1965-1966 total includes the Graduate School of Arts and Sciences. By 1912-1913, the college and graduate school had obtained 79 percent of the total. Clearly, other professional schools gained relatively since 1912-1913. Striking also is a rise of 117 times in this aid over a period of 43 years. The government provided more than one-third of the 1965-1966 total.[61]

The Impact of Inflation

Scholarship holders suffer especially in periods of inflation. Costs rise and scholarship stipends lag. But an offset is the failure of tuition to increase as much as prices. At any rate, in the great inflation of the 1725-1750 period and during the Civil War the purchasing power of aid money tended to fall. Knowing that a rise of tuition would further damage the economic status of students receiving aid the president in 1863 said that those "whose means are small, and

60. *Budget 1912-1913; Payment of Fellowships and Scholarships; Four American Universities,* p. 25.
61. *Financial Report to the Board of Overseers of Harvard College,* 1965-1966, pp. 10-11, 14-15; also see chapters on the medical and law schools.

who are aided by the scholarships and exhibition funds are now, it must be remembered, aided to a less extent than three years ago owing to the unavoidable depreciation of the currency in which the income of those funds is paid and disbursed. . . ."[62] Later Conant also was to complain of the erosion of scholarship funds as prices rose.

The Class of Views: Eliot vs Conant

From President Eliot's inaugural address certain principles of scholarship policy are evident. Later he implemented his original statement. Eliot was anxious that the student should be helped for only part of his costs. The disciplinary gains of working for part of the needed money greatly appealed to the president.[63]

Eliot continued to raise questions about the excessive use of scholarships and fellowships, and also disliked their use for attracting students from competitors.[64] He believed that they attracted docile youths, and not the vigorous and aggressive ones Harvard needed.

Ordinary scholarships . . . can be given in cases of poverty, but it would seem that they should be given sparingly in graduate schools, because by that time an energetic student ought to be able to provide in large part for his own support; and to give them for the purpose of bringing students who would otherwise go elsewhere, though tempting, is probably in the long run an injury to the cause of education. The danger of giving scholarships too freely is insidious.
Excessive generosity for divinity students resulted in their pauperization. So long as they receive too much help, the School will not command the respect which the other professional schools of the University command, and it will not contend, as it might, against the common impression that members of the clerical

profession are semipauperized,—in their early years by the habit of accepting complete support during the long period of education, and in their later by half-fares, free admissions, gratutious services from physicians, special discounts from tradesmen, and spasmodic gifts from their churches instead of punctual payment. . . ."[65]

Eliot's theories remained relatively undisturbed until Conant, in 1933, made a frontal attack on them. For Conant the important objective was to free the able student of all financial cares, in the belief that outside work was at the expense of studies. He wanted to provide students of ability with funds adequate to cover all their needs. Hence, the National Scholarships both in the college and in professional schools. Under Conant the policy was to merge funds and offer larger scholarships for those in need and honorary scholarships to those with ability but adequate resources. That the Conant policy has been successful is attested by the excellent record made by the National Scholars. More than 65 percent of the scholars in the class of 1938-1940 graduated Summa or Magna Cum Laude, a ratio about 4 times as great as in the college generally.[66]

Trends in Value of Scholarships Vis-à-Vis Tuition Costs

In the latter part of the seventeenth and eighteenth centuries, scholarships amounted to between 10 and 11 percent of tuition payments, or, with the exclusion of payments for work, roughly 7 percent. Some rough figures are shown in the following table. This table reveals the fact that scholarship money was scarce in the first 235 years of Harvard's history and especially in the eighteenth century. A spectacular advance occurred in the 1860s. After that, interest in

---

62. *Report of the President of Harvard College*, 1862-1963, p. 13.
63. *Ibid.,* 1898-1899, pp. 22-23.
64. *Ibid.,* 1908-1909, pp. 22-23.

65. *Ibid.,* 1890-1891, p. 19.
66. See especially *Report of the President of Harvard College*, 1933-1934, pp. 14-15, 117-124; 1934-1935, pp. 13, 23-25; 1935-1936, p. 19; *Harvard Alumni Bulletin,* vol. V, no. 44, p. 90, 1941; Morison, *Three Centuries of Harvard, 1636-1936,* pp. 486-487.

aid to poor students continued to grow, and scholarships tended to stabilize at about one-quarter of tuition income.

Table 8-1.

Comparison of Aid (Exlusive of Work) with Tuition

Period	Tuition income	Scholarships etc. (gift aid)	Percentage aid is of tuition
1693-1712	£89	£6.2	7.0
1860	$ 88,225.83	$ 2,667	3.0
1870	82,463.00	19,686	23.8
1890	194,236.00	49,292	25.3
1923	734,291.00	178,094	24.3*
1963	6,812,458.00	1,585,900	23.3†

* 26.1 if loans are included.
† 31.9 if loans are included.

Sources: Foster, *op. cit.,* for row 1; *Report of the Treasurer of Harvard College,* 1859-1860, pp. 8-17; 1869-1870, pp. 32-33; 1889-1890, pp. 44, 48-49, for rows 2-4; H. Doermann, *The Economics of Undergraduate Diversity,* paper in S.E. Harris seminar, 1963, for rows 5-6. My calculations.

The Relation of Student Aid to Total Student Expenditures, 1723-1963

It is of some interest that in 1723 Harvard students' aid accounted for 11.6 percent of the *expenditures at Harvard,* a figure never reached again. By 1750, the aid/expenditures ratio had dropped to 3.3 percent, falling to 2 percent in 1781-1782, a year of great inflation. But the percentage did not rise above 5 percent in any of the years 1789-1800 through 1859-1869 (estimated at ten-year intervals). A spectacular rise occurred from 1859-1860 (2.3 percent) to 1869-1870 (7.85 percent). Then there followed a gradual decline to 5.0 percent in 1919-1920. In general, the college (or university) tended to be less than

generous in providing student aid in the 140-year period 1720 to 1860, and somewhat more generous in the about a hundred years ending in 1962-1963. By 1967 there was a large gain. One factor that contributed to the unsatisfactory 140-year record was the rising importance of the graduate and professional schools, which accounted for rising expenditures, but with student aid at a smaller percentage of expenditures than in Harvard College.

Table 8-2.

Percent Harvard Student Aids to College Expenditures,* Various Years

1723	11.6
1781-1782	2.0
1809-1810	0.8
1859-1860	2.3
1869-1870	7.8
1909-1910	6.7
1939-1940	5.0
1959-1960	7.0
1962-1963	7.0

*Actually, ratio of scholarships to all students in arts and science to their expenditures. Coverage varies to some extent.

Sources: Treasurers' Journals; *Report of the Treasurer of Harvard College; Stewards' Quarter Bill Books;* "Legislative Records of the Council," in *Acts and Resolves passed by the General Court of Massachusetts; Financial Report to the Board of Overseers of Harvard College.* (Since for many of these years the treasury did not consolidate expenditures, we had to do so. The comparison over long periods is subject to some reservations since the treasurers varied bookkeeping procedures at different times.) My calculations.

Loan Funds

There is much to be said for loan financing. A given amount of money used for lending is much more productive than an equal sum disbursed as scholarships, for the loan fund is a revolving one. Other arguments used on behalf of loans are (1) the student appreciates his education more if he pays part of the costs, (2) the burden of repayment is reduced as incomes rise in the period of repayment (in this manner society is forced to pay part of the bill), and (3) the availability of loan funds enables many and especially the middle-income group to achieve an education which otherwise might be denied.[67]

President Lowell was critical of the loan programs.

They . . . [loans] are virtually debts of honour; but it has been supposed that after a man has thus been enabled to enter upon a successful career he will gladly repay the money lent him and open the door to someone else. It is disappointing, therefore, to learn how small a proportion of the recipients actually pay these debts. Taking the college loans that have fallen due, 295 men have paid in full, 259 have not paid at all, and 37 have paid in part. . . .[68]

Dependence on loans varied from school to school. In general, the professional schools relied more heavily on them than the college, the reason being lack of scholarship funds and the greater likelihood of earned income in the *near* future. Thus, in 1929-1930, the business school provided 4 times as much loan money relative to tuition charges as arts and science, and all the other major schools other than education relied more on loans. [69]

The Fund for Assisting Students at Harvard College

As noted earlier, officially, Harvard became increasingly interested in loan-financing of students in the nineteenth century. In 1847, the corporation had asked the treasurer to investigate the extent to which scholarship grants might legally be converted to loans. The response was that about $15,000 (with $750 a year of income) might thus be converted. The corporation approved measures to induce a corresponding conversion of grants to loan.[70]

The Creation of a *Fund for Assisting Students at Harvard College* in 1838, following a proposal of President Quincy, who had been concerned over the loss of students to rival institutions favored by a large central loan fund, brought attention to the advantages of loan financing of students.

Under the leadership of Samuel Eliot, the father of Charles Eliot, subscribers provided $11,350. In the early years, the trustees invested in bank stock primarily; but after the Civil War, until recent years, bonds were the major investments. Of late, a substantial part of the funds were put into equities. It is, therefore, surprising that by 1889, the assets had climbed to $87,000, by 1939 to $486,600. In 1959, the trustees turned this fund over to the college. Its value in 1965-1966 was $1,599,000. C. Eliot was critical of the fund. He wanted improved investments and accelerated repayments. He even suggested to a new member of the corporation that he consult with the trustees and raise issues of bad management. [71]

What is the explanation of a rise in the value of the fund from $11,350 in 1838 in the face of the large defaults, to its present value of more than $2 million? Has the investment record been phenomenal? Investment in bank stocks at first, bonds primarily for between 60 and 70 years and in recent years, a roughly equal investment in bonds and equities, does not seem to suggest a brilliant or a poor investment record. Policies were surely sound. The large investments

67. See Harris, *op. cit.,* Part IV, for full discussion of the loan problem, also see chapters on the medical and law schools in this volume.

68. *Report of the President of Harvard College,* 1913-1914, p. 22.

69. *Ibid.,* 1929-1930, pp. 128-129; *Harvard University Catalogue,* 1929-1930, pp. 577, 862-863; cf., *Treasurer's Statement,* 1909-1910, pp. 74-140; 1919-1920, pp. 171-248; *Report of the President of Harvard College,* 1921-1922, pp. 84-85.

70. Treasurer to the Corporation of Harvard College, February 27, 1867 (" . . . to ascertain whether anything would prevent the income from being used in the shape of loans instead of gifts.").

71. C. W. Eliot to Miss Mary Willets, October 15, 1896; C. W. Eliot to T. Nelson Perkins, February 1, 1907; Acting Comptroller to F. W. Galloway, December 29, 1910, in A. L. Lowell Letters; *Financial Report to the Board of Overseers of Harvard College,* 1965-1966, p. 198; Fund for Assisting Students at Harvard College, reports of January 13, 1858 and January 8, 1899.

in bonds from 1865 to 1929 suggest large capital gains as the rate of interest generally declined.

Yet the advance of two hundred times is explained primarily by the workings of the compound interest law, not by brilliant investment policies. Over a period of 121 years, a return of 5 percent per year should increase the capital sum roughly by 200 times or from $11,350 to $2,270,000. Defaults primarily and any failure to earn 5 percent on investment would reduce the value of the assets below $2,270,000.

In its first hundred years, the funds for Harvard College Students loaned $450,000 to 6,350 Harvard men, or one-fifth of living Harvard alumni. In 1939 the average advance per man was $71. Among the beneficiaries were a future Harvard president, two famous law school professors (C. C. Langdell and J. B. Thayer), a writer (Horatio Alger), two governors, eight deans, a president of the University of California, six other college presidents, a major general, fifty-sixty distinguished professors at major universities, four judges, nine overseers, and a nationally known poet.[72]

Employment

Work while at college has been traditional at Harvard for the large numbers without adequate means to support themselves. Many famous Harvard alumni devoted much of their time while at college to earning money.[73]

The great financier Thomas Lamont (1892) also reviewed an interesting experience as a member of the labor market.

Soon, however, I made up my mind I would go out strong for an editorship of The Crimson, *the students' daily newspaper.... After a few months I was lucky enough to be elected as the first freshman editor.* The Crimson, *prudently run was not an unprofitable enterprise, and at the end of each year the editors "divvied" up a few hundred dollars among ten or a dozen of us. Also, the practice was for one of the editors who could do with the money to come every night to the office about midnight to correct the final proofs and put the paper to bed. A few dollars a week was the reward for this, and the job was left in my hands for the next three years....*

The amateur journalism of the college daily led naturally to other chances. The Boston Advertiser, *an evening newspaper, asked me to be its Harvard correspondent at about five dollars a week. And I was in transports when a year or so later the Boston* Herald *bid me away with a regular stipend of fifty dollars a month. For me this was a bonanza. In one way or another I could relieve the family exchequer of two thirds of my college expenses.*[74]

As I mentioned elsewhere, students were encouraged to take some extra time off in order to earn money teaching in the schools during the winter. President Sparks and David Thoreau, among others, taught in country schools while at college.

Meritorious students, whose circumstances require the dispensation, may be excused from returning to College, after the Thanksgiving recess, for the remainder of the term, provided they are engaged in keeping schools. The time of such absence is commonly about three weeks, making their schools last ten weeks, including the winter vacation.... Their compensation is from sixteen to twenty dollars a month

---

72. See the excellent essay by D. McCord, *In Sight of Sever,* 1963, pp. 154-167; F. Gruber and H. Alger, Jr., *A Biography and Bibliography,* pp. 15-20; *Report of the Visiting Committee of the Board of Overseers of Harvard College,* 1924-1925, pp. 24-25. A loan to Alger helped him get through Harvard College which he entered at age 16. He also became a president's freshman (as was Emerson), an appointment which gave him a room without charge and $1 per week. Beyond this, he was allowed to extend his vacation so that he could teach in the winter. Despite these demands on his time, he finished eighth in a class of 88, won the Bowdoin prize, and excelled in English.

73. F. Rudolph, "The Progress of Student Aid in the United States," in *College Entrance Examination Board,* Financial Aid and National Purpose, 1962, pp. 1-11.

74. T. Lamont, *My Boyhood in a Parsonage,* 1946, pp. 173-174.

besides board and lodging. The average number of our Students, who are thus employed, is fifty. . . .[75]

Since College classes were fairly small, it appears that anywhere from one-third to one-fifth of the students taught school to earn their way through college.

Even as late as 1890-1891, the Bussey Institution of Harvard encouraged young men of meagre means to supplement their incomes by obtaining manure to keep the fields in good condition, by caring for animals taken to board at the institute farm, and by processing wood on the farm.[76]

In the seventeenth century, it will be recalled, the scholars had all kinds of tasks to perform. Throughout the eighteenth century the college paid six students (called scholars) to take care of the buildings while the college was in session. Even in the nineteenth century President Kirkland introduced a number of petty offices, e.g., bell ringer, so the pay received from these tasks could help these students meet part of their expenses.[77]

As was noted earlier, jobs contributed a substantial part of students' income in the post World War II period. But this source of income was also important throughout the twentieth century. In 1902-1903, the president noted that students in term-time earned from 25 cents an hour for a few hours a week to $1,500 or more a year. During the year ending September 1911, one-quarter of the students registered applied for temporary work from the Harvard Employment and Teachers' Agency. The students reported earnings of $137,000, and in 1912-1913, the president complained that the public was not aware of the numbers of students of small means at Harvard. They had earned $184,643.82 in that year,

one-half of which was obtained by work found for them through the employment office.[78]

Scholarships in the University

Over the years, the scholarships in the college have been the dominant ones. Next to the college, the Graduate School of Arts and Sciences has been the school with the largest funds for scholarships, or better, fellowships.[79] The reason for this is largely the fact that students in the graduate school come from homes with low incomes, and also because the college authorities learned early that teaching fellowships provided low-cost instruction. Students in law and medicine tended to come from higher-income homes than those in the Graduate School of Arts and Sciences. The pressure for fellowships in the graduate school is evident in the transfer of scholarship funds from the college to it.

A good indication of the dependence on aid is given by a comparison of fellowships and scholarships in 1908-1909 per student *enrolled.* A more detailed table is deposited in the archives.

Aid Given to Each Student, 1908-1909

Divinity school	$200.35
Graduate school of arts and science	90.94
Harvard college	20.72
Medical school	16.25
Law school	8.78

By the twentieth century, fellowships to graduate students had become substantial. By 1908-1909, the Graduate School of Arts and Science was approaching the college in funds available and its per capita stipend exceeded the college's. Other large professional schools did not do so well in the first half of the twentieth century. The divinity school and gradu-

---

75. *Report of a Special Committee of the Overseers of Harvard College,* Januuary 6, 1825, p. 37; for similar practice at Brown, see W. C. Bronson, *History of Brown,* p. 200.

76. *Report of the President of Harvard College,* 1890-1891, pp. 22-23.

77. See especially, *Corporation Records,* vol. I, p. 182, 1724; vol. II, p. 231, 1765; *Treasurers' Journals,* 1777-1807; *Harvard University Catalogue,* 1849-1850, pp. 76-77; Morison, *Three Centuries of Harvard, 1636-1936,* 201.

---

78. *Report of the President of Harvard College,* 1902-1903, p. 45; 1912-1913, p. 11; *Harvard Graduates Magazine,* vol. V, no. 19, pp. 546-547, 1911.

79. *Report of the President of Harvard College,* 1908-1909, p. 20.

ate school offered large stipends in response to the low income of students in these schools.[80] In these years scholarship aid as a proportion of tuition tended to be high especially for the college, graduate school, and divinity school, and low for the others— e.g., 28 percent for divinity in 1929-1930 and 2 and 7 percent for law and medicine respectively.[81]

Some General Observations

It is well to realize that the college's contribution is given not merely by aid but is related to how effectively the administration raises gift money and runs the college or university. A highly efficient administration will keep costs, and to this extent tuition down. The availability of philanthropic funds will raise income and thus reduce dependence on tuition. How much student aid is needed will depend on the incomes of the parents of the student, the costs of operation (and colleges generally do not include the return on capital for buildings and equipment as part of costs), the extent to which the faculty is exploited, and the contributions from endowment and gifts.[82]

Student aid is important not only because it enables many to go to institutions of higher learning who otherwise might not be able to continue their education but (related) also because aid precludes a student body determined very largely by capacity to pay, rather than capacity to learn. In the last generation or so there has been much concern that costs were rising more rapidly than capacity to pay and hence that the college was becoming more and more a haven for the affluent and mediocre. The rising trend in the ratio of family income of scholarship holders and non-scholarship holders to the per capita disposable income of the nation suggests this conclusion to many, as does the increase of the ratio of tuition and all costs to scholarship stipends.[83] In dispensing aid, one has to be clear on the objectives. Throughout Harvard's history the criterion of need has been important. But in the first hundred years, help was likely to be forthcoming to descendants of donors. Under Eliot the student had to show both need and capacity. During this period of large expansion of aid funds, the college authorities became sensitive on the issue of the relation of aid and educational achievement. They even went so far as to defend nonscholarship students on the grounds that they had commitments beyond their studies.

Despite the emphasis on need, Harvard for generations has not been able to finance those most in need of help, the low-income group—the bottom 20 percent in family incomes, those from families with incomes of less than $3,000 a year in the early 1960s. Obviously with annual student costs averaging between $3,000 and $3,500, or an amount equal to or more than the income of 20 percent of families, and with wider geographical exploration of scholarship prospects and hence the declining importance of the commuter class, the scholarship holder tends to come from parents with incomes in excess of the median income of the nation, and increasingly so. When the median income of families with scholarship holders is about $8,000 and for the nation $6,500, obviously the scholarship holder comes from a high-income class. The scholarship need cut-off level at Harvard for a family with three children is in excess of $15,000, an income level recently equal to that of the top 5 percent of the nation.

Obviously with costs at $3,500 in 1966-1967, it is not likely that the average stipend of $1,200 would attract many of the students from the low-income

---

80. *Ibid.*, 1908-1909, p. 20; 1950-1951, pp. 95-96; *Harvard University Catalogue,* 1919-1920, pp. 270-287.

81. *Treasurer's Statement,* 1909-1910, pp. 79-140; 1919-1920; 1929-1930, pp. 128-139; *Report of the President of Harvard College,* 1929-1930; Harvard University Catalogue, pp. 577, 862-863; see also chapters on the law and medical schools.

82. Cf., the interesting statement by F. Rudolph, "The Origins of Student Aid in the United States" in College Entrance Examination Board, Student Financial Aid and National Purpose, 1962, p. 10.

83. Elsewhere I have compared costs at Harvard with economic standards of the population as guides to Harvard's move toward luxurious and costly standards.

classes to Harvard. Should the stipend be raised to say between $2,000 and $2,500, then the number of students to be helped would be greatly reduced. In his interesting discussion in his 1960 report, Bender suggested that excessive emphasis on grades and apptitude tests would mean very heavy burdens on scholarship funds. The problem of enrolling more students from the low-income groups is not only a financial one; it is partly that the college seeks students with middle-class values; and those from the low-income families often have inadequate preparation.

Recent rises of per capita income in the nation and the growing prestige of Harvard have resulted in large increases of demand for entry to Harvard. Thus from 1954 to 1964 the total of applicants rose from 3,089 to 5,048, and the rejection ratio from 37 to 70 percent. These trends have enabled the college to attract more students of given ability from higher-income classes, and concentrate aid on those with low but not lowest incomes. It is clear from Doermann's figures that Harvard has gained disproportionately from the rise of interest in higher education and from the growing income of the American people. The college has exploited these developments by improving its product (e.g., through higher salaries and improved physical facilities), raising tuition, using about 25 percent of the additional tuition income for aid (though the addition of scholarship money is financed in part by additional endowment funds), and to some extent by obtaining scholarship and non-scholarship students from families with incomes that tend to rise relative to national levels.

9

Admissions, Enrollment and Attrition

Trends

During most of Harvard's history, enrollment was considered an indication of the quality of a Harvard education: "The number of students in College for a long term of years may perhaps be considered as in some degree a test of its prosperity or decline, and of the public favor which it enjoys."[1] Yet throughout the first two centuries enrollment expanded slowly. In 1652 the college had but 50 students; at the end of the Puritan period, in the early eighteenth century, it had 54. In 1819 enrollment was still only 249. In the later 1840s the authorities boasted of an average college enrollment of just 293, with 447 in the university.[2]

Even this gradual growth was disturbed by fluctuations of enrollment. For example, near the end of the seventeenth century a disturbing decline of enrollment occurred. Some classes graduated only three members; and in 1672, 1682 and 1688 there were no graduates. In late 1674 the exodus was so large that only three students remained, and they stayed only because they had friends in Cambridge. In that year Harvard almost died:

Its reputation and good name were sinking as fast as the attendance; the discipline (including flogging) was outrageously severe; . . . the Corporation were resigning right and left; the Treasury was empty . . . the managers were preposterously successful in antagonizing prospective benefactors; the salaried officers were all dismissed except the president (Hoar).[3]

Percentagewise the increases were large in the years 1650 to 1819. But the large absolute rises occurred under Eliot, Lowell, and Conant. Under the first the increase was about three thousand, or 300 percent; under Lowell, about four thousand, or 100 percent; and under Conant about three thousand, or 40 percent. (Undergraduate enrollment, however, rose only about one-half as much as total enrollment from Eliot's inauguration to 1964.) Whereas in the first 224 years total enrollment rose by less than 1,100, in the next 98 years the rise was more than 14,000— roughly 29 times as large an absolute rise *per year.*

The trend has thus been upward, though at varying rates, but there have been periods when enrollment actually declined. Thus, undergraduate enrollment reached an early peak at 255 in 1829; between 1835 and 1856 it had dropped to 210. There had been too much washing of dirty linen in public, and Yale, Princeton, and others were forging ahead. In 1834, the whole sophomore class was dismissed for rowdy behavior, and the class of 1836 was the smallest since 1809.[4] Another peacetime period of serious declines was in 1903-1904 and 1905-1906.

---

1. *Memorial Concerning Recent History and the Constitutional Rights and Privileges of Harvard College Presented by the President and Fellows to the Legislature,* 3d. ed., January 17, 1851, p. 6.
2. *Ibid.,* p. 15.

---

3. Batchelder, *op. cit.,* p. 133.
4. Relevant *Reports of the President of Harvard College; Harvard University Catalogues;* Morison, *Three Centuries of Harvard, 1636-1936,* p. 253.

The Revolutionary War, of course, cut numbers. When in 1775 the college moved to Concord for sixteen months, only 125 students migrated with it.[5] Yet it was invasion, inflation, and serious financial problems, rather than direct loss of students to military service, which seriously cut down enrollment. (In the decade 1762-1772 undergraduate enrollment averaged 177. In 1772-1777 this fell to 152, and in 1777-1781 to only 122.)[6] Harvard men showed little interest in the War of 1812. In the Civil War there was little expectation of service from college students. It is of some interest that enrollment at Harvard, which was 839 in 1859-1860, remained at 799 in 1864-1865. The crew races were held in June, 1864, a time of desperate shortage of men in the Union Army, but no member of the crew enlisted. In World War I and World War II the demands on students were much more compelling. Morison notes that enlistments by Harvard men in the Civil War were 1,568, with alumni numbering 7,440 in 1863 (10 percent casualties in the Union forces and 25 percent in the Confederate armies) and 11,319 in World War I (3.3 percent casualties). These figures do not suggest such large avoidance for Harvard men as for Harvard undergraduates.[7] In 1916, Harvard enrollment was 5,656; in 1917, it dropped to 3,684, an indication of war demands.

On January 1, 1944, enrollment was 1,826 as compared with a normal enrollment of 8,078. Between November, 1940, and December, 1945, approximately 3,600 students had left Harvard for war and 2,500 had returned.[8] The large losses were of course made up to some extent in the postwar years: enrollments rose far above normal. At one point veterans accounted for 80 percent of enrollment.[9]

Table 9-1 gives some statistics.

5. Quincy, *op. cit.,* ch. 28.
6. *Stewards' Quarter Bill Books.*
7. D. J. Pratt, *Statistics of Collegiate Education,* 1866, p. 2.
8. *Report of the President of Harvard College,* 1916-1917, p. 21; 1942-1943, pp. 5-7; 1946-1947, p. 151.
9. *Ibid.,* 1945-1946, pp. 6, 107; 1946-1947, p. 112; 1947-1948, p. 131.

Numbers of Graduates

At the celebration of Harvard's two hundred and fiftieth anniversary in 1886, the university released some interesting statistics on graduates *(A Bundle of Statistics Relating to the Graduates of Harvard University,* November 5-8, 1886).

The average annual number of graduates quadrupled during the college's second century and nearly tripled again during the first eighty-six years of the nineteenth century:

Number of Harvard Graduates

Century	Number of Graduates	Average per Year
17th	446	7.5
18th	3,069	30.69
19th	7,418	86.1

Yet the yearly average of graduates of the college revealed periods of decline as well as expansion:

Years	Number of Graduates	Years	Number of Graduates
1642-1650	23.9	1771-1780	40.8
1671-1680	4.9	1801-1816	46.5
1700-1710	12.3	1841-1850	62.8
1721-1730	36.5	1861-1870	100.0
1741-1750	23.9	1881-1886	198.5

By 1836, the college had 5,386 graduates. By 1886, it had 10,933 — a rise of more than 100 percent.

Historical Analysis of Enrollment Trends

Especially important in determining the trend of enrollment are costs, population movements (both for the nation and especially in the area of the college), competition of other institutions of higher learning, and the growth of the economy. On the basis of these and other relevant criteria, we may try to explain the rising enrollment at Harvard.

Table 9-1.

Enrollment and Costs to Students, Various Years

Year	Numbers*	Undergraduate	Graduate	Annual Cost to Students†
1636	0			
1652	50			
1712	54(44)			£16
1771-1772	172			£12 19s 6d
1819	383‡	272	111	$ 230.25§
1859-1860	839	431	408	273.00
1869-1870 (Beginning of Eliot period)	1,097	563	534	349.00
1909-1910 (Beginning of Lowell period)	4,046	2,265	1,781	324.00
1929-1930 (Near end of Lowell period)	8,312	3,202	5,110	1,100.00
1949-1950 (Near end of Conant period)	11,105	5,030	6,075	1,430.00
1967-1968 (15th year of Pusey period)	15,215	6,043¶	9,172	3,600.00

* Excluding Radcliffe, except 1967-1968.

† Coverage and estimates vary to some extent from totals given elsewhere in this volume.

‡ Another estimate is 249.

§ 1818

¶ This figure includes 1,209 Radcliffe students. The Harvard undergraduate enrollment was 4,834, a decline from inflated 1950 figures, which included overage veterans.

Through 1818, this represents the average cost of education. Thereafter, through 1900, it is the minimum stated by the college for a year's work. For 1909-1910 and 1919-1920, it includes tuition, medical fees, rooms, and board. From 1920, it includes tuition, medical fees, rooms, and board. From 1920 on, estimates include clothes, transportation, books, laundry, etc.

Sources: Foster, *op. cit.,* p. 35; *Harvard University Catalogue,* 1820, 1860 to 1968; *Report of the President of Harvard College,* 1830, 1841, 1850; *Stewards' Quarterly Bill Books; Official Register; University News Release,* October, 1967; *Treasurers' Journals; Treasurers' Ledgers; Steward's Reports;* F. Glimp to S. E. Harris, March 15, 1967

FROM THE BEGINNING TO THE CIVIL WAR

For the period before the Revolutionary War, we cannot say much, since too many of the necessary facts are not available. The rise of enrollment in the Puritan period was modest indeed — the French Wars in 1745 and 1756 tended to depress numbers, though the economic recovery after the wars brought rising numbers,[10] and even by 1771-1772 enrollment was roughly only 172. The percentage rise was large, but that of absolute numbers was not spectacular. The slow absolute gain of population is relevant here as well as the modest economic gains. Even by 1790, the population of the country was but four million — a gain in about 160 years equal to only 2 percent of the rise of the next 170 years. Moreover, competition was beginning to be felt. By 1769, Harvard had eight competitors of varying significance, beginning with William and Mary in 1692 and Yale in 1701, and ending with Dartmouth.

10. J. Qunicy, *op, cit.,* vol. II, p. 100.

Disapproval of Harvard's religious position also hurt enrollment. The impact of the celebrated itinerant preacher, George Whitefield, in the 1740s undoubtedly contributed to Harvard's losses. According to Whitefield, tutors "neglect to pray with, and examine the hearts of their pupils. Discipline is at too low an ebb. Bad books are fashionable among them. . . . As for the universities,. . .their light has become darkness; darkness that may be felt and is complained of by the most godly ministers."[11]

It has frequently (though inaccurately) been said that a rise of costs inevitably cuts enrollment. In 1762, the college strongly supported this viewpoint:

That if any addition be made to the sums paid for tuition, and at the expense of education be increased, it would probably cause many persons to send their children to the colleges of the other governments where they may be maintained and instructed with less charge. That this would not only be dishonorable to the Province, but also by carrying monies into the other governments, would in a course of years occasion a real loss, equal to the expense of additional buildings for the accommodation of the students here.[12]

A few statistics on costs for the eighteenth and early nineteenth centuries follows:

Annual Cost to Student

Years	Amount			Reason for increase
1712-1722	£14	0s	2d	
1742-1752	28	1	1	Inflation
1752-1762	11	1	1	Currency reform
1780-1781	634	8	0	Revolutionary War inflation
1781-1793	29	12	5	
1793-1806	$115.91			
1816-1826	$210.74			

11. *Ibid.*, pp. 40-42, 462.
12. Quoted in Pierce, *op. cit.*, p. 267.

Even in the years 1779 to 1819 Harvard's expansion was modest – an enrollment increase of 211 (123 percent) over the forty years. Rising competition was an adverse factor. Another adverse factor was the economic trend. The Revolutionary War had a serious impact on the economy, and for the first twenty years of the nineteenth century the economy showed little gains other than a substantial rise of population. In fact, the crude figures available reveal a substantial decline in real income per capita, for prices were roughly unchanged and population increased much more than income. Against these unfavorable factors we can put only the relatively unchanged cost of a Harvard College education.

The next period to be surveyed is the forty years before the Civil War. In these years, enrollment increased by about 450, or 119 percent – as in the earlier period, about 3 percent per year, noncompounded. This was a period of great economic advance, with income rising about twice as much as population; the real income gain is still greater when correction is made for a decline of prices of about one-third. The large population rise, the gain of real income per capita, and the stability of college costs (though a rise when corrected for the general decline of prices) all contributed to rising enrollment. Yet the increase in numbers at Harvard was but one-half that of the rise of population in the nation and in the Northeast.

THE IMPACT OF THE CIVIL WAR

On the whole, the Civil War does not seem to have reduced enrollment substantially. The university authorities were inclined to seek exemption of students. E. R. Hoar, a member of the corporation, in particular, pressed the university and the state attorney general for exemption for college students. The attorney general and the governor were fearful that any general exemption would arouse hostility against the college, and the governor hesitated to commit himself. An acting president apparently said "The students of Harvard College are too valuable food for powder and ball."

On October 1st, 1862, the governor wrote to Acting President Peabody apprising him of his reluctance to assess college student's relation to the draft. But he offered his own view:

Such exemption cannot be successfully pleaded. . .In the absence, or in advance, of any specific case of a student of the college being drafted and exemption refused, and with so long a margin of possibility or probability that no student may be drafted at all, I feel unwilling to bring the question before the Supreme Court, ex parte. [13]

In the generation before the Civil War, Harvard had made substantial gains, while others had not done so well. During the war Harvard's enrollment continued to rise substantially; that of the other eleven institutions of higher learning in New England actually declined. In 1860-1870, the pre-Eliot decade, enrollment rose an average of 3 percent.

Despite the Civil War, the economy grew in the 1860s. The increase in costs per student was substantial, though less than that in prices; that is to say, a college education had become somewhat cheaper relative to the general price level. The cost of a Harvard education declined 9 percent. But this was more than offset by a 15 percent reduction of real per capita income. In other words, a Harvard education had become somewhat more expensive in relation to the real income of the American people.

Despite this fact and in contrast to the preceding forty years, enrollment increased almost twice as much as the rise of the population in the Northeast and somewhat more than the nation's population, and this despite rising competition. The gain of Harvard enrollment, relative to population trends in the Northeast, was four times as great as in the preceding forty years.

THE ELIOT PERIOD (1869 to 1909)

Now to the crucial Eliot period, when Harvard established its unique position in numbers and prestige. Enrollment figures reveal the remarkable advance: despite increasingly stiff competition, enrollment rose by 269 percent, or about 3,000, in these forty years — a rise that was twice that of population, relatively, and 2 2/3 times that of the Northeastern population. The enrollment gain even outstripped the 3 percent average per year of the post-Revolutionary period. The Eliot figure was almost 7 percent per year.

A favorable factor was the great economic advance during this period. Despite a 21-percent price decline,[14] total income rose 2 1/3 times as much as population. The real per capita income, corrected for the price decline, grew by the large amount of 95 percent.[15] Relative stability of student costs and the great advance of the graduate schools were important contributory factors. Higher education had become a much less costly service by 1910 than in 1870. It was likely to appeal increasingly to the middle income group.

THE LOWELL PERIOD (1910 to 1930)

These years, roughly the Lowell period, also witnessed large rises in enrollment — even larger vis-à-vis population than during the Eliot period — but the average annual gain was less, 5 as against 6 to 7 percent. This was a period of very large increases in costs to the student — 240 percent, compared to a wholesale price rise of roughly 25 percent and a consumer price rise of 25 to 70 percent, depending on the index used. Meanwhile, in this period of rapid economic advance, income (corrected for population change) was increasing 82 percent. This rising real income per capita tended to bring more students within the Harvard's range, but these gains were more than nullified by the rise of costs. In view of these price and income trends, the 105 percent increase of enrollment was

---

13. Commonwealth of Massachusetts, Executive Department, to Reverend A. P. Peabody, October 1, 1862; Provost Marshall's Office, 4th Congressional District, to President Thomas Hill, July 20, 1863; E. R. Hoar to the Reverend Dr. Hill, September 15, 1862; J. Clarke to President of Harvard College, October 26, 1861; E. R. Hoar to Reverend Dr. Hill, (date not given).

14. Three indices yield varying results. A decline of 21 percent and rises of 6 and ½ of 1 percent.
15. This is reduced to 66 percent on the assumption of a 6 percent price rise. Two indices give different results.

striking indeed. Here the unusual national rise of interest in higher education is especially relevant.

In the early 1920s the college imposed a limitation of enrollment: 1,000 for the entering freshman class. A committee examining this restriction noted especially the shortage of faculty and of classrooms, and also the adverse effects on quality of large classes. Despite the substantial increases in faculty, the student-faculty ratios had not greatly improved in the preceding twenty years. Limitation of numbers was gaining support at most good institutions.[16]

THE CONANT PERIOD (1930 to 1950)

Trends in the period roughly covering the Conant administration are interesting. The Conant policy on tuition was in the Eliot rather than the Lowell tradition. The cost rise for students was held to 30 percent – a surprisingly small amount for a period when the wholesale price level rose by 84 percent, consumer prices by 43 percent and per capita income by 217 percent. A Harvard education had again become a bargain, especially when compared with the best measure of capacity to pay, per capita income. Despite the Great Depression, the net improvement of per capita income, corrected for price change and rise of personal taxes, was 46 percent, an indication of a greatly improved economic situation.

In these years the over-all rise of enrollment was modest in relation to population growth, the increased capacity to pay and the "cheapness" of the Harvard charge. In the post World War II period a large escalation of college population had emerged, and the outstanding institutions of higher learning increasingly treated unusual demands for entry by improving the quality of the entrants rather than by increasing their numbers greatly.

RECENT YEARS

From 1949 to 1968, primarily Pusey years, the costs of a Harvard education rose greatly – an average of about 8 percent of a year, especially through a

---

16. *Report of the Special Committee Appointed to Consider the Limitation of Numbers, 1926.*

substantial rise in tuition charges. About two-thirds of the increase of costs could be related to general inflationary forces and one-third to a rise of payment for services tied to higher real incomes. The exploitation of Harvard teachers had reached a point by the early 1950s where the pressure to raise salaries and tuition became irresistable.

In this period the rise of costs roughly matched that of per capita disposable income, i. e., income after payment of direct taxes. Hence, the burden of financing a Harvard education had not increased. Despite the stability of the real burden, demand for higher education greatly increased – a trend related partly to the rising interest of America in higher education generally and in Harvard in particular. Although undergraduate enrollment actually dropped, this is explained primarily by the large veteran enrollment in 1949-1950. But graduate enrollment continued to rise. Harvard's policy was to exploit rising demand by increasing the charges and improving the quality of its student body.

Graduate Enrollment

A large part of the explanation of the rise of enrollment in the nineteenth and twentieth centuries has been the blossoming of the graduate schools. In 1830-1960 graduate enrollment rose more than undergraduate. In percentages, the rise of graduate enrollment exceeded that of the college, though not between 1930 and 1960.

There were no graduate schools in the eighteenth century. The first hint of one came in 1772, when Ezekiel Hersey donated funds for a professorship of anatomy and physics. In 1782, with supplementary financing by the college, the post was filled. The three medical school professors who taught in the last part of the eighteenth century had no regular salaries, but depended on fees.

By 1819-1820, graduate schools accounted for 111 of 383 students, or 29 percent. But until the latter part of the nineteenth century, these graduate schools were really professional schools. It was only under Eliot that the professional schools became true

Table 9-2.

Annual Average Rise in Enrollment Harvard University,
1830 to 1960, 1900 to 1960 and 1930 to 1960

Years	University		College		University Except College	
	Numbers	Percent*	Numbers	Percent	Numbers	Percent
1830-1960	84	2.0	33	13	51	30
1900-1960	120	3.0	45	2.2	75	3.5
1930-1960	100	1.2	46	1.4	54	1.1

* These percentage figures are averages. Thus for 1900 to 1960 the rise of enrollment was 180 percent. Hence the average for 60 years was 3 percent. But in 60 years an annual gain of 1 3/4 percent would, if *compounded*, yield a rise of 180 percent.

Source: *Harvard University Catalogues.* My calculations.

graduate schools. Between 1850 and 1870 professional and graduate enrollment was close to 50 percent of total enrollment. By the end of the Eliot regime graduate enrollment had declined to 44 percent, but after World War I it rose substantially above the 50 percent level.

Eliot was a strong supporter of the graduate school, and though the proportion of graduate students declined in his administration, there was a very large absolute rise of graduate as well as undergraduate enrollment. A large decline of medical and dental enrollment contributed to the relative reduction of graduate students. Here the issue was standards, and the president was prepared to accept a 50 percent reduction in medical school attendance as the price for revolutionizing medical education and greatly improving standards. Another striking aspect of Eliot's period was the great emphasis on graduate arts and science. Enrollment rose from 9 in 1869 to 425 in 1910.

One does not always find the results expected. Lowell's major interest was in the undergraduate, yet it was particularly in the Lowell period that graduate enrollment escalated. Whereas undergraduate enrollment rose by less than one-half, graduate enrollment trebled. These trends can be explained by various factors. One was the restrictive admission policies for undergraduates. A second was the increasingly widespread interest in graduate instruction. From 1910 to 1930 master's degrees granted nationally rose from 2,100 to 15,000 and Ph.D.s from 440 to 2,300. By 1940 the totals were 26,700 and 3,290.[17] A third factor was the growing autonomy of the administrations of the graduate schools.

GRADUATE ENROLLMENT BY SCHOOLS

Table 9-3 gives the graduate enrollment total, and by schools, over ten-year periods from 1800 to 1960 and for 1967.[18]

17. B. Berelson, *Graduate Education in the United States,* 1960, p. 26.
18. I have not reproduced material on the number of degrees granted by schools. (These statistics are available from catalogues or various dates, Report of the President of Harvard College); In 1849-1850 the university conferred 177 degrees, of which the B.A.'s numbered 65; M.A.'s (really unearned), 40; medicine, 33; law, 36; divinity, 3. By 1930 there were 26 different degrees conferred on 1,300 students and many more sub-degrees (15 variants of the B.S. alone). F. C. Waite of Western Reserve estimated the degrees before 1801 as follows, though the accuracy of the estimates has been questioned: Harvard, 6,489; William and Mary, 39; Yale, 4,134; Princeton, 1,427.

Table 9-3.

Enrollment, Graduate and Professional Schools, by Ten Year Periods, 1800-1960[a]

Year	Divinity	Law	Medicine	Public Health	Dentistry	Engineering and Science	Business	Design and Architecture	Education	Public Administration	Arts and Science	Total Graduate and Professional
1800	33	13	54									100
1810												
1820												
1830	54	27	91									172
1840	20	85	87									195
1850	17	94	127									277[b]
1860	21	166	140									408
1870[d]	36	120	306		16	52					c	534
1880[d]	12	156	241		18	37					c	
1890[d]	35	254	290		35	65					107	808
1900[d]	27	613	558		131	495					326	2,189
1910[e]	49	763	279		87	100	78				425	1,781
1920	58	879	419		189	126	—	65			531	2,739
1930	85	1,639	516	21	108	283	1,011	137	289		945	5,110
1940	71	1,390	522	85	159	155	929	95	235	14	1,082	4,772
1950	107	1,530	502	94	51	—	1,361	187	213	84	1,827	6,075
1960	204	1,601	506	113	52	—	1,591	212	502	66	1,780	6,737
1967	248	1,707	556	165	51	—	1,904	265	479	100	3,201[f]	9,172[f]

a   I have not itemized students in the Veterinary School, Bussey Institute, Junior Fellows, Nieman Fellows, and Trade Union Fellows, but they are included in the totals.

b   Includes 34 special students attending Scientific School and 4 resident graduates.

c   President Eliot announced that there were 8 graduate students in 1868-1869, 28 in 1872-1873, and 67 in 1877-1878.

d   See C. W. Eliot Memorandum . . . Salaries, April 1903, for some differences.

e   For 1909 and enrollment in other schools, see Harvard University History. . . . Fees, 1909.

f   Includes Radcliffe

Sources: Harvard University Catalogues; Reports of the President of Harvard College; Samuel Eliot Morison (ed.), The Development of Harvard University, 1869-1929, 1930, p. 455; released from the University News Office, October, 1967.

In 1800, medicine, divinity (theology), and law were in the lead in that order. By the mid nineteenth century law and medicine accounted for 91 percent of graduate and professional students. But new schools emerged, and by 1960 law and medicine together held less than one-third, graduate arts and science more than one-quarter, and business and education together almost one-third.

Some Variables: Costs to Students, Population, Competition

Table 9-4 presents enrollment trends and related variables for the years 1771-1960. A close correlation between enrollment increases and rise of costs is not suggested, for reasons which are made clear in the discussions of the Eliot, Lowell and Conant periods above. One particular aspect of costs, however – the provision of housing – has a special impact.

Inadequate housing tends to limit enrollment. Increasingly students want to live away from home. They want to get away from parental pressures, they learn (or think they can learn) more by living at the college – and with higher incomes they can afford the additional expense. Not undergraduates alone but graduate students, especially the married ones, want more housing provided by the institutions of higher learning. The required funds are not easy to get, especially if the institution is not prepared to borrow from the government and pass on the costs to the student. Even without charging capital costs to undergraduates, the average annual rooming cost for each student is on the order of $500 per year.

As early as the 1920s President Lowell tied restrictions of enrollment to inadequacy of college housing. In the later 1930s President Conant—stressing the rising demand for a Harvard College education, the increased desire for living in, the improved economic situation, the wider geographic base of Harvard students and the reduced mortality of freshmen—concluded that the solution lay in a restriction of the college entering class to a thousand students. Provision of additional dormitories proved less difficult than Conant had anticipated, however.

As population and wealth increase, enrollment should rise. Only an intensification of competition should preclude such a trend. Yet from 1652 to 1693 enrollment was almost unchanged, despite a rise in the Massachusetts population from twenty thousand to fifty thousand and despite Harvard's monopolistic position.

In a review of Samuel Eliot's *Sketch of Harvard College*,[19] one writer was critical of Harvard's policies. As evidence of failure, he commented on the number of graduates. Between 1815 and 1824 there was an average of sixty-two. In the 1840s there were only fifty-eight.

"Yet in the interval between these two periods, the population of Boston had increased from 40,000 to nearly 120,000; and the increase in wealth and general intelligence, and the desire for a thorough education for the young, have been at least in equal proportion." In this view, numbers would have been at least half again as large in the 1840s between 1815 and 1824 if the task had been well performed.

President F. A. P. Barnard of Columbia College was disturbed when he found that the ratio of New England college attendance to New England population had declined from 1 in 1,294 in 1838, to 1 in 1,689 in 1855, and 1 in 1,927 in 1869. In these years, the population increased relatively 5 times as rapidly in New England as enrollment in twelve New England colleges.

But Harvard stood out in these tabulations. She alone accounted for more than the increase of the combined twelve. . . Harvard had, he [Barnard] *remarked, been progressively more and more completely identifying herself with the cause of new education.*[20]

(Enrollment figures vis-à-vis population vary, of course, according to the period and region considered.)

Fear of competitors kept tuition down throughout Harvard's history. It was generally believed that higher tuition meant reduced enrollment. But this is not

---

19. *North American Review*, 1849, pp. 102-125.
20. James, *op. cit.*, vol. I, pp. 206-207.

Table 9-4.

Enrollment Trends and Related Variables, 1771 to 1960

Years	(1) Percentage of Enrollment Increase at Harvard	(2) Percentage of Rise in Costs to Harvard Students	(3) Percentage of U.S. Population Increase	(4) Percentage of Population Increase, Northeast, Middle Atlantic and New England States	(5) Massachusetts population	(6) Percentage of Income Increase	(7) Competition (No. of Institutions of Higher Learning)
1. 1771-1819	123	Little Change			1770 235,000 1790 378,000 1810 472,000	—	9 By Rev. War
2. 1819-1860	119	Little Change	236	243	1820 523,000 1860 1,231,000	478	280 1776-1865
3. 1860-1870	30	30	27	16	1870 1,457,000	53	
4. 1870-1910	269	No Significant Change	132	102	1910 3,366,000	307	588 1865-1915
5. 1910-1930	105	240	33	33	1930 4,249,000	142	
6. 1930-1950	34	30	23	15	1950 4,690,100	290	
7. 1950-1960	1	67	19	13	1960 5,142,000	71	

Sources: Col. 1, 2, Earlier tables, with further calculations. 3, 4, 5, 6, *Historical Statistics of the United States, 1789-1945; Statistical Abstract, 1962; Economic Report of the President*, January 1, 1964. (My calculations.) Col. 7, J.B. Sears, *Philanthropy in the History of American Education,* 1922, esp. pp. 10, 36.

always accurate: higher costs attract many who assume that higher prices mean a better product. In a famous paper early in the twentieth century Charles Francis Adams urged higher tuition.

Degrees, in his view, have varying values. Harvard holds a recognized place, and the degrees of others: "have not at all the same market value as that of Harvard. . . .Some degrees if not legal tender are at least current money. Students everywhere will end off with a shorter or longer course at Harvard to receive the educational mint-mark or tower-stamp."[21]

Colleges competed strenuously for students, and in 1851, in a presentation to the Legislature, the corporation dwelt on the effects of rising competition upon enrollment. Fifty years earlier, they reminded the Legislature, there had been only 25 colleges in the country, some of the inoperative. Now there were 120. This factor, together with higher admission standards, later age of entry, and the high cost of living in Cambridge, was adversely affecting enrollment at Harvard.[22]

In 1840 President Quincy commented:

In every section of the country, which is great either from extent, or numbers, or wealth, there is a natural ambition to concentrate within its own immediate vicinity or influence, as far as possible, all the great institutions of society; . . . But the great interests of the public, in respect to the advancement of the intellectual power, require a conduct regulated by different principles.[23]

One aspect of competition among institutions for students—through victories on the athletic field—has been of much interest in recent years. Eliot compared Harvard and Yale's athletic achievements and enrollments 1891 through 1901 and concluded:

. . . Looking at the whole period, the Freshman Class at Harvard gained a much larger percentage than the Freshman Class at Yale, although Yale has been decidedly more successful in the athletic sports, and particularly in football and rowing, which are the sports in which colleges and schools, and the general public take the strongest interest.[24]

Admission and Rejections

Enrollment depends upon the numbers admitted and how long the students stay. As has been noted, the rise of enrollment was not large in the first two hundred years, despite the early age of students at entry.

Morison reports that the median age of entering freshmen was 17 under Dunster (1640-1654) and little more than 15 under Chauncy (1654-1672). It averaged 15.75 in 1673-1707, returned to 17 years in 1769 and stayed at that point during the rest of the century.[25]

Even as late as 1848 the president complained of the immaturity of college students. But the average age of freshmen tended to rise to 17 years, 11 months, between 1856 and 1860 and to over 19 between 1886 and 1900.[26]

As early as the mid-1640s the college set admission requirements,[27] and throughout most of its history, students have had to take examinations as a condition for entry. Yet Harvard was not inclined, certainly before Eliot's days, to overstress the point that Harvard was to be a haven for men of the highest scholarly aptitude and attainments.[28]

In the early 1800s, with the increased resources of public schools and the rising availability of students

21. "The Harvard Tuition Fee: Its Proposed Increase," reprinted from the *Harvard Graduates Magazine*, 1904, esp. pp. 15-17.
22. *Memorial. . . .Privileges of Harvard College. . .to the Legislature*, January 17, 1851, pp. 7-9.
23. J. Quincy, *op. cit.*, vol. II, p. 452.
24. *Report of the President of Harvard College*, 1900-1901, pp. 15-17.
25. Morison, *Harvard College in the Seventeenth Century*, pp. 75-76, 450.
26. *Report of the President of Harvard College*, 1847-1848, p. 14; 1899-1900, p. 339; 1900-1901, p. 309.
27. For a discussion of early requirements, see *Admission to Harvard College*, A Report by the Special Committee College Admission Policy, 1960, pp. 2-3.
28. *Reports and other Papers Relating to Harvard College During the Administration of President Jared Sparks . . .* , p. 49.

from the West and South, the reservoir for Harvard students grew. At various times the issue of making entrance exams more difficult arose. Thus in 1836 a committee of the college proposed to raise the standard of scholarship. "by introducing gradually . . . a greater degree of exactness and thoroughness into the examination for admission." But the committee was fearful of the results on enrollment.[29]

An overseers, committee in 1859, which also seemed to favor more difficult examinations, was nevertheless concerned over the effects on enrollment. But this committee insisted that the "object of the university should be the production of the highest scholarship consistent with its general prosperity, rather than an accumulation of numbers."[30]

In 1889 Eliot was still concerned over the small number of public schools that prepared students for Harvard. Only 97 out of 352 students admitted (27½ percent)came from free public schools.[31]

Meanwhile, Eliot was steadily guiding a revision of admission requirements in the direction of flexibility and quality, allowing a much greater choice of subjects, but requiring higher levels of performance.[32] By 1898, the college had to choose between those who could pay the bill and those who met all the prerequisites.[33]

After the revolutionary Eliot reforms, other changes were made which tended to increase the sources from which Harvard could draw students. The first was the admission of special students—largely students with ability who had not specifically prepared for Harvard but who were given an opportunity to reveal their ability and achievements at Harvard.

An important innovation was the New Plan for Admission introduced for the class of 1911. This plan had many advantages. First, it allowed the schools greater freedom in providing a curriculum without excessive emphasis on college requirements for admission. Second, attention was diverted from quantity (the number of exams passed) to quality. Third, the recognition of schools that might provide students for Harvard was greatly expanded.

Examinations under the New Plan rapidly became increasingly important. Admission under the New Plan jumped from 14 percent in the class of 1911 to 34 percent in the class of 1913.[34]

Another important reform was the admission of the top seventh of high school graduating classes. In this manner Harvard opened its doors to students with high achievement everywhere. In 1922-1923, the college accepted 212 freshmen under these conditions, or almost 25 percent of the entering class.[35]

With this liberalization of entrance requirements, and in part for this reason, the college was also confronted with the problem of excess demands.

Unavailability of staff, dormitory space, and academic plant brought serious restrictions on admissions in the 1920s. The disposition was to keep up quality, avoid overcrowding, and restrict entry. The professional schools were disposed to increase admissions, but only after the required resources became available.

In the college in 1928 the disposition increasingly was "to make its choice on all the evidence it can procure." The college considered the curriculum of the secondary school, the student's record in his senior year at school—a helpful guide in estimating his college performance—and aptitude tests. The trend was away from emphasis on acquired knowledge. It was essential to consider the student's apparent capacity to reason and apply his knowledge. For some graduate schools, entrance requirements were raised.

29. *Report of the Committee Appointed by the College Faculty to consider in what manner the examination shall be conducted for the admission of the next class in the college. . ., May 7, 1836.*

30. *Overseers Committee for Visiting Harvard College,* January, 1859.

31. C. W. Eliot, "The Gap Between Common Schools and Colleges," in *C. W. Eliot Papers,* pp. 198-199.

32. For details, see *Harvard College Reports* in Harvard University Archives., pp. 93-97.

33. See *Admission to Harvard College,* 1960, pp. 4-5.

34. *Harvard University: History, Constitution, Organization. . .1910; Report of the Committee on Admission on the New Plan of Admission,* 1914.

35. *Report of the President of Harvard College,* 1922-1923, p. 6; 1929-1930, pp. 333-338.

Applications for enrollment increased so sharply that despite rising enrollments, the upward trend of the percentage of rejections is clear.[36]

Percentage of Harvard College Applicants Rejected by Class

1847-1848	16*
1910	22
1930	20
1944	25
1946	45
1955	34
1963	62
1964	70
1969	79

*Rough estimate based on 1849-1850 college enrollment.

Years at College and Attrition

Enrollment is largely determined by the number of years a student must stay at a college to earn his degree. Eliot in particular tried to encourage graduation in three years (and to lower the entering age from 19 to 18). He was supported by some of the professional schools which wanted access to students at an earlier age. Eliot considered it important that otherwise "the average college graduate who fits himself well for any of the learned professions, including teaching, can hardly begin to support himself before he is twenty-seven years old."[37]

Enrollment was clearly kept down in the Eliot period as the practice of graduating in three years became more popular. In the class of 1894, 5 percent graduated in three years; in the class of 1906, a record 36 percent. But President Lowell was less disposed to push graduation in three years and the percentage declined.[38]

In the professional schools, the tendency was to increase the years of instruction and thus to raise the numbers enrolled. One observer in the 1890s noted "the time of study in the professional schools now needed to equip the student for his work is larger by one year at least, often by two years, than was deemed necessary thirty years ago."[39]

Enrollment is also greatly affected by the rate of attrition. When admission policy is faulty, one effect is likely to be a large number of drop-outs. At Harvard, the proportion that continues an education to the senior year or to graduation has tended to rise over the years, though unevenly. The following statistics show the proportion of the senior to the freshman class over a period of 140 years.[40] (The ratio of graduates to freshmen is somewhat smaller).

Percentage of Seniors to Freshmen

Year	Percentage
1803	107
1810	81
1820	69
1840	57
1850	75
1890	86
1900	62
1910	48
1916	62
1920	51
1938	75
1940	75
1951	75

Sources: Generally *Reports of the President of Harvard College,* occasionally *Harvard University Catalogues.* (My calculations)

Statistics for earlier years are sporadic. George Ticknor estimated that in the seventeen years ending 1824, the whole number "of students expelled, rusticated, dismissed and suspended, was three hundred

36. *Ibid.,* 1847-1848, p. 14; 1909-1910, pp. 254-256; 1929-1930, pp. 333-338; 1945-1946, p. 146; *Admission to Harvard College,* 1960, p. 47; *Admission and Scholarship Committee,* 1959-1960, p. 2; *Report of the President of Harvard College,* 1964-1965, p. 2.
37. C. W. Eliot, "School Programmes Be Shortened and Enriched," in *C. W. Eliot Papers.*
38. Morison (ed.), *The Development of Harvard University,* pp. xliii-xlvii.

39. *Four American Universities,* p. 10.
40. For a somewhat different approach, tabulating all law school students of 1870-1871, 1880-1881 and 1890-1891 and those present only part of the year, see F. Bolles, *Harvard University,* 2d. anniversary ed., 1892, p. 33.

and fifty-four," compared with a generous estimate of 1400 admitted. This is indeed evidence of waste.[41]

President Eliot was also greatly concerned over the rate of attrition. In the decade 1870 to 1880 the losses were 9 percent of enrollment, half due to faulty scholarship and half to other causes. In 1876-1877 the college "suffered abnormally net reductions, i.e., losses from their original number." Again in 1900-1901, the loss of sixty freshmen, roughly 11 percent of the class, was an occasion of comment by the dean, who also noted that the survival rate of public school students was higher than that of private school students, though the record of Boston schools was not good.[42]

If the percentage passing the general examinations or the number receiving honors through general examinations is accepted as a criterion, the quality of students seems to have improved steadily in the 1920s and 1930s. In the 1920s, the percentage who failed tended to deline, with an average of 8.8 percent; and the percentage of honors based on examinations rose with an average of 23.7 percent. In the 1930s the failures averaged only 3.7 percent, while the honors based on general examinations were up to 36 percent.[43]

The survival rate has tended upward though unevenly, especially in recent years. To some extent the results are influenced by shifts in the rate of enrollment. When the rise is very rapid, the ratio of seniors to freshmen tends to be small. In 1803, on the other hand, the senior class was actually larger than the freshman class, an outcome that may be explained by an unusually small freshman enrollment. The low figure for 1919-1920 is related to the reduction in the senior class arising from World War I.

Another approach is to compare enrollment and degrees granted. A large ratio of degrees to enrollment suggests a high survival rate and, presumably, smart admission policies.

Over the nation, graduates tend to average about 10 percent of enrollment. At Harvard over a period of sixty years (1830 to 1890) the ratios do not vary greatly. The maximum is 14 percent in 1890; the minimum, 10 percent in 1840.[44]

In the earlier period of Harvard's history the statistical deficiencies rule out any definitive treatment of this problem. Morison, however, estimates the number of A.B.s from 1642 to 1700 at 446 and the nongraduates at 97, yielding a graduate/nongraduate ratio of 4.6. This seems like a very high ratio of graduates to enrollment (80 percent); apparently the nongraduate estimate is low. The average for one year in each decade of the period between 1830 and 1890 was roughly 50 percent of original enrollment graduating.[45]

In the 1930s President Conant interested himself in reducing the failures in the freshman class by improving admission procedures. Freshman failures dropped from 30 percent in the pre-1938 period to 22 percent in 1938.[46] The law school, disturbed by the fact that failures had risen to 30 percent, began in the 1930s to study the correlation between the performance of law school students and the colleges from which they had obtained their degrees. The improved admission policy, related to the fruits of this study, cut failures to 20 percent. The medical school over the years has also increased educational requirements for entry and gradually squeezed out the marginal students.[47]

---

41. G. Ticknor, *Remarks on Changes Lately Proposed or Adopted in Harvard University*, 1825, p. 10.
42. *Report of the President of Harvard College*, 1876-1877, p. 27; 1880-1881, p. 21; *Report of Dean Briggs*, 1900-1901, p. 93.
43. Based on *Report of the President of Harvard College*, 1922-1923 through 1939-1940.
44. Degrees from *Quinquennial Catalogues* and *Reports of the President of Harvard College*.
45. If 50 percent graduate and assuming a constant absolute enrollment, the ratio of graduates to enrollment is 12½ percent. The actual average was 12 percent.
46. *Report of the President of Harvard College*, 1937-1938, pp. 194-197.
47. *Ibid;*, 1943-1944, p. 170.

PART

2

FACULTY

10

Faculty: Growth and Structure

Trends in Faculty Growth

The growth of the faculty and its changing structure throw some light on the development of Harvard. At first the growth was slow. In 1643, the president and two fellows, as tutors were then called, were responsible for the instruction, but even at the end of the Puritan period seventy years later, the number had increased only to three fellows and the first professor still had not been appointed. As late as 1829-1830, after almost two centuries of Harvard's history, the number of faculty for the whole university—the professional schools had begun to make an impression— was 25: 17 professors, 1 lecturer, 2 tutors and 5 instructors.[1] At this early date in the development of the professional schools, they accounted for 11 professors. (Note the double counting, for by eliminating duplications, we obtain a total of 17.) Divinity accounted for 4; medicine, 5; law, 2; and the college, 11. From 1810 to 1826, the college appointed 26 professors, but 9 were not new. By 1840, President Quincy counted 3 professors of law, 7 of medicine, 10 other professors, 5 instructors, and 7 proctors.[2]

At the midnineteenth century, college authorities boasted of the growth of the faculty in the preceding fifty years.[3] In 1801, the faculty had consisted of 6 professors and 4 tutors, with 1 professor in each of six departments inclusive of two medical departments. But in 1851, there were 10 academic professors, and two unfilled vacancies, each at the head of a department, 4 tutors, and 3 instructors, "thus ensuring the thoroughness of teaching in as many studies as can be usefully embraced in a course which continues no longer than four years . . . Moreover, 17 courses of lectures are given during the year in advanced courses. . . . "

The corporation reflected also on the great advance in the quality of instruction: ". . . in fact, the quality of the instruction has improved to a degree which can scarcely be explained to persons who have not made it a particular subject of inquiry. . . ." Aside from the 12 academic professors the university could boast of 13 professors in the four professional schools, three of which did not exist in 1800. But growth was spasmodic. The total number of professors was 19, 23, 15, and 21 in the years 1839-1840, 1849-1850, 1859-1860, and 1869-1870.

Growth accelerated after the first quarter of the nineteenth century, and especially following the

---

1. I have relied primarily on the *Harvard University Catalogue* for estimating the numbers and ranks of faculty. But the treasurers' and presidents' reports also frequently give the faculty numbers. At times estimates diverge, though the explanation is generally either that some faculty are counted more than once if a member of more than one faculty or that the estimate may be made at different times of the academic year.
2. Josiah Quincy, *The History of Harvard University*, 1840, vol. II, pp. 555–556, 635–636.

3. *Memorial Concerning the Recent History and the Constitutional Rights and Privileges of Harvard College Presented . . . to the Legislature, January 17, 1851*, 3d. ed., pp. 10–11, 15.

inauguration of President Eliot in 1869. A concise presentation of growth in the first 200 years as against that of the next 50 years is revealed by a document presented in conjunction with the 250th anniversary proceedings (1886) of the university.[4]

Growth of Harvard through 1885

	Up to 1836	Up to 1885
Presidents	16	22
Fellows, beginning with Hobart, 1707	56	73
Treasurers	13	20
Appointments to professorships, etc.	63	279
Appointments to tutorships, beginning with Flynt, 1699	117	196
Appointments as instructors	10	220
Appointments as lecturers	3	99
Appointments as librarians, beginning with Eliot, 1766	18	26
Professors holding office	17	90
Tutors holding office	3	3
Instructors holding office	4	57

In the years 1836 through 1885, the number of professors appointed equaled 4½ times the appoint-ments in the first 200 years or an annual rate of 18 times that of the first 200 years. The number of professors holding office was more than 5 times the 1836 figure in 1885. The rise of appointments of instructors and lecturers was even greater than for professors.

In 250 years, there were 22 presidents, or an average life of 11 years; 20 treasurers, or an average life of 12 years. There were 26 librarians in 120 years, or an average life of 5 years.

It was especially with the ascendency of President Eliot that the rate of growth rose in a spectacular manner. There were 70 professors in 1869-1870, 123 in 1909-1910. By the end of the Eliot regime, the number of full professors was almost 6 times that at the beginning of his administration. That the magic of Eliot was more effective than the improvement of the economy is easily to be shown.

The biographer of Charles Eliot reminds us that the faculty of most institutions of higher learning at the time of the accession of Eliot generally consisted of between 10 and 15 men, the lower limit determined by the requirements of a four-year curriculum and the upper by budgeting restraints. Harvard had the largest number with a faculty exceeding twenty.[5]

Table 10-1.

Percent of Professors, Population, Enrollment, Total Income, Per Capita Income, and Prices by Ten-Year Periods, 1869-1970 Through 1909-1910 and 1869 Through 1909

10-Year Periods	Professors	Population	Enrollment	National Income	Per Cap. Income	Prices
1870s	143	26	24	5	$ - 16	−24
1880s	27	26	53	43	43	− 2
1890s	42	21	97	44	20	− 1
1900s	30	21	−1	87	49	+25
1869-1909	486	132	269	297	70	− 9

Sources: *Harvard University Catalogues* and *Historical Statistics of the United States 1789-1945* (my calculations.)

4. *A Bundle of Statistics Relating to the Graduates of Harvard University*, November 5–8, 1886.

5. Henry James, *Charles W. Eliot: President of Harvard University*, 1930, vol. I, p. 213.

What is especially striking is the tremendous growth of faculty as evidenced in the percentage rise in the number of professors in the 1870s, a decade when the improvement of income was disappointingly small and the standard of living (cf. income per capita and price movements) improved very little. In the 1880s, with a percentage increase of professors less than one-fifth as large as in the 1870s, the relative gain of income was 8 to 9 times as great as in the 1870s, and the improvement of the standard of living much greater than in the 1870s. From 1880 to 1910, the total faculty grew from 150 to 618.

In the first ten years of the Eliot administration the number of professors increased 6 times as much as enrollment, but in the 1880s and 1890s the percentage rise of professors in ten-year periods lagged behind that in enrollment. In the 1900s (1900 to 1909), and in 1869 to 1909, the whole Eliot period, the number of professors increased more than enrollment.

I would draw the following conclusions from the spectacular developments under Eliot. The major gains do not check too well with economic developments, although an improving economy contributed to them. The genius of Eliot was decisive. The rise of the numbers of professors was 3 to 4 times that of population, and more than 1 4/5 times that of enrollment. The unusually rapid rise in the number of full professors in the first ten years resulted in heavy fixed charges which had to be covered by large rises of enrollment (until 1900), and increased proportions of junior faculty.

From 1880-1881 to 1905-1906, the faculty of the college rose by almost 2 times, but teachers of lower grade in this faculty by 9 times, a rise pointing to the progress of Eliot's policy of reducing the chores—e.g., grading papers. As might be expected, the rise of teachers in other departments exceeded substantially that in the college. In part the explanation was the large increase of *students* in other departments.[6]

Rise of students in the faculty of arts and sciences

1. Harvard college	1.3 times
2. Graduate school	8.2 times
3. Scientific school	12.6 times
Faculty arts and sciences (includes 1,2,3)	2.1 times

Over a period of twenty-five years—1881 to 1906—18 of 56 members in 1881 survived in the 1900 faculty then numbering 149.

Growth continued under Presidents Lowell and Conant in the forty years following the Eliot administration. An indication of the trends is given by the statistics for the College of Arts and Science. The faculty continued to grow at about 25 percent per decade, and even increased substantially in the Great Depression. The constraints imposed by the depression are reflected in the small rise of 15 percent in professors and associate professors in the 1930s. As we shall see, the college had to take account of economic pressures in slowing up promotions and removing many from the academic ladder.

In contrast to the 1930s, from 1940 to 1960 the rise of the number of professors and associate professors was 122 percent, with professors increasing from 45 percent of the faculty in 1940 to 64 percent in 1960.[7]

In the Eliot period, enrollment rose by 269 percent and the number of professors by 486 percent, a comparison suggesting a large improvement (decline) in the student-faculty ratio. These figures are of limited comparability because of changing definitions of a member of the faculty and because of trends in the structure of the faculty—e.g., the relative rise of junior members. Against the large rise of professors, we should consider the very large gains of junior members of the faculty, a phenomenon of the Eliot period.

6. W. C. Lane, *The University During the Last Twenty-Five Years*, 1906.

7. These statistics are subject to some reservations. By 1960, the number of teaching fellows (part student and part graduate student) had risen to 519, and were equal to 168 full-time equivalent faculty. (They are excluded from these totals.) However, in 1960 all instructors, since they were no longer technically members of the faculty--they were not eligible to go to faculty meetings--were excluded. Also see *Economic Status*, p. 22. The relevant table is deposited in the Harvard archives.

Faculty numbers in the professional schools seemed to increase more rapidly than in the college (arts and sciences). For example, from 1910-1911 to 1951-1952, the numbers of faculty in the college rose 2 times but from 1910-1911 to 1949-1950 the rise for the university exclusive of arts and science was 4 times.

Ratio of Students to Faculty

The ratio of students to faculty is an important index of the quality of education and of economical operation. This ratio rises as enrollment grows more than faculty. In periods when proliferation of courses prevails the result will be either increased teaching loads, or (more likely) reduction of the student-faculty ratio. Such a development is to be noted in the period 1869-1870 to 1889-1890 in Harvard College, a period during which Eliot greatly expanded the faculty, and in part in response to the needs of the elective system. The steady decline in the student-faculty ratio for the college is to be associated also with the rise of assistant professors and instructors on the faculty. The high cost of professors in a period of rapid expansion, and the increased emphasis on sparing professors chores, accounted for the reversal of the downward trend in the ratio of junior faculty members.[8]

From 1840 to 1900, the proportion of professors and associate professors (the latter of recent origin) to the total on the faculty in the university (generally inclusive of instructors) greatly declined. An important part of the explanation is the heavy recourse to junior appointments in the medical schools (and to some extent in the college). For the college, the percentage of professors and associate professors to the *total* faculty exclusive of teaching fellows was 54 in 1859-1860 and 64 in 1959-1960. By 1960, the college provided as mature a faculty as a hundred years earlier, and in addition relieved this faculty of heavy burdens through rising recourse to junior members, with the result that more time of the senior members was available for important teaching assignments and research. Under Eliot, with substantial fluctuations, the net change in the ratio of professors to faculty in the college was not large, though in the university the trend was clearly down, a decline that continued until 1900. But under Conant and Pusey the ratio of professors rose substantially.

The student-faculty ratio should be used with discretion. The large decline for the university student-faculty ratio, for example, is related to the changing faculty structure. Thus in 1829-1830 the university student-faculty ratio was 16½ to 1, and the proportion of professors to faculty was 68 percent. In 1949-1950, the ratio was 4 to 1 and the percentage of professors (and associate professors) was 16. Obviously, if the structure of the faculty were unchanged, the decline from 16-to-1 to 4-to-1 would reflect a great improvement in the faculty-student relationship. But with professors only about one-quarter as numerous relatively in the later years, the gains are greatly reduced if not wiped out.

Here I do not deal with the issue of the quality of each faculty member. Surely the average is more highly trained and much more productive today than 150 years ago. The smaller decline in the student-faculty ratio for the college reflects perhaps a greater improvement than the much larger reduction in the student-faculty ratio for the university, the main reason for this conclusion being that the ratio of professors to faculty remained relatively stable for the college.[9]

Two tables follow, one for the university and the second for the college. They give student-faculty ratios and the percentage of professors and associate professors to total faculty over much of Harvard's history.

---

8. *Report of the President of Harvard College,* 1895–1896, pp. 13–14.

9. Even the student-faculty ratio of the college is subject to reservations. For example, the large drop from 1940 to 1960 might be offset to some extent if allowance were made for Harvard's assumption of responsibilities for Radcliffe students in the 1940s. But it is not clear that this correction need be made since unofficially the Harvard faculty had taught Radcliffe students. Again, though I have tried to be consistent and included as faculty professors through instructors, this has not always been possible.

Table 10-2.

Enrollment, Faculty, Student-Faculty Ratio
Various Years, 1654-1950

Year	Number of Students	Number of Faculty Members	Student-Faculty Ratio	Percentage of Professor and Associate Professors of Faculty
1654	50-60	3-4	16 approx.	0
1809-1810	188	12	16	17
1829-1830	412	25	16 1/2	68
1839-1840	432	25	17	76
1849-1850	577	23	25	70
1859-1860	839	30	28	50
1869-1870	1,097	41	27	51
1879-1880	1,356	150	9	34
1889-1890	2,079	217	10	30
1899-1900	4,091	545	7 1/2	18
1909-1910	4,046	618	6 1/2	21
1919-1920	5,273	782	6 1/2	22
1929-1930	8,312			
1939-1940	8,379	2,104	4	19
1949-1950	11,105	2,714	4	16

Sources: Harvard University Catalogue, Report of the President of Harvard College, Report of the Treasurer of Harvard College, various years. My calculations.

Table 10-3.

**Harvard College, Student-Faculty Ratio, and Percentage of Professors
and Associate Professors through Instructors to Total Faculty,
1849-1960, Various Years.**

Year	Student-Faculty Ratio	Percentage of Professors and Associate Professors to Total Faculty
1849-1850	15	55 (6 of 11 professors also associated with other faculties)
1859-1860	18	54 (Based on 1856-1857)
1869-1870	27	54 (Based on 1866-1867)
1879-1880	16	38 (Based on 1876-1877)
1889-1890*	19	72 (Related to professors and asst. professors only)
1899-1900*	18	52
1929-1930*	13	49 (Through instructors)
1939-1940*	11	45 (Through instructors)
1959-1960*	9	64 (Excludes instructors and lower ranks)

*Includes Graduate School of Arts and Sciences and Lawrence Scientific School (until closed) and undergraduates.

Sources: Harvard University Catalogue, Report of the President of Harvard College, Report of the Treasurer of Harvard College, various years, 1959-1960, Dean Bundy.

By 1899 President Eliot claimed:

Statistics show the fear to be unwarranted that the recent growth in the number of students has not been accompanied by a corresponding growth in the number of professors and instructors. The teaching force has, as a matter of fact, grown proportionately stronger in numbers, and the average number of years out of college of the members of the Faculty has decreased only seven-tenths of a year since 1869.

In 1901-1902, Eliot boasted that with the large rise of faculty, "the percentage of expenditure on salaries for instruction in this faculty ought to rise during the current year to the highest percentage of the ten years past, unless some unexpected expenditures on buildings or their maintenance shall become necessary." [11]

The college had 19 instructors, assistants, and Austin Teaching Fellows in 1880-1881; by

10. "President Eliot's Report", *The Harvard Bulletin*, 1899, p. 3.

11. *Report of the President of Harvard College,* 1901–1902, pp. 37–38.

1902-1903, the number was 176, and in response to deficits, was reduced to 159 in 1904-1905. The president said that the rise was "due in part to the increase in the number of students, but chiefly to the desire of the faculty to have the instruction given by professors and assistant professors followed up and repeated by young instructors who come into close personal relation with the individual students." [12]

Both Eliot and Lowell had commented on the large increase in numbers of junior faculty and the resultant expected rise of professors. The Great Depression brought a crisis for Conant. Expectations of junior members were to be disappointed as the depression greatly reduced the rise of numbers of students and inflow of gifts which might have financed an expansion of the professorial group.

In his 1937-1938 report, Conant called attention to the budgetary limitations which precluded the promotion of all young faculty men worthy of tenure. [13] This was the period of the Walsh-Sweezy case when the authorities decided not to promote two of the most popular teachers in the college. The resultant crisis led to the appointment of the Committee of Eight to study the supply and demand situation. This committee, in turn, in its 1939 report proposed a rigid formula which provided each department with a tenure appointment every x years, the value of x depending primarily on its number of tenure appointments in the base year. A large department might appoint a new tenure member every three years; a small one, every ten years. The system is of course rigid, and flexibility is obtained only in so far as new chairs are had, or the formula is not followed closely.

In his 1951-1952 report, President Conant expressed satisfaction with the workings of the so-called Graustein formula, upon which the intervals for new appointments were based.

It seems strange to me that in all the discussion of academic finance so little is said about the commitments, legal and implied, to the young teachers who, *if they stay on, will soon be middle-aged and far from contented with their present salaries. No business could stay solvent without a careful and continuous inventory of the "materials in hand and in the process of manufacture." Solvency for a university depends on far more than balancing the dollar budget each year—essential as such balancing is, of course. Solvency depends on a stable personnel policy....* [14]

Of course the Graustein formula imposed a rigid system on the faculty of the college. Thus if a department were alloted 17 tenure appointments, that would mean that the department could appoint a permanent member every 2 years. (The assumption is that a tenure member stays on for 34 years: 34 divided by 17 equals 2.) But to some extent, the administration has been able to introduce some flexibility. Out of new resources or general funds, the changing needs by departments can be treated to some extent. Also, appointments can be anticipated or, when demand is not great or talent is unavailable, at least temporarily a position may not be filled. In 1937, there were 141 professors and associate professors. The Graustein formula became effective in 1941. By 1963, the professors and associate professors had risen to 452. In this manner departments or new programs, under financed as needs change, obtain required resources. [15]

Eliciting the Required Supply

The market for college professors is not a perfect one. Shortages do not necessarily bring higher rewards. Presidents in particular seem to be in short supply. Rewards have been too small and uncertain to attract the necessary talent.

Thus, in December 1698, Increase Mather, president of Harvard said:

... Should I leave preaching to one thousand five hundred souls (for I suppose that so many ordinarily

---

12. *Ibid.,* 1904–1905, p. 19.
13. *Report of the President of Harvard College,* 1937–1938, p. 38.

14. *Ibid.,* 1951–1952, pp. 10–11.
15. Faculty of Arts and Sciences; *Committee on Appointments, Promotions and Retirement,* March 14, 1956, especially pp. 2–6.

to attend in our congregation), only to expound to forty or fifty children, few of them capable of edification by such exercises . . . . [16]

Eliot was convinced that the ordinary laws of supply and demand were not relevant. In his inaugural address of October 19, 1869, Eliot had something to say on this issue:

. . . The law of supply and demand, or the commercial principle that the quality as well as the force of good is best regulated by the natural contest between producers and consumers, never has worked in the province of higher education. . . . The reason is that demand for instructors of the highest class on the part of parents and trustees is an ignorant demand and the supply of highly educated teachers is so limited that the consumer has not sufficient opportunities of informing himself concerning the real qualities of the article he seeks. . . . [17]

---

16. Quincy, *op. cit.*, vol. I, p. 499.

17. Samuel Eliot Morison (ed.), *The Development of Harvard University, 1869–1929*, 1930, p. ixxii.

11

Inbreeding

Since there were no training programs for college faculties, it would be expected that the first colleges would depend upon their own graduates for recruiting teachers. The Ph.D. had not become an established institution until the latter part of the nineteenth century. At Yale, from 1801 to 1877, only one non-Yale man was appointed to a professorship. In the total active Yale faculty in the early 1900s, 37 percent had taken their undergraduate work in other colleges as compared with 33 percent of the Harvard faculty.[1]

In his 1880-1881 report, President Eliot had something to say about the source of Harvard professors. He discussed:

The relative advantages of the three recognized modes of filling professorships: namely, by promoting gentlemen who had served him successfully in lower grades; by inviting professors in other institutions; and by calling to professorships gentlemen who have never been teachers but who have otherwise distinguished themselves. . . .

Eliot clearly sought the best talent irrespective of origins. His study yielded the following results:

1. Twenty-one professors and two assistant professors had not previously served at Harvard in lower grades. Of these twenty-three, nine had held appointments at other institutions.

2. Thirty-five professors and thirteen assistant professors were appointed after having served successfully at Harvard in lower positions. Of these forty-eight appointments, five had held appointments at other institutions.

3. Out of fifty-six professors, thirteen, nearly one-quarter, were not Harvard graduates. Out of fifteen assistant professors, six, or two-fifths, were not Harvard graduates.

4. Out of seventy-one appointments recorded, fifty-five had been made since 1869. Of this number, fifteen were appointments not based on previous service at Harvard.[2]

In an official report of 1939, a Harvard faculty committee revealed that from 1904 to 1938, 4.8 out of every 7 tenure appointments or roughly 70 percent were filled from the inside. "During the 34 years, including the last part of President Eliot's, the whole of President Lowell's and the first part of President Conant's administration, for every 2.2 men the university appointed from within, it took one from the outside. . . ."[3]

President Eliot expressed well the problem of selecting the best men and averting excessive inbreeding.

---

1. G. W. Pierson, *Yale College, 1871-1921,* 1952-1955, pp. 291-293; M. deWolfe Howe, *Classic Shades,* pp. 136-137.

2. *Report of the President of Harvard College,* 1880-1881, pp. 8-14.

3. *Report of Some Problems of Personnel in the Faculty of Arts and Sciences,* 1939, pp. 20-25.

A university president, or a selecting committee, in search of a new professor, or of new professors, has means of forming a judgement which are fairly trustworthy, if patiently collected and sifted. In the first place, there is the candidate's record as a student at his college or university; secondly, his reputation as a teacher, wherever he may have been employed; thirdly, his activity in the learned societies with which he has been connected; fourthly, his productiveness as an investigator and author; and fifthly, his general repute as a man of character and influence. Experienced officials pay but scanty attention to testimonials and letters of recommendation, particularly if they have been forwarded through the candidate or procured by him. Americans are apt to be too charitable and good-natured when writing letters of recommendation. They are also fond of superlatives, and are too apt to deal only with merits, omitting defects, when they write testimonials at the request of a candidate ....[4]

Within twenty years past, numerous learned societies have arisen in the United States, each of which is devoted to some special branch of knowledge .... The professor, or professors, of these several subjects in any one university will gradually have opportunities to measure and weigh all the other active members of the same society, and particularly to see and hear the younger members of the society. ...

In selecting university teachers, young or old, it is always a question what sort of qualification should have most influence on the selection,—knowledge of a subject, capacity to expound it in an interesting manner, published works, success as an investigator, or the total personality, including manners and customs, temper, bearing, and quickness of sympathy. In every case there must be a balancing of these different qualities, which are rarely combined in a single individual, and a comparison with like balances in other candidates.

Every selection and promotion, according to Eliot, should be a joint effort of the president and interested faculty members. "... This method of selecting and promoting University teachers offers the best securities possible against the danger of 'breeding in and in,' a danger which is very real whenever a faculty has full authority over appointments and promotions...." The danger of inbreeding is great just because it is natural to support graduates of the college. They are well known to the incumbent faculty.[5]

One can raise some questions concerning the appropriateness of the 2.2 to 1 ratio estimated by the Committee of Eight in the late 1930s. Harvard's output of Ph.D.s in 1957-1958 was 371 or 6.7 percent of the output of 28 institutions of higher learning that gave Ph.D.s by 1940. For the period 1900 to 1940, Harvard may have given as much as 10 percent of all Ph.D.s, or on the basis of statistics from Berelson, I would put its Ph.D.s in these years very roughly at 500.[6] Its tenure appointments from within were roughly 7 times as great as its proportion of Ph.D.s. Even if one allows for the high caliber of Harvard Ph.D.s, the degree of inbreeding seems high.

Yet there had been some improvement in earlier years. Of 23 faculty members in the college in 1869, only two were not graduates of Harvard; by 1897 the college had one-third of its faculty trained elsewhere.[7]

According to the *Faculty Committee on Economic Status* (1950), 75.4, 79.3 and 88.2 percent of assistant, associate, and full professors respectively were recruited from within the university in the years 1946 to 1949. The significant figure is that for associate professors, for that is the point of entry to tenure, inbreeding continues to be high. On the assumption that most associate professors attain the ultimate position, it would be expected that the authorities would select most full professors from within.[8]

4. James, *op. cit.* especially Chap. 8.
5. Charles William Eliot, H. A. Neilson (ed), *The Man and His Beliefs*, pp. 226-227; and C. W. Eliot, *University Administration*, 1908, pp. 90-91.
6. B. Berelson, *Graduate Education in the United States*, 1960, pp. 26, 93.
7. *Universities and Their Sons*, 1900, p. 113.
8. *Economic Status*, table 9.

12

Rank Structure

Before discussing salaries, it is necessary to consider the rank structure of the faculty, e.g., the relative numbers in each rank. The next table gives the facts. of Harvard history.

From 1904 to 1917, despite the general inflation (with adverse effects on the budget), the proportion of professors to total faculty (exclusive of assistants) rose from 31 to 44 percent. The explanation of this reversal is in fact a decline in the number of instructors, for which Eliot was partly responsible; and I suspect a tendency to accelerate promotions as a means of contending with the inflation. From 1904 to 1917, the growth reflected the influence of both Eliot and Lowell. The proportion of professors increased in response to improved economic conditions, and also under the pressure of several deficits, to Eliot's dropping of many junior faculty members. As inflation proceeded the authorities tended to accelerate promotions (see table). Since Harvard had a fixed scale, the jump of rank was not what one might call a dry increase (i.e., without increase of pay). But in a period of inflation, the college administration might neutralize the effects of inflation by raising the pay of all faculty members. Policy from 1904 to 1917, however, was somewhat different. The college economized on its salary funds by providing merit increases through accelerated promotions rather than favoring general increases.

By 1960, the situation had greatly changed. The country had experienced unparalleled prosperity for twenty years and Harvard's prestige had greatly increased. The famous report the Committee of Eight issued in 1939 had called for shorter probationary periods for faculty, and also for smaller numbers of assistant professors, their work to be done by an increased number of instructors and faculty instructors.

In fact, developments have been far out of line with those recommended and anticipated by the committee. They anticipated little change in the numbers on tenure. Actually the number of professors and associate professors rose from 141 in 1937 to 318 in 1960, equal to 60 percent of the total, exclusive of assistants. Prosperity and the related program for Harvard College, rising enrollments, and increased attention to research are relevant here. Despite the committee's wish for a decrease of assistant professors, the number was roughly unchanged. (In 1937, 101 inclusive of faculty instructors and 98 in 1960.) But the number of instructors (full-time equivalent) declined from 108 to 60, a decline associated in part with the elimination of graduate students from this category. Perhaps the most striking change was in teaching assistants (non-Ph.D. teachers principally), an increase from 147 to 500 (186 full-time equivalent). Hence, the general picture is a very large relative rise of senior (tenure) members of the faculty and of the teaching assistants and a decline in the middle ranks, i.e., assistant professors, instructors, and lecturers. By 1963, Pusey revealed a rise of teaching assistants to 776.[1]

---

1. *Report of the President of Harvard College* 1963, p. 45.

Table 12-1.

Numbers of faculty (exclusive of president), 1643-1963
by rank, various years

Year	Total	Professors	Assoc. Prof.	Assist. Prof.	Instructors	Tutors or Fellows	Assistants	Various Types of Lecturers
1643	2					2		
1712	3					3		
1722	6	1			1	4		
1765	7	3				4		
1788-1790	24	(3 med)¶			1	4		
1826	24	16			2	4		2
1867	24	13		3	2	5		1
1873	51	20		8	12	6		5
1904	183 (318)*	57		38	88		135**	
1917	196 (326)*	87		41	68		130**	
1937	350 * (497)*	102	39	54 47‡	108†		147	
1960	534 (1034)*	264	54	98	60 (Est.)	5	500 (186 Full Time Equivalent)	53
1963	682 §	392	60	157	73			
1963	(1438)*						776	

* - Bracketed figure includes assistants, various types.
** - Obtained by deducting numbers in other ranks from total.
† - Full-time equivalent of 152 appointees.
‡ - 47 represents faculty instructors, a rank similar to assistant professor.
§ - Unlike the 1960 total, this includes all units except medical, dental and public health.
¶ - 3 Medical Professors. The distribution is erroneous.

Sources: 1643, Margery Somers Foster, *"Out of Smalle Beginnings..." An Economic History of Harvard College in the Puritan Period (1636-1712),* 1962, p. 131; 1712, 1790, *Corporation Records;* 1826, 1860, *Harvard University Catalogue, 1825-1826, 1859-1860;* 1867, 1873, *Report of the President of Harvard College, 1871-1872,* p. 10; 1904, 1917, "Harvard Salaries and the of Living," in Harvard Alumni Bulletin, vol. XIX, no. 17, p. 324, January 25, 1917; 1937, *Report on Some Problems of Personnel in the Faculty of Arts and Science by a Special Committee Appointed by the President of Harvard University, 1939, p. 159;* 1963, "The Economic Status of the Faculty, 1963-1964," in *AAUP Bulletin,* June, 1964, p. 166; N. Pusey, *A Decade in Review, 1953-1963,* p. 15.

A somewhat different conclusion is reached by comparing 1946-1947 and 1966-1967. Tenure members—professors and associate professors—dropped from 68 to 60 percent.[2]

Many are critical of the universities for their large dependence on teaching fellows. But even in 1960 this number of teaching assistants (full-time equivalent) equaled only 25 percent of the faculty. In teaching hours, the ratio was somewhat higher since the full-time equivalent at the lower ranks involves more hours of teaching than at the higher ranks. But in another sense, the teaching fellow accounts for a smaller relative contribution, that is, in the number of student man hours. The large lectures and classes generally go to the senior member and the small classes, inclusive of tutorials, to the junior member.[3]

An appraisal of salary levels also requires some attention to the age at which different ranks are achieved. In Harvard's early history the fellows or tutors were very young, for they were just out of college; and frequently awaiting a call to the ministry. They were out in a few years. Analyzing the low level of pay, one should allow for the youthfulness of the tutor or fellows in the seventeenth and eighteenth centuries, as well as their lack of graduate education. The teaching assistant today is likely to be aged 25 to 30 and to have had two to four years of graduate work.

In a period of thirty-three years, 1905 to 1938, the average age at appointment to a member of the permanent staff varied from age 39.0 to 44.10. In the years 1905 to 1919 the average was 42.59; between 1920 and 1938, 40.52, or a reduction of 2.07 years. Hence, it was hoped that a shortening of the probationary period proposed in 1939 and acted upon would reduce the age of receipt of tenure.

With the improved economic situation and the rise of competition, the college was forced to appoint to permanent posts at an earlier age than was contemplated by the Committee of Eight. I do not have the exact figures but my guess would be a maximum of 35 in the 1960s.

The Report of the Committee on Recruitment and Retention of Faculty (1968) includes the following: "The period between appointment as associate professor and professor has been reduced in the last decade and over ages between three and four years." Such a change in age of elevation to permanency, e.g., 7 to 8 years lower than between 1905 and 1919, suggests that the rise of pay since 1905 has been larger than revealed by the crude pay structure.

2. Faculty of Arts and Sciences, Harvard University, *Report of the Committee on Recruitment and Retention of Faculty,* p. 54.

3. Cf., *Teaching Fellowships in Harvard College;* 1960 especially pp. 7-11.

13

Salaries

Pay and Age of the Faculty

Throughout Harvard's history, the problem of adequacy of faculty salaries has been a crucial issue. Salaries of tutors gradually rose from £4 in the early days to a maximum of over £80 by the early part of the eighteenth century. Of particular importance was the salary of the president, varying from 54 percent of the total budget between 1638 and 1650 (cf., about 1/40 of 1 percent in 1965) to 21 percent for the entire Puritan period (1638 to 1712). For faculty members the corresponding figures for these years were 13 and 29 percent.[1]

In the mid-1960s faculty salaries accounted for about 25 percent of the budget and the average pay was in excess of $16,000. But one should not overestimate the progress made. That the gains have been large is evident in the comparative standards of living in the Puritan period and today. But in comparing incomes in dollars we have to allow for price movements, for the change in the quality of the teacher, and in his general productivity, that is, the rise in the cultural and income product received by the student, for which the teacher should receive much credit.

Over the years age and experience are relevant. Thus, in 1904-1905, there were 138 faculty members in the college. Of these, only 10 were full professors at age forty or less. Promotions were slow. In 1966-1967, with full professors equal to about 50 percent of the full-time faculty, the relative number of full professors aged forty or less is considerably higher than the 7 percent early in 1904-1905.[2]

In the unsatisfactory economic conditions of the first half of the eighteenth century, a period of warfare and inflation, the economic status of the faculty was precarious indeed. The rise of salary did not keep up with the inflation.

An abridged table giving some indication of trends in pay has been deposited in the Harvard University Archives. Of some interest is the high pay of the mathematics and divinity professors and the low pay of the Hebrew professor. The tutor consistently received higher pay than the professor of Hebrew. In these years the inflation was so great that in 1750, 7½ units of the old tenor were exchanged for 1 of the new. Incomes clearly lagged behind this implied rise of prices. The average pay of three professors dropped from £566 in 1749 to £69, a reduction associated with the issue of new money when 7½ old tenor equaled 1 new tenor.

It is characteristic of faculty salaries that they lag far behind the rise of prices.

In the first half of the eighteenth century the college periodically increased salaries in response to rising prices. But the rise lagged. For example, the first tutor received £140 in 1727 and only £400 in 1749.

---

1. Margery Somers Foster, *"Out of Small Beginnings..."—An Economic History of Harvard College in the Puritan Period (1636-1712),* 1962, pp. 135, 149.

2. Report of the President of Harvard College, 1904-1905, p. 14; *Economic Status of the Faculty of Arts and Sciences,* Harvard University, 1950, pp. 20-21. (By Ad Hoc Committee.)

Yet in 1750, 7½ units of the old tenor were exchanged for 1 unit of new tenor. The college increased the basic pay at intervals—e.g., 1727, 1735, 1742, 1749—to compensate for the rise of prices. In 1727, they allowed £50 additional and in 1742, £31. Apparently the theory was that the rising prices would not persist and hence the bonus would be temporary.

At one point in 1747, the college gave a special increase:

Whereas the Report of the Treasur^r we find that the nominal sum of the Money, given by Mr. Hollis for the Salaries of the Profess^rs, is increased (by a part of it being lett upon silver money Bonds) so there may be allowed Ten pounds in Addition to Each of the said Profess^rs. . . .

Failure of students to pay their bills proved embarrassing to the college:

Order'd That for the year current ye Treasurer be directed to pay out of the Treasury to Mr. Flynt, and Mr. Robie [Tutor] what their Tuition money falls short of making up their Salaries (the Stewart finding it exceeding Difficult to get in the Tuition money as well as other College dues). . . .[3]

President's Salary

The president's salary was a source of trouble throughout the seventeenth century and most of the eighteenth century. It is well to remember that the president also had teaching responsibilities and his salary even as late as 1750 was about one-half of the teaching budget.

President Quincy described the financial problems of the president from the very beginning.

At this period the prospects of the College were affected by pecuniary embarrassments. Its funds were scanty and, almost the whole of them, specifically appropriated. The support of its President, even in the humble style which the simple state of society then required, was dependent upon the favor of the General Court, who made an annual grant of one hundred and fifty pounds, Massachusetts currency, generally without regard to the depreciation of the circulating medium. The insufficiency of this grant had been strikingly manifested by the fate and fortunes of Leverett; and the friends of the College now resolved to attempt, if possible, to enlarge the amount and, by connecting it with the acceptance of the office, to give the transaction the aspect of a contract, and thus place it upon a surer basis than the precarious favor of the General Court.

He knew that Dunster, after long, faithful, and most successful services, had been compelled to resign by the prevailing Paedobaptist fanaticism, under circumstances of great pecuniary embarrassment; and the application of the Corporation for his relief, rejected by the General Court with a cold and somewhat contemptuous denial. He knew that Chauncy, after accepting the office of President on a promise of liberal maintenance by the General Court, had been stinted in his resources, and his touching appeals to their humanity and good faith neglected; and that, after a long, laborious, and useful life, he left a helpless family, who were compelled to expose to the world their utter poverty, in order to awaken that body to the performance of a simple act of retributive justice.[4]

In October, 1681, the general court provided pay for Increase Mather to the amount of "one hundred pounds money per annum, and fifty pounds country pay. . .and this to be continued so long as he shall supply the place of President. . . ."[5]

In an attempt to entice Benjamin Wadsworth to accept the presidency in 1725, the general court allocated to the president £40 of rent from Massachusetts Hall and a total pay of £400. But it is clear from the next quotation that the government was anxious that

---

3. See *College Books*, Vol. II, pp. 456 (1720), 555 (1727), 638-639 (1735), 727 (1742), 767 (1747), 803 (1749) for last few paragraphs.

4. Quincy, *op. cit.*, vol. I, pp. 334-336.

5. At the General Court Held at Boston, 12th of October, 1681, in Harvard University Archives.

the college pay a substantial part of the bill in the future, a privilege not sought by the college.

On December 31, 1725, the House of Representatives of Massachusetts voted:

Resolved, That the Sum of Seventy Pounds *be allowed and paid out of the Publick Treasury, to the Reverend Mr.* Benjamin Wadsworth, *President of* Harvard College, *which with the Sum of* One Hundred & Fifty Pounds, *granted to the said Mr. President Wadsworth, the last Session of this Court, and the Sum of* One Hundred and Thirty-nine Pounds, *so much Remaining in the Hands of the Corporation of the said College, being for the Rent of* Massachusetts Hall *for the first Five Years, Exclusive of all Charges and Repairs thereon, together with the Sum of* Forty One Pounds *of the Rent of the said* Massachusetts Hall *for the Year Currant, which this Court do hereby Appropriate and Order to be paid to the said Mr. President Wadsworth, making in the whole the Sum of* Four Hundred Pounds, *the Court are of Opinion is a Sufficient and Honourable Support and Maintenance for him the said President for One Year; and that the said Mr. President Wadsworth may be further Encouraged cheerfully to go through the Momentous Affairs of his Office, It is further Resolved, and this Court do freely Give, Grant and Appropriate the future Annual Rents, and Incomes of Massachusetts Hall to him the said Mr. President Wadsworth. . . .It is also Resolved, That the Sum of* One Thousand Pounds *be allowed and paid out of the Publick Treasury to the Corporation of* Harvard College, *and by them to be forthwith used and disposed of, for the Building and Finishing a handsome Wooden Dwelling House, Barn, Out-Housen,&* c.[6] *for the Accommodation of the Reverend the President of* Harvard College.

The college thanked the court but added, "we are heartily willing to do what we can towards the annual support of a President, yet we shall not be able to do anything considerable therein without diminishing the College stock or principal."[7]

Quincy commented:

Notwithstanding these flattering appearances accompanying the commencement of this presidency, Wadsworth, like his predecessors, soon found other thorns in his path besides those strewed by official duty and College discipline. By the appropriation of the rents of Massachusetts Hall, the legislature had indeed placed a portion of his compensation upon a somewhat more solid foundation, than former Presidents had enjoyed; but the unappropriated funds of the College were wholly inadequate to supply the residue, and, with the depreciation attendant on a currency chiefly paper, soon reduced his efficient income nearly to the same level with that of his predecessors. . . .[8]

In June, 1737, the house, in setting up a salary for the newly elected President, Edward Holyoke, stated:

They have at all times readily afforded their aid and assistance in Supporting of, the President, as the matter required, and that now there be allowed to the President a suitable and ample support. A salary of two hundred pounds of the Bills of Credit in this Province of new tenor [1 new equaled 3 old] *over and above the rents of Massachusetts Hall for a space of one year* [will be paid] *from the time of his installment. . . .*[9]

President Holyoke was in difficulties. On January 18, 1739, he sent a memorial to the house complaining of the inadequacy of pay, which he pleaded in person. The court granted him £100, new tenor.[10]

The president's salary did not respond well to the inflation. Whereas in 1715, the president's pay was a little more than two-thirds of that of the governor and justices, in the years 1740 to 1750 his pay varied

6. *Proceedings and Collections of the Massachusetts Historical Society,* vols. I, VI, pp. 444-445.
7. Quincy, *op. cit.,* vol. I, p. 379.

8. *Ibid.,* p. 380; also see I, VII-XIV, various pages; Society, vols. *Massachusetts Historical Proceedings and Collections of the Corporation Records,* vol. I, p. 202.
9. *Proceedings and Collections of the Massachusetts Historical Society,* vols. I, XV, pp. 59, 168; vol. XVI, pp. 224, 231.
10. *Ibid.,* vols. I, XVI, p. 231.

between 1/6 to 1/11 and 2/5 to 1/4, respectively, of the pay of the governor and justices respectively.[11]

Pay in the Revolutionary Period

The third quarter of the eighteenth century was relatively prosperous, with incomes generally rising in the nation; and the inflation had been temporarily contained. Yet in 1773, the salary of the divinity professor had actually declined by 22 percent from the 1750 level and that of the mathematics professor by 5 percent. Clearly the income of the academic world was lagging vis-à-vis that of the economy.

The three professors of this period received part of their income from appropriated and part from unappropriated funds of the university, and in part from the government. In all, the three professors received £200 each, with the college providing £350 and the general court £250. The general court in determining its grant took into account the varying returns of the endowment of each professorship, and in September, 1777, the corporation announced a program to equalize professors' salaries. Moreover, the college tended to equalize pay through assessments on students.

Depreciation of the currency and unavailability of funds for the college put a burden on the government or on the students. A tripling of the income of the modal salary from 1756 to 1778 was far from enough to offset the inflation of the period.[12]

In the midst of the Revolutionary War, the overseers proposed that the corporation enact some measures to increase salaries "in a way that will not lessen the College funds, nor increase the quarterly payments of the students in such a degree as to prevent the growth and increase of the College." It is clear that the college did not have the resources to finance the needed rise of pay and was unwilling to raise the charge to the students.[13]

In 1779, the college, embarrassed by the lack of funds to pay the faculty, attempted to increase the charges on the students, who profited as prices rose greatly by paying their quarter bills three months after receipt of food and seminar. Hence the corporation demanded payment in quarterly bills, which took account of the rise of prices of provisions over a quarter.[14]

On one occasion, following a large depreciation of the currency, when the permanent tutor applied for an increase of pay, the professors also protested. They averred that the:

grants made in consideration of the depreciated state of the currency did not supply the deficiency; that they had been subject to many difficulties and hardships, and experienced a painful inability to support their families in a comfortable and decent manner; and that, with the most rigid economy, they were not able to make any savings . . . .[15]

Pay, 1800 to 1860

After the Revolutionary War, the economic status of the professors improved. Thus the modal salary moved as follows:

Economic Status of Professors, 1777 through 1860	
Year	Salary
1777-1778	£200 ($633)
1809	$1,500
1829-1830	1,500
1849-1850	1,800
1859-1860	2,300

Source: Report of the Treasurer of Harvard College, relevant years; *Report of the President of Harvard College,* 1829-1830.

11. *Journal of House of Representatives of Mass.,* vols. 1, 2, 6, 9, 13, 18, Ed. by *HSM,* 1919-1945; *Journal of House of Representatives of His Majesty's Province of Mass. Bay in New England.* (Harvard College copies of original prints of 1745-1750)
12. See Quincy, *op. cit.,* vol. II, pp. 245-246; *Corporation Records,* vol. III, pp. 141-142

13. *Corporation Records* vol. III, 1778, pp. 19-20. pp. 242-243.
14. Quincy, *op. cit.*
15. *Ibid.,* p. 282.

In the period 1809 to 1859 prices had fallen by 38 percent, but the income of Harvard professors had improved by 53 percent. Hence in stable dollars the pay of professors had improved by 148 percent. This gain for Harvard professors was much greater than that in per capita income, which rose by only 3 percent in these fifty years.16

But even as late as 1866, President Felton complained "that salaries are insufficient for the support of the Professors' families, so that it is necessary for those who have not independent means to engage in some paying work besides their college duties. . . . "17

This unusual advance in these fifty years must be related to an improved supply and demand situation for faculty, the rising demand related to the increase in the college population, the emergence of more competitors for faculty members, and the rising income of Harvard. The sources of supply of potential professors were still relatively narrow.

The crises of the 1820s underlined the problems confronting the college in meeting the bills for faculty salary. Prof. George Ticknor accepted a cut from $1000 to $600, though he made it clear that the college could not unilaterally impose this reduction on him.

That the sacrifices proposed in the report of your Committee are among those required, the unfortunate state of College, means, as set forth in the report itself leaves no doubt. But these sacrifices are not all that is demanded. On the contrary, if great changes are not made in the . . . instruction of the students, these very sacrifices, I fear, will be found ineffectual by reducing the whole tone of the college. . . . 18

In the crises of the 1820s not only Professor Ticknor but most of the faculty had to accept substantial cuts, and also increases in their work loads. In urging the Legislature in 1824 to provide continued subsidies, the corporation emphasized the low pay of Harvard faculty, the difficulties in cutting their salaries and the much larger salaries they might have had if they had abandoned academic life.19

Perhaps one of the most interesting episodes is found in the medical school. The school protested at the university appropriating the school fees to be used for other branches of the university. Moreover, the faculty have "voluntary expended . . . from their own resources within the last three years [1824 to 1827] for the purposes of the Medical School . . . of which welfare the present members of the faculty may never be partakers nor even witnesses. . . . "20

In 1840, a committee discovered that only $3,150 were available for theological instruction. The relevant committee recommended that the Hollis Chair of Divinity not be filled since the entire cost was assessed on the general funds of the university. The duties performed under the Hollis chair would be transferred to other foundations.21

The Eliot Period

In 1869, Pres. Charles Eliot took over. Nine years earlier in a letter to Charles Eliot Norton he had expressed clearly his dissatisfaction with his pay as a teacher and with the burdens imposed on him.

. . . I generally experience a slight disgust at recitations at the beginning of a term, particularly at Mathematical recitations. . . . Sometimes too the smallness of College pay grinds me, particularly when I see other young fellows getting twice as much pay

---

16. The income and price statistics from *Historical Statistics of the United States,* 1789-1945. (I should warn the reader that income statistics of this early period provide only the roughest kind of results.)

17. *Report of the President of Harvard College,* 1859-1860, pp. 4-5.

18. Committee on Reducing the Expenses of Education; G. Ticknor to the President and Fellows of Harvard College, December 30, 1826.

19. Memorandum of February, 1824.

20. Dean Walter Channing, to President and Fellows, July 25, 1827, *Agreement of August 9, 1827 of Committee of Corporation, and Medical Faculty* [on use of Medical Fees].

21. *Report of the Committee (J. Walker, Chairman)* to which was referred the *Theological School, Generally,* April 25, 1840.

for less work of inferior quality. And yet the College demands so much of my time that I can do original scientific work only by working up to the very limit of my physical endurance. . . . Lest you should think from these remarks that I have some reasons to complain of my lot, I may as well state distinctly that I don't know a person in the world who is happier than I am, or who has such good reason to be. . . . [22]

Despite his interest in higher salaries in order to attract able men into college teaching, Eliot emphasized the relatively limited economic incentive:

. . . It should be distinctly understood that the profession can never be properly recruited by holding out pecuniary inducements. In drawing good men from one institution to another, the prevailing inducements are apt to be, not increase of salary, but wider companionship, better access to books, better schools for the children, a wholesome life for the family, more social and educational advantages and the general prestige of the inviting institution. . . . [23]

The new president announced in his 1869-1870 report that the pay of a full professor had been raised that year from $3,000 to $4,000, the assistant professor to $2,000 (a rise of but $150), and the pay of tutors was left unchanged at $1,000. This unusual move contributed greatly to the dramatic rise of Harvard to its eminent position. Moreover, it was a courageous move in that the highest pay increases went to the top talent, which the president wanted to hold and attract.

By increasing tuition fees from $104 to $150 and obtaining $10,000 yearly additional from the rent of a dormitory and $50,000 from a class subscription fund, the president was able to increase salaries and create seven new professorships, and in fact thirteen by 1871.[24]

Eliot needed money not only to raise the pay of his faculty but also to increase its size, improve its quality, and also to finance his costly elective system.

Despite the dramatic salary increase, there were many grumbles. The president was determined to stretch every dollar as far as it would go. Henry James commented thus:

He was called parsimonious and it appears that his judgment concerning salaries could hardly be called generous. There was, to be sure, never enough money to satisfy his ambitions for the enrichment of the curriculum. But, thriving as he did on the hardest work and the longest hours and finding it easy to live plainly and to manage frugally his own affairs, he made insufficient allowance for the fact that many men were not so well fitted to grow old serenely on a meagre stipend. The best salaries that the University paid were modest and there are more instances than it is pleasant to consider of instructors who were kept waiting for full pay until middle age, or until some other institution began to bid against Harvard for their services and reputations. Theodore Richards, recipient of a Nobel Prize in 1914, has left a record of one such bidding that occurred in 1900 or 1901. . . . [25]

In 1877 Henry Cabot Lodge was finishing his first year as an instructor when Henry Adams resigned. President Eliot coaxed Lodge into assuming the responsibility of teaching American history and though Adams had received $2,000 as an assistant professor, the president would offer only $1,000 to Lodge, who now would teach both colonial and modern history. The president dwelt on the poverty of Harvard. "None of our college salaries are adequate . . . The Corporation will be glad to be further indebted to you . . . and they will regard the $1,000 not as a proper compensation but as an inadequate honorarium." [26]

Col. Henry Lee, a generous benefactor of the college, was critical of Eliot especially for putting resources into growth rather than concentrating on raising salaries.

22. Henry James, *Charles W. Eliot: President of Harvard University,* 1930, vol I, p. 87.
23. Eliot, *University Administration,* p. 99.
24. James, *op. cit.,* vol. I, pp.252-257.

25. *Ibid.,* vol. II, pp. 80-81.
26. *Henry Cabot Lodge, A Biography,* New York, 1953, p. 53.

. . . he [Eliot] is a fanatic, and we run Harvard College trusting to fanatacism, picking up here and there enthusiastic scholars willing to take the vows of perpetual poverty; and this policy seems to me dangerous and derogatory to a great University, which we are striving to build up. The compensation should be such as to invite men of scholarly tastes and enthusiasm, who long to become teachers of men, to adopt that profession, without feeling that by this choice they are depriving their wives and children of the social and educational privileges of the families of lawyers or physicians, or of average merchants. . . . [27]

In 1913, years after his resignation, President Eliot replied to the critics who accused him of ascetic propensities in relation to his faculty. He emphasized the rise of pay and the introduction of the first retirement system in America.

In his "Story of Harvard University" Mr. A. S. Pier said (page 199) that Harvard's professors "are not highly paid . . . Perhaps President Eliot was never deeply moved by their pecuniary difficulties. To his ascetic and devoted spirit, ascetism and devotion were required of the teachers of youth, and it mattered little if they were prescribed by poverty instead of being elective." Protesting mildly against these remarks Eliot said, "As to the pecuniary difficulties of Harvard Professors, I took a keen interest in them, and one of the achievements of my first year as President was the raising of the full Professor's salary from $2,400 a year, with a precarious grant of $600 annually, to $4,000, and the raising of the Assistant Professor's salary from $1,500 a year to $2,000. I was interested during my whole term in getting all possible improvements made in the College salaries from bottom to top, and the increases were numerous, although never large after the one effected in 1869-1870. . . . [28]

Perhaps a more supportable appraisal of Eliot's crucial contributions are suggested by two other estimates.

It is a point insufficiently noticed by Harvard's historians that, before the College could put out so magnificently, it had to take in. Thus, if Eliot was able to expand the elective offerings, it was because he first was financially able to expand his faculties. By contrast, Princeton and Yale remained plain and poor and other hopeful colleges more pinched and impecunious still. [29]

Eliot's first great step was not the introduction of the elective system (that came gradually over a period of fifteen years), but the strengthening of the faculty. . . . by increasing salaries, by setting scholars free from the traditional dull routine, and by seeking unusual men from all over America and even in Europe. . . . The same year that Harvard professors went up to $4,000, those at New York University were advanced from $1,500 to $3,000. By means of this one action Eliot had placed Harvard in a position to get almost any man it wanted in America. [30]

Eliot continued to experience difficulties in keeping salaries high enough to isolate Harvard faculty from increasing offers from the outside. In 1892, the president commented on the problem:

During the year seven universities and colleges made ineffectual efforts to draw teachers of this University into their services. Four professors, four assistant professors, and six instructors declined offers of higher pay and higher titles at other institutions. The influences which bind its teachers to the University are chiefly these: The dignity and stability of the institution; the perfect liberty of opinion; the freedom in teaching the great resources of the University in books and collections . . . the separation of Cambridge from the luxurious society of great cities; the propinquity to the resources of Boston for the gratification of aesthetic and musical tastes; the healthfulness of Cambridge, and the facilities for bringing up children in a wholesome way, which learning and high character traditionally enjoy in

27. J. T. Morse, *Memoir of Colonel Henry Lee,* 1905, pp. 134-135; cf., 124-126.
28. James, *op. cit.,* vol. II, pp. 81-82.
29. G. W. Pierson, "American Universities in the Nineteenth Century," in Margaret Clapp (ed.), *The Modern University,* 1950, p. 86.
30. E. Earnest, *Academic Profession,* 1953, pp. 154-155.

eastern Massachusetts, independent of pecuniary conditions.[31]

One instance of competition from outside was the philosopher Hugo Munsterberg who was invited first by Oxford and then by Konigsberg, the latter near his beloved Danzig home. He was ready to accept, but a day later after a long Sunday morning talk with Royce he changed his mind.[32]

Modal salaries of professors from 1870 to 1900 had risen only by $190 or about 5 percent. Hence the gains since 1870 seemed modest indeed. One explanation is the large increase in the number of appointments.[33] The faculty also profited from a large drop in prices.

An explanation of why Eliot moved so little beyond the 1870 position can be had by examining a table.

2. Despite the increase in enrollment, endowment per student rose by about 50 percent, and even more in stable dollars.

3. With the rise of enrollment and the yield of investments declining drastically—the return on government bonds fell from about 4 percent in the late 1870s to 2.18 percent in 1900—the rise of endowment per student was accompanied by a decline of endowment income per student.

4. Despite the large decline of endowment income and total income per student, the cost of a Harvard College education to the college actually increased from $349 to $358.

Here the enrichment of the Harvard College curriculum and staff and higher salaries are relevant. The substantial gain of enrollment in the professional schools was especially reflected in reduced unit costs.

Table 13-1.

Harvard College and University, Various Indices, 1870 and 1900

	Enrollment H.C.	Enrollment H.U.	% of H.U.	H.U. Income per Student	Endowment per Student	Endowment Income per Student	H.C. Costs per Student
1870	563	1,097	51	$364	$2,176	$169	$349
1900	1,902	4,091	46	278	3,083	130	358

Sources: See original tables elsewhere in this book.

This table reflects the following:

1. The large rise of enrollment, and especially in the professional schools, helps account for the resultant decline of college income available per student. This is, however, not so serious as it seems as the value of the dollar increased substantially as prices fell.

President Eliot's major achievement in improving the economic status of the profession was the rise of Harvard professors' salaries from $3,000 to $4,000 in 1869-1870, his first year of office. Against a 12 percent rise of income per capita in the nation from 1870 to 1900, Eliot could offer but a 5 percent rise in the professors' salaries. But it is well to remember that if Harvard's salaries lagged behind the rise in the economic standards of the nation, there was, however, a substantial gain of 5 percent plus the improvement reflected in a decline of prices, which, on different indices, equaled 13, 35 and 36 percent, or on the basis of an average figure, the 5 percent gain

31. *Report of the President of Harvard College,* 1891-1892, pp. 8-9.
32. *The Economic Status of the Faculty of Arts and Science,* pp. 12-13.
33. *Report of the President of Harvard College,* 1883-1884, pp. 45-46; see Chapter 10.

was equal to one of more than 40 percent in purchasing power. This episode once more underlines the point that faculty improves its status when prices fall, not when they rise.

Before the onslaught of the inflation of the first half of the twentieth century, the Harvard faculty had attained a comfortable standard of living related both to the moderate rises of salary and falling prices. The high standard was reflected in the availability in 1900 of a six-room house on Wendell Street for $14 a month, a nine-room house on Dana Street for $37.50 a month, a comfortable house in a good neighborhood which might cost $70,000 to $80,000 today sold for between $4,000 and $9,000; eggs, 25 cents a dozen; corned beef 5 cents a pound; porterhouse steak, 25 cents; at the Colonial Club where could be found the "quintessence of Cambridge, the literary and academic elite, luncheon cost 50 cents and dinners 75 cents;" the finest suit could be made to order at the Harvard Cooperative for $35; domestics cost $3 to $5 dollars a week; coal, $6.25 a ton; and woolen socks cost 15 cents.[34]

The 1904-1905 Program

In 1904-1905 came the next frontal assault on the salary problem. This attack stemmed in no small part from the increasing competition for Harvard faculty, and especially from the University of Chicago. Eliot's first treatment of this problem in 1869-1870 could also be related to the competition of other institutions of higher learning, but not so much as in the early twentieth century. The 1904-1905 campaign, which called for an unprecedented $2,500,000 appeal for a teachers' endowment fund to yield $100,000 annually, could be supported as a move to further strengthen Harvard's competitive position. On an absolute scale, the Harvard faculty had done well, though not so well as the whole population. On the competitive issue, the following is a statement of Bishop Lawrence, the effective fund raiser.

When he became President of the Alumni Association in 1904, William Lawrence, '71, Episcopal Bishop of Massachusetts saw trouble ahead for Harvard if teachers' salaries were not raised. Annual deficits had been running for several years. Other universities, especially Chicago, were offering much larger salaries, which, however, several Harvard men had declined: other teachers were becoming restless. The Corporation had lately cut down the salary list by thirty thousand dollars; and the Overseers had resolved to call a halt. There was strong and reasonable pressure for the increase of the tuition fee, a step to be avoided, if possible, for State universities with free tuition were springing up over the country, and Harvard had a responsibility to the people of Massachusetts which had no state university.[35]

A statement by a special committee of overseers in 1904 stressed that between 1869 and 1904 enrollment had increased greatly, a declining proportion was financed by the students, and the pay of those engaged in teaching these students had been greatly reduced.[36]

At this point in Harvard's history, the clash of interest between the college and professional schools emerged as a serious problem. An official statement stressed the increasing competition of professional schools for funds.[37]

In his 1903-1904 report the president also said that "the new endowment should be confined to the uses of Harvard College, and within the college to salaries and retirement allowances."[38]

A vital decision was that the $2,500,000 would be used for salaries, not buildings. This in itself was an advance. The overseers' committee, stressing the sacrifices which had been made by teachers, would

34. *The Economic Status of the Faculty of Arts and Science,* pp. 7-9.

35. William Lawrence, *Memories of a Happy Life,* 1926, p. 214.

36. *Report of a Special Committee of the Board of Overseers on the Financial Requirements of the University and the Deficit Incurred During Recent Years,* 1904.

37. *Harvard Teachers' Endowment Fund, General Correspondence,* 1904-1905.

38. *Report of the President of Harvard College,* 1903-1904, pp. 51-52.

have liked a rise in salaries of 50 percent if this were possible and concluded that "the expense of student life at Cambridge may have been kept down by an undue sacrifice imposed on those whose lives are professionally devoted to student instruction." [39]

One reason for the increasing cost of higher salaries was the increase in the number of faculty members. But the change in structure—professors declined from 54 to 21 percent from 1867 to 1905—points to a smaller average rise of pay than would otherwise be estimated.[40]

At the time of decision early in the twentieth century, the average pay was as follows:

Average Pay Early in the Twentieth Century	
57 professors	$3,980
38 assistant professors	2,130
88 instructors	990
All teachers	$1,570

President Eliot, anticipating further promotions with so many young faculty members, set aside part of the proceeds of the drive to cover the cost of these promotions. The net effect was a rise of salaries of $500 for each of the three top ranks, with the assistant professor receiving the maximum percentage rise, 25 percent in his first five years. But the average rise of salary was 13 percent. In contrast to 1869-1870 policy, the president now favored the low-income group.

In comparing the growth of the nation's per capita income with that of the faculty, I conclude that the rise for the faculty of 13 percent (plus 4 percent for full professors) was much below what might have

been expected. Per capita income had risen by 46 percent in the years 1870 to 1905, as compared to 13 percent for the Harvard faculty (plus a few percent for full professors), and the faculty gained also (as did others) from a small decline in prices. But it took a major effort after thirty-five years of losing ground relatively for the faculty to achieve one-third of the gain of the average American.

One comment from a nonacademic person who was asked to contribute follows.

My annual income has never been anything like so large as the lowest sum mentioned in your list, $925. I have managed to live very comfortably, keep my debts paid up, help others a little, and indulge in an occasional winter in Florida or similar luxury. I think the poor professors and instructors, with their short hours of labor and long vacations will manage to take care of themselves, but it makes me tired to see any one begging for them, when so many thousands of others need the money so much more. [41]

Inflation, 1906 to 1919

In 1906, the new salary scale was in effect, and it remained in effect as late as 1919. Meanwhile, the country had experienced a great inflation and an even greater rise of per capita income. The 1906 scale provided a maximum salary of $3,500 for assistant professors, and a rise to $4,000 at the full professor level, with $500 additional every five years until the ceiling of $5,500 was reached.[42]

As in the early nineteenth century, an additional stimulus to getting salaries up was the increased salaries of competitors. Thus in 1919 Yale raised the scale for professors to a range of $5,000 to $8,000, claiming this was the highest in the nation.[43]

It is not surprising that the Harvard faculty suffered greatly in the World War I inflation. The salary structure of 1906 still prevailed in 1919. Yet

39. *Report of a Special Committee of the Board of Overseers... And the Deficit*, 1904.

40. "Teachers' Endowment Fund," *The Harvard Bulletin*, vol. VII, no. 32, pp. 4-5; *Report of the President of Harvard College*, 1871-1872, p. 16; 1901-1902, pp. 37-38; 1904-1905, pp. 344-346; *The Economic Status of the Faculty of Arts and Science*, pp. 20-21.

41. Teachers' Endowment Fund, General Correspondence.

42. Harvard Salaries and the Cost of Living, *Harvard Alumni Bulletin*, vol. XIX, p. 326, January 25, 1917.

43. Pierson, *op. cit.*, pp. 536-537.

per capita income in the nation had risen by 115 percent, a rise closely paralleling the increase in the cost of living. Hence, the real income of the American people had been maintained despite a large war, but the real pay of Harvard faculty had fallen by more than one-half. In the years of World War II and later the same experience prevailed except that adjustments of salaries were made more quickly, but there were still delays and the relative position of the Harvard faculty deteriorated greatly.

It is not unexpected that the 1919 endowment drive of more than $15 million was to go primarily for a rise of faculty salaries. The expectation was that prices would remain at 50 percent above the 1913 level—a projection—and, therefore, that salaries ought to rise by 50 percent. The forecast proved to be correct.[44]

Harvard officials noted that low pay meant large sacrifices by faculty members, "pot boiling" jobs, seduction by industry, and a deterrence of the young from teaching. No better statement of the issues was made than that by President Lowell.

After noting the increase of prices during and after the war, President Lowell said:

Men who had been comfortable found that they could not live as they had done. Professors do not expect to acquire wealth. Their reward comes in other forms; but they do desire, and for its own interest the University desires them, to live comfortably, in a style reasonably appropriate to their position and duties; to lay by enough for illness and old age; to provide in case of their death for those dependent upon them; and to give their children as good an education as they received themselves. . . . The cry that teachers are now under paid is universal throughout the land, and everywhere efforts are being made to raise their salaries. . . .[45]

These inflationary forces have continued with some exceptions up to the present. But in more recent years upward adjustments in faculty salaries have prevailed. Indeed the results of such lags as between 1904 and 1919 or between 1940 and 1955 meant that real wages declined at least temporarily, and the rise of faculty salaries fell far behind those of *all* workers. From 1912 to 1967, for example, faculty salaries at Harvard rose by 300 percent. In stable dollars the rise was from $8,000 to $18,000, or an increase of 125 percent in dollars of stable purchasing power. The gain was real, but much less than for the whole population.[46]

More money was needed for salaries, primarily to offset the ravages of inflation. But there were other problems also. A 10 percent contribution to pensions was now necessary. The law school wanted to increase the faculty-student ratio. In the dental school, 100 faculty members were giving free services; 23 receiving only traveling expenses; 24, a small salary for part time; 2 receiving a small salary for all their productive time. The 123 were not even receiving "the complimentary $100 gold piece."[47]

Interwar Period

In the 1920s the average increase of faculty pay was 5 to 7 percent. Since prices declined by 18 percent, the real gains were much larger. Against this improvement, the income of the average American seemed to have fallen by 13 percent. More surprising is the fact that in October, 1930, by which time the depression had blossomed, the corporation announced a substantial rise of salaries. The range of full professors' salaries increased from between $6,000 and 9,000 to between $8,000 and 12,000, or a 33 percent increase, with commensurate increases in other ranks. Since prices were to fall 17 percent more in he 1930s, the faculty improved its position by 60 percent. Despite this large gain and increased costs to the university of the rise of salaries, and despite the decline of return on investments from 5.5 percent in 1929-1930 to 4.1

---

44. *Harvard and the Future*, p. 9, *Harvard Endowment Fund*, 1919; *Report of the President of Harvard College*, 1919-1920, pp. 5-6.
45. *Ibid.*, 1918-1919, p. 22; cf., *Harvard and the Future*, 1919, pp. 2-4; *Harvard University Endowment*, 1919.

46. Cf., *Harvard and the Future*, p. 3.
47. Draft of Fund Pamphlet, pp. 12-13 in *Endowment Fund Record; Report of Proceedings, Old Grads' Summer School*, July 28-30, 1919; Harvard Endowment Fund Committee.

percent in 1932-1933, the university maintained its tradition of not cutting salaries. Some economies were necessary, however.[48]

President Lowell expressed the issues well:

When hard times came, in and after 1929, some friends of the University thought professors' salaries should be reduced. Against any such action Lowell stood firm. Consistent as usual, he reminded his critics that he had never in good times favored salaries as high as those which members of the Faculties might have obtained outside the teaching profession. Now in bad times they should receive a corresponding protection against reductions due to economic stress.[49]

In gratitude, President Conant expressed his thanks to his predecessor for saving in the prosperous years in order to exclude cuts of salaries in depression. In saying that Harvard "*never* has had to cut the salaries of its staff," (my italics) however, President Conant was claiming too much.[50]

After 1940

Whereas the Harvard faculty greatly improved its position in the 1930s while the population on the average accepted a large cut in standards, the reverse was its history after 1940. An indication of the net change is suggested by a rise of per capita disposable income (after direct taxes) in current dollars for the country of 175 percent from 1930 to 1955, as against a rise of 30 percent for a full professor at Harvard.

I expressed the issue as follows in 1955.

All interested in higher education and the preeminence of Harvard should be greatly concerned that the average real *income before taxation of a Harvard full Professor has declined by 20 percent in 25 years, 1930-1954-55; that his money income before taxes has risen but 1/6-1/7 as much as that of the average worker, or the average American, or physician; that in a generation the full Professor at Harvard has suffered a* relative *loss of income more than half in relation to the working population, and 59 percent vis-à-vis physicians. What is more, Harvard has lost ground relatively to other institutions of higher learning.[51]*

In this period of twenty-five years, the full professor's average salary, increased from $10,000 to $13,000, a rise of 30 percent; the cost of living rose by 62 percent; hence, the purchasing power of a Harvard professor's salary in 1955 equaled $8,026, 1930 dollars, or 20 percent less than his pay in 1930.

In this same period, the pay of a Harvard full professor declined vis-à-vis others as follows:

Percent Harvard Professor's Pay Decreased in Relation to Other Workers, 1930 to 1955

Type of Worker	Percent of decline
Nonagricultural employees	56
Practicing physicians	59
Dentists	38
Lawyers	34

Source: S. E. Harris article in *Harvard Alumni Bulletin*, April 9, 1955.

One criticism may justly be made of this approach, namely, that in view of the large gains resulting from the 1930 increase, a comparison with the year preceding this large increase may be in order. On this basis, from 1929 to 1955 I find that the real income of the full professor at Harvard rose by 11 percent instead of declining by 20 percent. I make one comparison on this basis. Again the Harvard professor loses, but not as much relatively as on the basis of the comparison with the 1930 increase.

1. Rise of real income of a Harvard full professor, 1929 to 1955, 11 percent.
2. Per capita disposable personal income rise in stable dollars, 1919 to 1955, 49 percent.
3. Relative decline of a Harvard full professor's pay, 25 percent.

---

48. *Report of the President of Harvard College*, 1929-1930, p. 13; Morison, *op. cit.*, p. 151.
49. H. Yeomans, *Abbott Lawrence Lowell, 1856-1943*, p. 303.
50. *Report of the President of Harvard College*, 1951-1952, p. 8.
51. *Harvard Alumni Bulletin*, April 9, 1955, pp. 513-514.

Post World War II

From 1955 to 1964, the Pusey-Bundy administration greatly improved the economic status of the Harvard faculty. The rise of pay greatly exceeded the gains for the average American, and also a fortiori that in the price level.

Percent of Increase, 1955 to 1964	
Item	Percent
Full professor's pay	61
Per capita disposable personal income	33
Consumer prices	14

Again the faculty thrived in a period of relative price stability. The increase in pay was made possible by the success of the program for Harvard College, by the $5 million gift by the Ford Foundation, and by continued rises of tuition.[52]

From 1929 to 1963-1964, Harvard salaries improved, though they still lagged behind the gains of the general population.

Percent of Increase, 1929 to 1963-1964*	
Item	Percent
(1) Per capita disposable income	223
(2) Harvard full professor's pay	180
(3) Consumer prices	81

*Allowance for taxes paid under (2) would substantially increase difference between (1) and (2).

In 1950, a Harvard faculty committee also studied the trends in Harvard pay. They found that from 1900 to 1950 per capita income of the country rose by more than 5 times, the pay of a full professor at Harvard by only 2.7 times. At age 30, they pointed out, Harvard salaries for instructors were $3,500 as compared with scientists under 30 in industry at $5,560 and in government $5,050. This study also showed that for the period considered Harvard pay had increased much less than the cost of living.[53]

An interesting approach of the faculty committee was the following:

a. Salary, 51 full professors, $10,070 in 1939; $12,167 in 1948, or a rise of 21 percent.

b. Salary, 19 full professors who were associate professors in 1938, increased more than 55 percent.

c. Salary, 21 full professors who were assistant professors in 1938, increased more than 82 percent.

The average rise for b and c was 21 percent on the basis of Harvard's salaries above, and 15 percent when allowance is made for Radcliffe. Pay of 138 identical members in 1938-1939 and 1949-1950 rose by 44 percent. But this reflects promotions as well as a rise in the pay scale. The increase is understated because the average age of appointment was reduced and the teaching load cut by 20 percent.

Above I noted that the average age of attainment of rank has been declining. The economic status report shows that this holds for all ranks.[54]

In relation to competitors, Harvard lost ground in the 1940s. Its pay at the full professor level was still best, but at lower ranks its position deteriorated.[55]

Conant Policy

President Conant was not so much interested in raising money as he was in theories of education. He was mainly an idea man though also a good administrator and an outstanding educator.

Conant was not highly successful in raising funds, in part because his great abilities lay elsewhere and in part because the depression and war aggravated the difficulties of raising money. Faculty salaries lagged in his administration both because of the difficulties

52. *A Program for Harvard College; The Case for a Program for Harvard College*, pp. 4-5; *Newsletter #151*, July, 1959.

53. *The Economic Status of the Faculty of Arts and Science*, pp. 49-54,

54. *Ibid.*, table 4.

55. *Ibid.*, pp. 21, 32.

of obtaining additional funds and because tuition was kept at a low level. But Conant introduced some new programs, notably the national scholarships and university professorships, which were of great importance though the response of donors was rather disappointing.

Faculty salaries suffered in the 1930s and 1940s, in part because of the obstacles to fund raising, and in part because of the failure to raise tuition significantly in a period when per capita disposable income rose by about 300 percent.

Pusey (with the important help of Bundy) exploited the rising incomes of Harvard families and, prepared to give everything to a large drive, brought Harvard salaries back to a respectable level after the large losses in the 1940s.[56]

Reservations on Faculty Pay

Generalizations on faculty salaries should not rest only on the pay of the full professor, though this is the most important part of the structure. If pay of the professor rises *vis-à-vis* other groups, we may get an exaggerated view of the gains in compensation. Also relevant is the proportion of professors to all faculty members. If the pay of the former rises greatly, but the proportion of professors declines, then one may be misled by concentrating on the changes in pay in each rank. In its appraisal of faculty salaries the Association of University Professors tries to cope with this problem to some extent by studying the average compensation for full-time faculty members per student equivalent. Where professors are relatively numerous compensation on this basis should be relatively high. Yet this is not necessarily so. Harvard's full-time faculty compensation per student equivalent in 1963-1964 was $865. Leaving out graduate schools and medical schools, I found 25 institutions of higher learning with higher averages than Harvard. These were primarily first-class institutions such as Wesleyan, MIT, Amherst, Princeton, Chicago, and Haverford. But when I compare

Harvard's ratio of 58 percent of professors to all faculty with these other institutions the explanation seems to lie not in the ratio of professors to all faculty—the proportion is invariably lower than for Harvard—but rather in larger numbers of faculty to students. These are often small institutions with large costs because their faculties are large in relation to the number of students.

Another issue of significance is the age of the faculty. As I noted elsewhere, the age of attainment of professorial rank is lower than in the nineteenth century, and especially under the unusual market conditions of the post World War II period. In a significant article, the brilliant dean of the Harvard faculty, McGeorge Bundy, spelled out effectively the case for higher pay at Harvard. Unlike most college administrators he was aware that the measuring rod had to be not only price movements but also the gains of real income by the rest of the population. In his presentation, he showed that at age thirty, Harvard College teachers earned $5,500, but at the same age Harvard Law School graduates earned $7,000; Harvard Business School graduates, $9,000; and Harvard B.A.s (non technical) $8,000.[57]

Competitive Aspects

One aspect of Harvard's salary position requires a little amplification. Its competitive position is strong, though I suspect it has declined in the last generation.

Over the years Harvard's salaries have been higher than those of its competitors. Exact comparisons are not easy; in part because fringe benefits vary, though these were of little importance until recent years; in part because before the twentieth century, professors depended partly on fees. Yet it is clear that Harvard is generally the high-pay institution. A comparison for five periods in the nineteenth century sheds some light on the competitive conditions. In all years but 1830, soon after the Kirkland-Davis crisis, Harvard's salaries were much higher. The figures below are for full professors:

56. *Report of the President of Harvard College,* 1955-1956, p. 9.

57. McGeorge Bundy, *What Should Harvard Pay Its Faculty,* 1957.

Table 13-2

Annual Salaries of Professors at Several Institutions of Higher Learning, Various Years (1809 to 1900)

Year or Closest Available	Harvard	Yale	Dartmouth	Cornell	Columbia	Brown	Amherst	William & Mary	Princeton
1809	1500	–	770	600	500	600	--	--	1000
1830	1500	–	900	--	--	1000	1000	1000	1000
1850	2000	1200	1100	--	1600	1250	1200 (in 1860)	--	1300
1870	4500	–	3000	2250	–	1800	2000	--	–
1900*	5000	–	2400	--	–	--	3000	--	–

*At this time, a few colleges were paying as much as $7,000. C. F. Thwing, *College Administration*, 1900, p. 165.

Sources: J. Maclean, *History of the College of New Jersey*, 1746-1854, vol. II, pp. 118, 299, 316; *History of Columbia University*, 1754-1904, 1904, p. 85; Report of the Trustees of Columbia College in Reply to the Senate Committee in *Columbia College, 1799-1879*, p. 9; W. C. Bronson, *History of Brown University, 1764-1914*, 1914, pp. 177, 232, 259, 331; L. B. Richardson, *History of Dartmouth*, 1932, vol. I, pp. 236, 406; vol. II, pp. 706-707; *Sketches of the History of Dartmouth*, p. 62; C. Fuess, *Amherst, The Story of a New England College*, Boston, 1935, pp. 94, 183, 269, 293; *William and Mary College Laws*, 1830; and Harvard sources given elsewhere.

Harvard continued to pay higher salaries in the twentieth century. Eliots' famous increase in 1869-1870 gave Harvard a large advantage for years to come. Even when Chicago began to be a troublesome competitor in the early twentieth century and offered much higher salaries, Harvard was able to withstand raids, partly because of the increased prestige related in part to Eliot's policies.

In 1963-1964, the American Association of University Professors found that Harvard was one of four universities with average pay of $14,000 or over, and the only institution of higher learning with an average pay for full professors in excess of $20,970.[58] (In 1967-1968 top salaries in the college were $28,000.) But despite that fact Harvard is losing ground. It does not have the economic superiority of Eliot's day. Even in the 1920s, when I was a young faculty member, an offer from Harvard was almost

certain to attract a professor from another institution. Today the proportion that turn Harvard down is much larger than in the past. One reason for this is that public institutions of higher learning with large tax funds behind them have greatly improved in recent years, as have some leading independent institutions. A second relevant factor is that competing institutions, instead of sticking to a fixed scale, now increasingly go away out of line to induce a Harvard professor to leave. Effects on morale in the scouting institution may be bad, but the Harvard product is lost. Bundy reminded us, as Eliot had before him, that senior faculty members do not move despite (in Bundy's period) an enticement of $3,000 over the Harvard salary. But more move than did in the past.

In response to concern over Harvard's deterioration of competitive position, Dean Franklin Ford examined the issues in 1966-1967. He found that Harvard attracted many more faculty members from competitors in recent years than they in turn weaned

---

58. The Economic Status of the Profession, 1963-1964, in *Bulletin of the AAUP*, June, 1964, pp. 139-185.

away from Harvard. This does not answer the question of the numbers who, when questioned about interest in Harvard, ask that they not be considered. I suspect this number is larger than in the past. Some loss in competitive position is inevitable. I do not think relative pay is the only crucial issue. Among sixteen strong rivals, Harvard still has the highest average pay for full professors, and a large proportion of full professors in its faculty. At $18,700 average full-time compensation in 1966-1967, Harvard's pay was more than $5,000 in excess of that of the University of California, probably its most potent rival, and substantially above its fifteen other competitors, the last with an average of about $14,500. In fringe benefits included in the above, Harvard allocates 19 percent of pay as compared with 11 percent for the University of California and 13 percent for fifteen other competitors.[59]

With the opening of Johns Hopkins University and the University of Chicago, Harvard was confronted with increased competition. Pres. John Gilman of Johns Hopkins proved to be a formidable competitor. Gilman tried to attract Wolcott Gibbs, William James, F.J. Child, G.M. Lane, and J. Trowbridge, all stars on the faculty of Harvard. In 1881, William James, after some negotiation, decided to stay at Harvard. Professor Child exploited an offer from Johns Hopkins University to demand and receive relief from the drudgery of grading papers. In seeking to enlist Professor Münstenberg, it was necessary not only to apply part of Professor James' salary but also to squeeze Santayana out. Professor James, helping in the negotiations, in 1892 urged a committment of 3 years for Münstenberg, saying "I am afraid that these Chicago devils may get after him."

President Eliot may have been annoyed at Gilman's fishing in his waters and "casting his lures whenever he saw the man he wanted." But he wrote Gilman, whom he greatly admired, "Please don't think I feel in the least annoyed at proposals made by you to Harvard men. On the contrary, I should have thought it very odd if there had been no men here whom you cared to try for. . . ." [60]

Quality

We have already noted that the faculty members were better trained in later Harvard history than in the first 150 years. Indeed Harvard was fortunate in finding, even in the first years of endowed professorship early in the eighteenth century, such men as John Winthrop in science and G. Wigglesworth in divinity. But later Harvard seemed even more fortunate. Eliot wondered how it happened that among the graduates of Harvard in the first half of the nineteenth century there appeared historians such as Jared Sparks, John G. Palfrey, William H. Prescott, George Bancroft, Francis Parkman, and Justin Winsor; such poets and essayists as William Ellery Channing, Frederick Henry Hedge, James Freeman Clarke, Ralph Waldo Emerson, James Russell Lowell, Oliver Wendell Holmes, Thomas Wentworth Higginson, and Charles Eliot Norton; orators including Edward Everett and Robert Charles Winthrop; jurists Joseph Story, Lemuel Shaw and Richard Henry Dana; and such scientists as Benjamin Peirce, Jeffries Wyman, and Benjamin Apthorp Gould.

At the 250th anniversary of Harvard's founding, J.L. Lowell noted that Harvard had "received the new learning from Germany at the hands of Everett, Bancroft, and Ticknor, and also that Everett's "translation of Battmann's great grammar was reprinted in English, with the Massachusetts omitted after Cambridge . . . to conceal the American origin."[61]

59. From a memo (September 28, 1967) sent to a committee at Harvard studying these problems. The original material is obtained (though reworked) from the American Association of University Professors report on salaries for 1967. The University of California salary average is depressed in part because its faculty is an especially young one.

60. James, *op. cit.,* vol. II, pp. 13-15. W. James to C.W. Eliot, April 25, 1881, C. W. Eliot to W. James, April 5, 1892; W. James to E. W. Hooper, April 30, 1892.

61. See *History of Harvard College,* pp. 72-73; *Report of Visiting Committee of Harvard University,* January 1849, p. 9; F. W. Clarke, *Wolcott Gibbs, 1822-1908,* p. 7; Harvard University, *Record of the Commemoration of the 250th Anniversary of the Founding of Harvard University,* 1887, p. 213; James, op. cit., vol. I, p. 216; A. MacLeish, *The Next Harvard,* 1937, p. 4.

In the twentieth century Harvard continued to lead the nation in the quality of its faculty. A number of surveys in the first sixty-seven years of the century, based on the appraisals of experts, revealed that Harvard had the highest standing in the country.[62] In the last, the University of California at Berkeley was close behind. Harvard's eminence sprang from resources, prestige, and the good fortune of the appointment of a number of outstanding presidents, with Eliot undoubtedly the major factor.

The Radcliffe Reform and Teaching Burdens

One important reform of great importance we owe largely to the wise Dean (Provost) Paul Buck, who raised salaries by 20 percent (with some exceptions) in the middle of World War II. This was really a shuffle. The faculty was to combine Harvard and Radcliffe instruction. Some teachers at Radcliffe would now have less work for the same pay. Others would have more pay with the same work. Here is a disguised increase in pay.[63]

In comparison with the teaching burdens a hundred years ago, it may be argued that per hour of teaching, or, better, per hour of pleasurable teaching, pay has increased much more than is suggested by pay scales alone. Hours of drudgery have been greatly reduced. President Eliot, in enlisting many young faculty members, greatly reduced the burden of teaching for the older members of the faculty. I recall as a young instructor or assistant professor in the 1920s repeating a Harvard course for an additional $750 or thereabouts and adding several hundred dollars additional through tutoring Radcliffe students.

Before moving on from the problem of teaching burden I compare the teaching burden of today—about four to five hours per week for twenty-five

weeks—for senior faculty members with the requirements in the first quarter of the nineteenth century. The mathematics tutor had a teaching assignment of three hours and thirty-three minutes *per day;* the professors of Greek and Latin, three hours per day; the Hollis Professor of Mathematics, three hours thirty-three minutes; average daily time for eight officers, two hours, thirty-six minutes.[64]

The Faculty Finances the College

In assessing college salaries one should allow for the contributions of faculty members to the financing of higher education. In a good part of the nineteenth century, during which Harvard was in a precarious financial state, the faculty discovered that they could often obtain buildings, space, or equipment only by assuming the costs themselves.

Thus, in 1837, Professor John Warren of the medical school owned all "the anatomical apparatus in the Medical College . . . the materials were purchased with my money and elaborated with my hands." The materials were very expensive and "the labor bestowed upon them in the space of thirty-five years has been very great." Warren added that all the movable furniture in the medical college belonged to him, and also that a few medical school professors were instrumental in obtaining the $100,000 gift of the Legislature in 1814. ". . . The desire of elevating the Medical School and the hope of doing some honor to the university have been the incentives to my labor" he said.[65]

Particularly in the medical school, the faculty had to carry a large part of the financial burden. For example, the building on North Grove Street that was occupied by the medical school in the 1840s and 1850s cost $45,000, but $16,000 were still unpaid during President Walker's incumbency (1853 to 1860). On this the "professors pay annually to the

62. B. Berelson, *op. cit.,* p. 126.
63. Memorandum of *Remarks Made by Dean Buck at the Faculty Meeting of March 3, 1943; Report of the President of Harvard College,* 1942-1943, pp. 18-19, 38-39.

64. S. E. Morison, in *Publications of the Colonial Society of Massachusetts,* The Great Rebellion in Harvard College, April, 1928, p. 107.
65. John Warren to the President of Harvard University, May 18, 1837.

Corporation six percent as interest, and one percent towards the gradual liquidation of the debt."[66]

Others including L. Agassiz, the great naturalist, W. C. Bond, the astronomer, and G. Palmer, the philosopher,[67] also contributed greatly to the financial support of their teaching.[68]

Fees

Until relatively recent years, Harvard depended heavily upon the fees it charged students for financing the faculty. By fees, I mean payments that related to enrollment, and not a fixed sum of (say) $1,000 that we designate as tuition. In the professional schools, where endowed chairs were not numerous, the dependence on fees tended to be especially great. When the college wanted to attract a promising professor or undertake teaching of additional subjects, if endowment income was not available and general funds were low, and additional tuition was deemed unacceptable, the procedure would likely be a fee imposed on the students, for certain courses with the professor usually the beneficiary. In the course of Harvard's history, many differences broke out over the distribution of these fees. In the crisis of the 1820s, the corporation cut salaries, but promised additional pay which was to be related to rises in enrollment. The system of fees was not always accepted without criticism. Some objected because tying fees to the professor's compensation encouraged the acceptance of poor students.

In the early years of the medical school, the faculty depended almost wholly on fees. In fact, the medical school operated like a small business, with charges assessed to yield the maximum revenue and the faculty then dividing the net income among themselves on an agreed formula.

Anxious to obtain the services of George Ticknor, the corporation offered him in 1817 the Smith Professorship of Belles Lettres. But the pay of $1,000 was considered inadequate. Hence, Ticknor would not be asked to reside in the college and he would be entitled to fees.[69]

In the 1826 statutes, the following appeared:

The emoluments of the president and of all the professors and instructors, shall be made to depend, when it can be done consistently with the statutes of their respective foundations, in some measure on the number of students; and for this purpose, whenever a new appointment is made to any of these offices, or whenever the present incumbents shall assent to the arrangement, these officers shall receive a certain fixed salary, and shall be entitled, in addition thereof, to a certain sum for every undergraduate.[70]

Moonlighting

Through much of Harvard's history, the administration had to deal with the problem of outside work by the faculty. That the problem was not more acute is to be explained by the fact that the teaching and other responsibilities imposed on the faculty were so severe that outside work was frequently out of the question. Yet when the faculty member found his pay inadequate to cover necessary expenses, he often assumed additional responsibilities ranging from taking in boarders to tutoring students. It is not clear that the college always was consistent in its treatment of these problems. Even in the twentieth century, the college would invite new faculty members and offer

66. *Circular on Request for $50,000, by the Medical School* (no title or date given, but signed by medical school staff and President Walker).

67. L. Agassiz to President James Walker, October 9, 1856; W. C. Bond to President Walker, March 2, 1854; R. W. Brown, *Harvard Yard in the Golden Age*, p. 72.

68. O. W. Holmes, J. Bigelow, and J. P. Cooke, Jr., to the President and Fellows of Harvard College, November 24, 1855; J. A. Cooke, Jr., to the Corporation of Harvard

College, July 26, 1856; J. P. Cooke, Jr., to John E. Thayer, August 11, 1856; J. P. Cooke, Jr., to the Corporation of Harvard College, January 1, 1858.

69. *Statutes and Laws of the University in Cambridge, Massachusetts*, 1826, p. 9. Meeting of the President and Fellows of Harvard College, May 3, 1817 (on Ticknor): *Ibid*, May 14, 1817.

70. *Statutes and Laws of the University in Cambridge, Massachusetts*, 1826, p. 9.

the bait of Radcliffe teaching as a lure for assuring acceptance.

Barrett Wendell, a professor of English, expressed the issues well when he wrote:

Harvard salaries are necessarily low, particularly during the early years of service. Harvard instructors who are not fortunate enough to possess independent means are therefore compelled to do outside work or to leave their bills unpaid. They tend more and more to become mere schoolmasters. So while Radcliffe has undoubtedly helped Harvard instructors to increase their scanty earnings, there can be as little question that it has on the whole impaired their original power. It has thus tended to diminish the reputation which they might have won both for themselves and for the old college to which they owe prime allegiance.[71]

There was concern that excessive work for money would reduce the contributions to teaching and research. In the twentieth century, and particularly since World War II, faculty members' outside work has become much more important, the explanation in part being the scarcity of trained personnel and inadequate pay. In order to function more effectively as a medical school professor or as an engineer or economist, outside activities are often helpful and even necessary. The crucial issue is how much, and to what extent, the rewards are merely monetary.

The statutes of 1826 provided:

No person shall hold any executive office in the university, who has the pastoral care of a church; or who holds any civil office, except the office of Justice of the Peace; and whoever shall accept such pastoral care, or any civil office except that of Justice of the Peace, shall be considered as resigning his place in the university, and the same shall be void, and a new election shall take place.[72]

Again, when Radcliffe was being launched in 1878, they wanted the help of Harvard faculty. Agassiz wrote to Eliot:

My plan obliges me to obtain the services of some of the professors, and I address you before approaching them, in order to assure myself that I am correct in supposing that their relations to the university are such as to permit of their giving instruction to those who are not connected with it.[73]

President Eliot allowed the use of Harvard faculty.

In the midst of the crisis of 1825, the issue of outside activities brought recriminations. John Farr, the Hollis Professor of Mathematics, resented a ruling of a committee of the corporation that to save money, he would have to tutor. Whereupon Mr. Bowditch, a member of the committee, noted that Farr had been teaching only one hour a day "and making $2,000 a year by translating and publishing French textbooks; and that if he was not willing to do his proper share of teaching he could resign. . . ."[74]

Over-all Trends

In an appendix to this chapter, I have included a table which gives faculty salaries over a period of about 250 years. The large rise in salaries occurred especially in inflationary periods: e.g., 1723 to 1755; 1771 to 1778 (and later years in the Revolution); 1849-1850 to 1870; 1900 to 1919-1920; 1940 to 1958-1959.

The rise from 1860 to 1870 reflects the special efforts of President Eliot; and those of 1920 to 1930, the improving economy of the nation as well as the failure of the faculty pay to catch up with rising prices in the period 1900 to 1920.

On the whole, in the first 150 years of Harvard history, faculty salaries responded to rising prices better than in the great inflations of World War I and

---

71. M. A. de Wolfe Howe, *Barrett Wendell and His Letters,* pp. 88-89; cf., Graduate School of Education, in *Report of the President of Harvard College,* 1927-1928, pp. 165-166.

72. *Statutes and Laws of the University in Cambridge, Massachusetts,* 1836, p. 9.

73. *Elizabeth Cary Agassiz,* pp. 194-195, 200-201.

74. S. E. Morison, "The Great Rebellion in Harvard College," in *Publications of the Colonial Society of Massachusetts,* April, 1928, p. 107.

World War II. I suspect two explanations of this difference. First, in the earlier period salaries were so low that a lag in pay would reduce the standard of living to an unacceptable position. Second, the college investment officers were quick to adjust investments to the rising price level in the seventeenth and eighteenth centuries. They would demand a return on investments adjusted to the rising price level. By World War II, Harvard also began to adjust to inflation by investing more heavily in equities.

One of the explanations of the losses that Harvard faculty accepted in the great inflations of World War I and World War II was the lack of organization of faculty members, not only at Harvard but also at most institutions of higher learning. In contrast, school teachers were much better organized, and therefore achieved an adjustment not only to rising prices but also to rising per capita income, which the faculties in higher education had far from achieved even as late as 1967.

From all of this I do not mean to suggest that the Harvard faculty's pay did not reflect the rising standard of living, e.g., the rise of per capita or per family incomes of the nation. After all, the gains from $260 pay of a full professor in 1723 to $21,000 in 1964, or a rise of 80 times, reflects the real gains of the economy much more than rising prices. Yet there is much evidence that faculty salaries have lagged far behind incomes of other groups and notably in the last 150 years.

One writer tells us that a college president with an income of $2,000 plus a house could live well early in the nineteenth century. Evan a $600 income was acceptable when a quart of milk could be had for 1½ cents, and thirteen chickens for 63 cents.[75] Eliot's comments in 1902 were especially germane.

... The mode of life of professors in Cambridge has not changed so much in relation to the mode of life of other residents in the vicinity of the University, as the mode of life of the student has changed in refer-

ence to that of their predecessors. One hundred years ago the professors' houses in Cambridge were the best in the village. Professors' houses are no longer the best; they are undoubtedly more comfortable than professors' houses were one hundred years ago, but the houses of many other residents now much surpass theirs in size and style. The rise in the scale of living is general throughout the American community, and is by no means peculiar to university life."[76]

While the hourly wages in manufacturing increased 1071 percent between 1870 and 1963, Harvard full professors' wages only increased by 425 percent. Between 1869 and 1938, net per capita income rose by 231 percent; Harvard full professors' income rose by 156 percent. From 1929 to 1963, the comparison is similar, with per capita income increasing by 251 percent and Harvard full professors' income rising by 110 percent.[77]

Another indication of the unsatisfactory relative pay of a full professor is a comparison of that variable and tuition charges at Harvard. In recent years the professors' pay has tended to be low compared to tuition charges. (A low ratio may reflect low salaries as well as high tuition.) Thus, in 1723, the ratio of salary to tuition was 43 to 1; in 1964, 14 to 1.

How Much for Faculty?

How much should a faculty member be paid? This is not an easy question to answer. On the assumption that in the base year his pay was satisfactory, then it might be argued that pay should keep up with the income of the average member of the labor market. Pay should also be adequate to attract faculty members in needed numbers and quality. That means that income should be high enough to put institutions of higher learning on a strong competitive basis with other professions and employments that require as much training and ability. In the United States in the 1960s, the pay of a practicing physician is about 3

75. G. P. Schmidt, *The Old Time College Professor*, 1930, pp. 71-72; *Report of the President of Harvard College*, 1901-1902, pp. 58-59.

76. *Ibid.*

77. From U. S. Census, *Historical Statistics of the United States*, 1789-1946; *Economic Report of the President* and various tables in this book on faculty salaries.

times that of the average college faculty member. In Great Britain the physician earns only about 20 percent more than the average college teacher. Obviously the institution of higher learning in this country is in a weak competitive position for attracting faculty vis-à-vis physicians. College officials, determining their salary scales, will of course also watch the pay of competitors. If they fall far behind they will lose faculty members. Finally, pay should be high enough to assure the faculty member a standard of living commensurate with his position and without recourse to excessive outside work.

In Eliot's day the president often commented on the unwillingness of Harvard faculty members to leave, even though they were being tempted by higher pay elsewhere. More recently, Dean Bundy wrote:

Men work for many other things than money, and in my three years as Dean I have repeatedly learned of distinguished colleagues who have refused invitations from other institutions at startling increases in salary; I think it is fair to say that in recent years no senior man has left this Faculty for money.[78]

Rudolph commented well on the practice at Harvard and Yale of exploiting the affluent professor. The governing boards counted on the "durability of the Professor or Professors who did not depend upon salary to keep body and soul to-gether."[79]

In his inaugural address President Eliot said: "The poverty of scholars is of inestimable wealth in this money getting nation. It maintains the true standards of virtue and honor. The poor friars, not the bishops, saved the church. . . ."

The Harvard 1968 Report on Recruitment and Retention of the Faculty

Soon after finishing this manuscript, Harvard's *Report of the Committee on Recruitment and Retention of the Faculty* (May 1, 1968) appeared. This report throws some light on the problems discussed here. There are a few relevant points. In the last twenty years, Harvard's competitive advantage in pay for tenure members has been eroded to some extent. But except in the instructor and especially the assistant professor levels, Harvard's salary scale is still above that of its competitors. Since 1951-1952, tenure positions declined from 25 percent of the faculty to 17 percent in 1967-1968. Whereas the numbers of tenure members increased by 33 percent in these years, all faculty except teaching fellows rose by 51 percent. Teaching fellows increased from 45 to 48 percent of the total. All of this points to a larger proportion of Harvard's work being done by younger members of the faculty.

Harvard has serious problems despite its high pay. Perhaps the most troublesome one arises from the policy of competitors offering salaries, in individual cases, away above those consistent with Harvard's scale. Harvard finds it more difficult than in the past to attract faculty from the outside, and to keep its faculty from leaving in response to offers involving higher pay and reduced teaching loads. Harvard has to depend heavily on its own products to recruit its faculty. Thus, on July 1, 1967, almost 50 percent of the appointees to tenure positions at Harvard had been employed at Harvard previously to the time of tenure appointment.

A census of Harvard faculty receiving offers outside revealed that 9 percent found income at Harvard higher, 6 times as many found income at the competing institutions superior.

Competition is much more serious than it used to be, a fact reflected in the age at which tenure is given at Harvard: thirty-nine in 1939 and thirty-five currently. (This is a disguised rise of pay.)

One point needs special emphasis. In the twentieth century the demand for a Harvard education rose by several times, and that for all institutions of higher learning even more. Yet the pay of the faculty, though it increased both in current and real dollars, nevertheless rose much less than in the economy. Even so, the rising demand for higher education increased much more than that for all goods and services.

78. McGeorge Bundy, "What Should Harvard Pay Its Faculty?," in *Harvard To-Day*, Spring, 1957.
79. F. Rudolph, *The American College and University: A History,* 1962, p. 195.

Year	Professor	Associate Professor	Assistant Professor	Instructor
1712–1713	None	None	None	None
1714–1715	None	None	None	None
1722–1723	£80	None	None	£70.00
1765–1766	206–252	None	None	104
1771–1772	171–290	None	None	None
1777–1778	361.10–488.	None	None	None
1809	$ 1,500	None	None	None
1818	1,200–$ 1,700	None	None	None
1829–1830[7] Retrenchment	600– 1,500	None	None	$ 500–$1,200
1839–1840	1,000– 2,000	None	None	500
1849–1850	500– 2,000	None	None	500
1859–1860	800– 2,500	None	None	500– 722.50
1869–1870	1,500– 4,500	None	None	700– 1,200
1879–1880	500– 4,500	None	$1,500–$ 4,000	250– 1,500
1889–1890	500– 4,500	None	1,500– 3,000	600– 2,000
1899–1900[3]	1,000– 5,000	$ 4,000	400– 3,125	200– 2,000
1909–1910[4]	4,000– 5,500	3,500–$ 4,500	2,500– 3,000	1,200– 1,500
1919–1920	6,000– 8,000	5,000– 5,500	3,500– 4,500	1,600– 2,750
1929–1930	8,000– 12,000	6,000– 7,000	4,000– 5,500	3,000
1939–1940	8,000– 12,000	6,000– 7,000	4,000– 5,500[2]	3,300[2]
1949–1950	9,000– 15,000	5,000– 7,500[1]	4,500[1]	3,500[1]
1958–1959[8]	12,000– 20,000	8,000– 11,000	6,500– 7,700	5,500– 6,000
1966–1967	$15,000–$26,000	$11,000–$15,000	$9,000–$10,600	$7,800–$8,600[9]

	1903–1904	1917	1963–1964
Average: Professors	$3,380	$4,671	$20,970
Associate professors	–	–	
Assistant professors	2,130	2,841	
Instructors	990	1,252	
All faculty			11,780

Sources: 1712–1818, *Treasurer's Ledgers and Journals;* 1829–1967 *Treasurer's Statements, Journals and Ledgers;* 1909–1949; "The Economic Status of the Faculty of Arts and Science," (a report of Ad Hoc Committee) 110, September, 1950, p. 28; "Harvard Salaries and the Cost of Living," in *Harvard Alumni Bulletin,* vol. V, no. XI, p. 324; January 25, 1917; 1963–1964, *A.A.U.P.,* June, 1964; The Economic Status of the Profession, 1963–1964.

to 1967 Minimum and Maximum by Rank

Lecturer[3]	Assistant[4]	Tutor[5]	Proctor[6]	Average Compensation All Faculty
None	None	£50–£60	None	
		50–80		
		70–90		
		68–66		
		100		
		$ 660 –$1,400		
		660 – 1,400	$150	
		645	112.50–$171.80	
		645 – 1,000	50 – 116	
		215 – 1,025	16.67– 100	
		722.50– 800	100	
		1,000 – 1,200	$100	
		1,000 – 2,000		
$300		$1,000		
$750–$1,500				$ 1,565 (1903–1904)
				1,840 (1917)
				$14,000 (1963–1964)

1 Data is for 1947.

2 Data is for 1938.

3 The rank, of uncertain date, can be given a salary range only for the years shown. Otherwise it varies considerably.

4 Does not say so, but it is presumed that its data represents college only. It cannot be determined if part-time teaching staff is included in some categories because of the treasurer's books' format.

5 Does not represent the teaching fellow rank; 50–80 means range of 3 tutors, with pay 50, 70, 80 for 3 tutors.

6 Administrative duties only.

7 The number of faculty was in 1826–1827 reduced from 27 to 20.

8 From data supplied by Dean Bundy's Office.

9 Faculty of Arts and Sciences, Harvard University, Report on the Committee for Recruitment of Professors . . . , May 1, 1968.

14

Structure of Pay

At the outset, the pay of all faculty members was low indeed. President Dunster received £62 and the fellows, with whom he shared teaching responsibilities, obtained only £4 or less than one-fifteenth as much. Clearly in comparison with the past hundred years the fellow (or tutor) was being exploited. But to offset their low pay, I should mention that their lack of training beyond the bachelor's degree partly justifies the low pay. Tutors or fellows, or those with similar responsibilities, would today receive about one fourth of the president's salary. By the end of the seventeenth century, the president's income had risen to $178 plus some part of the tuition money, and the fellows were receiving about one quarter as much.[1]

The structure of pay in 1714 is difficult to understand. Whereas the annual pay of three tutors was £80, £70 and £50 respectively, the treasurer's pay was out £40 and the library keeper, apparently already in the exploited class, received the magnificent pay of £6. By 1750, the respective salaries were treasurer, £27; four tutors, £59 to £61 each; mathematics professor, £98; and Hebrew professor, £46.

Apparently, the treasurer had improved his status, but he was still not in the high-income class—perhaps partly because the job of the treasurer was to some extent an honorary position. At this time the tutors had much more income status vis-à-vis the professors than they have had in more modern times.[2]

By 1800, according to one observer, President Willard, with an income of $1,830, was the highest paid educator in the nation. Professors received about two-thirds as much and tutors about half the pay of professors. The ratio of 7:5:2 was not much out of line with what might have been expected in recent times.[3]

By the middle of the nineteenth century, the structure had not changed greatly. The president's salary was $2,500 a year, with most professors receiving $1,800. The pay of junior members was rather low, ranging from $430 to $1,025. A salary of $1,000 for the librarian, $1,200 for the steward, and $600 for the treasurer reflected their improving status.[4]

The influence of President Eliot is evident in the large relative gains of the professors vis-à-vis others. In the years 1869 to 1904, professors' salaries rose by 25 to 40 percent, but those of instructors declined by 40 percent.[5]

1. Foster, *op. cit.,* pp. 131–135.
2. *College Books,* vol. IV, pp. 52–74; 234–316; *Publications of the Colonial Society of Massachusetts,* vol. 16, pp. 420–464, 469–586.
3. P. Oliver, "Notes on Education in the United States in the year 1800," in *Bulletin of New York Public Library,* January, 1944, p. 9
4. *Report of the Treasurer of Harvard College,* 1849–1850, pp. 6, 8; cf., 1839–1840, p. 8.
5. C. F. Adams, "Proposed Increase of the Tuition Fee," in *Harvard Graduates Magazine,* vol. 13, 1904, pp. 9–10.

The range of salaries for professors and assistant professors in 1889–1890 follows:

Source: Treasurers' Journals, 1887-1894, p. 207.

Full-time Professors' and Assistant Professors' Pay, July, 1890	
Number of Professors	Amount of Pay
7	$ 4,500.
8	4,000.
6	3,500.
5	3,000.
4	2,500.
3	2,250.
1	2,150.
10	2,000.
1	1,500.
45	$139,900.
Mean	3,110

From 1904 to 1964, the largest gains were made by instructors—here the squeeze of inflation helps account for these large rises. Assistant professors did not do nearly so well. The gains of professors were roughly midway between those of instructors and those of assistant professors.

One problem troubles college administrators. They announce a particular scale of pay at different ranks and subranks. Under these scales they may treat all faculty members in a like manner; that is, they allow automatic increases to all with the passage of time. The alternative is to adjust rises of pay to merit. In this way funds can be saved. In periods of inflation, when adjustments to rising prices are made, the administration can deny increases to the less meritorious faculty members and thus pay according to merit and also save funds. It is of some interest that Eliot was against this kind of discrimination even if based, presumably, on the varying contributions of the faculty:

In the practice of some American Universities advances of salary are not invariably automatic, *that is, so many dollars of salary additional for so many additional years of service, the trustees exercising some discretion in delaying or on accelerating in special cases. . . . These cases always give rise to grave complaints from some section or other of the staff, and sometimes impair confidence in the justice and good feeling of the trustees. . . .*[6]

But in the large inflation of the years 1900 to 1919, the corporation relied on selective increases rather than on across-the-board rises. They thus saved funds.

In the Puritan period (1636 to 1714) labor was scarce. Daily wages were about 2s 6d and at three hundred days this would come to about £35. But a more realistic figure might be £25. Hence, the fellows earned about three times as much as the laborer, and the president 6 times as much. The ratio in the Puritan period and (say) 1963 may be put as follows:

Table 14-1.

Relationship Between Incomes for Different Positions

	Puritan Period Index	1963 Index
Laborer	100 (£25)	100 ($ 5,000)
Fellow	300 (£75)	150 ($ 7,500)
College or university president	600 (£150)	400 ($20,000)
School Teacher	80 (£20)	100 ($ 5,000)

It is clear that the relative positions of fellows (e.g., assistant professors' rank) and presidents have deteriorated; and that of teachers has improved. The great rise of education has increased the demand for teachers.

Salaries between 1638 and 1652 accounted for 29 percent of disbursements; between 1693 and 1712, about 60 percent; and for the whole Puritan period, 53 percent. The small percentage at the outset is related to the heavy disbursements for buildings and repairs, an amount relatively 3 times as high in 1638 to 1652 as between 1693 and 1712. In the first period the president's salary was 4 times as large in

6. Eliot, *op. cit.*, pp. 222–223.

relation to all disbursements as the pay of fellows, but with rising numbers of fellows and relative increases of pay by 1693 to 1712, the fellows' pay consumed twice as much as the president's, or a relative gain of 8 times for the former.[7] Salaries are a much smaller share of expenditures in the 1960s than in the first 250 years.

It is of some interest that whereas the president's salary was almost one-quarter of total disbursements in the years 1638 to 1652, by the 1960s it was only about one-three thousandth of the disbursements of the university.

7. Foster, *op. cit.*, p. 149.

15

Fringe Benefits

Fringe benefits are a phenomenon of modern economics. In the early 1960s, for example, a Harvard full professor's average income in the college was $21,000, of which sum $3,000 were fringe benefits, e.g., contributions of the university to annuity funds and medical subsidies. By 1967, fringes accounted for 19 percent. In studying the trend of Harvard pay, it is wise to allow for the larger rises of fringe benefits than of basic pay.

Early in Harvard's history, the college offered fringe benefits to its faculty. Provision of houses or rooms were an early form of fringe benefit, with the president especially the beneficiary. In the early history of the law school, the college anxious to encourage residence in the college, offered rooms to the law school professor. When President Kirkland accepted the presidency of the university in the early nineteenth century, the college financed his moving expenses, as it did for professors at times. On behalf of Kirkland, the college also instructed the treasurer to purchase a "sideboard, mahogany tables, looking glasses, floor clothes, andirons, shovels and the Rumford apparitus . . . and to deliver the same to the President taking his receipt therefor . . . ."[1]

A fringe of some significance in the hears of financial stringency was loans by the corporation to both president and professors.

Pres. Joseph Willard (1781-1804) sought advances from the treasurer on more than one occasion. In one letter he wrote that it was very "disagreeable to me to ask the anticipation of a quarter's salary or grant, even for a day; . . . If you could, at this time, without inconveniencing to the College, let me have the two grants of the present quarter (amounting to $107.50) which do not come due till the end of the next month, you would much oblige me . . . ."[2]

An interesting episode was an advance to the great Greek scholar, Prof. (later President) Edward Everett. In their anxiety to get Everett on the faculty, the corporation allowed him to go to Europe to prepare himself and provided him with $2,000 a year for 4½ years, part ($1,200 a year) a grant for support, and part a loan of $800 a year. But there was much misunderstanding about this outlay of $9,000, an impressive sum at this time.[3]

Henry Longfellow, the successor of Professor Ticknor, had an experience not unlike Everett's. He also was given permission to study in Europe at some cost to the college before assuming his responsibilities in Cambridge. But when he sought permission to extend his stay by a year, President Quincy was clearly annoyed.

---

1. Meeting of Corporation of Harvard College, October 16, 1810, J. Lothrop, Chairman; *Foundations and Statutes,* vol. II, p. 32; *Corporation Records,* vol. I, p. 149.

2. Letter of President Joseph Willard to Treasurer Storer, January 27, 1800.
3. Prof. Everett to the Honorable and Reverend, the Corporation of Harvard University, Sept. 6, 1823 (Records of October 6, 1823); Everett to Pres. Kirkland, September 12, 1823; Everett to Judge Davis (Treasurer), March 14, 1825; President Kirkland to Judge Davis, March 21, 1825.

... and the objections [against the initial leave] *were surmounted only on your assurance that you would return in October, and that the benefit of your instruction should not be lost by any* [class] *of the college ... but as trustees of the funds under their control, cannot deem themselves justified in paying the salary of the Professorship to a Professor, not resident and not performing its duties. They value your services highly ...* [and will] *keep the Professorship open for your return ... your salary must cease at the end of the current quarter ....* [4]

A fringe benefit that is not always recognized as such is pay during periods of illness. But as late as 1828, the university did not seem disposed to provide pay during periods of illness. Prof. Andrew Norton was clearly irritated with the corporation's attitude toward his illness which required a leave of absence. [5]

In 1743, the corporation had clarified its position toward differential pay for married faculty.

That, with regard to his [Professor Winthrop] *present circumstances (being a single man) his salary for the Present is sufficient, but that if his Condition Should be alter'd, w^r by He shall stand in Need of an Jncrease of his Salary, we shall make such an addition to his Salary, as shall be tho't reasonable.*

In the next year the corporation was more specific. The professor in the married state would receive £100 additional so long as he shall continue "in the faithful Discharge of his Office ...." [6]

Fringe benefits are of increasing importance. But it is well also to stress the point that in denying to the faculty income beyond the regular schedule of pay for additional work, the corporation was offering a negative fringe. Thus, on one occasion in 1831, a professor requested of the corporation compensation for special chapel and similar services. But in response the corporation stated:

... officers, having a stated salary in the college, ought to perform all the duties, which might be from time to time required of them, within the general scope of this office, without additional compensation and that the practice of making an allowance for every particular service must be discontinued .... [7]

In general, the corporation has tended to favor the unmarried faculty members in its increasing offers of free rooms to the unmarried. [8] In 1782-1783, the French instructor was allowed to use a chamber in the college, the library, and commons at the tutors' weekly rate. [9]

Another fringe benefit is housing subsidies. Throughout Harvard's history in the seventeenth century and a large part of the eighteenth century, the Harvard faculty received special exemptions from property tax, and the college at one point provided housing at special rates, though Harvard has not systematically assumed responsibility for housing for faculty.

Over all Harvard's record on faculty housing has not been distinguished. President Lowell showed some interest and even alerted the faculty to the possibility of a reasonably low cost cooperative housing project at Coolidge Hill, a mile or so from the yard. But the faculty seemed uninterested. It is surprising that Eliot, with his great interest of keeping costs down for students and faculty, never sought faculty housing. [10]

A fringe benefit of increasing importance is the sabbatical year. Professor Morison noted that except for the first three presidents and the first Hollis Professor of Mathematics, the importation of foreign scholars had ceased. An alternative attracted the

---

4. T. W. Higginson, *Henry Wadsworth Longfellow,* 1902, pp. 158–161.
5. Andrew Norton to President Kirkland, October 16, 1828.
6. *College Books,* vol. IV, p. 741, October 10, 1743; p. 743, February 9, 1744.
7. *Report of the Committee to Whom was referred the Memorial of Dr. Ware (C. Jackson and F. C. Gray),* April 21, 1831.
8. *College Books,* vol. IV, p. 257.
9. *Corporation Records,* vol. III, p. 150.
10. C. Killam to A. L. Lowell, August 7, 1915; F. W. Hunnewell II to Professor C. Killam in *A. L. Lowell Papers, 1914-1917,* F. 766; Housing, F. 454; *Acts and Resolves passed by the General Court of Massachusetts,* vol. XIII, p. 667; *Report of the Treasurer of Harvard College,* 1843-1844, pp. 3-4; Corporation Records, vol. I, p. 261.

interest of the governing boards. A brilliant student, the Reverend Edward Everett (A.B. 1811), was offered a Greek professorship, with the stipulation that he could study abroad at full pay of $1,200 per year for two years before he assumed his active duties. Everett took his Ph.D. in 1817 and obtained another two years leave. The financing of foreign travel and study proved to be fruitful. "Emerson recorded that Everett's influence in Cambridge was comparable to that of Pericles in Athens." [11]

Of all fringe benefits, the most important is the payment by the institution of higher learning of funds on behalf of the faculty to finance annuities after retirement. With salaries rather low, the case for retirement pay is strong indeed. Yet the availability of annuities is a relatively modern development. In the eighteenth century the college often allowed the retiring professor or his heirs a sum of money for services rendered, but this was not the rule. When Professor Sewall retired from the Hancock chair he occasionally worked for the library for a modest compensation. In 1791, Prof. Edward Wigglesworth resigned the Hancock professorship and the corporation voted him an annuity of £132. In 1840, following a retirement from the same chair, the corporation offered Prof. J. Ware a choice of a payment of $3,000 all at once or $600 per year for his lifetime. [12]

An unusual transaction followed the death of Prof. Joseph Winlock, Director of the Observatory, on June 11, 1875.

In consideration of the fact that Professor Winlock's ingenuity and perseverance secured for the Observatory a permanent income from the sale of the exact time to cities, railroads, and watchmakers,—an income which now amounts to about $2,000 a year,—the Corporation ordered that one-half of the receipts from the sale of time be paid for five years to Professor Winlock's widow and children. [13]

President Eliot here, as in many other areas, was an innovator. In the 1870s he increasingly urged an annuity program. By 1889-1890 a reserve fund, apparently donated, amounted to $242,211.97. The corporation was providing retirement allowances to a few faculty members by 1896-1897.

A right to retirement allowance would greatly enhance the value of all University positions. . . . In the opinion of the President there is no way in which a given sum of money,—like $100,00 or $500,000—can be applied so productively for the University, accelerating the time when a thorough system of retiring allowances can be adopted.

In such a system the president also saw an opportunity to offer security to the faculty, to hasten the retirement of some members of the faculty, and accelerate the promotion of others. [14]

In 1898-1899, the president proudly announced a formal program, under which faculty members with 20 years of service at age sixty could receive retirement benefits equal to 20/60 of their last pay. The maximum benefit was to be 40/60 of pay. [15]

Unfortunately, the program was incurring deficits within five years. But the president was not too discouraged. The losses could be financed by the gains from substituting younger instructors for the older members of the faculty. [16]

Fortunately by 1906 the Carnegie Foundation provided some help. Yet throughout its history the retirement program has been confronted with successive crises. [17] By World War I, the Carnegie Fund was in trouble; academic longevity had exceeded expectations. The university had to divert free funds to save

11. Samuel Eliot Morison, *Three Centuries of Harvard, 1636-1936*, 1937, pp. 224-230.

12. *Report of the Committee on the Theological School*, April 25, 1840; *Corporation Papers; Report of the Treasurer of Harvard College*, 1840-1846.

13. *Report of the President of Harvard College*, 1874-1875, p. 3.

14. *Ibid.* 1879-1880, pp. 20-21; 1889-1890, p. 36; 1896-1907, p. 17.

15. *Ibid.* 1897-1899, pp. 12-13; cf., *The Harvard Bulletin*, vol. I. no. 15, 1899.

16. *Report of the President of Harvard College*, 1902-1903, p. 46.

17. *Ibid.* 1906-1907, p. 7; 1907-1908, pp. 39-40; *Report of the Treasurer of Harvard College*, 1907-1908, p. 9.

the program. Continued inflation and rising standards of living reduced its effectiveness. At times unwise management also impaired effectiveness.

A post World War I committee chaired by Prof. F. W. Taussig recommended a program with contributions by the faculty, administrative costs financed by the Carnegie Corporation, an operation accommodating a large number of institutions and subject to actuarial principles.[18]

A goal may well be a minimum of 50 percent of the salary just before retirement. But this is not easy to achieve. Much of the accumulation is at income levels far below those at the retirement age. Should one start in the year 1960, for example, and accumulate until the year 2000, then on the reasonable assumption of a 5 percent rise of per capital income per year (2 percent inflation and 3 percent rise of productivity), the costs of an adequate benefit to the account of a full professor at Harvard ($20,000 per year salary in 1960 and $140,000 in the year 2000), would be greatly increased as benefits decline relatively to rising incomes.

Management is sometimes poor. Harvard, for example, stuck to Teachers' Insurance Annuity (TIA) through the 1940s, with investments of the retirement fund yielding a little more than 2 percent. As a member of a university committee representing the College of Arts and Sciences, I persuaded the Harvard faculty at the third university faculty meeting in its history to recommend a diversion of at least half of its payments to the university, where its treasurer was investing much more wisely. Harvard's partial desertion of TIA contributed greatly to the highly successful equity program of TIA, which involved investments in equities.

Even with these advances Harvard's annuities are not adequate. After forty-two years of service at Harvard, I received an annuity equal to but one-third of my last salary. The committee on pensions, of which I was a member, rightly urged the university to pay the whole "tax" or premium as a means of achieving a tax gain. But it would be better to have the university pay 10 to 15 percent and the faculty members at least 10 percent. Then an annuity after forty years of service could well reach more than 75 percent of retirement pay. In recent years, the university has increased its contribution to the retirement reserves of older faculty members as a means of raising annuities to a respectable level, and in 1967 it guaranteed faculty members with 25 years of service an annuity equal to 50 percent of their pay in their last years of service.

18. *Report of the University Council of the Committee on Proposed Changes on the Pension System*, F. W. Taussig, Chairman, (undated); *A. L. Lowell Papers*, 1909-1914, F. 1374; A. L. Lowell to R. B. Perry in *A. L. Lowell Papers*, F. 1292.

16

Inadequate Salaries

In Chapter 13 we have suggested numerous reasons for increasing salaries. Among the important causes were rising prices, the need of matching the gains of other professions and the economy generally, discouraging of excessive outside activities to supplement income and maintaining and improving the competitive position of Harvard. The problems were well summarized in a letter to alumni in 1905. The aim of the Teachers' Endowment Fund was to raise salaries of teachers in order that:

"the teachers in the College should be the best in the land; that the older professors should be free from the cares of a straitened income; that the younger teachers should be able to give themselves without distraction to their work; that the best men should not be drawn away to other Colleges but should see before them reasonable promotion in work and salary. . . . [1]

Inadequate pay to teachers is an old disease in Anglo-Saxon colleges and universities. Dr. Johnson well discussed the problem some two hundred years ago.

An occasion for unhappiness was the failure of the college to supplement incomes as in response to rising prices and standards of living, the yield of the original endowment for a professorship became inadequate.[2]

From a letter of John Winthrop to the general court, dated December 28, 1764:

It is true, that the pious founder of this Professorship appointed a salary for it; which proving insufficient for a maintenance, the government of the College have from time to time (the last settlement made my salary, including Mr. Hollis's, to be £97 14s 10½d) done what they could for my support and encouragement, but this notwithstanding for several years, together with what the General Court were pleased to allow me, which I thankfully acknowledge, my income was so scanty, that I was obliged to contract considerable debts for the necessary support of my family. . . .

This inadequacy of yield of a fund for a chair continued to plague the college. With the great inflation of the Revolutionary War the problem became so serious that in his 1782 report President Willard proposed that the students make up the deficiency in the salary of the Hancock professorship. It was proposed by the president that Mr. Hollis's gift statute "which disallows of any assessments to be made upon the students towards the support of his Professor of Divinity . . . " should be disregarded. The corporation did not concur.[3]

Harriet Martineau, a famous British traveler in the 1830s wrote:

---

1. Letter to the Alumni from the Committee to Raise the Teachers' Endowment Fund, May 18, 1905.
2. Quincy, *op. cit.*, vol. II, p. 533 (appendix); cf., *College Books*, vol. II, pp. 11, 30-35 (1727-1738).

---

3. *Corporation Records*, vol. III, pp. 141-142, 173; cf., Quincy, *op. cit.*, vol. II, p. 306.

When I was at Boston the state of the University was a subject of great mourning among its friends. Attempts had been made to obtain the services of three gentlemen of some eminence as professors, but in vain. The salaries offered were insufficient to maintain the families of these gentlemen in comfort, in such a place as Cambridge; though, at that very time, the managers of the affairs of the institution were purchasing lands in Maine. The Moral Philosophy chair had been vacant for eight years. . . . Every one was questioning what was to be done next, and anticipating a further vacating of chairs which it would be difficult to fill. I heard one merry lady advise that the professors should strike for higher wages, and thus force the council and supporters of the university into a thorough and serious consideration of its condition and prospects in relation to present and future times.

In President Eliot's period the inadequacy of pay plagued him greatly, despite the generous rise of 1869-1870.

Eliot treated the problems in various ways. In the *midst* of a crisis in 1894, he preferred dismissals to a general cut in salary.

. . . I cannot help but think that to diminish the number of salaries by five percent is a great deal wiser than to cut down all salaries five percent, particularly if the selection of the individuals asked to resign is wisely made.[4]

Eliot also stressed the nonpecuniary motivation of faculty members.

A great University contains hundreds of men— teachers, librarians, and curators—who live on modest salaries with full knowledge that they can never be rich, and that they can leave no considerable inheritance to their children. They seek happiness in other and higher ways than in the prevailing pursuit of wealth. . .they are persons of consideration in the community where they live. . . . The luxurious classes find it difficult to understand the delights of such men; and the scholars find it as difficult to imagine the gratification of luxurious idleness. . . . [5]

Longfellow intervened when the college wanted to fire a sixty-seven-year-old instructor in French and Spanish who was unable to handle mischievous boys. The corporation then reduced the instructor's pay from $1,000 to $500 and allowed him to stay on until age eighty-three. But treatment of another modern language instructor, Pietro Bachi, was not equally generous:

For twenty-one years he had received only $500 per annum. He had not squandered this pittance by gambling, drinking or speculating. He had a family of several children, as well as aging and ailing relatives. . . . He was charitable, impractical and naive— exactly the contrary of his employers, who were guided by rigid business principles and a time-honored salary scale.

Bachi was fired for getting into debt and Longfellow added to his burdens the teaching of Italian.

A problem of increasing severity was competition for talent from other institutions of higher learning. At the outset of his administration President Eliot inquired: " . . . Does the Treasurer's report of Yale give the salaries of the professors? Or where can I get that little piece of information? . . . It is essential to command the services of young men of the best ability. Meat three times a week does not attract such."[6] Another commentator reflected on the offer of the new University of Chicago of a salary of $7,000 to John W. White and $12,000 to George Palmer and his wife.

President Eliot complained in 1871-1872 of the numerous resignations.[7] From time to time professional schools also complained of losses of talent to other institutions offering larger salaries.[8]

---

4. C. W. Eliot to Barrett Wendell, January 16, 1894.
5. Eliot, *op. cit.*, p. 93.

6. Charles W. Eliot to George Brush, June 24, 1869, in Eliot, *op. cit.*, vol. I, pp. 249-250; F. Bolles, "The Academic Year, 1891-1892," in *Harvard Graduates Magazine*, vol. I, p. 110, 1892.
7. *Report of the President of Harvard College*, 1871-1872, pp. 3-5; 1903-1904, p. 50.
8. *Ibid.*, 1929-1930, p. 207.

A common thread in the discussions of Harvard salaries has been the sacrifices made by Harvard professors. James Bryce, writing in 1891, said it is "surprising that so many able men are to be found on the teaching staffs.... The reason is to be found partly in the fondness for science and learning which has lately shown itself in America, and which makes men of intellectual tastes prefer a life of letters with poverty to success in business...."[9]

Again and again the stress was on sacrifice, but also on what we now call psychic income. Henry Adams explained the issue well at the time he was induced to accept an assistant professorship at Harvard.

The degree of Harvard College might bear a value as ephemeral as the commission of a President of the United States; but the Government of the college, measured by money alone, and patronage, was a matter of more importance than that of some branches of the national service. In social position, the college was the superior of them all put together. In knowledge, she could assert no superiority, since the Government made no claims, and prided itself on ignorance. The service of Harvard College was distinctly honorable; perhaps the most honorable in America; and if Harvard College thought Henry Adams worth employing at four dollars a day, why should Washington decline his services when he asked nothing?[10]

An interesting case is that of Joseph Story, an Associate Justice of the United States Supreme Court, who also served as a professor of law at Harvard from 1829 to 1845 at a salary of $1,000 a year. Apparently his Harvard work was virtually full-time since the Supreme Court required little time. His son, writing in 1851 when law school professors earned $3,000, estimated that Justice Story had contributed $32,000 to the law school (16 times $2,000).[11] The committee of the overseers concurred. Interestingly, the law school's income from students in these sixteen years was only $105,000.

George Santayana, the great philosopher, was not prepared to sacrifice greatly to stay at Harvard. Graduated in 1886 and a student in Europe the next two years, Santayana received an appointment in 1889 as an instructor to give two courses at a compensation of $500. It was not until eighteen years later that he became a full professor at $4,000. For a man of his quality the pay was inadequate and by modern standards promotion was altogether too slow.[12]

9. J. Bryce, *The American Commonwealth,* 1891, pp. 549-550.

10. H. Adams, *The Education of Henry Adams,* 1930, pp. 296-297.

11. W. W. Story, *Life and Letters of Joseph Story,* 1851, pp. 529-533.

12. G. Santayana, *The Middle Years,* 1945, ch. VIII; G. Santayana, *Persons and Places,* vol. II, pp. 157-159; D. Cory (ed.), *The Letters of George Santayana,* 1955, pp. 103-104.

17

Dissatisfaction with Salaries

Elsewhere in the discussion of faculty problems, I have dealt with the general relative deterioration of faculty economic status at Harvard. The explanation may be failure of the government to adhere to its committments, the onslaught of inflation, the general lag of faculty salaries behind the rising income of the nation or of professional workers generally, or the emergence of strong competitors determined to mobilize a faculty.

Here, I am concerned with a somewhat different problem, namely, the complaints of faculty members to the president or the corporation of inadequacy of pay. In some instances, the explanation is the rising price of necessaries of life; in others the failure of the salary of the faculty member to cover the minimum expenses of his household. They may also complain that pay is too low in comparison with that of other faculty members or too low at current work loads. Faculty complaints were especially numerous in the nineteenth century, reflecting in part the financial problem of the university.

In 1722, the college hired Judah Monis to teach Hebrew at £50 salary per year. Monis complained that the salary was inadequate:

... I hope you will give me leave to say that the salary you have voted me as an Encouragement or Reward for my Labour, is not sufficient to support me in my Single State, much less if I should enter a married state. ... [1]

A committee of the corporation in 1781 urged more adequate financial help from the state government as a condition for finding a president of quality. Depreciation of the currency had greatly impaired the financial condition of the college.

Benjamin Waterhouse, who quite consistently was in trouble with the authorities, though a valued innovator, sought finance from the university to cover the expenses involved in caring for and showing his natural history specimens. The visitors he wrote, "never stay less than 3, or 4 hours, and very often all day. ..." [2]

The son of Joseph Willard, who was president of Harvard from 1781 to 1804, intervened on behalf of his widowed mother, requesting a grant from the college since President Willard had spent $7751.50 in excess of his income during his incumbency. [3]

A number of instructors early in the nineteenth century addressed the college, stressing the arduousness of their duties, the increase of numbers of students and also the increase of salaries of other officers. They wanted an increase in pay. [4]

In 1814, President Kirkland referred to a meeting of the corporation:

A memorial of the Professors, stating the inadequacy of their respective salaries for their support, especially

---

1. Judah Monis to the Right Reverend President ... Corporation of Harvard College, May 22, 1722; Morison, *Three Centuries of Harvard, 1636-1936*, pp. 57-58.

2. Benjamin Waterhouse to the Rev. President Willard, March 8, 1801.
3. J. Willard to the Hon. and Rever ... Corporation of Harvard College, September 12, 1806.
4. To the Corporation and Overseers of Harvard College (apparently 1805), names of petitioners not available.

within a few years past, with respect to those of them having families, it was Voted, That three hundred dols be granted to the President, two hundred to each of the professors, aforesaid, . . . [5]

The Memorial stated:

Some of us having large expensive families, have been under the necessity of resorting to other means, precarious in their nature, and burdensome to their families, in order to supply the deficiency when they think it ought to be in their power . . . to obtain a present support but also to make some provision for future exigencies. . . . [6]

At about the same time, a group of faculty men urged the corporation to consider the inadequacy of college salaries:

And that with a given sum the same quantity of necessaries of life cannot at the present time be purchased. And consequently the nominal salaries are insufficient to furnish such support or to answer the national expectations, which have been formed. [7]

In 1816, Mr. Norton, the librarian, requested a raise in pay. He informed the authorities that his expenses exceeded his income by $60 or more.[8]

Prof. Jacob Bigelow, the holder of the Rumford chair, the funds for which were held in France, complained of the losses incurred as a result of the delay involved in converting French francs into dollars. The delay was often a year and cost him about $60 interest.[9]

Not only the faculty, but others also complained of their inadequate pay, inclusive of the janitor.

The Janitor would respectfully state to the Corporation, that during the time he has been employed by the College, his wages have been only ten dollars per month, and considering, beside his other duties, he has been very much employed during the vacations as well as in the term time, in assisting Mr. Peirce in preparing the Library Catalogue for publication; by bringing books to him and returning them to places, he thinks that to have two dollars per month added to his wages would not be an unreasonable addition . . . [10]

Complaints over the inadequacy of salaries were especially numerous following the cuts during the crises of the 1820s. Three outstanding faculty members, professors Ware, Willard, and Everett, inquired whether some of the retrenchments were expedient. At any rate they expressed the hope that "enough remains, about the expediency and propriety of which there can be no question, to relieve the college from present embarrassment. . . ."[11]

A corporation committee examined the demand of the Reverend Dr. Henry Ware for additional compensation for his work as acting president for four months. The committee contended that the corporation are:

trustees disposing of property not their own and that their doings will be a precedent in similar cases, unless they can act on grounds peculiar to this case alone. . . . To proceed on the assumption that a Professor's salary is not sufficient for his support would invite applications from all the other Professors, which could not be rejected. . . . [12]

Dr. Ware had complained especially of his inability to support his family during his twenty years of incumbency of the Hollis professorship. The deficit

---

5. Meeting of the President and Fellows of Harvard College, May 9, 1814.
6. Henry Ware et als, to the Hon. and Rev. Corporation of Harvard College, April 21, 1814.
7. To the Reverend and Honorable Corporation of Harvard College, (date and names of memorialists not available).
8. Mr. Norton to The Corporation of Harvard University, January 1, 1816.
9. Jacob Bigelow to Hon. John Davis, Treasurer of Harvard College, July 22, 1818.
10. Servant F. Willard to Ebenezer Francs, Esq., August 14, 1828.
11. Statement by Professors Ware, Willard and Everett, 1824.
12. *Report of Committee on Communications from Rev. Dr. Ware in relation to his compensation*, (F. C. Gray and C. L. Jackson), December 16, 1829; Henry Ware to the Honorable and Reverend Corporation of Harvard College, January 22, 1829.

averaged $200 a year. "That deficiency I have been able to supply by taking boarders, to the great loss of domestic comfort—and by receiving compensation for the supply of the pulpit in vacant parishes. . . . [13]

In 1830 J. W. Webster, professor of chemistry, asked the corporation to increase his pay. He had been led to believe that his initial pay was low and that it would be increased. Moreover, his teaching duties had been increased and unlike his counterpart at Yale who gave this course, he had to repeat his course, and did not profit from a large amount of assistance that was to be had in New Haven. Whereas his salary was $1,000, in the last three years, his expenses had averaged $890.

This is an especially interesting episode, for Dr. Webster had the reputation of being extravagant. He was hanged on August 30, 1850, for murdering his colleague, Prof. G. Parkman, who had advanced him a loan. Parkman discovered that Webster had mortgaged the same property for two different loans and thereafter pressured Webster relentlessly. Webster finally disposed of him.[14]

Henry Ware, Jr. raised a man-vs-bricks issue in 1836, one that has had a long history since.

I beg you to consider whether the building of new and expensive fences around the grounds and the preparation for a library might not safely be deferred for a few months and the money they would cost be devoted to supply the wants of some of the servants of the college. [15]

Simon Greenleaf, the Royoll professor of law, appealed to the corporation for an increase of pay in 1845. His original assumption had been that the university would pay him $1,500, and private practice yield $1,500. But the rising burden of instruction gradually shut off his private practice so that even a $2,500 salary then received was $500 less than had been anticipated, and $1,000 less than he needed. Besides, Justice Story presumably was to return from the bench and become the Dane professor of law at $4,000.[16]

A report to the overseers of 1869 said:

. . . the College must in some way find the means of being just and liberal to its officers of instruction and government. Absolutely the most disastrous thing which can befall this University is the failure to offer such compensation for educational service as will command the highest educational talent in the country. [17]

A faculty committee of 1950 also appraised the situation. Its conclusions were that Harvard salaries had suffered greatly from 1912 to 1949 as inflation continued. In general, they did not keep up with earnings in the economy generally, and there were even some losses vis-à-vis competitors.[18]

In 1968, the problem of salaries once more came under scrutiny. Aside from a number of proposals which would have the effect of raising salaries, the committee recommended "that the level of salaries of professors should continue to be increased steadily in order to maintain this faculty." The report reflected some concern over Harvard's competitive position;[19] though another conclusion was that salary differentials were not as decisive as had generally been assumed.

13. Henry Ware to the Honorable and Reverend Corporation of Harvard College, January 22, 1829.
14. G. W. Webster to the President and Fellows of Harvard University, September 10, 1830; Morison, *Three Centuries of Harvard, 1636-1936*, pp. 282-286.
15. H. Ware, Jr., to unknown recipient, December 8, 1836; George Noyes to the Rev. Dr. Walker, May 15, 1840.
16. Simon Greenleaf to President Quincy, July 17, 1845.
17. *Report to the the Board of Overseers of Harvard College, on the Tradition, Needs, and Profits of the University*, 1869, p. 37.
18. *The Economic Status*, 1950, pp. 27-30, 39, 49-50.
19. *Report of the Committee on Recruitment and Retention of Faculty*, 1968, pp. 34-38, 94-96.

18

Salaries—Sources

Dependence on the Government

In the first 150 years of Harvard history, the college depended substantially on the government. This is suggested by Foster's summary which shows that whereas students accounted for 18 percent of the income of the college from 1638 to 1712, exclusive of six years, the government provided 37 percent.[1] With salaries of the president and fellows accounting for 49.5 percent of disbursements in the years 1638 to 1712 it is evident from these crude figures that the government contributed greatly to the support of the faculty.

In 1782, John Lowell analyzed the source of revenues to finance faculty pay. The president received £120 rent, half of the rent of Massachusetts Hall and Hollis. Mr. Lowell expressed a hope that the availability of the facts would induce a greater degree of generosity by the government, "for if they do not, there must be further assessments on the students, which will greatly increase the expense of education." [2]

During the early period of the war, each of the three professors who were established officers of the college:

derived his support from three sources, the appropriated funds, the unappropriated funds, and the annual grant of the General Court. The amount of the salary, received by each Professor from the college, was in proportion to the appropriated incomes of the funds of his professorship, and to the difference in these the legislature always had reference in their annual grants; the two Hollis Professors being accustomed to receive one hundred pounds each, and the Hancock Professor only forty or fifty. . . .

But the government was not always reliable. Its treatment of the presidents has already been discussed.

Again in February, 1743, a motion was made to the government on behalf of Professor Winthrop, a distinguished professor of mathematics. But the motion failed.[3] The Revolutionary War period was an especially troublesome time when the government failed to meet its commitments.[4]

After the war the situation did not immediately improve.

Ordinarily student fees contribute a large part of the total income of independent colleges and universities. Hence, to this extent, students carry a large part of the load of faculty salaries. In the first 150 years of Harvard history, the government assumed relatively more burdens in financing the president and faculty than in covering all disbursements. But as the cost of the faculty rose and as the contributions of the government proved inadequate or unstable, the college pressured students more and more to fill the gap.

---

1. Foster, *op. cit.*, pp. 127-149
2. John Lowell, *Respecting the College Estate*, October 31, 1782.
3. *Proceedings and Collections of the Massachusetts Historical Society*, vol. I, no. "", pp. 354-355.
4. Quincy, *op. cit.*, vol. II, p. 246; *Corporation Records*, vol.

Hence, government, the college, and students shared the costs. Thus, in the years 1714-1715 it was announced that the salaries of fellows were paid out of the pupils' tuition money, the rent of the Charlestown Ferry, and the college treasury including Mr. Penoyer's donation.[5] Endowments paid the bills of professors, with additions generally necessary.

Tutors in the early eighteenth century received pay from the treasurer in bills, partly from the individual students at a charge of 10 shillings per student, and partly by the treasury writing out a bill on the ferrymen.[6]

Fees

As financial problems became more troublesome, the college increasingly required students to attend lectures and pay the professor for the privilege. Thus, on October 30, 1727, the corporation voted that pending approval of Mr. Hollis, Mr. Greenwood begin his duties as Hollis professor of mathematics, and that all undergraduates and graduates attending his lecture pay him ten shillings per quarter. From time to time for the next twenty years this charge was renewed and at varying rates.[7]

In 1742 it was voted that each candidate for his first or second degree should "pay to the Pres^dt for his Degree fourty shillings in the old tenor, or equivalent in the new, any former Law notwithstanding."[8]

As late as the 1770s fees by students continued to be a factor of some importance in financing professors, though in 1796 the corporation refused to put upon students the deficiencies of the Hancock professorship and the Hollis professor of mathematics.

In the first 150 years of Harvard's history, the point was frequently made that preference in financing should be from the government or foundations. But in so far as these were inadequate, the faculty was exploited, additional assessments had to be made on students, or income from endowments was used. In its early years the medical school depended heavily on fees. In 1809, four professors had to share $1,095, the annual return of foundations. Hence, the heavy reliance on fees, and to some extent on nonappropriated funds of the university.

In 1810, a professorship of clinical medicine was established. The incumbent was to received compensation only from fees, whereas the other three professors were dependent on their foundations, though in 1811 the corporation voted $500 to $700 for each out of university funds.[9]

As the university expanded, fees continued to be important. Thus, in the period 1810 to 1826, the university added fifteen new professorships; three of these were titular, conferred on tutors after six years experience; four were dependent on fees; and eight rested upon foundations more or less adequate to their support independent of the general unappropriated funds of the college.[10]

In 1841-1842, however, the treasurer announced that fixed compensation would be substituted for the inconvenient practice of paying various additions dependent on the amount of voluntary students.[11] But to some extent fees continued. In 1846, Longfellow complained that the $10 fee collected from law and divinity students for language instruction should be given to the instructors and not be appropriated by the college treasury. The corporation did not concur.[12]

At about the same time, Mr. Lawrence donated to the college a large sum of money to finance a scientific school. He would allow the professors one-half of tuition received. But "the Professors. . .should

III, pp. 141-147.

5. *Publications of the Colonial Society of Massachusetts*, vol. 16, pp. 405, 421; *Corporation Records*, vol. I, pp. 93, 95, 104-106.

6. *Harvard University Archives*, I, 50.15.86.

7. *College Books*, vol. VI, p. 11; cf., *Ibid.*, pp. 30, 35.

8. *Ibid.*, pp. 240, 268, 299; *Publications of the Colonial Society of Massachusetts*, vol. 16, pp. 240, 758, 801.

9. Quincy, *op. cit.*, vol. II, pp. 306, 308; *Corporation Records*, vol. III, p. 173; *Legacies Appropriated to Medicine*, 1809.

10. Quincy, *op. cit.*, vol. II, p. 334.

11. *Report of the Treasurer of Harvard College*, 1841-1842, p. 2.

12. C. L. Johnson, *op. cit.*, p. 100.

depend to a considerable extent upon fees—it is the best guarantee to exertion and fidelity—and the permanent prosperity of the Institution."

The fee system tended to depress standards. Southgate Shaler, class of 1862, a later distinguished geologist, noted that few or none who had any semblance of education failed to receive entry to Agassiz's laboratory. Fees served as an incentive to admit students.[13]

Perhaps one of the more interesting fee problems arose in 1863 when the college tried to induce Charles Eliot to accept a $1,500 professorship of chemistry. It was a peculiar offer. Mr. Eliot was to receive a guarantee of $1,500 and up to $900 from receipts of the laboratory. But both the $1,500 and $900 were to be available only after all expenses had been met inclusive of the $1,500 "guaranteed" salary. Mr. Eliot objected.[14]

Eliot was greatly annoyed when he discovered that the college was seeking help from his family to get him a professorship. "... I do utterly object to receiving any salary which is raised by subscription *for me,* directly or *indirectly.* I want a professorship on the usual salary, paid in the common way . . . . "[15]

Financing in Inflationary Periods

In inflationary periods, salaries tend to lag behind the rise of prices, and hence real income declines. The return on investment also responds inadequately to the rise of prices. The college offsets the decline of investment income (in stable dollars) by reductions in the *real* income of faculty. As the investment income in stable dollars falls, the college, with modest success, ties income on investment to the rising price level.

In the numerous inflations of the twentieth century, the policy—if it could be called a policy—

generally was to allow salaries to fall far behind the rise of prices, and then periodically to seek additional funds to finance rises of pay. The lag of pay behind the rise of prices was especially serious in the three major wars of the nineteenth and twentieth centuries. The college depended primarily on three major endowment drives to bring salaries up in response to rising standards and to ising prices—the 1904, 1919, and 1956-1958 campaigns. Increases of tuition contributed also, and especially during the Pusey-Bundy period, and to some extent under Lowell.

In one other respect recent policy diverged from that of the Eliot period. Whereas he balanced his accounts especially by squeezing junior faculty absolutely and even a fortiori, relatively, Harvard policy in the last generation at any rate has been to narrow the salary range, that is, to increase salaries to junior members more than senior. When in inflationary periods the lag of salaries becomes large, the income of the junior members falls to an unacceptable level, and the authorities have to make account of this deterioration.

The Impact of the Faculty Payroll

How much is available for salaries of faculty also depends upon other demands on the college and university. In a table which has been deposited in the Harvard University Archives, I have put together for various years beginning in 1724 the percentage of salaries to total expense. The figures are not strictly comparable, and I have therefor indicated by horizontal subdivision lines the parts of the series which are to some extent comparable.

It is not always easy to explain the variations in the percentage of faculty salaries to all expenditures. One important factor is the changing significance of auxiliary services, e.g., dormitories and food service. Thus, the relative decline of salaries from 1930 to 1940 and later years may be explained in part by the increased importance of these services. The rise of outlays on services is reflected in an increase of the importance of wages and equipment and supplies. But

---

13. *The Autobiography of Nathaniel Southgate Shaler,* 1909; p. 95.

14. Eliot, *op. cit.,* vol. I, pp. 99-102.

15. *Ibid.,* pp. 107-108.

the gains of wages are also related to the improved organization of nonfaculty employees in the university and with rising wage rates and the higher ratio of wages to all expenditures.

Other factors that may explain variations are the lag of salaries behind price rises—cf., 1910 and 1920, and 1940 and 1950; the increasing emphasis on men against buildings—e.g., between 1860 and 1890, a reflection of Eliot's vigorous manpower policies. The relative decline of faculty salaries from 1940 to 1962 may also reflect to some extent the rising burden of plant.

19

The Rising Cost of Professorial Chairs

Professors have become much more costly over Harvard's more than three hundred years. On December 10, 1643, at a meeting of the governors of the college it was voted "that 2 Batchelours shall be chosen for the present helpe of the President, to read to the Junior pupills as the President shall see fitt, and be allowed out of the Colleadge Treasury £4 per Annum [$13] to each of them for their paines." By 1654, the salary had risen to £11 average and from 1693 to 1715 fluctuated between £70-100 or roughly an average of less than $300 per year.[1]

Over a period of 330 years, the average Harvard salary has risen by about 78 times in dollars of current value. Indeed we are comparing different products. The average faculty man is much older now, better trained, and provides a much improved product. Moreover, there have been substantial changes in prices and incomes since the early days of Harvard.

As salaries rise, it becomes much more costly to endow a professorial chair. In 1721, Thomas Hollis provided endowment of the first Harvard chair, a divinity professorship. In 1947, this endowment was carried at $32,666 on the treasurer's books. But Hollis's gift was much smaller. Additions had been made to this chair by others, and part of the proceeds had been invested for appreciation. In fact, Mr. Hollis in 1720 donated £80 (around $270) per annum to be

paid to a professor of divinity. This was the equivalent of a capital sum of about $4,600.

Even as late as 1765 to 1816 seven chairs were financed by average capital gifts of but $9,000, with $4,000 to 5,000 averages sufficing in the years 1765 to 1791, and two chairs being endowed with $20,000 in the early nineteenth century.

Reporting in 1901-1902, President Eliot summarized the flow of endowed professorships as follows:

Endowed Professorships at Harvard	
Early 18th Century	2
1765-1800	6
1814-1819	4
1829-1892	18
1895-1901	10
	40

In the early 1800s, a professorship could be endowed with $20,000. By 1855, that cost had risen to $50,000; in 1895, it was $100,000; and in 1904, the cost could range from $100,000 to $125,000.[2]

Eliot was inclined to be critical of the expansion of professorial appointments without adequate provision of endowments to finance them. "During the Presidency of Dr. Kirkland no less than seven new professorships were founded in Harvard College; and

---

1. Foster, *op. cit.*, pp. 131-135.

2. *Report of the President of Harvard College*, 1895-1896, p. 43; 1901-1902, pp. 61-62; 1903-1904, p. 52.

five of these were filled, in spite of the fact that not one of the seven had an endowment sufficient to provide a full salary for the Professor appointed."[3]

Institutions of higher learning seek funds for endowed chairs with great pertinacity. University administrators may seem greedy when they undertake to finance an endowed professorship in exchange for a gift of $500,000. At a yield of 5 percent, $500,000 produces $25,000 income. Such a gift suggests to an administration the end of concern, for the professor's pay is financed once and for all. Yet this is an over-simplification of the problem. With persistent rises of prices and a fortiori of per capita incomes, the $500,000 or $25,000 salary becomes increasingly inadequate. In fifty years, on the assumption of a 3 percent rise of productivity per year and a 2 percent inflation—reasonable projections on the basis of past history—per capita income would rise 10 times, that is, from, say, $2,500 to $27,500. If college salaries are to rise *pari passu,* the pay of the professor would have to rise from $25,000 to $275,000, and endowment per chair to $5,500,000. (Assume a 5 percent yield.)

If this seems like a "mad" projection, compare the $4,600 endowment of the first professorship and the $500,000 required in 1965, a rise of 109 times. Or consider the $100,000 required fifty years ago against the current $500,000 to $600,000. The rise was less in the past fifty years, a fact explained by the relative declines of professional pay and the Great Depression.

The responsibility for financing a chair permanently is indeed a serious one. Professorial endowments of $20,000 in the early nineteenth century, which would yield about $1,000, now cost the university $20,000 to $28,000 per year. Hence the university has to provide the cash in 1967 in income or capital sums to yield the difference between the original pay (and yield of original endowment) and current salaries. Where the university would incur such expenditures in any case there is no serious problem. Thus, in 1834, the college received its first

endowed professorship in history, the John McLean Professorship of Ancient and Modern History. The present incumbent surely receives more than $20,000, but McLean's gift, large for the period, was $20,000, the equivalent of $1,000 income. In 1947 the McLean Fund amounted to $40,062, a rise explained by reinvesting part of the earnings, or additional gifts by friends of the university, or transfers by the university. Hence income is roughly $2,000, and costs probably in excess of $25,000. But since the university has at least twenty professors of history, there is no problem here. The university will have to finance at least one professor of history. The return on the endowment reduces the burden on other university funds to finance a professor of history.

But with changing values endowments may prove embarrassing. A commitment to pay $20,000 salary, say, in the year 2010 following a gift of, say, $400,000 in 1960 for a professor of divinity or paleontology or classics may conceivably be embarrassing. It may well be costly to assume the responsibility of paying appropriate salaries in later years for large numbers of endowed chairs. The university may find more flexibility if the proportion of endowed to total positions were not too high.

One way of protecting the university is to use a new endowment to pay the salary of a professor already on the payroll. But this technique although frequently used, at times arouses criticism.

In 1927, the law school sought to raise an endowment of $5 million. Among its requests were additions to the endowment of old professorships—Royall, Dane and Bussey—to make them $150,000 each. At this time the school also sought five new professorships at $200,000 each. The three old chairs were as follows:

Professorship	Year	Endowment
Royall Professorship of Law	1781	$10,307.
Dane Professorship of Law	1829	15,000.
Bussey Professorship of Law	1862	29,837.

Source: Endowment Funds of Harvard University, published by the university, 1949, pp. 229-230, 282.

3. C. W. Eliot, *Harvard Memories,* 1923, p. 50.

Costs of endowing a professorship at Harvard have risen not only because of the rise in salaries of professors but also because of the long-run downward trend of returns on investments. With interest rates at 6 percent, the average during the greater part of Harvard's history, a $20,000 salary could be financed with an investment of about $330,000 but with recent interest rates of 3 to 4 percent, the cost would be $500,000 to 660,000. Hence with the reduced rates costs rise by 50 to 100 percent.[4]

From the eighteenth and nineteenth centuries to the 1940s the decline of yields roughly doubled the cost of an endowed chair. Against these factors making for higher costs, we should note that since the end of World War II, the long-term rates have been rising again.

---

4. $20,000 \times \dfrac{100}{6} = 333,000$ ($333,000 at 6 percent yields $20,000)

$20,000 \times \dfrac{100}{3.5} = 571,430$ at 3½ percent rate

20

Work-loads

Complaints

Complaints of excessive work loads were not unknown in the seventeenth and eighteenth centuries. But the faculties were small and the number of complaints correspondingly few. In the nineteenth century, expressions of dissatisfaction escalated. In this period, the question of hiring assistants and the distribution of work among instructors, tutors, and professors became matters of concern.

Potential faculty members wanted to be assured that their health would not be jeopardized by excessive teaching hours. Men already on the faculty watched with displeasure the rising work load. Others wanted to be free to participate in other activities. Still others sought aid or assistants to lighten their loads.

In 1816, Prof. John Gorham hired an assistant, J. F. Dunn, who was promised $410 a year or $4.33 per diem, for his chemical laboratory. This was one of the earliest appointments of this kind. For this sum, the assistant was to perform the experiments, dry and clean the apparatus after the experiments, prepare the lecture room and laboratory, keep the keys, and deliver them without special permission only to the professor of chemistry, members of the governing boards, and the president.[1]

The college preferred that its professors live in the college. By living in, they assumed responsibilities. But in some instances, there were serious objections to living in. The university offered Justice Story of the Supreme Court a professorship of law. He said he would only accept the professorship "if the duties are so arranged as not to interfere with my judicial duties which are and ever must be of permanent obligation and interest...."

Crisis and Work Loads

In 1825, the college was confronted with a financial crisis. A committee of the corporation proposed all kinds of economies, inclusive of increasing work loads. One suggestion was that the professors on foundations should be asked to perform other duties as well. Thus, the "Professor of Metaphysics, etc., might be appointed Alford Professor and perform all those of his present duties, which are consistent with the statutes of the Foundation and also give instruction in Natural Religion and whatever else the statutes require...." They would also ask professors on foundations to give more private lessons.

The committee of the corporation recommended (1) merging of professorships, when consistent with the foundations supporting them; (2) professors assuming the work of tutors; and (3) generally increased work for reduced salaries. The net result of this crisis was felt for at least a generation in heavy and almost unacceptable burdens on the faculty.[2]

---

1. John Gorham, Agreement with J. F. Dunn, February 28, 1816.

2. Report of Committee on Economies, 1825 and 1826.

In considering work loads, the corporation in 1825, requested

...that as a general rule each instructor should employ from three to five hours each day in personal instruction. But considering the difference in the kind and degree of labour, which would occupy the same space of time, it is judged expedient to leave this point for occasional regulation by the Corporation or faculty....

Teaching Hours

The corporation requested information in 1846 on the number of hours each professor spent teaching.[3]

Although work loads in the classroom have been reduced greatly for older members of the faculty, and in large part because of Eliot's provision of young faculty members who assumed much of the drudgery involved in teaching assignments, there have been increasing complaints of senior faculty members diverting responsibilities excessively to the younger faculty. Eliot commented on the need of the president protecting the interests of the younger faculty members who might otherwise be exploited by the older faculty members.[4]

Under President Lowell in the years just before World War I, the tutorial system emerged as a large program requiring much manpower. The tutorial work became the responsibility primarily of young members of the faculty. In many respects they were exploited because the techniques were new, the hours of teaching heavy, and recognition through promotion at Harvard was not frequent, nor was tutorial work recognized elsewhere. In fact, very few tenure members of the faculty were prepared to participate in the program. It seemed like a heavy burden for older members to assume.

Of some interest here is an exchange of letters from Samuel Morison, the great Harvard historian, who in 1914 was just beginning his distinguished career. Urging Morison to undertake tutorial work, President Lowell wrote him in 1914: "...Success in that work (for which I think you are especially fitted) keeps you in the mind of the departments concerned. You have many friends who would gladly see you tested here...."

Morison replied he would better stick to lecturing and writing with which he was accustomed. It would be a "mistake for me to begin again at the bottom of another branch...." Incidentally, Morison advanced at a spectacular rate nevertheless. As I recall, he left Harvard as an instructor to become the first incumbent of an Oxford chair in American history and returned as a full professor.[5]

The hours of teaching tended to decline in the last hundred years. But as late as 1895, for free tuition and $300, Mr. A. L. Cross, an assistant in history, was to read theses and blue books and spend 6 to 12 hours in conferences per week. Three other assistants were to receive $150 or $200 for 9 hours of conferences per week each and to read 110 blue books.

In 1960, teaching fellows—generally with 2 to 3 years of graduate work behind them—received $4,800 a year for full-time, but generally were limited to 3/5 time teaching. For one-quarter time ($1,200) a teaching fellow would, for example, take one section of an introductory course three times a week throughout the year (e.g., Economics 1 or a language course).[6]

One reason for excessive teaching loads was that through a large part of Harvard's history faculty members had to teach in many fields. In 1766, however, the board of overseers was responsible for an important modification of assignments:

...the same tutor should no longer teach all the branches to one class, but one branch to all classes.

---

3. Committee of the Corporation Appointed to consider certain votes of the Overseers, June 1, 1825; J. C. Merrill to the President, October 13, 1846; H. W. Torrey to President Everett, October 13, 1846; James Walker to President Everett, October 19, 1846; E. T. Channing to the President, October 29, 1846.

4. Eliot, *The Man and His Beliefs*, p. 234.

5. A. L. Lowell to S. E. Morison, November 3, 1914; S. E. Morison to A. L. Lowell, November 1914, in *A. L. Lowell Papers*, F. 199.

6. Charles Gross, Chairman of the History Department to the Dean (presumably), October 10, 1895; and Faculty of Arts and Sciences, *Teaching Fellowships in Harvard College*, 1960, p. 10.

This was the origin of the old and long continued plan of instruction, which consisted in having four tutors—one for Latin, another for Greek, another for mathematics and physics, and another for the intellectual and moral sciences.... [7]

Burdens on Distinguished Faculty

Ticknor was not pleased with the teaching loads. The instructor in French and Italian had to teach 113 persons daily. Enrollment in each section was 19 to 24 persons, though a class in excess of 12 cannot be taught well. [8]

In 1830, a committee considered the problem of twelve sophomores who were deficient in mathematics. The president proposed private instruction for them, but the committee of the corporation thought otherwise. They would require the staff to spend six hours a week on this task:

...and the whole of it might be given either by the professor or by the tutor, without increasing his duties beyond what the Overseers and this Board have declared to be reasonable.... No instructor could be dissatisfied at being required to pass at least 25 hours a week or an average in the presence and actual instruction of the students.... [9]

Clearly, work loads have declined since 1830. A junior member of the faculty today may teach eight hours a week; a senior member, four to six hours. Today, however, the faculty devotes much more time to research.

Members of the mathematics department were no more pleased than those in modern languages. A mathematics tutor had to teach six hours a day and "independently of any time employed by the incumbent in extending his acquaintance with the subject." Moreover, they spent much time on private assistance, and notably with delinquents, and on helping volunteers who wished instruction at higher levels.

...This effort of mind during the whole of an exercise [in mathematics] *must equal that required by a continued demonstration.... These* [Explanations and Illustrations] *must be repeated and varied till the most of them comprehend the truths to be elucidated.... From such a service the instructor returns to his chamber fatigued and exhausted in mind and body beyond the power of any effective intellectual exertion....* [10]

John Quincy Adams, when offered the professorship of rhetoric and oratory in August, 1805, would accept the appointment only under certain conditions. "...Avocations from which I do not feel myself authorized or inclined to seek a dispensation call me to a distant part of the country during half the year...."

In view of Adams' proposed absence from Cambridge half the year, the corporation proposed an assistant to the professor. But Adams reacted strongly against this proposal:

...the exercise of any control over the principles or practice of an instructor would in my mind be inconsistent with the delicacy of deportment due from one gentleman to another, even if the power of such control were absolutely given.... [11]

Professor John Popkin, early in 1822, replied for the faculty to a series of questions put by a committee of the corporation in the general areas of discipline, instruction, and morals. The general tenor of his unusually long report of about 12,000 words was that older members of the faculty were overburdened with disciplinary problems and would like to be

7. *Report of the Board of Overseers of Harvard College on the Condition, Need and Prospects of the University,* 1869, p. 8.
8. George Ticknor, To the Corporation of Harvard College, April 6, 1829.
9. Charles Jackson to President Quincy, [Concerning] Twelve Students Deficient in Mathematics, February 17, 1830.

10. James Hayward to the Reverend and Honorable Corporation of Harvard College, September 5, 1825.
11. John Quincy Adams to Samuel Dexter, Chairman of the Committee of the Corporation and Overseers of Harvard University, August 6, 1805; John Quincy Adams to the Corporation of Harvard College, October 11, 1805.

relieved. They preferred to occupy themselves with their subjects and teaching. Yet he would impose on the faculty additional responsibilities such as greater visitations in the college rooms, increased checking of spending by students, and of absences from class.[12]

Protests in the Nineteenth Century

During the nineteenth century, the issue of work loads came up again and again. It will be recalled that Professor Waterhouse brought to the attention of the corporation the heavy burdens involved in showing his specimens. In 1805, six instructors inclusive of a future president expressed surprise that others had received increases in pay but that they, who were responsible for the behavior of students, were not equally fortunate.[13]

Upon being offered the Boylston Professorship of Rhetoric and Oratory, Professor McKean raised some questions of the work load:

...Nor can I omit soliciting your consideration to the extent of services assigned by the statutes. I have not the slightest arrogance to expect nor the presumption to ask, any modification of the institution for my particular accommodation. Nor do I wish if it were in my power that it become a sinecure. But if, on examination it shall appear that more is required than can be effected, by usual talents and industry, may I hope for your influence in obtaining some alterations? [14]

Many famous professors complained of the extreme burden of their Harvard work. Henry Longfellow was vocal on these issues. He did not like the official plan.

...You have given hardly weight enough to the consideration that the kind and amount of preparation necessary for an ordinary recitation, is different from that required by a lecture on even the simplest oral lecture. Besides I seriously object to having my usefulness in the college computed by the number of hours occupied with the classes...many days of hard study are often necessary for the preparation of a single lecture. [15]

E. A. Horsford, Rumford professor in the sciences, also was unhappy. Responsible for both the elementary and advanced instruction in chemistry, Horsford complained of his excessive burden. Professor Horsford wondered what would have been the fate of his distinguished colleagues, Agassiz, Gray, and Wyman, if they had to carry those students of poor quality, and if they were not able to give public lectures which financed their operations and their families.[16]

Francis Bowen, the professor of natural religion, moral philosophy, and civil polity from 1853 to 1889, was also unhappy. The reforms of 1825-1826 were reflected in heavy duties:

The number of hours occupied by my college duties already exceeds by about one-third the average time required of the other Professors. [For] *each of them also, teaching not more than one or two subjects, much less collateral labor is necessary than in my case....* [17]

A committee of the overseers in 1845 considered the problems of costs of a Harvard education, and incidentally also the possibility of economizing through increases of faculty work load. The majority of the committee recommended that faculty members teach at least 3 hours a day, during the thirty-nine weeks of activity. The majority was not pleased that the president did not teach at all whereas at Yale the president had a heavy teaching schedule; that the Perkins professor taught only 11½ hours a week; that

12. John Popkin to Messrs. E. Porter, W. Prescott and J. Lowell, in Reply to Serious and Important Questions of the Committee of the Corporation. . . , January 1, 1822.
13. Memorial of Professors and Tutors Communicated to the Corporation and Overseers, July, 1805.
14. Joseph McKean to the Committee, Honorable John Phillips, et als, September 28, 1809.

15. H. Longfellow to President Quincy, August 5, 1837; H. W. Longfellow to the President and Fellows of Harvard College, September 28, 1839; The Committee on the Memorial of Henry Longfellow, October 26, 1839.
16. E. Horsford to the President, April 26, 1854.
17. Francis Bowen to President Walker, November 29, 1859.

the McLean professor averaged only 2 hours a week; the classic professor, only 2 hours a day; the Smith professors of modern languages lectured only 2 hours a week with no lectures in one term; the Erving professor, only 1¼ hours of teaching for undergraduates.[18]

Teaching burdens, according to the minority of the overseers committee, were not easily comparable. "The different nature of the branches taught may render this work far more toilsome in one branch than in another....[19]

Recent Trends

Work loads continued to be a problem. In the later 1840s, President Everett had discovered that some faculty members had spent as much as 38 hours a week with students. By the end of the nineteenth century, faculty members became responsible for increasing numbers of undergraduates, for a substantial number of graduate students, for Radcliffe, and for other parts of the university. The proliferation of committees had also become a matter of increasing concern. President Eliot noted that with these responsibilities it was not easy to progress with research, and made strong efforts to reduce the burden of committee work.[20]

Despite the additional responsibilities by Eliot's days, I doubt that the *burdens* were as large as in the first half of the nineteenth century. Faculty men may well have put in more hours in, say, 1900. But research had become much more important, and the methods of teaching had greatly improved. Moreover, the professor had been freed from most of the unpleasant and sterile recitations. Young assistants had largely freed them of the task of going over the readings with students and from grading.

Burdens on Presidents

Earlier I referred to the view held by some that the president should not be spared the responsibility for

teaching. But in general the president's tasks have been impressive. Even today, he must raise money, help allocate resources, be an intermediary between the faculty and governing boards, assume some responsibility for educational objectives and curriculum, and deal with students, the faculty, alumni, parents, the government, and the general public. In fact, he has little time left for the purely educational function.

It was not easier in the days of Harvard's first president, Henry Dunster. For the committee of the general court of 1653, Dunster:

reviewed his election in 1640, and the promise that he should have no further distraction...but to instruct; mentioned the other duties–presidential, financial, procuratorial–that had fallen upon him; adverted to the Colonies' failure to grant adequate supply, which resulted in the tutorial staffs 'being so unsettled, and so often changed, that ever and anon, all the work of teaching and managing fell on the President's shoulders'....

Presidential burdens were large at the outset and are today, but they were also in between. Thus, in 1798, the president requested of the treasurer lime and laths and detailed the manner of obtaining them.[21]

On June 7, 1798, President Willard wrote the treasurer:

I have sent the Bearer, Mr. Road, for the oil and paints wanted for the college use–you will please procure one barrell of oil, two hundred weight of white lead mixed, half one hundred of yellow paint unmixed, and half a dozen brushes of the size No. 1....[22]

Relevance of Residency

According to an early nineteenth century issue of *Foundations and Statutes*, professors, unless specially

---

18. Board of Overseers, *Report on Diminishing the Cost of Instruction*, 1845, pp. 6-9.
19. *Ibid., Minority Report*, J. C. Gray, pp. 18-20.
20. *Economic Status of the Faculty*, pp. 14-15; Morison, *Three Centuries of Harvard*, 1636-1936, p. 378.
21. Joseph Willard to Ebenezer Storer, June 12, 1798.
22. *Ibid.* June 27, 1798.

exempted, were to be resident in Cambridge in the college or nearby. Lesser officials, e.g., tutors, regent, and proctors, had chambers in the college. Officers living in the college, unless exempted, were to dine in the commons.[23]

This requirement of residency was the occasion for many differences between the faculty and the administration, for residency in Cambridge and especially in the college meant more work and more participation in the immediate government of the college. Some professors succeeded in being relieved of the residency requirement. Others did not.

Professor (later president) Everett in 1821, for example, sought permission as Eliot professor of Greek to escape the burdens of residency. Everett dwelt on the additional responsibilities involved in living in Cambridge, of the loss of friends who mostly resided in Boston, and the absence of any necessary close relations between students and the holder of the Eliot chair.[24]

The corporation refused permission even to this distinguished scholar. In their view, the Eliot professor had special obligations; and, moreover, permission to Everett would have made it difficult to deny the privilege to several other professors.[25]

In March, 1837, Prof. Simon Greenleaf of the law school asked for a suspension of the statute on residence in Cambridge. Professor Greenleaf again asked for relief from the residency requirement as a necessary condition for his practice in Boston. He supported his request by revealing the favorable financial position of the school which would allow a professor in residency to be appointed. This request was granted, for the corporation did not want to lose so eminent a faculty member.

One reason for insisting on a residency requirement was that the authorities, harrassed by student outbreaks, wanted the faculty to dine with the students as often as possible.

This problem of getting faculty to dine with students is one that still confronts the college under the House Plan. I recall that in the early days of Dunster House special efforts were made, with some success, to encourage faculty members to dine with students.[26] I also recall that one of the students who profited greatly from this practice was Lincoln Gordon, former Assistant Secretary of State and recently appointed president of Johns Hopkins, and another was David Riesman, the eminent social scientist.

Final Comments

Work loads have been a problem throughout Harvard's history. In 1720, President Leverett defended himself against the charge that "there had not been in the College Hall above or more than three expositions performed by the President for this twelve month." The four fellows (teachers) would not support this charge, though the Legislature had been informed one would swear to it.[27]

In the first two hundred years of Harvard history, faculty members had to spend an excessive part of their energies on nonacademic matters. For example, in 1734, the steward would turn over the food bill to the tutor "whose turn it shall [be] to make up such bill; who shall fill up the other columns...and the said Tutor shall enter the said bill Immediately in the college Book of Quarter Bills....[28]

By Eliot's days, there was much less complaint of excessive teaching burdens than there had been in the first seventy-five years of the nineteenth century. Gradually, and especially from Johns Hopkins, Eliot learned much about the need of relieving faculty of chores. Moreover, he gave faculty considerable

23. *Foundations and Statutes* (undated), p. 53.
24. E. Everett to the Reverend and Honorable, the President and Fellows of Harvard College, April 27, 1821.
25. President Kirkland to Professor E. Everett, May 5, 1821.

26. S. Greenleaf to Joshua Quincy, March 6, 1837; S. Greenleaf to the Corporation, April 6, 1842; Meeting of President and Fellows of Harvard College, August 4, 1806.
27. Quincy, *op. cit.*, appendix LIII, p. 543.
28. *College Books*, vol. I; *College Laws*, 1734, p. 156.

discretion in what they taught and how they taught.[29]

Aside from excessive work loads, working conditions were not all that they might have been. Both physical facilities and equipment were often far below an optimum. An excellent example of the deficiencies is given by a note from William James, the great philosopher and psychologist, to President Eliot. James asked for part of the athletic building for a laboratory:

If we could have the Western part of it, with the partition between the hand ball courts extended to the ceiling, it would be a tremendous improvement over our present quarters, where noise, dust, and vibrations alike prevent the carrying on of most of our work successfully. There is no department in the college to which quiet and isolation are as essential as they are to ours; and it seems an irony of destiny that we should be kept in the noisiest spot in the whole College Yard.[30]

---

29. James, *op. cit.*, vol. II, ch. XI, and C. W. Eliot to Bishop Lawrence, May 3, 1905.

30. William James to C. W. Eliot, January 21, 1897.

21

Some Problems of Tenure and Retirement

Tenure, Retirement, and Economic Status

Obviously a faculty member's economic status is improved the longer he is allowed to remain active in the university and the more he is protected by tenure. Few faculty members would choose an annual salary of $15,000 subject to termination at a few months' notice to a guarantee of tenure at age 30 for thirty to forty years or more at an average pay substantially less than $15,000. He is likely to want tenure for another reason, namely because it gives him freedom in expression of unpopular views.

As Morison once said:

...Many things that members of a university write, do, and say, must be unpopular; for it is a university's business to be wiser, more liberal, and more hospitable to new ideas, and more critical of them, than the community. Badgering, bridling, and blindfolding the universities is cheap and popular, although its community hurts itself in the end more than the college...[1]

On the importance of tenure Eliot had much to say. It is a great boon in yielding freedom from anxiety for the future, and especially after the middle years when mobility is greatly reduced. Moreover, with annual appointments, the faculty tends to become excessively cautious and hence the public loses much good advice. Tenure appointment at age 30 to 32 will yield "a tranquil, independent and honorable life, such as promotes longevity and favors

the prolongation of mental and bodily activity...." The schools need not then be filled with teachers at advanced ages, for a generous retirement system would remove the tired, inefficient, and obstructive.[2]

Eliot was a pioneer in supporting retirement income, saying: "...the right of a college official [retired] at an age named seemed to involve a corresponding right of the official to claim a retirement allowance at a specified age."[3]

Tenure: Conditions

Tenure raises tough problems. At what point should tenure be offered: To what extent does the university retain the right to drop a faculty man with tenure?

From the very beginning, Harvard retained the right to discharge a faculty member for cause. The first chair, the Hollis Divinity Professorship (1721) provided for services of the professor; but he was to be appointed for five years only. Hence, tenure was not involved. But the Hollis Professor of Mathematics and Natural Philosphy (1726) was to be appointed without limit of time. The professor "shall not be displaced by them [governing boards] during his capacity for service except for some just and valuable causes."[4]

---

1. *The Harvard Book*, p. 23.

2. C. W. Eliot on *Teachers' Tenure of Office*, pp. 54–55.
3. C. Eliot to President Dwight, June 17, 1896.
4. *Endowment Funds of Harvard University*, pp. 55–56, 208–209.

By 1765, the governing boards were more precise. ". . . the said professor shall hold his office during good behavior, and . . . he [will] be removable from it by the said President, Fellows and Overseers for want of ability to execute its trust, or for misbehavior in *that office,* or for immoral and scandalous behavior out of it . . ."5

In 1874, Eliot announced that "all appointees should of course be subject to removal at any time for inefficiency or misconduct." But he was equally clear that arbitrary dismissals were not supportable.

In 1901, Eliot was highly critical of Stanford for firing Professor Ross, who had written an able defense of silver money. Apparently Stanford was under the control of Mrs. Stanford who had husbanded $24 million for Stanford. This was, in Eliot's view, an extenuating circumstances. But if her mind should weaken before her body, great harm might follow.6

Perhaps the most interesting tenure episode was that concerning Henry Flynt. He was born in 1676 and died at the age of 84 in 1760, he had been a tutor 55 years and a fellow (member of corporation) for 60 years. He also served as a clerk to the board of overseers. "His learning and ability were sufficient for the several stations he occupied, and his zeal and fidelity in the discharge of his duty was unsurpassed."

A tutor 79 years of age was, however, inconvenient and soon after Flynt's resignation, a vote was passed by both boards that "no person chosen henceforth into the office of Tutor, shall abide there more than eight years." Obviously a conflict of interest prevailed, when the same man was both a member of the governing boards and a tutor.7

Early in Harvard's history, professors received appointments for life and tutors or fellows for three years. On April 9, 1716, the corporation voted that no tutor or fellow should hold a fellowship with salary longer than three years except if continued by a new election.8

The theory behind tenure is that unless a faculty member receives it within a reasonable time, his freedom to speak the truth is impaired. With tenure he is less restrained in presenting unpopular or unpalatable statements. The forced resignation of President Dunster, the second head of Harvard, because he held unpopular views on baptism, could not have occurred if tenure were as strictly adhered to as it is now. One must not, however, assume that the governing boards do not have some control over faculty members, even with tenure. Wide variations in possible salaries of tenure members — say, $12,000 to $25,000, discretion concerning retirement age, access to research funds — in all of these areas the professor with unpopular views may suffer.

Problems of tenure have plagued Harvard on numerous occasions. In 1727, the corporation, with some doubts, appointed Issac Greenwood, at the suggestion of Mr. Hollis, to the Hollis Chair in Mathematics. Greenwood's behavior was not acceptable.9 By November 25, 1737, the Corporation declared that the mathematical professor:

notwithstanding repeated warnings and admonitions given him by the Corporation and Overseers, had been guilty of many acts of gross intemperance, to the dishonor of God, and the great hurt and reproach of the society of which he had made a free acknowledgement...and if said professor shall not manifest his repentance by such a reformation as shall give us a hopeful prospect of his future usefullness, in the said college, we do judge it will be necessary that he be removed from his office within the space of five months at farthest.10

5. *Ibid.,* p. 32; Cf., Memo of C. W. Eliot in *C. Eliot Papers,* Vol. 68, 1874 (?); C. Eliot to W. Denman, October 5, 1905.

6. C. W. Eliot to President Jordan, June 4, 1901.

7. Statutes Meeting President and Fellows, in *C. Eliot Papers,* May 1872; Memo of Charles Eliot, 1874 (?) in *Eliot Papers,* vol. 68; C. White to Treasurer E. Hooper, July 15, 1880; C. W. Eliot to J. S. Diller in *C. Eliot Letters,* vol. 90; *Historical Register of Harvard University,* 1937, p. 458; Quincy, *op. cit.,* vol. II, pp. 82–83.

8. Quincy, *op. cit.,* vol. I, p. 281; *Corporation Records,* vol. I, pp. 104–105.

9. See especially Samuel Eliot Morison, *Harvard College in the Seventeenth Century,* 1936; Morison, *Three Centuries of Harvard, 1636–1936,* pp. 18, 70–73, 80–81, 233–234; 309–310; *Corporation Records,* vol. I, pp. 404–405.

10. Quincy, *op. cit.,* vol. II, pp. 12–21, especially p. 12.

Continued misconduct led to a corporation vote on December 7, 1737, removing the culprit from office.

A most interesting case was that of Prof. Benjamin Waterhouse, who was dismissed from his post as professor of theory and practice of physick in May, 1812. His colleagues at the medical school expressed a lack of confidence and declared it was not safe to engage in any free discussion respecting the affairs of the institution with that professor. "Waterhouse," his colleagues claimed, "had repeatedly published in the newspapers without his proper signature suggestions and insinuations injurious to our character and highly opposing to our feelings . . . ."

It was revealed that Waterhouse was the leading figure in an attempt to establish a rival medical school, but had also tried in devious ways to conceal his relationship with that enterprise.

It appears from that evidence adduced that Dr. Waterhouse:

did in the New England Palladium of May 3, 1811, over the signature of 'Novum Organum' without any reasonable provocation, publish a false, scandalous and malicious libel against the Professor and Adjunct Professor of Anatomy and Surgery, which had a tendency to injure their character. . . ."

The corporation, (Lowell not voting) voted to dismiss Waterhouse on grounds of lack of veracity, on his contribution to the breakdown of confidence between colleagues, and on his concealed support of a rival medical school: ". . . notwithstanding that at his inauguration he declared and promised in writing that he would not only endeavour the advancement of Medical knowledge in the University but would consult its prosperity in every respect." [11]

In 1825, the corporation faced a financial crises. An obvious way out was to cut salaries; another was to drop personnel. Tutors could not understand why they should lose both income and position whereas others suffered only a cut in salary. Moreover, they claimed tenure with the assumption of a third three year appointment.

A tutor accepting a third term "must be assumed to have calculated upon its permanency, have conformed his plan of life and occupation on such calculation, to have relinquished other pursuits. . .,"[12] one complained.

At times the college would be quite arbitrary in its dismissals. Luigi Monti, instructor in Italian, wrote a long memorial to the board of overseers complaining that he had turned down an excellent position paying much more than Harvard; and though the authorities allowed that his performance was satisfactory, he was dismissed without explanation. [13]

Academic Freedom

Professor Morison in his inimitable style discussed the failure of Prof. Francis Bowen to be confirmed as McLean Professor of History by the overseers in 1851, the major factor apparently being his lack of sympathy with the Magyar uprising in Hungary.[14]

Bowen, himself, made it clear that he had not been confirmed for the McLean professorship in 1851 because of his views on the slavery issue. [15] A few years later Bowen received the appointment as the Alford Professor of Natural Religion, Moral Philosophy and Civil Polity, and served from 1853 to 1889. Bowen was in trouble again in 1870. Apparently he had published some views on the national debt which were not generally acceptable. Under pressure he recanted. He acknowledged that the corporation was the final judge whether a publication of a college teacher "is

11. Meeting of President and Fellows of Harvard College, May 20, 1812. (Six of seven members present though seventh member supported decision); The Committee to Consider the Memorial of Dr. Waterhouse. . . Removing Him from the Office of Professor of the Theory and Practice of Physic in Harvard College, *Records of Overseers,* vol. 402, June 25, 1812.

12. G. Otis and J. Haywood to the Honorable and Reverend, the Corporation of Harvard University, 1826.
13. Memorial to the Honorable and Reverend Board of Overseers by L. Monti, January 17, 1859.
14. Morison, *Three Centuries of Harvard, 1636–1936,* pp. 290–293.
15. F. Bowen to President Sparks, March 27, 1851.

likely to be injurious to the interests either of the college or of sound morality." [16]

The Bowen case was not unique. There were other episodes where the president or the governing board violated principles of academic freedom.

Thus, in April, 1776, a committee of the board of overseers was appointed to inquire into the political principles of the governors and instructors. Their principles proved to be satisfactory. [17]

Samuel Eliot, treasurer of Harvard and Charles' father, was not very happy in 1856 about the intrusion of Harvard faculty into political issues. In a note to the president he said:

It seems to me that the expression of their feelings may be safely left to those who have no such reasons for abstinence as the officers of the college have, remembering that it is an institution intended for the instruction of all who offer themselves and that abstinence from denunciation on their part will give tenfold weight to the doctrines of political right they may teach to their pupils.... [18]

Harvard's record on academic freedom over the years has been excellent. But there have been some deviations − e.g., the Bowen case. I can with intimate experience vouch that possibly at least one able teacher and scholar failed of promotion because he was a Marxist. Indeed later he also became a Stalinist, propagandist, and experienced a deterioration of scholarly standards. But there is little doubt had he not embraced Marxism, he would have attained tenure. President Conant in 1948 expressed well the issue of free inquiry:

The bedrock in which the scholarly activities of a university are founded is a charter of free inquiry; without this you may have an institution of advanced education, a technical school or a military college.... The nation has a right to demand of its educational institutions that the teacher dealing with

controversial subjects shall be fearless seekers of the truth and careful scholars rather than propagandists.... [19]

Doubts in Tenure

Much is to be said against tenure. At present a first-class university offering tenure at age thirty is committing itself to a payment of $1 to $2 million dollars. Should the professor prove to be a disappointment either as a teacher or as a researcher, the institution of higher learning loses much. To deal with this problem, institutions of higher learning increasingly rely on *ad hoc* committees with outside members to protect the institution from serious mistakes. Undoubtedly these committees reduce the dangers, but they do not nearly eliminate them.

In the troublesome days of the first forty years of the twentieth century, the issue of tenure and academic freedom became increasingly troublesome. The Sacco-Venzetti case, with some faculty members pitted against President Lowell, invited much agitation of alumni to get rid of such "radicals" as Prof. Harold Laski.

Writing in 1917, President Lowell spoke out nevertheless for academic freedom. In the field of his competence, the professor has every right to pronounce the truth and write about it as he sees it, he said. But outside this area, the faculty member must be restrained. He talks to a kept audience of students and in these areas where he cannot claim expertise, he should not pontificate and subject his listeners to remarks which may be offensive or injurious to them. [20]

In the early years of the Conant regime, the president was confronted with troublesome problems

16. F. Bowen to President Eliot, March 3, 1870.
17. Quincy *op. cit.,* vol. II, p. 168.
18. S. A. Eliot to President Walker, September 16, 1856.
19. *The Harvard Book,* pp. 32, 38.
20. *Report of the President of Harvard College,* 1916−1917, pp. 17−18; cf., Morison, *Three Centuries of Harvard, 1636−1936,* pp. 254, 259, where Morison discusses the importation of Lehrenfreit from Germany in the second quarter of the nineteenth century. But this freedom was not extended to the political field.

of academic freedom and tenure. The number of young faculty members eligible for promotion had increased far beyond the openings available in a depression decade. Many able young men had to be dropped, and among them Alan Sweezy and Raymond Walsh, first-class teachers and adherents to a liberal philosophy. The charge was made that appointments of these men were not renewed because of their views. A careful survey of the problems involved was made by the famous Committee of Eight appointed by the president. The major advance was to require that a man be dropped within a short period if a tenure appointment were not likely to be available. [21]

The committee expressed itself thus:

This Report is premised on the principle that permanence of tenure is desirable once the stage of apprenticeship is passed. The arguments in favor of this principle seem to the Committee unanswerable. Suffice it to enumerate three. First, it safeguards liberty of thought and teaching against undue influence. This is of vital importance, especially to men of originality of mind. Second, it makes the profession attractive to men of ability despite the fact that what it yields financially is a fixed salary rather than an opportunity to amass wealth. Third, it creates a sense of security which enables a scholar, after he has given evidence of an internal principle of growth, to devote himself singlemindedly to the advancement of knowledge unharassed by one of the major anxieties of life. [22]

Annuities

Earlier we discussed the problem of retirement income. But some additional attention should be given

to this problem here as we deal with tenure and retirement.

As noted earlier, some beginnings were made in providing retirement income even before President Eliot began pushing such programs in 1880. Thus, in 1791, Dr. Edward Wigglesworth, professor of divinity, when confronted with serious illness, announced that he was prepared to retire if provision were made for his comfortable support. The corporation voted him an annuity. [23]

Again in 1840, Prof. Henry Ware, who had been acting president, sought to "be retired in future from all duties of the office of Professor of Divinity in Harvard University on account of an infirmity by which I found myself disabled from performing with satisfaction to myself the duties of that office." As noted earlier, the corporation offered him a choice between an annuity and a fixed sum. [24]

In 1875 Prof. Joseph Winlock, a distinguished astronomer died prematurely. A friend commented that as his widow went:

... almost in a single day from a happy wife surrounded with the comforts of life to an endowed mother with a family of children helpless and dependent on her support, I most sincerely hope a fund may be raised for her relief.

A fund of $30,864 was raised. [25]

Eliot, more than anyone else, was responsible for the introduction of a retirement program. What especially interested Eliot was the responsibility of the college to provide a decent living for any professor who because of advancing age should be retired. The 1879–1880 plan provided that the college could retire a faculty member at age 66.

In this early formulation, Harvard provided that where a faculty member had been appointed at an advanced age, the college could give credit for additional years of service. In the 1950s, the university

21. *Report of the President of Harvard College,* 1937–1938, p. 38; 1951–1952, pp. 10–11; A Special Committee Appointed by the President of Harvard University, *Report on Some Problems of Personnel in the Faculty of Arts and Sciences,* 1939.
22. *Ibid.,* p. 25.

23. Quincy, *op. cit.,* p. 260.
24. Henry Ware to President Walker, August 14, 1840.
25. J. Henry to A. Agassiz, June 21, 1875; C. F. Choate to C. W. Eliot, July 26, 1875.

rediscovered this provision, apparently without being aware of the similar item in the 1879-1880 program. Actually the Harvard retirement system did not go into effect until 1899-1900, because the necessary resources were not available until that time.[26]

In the course of developing the program, numerous problems emerged. Perhaps the most troublesome was finance. Carnegie's foundation entered the retirement field with subsidies for faculties. But they had greatly underestimated costs. Teachers apparently have long lives. Not only the longevity of the faculty members, but also the steady rise of prices and incomes jeopardized the fulfillment of commitments. Benefits lagged far behind incomes of the average American.[27]

For various problems on retirement income in the Eliot period, see references below.[28]

In the 1950s, the university authorities once more considered the issue of retirement income. The occasion was undoubtedly the dissatisfaction of the faculty with the level of annuities. With the great inflation of the 1940s and 1950s, and the large overall gains of per capita and family income, annuities just did not provide an adequate income on retirement. Not only were these incomes low compared to the average income of the nation, but as prices and incomes continued to rise after retirement, these incomes became increasingly deficient.

In the 1950s an attempt was made to correct this situation both by the university joining the Federal Old Age Insurance program–this especially helped older members of the faculty since benefits vis-à-vis contributions were especially high for the older faculty–and by increasing the contribution of the university.

To achieve substantial results it was necessary to increase the return on the investment of faculty contributions. The Teachers Insurance Annuity, which was responsible for investment policy, was paying little more than 2 percent. In the 1950s returns on retirement funds were increased as the university invested increasingly in the retirement fund.

Another source of additional income was to be had by reducing tax burdens. In so far as the university rather than the faculty assumes the responsibility for financing the contributions, the tax burden is greatly reduced. The annuitant would pay taxes later on the university contributions, but with retirement income much less than income during active work, taxes would be saved. Besides, an equal amount of taxes paid twenty years later are much less costly than taxes paid today.[29]

Despite the gains associated with larger university contributions and the shift to more lucrative investments, and despite the savings on taxes, annuities continued to be inadequate in the 1950s and 1960s. In 1967, the university acknowledged this fact by guaranteeing faculty members with twenty-five years of service a return equal to 50 percent of pay of years before retirement. This income had not risen to the 50 percent of last pay expected under the 1950 Retirement Plan. This provision also provided an incentive for the faculty member to stay at Harvard until retirement.

26. Pension System, Corporation Meeting, June 14, 1880; C. W. Eliot to F. Storer, February 15, 1907; Meeting of University Council, October 24, 1916 . . . Resolutions to the Trustees of the Carnegie Foundation; C. W. Eliot, *University Trustees,* pp. 14–15; C. W. Eliot to Mr. Pritchett, September 24, 1905; System of Retiring Allowances in Harvard University, Adopted March 27, 1899; C. W. Eliot to President Dwight, June 17, 1896; C. W. Eliot to Mr. Ashley, August 5, 1907.

27. *Report to the University Council of the Committee on Proposed Changes in the Pension System,* 1916 (?); Commission to Report Upon A Plan of Insurance and Annuities, 1917; C. W. Eliot to G. Goodale, December 2, 1908.

28. C. W. Eliot to A. L. Lowell, May 22, 1914, and May 26, 1914; C. W. Eliot to Professor C. C. Langdell, September 27, 1900; C. W. Eliot to Professor J. W. White, November 1, 1900; J. K. Paine to President and Fellows of Harvard College, June 20, 1905.

29. For recent developments see especially *Report of Faculty Committee on Academic Pensions,* May 5, 1949; *Retirement Plan for Officers of Instruction and Administration,* July 1, 1950; Faculty of Arts and Sciences, *Report of the Committee on Compensation,* February 10, 1956; *Committee on Appointments, Promotions and Retirements,* March, 1956; *Report of the Committee on Retirement and Retention of Faculty,* 1968, pp. 69–73.

22

Faculty Status: Other Aspects

Competition Among Institutions of Higher Learning

Elsewhere we have noted that the rising competition of new institutions of higher learning put pressure on the Harvard corporation to improve the economic status of faculty. The drive early in the twentieth century to raise $2,500,000 for the purpose of increasing salaries is a case in point.

As early as 1929-1930, President Lowell commented on a tendency of several institutions of higher learning to offer salaries out of line. The 1968 committee returned to this issue.[1]

Lowell expressed his views in 1929-1939 as follows:

There are two methods of dealing with the question of academic salaries; one that of the public services, and the other that of the higher positions in business concerns. In the former there is a fixed scale, and the individual is placed at the point in the scale that his talent, experience and service seem to demand. In the latter the appointee is offered the remuneration necessary to obtain him. Each method has its merits, and each is appropriate to a definite kind of occupation. Traditionally, the fixed scale has been in use for universities and colleges, and in the long run would seem to be the best both for them and for the members of their staffs . . . . The two systems can hardly co-exist. Special large offers to particular men are inconsistent with a fixed scale which hereafter the

institution making such offers is likely to desire to maintain.[2]

Control of Appointment by Donors

It is not a generally accepted practice for leading institutions of higher learning to accept a gift on the condition that a particular person should receive the appointment financed by the gift. In the early eighteenth century, Thomas Hollis, one of Harvard's first large benefactors, insisted on and received the right to propose a candidate for a professorial chair. As noted earlier, when Charles Eliot was a young faculty member, an attempt was made, much to Eliot's annoyance, to find a chair for him through soliciting funds from his friends and family.[3]

The Impact of Inflation[4]

With pay during most of Harvard's history little above the minimum required for an appropriate living standard, inflation was costly. Perhaps this explains a disposition of the authorities to contend with inflation

---

1. *Report of the Committee on Recruitment and Retention of Faculty*, 1968, pp. 67-68, 95.

2. *Report of the President of Harvard College*, 1929-1930, pp. 13-14.

3. Morison, *Three Centuries of Harvard, 1636-1936*, p. 254; Corporation Records, 2d series, vol. VI, no. 172; *Treasurers' Ledgers*, 1831; *Report of the Treasurer of Harvard College*, 1835, p. 8; *Report of the President of Harvard College*, 1835-1836, p. 9.

4. See especially Chapter 34 for further discussion of the relation of inflation to Harvard's economic status.

by adjusting pay more readily than has been the practice in the twentieth century.

As early as 1715, the corporation announced that "in consideration of the expensiveness of the time," they would allow each of the fellows £5 additional to their regular salaries," and in September, 1718 and later years, the corporation voted £10 each additional to the fellows "by reason of the depression of the value of the bills of credit."[5]

Beginning in 1782, the corporation made grants to the faculty "on account of the dearness of living, compared to what it was before the late war, and are not to be drawn into precedent.[6]

In these first 250 years of Harvard history, the managers of the college watched price movements and tried to treat the inflation by special grants to faculty. In contrast, from 1904 to 1917, salaries rose only by 17 percent although the cost of living had increased by 69 percent. By 1919 the situation was even more precarious. And from 1930 to the early 1950s, the real income of a Harvard professor had dropped by 20 percent although that of the average American had risen by 50 percent.[7]

The Research Problem

For the most part the Harvard faculty in its first two hundred years had little time or enthusiasm for research and scholarship. The faculty had to concentrate on recitations and discipline.

By the second quarter of the nineteenth century the issue of research responsibilities of the faculty began to emerge. According to Morison, Thomas Nutall, curator of the botanical garden in the years 1822 to 1832, was the first faculty man given an appointment with the privilege of devoting most of his time to research. Again in the appointments of the Historian Jared Sparks and the Botanist Asa Gray in 1839 and 1842, Harvard had become the first institution of higher learning to acknowledge a responsibility for the production of knowledge as well as its dissemination. Sparks could only be had on the condition that he would have substantial time to devote to his pioneering work on history. The president informed Gray that his appointment as a professor of botany at $1,000 per year "would leave you time to prosecute the important work in which you are engaged."[8]

It was during the Eliot regime that the issue of research vs teaching emerged as an important one. At the age of 20, Eliot had written his mother that a distinguished teacher, "whose precepts impart the truth, which his example makes attractive, who has control over the standard of education in the community, and who, moreover, sets a high example of scholastic attainments, is a man of influence, of reputation, and of usefulness. . . ."[9]

In his 1869 inaugural address Eliot was not disposed to accept research as a responsibility of the faculty.

Experience teaches that the strongest and most devoted professors will contribute something to the patrimony of knowledge. . . . Nevertheless, the prime business of American professors...must be regular and assiduous class teaching. With the exception of the endowments of the Observatory, the University does not hold a single fund primarily intended to secure to men of learning the leisure and means to prosecute original researches.[10]

In the 1870s Eliot refused a chemistry professor a few hundred dollars and a semester off for research.

5. *Corporation Records*, vol. I, p. 104, October 25, 1715; *Publications of the Colonial Society of Massachusetts*, vol. 16, pp. 454, 461.

6. *Corporation Records*, vol. III, p. 305 (1782-1788).

7. Cf., "Harvard Salaries and the Cost of Living," in *Harvard Alumni Bulletin*, vol. 19, p. 325, January 25, 1917.

8. Morison, *Three Centuries of Harvard, 1636-1936*, p. 217; H. B. Adams, *Life and Writings of Jared Sparks, passim*; A. H. Dupree, *Asa Gray*, 1859, pp. 110-111.

9. James, *op. cit.*, vol. I, p. 61; *Addresses at the Inauguration of Charles William Eliot*, 1869, p. 54.

10. Morison (ed.), *The Development of Harvard University, 1869-1929*, p. lxxii; H. Orlans, *The Effects of Federal Programs on Higher Education*, 1962, p. 55.

It would not, he said, do the university any good. But Eliot was increasingly aware of the need of research and also of the difficulties of diverting resources from teaching for research. In 1888, he wrote:

The Corporation would gladly prevent . . . sacrifices [Eliot refers to paying part of assistants' salaries] *on the part of Professors; they would gladly relieve scholars capable of the highest work of all the mechanical or clerical labor which expert assistants might do under their direction; they look back with regret at the days and years spent by men like Louis Agassiz, Jeffries Wyman, Ezra Abbot, Ephraim Whitman Gurney, and Asa Gray (to mention only the dead) in such mechanical or clerical labors; but they are absolutely unable completely to prevent the recurrence of such losses. They must use the resources which the community places in their hands, primarily, to provide the instruction and guidance, and the aids to instruction, which are demanded by the hundreds of students who throng the College halls, and only secondarily to promote research and the advancement of learning.* [11]

By 1891, he clearly recognized research as a factor determining the professor's value to his institution and in 1901 he commented on the increasing disposition of men of wealth to endow research. [12]

In his 1891-1892 report, Eliot wrote:

There seem to be three main considerations which affect the exchangeable value of a professor's services. The first is the success of his regular teaching, or, in other words, the success with which he gives instruction from six to ten hours a week during term time. The second consideration is his capacity for usefulness outside of this regular teaching, as, for example, in administrative work, scientific investigation, literary production, or in the varied activities which give social or public influence. The third is the length of his service. [13]

By 1900-1901, though still suggesting some reservations, Eliot had moved far:

Prof. Theodore Richards, a member of the staff for 12 years and an assistant professor of chemistry, was offered a full professorship at the University of Gottingen. The desire of the Corporation to retain the services of Professor Richards caused them to consider the conditions under which it was reasonable to expect professors engaged in instruction to be also successful original investigators. To determine the just relation between instruction and research is one of the most difficult of modern university problems. It is clear that a man of letters or science, whose time is to be chiefly given to private study, and who is supported on an endowment must have contact with advanced students of his subject, else he will have no competent assistants in his researches, and will bring up no body of disciples. He should also be required to give stated lectures, or prepare stated reports, or perform other duties which will give public evidence that he is hard at work on his subject, and is producing results which can be imparted to advanced students, to an Academy, or to other competent audience. [14]

From 1900 to 1965, research has become increasingly important. [15] In 1932, President Conant in his first report wrote, ". . . In the future as in the past, our teachers must be scholars who are extending the frontiers of knowledge in every direction. I hope there will never be a separation of our faculty into those who teach and those who carry on creative work. . . ." [16]

The famous Committee of Eight also was eloquent on this issue.

Harvard University is an institution of learning, devoted to the promotion of knowledge and to its dissemination. A part, at least, of the salary which is paid to a member of its Faculty of Arts and Sciences

---

11. *Report of the President of Harvard College,* 1887-1888, pp. 21-22.

12. *Ibid.,* 1900-1901, p. 35.

13. *Ibid.,* 1891-1892, p. 8.

14. *Report of the President of Harvard College,* 1900-1901, p. 34.

15. Cf., F. Rudolph, *The American College and University: A History,* 1962, pp. 395, 399-402, 405-407.

16. *Report of the President of Harvard College,* 1932-1933, pp. 6-7.

*is designed to compensate for the labor of intellec-
tual inquiry, which is therefore a duty as well as a
privilege. To promote this activity the University has
invested heavily in libraries, laboratories, publication
and clerical or other assistance. It limits the burdens
of teaching and administration in order that the members of the Faculty may take advantage of the
opportunity which these facilities provide. . . .
Whatever be the special technique by which knowledge is advanced, or mastery attained, in the field to
which he devotes himself, he must possess that technique and be able to put it to use. . . .* [17]

In the post World War II period the problem has
become more serious. Research funds are increasingly
available. Professors in major universities give of their
time and effort increasingly to research and graduate
students and less to undergraduates. The function of
teaching undergraduates falls increasingly on the
four-year colleges and the junior colleges. Even at
Harvard, where undergraduate teaching still receives
considerable emphasis, government contracts and
grant receipts availed of amounted to $41,700,000 in
1964-1965 or 30 percent of all receipts.[18]

17. *Report on Some Problems of Personnel in the Faculty of
Arts and Sciences,* 1939, pp. 52-53.

18. Department of Health, Education, and Welfare, *Statistics
of Land-Grant Colleges and Universities,* June 30, 1962,
pp. 54-57, and *Financial Report to the Board of Overseers of Harvard College,* 1964-1965, pp. 12-13.

PART

3

EXPENDITURES AND FINANCE

23

Costs, Seventeenth Century and 1965

Of some interest is a comparison of costs of a number of important items in New England pounds sterling in the seventeenth century and in dollars in 1965.[1]

Table 23-1.

Relative Costs, Seventeenth Century and 1965

	17th century (£1 N. E. = $3.33)	1965 $	Historic multiplier ($/£ price)
Bushels wheat	£25	$ 2.50	10
Small house	60	10,000	170
2 average books	1	7.92(1965)‡	8
Annual tuition fee	2	600*	300
Annual charge for food at college	10	500*	50
Faculty member's salary (1 year)	75	10,000†	133
Laborer's wages (1 year)	25	4,500	180

* Estimate based on the Department of Health, Education, and Welfare publication, *Management, The Economic Status of the Profession.*

† Estimate based on *AAUP Bulletin,* June, 1964.

‡ From American Textbook Publishers Institute, courtesy of Pres. Edward Booher, McGraw Hill Book Company.

1. Cf., Margery Somers Foster, *"Out of Smalle Beginnings..." — An Economic History of Harvard College in the Puritan Period (1636-1712),* 1962, p. 58.

This table is subject to all kinds of reservations. Perhaps the most important is the point that all these items have experienced major changes in quality over the years. Had the changes been uniform, this would raise no serious problem. But they were not. Thus, the worker is much more productive than three hundred years ago; the training at college, greatly improved; the small house today, scarcely comparable with that of the seventeenth century; the food at college is more varied and much more nutritious. But who is to be sure that the educational product has improved more than wheat by 30 times? (Cf., multiplier of 300 for tuition and 10 for wheat.) To some extent I have deflated the differences in the product. I did not compare tuition at Harvard ($1,750) with the £2 tuition in the seventeenth century at Harvard, nor did I compare Harvard salaries ($17,000), but rather the much smaller tuition ($600) and salaries ($10,000) of all institutions of higher learning in 1965.

With these limitations, we can at least conclude that the price of books as well as wheat is *relatively* low today. But labor is very expensive, as are houses, and annual tuition fees. Even more high priced as compared with their relative positions three hundred years ago, faculty members' salaries are costly and food at college is expensive.

To some extent these differences may be explained by varying rates of change in quality. Thus undoubtedly the quality of a college education has improved more than a bushel of wheat. The high price of labor is surely related to the tremendous rise of productivity. Faculty salaries were very high, relatively, in 1965. Why? Perhaps a crucial factor is not so much rising productivity in general as the unusual increase of demand for education, a factor related to productivity.

Annual tuition was but 3 percent of the average faculty salary in the early period and 6 percent in 1965. Hence, the student now contributes more toward salaries. Food at college was 5 times as costly as tuition in the seventeenth century, but is less costly than tuition now. That is to say, tuition is much more costly vis-à-vis food than three hundred years ago.

The average wage of a worker was one-third the salary of a faculty member but now it is 45 percent, a relative loss for the faculty.

Laborers received about £25 for a year's work in the seventeenth century. During most of that period prices did not fluctuate very much or move net very much.[2] With wages fairly stable, we may conclude that the second half of the seventeenth century was not a period when productivity was rising greatly. The standard of living was relatively fixed. One explanation of this fact is undoubtedly the military activities of the period.

---

2. *I bid.*, p. 58.

24

Income and Expenditures[1]

The Puritan Period: (1636-1712) And a Comparison with the 1960s

Income[1]

Dr. Margery Foster studied the Puritan period well. I summarize some of her statistics as follows:

Table 24-1.

Harvard College Income, Puritan Period

	October 1636-May 1652			1693-1712			1636-1712 (excluding 1652-1654 and 1682-1686.)		
	£	s	d	£	s	d	£	s	d
Students	347	4	8	2,519	6	10	5,396	10	1
Government	1,170	18	8	2,956	0	0	10,926	18	2
Individuals' gifts	1,441	11	0	2,161	18	0	7,101	4	11
Endowment	125	11	6	3,136	2	6	5,746	18	5
Related activities	88	11	1	166	5	2	332	3	3
Total income	3,176	16	11	10,956	8	6	29,520	10	10

Source: Ibid., pp. 126-127.

Foster estimates income from students at about 18 percent of average annual college income in the Puritan period. In the years 1636 to 1652, the average was only 11 percent. But if for the whole period

1. Numerous tables have been compiled and deposited in the Harvard University Archives.

capital items are excluded, the total *student contribution* is raised to 22 percent. *Tuition* (part of student contribution) is then only 16 percent of current income. But the Foster figures exclude gross income from commons. Only the net income paid to the treasury by the steward is included.

A document presented by the corporation and overseers to the court in 1655 was not optimistic:

. . .All the estate. . .the college hath. . .is only its present building, its library, and a few utensils, with the press and some parcels of land . . . and in real revenue about twelve pounds per annum (which is a small pittance to be shared among four fellows), besides fifteen pounds per annum which by the donor's appointment is for scholarships.

Clearly, scholarships were a major outlay at this time. College Books I, II, III, give the details of the early receipts and disbursements of the college.

Dunster's accounts of 1654 revealed receipts of £269 18s 8d; disbursements of £298 5s 2½d. Due him were about £29 lawful money.

Under Dunster, available funds went increasingly to faculty members and decreasingly to buildings. But in 1655 the corporation and overseers complained of the dangerous state of buildings. In reply, the government promised to repay £150 due to the college "to be improved for the repairing of the college, and to satisfy Mr. Dunster what shall be truly due to him in account on him . . . ."

In the years 1693 to 1713 Thomas Brattle was treasurer. In these years (inclusive of two additional years when the Reverend William Brattle was temporary treasurer), the college personal estate increased from upwards of £1,550 lawful money and £100 income from real estate to nearly £3,800 personal and real estate yielding £280.[2]

A comparison for 1636 to 1712 and 1963 to 1964 follows:

Table 24-2.

Percent of Income from Various Sources

	1636-1712	1963-1964
All student income	22	36
Current gifts, government and private	54	21
Endowment	23	30
Other	1	12
	100	99

Source: Foster, *op. cit.,* pp. 148-149; *Financial Report to The Board of Overseers of Harvard College,* 1963-1964, pp. 12-13. Some part of the private gifts were for endowment in 1636-1712. I have excluded government contracts and grant receipts availed for 1963-1964.

Tuition is much more important now than in Harvard's early days. The small contribution of the student in the early years is explained by low incomes. Current gifts were more significant in the seventeenth century, as might be expected. In periods of stress, they tend to be more important relative to endowment income. The contrasts are even greater if we go back to 1636 through 1652. Endowment was only 5 percent and tuition less than 10 percent.

Over the Puritan period, endowment income tended to become of increasing importance. As endowment grows year by year, endowment income tends to rise to an increasing part of income—unless inflation or some other external force interferes. Miss Foster found that endowment income rose from £18

2. *College Books* vols. I, II, III; Josiah Quincy, *The History of Harvard University,* 1840, vol. I, pp. 22, 410-411, 452-466; *Universities and Their Sons,* 1897, p. 72.

average income between 1636 and 1653 to £156 from 1963 to 1712. This rise of $8\frac{2}{3}$ times is to be compared with an average rise of all income of less than $1\frac{1}{2}$ times.

In the early Puritan period, the major source of endowment income (83 percent) was interest on loans. By the late period, rents had increased from 6 to 22 percent, reflecting land gifts and some investments in land; annuities rose from 11 to 17 percent; and interest declined from 83 to 61 percent.[3]

Disbursements

The first point to observe is that accounting methods in some respects were better in the seventeenth century than those of today. The eighteenth century's accounting gives us the cost of particular types of services, e.g., teaching, plant, student aid. We get some idea on what the money is spent. But the 1963-1964 breakdown does not tell us how much goes for teaching, research, building, maintenance, etc. This is the kind of information we ought to have. What, for example, do the $27 million of salaries and the $27,600,000 of wages finance in 1963-1964? In the early seventeenth century, salaries and allowances accounted only for one-quarter of disbursements. In the founding years, new capital plant, equipment, and repairs required unusually large outlays. They accounted for almost two-fifths of disbursements in the years 1636 to 1652. For the whole Puritan period, as most essential capital needs were met, salaries and allowances rose to 53 percent and the plant declined to 20 percent.

In 1963-1964, salaries and wages *each* accounted for about one-quarter of disbursements. Wages are surprisingly important. They could not have been nearly so important in the seventeenth century. The explanation is undoubtedly the increasing complexity of the modern university.

The ratio of wages to salaries is much higher for twenty-five *other* departments than for the university

3. Foster, *op. cit.* pp. 123-198 (my calculations).

and its ten schools. The high ratio in other departments reflects the increasing importance of noneducational activities.

The Eighteenth Century

The college continued to grow. In the ten years from 1712 to 1722 expenditures amounted to £13,970 (about $47,000) and by the thirteen years between 1793 and 1806 to $354,000, or a rise of 6 to 7 times in ninety-three years. Incomes rose from about $87,000 between 1721 and 1732 to $435,000 between 1793 and 1806. The relative rise (per year) was roughly equal in the eighteenth century to that in the seventeenth century.

An examination of trends reveals the effects of both rising enrollment and inflation. Thus the gains of income and expenditures were especially large in the 1730s, 1740s and 1777 through 1781. The first two periods were of course, years of large inflation, and the last, hyperinflation. But these years were also followed by adjustments of currency values upward. Thus we can explain a reduction of current income from £51,167 in the 1740s to £23,001 in the 1750s and a decline from £463,000 in the three years 1777-1778 to 1780-1781 (an average of £154,000) to £62,186 in the twelve years 1781 to 1793 (an average of £5,200).

Once the government acknowledged a decline in the value of old tenor so that 7½ old equaled 1 new in 1750, the incomes and expenditures would reflect the high value of new tenor and therefore deflated levels of incomes and expenditures. Similarly with the transition from hyperinflation in the Revolutionary period to a relatively stable currency in the early nineteenth century.

Changes in enrollment contributed substantially to rising operations as expressed in money. Thus, average enrollment seemed to rise by more than 40 percent in the 1720s (1722 to 1732) and expenditures doubled. Inflation was also a factor. A major item was a very large rise in salaries, related to increased numbers on the faculty. In the 1730s and 1740s, enrollment declined. Hence, in these years the troublesome problem was inflation. The total operation seemed to decline, and pay for faculty members and the value of scholarships in stable currency units actually declined.

The 1750s and 1760s were years of monetary stability. Enrollment rose by 83 percent over the 1740s by the 1760s. In the 1760s, expenditures had declined by one-half from the 1740s, but in stable currency this amounted to a very large rise. Enrollment seemed to reflect not only the economic conditions, inclusive of monetary stability, and attitudes toward Harvard, but also availability of housing. In the 1720s and 1760s the rise of enrollment was marked: these were the years when first Massachusetts Hall and then Hollis Hall became available. In the war period, students, relative contributions to income rose greatly despite a large drop of enrollment. Here the great inflation and loss of endowment income were relevant.

Basing himself on *College Papers* and *Corporation Records,* Josiah Quincy presented some interesting statistics on Harvard's finances. Its income rose, though at an uneven rate, he found. For example, income was but £27 in 1654, of which £15 were restricted to student aid. But in the next fourteen years income averaged £187 and expenditures only £125. By 1746, income had risen to £1,900 and expenditures to £1,781 an increase of income that greatly exceeded the large rise of prices. A feature of this whole period was a tendency for income to exceed expenditures, a rather remarkable fact for a new college in a rather stagnant economy.

The rise of income was related to a large increase of funds (capital): less than £900 in 1654, £2,141 in 1682, £1,530 in 1693—the last a drop associated with inept management by Treasurer Nowell—£3,767 in 1715 and £11,150 in 1746. But with the devaluation of 1750, the value of the property was reduced to £4,576 in 1755.[4]

4. Quincy *op. cit.,* vol. II, pp. 231-237.

Structure Of Income—Eighteenth Century And Other Periods

What of the breakdown of income during the eighteenth century? The relative contribution of students was clearly on the rise compared to the Puritan period. Over the period as a whole students contributed more than one-half of total income. But the rise shown by these statistics overdoes the gain, for in the Puritan period, a large part of the commons bill was not included in the college's income. The contribution of students was low (42 percent) in the years 1742-1743 to 1751-1752, in large part because the commons was closed for five years. Students financed an especially large part of costs in the years of the great inflation, e.g., the Revolutionary War and postwar periods. Here the losses on endowment in inflationary periods are relevant.

The contribution of students should be broken down further. The students clearly paid more relatively than in the seventeenth century. But when comparison is made with recent times, e.g., 1963-1964, allowance should be made for the breakdown of student payments. Tuition income was only 22 percent of the total student income in the eighteenth century, and hence little more than 10 percent of total income.

An examination of the contribution of endowment shows that endowment was more important in the eighteenth than in the seventeenth century. The rough figure yields 33 percent of income from endowment for the eighteenth century.[5] It would be expected that with continued gains of endowment funds, the share of endowment would greatly rise. That it did not rise more is to be ascribed to the large inflations of the eighteenth century. Endowment's contribution stayed up very well in the first half of the century despite the large inflation. Here Harvard's smart policy of loans requiring repayment in an equal weight of silver undoubtedly helped. But Harvard was not equally fortunate in the Revolutionary period.

The contrast in the importance of student income is great. In the eighteenth century student income was much larger relatively than today and endowment income roughly of equal proportion, but gifts for current use were much larger in the Puritan period and in recent years.

Table 24-3.

A Comparison of Income Structure of Harvard, in Percentages

	All Income						Students' Income				
	Students	Endowment	Government	Current private	Misc.	All	Tuition	Food	Rent	Fines, etc.	All
Puritan period*	22†	23		54	1	100	73		27		100
18th century	55	33	11	2		101	29	51	10	9	99
1963-1964	36	30		21	12	99	75		25		100

*Obtained by eliminating capital items from the total.

†This comparison is not very helpful since the figures for the Puritan period include only the net income turned over to the college by the steward, not the total outlays for food. Hence, the total income from students and total income were understated by virtue of the inclusion only of *net* income on food, rather than gross income.

Sources: Puritan period, Foster, *op. cit.*; eighteenth century (1712-1806), see Tables A and B in Appendix; 1963-1964, *Financial Report to the Board of Overseers of Harvard College,* 1963-1964, p. 10 (my calculations throughout).

5. I omit 1778-1781 because in current dollars this period is excessively weighted.

A student today pays $2,000 for tuition and about $1,100 more for room and board. The structure has changed greatly:

Percent of Student's Costs

	18th century	1966-1967
Tuition	29	56
Rent	10	14
Food	51	17
Other	10	13

In comparison with the eighteenth century, tuition provides a substantially larger part of student income, food much less, rent substantially more. Educational costs have become greater to the student—he can afford to pay much more now—and whereas food was five times as costly as housing in the eighteenth century, by the 1960s food was only one-fifth more costly. To some extent relative costs of food and housing depend on the numbers consuming college food and housing as well as relative costs of these items in the two periods. The large outlays on food in the eighteenth century may largely be explained by the high relative costs of food.

A breakdown of endowment income by decades reveals heavy dependence on interest, i.e., on loans, with the percentage varying from 76 (post Revolution) to 56 to 63 percent. In the three highly inflationary years 1777-1778 to 1780-1781, the interest share dropped to 24 percent. In periods of substantial inflation the college seemed able to protect itself substantially against depreciation of the currency used to repay loans but not so in hyperinflation. Rents, on the other hand, declined steadily in their relative contribution during the large inflation of the first half of the eighteenth century. But their share rose from 18 percent from 1762-1763 to 1771-1772 to 76 percent in the Revolutionary War years. Apparently in periods of hyperinflation the adjustment of income to rising prices proved easier for investments in property than in loans.

EXPENDITURES

In the eighteenth century salaries became a much more important item than in the Puritan period. One reason clearly was the increase in numbers of faculty members. For the period under consideration, expenditures averaged as follows:

Percentage of Expenditures on Several Items, Eighteenth Century

Salaries	51
Scholarship	5½
Repairs and maintenance	5½
Equipment and supplies	32
Other	6

(See Tables G and H which have been deposited in the Harvard Archives.)

Of more interest were the variations by decades. In one period, the 1740s, salaries were 70 percent of all expenditures; between 1712 and 1722 they accounted for only 34 percent. In the inflationary first half of the eighteenth century, the importance of salaries steadily increased. The total amount paid roughly rose with prices, but since the number of faculty members had increased, there clearly was a squeeze on salaries. Once new tenor had been issued (1750), the *real* value of salaries actually had increased. In the Revolutionary War period, salaries in real terms plummeted. Here, the response of pay to rising prices was most inadequate. But in the quiet post Revolutionary War period, disbursements on salaries rose, though their share of the total outlays declined.

Perhaps the most interesting aspect of salary trends was the high inverse association of the percentage going to salaries and to equipment and supplies. This association was remarkable. For example, apparently as the college suffered from declining real incomes in periods of rising prices, the college economized on equipment and supplies. They concentrated on the most essential item, faculty pay. Thus, from on 1730s to the 1740s salaries rose from 52 to 70 percent; equipment and supplies dropped from 32 to 15 percent. For the period as a whole, the large outlay on equipment and supplies is rather unexpected, though growth explains this trend in part.

During this period, scholarships seemed to bear part of the brunt of rising prices. They accounted for a declining share of income. Undoubtedly the tie-in of scholarship to endowment contributed to this result—endowment income suffers in inflationary periods. Repairs and maintenance rose steadily as a percentage of expenditures, a trend associated with the growth of the plant.

Perhaps the most interesting aspect of gifts was the attempts of Cottom Mather to divert the Hollis gifts in the 1720s to Yale. A period writer discussed at length:

... Mather's avowed, new-born affection for that "dear infant Yale and his disgust with Harvard—the many motives which Mather must have had to conceal any attempt of his to turn bounty of Hollis away from Harvard—the ceaseless activity which characterised him, and his capacity to resort to underhand measures to gratify his passions...."[6]

Some Persistent Problems in the Nineteenth century

Even by the first half of the nineteenth century, college officials were complaining of the anticipated large deficits to be faced. Professors were becoming more numerous and their pay was rising. Appointment of new professors under foundations especially concerned Treasurer Thomas Ward in the 1830s. He would urge contributions to the general fund instead of setting up foundations that would ultimately be a drain on the general fund, as the income of the foundation increasingly yields less income than the pay of the professor. Eliot also was aware of the threat of new foundations to the general fund. But Eliot, unlike Ward, wanted to greatly increase the number of professors and thus contribute to low levels of pay.[7]

In Eliot's day the exploitation of faculty through pay adjusted to the faculty member's economic status—that is, to pay little to the affluent—was quite common. But even in the first half of the nineteenth century it was clear that professors would carry part of the financing burden.

1800 to 1870

This is the pre Eliot period. Enrollment rose from 179 in 1800 to 1,097 in 1869-1870, or a rise of 5 times. Harvard's income increased by almost 8 times in the years, 1800 to 1870. Prices were generally lower in this period, and hence the gains of university income were real. The income per student rose substantially, for whereas enrollment increased by 5 times, income rose by 8 times. With net prices declining until the Civil War, these gains over most of this period reflect the higher standards in the economy and the university.

During this period, endowment income grew from 37 to 61 percent of total income, and students' contributions declined from 52 to 38 percent. That this result prevailed is explained partly by the price history, for prices declined during most of this period, though as a result of Civil War inflation they were moderately higher in 1870 than in 1800. With falling prices, the real value of endowment income, *ceteris paribus,* rises. Hence, endowment was not greatly eroded by price trends; and the substantial rise of endowment contributed partly to Harvard's improved position.

In these seventy years, endowment per student doubled despite a rise of enrollment of about 5 times. That endowment *income* per student rose by 142 percent against an increase of only 100 percent in

---

6. *Endowment Funds of Harvard University,* published by the University, 1948, pp. 55, 208; Quincy, *op. cit.,* vol. I, pp. 224-237.

7. Treasurer T. Ward to the Corporation ... Present and Prospective Income and Expentirues of the College, July 24, 1838.

endowment per student points to much higher returns on investments in 1870 than in 1800. Part of the explanation is undoubtedly satisfactory economic condition in 1870. The rising returns from investments had eased the problems for students.

The Last Hundred Years

I shall be brief here since in Chapter 52 on Growth I discuss rather fully the rise of Harvard's budgets in the last hundred years. In the Eliot years, roughly 1870 to 1910, enrollment increased by 3 times and income by 6 times. The gains per year greatly exceeded those of 1800 to 1870. In the Eliot years, moreover, the value of the dollar tended upward. But the spectacular enrollment gains tended to depress the relative contribution of endowment to expenditures.

Under Lowell (roughly 1910 to 1930), income per student in stable dollars roughly doubled, a record more impressive even than under Eliot. Lowell profited especially from the large rise of endowment, which together with the stoppage of the decline in yields on investments contributed to much higher endowments and endowments per student under Lowell. The gains of endowments, and to that extent in income and expenditures in real terms, prevailed despite the large rise of prices.

Harvard, a Haven for the Rich?

One point of importance is the following: In these twenty years (1910-1930) per capita income of the nation in current dollars rose by 82 percent; in the same period income received by Harvard per student rose by 225 percent. Harvard was clearly running away from the standards of the nation. In this sense, Harvard was on its way to becoming a rich man's college, though the large gifts and endowment income kept student costs down.

These results may be compared with the Eliot period, when the nation's income per capita rose 77 percent and the income per student at Harvard rose 85 percent. Clearly, Harvard under Eliot was adhering

to national economic standards, not running away from them as under Lowell.

In the first quarter of the nineteenth century there had also been complaints of the extravagance of Harvard's education. But from 1800 to 1830 there were substantial reductions of both per capita income in the nation and income per student at Harvard. The decline was greater for income per capita. Hence, Harvard was becoming a relatively expensive place. In the years 1830 to 1870, the rise in both variables was roughly equal:

Percentage Movements of Three Indices, 1800 through 1870		
Per capita income, U.S.A.	Income per student, Harvard	Wholesale prices
1800-1830 − 57	− 33	−41
1830-1870 +112	+122	+32

Sources: Historical Statistics of the United States, 1789-1945; Report of the Treasurer of Harvard College and *Treasurer's Ledgers,* various years (my calculations).

Once a correction is made for price movements, it becomes clear that Harvard's income per student rose somewhat in real terms between 1800 and 1830, and rose less from 1830 to 1870 than is suggested by figures in current dollars.

Perhaps a more effective way of putting the issue is to compare not the Harvard income per student but rather the cost of education to the Harvard student and per capita income of the nation, for to some extent the income of the college per student does not reflect exactly costs to the student. The college can finance a varying part through gift income. (The statistics are not always available for the years under consideration.)

This table is revealing. In relation to the advance of the economy, Harvard was becoming an expensive place in the early part of the nineteenth century; a relatively less costly operation for students in the years 1830 to 1870; a bargain in Eliot's days; a much more expensive experience under Lowell; a bargain again under Conant; and a relatively more expensive institution under Pusey. Eliot and Conant were clearly of the low-cost, poor-boy tradition; Lowell and Pusey, of the high-cost tradition. But in Pusey's defense it should be said that salaries and even physical facilities had lagged in the periods of the Great Depression and the war. The large rise of costs, absolute and relative, reflects to a large extent catching up on salaries and the physical plant.

Percentage of Change

	Annual costs of education to students at Harvard College	Per capita income, U.S.
1807-1830	+ 20	– 47
1830-1870	+ 73	+118
1870-1910	– 7	+ 76
1910-1930	+230	+ 82
1930-1950	+ 29	+217
1950-1965	+100	+ 71

Sources: Annual costs of education, *Treasurer's Journals; Treasurer's Ledgers; Stewards' Quarter Bill Books; Harvard University Catalogue; Official Registers.* Per capita income, *Historical Statistics of the United States, 1789-1945; Economic Report of the President,* January, 1966 (my calculations).

General Trends, Eighteenth through Twentieth Centuries

In the eighteenth century, the relative contribution of students to total income was greater than in the nineteenth century, but tuition's share of income has tended to rise in more recent years. Greater recourse to gifts, private and public, tended to keep down the share of tuition in the last hundred years. By the 1960s, the share of tuition and all student income had risen greatly vis-à-vis the Puritan period.

As endowment funds and current gifts became increasingly important, the proportion of student payments to total income declined substantially in the first seventy years of the nineteenth century. But in the Eliot years, (1870 to 1910 roughly), the endowment share of income declined substantially despite the very large relative gains of total endowment. The major explanation of this trend was the large increase of enrollment, a factor tending to reduce the relative contribution of endowment; another factor was the reduction of the yield on endowments. The rise of enrollment combined with a low tuition policy kept the relative student contribution stable.

In the Lowell period—1910 to 1930, roughly—a large drop might have been expected in the contribution of endowment, with the very large enrollment and price increases, and therefore a large rise of tuition's share of income. But the relative decline of endowment income was small, a fact to be explained in part by the large gains of endowment and the beginnings of substantial investments in equities. Despite substantial increases of tuition charges, income from students was *relatively* unchanged.

In the years since Lowell, despite very large increases of investment funds with the total above $1 billion (market) in 1967, the contribution of endowment income tended to decline greatly relatively, and that despite the rising interest in equities. Inflation contributed to this result, as did the increase of current gifts (inclusive of government grants), and the rise of enrollment.

The decline of tuition's relative share of university income under Conant and Pusey is explained in part by the large gains of government income. From 1910 to the early 1960s, tuition income tended to decline relative to all income; and this occurred despite the fact that room and board, an ingredient in student income, became of increasing importance. Note that in these years endowment's relative share dropped by one-third and student income by one-half. But income from gifts and government contracts rose from 8 to 45 percent.

The Last Hundred Years

In a table covering almost a hundred years, I examine again the structure of income and the importance of two categories of expenditures, salaries, and student aid.

Table 24-4.

**Various Income Sources and Expenditures, Percent of Total,
1869, 1889, 1909, 1928, 1966, Years Ending June, July, or August**

| | INCOME | | | | | EXPENDITURES | |
	Investment	Tuition	Term bills	Misc.	Current gifts	Salaries	Student Aid
1869	58	19	23	<1	<1	45	5
1889	52	27	7	2	9	45	8
1909	45	31	8	3	13	37	5
1928	43	21	13	8	16	30	4
1966*	30	19	6 †	7	14	25	9

*Reimbursement of direct and indirect expenses related to grants and contracts equaled 34.7 percent.
†Board and lodging.

Sources: Samuel Eliot Morison (ed.), *The Development of Harvard University, 1869-1929,* 1930, p. lxxxix (my calculations); *Financial Report to the Board of Overseers of Harvard College,* 1965-1966, p. 10.

This table suggests the following conclusions:

1. A steady decline in the contribution of investment income, and despite the rise of endowment from $2,400,000 in 1869 to $963 million (market value) on June 30, 1966. By 1966, investment income was providing only one-half as much relatively as ninety-seven years earlier.

2. Tuition contributed relatively as much in 1966 as in 1869, but despite Eliot's concern for the poor boy, tuition amounted to 19 percent in 1869 and had risen to 31 percent in 1909, the end of Eliot's term. (The large rise of enrollment is relevant.) The ensuing decline in the next fifty-seven years reflects the gains (see 4 below) of other items.

3. Current gifts began to be a factor of great significance in the 1880s, and their relative importance has clearly been upward (even without the Federal grants).

4. To some extent the rising importance of Federal grants and contracts and of current gifts account for the reduced relative significance of investment income and tuition. Even allowing for that, however, the reduced relative contribution of tuition in the face of a very large rise of per capita income (and a much smaller increase of unit costs in higher education) is surprising.

5. The importance of salaries steadily declined. Here I would point to the large gains of wages (in 1966 as important relatively as salaries), and also the lag in faculty salaries vis-à-vis incomes of all members of the labor market.

6. If allowance were made for federal grants, then tuition and investment income would have fallen much more since 1928.

A Comparison of 1840 and 1965

By 1840, Harvard was on its way to its third century, and 1840 may be taken as an example of Harvard's condition after two centuries. Hence, the 1840 *Treasurer's Statement* deserves some space.

Receipts and Income	
1840	$ 177,902
1965	135,322,877

After two hundred years Harvard's income was but $178,000. In the next 125 years, income had grown by 750 times as much as in the first 204 years. Only a small part would be lopped off to allow for price increases since 1840.

Actually, 59 percent of the $72,729 income was from capital items.

Percentage of Income from Different Sources 1840 and 1965

	1840	1965
Charges to students including housing	38	
Receipts from commons	7	27
Sales of wood	9	
Dividends	10	
Interest	27	22
Rents	8	

In comparison with the recent structure of income at Harvard College, receipts from students were high in 1840 (inclusive of commons), from sales of wood very high, and even the income from investments and especially rents was high. Dividends were, of course, low, for the period of large-equity investments was still far off. It is of some interest that income on investments was about twice as high relatively in 1840 as in 1965.[8]

Twelve faculty members of professional rank averaged over $1,400 per year in 1840. This compares with an average of about $20,000 now or 14 times as much. Ten instructors and tutors averaged $520 in 1840; and there were ten proctors earning generally from $300 to $500.

In capital values the differences between 1840 and 1966 are even greater than income differences. Harvard's property in 1966 was about 1,500 times as valuable in dollars as in 1840, but income differences were only half as great.

Table 24-5.
Harvard University — Total Income and Sources of Income as Percent of Total, 1809-1963

Period	Total income	Endowment fund Income	Gifts for current use	Student income	Gov't. contract and grant receipts	Other income
1962-1963	102,896,078.00	21.2	14.6	26.3	30.3	7.6
1959-1960	74,552,070.00	22.5	16.9	29.7	24.3	6.6
1949-1950	30,311,683.54	24.9	16.1	40.6		18.4
1939-1940	14,115,497.61	36.3	11.9	24.9		26.9
1929-1930	13,911,720.54	38.4	15.1	36.1		10.4
1919-1920	4,183,492.00	45.3	10.1	35.1		9.5
1909-1910	2,035,107.90	39.5	8.2	38.1		14.2
1899-1900	1,487,635.95	35.9	4.1	50.7		9.3
1889-1890	1,005,143.61	41.2	16.1	37.9		4.8
1879-1880	574,401.36	44.0	12.1	42.2		1.7
1869-1870	305,079.31	60.8	1.2	37.5		.4
1869-1860	156,171.08	46.8	5.1	46.9		1.2
1849-1850	92,214.02	43.5	1.6	51.8		3.1
1839-1840	90,608.75	34.3	1.2	58.3		6.2
1829-1830	51,605.17	43.2	–	49.8		7.0
1819-1820	83,805.39	20.8	.7	76.83		1.9
1809-1810	35,592.02	46.4	–	47.7		5.9

Sources: Deposited in Harvard Archives

8. *Treasurer's Statement,* 1840; *Financial Report to the* *Board of Overseers of Harvard College,* 1965-1966.

25

Patterns of Expenditures[1]

The structure of expenditures in Harvard's early history differed greatly from that in more modern times. Here, for example, is a breakdown from 1636 to 1652 and the whole Puritan period, 1636 to 1712, exclusive of 1652 to 1654 and 1682 to 1686, and of 1964-1965. In these early years, capital expenditures are included in disbursements, and the payments to the steward's department are net (payments of treasurer to steward), not gross.

Table 25-1.

Percent of Disbursements

	1636-1652	1636-1712	1964-1965
1. Salaries, wages and allowances	29	53	50.3
2. Steward (net)	0	1	6.1
3. Buildings, repairs, and equipment	39	20	
of which repairs and equipment	1½	3	20.4
4. Scholarships, etc.	7	7	8.7
5. Miscellaneous	16	4	14.5
6. Capitalized gifts or incomes, rents, and annuities	9	15	0
	10½	103	100

Sources: Calculated from Foster, *op. cit.,* pp. 146-147; *Financial Report to the Board of Overseers of Harvard College,* 1964-1965.

1. Tables on disbursements, inclusive of sources, for 1723 to 1965 are deposited in the Harvard Archives.

A comparison of the Puritan period and 1964-1965 can have only limited significance. Clearly, wages and salaries are now about 1-2/3 as important relatively as in the early Puritan period, and about equal importance vis-à-vis the whole Puritan period. But in the current situation wages as against salaries have become much more important, a fact to be explained by the growing complexity of the modern university. Should we eliminate capital items in the two Puritan periods, which are not included as disbursements in 1964-1965, then salaries would be much larger relatively in the years 1636 to 1712 than wages and salaries in 1964-1965. This elimination also results in larger relative disbursements for student aid in the seventeenth century than in the 1960s. In recent years, what stands out are the large wage outlays (25 percent in 1964-1965) and equipment and supplies (21 percent in 1964-1965) compared to 3 percent for equipment and repairs in the Puritan period. But buildings, repairs, and equipment accounted for 20 percent in the Puritan period as against 20 percent for equipment and supplies in 1964-1965.

In the eighteenth century, the pattern of expenditures was greatly influenced by the instability of the currency. Salaries generally stayed at levels of 50 percent or more of outlays, though there were some exceptions. The exploitation of the faculty in inflationary periods is suggested by a drop of salaries from 63 percent in 1771-1772 to 41 percent in 1781-1782.

Scholarships, tied to a considerable extent to endowments, also tended to account for a declining share of outlays. Here again rising prices, with adverse effects on endowment income, were relevant. As is typical of all growing enterprises, the expansion of the plant was reflected in an upward tendency in the relative outlays on maintenance and repairs. There is also some evidence of relative declines of this factor as economies are pressed on the officials in periods of financial stress. Unfortunately, the conclusions to be drawn for the eighteenth century are imparied by the large and fluctuating outlays in the "other" category. The extremes are 8 percent in 1771-1772 and 52.4 percent in 1723-1724.

A comparison of expenditures over most of the nineteenth century reveals a relatively stable structure. In the period from 1810 to 1890, total expenditures rose from $11,623 to $826,000, with the largest absolute rise occurring in the first twenty Eliot years, an increase of $540,000. But relatively, the large gains occurred earlier. The relative outlays on salaries fluctuated greatly: extremes were 64 percent in 1829-1830 and 33 percent in 1819-1820. The average for the nine years (one year per decade) covering a period of ninety years was 47 percent, a figure not much out of line with Harvard's historical experience for wages and salaries.

The most important explanation of the substantial fluctuations in the percentages spent on salaries is the inverse movement of the catchall, "other expenditures." These varied from 17.9 percent in 1829-1830 to 56.9 percent in 1819-1820, but in the other years the extremes were from 30 in 1849-1850 to 41.3 in 1889-1890.

The trend of scholarships was upward, reaching a maximum of 8.1 percent in 1889-1890. Repairs were relatively stable, though in 1859-1860 a value of 20.12 percent was much out of line.

I have divided the twentieth century into two periods; the first, 1900 to 1920; the second, 1920 to the present. This was necessary because of changes in accounting methods. In the first period, the treasurer gave a breakdown that included administration and library as special items. The total of this item plus instruction and research fluctuated from 48.7 in 1899-1900 to 58.6 percent in 1909-1910, a total not much out of line with earlier salaries or later wages and salaries. Inclusion of library and administration cut to some extent the general expense item. The most unexpected total was 15.1 percent for buildings in 1919-1920 as compared with 6.4 percent in 1909-1910 and 7.40 in 1889-1890 for repairs alone. This 1920 total includes repairs and equipment and caretaking. By 1919-1920, the university had very large investments in buildings.

In the last thirty to forty years, accounting changes again were such as to require separate treatment. Now, we have a breakdown of salaries and wages, a new special item, equipment and supplies (not buildings), and pensions.

Wages really escalated from 9.2 percent in 1930 to 33.3 in 1950 and 25.8 percent in 1962-1963. One important explanation of the large jump in the 1930s and later is the introduction of the House Plan, with its heavy costs for dormitories and commons. Salaries tended to decline relatively: 32 percent in 1929-1939, to 25.0 percent in 1965-1966, a decline that reflected the increasing complexity of the system. The equipment and supplies item rose from 6 percent in 1929-1930 to 20.1 percent in 1965-1966. Operations of the House Plan and the increasing needs of organized research help explain these increases. In part, this item is a substitute for the buildings item used earlier—15.1 percent in 1919-1920.

The relative outlays on salaries and wages combined fluctuated in these years, and even more so, wages. The combined total varied from 41 percent in 1930 to 66 percent in 1940 and 50 percent in 1965-1966. A new item now included, varying from 3.1 to 6.1 percent, was employee benefits. These might be added to salaries and wages. With specific evaluations for equipment and supplies, wages and pensions, the over-all miscellaneous dropped from 44 percent in 1930 to 14 percent in 1962-1963.

26

Deficit Finance

Approaches to Deficit Finance

How does a college deal with deficits? The obvious approach is to increase revenues or reduce expenditures. The college generally found it easier to cut outlays than to increase revenues. In the great crises of the 1820s, for example, the emphasis was almost wholly on reducing expenditures. The college would merge professorships, not fill vacancies, economize on student aids by demanding large services by recipients of assistance, dismiss the president's secretary, reduce salaries, and the like.

But the college would also rely in crisis periods on consuming capital. For example, in the 1820s Harvard sold its sloop that had been used for procuring wood as well as other capital items. From 1810 to 1821 the stock (capital) account of the college dropped from $149,000 to $67,000. On numerous occasions the college allowed its plant to deteriorate by postponing repairs. Such policies bring capital losses. Eliot refused to accept a professorship in the 1860s, in part because "the general condition of the School (Lawrence Scientific) steadily deteriorated;— its building and its apparatus were suffered to fall into a condition of decay and disorder. . . . " Later, he pointed out that repeated deficits were not welcome because they induced a consumption of capital.

Eliot's accounting theory helped keep deficits down. He would cover repairs out of current income, and improvements and extensions out of gifts. He would spend on the current generation of students all available income. He would not, like commercial firms, put aside depreciation or obsolesence funds. He believed that universities should not make reserves "for maintaining and replacing a wasting plant, such as a corporation whose object is to make money profits steadily generation after generation necessarily provides. . . . " [1]

At times the solution suggested was an increase of endowment. But over most of Harvard's history, an appeal for new funds in the midst of a crisis did not seem practical. When the situation became precarious, the authorities would use up capital in another sense: they would borrow. Thus, on February 21, 1814, the president and fellows voted that "the treasurer be authorized to borrow the sum of five thousand dollars of the Massachusetts Congregational Charitable Society at an interest rate not exceeding five and one-half per cent for one year." [2]

An example of the impact of deficits on capital consumption follows. From 1857 to 1862 Harvard incurred deficits of $18,561. The college also expended $12,197 on Appleton Chapel and the Boylston Museum. All in all, inclusive of a drop in another capital item, the college had a deficiency of income of $31,629. The stock account was credited with this deficiency of income and an equal amount was charged to the insurance and guarantee account.

---

1. Charles W. Eliot (Neilson, ed.) *The Man and His Beliefs,* pp. 235-236.
2. Asa Gray to Dr. Walker, President of Harvard University, December, 1854; C. W. Eliot to the President and Fellows of Harvard College, May 19, 1863; Meeting of President and Fellows of Harvard College, February 21, 1814.

This account was financed from the excess of investment income over the amounts paid out to endowment (stock) funds. An insurance and guarantee fund of this type has now continued for over a hundred years. This capital sum is available to cover any serious declines in investment income, e.g., in the 1930s. The general investment's gain and loss account amounted to $8,400,000 on June 30, 1966. This compares with $28,200,000 of endowment fund income availed of in the year 1965-1966.[3]

In the Great Depression of the 1930s, the university was confronted with serious deficits. Enrollment, tuition payments, and income on capital declined. Yet through the use of large savings in earlier years, the resultant capacity to consume reserves, and the postponement of maintenance expenditures—a form of capital consumption—the Lowell administration performed miracles. They were also helped by the decline of prices, which improved the finances of the dining hall. At one point the college put through a 10 percent cut in the budget. In 1932, budget officers were asked to budget for a 10, 20 and 30 percent drop in expenditures. But these precautions were not necessary. Even in the 1930s promotions and expansions of staff prevailed. In fact, at the outset of the depression, the faculty scale of pay was greatly improved, and as prices dropped 25 percent, the faculty gains were large.[4]

In early 1933, President Lowell refused to accept government loans, saying:

I hope that I have not been influenced by the fact that Harvard has had sufficient foresight to accumulate in good times some surplus for days which may not be so fortunate . . . the beginnings of government aid mean ultimately government supervision. . . . [5]

---

3. *Financial Report to the Board of Overseers of Harvard College,* 1965-1966, pp. 11, 19; N. Silsbee to the President and Fellows of Harvard College, September 26, 1863.

4. H. Shattuck to A. L. Lowell, July 11, 1932; A. L. Lowell to all Budget Officers, June 14, 1932 in *A. L. Lowell Papers, 1930-1933,* F-716, 755.

5. A. L. Lowell to Congressman Robert Luce, February 4, 1933 in *A. L. Lowell Papers, 1930-1933,* F-905.

Colleges or other administrative units in debt had recourse to different treatments. Thus in 1914-1915, the business and law schools, and the botanical gardens drew on reserves. The Bussey Institute relied on the McKay fund, and both the business and the dental schools borrowed from the university.[6]

Early Problems

Once a college is confronted with deficits it is likely to take corrective measures. But oddly enough, deficits became a serious problem for Harvard only in the latter part of the eighteenth century. In the first almost 140 years of Harvard history, the college could avoid deficits by putting the cost of instability on its professors and other members of the staff. The faculty did not even have a salary scale until the latter part of the seventeenth century.

In these early years there was no effective manner of financing deficits. Hence, the burden would be shifted to the students or the faculty, or even to the steward. It is not surprising that Miss Foster finds the average annual income and disbursements from 1638 to 1712 both £440.[7]

Or consider the *Report to the General Courts of the Committee on Harvard Coledge of May 3, 1654.*[8] In this report the committee analyzed receipts and disbursements under President Dunster: The "Comm[i]tee was to Consider what is fitt for an honerable and Comfortabl[e] mainteynance for the president both here and hereafter and how the same is to be raysed."

The committee also considered the sad state of the fellows who had done service but who had not been rewarded, one result being that they had not paid the steward, who in turn was in difficulties. One corrective was to force the "scollers" to pay their bills:

Remedy. That their bee a st[r]ict and martiall order made and duly executed that all scollers whose

---

6. Surpluses or Deficits, 1914-1915, in *A. L. Lowell Papers, 1914-17,* F-790.

7. Foster, *op. cit.,* pp. 148-149.

8. Reproduced in Samuel Eliot Morison, *Harvard College in the Seventeenth Century,* 1936, pp. 570-578.

214

arrears are not duly paid quarterly; or in convenient tyme affter, be sent to their Friends or turned out of Commons, and this to be without offense to anny.

Income vs Expenditures in the Eighteenth Century

In the eighteenth century, current income and general expenditures seemed to be in balance as a rule. The balance is clear for the years 1722-1723 to 1751-1752. But from 1752-1753 to 1761-1762 the college seemed to have a surplus of income of about £3,700 (about 15 percent), and from 1762-1763 to 1771-1772 a surplus of about £14,000 or 38 percent. These large surpluses are not easily explained.

With the great inflation of the Revolutionary War period, a similar excess of income prevailed. Between 1777-1778 and 1780-1781, income was £463,666 and expenditures only £314,602. Here again the idiosyncrasies of accounting in a period of great inflation may be relevant. From 1781-1782 to 1792-1793, there was a virtual balance though expenditures exceeded income by £1,600 or 2 to 3 percent. By this period, the value of the monetary unit had been greatly increased. From 1793-1794 to 1805-1806, the college experienced large surpluses, associated in no small part with its very successful investment experience. The income at £434,586 exceeded expenditures by £80,000.

Conditions would have been much more serious if the college had not greatly increased the burden on students. During the war their contribution to income had risen to the record level of 86 percent. Even in the years from 1781-1782 to 1792-1793, students' income remained relatively abnormally high.

The relatively heavy charges on students resulted from the inroads of inflation—despite corrective measures taken by the college in demanding compensation for inflation from borrowers of endowment funds. Whereas in successive ten-year periods beginning 1722-1723 to 1731-1732, endowment income

was 41 and 40 percent of the total, it dropped to 29, 26, and finally 9 percent in years beginning in 1777-1778, and 21 percent from 1781-1782 to 1792-1793.

That the budgeting balance was achieved in large part by exploiting the staff is suggested by the percentage of expenditures going to salaries in periods of stress:

Percent Salaries were of Expenditures	
1742 to 1752	70
1752 to 1762	56
1762 to 1772	64
1777 to 1781	38
1781 to 1793	41

Surprisingly, there were no deficits during the years of the war inflation. Increased tuition charges, adjustment of rents to inflation, and the exploitation of faculty members kept the budget balanced. But the adjustments following the war and the inflationary economy were difficult. In twelve years, 1781 to 1793, there were eight years of deficits on current account. This was a poor record compared to that of the period from 1722 to 1772. In these fifty years there were nine years of deficits, mostly in the 1720s and 1730s.[9]

Eliot on Deficit Financing

In his 1882-1883 report President Eliot presented a theory of university finance which came close to what we might term deficit financing. His general position was that the university should spend whatever sums were received in current income, with the

9. Sources for this section: *Stewards' Quarter Bill Books, Treasurer's Ledgers, Treasurer's Journals, Harvard College Papers, Acts and Laws of the Province of Massachusetts Bay* (to 1780), *Acts and Laws of the Commonwealth of Massachusetts* (1780-1800), *Legislative Records of the Council, Corporation Records, Steward's Audited Accounts,* for relevant years; *Treasurer's Journal* and *Treasurer's Ledgers,* 1807-1819.

result that occasional deficits would be inevitable. At one point he was also careful to point out that years of slow growth were those of surplus or small deficits. Three statements give Eliot's advanced views on university finance:

It is the general purpose of the Corporation to spend every year all their income. . . . As fast as new resources are placed in their hands, whether from increase in the amount of tuition fees, or from the income of new endowments, the Corporation incurs new permanent charges. . . . The financial policy proper to a University is, of course, entirely different from that of a corporation whose final object is to make money; it should be conservative in regard to the preservation of capital, but free in regard to the prompt and complete expenditure of income. For the future enlargement of their resources the Corporation rely upon the increase in the number of students and the influx of gifts.

While it is unsuitable that any school or department of the University should live beyond its means, it is not possible to avoid occasional deficits, unless the Corporation abandon their policy—now of many years' standing—of spending year by year all their properly available resources. To avoid deficits invariably would mean to aim deliberately at an annual surplus. . . . Accordingly, they believe that the University should be conducted as a growing, changing, expanding organization, losing here but gaining there, and always turning out from year to year the largest possible immediate product of well-trained men for the largest possible variety of intellectual work. If the general tendency of the institution is towards greater size, wealth, and usefulness, the various departments may from time to time experience deficits, or temporary diminutions of their resources, without occasioning serious anxiety. . . .

. . . Between 1832 and 1857 there were only four years in which there was not a surplus. Financially, this period might be called successful; but it was not a period of rapid development, either in the College proper or in the University as a whole. One may also

see . . . that the period during which deficits have been largest and most frequent is the period when the increase of the invested funds of the University by gift and bequest has been most rapid. *There seems to be no connection between the procuring of annual surpluses and general University prosperity, or between the occurrence of deficits and University decline.*[10]

President Eliot itemized the surpluses and deficits over the years 1826-1827 through 1903. From 1827 to 1866 surpluses amounted to $117,270 and deficits only $36,039. (About one-half during the troublesome years 1850 through 1863.) The years of serious deficits were Eliot's and Lowell's years. In the Eliot years, 1870 to 1903, there were sixteen years of surpluses and eighteen years of deficits. But surpluses were $90,000 and deficits $270,000, with the largest deficits in 1881, 1893, 1899, and 1903.[11]

On numerous occasions Eliot harped on the wisdom of spending every dollar received. In 1895, the corporation turned down a gift because the donor would not allow the money to be used until it had accumulated for a hundred years and had grown up to $500,000. Even as early as 1873, Eliot criticized a policy of accumulating a large sum of money by Harvard at compound interest through the intermediary of the Massachusetts Hospital Life Insurance Company. The result would be, in his view, reduced gifts for the college, as potential donors became aware of these accumulations.[12]

The Great Crisis in the 1820s

Perhaps Harvard's most serious financial crisis occurred in the first quarter of the nineteenth

10. *Report of the President of Harvard College,* 1882-1883, pp. 42-43; 1902-1903, pp. 53-54 (my italics).
11. These statistics from *Report of the President of Harvard College,* 1902-1903, pp. 326-327.
12. C. W. Eliot to the President and Fellows of Harvard College, March 8, 1873; C. W. Eliot to Professor Sylvester Waterhouse, December 3, 1895; *C. W. Eliot on University Trustees,* pp. 29-30.

Century. Many factors contributed to this crisis: President Kirkland's lack of economic wisdom, especially costly since he had been given greater discretion than earlier presidents; slipshod work by Treasurer John Davis; an inadequate accounting system; the unsatisfactory economic conditions in the second decade of the century; the large expansion with accompanying heavy burdens of fixed charges as the rise of enrollment flattened out and numbers actually declined; the growing opposition of the Calvinist elements, with repercussions on gifts and enrollment; the excessive response of spending to the receipts from the bank tax, which yielded $100,000 over ten years (1814 to 1824), but which then was not renewed. In the meanwhile Harvard had spent $150,000 on capital items and to finance some commitments imposed by the government.[13]

Quincy wrote that previous to the presidency of Dr. Kirkland the corporation had kept carefully within the limits of their incomes and seldom "ventured into expenditures until the means of reimbursement were in their possession." New demands for cash appeared in the first quarter of the century. A law was passed that tutors after six years of satisfactory service would be entitled to a college professorship. Immediately the roster of professors rose by two. At about the same time the building of University Hall had begun without the means of financing being available.

In the midst of this crisis, Kirkland had to resign, and a practical man had to be found to replace him. The faculty was asked to recommend economies, and they did. Not only a reduction in staff and reduced outlays on capital were necessary, but also increased working loads for university personnel. The corporation had to adopt more drastic measures than those recommended by the faculty. In assuming this responsibility Nathaniel Bowditch stood out.

No one was inclined to criticize Kirkland beyond stressing his ineptitude in financial matters. But an audit "showed that he had overdrawn his salary to the amount of $1,700 . . . compiled an extraordinary expense account, including outlays on post-

age, stationery and bridge tools on his visits to Boston for seventeen years past. . . . "[14]

An excellent statement of the problems under the Kirkland-Davis regime and the objective sought by the Quincy appointment follow:

The general community approved of the choice [Quincy] *with great unanimity, though there were some apprehensions that he might not be able readily to adapt himself to duties so different from those of his former life. But it was generally understood that the finances of the College had been in a state of great disorder. Dr. Kirkland, the model of a dignified clergyman, an accomplished scholar, a polished gentleman, bland and courteous in his intercourse with the students, by whom he was greatly beloved, and universally popular in society for his genial graces, was not a man of business, and no natural or acquired talent for management of money. Judge John Davis, of the United States District Court, who was treasurer of the College during the whole of Dr. Kirkland's Presidency, unfortunately was not fitted to make good his deficiencies in this particular. Between them both . . . the College finances had fallen into almost inextricable confusion . . . it was thought important that a man of the world, accustomed to business, should be placed at the head of the University. . . . [15]*

In response to the crisis the college introduced all kinds of economies. The corporation reduced President Kirkland's salary and deprived him of his secretary, cut professors' salaries from $1,700 to $1,500, required a minimum number of hours of teaching, reduced the number of instructors, sold the wood carrying sloop *Harvard* and purchased wood on the open market at a saving, disposed of the unprofitable printing press, and also sold land that involved net costs to the college. The corporation carried their

---

13. Quincy, *op. cit.*, vol. II, p. 356.

14. S. E. Morison, "The Great Rebellion in Harvard College," in *Publications of the Colonial Society of Massachusetts,* April, 1928, p. 109.
15. E. Quincy, *Life of Josiah Quincy,* 1874, pp. 430-431; cf., E. Hale, "A Group of Presidents," in *Harvard Graduates Magazine,* 1896, vol. 4, p. 563.

economies to the point of refusing to pay for the wine drunk on communion days by the faculty, or for the dinner of the examining committee (and hence the examining committee failed to appear); and upbraided students for paying the college 12 cents instead of 12½ cents due.

Some indication of trends is to be had from the condensed table here. Enrollment, especially of undergraduates, had responded badly and in part because of the rising and high cost of an undergraduate education. The growth of investment funds was also unsatisfactory in the years 1809 to 1819 though large rises prevailed in the next twenty years. Pressure to bring down costs for students is evident both in the stabilization of tuition rates and the decline in total costs.

Table 26-1.

Enrollment, Costs of Education and Investment Funds, 1809 to 1839, by Ten-Year Periods

	1809	1819	1829	1839
Enrollment	188	249	412	432
Undergraduate enrollment	?	272	248	237
Tuition	$ 51.96	$ 56.80 (1818)	$ 55	$ 55
Total annual cost of education, per student	167.60 (1807)	230.25 (1818)	201.50	217.50
General investment	281,100	289,900	398,900 (1830-1831)	515,800

Panicked by the large deficits, the corporation and overseers took as drastic measures as were ever taken in Harvard's history. Expenditures had been especially large for construction. University Hall alone cost $65,000, of which sum the bank tax financed $50,000. But since salaries accounted for nearly two-thirds of outlays by the late 1820s the great economies had to be found there. The corporation merged the four professorships financed out of university funds with the endowed professorships restricted income to the latter to the yield of relevant funds, and in general cut faculty salaries. The college greatly increased the teaching load, restricted beneficiary funds to the income of relevant funds, and required the recipients to be proctors, monitors, choristers, etc., services previously a charge on the budget, and failed to fill the vacancies in professorships.

In treating the deficits of the 1820s, the governing bodies not only introduced substantial economies; they also sought large educational reforms. They asked for large reductions in tuition and at the same time wanted to reduce financial aid for students. The authorities apparently sought to avoid the use of general funds as a means of financing student aid. They held that should general funds be used to finance student aid, the students who were charged full costs for their education would then also finance the indigent.

The overseers' committee reminded the corporation that "the college was not opened to serve the rich alone but rather as a place where persons with moderate property might have their sons educated on equal terms with the rich. . . . " 16

Economies were to be thrust upon students receiving financial aid, but especially on the faculty: cuts in pay, additional teaching responsibilities, denial of time for research, limitation of nonresident professor's pay to income from foundations financing a chair, refusal of additional pay to faculty members for additional services. There were protests from some faculty members.

16. Committee to Inquire into the Expenses and Income of the College . . . for Reducing the Expenses . . . to the President and Fellows of Harvard College, December 26, 1826.

17. For greater details, see last reference and J. Quincy, *op. cit.,* vol. II, pp. 353-369, 558-563; Committee . . . Settlement of All Accounts with Mr. Hilliard, October 18, 1827; Committee of this Board . . . Subject to the Appointment and Compensation of Proctors . . . Services of Beneficiaries, November 15, 1827; L. Hedge to the President of Harvard College, January 4, 1827; G. Ticknor to the President and Fellows of Harvard College, November 8, 1827.

That the economy campaign had some impact is revealed by the decline of the deficit from $4,037 in 1826-1827 to $353 in 1827-1828 and the attainment of a surplus of $9,710 in 1829-1830. But in 1831-1832 the deficit once more was at $4,438. By 1835-1836 the effects of Quincy's skillful administration were evident. The next five years brought substantial surpluses of $28,000 in all.[18]

In this period there was much concern, as there has been in later years, for the relationship between enrollment and tuition income. At this time the view held by the authorities was that a reduction of enrollment was costly, for revenues dropped more than costs.

From all of this it is clear that a university needs efficiency to management as well as able professors and a good curriculum. Kirkland was a great president, but he was unfortunate in not having the help of financial advisers who are available to the modern university president.[19]

The Relationship Between Enrollment and Deficits

One of the problems that emerged in the 1820s, and many times since, was discovering the relationship between enrollment and deficits. Prof. George Ticknor related the crisis to the high unit cost of higher education at Harvard. In 1823, he had pointed out that the cost of Harvard education was $69,000 ($230 per student for 300 students). What puzzled him was the better education provided in Europe at a much lower cost.

It might be assumed, since costs exceeded tuition, that the college would gain from a reduction of enrollment, or from a failure of enrollment to rise. But in every crisis—early nineteenth century, early twentieth century, the Great Depression, and World War II—adverse effects on enrollment were associated with increased deficits. College administrators had not learned the difference between marginal and average costs, a fact known to economists for a hundred years. Reduced enrollments would be expensive if costs declined less than the loss of tuition, a likely outcome if major costs were relatively fixed.

In the 1904 crisis a committee of the overseers showed that in thirty-five years the rise of outlay in relation to student tuition had increased by 28 percent per student (numbers had increased three times). Why should expenditures per student have increased so much with a rise of enrollment of 300 percent? The explanation was undoubtedly the large expansion of faculty and curriculum under Eliot, a trend that offset the economies of scale expected with a trebling of enrollment. The committee at least pointed to one favorable factor; namely, that rising enrollments reduced costs per student as enrollments in standard courses rose.[20] In 1849, however, as is revealed later, Samuel Eliot presented modern views of this problem.

In World War II, the college complained again of the losses of revenues associated with declining enrollment. The explanation of losses could only be that fixed costs were so heavy inclusive of commitments to the faculty that the loss of $400 tuition per student would not be matched by an equivalent reduction in unit costs. Indeed, the university took special measures to cut costs, such as a twelve-month

18. *Report of the President of Harvard College,* 1902-1903, pp. 326-327.

19. For this period see especially *Report of the President of Harvard College* and *Report of the Treasurer of Harvard College,* 1824 through 1830; *Committee of Overseers Report,* May 4, 1824, pp. 9-10; *Report of the Committee to Enquire into the Income and Expenses of the College,* Dec. 26, 1826; *The Ticknor Papers,* in Harvard University Archives; Samuel Eliot Morison, *Three Centuries of Harvard, 1636-1936,* 1937, pp. 219-220; S. Willard, *Memories of Youth and Manhood,* 1855, pp. 299, 300; J. Quincy, *op. cit.,* vol. II, pp. 362-369 and appendix XLI, pp. 558-563; S. E. Morison, "The Great Rebellion in Harvard College and the Resignation of President Kirkland," in *Publications of the Colonial Society of Massachusetts,* vol. 128, 1928, p. 108.

20. G. Ticknor, "Remarks on Colleges," August 20, 1823, in *G. Ticknor's Papers,* in Harvard University Archives; *Report of a Special Committee of the Board of Overseers on the Financial Requirements of the University. . . .* 1904.

year for the faculty, which reduced costs by $145,000 in one year. A subsidy of up to 40 percent of the faculty salary for professors migrating to Washington might be considered a fringe benefit, but it was also a means of encouraging faculty to take themselves off the university rolls.[21]

End of Depression: Aftermath of the Crises of the 1820s

After the crisis of 1825, the college recovered but the attacks continued into the 1840s. A member of the corporation, F. C. Gray, dispatched a brilliant defense of the college in a published letter to the Governor, April 16, 1831. After commenting on the high moral standards of the college, Gray said that at no other college "now obtain, I say it boldly and without disparagement or disrespect of others, an education nearly so complete ..." To the charge of small enrollment, Gray replied that there were more students in Cambridge than anywhere else but Yale. But "last year *one hundred and forty-four* undergraduates received charitable aid in Yale, and only *thirty-four* in Harvard." Gray also commented on the high cost of a Harvard education. His refutation consisted in blaming indulgent parents and friends who encouraged extravagances and also in showing that nowhere were books to be had as cheaply, and that board at $1.75 weekly was a subsidized bargain.

On the costs of instruction, Mr. Gray's defense was the quality of the product, and the subsidy by the college. "... There may be less money paid by students elsewhere, than in Cambridge, but they do not get so much of it in proportion to cost; and therefore it is not so cheap. ..."

To the charge of accumulating cash to meet future contingencies, Gray replied that with uncertainties it was necessary to prepare for future deficits. He would use resources for making education better, not cheaper, as demanded by Harvard's critics.[22]

An 1849 report of the board of overseers described the retrenchments imposed by the crisis of 1825. The committee expressed the view that in 1844 "the means of education are worth what they cost, that on the whole nothing is squandered. ..." [23]

Other Special Problems in the Nineteenth Century

In commenting on the large deficits of the six years 1866 to 1872 (not all Eliot years) of $27,570, Eliot added that the funds of the college were further reduced by losses on sales of stock and capital outlays. Income suffered further because of the exchange of $106,887 of productive assets for nonproductive land. In all, Eliot estimated the losses of income for the university, college, and library at $10,000 per year; against this the university had acquired 20 acres of well situated land that assured nonremoval of the college and avoided extensive repairs ($33,000). The university thus acquired assets that were worth more than $140,000.[24]

By 1872-1873, with the rise of tuition ($8,156) and a reduction of expenditures ($6,711), the deficit of $11,444 was converted into a surplus. Improved economic conditions were relevant, and the surplus was had despite the effects of a Boston fire that greatly impaired the finances of the university. Of some significance also was income from a new building, Matthews Hall. At this time the college did not hesitate to make profits on its dormitories. But the president noted a rise of salaries of $8,000 in 1873-1874, and probably in 1874-1875. He continued that falling prices help the faculty and they are pleased with a security of jobs in bad times.[25]

In 1877-1878, deficits still plagued the college. Once large committments had been made, a worsening of the economic situation was likely to be reflected in deficits. A few years later the treasurer commented:

---

21. *Report of the President of Harvard College,* 1940-1941, pp. 16-17; 1941-1942, p. 355.
22. Mr. Gray's Letter to Governor Levi Lincoln, April 1831, especially pp. 7-16.

23. *Report of a Visiting Committee of Harvard College Made to the Overseers,* January, 1849, pp. 17-19.
24. *Report of the President of Harvard College,* 1871-1872, pp. 35-42.
25. *Ibid.,* 1872-1873, pp. 30-31; 1873-1874, pp. 37-38.

The Corporation had to choose between the risk of consuming part of its unrestricted capital, and the certainty of crippling the University in its efforts to do the work reasonably expected of it. The risk was taken with the full understanding that consumption of capital could not be allowed to go on for more than one or two years. . . .

In 1898-1899, the major cause of a deficit was "heavy costs of installing bathrooms in the dormitories of the yard. These improvements were made necessary by the rising scale of comfort and sanitation in the community at large." [26]

Crisis in the Early Twentieth Century

In 1903-1904, the deficit amounted to the very high sum of $43,000, a result of excessive enthusiasm engendered by surpluses in the preceeding two years and a large rise of salaries justified by an expected increase of enrollment which never materialized. An accompaniment of this miscalculation was unexpected capital outlays. Losses of tuition income and reduction of rents impaired the financial position further.

By 1905, with deficits in seven of the last nine years, the corporation had cut expenses to the bone, and had reduced the salary list and the standard of salaries. But the overseers urged maintenance of salary levels and promotions. [27]

In this crisis the university experienced another financial setback, though not of the proportions of that of the first quarter of the nineteenth century. Here again the faculty had to take the brunt of the adjustment. President Eliot sought a cut of $25,000 from the salary list. He achieved this by postponing promotions, by not replacing professors who retired, but primarily by cutting the number of junior appointments as well as their pay. [28]

Apparently an attempt to eliminate courses was not a great success. Requested by a committee of the board of overseers to justify certain courses with less than ten students, the committee on instruction of the faculty of arts and sciences felt that nearly all the courses were worth having. The board of overseers voted in December, 1906, that no new subject or branch of instruction involving additional expense should be added "except after mature deliberation by the Governing Boards of the University." Moreover, the faculty of arts and science was requested "to undertake a comprehensive revision of the present scheme of instruction, with a view to securing more concentration of effort, increased educational efficiency, and, if practicable, diminished expenditure." [29]

A committee of the overseers explained that a deficit must reflect inefficiency or an attempt to educate too many persons at a cost for each greater than the trust can afford to contribute. Apparently the second explanation impressed the committee. But Eliot, though not greatly concerned over deficits, was in fact in favor of low tuition and, therefore, would depend on getting more nontuition income and seeking economies. [30] Thus in 1906-1907, the college reduced its deficit from $59,296 to $16,713. The sources of this improvement were increased fees, higher returns on investments, and a reduced number of appointments.

As deficits cumulated the college had to use up capital. In 1905-1906, the corporation wrote: "The Corporation have now used up capital sums amounting to $488,841 by this process of charging annual deficits to unrestricted funds. . . ." Both the stock account and the Insurance Guaranteed Fund were exhausted. [31]

26. *Report of the President of Harvard College*, 1898-1899, pp. 53-54.
27. *Ibid.*, 1902-1903, pp. 48-50; 1903-1904, pp. 49-50; 1905-1906, pp. 55-57.
28. *Report of the President of Harvard College*, 1902-1903, pp. 50, 55; 1903-1904, p. 50; 1904-1905, pp. 19, 61; 1905-1906, p. 58; 1907-1908, p. 53.
29. *Ibid.*, 1905-1906, pp. 10-11.
30. *Report of a Special Committee of the Board of Overseers on the Financial Requirements of the University*, 1904; *Report of the President of Harvard College*, 1906-1907, p. 55.
31. *Ibid*, 1905-1906, pp. 55-56.

In the discussions of 1903-1905 and even earlier, one of the subjects of controversy was the relationship of the graduate school to the college proper. Eliot's elective system and accompanying faculty expansion brought large increases in the number of courses, both undergraduate and graduate. Courses tended to be especially small, and hence costly, at the graduate level. One result of this development had been the clash of supporters of the college against those of the graduate school. Dean L. B. R. Briggs in 1903 raised this issue:

... I suspect that if the receipts and expenditures of Harvard College could be disentangled once more from those of the Graduate School and the Scientific School, the process would reveal some sacrifices of the College to its neighbors; and I believe with my predecessor that the time has come for peculiar attention to the welfare of Harvard College.... [32]

An interesting criticism of the Briggs position is to be found in a statement by Professor Charles Haskins.[33] His position was that one could not estimate the cost of an undergraduate and a graduate education. Each curriculum served the interest of both groups. Provision had to be made for undergraduate instruction for some graduate students, and graduate instruction for some undergraduates; and the graduate school was the magnet for outstanding scholars who served both graduates and undergraduates.[34]

In the first half of the nineteenth century the professional schools began their large growth, a development which aroused the opposition of the defenders of the college and liberal education. They resented the competition for funds, the inroads of science, law, and medicine and the presumed neglect of the college. The anonymous reviewer of Samuel A. Eliot's sketch of Harvard College written in 1849 well expressed the growing opposition to the emergence and advance of professional education.[35]

On the submergence of the college, the critic wrote:

Now it is hardly half of [the university]; so many professional schools and other establishments have sprung up around it, so many funds have been left in trust for various purposes, many of them having hardly any connection with the education of undergraduates at Cambridge, that it is no longer only a College, nor even a University, but a vast nondescript establishment for the general promotion of science and letters.... [36]

One of the features of this paper was an unusual understanding of the relationship among enrollment, fixed costs, and unit costs. A criticism of Harvard was its high costs and hence inadequate enrollment. Hence the writer suggested seeking more money for scholarships, and hence more students and reduced cost per student—not money for unwanted scholarships.[37]

A Summary of the Eliot Years

It is now clear that deficits were most troublesome under Eliot, with two periods especially difficult, namely, the 1870s and the early twentieth century. But deficits were substantial in later years also. From 1906 to 1916 the deficits amounted to $242,000 in all departments and $297,000 in the college, with surpluses in the college only in three years.[38] (These were not all Eliot years.)

Great expansion under Eliot contributed to periodic crises. Covering the period 1867 to 1903, C. F. Adams showed that the number of courses in the academic department had increased from 92 to 456,

32. *Harvard Graduates Magazine*, vol. XI, pp. 387-388, 1903.
33. C. H. Haskins, "The Graduate School and the Tuition Fee, " in *Harvard Graduates Magazine*, vol. 23, pp. 591-593.
34. See S. E. Harris, *Higher Education: Resources and Finance*, 1962, pp. 55-56, 516-517.

35. "Eliot's Sketch of Harvard College," in *North American Review*, vol. 68, pp. 102-125, 1849.
36. *Ibid.*, p. 107.
37. *Ibid.*, p. 124.
38. "Why Harvard Needs Money," in *Harvard Alumni Bulletin*, vol. XIX, p. 306, January 18, 1917.

that outgo per student had increased 28 percent more than income, and that the losses were related to 4 times as many students as in 1868, while the cost per degree had risen by 80 percent. The situation would have deteriorated further had not large gifts been received, the pay of instructors reduced, and the costs per student of many courses reduced with rising enrollment.[39]

With the 1870s, mostly a period of depression, the college showed elements of overextension. In his 1876 report, President Eliot boasted of a trebling of university income in the last fourteen years; the rise of buildings from eighteen to twenty-six and almost a doubling of land held in Cambridge. But inflation had been troublesome until 1873, and the ensuing depression required much higher tuition income to be attained by raising rates and increasing enrollment. By the 1870s the return on investments had begun to decline from 7.44 percent in 1873 to 5.19 percent in 1886. Such reduction of income was especially troublesome because of the rising committments of the college.[40] Again in the early twentieth century, accelerated expansion proved troublesome when incomes did not respond.

After Eliot

Deficits did not end with Eliot. In his 1913-1914 report President Lowell dwelt on a deficit of $52,009 for the university. One of the principal causes, apparently, was a number of young faculty members who had to be promoted, with resultant higher salary budgets. Lowell urged the need of higher tuition: "We are thus faced with the alternative of increasing our income, or of cutting down instruction severely, which would be most unfortunate. . . . We must strive to offer the best, even if it costs the students more." [41]

World War I further increased deficits. In December, 1917, the president complained of the declining enrollment, with 2,000 students lost at a cost of $400,000. By June, 1918, the drop of enrollment was from 5,592 (October, 1916) to 3,086.

Even in the prosperous early 1920s deficits prevailed. But soon increased tuition and gifts corrected the situation.

In the Great Depression Harvard was bound to suffer. But its over-all position did not deteriorate greatly in view of the extent of the decline of the nation's gross national product of almost 50 percent from 1929 to 1933, of gross national product in stable prices of about one-third, and of corporate profits from $10 billion to losses of $2 billion.[42]

Harvard had two important reserves. One was the accumulation of surpluses from prosperous times in the 1920s, and the second was the excess of applications from students over spaces available. By reducing the standards for entering students the university could maintain its enrollments to some extent, thus improving its income position.

In finance the most troublesome item was the reduction of income from endowment. In one year, 1932-1933, the return on general investments was reduced from 5.25 to 4.8 percent at a cost of approximately $450,000, a loss which affected especially the college and the medical school. Yet through careful husbanding of resources and acquisition of new endowments, the university expected a balancing of the budgets. Even collections on students' bills were normal.[43]

The university did not escape financial embarrassment. Early in the depression it was necessary to cut the library budget by 16 percent and cut the tutorial program. Another casualty was a decline of promotions resulting finally in the crisis of 1937-1938, which led to the report of the Committee of Eight. Fortunately the enrollment remained relatively stable, though students had great difficulties in pay-

---

39. C. F. Adams, "The Harvard Tuition Fee: The Proposed Increase," in *Harvard Graduates Magazine,* 1904 (reprint), pp. 8-9.
40. *Report of the President of Harvard College,* 1874-1875, pp. 30-31, 40-41; 1875-1876, p. 4; 1885-1886, p. 4; *Treasurer's Statement,* 1877-1878, p. 4; 1879-1880, p. 4.

41. *Report of the President of Harvard College,* 1913-1914, p. 12.
42. Estimates from *Economic Report of the President,* 1964.
43. *Harvard Alumni Bulletin,* 1932, pp. 732-734.

ing their bills. The stability of enrollment resulted from the unavailability of jobs, and also a continued secular trend towards higher education.[44]

Some Conclusions

Deficits have frequently prevailed in Harvard's history and especially in the last hundred years. In the eleven years ending 1900-1901, for example, deficits were incurred in seven years. An unsatisfactory state of finance prevailed in earlier years also, but by transferring the deficiencies to the faculty through cuts in salary, or allowing prices and incomes generally to rise much more than salaries, and through imposing higher charges on students, Harvard could conceal or treat the deficit. In the great crisis of the 1820s deficits were indeed troublesome. At this time the authorities would have had recourse not to higher but to reduce tuition on the theory that a cut in tuition would bring more students and higher revenues. In later years when confronted with deficits and consideration was given to the level of tuition, the medicine was likely to be a rise of tuition.

But the university was slow indeed to introduce increases of tuition when finances became troublesome. In the 1860s, however, the response of higher tuition was unusually quick and substantial, the occasion being both some losses of enrollment and a large inflation. In the World War I and World War II periods, the authorities were indeed slow in raising tuition, as they had been in the later Eliot years. In the midst of war and declining enrollment, a no-increase policy could be supported, but not in the postwar period. Harvard thereby suffered greatly because of its failure to adjust its price (tuition) to the great inflations. In the Lowell years, and to some extent in the Eliot years, this meant large and persistent deficits. Lowell sought higher tuition, only to encounter opposition, but Eliot belonged to the low-tuition school.

In the Great Depression, tuition remained unchanged. In view of the large drop in prices and a fortiori of family income, stable tuition was equivalent to a rise of tuiton. In the years 1940 to 1955, the response of tuition to the rise of prices and per capita income was most inadequate. The resultant deficit was revealed only in the sense that the impact was felt by the faculty members, who were exploited as prices and incomes generally rose and their incomes lagged far behind.

Throughout Harvard's history, when confronted with deficits, dismissal of teachers, increases of the teaching load, and reduction of salary of faculty were the first lines of defense against deficits. This was especially clear in the 1820s. Until relatively recent years the burden was shifted especially to the younger members of the faculty. Eliot could be much more cold blooded in dropping faculty members than modern administrators would be. At one point Eliot defended a policy of dismissing a number of faculty members rather than imposing a cut in pay for all.[45]

In the first two hundred years or so, the faculty bore the brunt of adjustment as faculty salaries lagged far behind the rise of prices in the long inflationary periods. Later direct assaults on salaries were frequent. Thus, the observatory, confronted with a deficit in the 1880s, would drop three members of the faculty and not replace two others; and would scrutinize new enterprises.[46]

There were occasions where attention was directed to other means of contending with deficits. In 1894, for example, the overseers carefully considered the problem. Eliot, never too troubled by deficits, announced that he had gone as far as he could in putting the burden on the faculty. Eliot was also worried over a decline of investment income. The majority of the overseers' committee wondered whether twenty-five years of progress had not brought the Eliot administration to a condition

44. *Report of the President of Harvard College,* 1931-1932, pp. 21, 22, 36, 176-177, 227-228; 1932-1933, pp. 27-29; 1935-1936, pp. 218-220; 1937-1938, p. 38.

45. C. W. Eliot to Professor Barrett Wendell, January 16, 1894.
46. E. Pickering Report, June 8, 1885, in *C. Eliot Official Papers.*

similar to Kirkland's in the 1820s. The majority of this committee would not raise tuition to cover costs fully, but would raise tuition by $50. In two earlier increases by one-half and one-third, enrollment had risen, not declined. They would provide scholarships for those who could not contend with higher fees. The majority proposed to pay professors well and they would seek teachers who could "inspire men, take them off their feet, withdraw them from the life of trifles and gain and comfort...." The minority committee also wanted higher salaries, but was not ready to pay for them by imposing higher tuition charges.[47]

---

47. *Report of the Board of Overseers,* January 10, 1894.

27

Every Tub on Its Own Bottom

The expression "every tub stands on its own bottom" means roughly that each college or (say) museum in the university finances itself. No college is responsible for the solvency of another, nor is the university. Indeed, the university has often advanced funds to a college, but the understanding is that interest is to be paid and the loan repaid. There have been exceptions to this rule. At crucial times, for example, in allocating funds, the university favored the impoverished school of education or the divinity school. Behind the tub theory was the idea that subsidies from other departments tend to destroy incentives which otherwise would assure balanced accounts.

Adherence to the tub principle has been reflected in numerous issues. For example, the problem arose of students in one college taking courses in other colleges, e.g., a college student taking courses in the science school. The science school demanded payment on behalf of students from other colleges taking courses in the science school. The problem became so troublesome that general rules had to be worked out which prescribed intercollege payments, and also the extent to which the practice of taking work in colleges other than the student's own would be allowed, and also rules on who should pay the extra amounts and who should receive the fees, e.g., the college offering the instruction sought by outsiders or the faculty member.[1]

One of the most persistent exchanges between parts of the university revolved around the payments for the public (i.e., the university) library. At one point fees of $10 per student were imposed on law school students. The law school faculty vigorously objected, holding that the student was being asked to pay one-ninth as much for the use of the general library as for all services of the law school.[2]

Financial problems harassed the divinity school throughout its history. It was in relation to the divinity school that President Kirkland in the first quarter of the nineteenth century first proclaimed "It is our rule here for every tub to stand on its own bottom!" In the official history of the divinity school, it was admitted that the school incurred deficits every year, which had to be financed by the university. Here was a serious break with the tub theory. The school also showed that it was on an export basis, that is many more students took work in the divinity school than divinity students took courses in other branches of the university.[3]

Financial problems were not unknown to the medical school. For a long time the college would collect important fees which rightfully belonged to

---

1. Memo of June, 1901, in *C. W. Eliot Official Papers*, Boxes 270-271; *Report of Committee of Scientific School . . . to Consider Fees, to the Corporation*, April 20, 1849 and June 30, 1849.

2. T. W. Harris to S. A. Eliot, January 13, 1846. *Report of the Committee . . . to Consider the Subject of Reducing and Equalizing the Charges for the Use of the Library . . .* March 28, 1848; J. Sparks to President Walker, February 12, 1853; J. Parker, et als, to the Honorable and Reverend, the Corporation of Harvard College, January 1853, "On a Subject of Vital Importance to the Law School."

3. G. H. Williams, ed., *op. cit.,* pp. 174-175, 212-213.

the medical school. The dean of the medical school demanded these fees and proposed to use them for janitorial service, maintenance of the plant, and related purposes.[4]

Special transactions affected the relations of the college and other parts of the university. For example, at the beginning of his regime, Eliot wanted to invest in unproductive land in order to be ready for later contingencies. The treasurer objected on the grounds that this would divert money from productive uses for the college. In short, the university might gain at the expense of the college.[5]

At this time the treasurer proposed a new system of accounting, the net effect of which would be to relieve branches of the university of charges which were then unfairly being imposed on the various schools. The university income would finance these charges.

Of course the college was thus relieved of some of its assessments. In later years, Eliot was solicitious that charges allocated to this account should properly be put upon the university account.[6]

In recent years, the theory has prevailed that every department is on its own. But, as in earlier years, the corporation has used its general funds to support schools in financial difficulties, e.g., education. Thus in 1951-1952 the president announced that $2 million of transfers of capital had been made in the last twenty years to the faculties of medicine, public health, and education. More would have been available if the library had not received so much—$7 million in fifteen years ending in 1947-1948. In Eliot's day the university liquidated schools—e.g., veterinary, Bussey. But the corporation also covered numerous deficits—e.g., of the medical school. A decision to liquidate rested not only on deficits but also on lack of large contributions to finance the objectives of a university.[7]

4. W. Channing to Eben Francis, Esq., Treasurer of Harvard University, August 27, 1827.
5. N. Silsbee to the President and Fellows of Harvard College, October 28, 1870.

6. C. W. Eliot to J. D. Greene, July 20, 1908, July 23, 1908.
7. *Report of the President of Harvard College,* 1900-1901, pp. 26-27; 1905-1906, p. 9; 1907-1908, pp. 31-32; 1947-1948, p. 14; 1951-1952, p. 35.

28

Miscellaneous Issues on Finance

The only unifying impact in this chapter is that each section has some relationship to expenditures. In some instances the issues are discussed briefly here and more fully elsewhere, e.g., tuition, high costs at Harvard, the crises of 1824 and 1849. The association of the level of expenditures and unit costs receives special attention here, though these issues are discussed in other parts of the book. Here is an appropriate place to consider the relationship between enrollment and costs; the elective system and research and costs; such special episodes as William H. James request for a $300 budget for research in psychology, and the conflict of interest involved when the university purchased its stone for Gore Hall from a stone cutter's firm owned by President Quincy. This is also a good opportunity to consider again the relation of salaries and wages to total payroll expenditures and such matters as the ratio of growth of the college and the university.

As early as 1650 the college authorities instructed the steward to keep informed of provisions available, of disbursements made (with the approval of the president), and to assure collections of money due the college, to restrict indebtedness to the college, and the manner of distributing receipts between the steward and the college.

Certain Orders by the Schollars
& officers of the Colledge
to bee observed.
written 28 March 1650

The Steward receiving a just & clear account of the Visible stock or Treasury of the Colledge as it is a society either in Visible pvisions or in debts acknowledged or prooved due by the members of the Society shall be bound wth sufficient security quarterly to give an account thereof wth in ten dayes to the Praesident when hee shall require it, together wth the just & necessary disbursements, wch by the Praesidents allowance have been issued out (for necessary pvisions) to the Steward himselfe, Butler, Cook, or any other officers of the house, as also to & for the necessary provisions of fuell, reparations of outworn utensils &c, towards all wch Charges, the steward is to see (besides the stock maintayned) that one third pt bee reserved of all payments to him by the members of the house quarterly made, & the other two parts in sutable pvisions to the Schollars to bee returned as the season & state of the year doth require, & answerably hereto shall deliver in such provisions to the Cook & Butler, or Brewer & Baker, & of them require weekly & Quarterly accounts:

fforasmuch as the students whose friends are most careful to discharge their due expences, have sundry times sorely & unjustly suffered by such as neglect to pay their debts; therefore the steward shal not pmit but upon his owne peril, any students to bee above Two pounds indebted.[2]

Concentration of Funds on Faculty

In the period from 1736 to 1775, the annual budget of free funds was £1188,08s.,1d. In contrast to modern days, virtually all the unappropriated income went for teaching.

Annual Budget of Free Funds, 1736-1755

Salary of four tutors	£ 651	0 0
Rents of Massachusetts Hall paid to president	55	8 1
Salary to president paid by corporation	147	0 0
Mr. Greenwood (professor)	135	0 0
Mr. Manis (Hebrew professor)	100	0 0
Librarian	20	0 0
Treasurer	80	0 0
	1188 08 1	

Of special interest is the higher pay of tutors than of other faculty members and the use of rents to help finance the president.[2]

Financial Problems, 1824

In the first half of the nineteenth century, the university issued a number of statements of an official or semiofficial nature. It is of some use to note the grievances presented in these documents.

In 1824, President Kirkland released a document of some interest. [3] The president began with a distinction between appropriated (i.e., restricted) and nonappropriated funds. Of $19,651.67 of income, $16,149.35 were appropriated. The $16,149.35 were

1. *College Books*, Vol. I, p.32.
2. *Treasurer's Collected Papers*, 1736-1755.
3. *Statement of the Income of Harvard College, and the Manner in Which it is Applied*, February 16, 1824.

divided into nineteen appropriations. (In 1963-1964, there were about twice as many departments for accounting purposes), the amounts in 1824 varying from $20 from a legacy for a professor of theology to $2,221.80 for a theological institute for graduates. The major items were endowments for teaching chairs. The appropriations included eight professorial chairs, with the highest yield only $1,619.28 going to the professor of rhetoric. The library was down for $360; the fund for permanent tutors, $850. Returns on eight endowed chairs averaged less than $1,000.

The president divided salaries for those immediately employed "in the government and instruction of the Students, and in their instruction especially by lessons and recitations." In this category, were six professors at $1,700. (Two received $150 additional for serving as registrar and inspector, respectively). Four tutors averaged $730; the librarian, $600; the steward, $1,250; the president, $2,550; and the treasurer, $751.20. Seven other professors (inclusive of French and Spanish instructors) received $8,558.04. (Included in the seven were medical professors.) The pay was generally in excess of the amount yielded by the relevant endowment. Thus the Eliot Professorship paid $1,700, but the income from endowment of this chair was only $1,200; and whereas the two Hollis professorships and the Hancock chair yielded $735.60 altogether, each of these three received $1,700, or $5,100 in all.

In addition to the sums already noted, the college was liable for $2,818 for repairs, (annual average over thirteen years), occasional expenses of $2,167.28, and for a small item of $60.10, the total roughly $33,000. Here again the concentration of funds on the faculty compared to later periods is striking.

How were these bills financed?	
1. Free money from gifts	$ 3,502.32
2. Restricted money	9,510.88
3. Assessments on students........	21,150.00
	$34,163.20
Difference in favor of the college ...	758.21

The president was not happy that students paid more than 60 percent of the costs, nor was he pleased at the heavy bills for the maintenance of buildings.

What especially troubled him was the deficiency in the yield of endowed chairs compared to payments to the relevant professors, an issue discussed elsewhere. However, some funds provided services that were peripheral to the main objectives of Harvard.

Kirkland found additional resources to finance the underfinanced professors.[4]

Another trouble to the President, and to all interested in the extension of the means of education, was in part the consequence of the growth of the College, which was so gratifying in other points of view, and which was the very object of efforts innumerable and unwearied. With the increase of officers, which was uncommonly rapid, there was an unavoidable increase of expense; especially, as in the eagerness of all parties, both the founders of the offices, and the governors of the College, it frequently happened that a professor was appointed, when the funds destined for him were quite insufficient for his support, and the deficit was to be drawn from the charge for instruction to the students. . . . [Kirkland] He distributed, with constant generosity, from his own income; he presented particular cases of promise to his wealthy friends, and secured their assistance; and, of course, he gladly availed himself of all the funds of the College which could be placed at his disposal for this purpose. From all these resources the amount he obtained and distributed was very considerable. . . .

1849: Inadequate Funds

In 1849, Pres. Edward Everett delivered a famous speech on Harvard's need of state funds. He hoped for some help from the commonwealth. The thrust was directed especially at the needs of the library. He insisted that "the majority [of Harvard students] are the sons of parents in moderate, narrow, and even straitened circumstances. . . ."

The duty of educating the people rests on great public grounds,—on moral and political foundations. It is deduced from the intimate connection which experience has shown to exist, between the public welfare and all elements of national prosperity on the one hand, and the enlightenment of the population on the other. . . .[5]

1849: The Intrusion of Science and Professional Schools

In the same year the *North American Review's* knowledgeable critic produced his famous paper on Harvard.[6] His main theme was that Harvard had abandoned its liberal tradition and had moved too far in the direction of the physical and natural sciences.

With many of Harvard's activities extraneous to its previous liberal traditions, the corporation was not only squeezing out the liberal curriculum but also putting heavy financial burdens on Harvard College, in that financial support and personnel were being diverted to noncollege activities. Moreover, sponsors of the new activities competed for funds. The Harvard College student was being asked to pay additional fees and being deprived of part of his faculty. Tuition, indeed, was only $75, but the additional expenditures of $300 and the loss of state scholarships frightened the poor away from Harvard and attracted the affluent.

According to the critic, the intrusion of the non-Harvard College operations was reflected in a reduction of the general stock from $218,000 in 1835 to $176,000 in 1849, in a rise of general expenses from $4,843 to $7,379; in a reduction of graduates from 62 average in between 1815 and 1824 to 58 average in the ten years from 1839 to 1849. Yet in the interval, the Boston population had risen from 40,000 to nearly 120,000.

---

4. *History of Harvard College*, p. 107.

5. E. Evertt in *Harvard's Needs for State Funds*, 1849. pp. 381-387

6. "S. Eliot's Sketch of Harvard College." in *North American Review*, January, 1849.

Relations with the Government

In the year 1849, a semiofficial report appeared in which thanks were given to the government for its past benefactions. The overseers' visiting committee stressed the point that the university had no discretion in the use of endowment funds.

There is a sacredness in these Trusts, which may not be violated, however obsolete the object of the trust may be "deemed," or frivolous in the eyes of modern reformers....
If, therefore, education is to be treated like merchandise, and knowledge like broadcloth, if the account current between instruction and ignorance is to be settled by the course of the market, they who are in search of cheap bargains, may seek them at this Great Workshop, when only half the cost of production is charged to the customer, when the Corporation gets no dividend and the Overseers work without pay.[7]

The visiting committee commented on the excessive charge for tuition at Harvard, i.e., $90 compared to $42 at Amherst and $40 in Williamstown. The committee, however, "disclaimed all comparisons with Colleges, which are doubtless doing all they can honorably to advance and extend the benefits of a liberal eduction."[8]

So far as nontuition costs were involved, the committee commented on the fact that when Harvard opened, Cambridge was a wilderness and Boston a village.

Here the University is located now and forever. Change is impossible.... But the daily expenses of life have increased and will continue to increase. Here is the very golden region of education, but it is pretty hard to get to it, and harder still to subsist there when the journey is made.... If Harvard University is, or is to be, as there is every prospect it will be, the El Dorado of Education, kindness and humility will smooth the passage and furnish a goodly

ailment for those who are laboring in its rich waters or working in its prolific mines.[9]

High Costs at Harvard

Criticism of Harvard for its high costs continued. But the treasurer in 1850-1851 pointed out that the funds appropriated to Harvard College were only $484,500, a sum that yielded $24,225. In comparison, West Point was spending $80,000 on a smaller number of students and this sum was independent of the pay of cadets and appropriations for books, building and apparatus.[10]

Standards, Enrollment and Income

Does a rising enrollment improve or hurt the financial position of the college? In 1872-1873, President Eliot suggested that with 12 percent additional students, the college gained, for the teaching staff did not have to be increased.[11] In 1874-1875, the president again commented on the improvement associated with rising enrollment: "yet a principal reason for the good condition of the University Treasury is the increased volume of receipts from students exclusive of rents."[12]

What is the relationship between standards and the demand for places in an institution of higher learning? Here Eliot was prophetic. He denied the argument that raising the standards of the medical school and the law school would result in a loss of income.

An institution which has any real prestige and power will make a money profit by raising its standard, and that either at once or in a very short time. Its demand for greater attainments on the part of its students will be quickly responded to, and this improved class of students will in a marvellously short time so increase

7. *Report of the Visiting Committee of Harvard University Made to the Overseers*, January, 1849, pp. 14-29.
8. *Ibid*, p. 21

9. *Ibid*, p. 29
10. *Report of the Treasurer of Harvard College*, 1850-1851, p. 3.
11. *Report of the President of Harvard College*, 1872-1873, p. 36.
12. *Ibid.*, 1874-1875, pp. 40-41.

the reputation and influence of the institution as to make its priviliges and its rewards more valued and more valuable. . . . [13]

Expansion and Costs

Expansion and rising costs were a problem throughout Eliot's administration. Soon after his assumption of power, a combination of expanding curriculum, related to the advance of the elective system, the related large rises in the number of faculty members and the initial salary increase in 1870, all brought serious financial problems.

Eliot was aware of the high costs of the elective system when he wrote:

There is no doubt that a prescribed system is indefinitely cheaper than an elective system; for with only one curriculum of elementary courses to provide, a college can get along with a comparatively small number of inferior teachers. A broad elective system requires many teachers of high quality. . . .

Rising costs were also the result of a growing acceptance by Eliot of the view that research by professors is indispensable. He had not started with this view. But more research also meant vast increases in the junior staff, who would relieve professors of routine tasks so that they could carry on research. Aside from the university serving as a storehouse of knowledge, the university must seek new truth:

. . . each prepared to push forward a little the present limits of knowledge; each expecting and hoping to clear up some tangle or bog on the frontier. . . a university which is not a place of reasearch will not long continue to be a good place of teaching. . . . [14]

Research needs continued to trouble those responsible for Harvard's financial and educational policies. In a study during the 1950's of the behaviorial sciences, a Harvard committee devoted much time to the inadequacy of funds for facilities and research in the social sciences.

Contributions by special funds, e.g., the Milton Fund, the Clark Fund and the Harvard Foundation for Advanced Study and Research, provided moderate amounts. A 1950 study revealed that 29 percent of its social scientists, 27 percent of the humanists, and 30 percent of the natural scientists definitely needed more research funds, and 38 to 39 percent could use more.[15]

Confronted by continued deficits, the Eliot administration sought to economize in some areas. When offered a female medical school, Eliot was agreeable to absorbing it, but only if $600,000 were made available to cover debts, purchase needed equipment, and establish an endowment fund. Eliot also would have welcomed some help from the state, and in part because higher education was not limited to a small elite group.[16]

Eliot warned that economies had to be introduced in repairs and improvements, wages, printing, appropriations for collections, and laboratories. In the face of unsatisfactory economic conditions and hence anticipated reduced income on investments, these economies were all the more important.[17]

Expansion and resultant financial problems continued to concern Harvard under Lowell. Just before World War I, President Lowell asked each department to assess its unfilled needs. Virtually every department proclaimed large additional outlays needed.[18]

To cope with increased demands for funds, Lowell tried to conserve unused balances. Unexpended balances were not to be available for the next year. If new equipment were needed, authorization was required, and departments were not to pay for new equipment out of unexpended balances.[19]

13. *Ibid.,* pp. 26-27.
14. Eliot, *op. cit.,* pp. 78-79.

15. *Historical Development of the Behaviorial Sciences at Harvard,* pp. 269-275.
16. C. W. Eliot to E. S. Joynes, December 18, 1875; *C. W. Eliot Papers, 1874-75,* vol. 68; C. W. Eliot to President of Massachusetts College of Pharmacy, February 10, 1885.
17. *Board of Overseers Report,* January 10, 1894.
18. Memorandum in *A. L. Lowell Letters,* undated, but probably around 1912.
19. A. L. Lowell to Dean H. A. Christian, November 16, 1910, in *A. L. Lowell Letters.*

Lowell was troubled by the increasing personnel costs other than salaries—just as Eliot had been. It will be recalled that by 1966 wages accounted for 25 percent of disbursements, as did salaries. During the seventeenth and eighteenth centuries and a good part of the nineteenth century, wages were relatively much less than salaries. Even as late as 1914, of $1,562,780 of wages and salaries, the corporation payroll for teachers and administrators accounted for 71 percent of the total, or almost 3 times the wage bill. Especially since 1914, there have been really large relative gains for wages.[20]

Priorities

Pusey in the 1956-1958 campaign established priorities of the college. In 1898-1899, the corporation had at its disposal the Pierce Fund. They had allocated $750,000 as follows: The major allocations were for buildings, $275,000; $100,000 for a permanent fund for the purchase of books; $100,000 for a curator of the Museum of Comparative Zoology; $100,000 for an endowment of a medical laboratory; and $100,000 for a professorship of comparative medicine. Clearly the corporation was then especially interested in science and in buildings, and apparently not primarily in increasing and improving the faculty.[21]

On priorities of payments, Eliot had interesting views, as he did on many other subjects. He inquired what proportion of expenses should go to salaries and what proportion to other expenses, saying; "The large part of a university's income which must go to other objects than salaries is often a disagreeable surprise for inexperienced trustees." Rising costs of maintenance and supplies contribute to this result. In the early days of the university, with some exceptions, as noted earlier, the college concentrated its payroll on salaries.

Low Tuition

President Eliot was a supporter of low tuition. He considered "increased dependence on fees . . . . extremely undesirable, because it threatens the stability and just independence of Harvard College . . . ."[22] One reason for the rise, of course, is increasing enrollment; another, reduced return on capital; and another, the introduction of fees of all kinds.

Pessimism of the 1940s

In his 1940-1941 report the dean of the business school wrote: "Large fortunes are rapidly disappearing. The Middle Class is far weaker than it was twelve years ago. It will not be able to support as long or as expensive education in the future as in the last thirty years. Income from endowment is shrinking and the future uncertain."[23]

The law school expressed its concern in another way. Payments for its major plant inclusive of Langdell Hall came largely, not from endowment or gifts, but from tuition.[24]

In 1947-1948 President Conant agreed that Harvard had a splendid plant and an endowment capital which yielded approximately $6,500,000 or 25 percent of outlays. The salary roll of 460 permanent members was $4 million. But services and facilities, he seemed to complain, cost 2 or 3 times as much.[25]

What especially concerned the authorities was the declining contribution of endowment. A comparison of the structure of income in 1931-1932 and 1951-1952 suggests the trends. Endowment's share of income dropped for seven out of nine of Harvard's schools. But a large part of the explanation was the new vogue of gifts for current use and especially from the government. For example, endowment income of

20. Memorandum of Interview with Mr. Burke, in *A. L. Lowell Papers,* 1914.
21. *Report of the President of Harvard College,* 1898-1899, p. 44.

22. *Ibid.,* 1903-1904, pp. 50, 345.
23. *Report of the President of Harvard College,* 1940-1941, p. 250.
24. *Ibid.,* 1946-1947, pp. 410-411.
25. *Report of the President of Harvard College,* 1947-1948, p. 12.

the medical school dropped from 55 to 25 percent. But annual gifts rose from 14 to 35 percent and government grants from 0 to 8 percent.[26]

Some Aspects of Faculty-College Relations

In 1883, an assistant professor of psychology asked the president and fellows of Harvard College to set aside a small room (preferably in the physical laboratories) to serve as a workroom for the psychological laboratory. William James, the assistant professor, also asked for an appropriation of not more than $300. He needed these items not only to show his students the most recent methods used by others for determining simple psychic facts, but to advance the science by new investigation. Among other items he wanted a new model of the course of fibres in the brain. The university granted his request. What is striking is how modest the demands of this great scientist were.[27]

Another interesting relationship involved a conflict of interest. President Quincy owned a stone cutting firm in Quincy. The university contracted with Quincy's firm to buy the stone needed for the new (Gore) library. Quincy then had some doubts. But the Rumford professor assured him that there was nothing irregular about the transaction. All respectable stone cutters had been invited to bid, and Quincy's firm had offered the lowest price.

26. *Ibid.,* 1951-1952, p. 34; the table is deposited in the Harvard University Archives.

27. W. James to the President and Fellows, November 20, 1883; W. James to A. Agassiz, Esq., Cambridge, December 4, 1883; *Report of Committee Appointed to Consider the Requests of William James.* December 6, 1883.

PART

4

RELATIONS WITH THE GOVERNMENT

29

Resources for Harvard: Public vs. Private

Sources of Income

A college or university must have income in order to pay its bills. The sources of this income are charges against the student, e.g., tuition; gifts from private sources; income from accumulated funds, i.e., endowment; and grants from the government.

Accounting of income is not complete. Any college or institution of higher learning also has a plant and equipment which yield income. But though the plant and equipment may cost millions, the institution of higher learning does not generally include the yield of its academic plant and equipment as income. At times, though, Harvard has declared that the non-income yielding plant should be considered in assessing costs of operation. In 1869, for example, the overseers estimated unproductive assets inclusive of land, buildings and the library, at $1,649,876.[1]

In 1949, it was estimated that Harvard's buildings had cost more than $100 million. In the thirty years ending 1949, building space had increased by 64 percent. Since then, investments in buildings have increased by tens of million of dollars. The replacement value of these buildings greatly exceeds the original costs. Construction costs rise much more than the rate of depreciation of buildings.[2]

How much each of these sources of income yields depends upon the stage of economic development, attitudes toward the government, and many other institutional factors. When a country is impoverished, for example, it cannot depend heavily upon tuition. In the current situation, the United States, the richest nation in the world, relies substantially on tuition, with charges to students contributing about one-fourth to one-third of the total costs. In the independent institution of higher learning, tuition accounts for half the income, the proportions varying from virtually no tuition charge (e.g., Rice until recently and Cooper Union) to 100 percent. At Harvard in the middle 1960s, tuition, endowment income, and current gifts provided 54 percent of income, with endowment yielding 40 of the 54 percent; tuition, 36

1. *Report of the Board of Overseers of Harvard College,* 1869, pp. 34-36.
2. From 1913 to 1945, construction costs rose by 208 percent or 4½ percent per year compounded. A rough estimate puts the rise of prices of materials and components for construction at 90 percent from 1945 to 1963. Hence from 1913 to 1963 the rise of construction costs was 380 percent or five percent per year compounded. On a forty-year life, which is conservative, depreciation would be about 2½ percent a year. See Harvard University, *Education, Bricks and Mortar,* 1949, especially pp. 7-8; for construction costs, *Historical Statistics of the United States,* 1789-1945, p. 172; see also *Economic Reports of the President.*

percent; and current gifts, 25 percent. Reimbursement of direct and indirect expenses related to contracts and grants accounted for 33 percent additional to the 54 percent.[3]

In studying government aid, we are likely to concentrate on financial aid and especially monetary gifts. But the state helps in many ways, e.g., tax relief. A student of this problem lists eight categories of aid.[4]

Termination of State Aid

By the end of the first quarter of the nineteenth century, the government had dissipated any interest in helping Harvard. Professor Morison has explained how the ousting of the Federalists, the party friendly to Harvard, had contributed to the termination of aid. The hostile Calvinists, in declaiming against a college that sponsored no private prayer meetings and had only a dozen professors of religion for 302 undergraduates, contributed to the separation of the state and Harvard

Two keen observers noted that:

. . . Harvard was under criticism in Massachusetts for all those reasons for which a good university might expect to suffer at the hands of an anti-intellectual democracy. The Calvinists still disliked it for its religious liberalism, the Democrats for the Federal-Whig tradition, the reformers for its alleged indifference to such issues as slavery . . . and the poor editoralists because it was aristocratic and offered a rounded liberal education instead of courses that would help young men to become better farmers or merchants.[5]

By the second quarter of the nineteenth century, the emphasis was increasingly on private enterprise and its contribution to Harvard. The issues were well expressed in a magazine article of 1842.[6]

Francis Bowen, editor of the *North American Review,* by drawing on Harvard history, attempted to explain why American colleges were less distinguished than European universities and why the states had ceased to support them in the nineteenth century. For the first eighty years of Harvard's history, he states, Harvard was a child of the state, and more importantly, of the people who gave to it far more than could be expected of them in view of the conditions of life in the colonies.

About the year 1720, a great change became manifest. The child had grown to a man's estate, and repudiated the authority of its parent. The College having increased so much in means and power, a contest for its management arise between the Corporation on the one hand, and the Overseers and the General Court on the other. . . . . After a long struggle, the Corporation established its independence, and reduced the visitorial power over them to the mere shadow, which it has ever since remained. . . . . The legislature ceased to cherish an institution, which it could no longer control.[7]

Early Difficulties

How serious the condition of the young college was is attested by a memo entitled Information Given by the Corporation and Overseers to the General Court, 9 May, 1655. After complaining of the injustices done to President Dunster, the governing board said:

It is absolutely necessary that it [the college building] be speedily new covered, being not fit for scholars long to abide in as it is. And without such

3. *Financial Report to the Board of Overseers of Harvard College,* 1964-1965, p. 10.
4. *House of Rep. Doc. No. 44,* 1837; F. W. Blackmer, *The History of Federal and State Aid to Higher Education in the United States,* Washington, 1890, pp. 24-25.
5. Samuel Eliot Morison, *Three Centuries of Harvard, 1636-1936,* 1937, pp. 217-219; Samuel Eliot Morison, "The Great Rebellion in Harvard and the Resignation of President Kirkland," in *Publications of the Colonial Society of Massachusetts,* vol. 28, p. 102, 1928; R. Hofstadter and W. P. Metzger, *The Development of Academic Freedom in the United States,* 1955, p. 252.
6. F. Brown, "Francis Wayland's Thoughts on the Present Collegiate Systems in the United States," in *North American Review,* vol. 60, p. 313, October, 1842; cf., *Encyclopedia Britannica,* "Harvard University," 1956, vol. II, p. 230.
7. F. Brown, *op. cit.,* p. 30.

reparation some time this summer both the whole building will decay . . . and the scholars will be forced to depart. So that either help must be had therein, or else (we fear) no less than a dissolution of the college will follow. . . .

They also discussed the uncertainity of the ferry income, the inability to sell the lands, the indebtedness of the steward, the small returns on the printing press, the diversion of study rents to President Dunster's salary. The college had other complaints also. Evidence was lacking that the £400 given by the general court in 1636 was ever paid out. In 1644, the county treasurer showed that the province's debts to the college had been £586 11s 9d and the government had paid out to the college only £227 12s. The debts were in fact larger, for the government diverted gifts to the college for its own use. No estimates of these debts were given.

For building a house, Dunster was supposed to receive £150 of the £400 grant to the college. But the evidence does not suggest that he ever received this money, for Dunster wrote of the president's house as "the place, which, upon very damageful conditions to myself, and of love to the college, *I have builded* . . . ."[8]

Perhaps the government was given too much credit—though it often saved the college in the first 150 years—if we do not allow for the colony appropriating for its own use funds meant for the college.

In the Puritan period, Harvard relied primarily on government and private benefactors. Thus Margery Foster finds that in the years 1636 to 1652, tuition yielded about 7 percent of income and for all the Puritan years (1636 to 1712) with a few years excluded, the contribution of tuition had increased to between 13 and 14 percent.[9] This is a surprisingly large proportion for a province so poor, and can only be explained by the primitive system of taxation available to the government.

In the Puritan period, the largest source of funds was the government, but private gifts and endowment were also large factors of a total income of £29,520, the major items were tuition and fines, 4,060; the government, 10,927; (private) gifts, 7,101; and endowment, 5,767.[10]

In seeking help from the state in 1849, an overseers' visiting committee of the university proclaimed:

The university is not theirs [the governing board] *but the country's. It has all the characteristics of a national institution, in the grandeur of its objects, and its powers to carry them into operation. . . . .*
The state which in the day of its feebleness and poverty opened a little rivulet in the wilderness, will . . . enable the people to drink of the waters now flowing in luxurious abundance. . . . [11]

In the assesment of the contributions of the state, time and again Harvard's representatives dwelt on the permanency of endowment and the ephemeral nature of the government's gifts. From 1636 to 1824, according to an overseers' report, the government had provided $216,000. But this was used largely in pay for the faculty and president and for buildings. Whereas the government had given $216,000, Harvard in 1849 had accumulated a stock of $459,000. If the grants of government had been preserved, the income would have been $13,000, but the endowment in 1849 yielded $27,000. What the state gave was for pressing, immediate uses.

The idea of grants for future use, in the poverty of the Institution and the State, of investments and endowments and laying up money at interest for future generations, which was wanted for daily bread, never occurred to the noble minded men who committed the future to Providence . . . They gave—that it might

8. Josiah Quincy, *The History of Harvard University,* 1840, vol. I, p. 473.
9. Margery Somers Foster, *"Out of Smalle Beginings . . . "*– *An Economic History of Harvard College in the Puritan Period (1636-1712),* 1962, especially pp. 126-127. Should we exclude income not relevant for this calculation, e.g., income from the steward, press, and Indians, and include fines assessed on students, the ratio of charges to income becomes 14 to 15 percent.

10. *Ibid,* p. 127.
11. *Report of the Visiting Committee of Harvard University Overseers,* January, 1849, p. 4.

be spent. . . . The Committee would speak with great respect and pride of the liberality of the State. The College was the child of its first love—nursed in its infancy with a kindness that can never be forgotten by gratitude or hope. But the gifts of the State to the College are not to be counted so much for their pecuniary amount as for their appropriateness in circumstances and time, and by a recollection of the poverty of the State itself when this liberality was manifested. [12]

Disagreements on the Contributions of Public Aid

Especially in the nineteenth century with the rise of a spirit of private enterprise, the Harvard authorities and even outside commentators tended to inflate the private and deflate the public contributions. Even President Eliot seemed to be forgetful of what the colony had done, but not always. In advising Johns Hopkins in 1898, Eliot stressed the need of a public aid:

. . . Harvard College was originally, and has always been an endowed institution; but in the seventeenth century Massachusetts habitually aided it, and during its first one hundred and eighty years the college was repeatedly indebted to the Province and State for substantial assistance. . . . [13]

Another grievance that the college had against the government was the interception of funds given to the college for its own use:

Some of these funds, although received by the Treasury of the Colony in 1647, were not paid over to the Treasury of the College, until 1713; then, indeed the college received an allowance of simple interest for the delay. [14]

Perhaps the most vigorous espousal of the view of greater gains from private than from public contributions is to be found in comments on a study by Samuel A. Eliot in the year 1845. [15] Undoubtedly the emergence of a free enterprise system and its accompanying spawning of millionaires contributed to the increasing acceptance of this view.

Denying the extent of the state contribution and considering period by period, the critic tried to demonstrate that private gifts were the dominant factor. " . . . But it is not so much in their corporate capacity of a Commonwealth as in their private character as individuals, that they (our forefathers) acquired reserves . . . ."

With the termination of the Revolutionary War began a new era in the history of the country, the importance of which is to be perceived in the change, not so much of the external political relations of the country as of the feelings and habits of thought within, the impetus given to the ambition, spirit of enterprise, and self-reliance of every individual composing the entire mass of the population . . . . Ambition, with all its mingled good and evil, has pervaded every hamlet, has entered every house and every bosom, has quickened the perception of every deficiency, and the desire to remove it. . . . The government has much less to do with the advance of the country here than anywhere else. The people act for themselves. They will not wait for the statesman, still less for the intriguing politician, to tell them what to do, and how to do it. . . . The legislature is usually so much afraid of being accused of extravagance, that it often falls far behind the real liberality of the public. [16]

An examination of the relevant documents does not support the pessimistic assessment of public aid in the years 1725 to 1752. I count thirty-two grants for the president and professors during this period. [17]

---

12. *Ibid.,* pp. 22, 24.
13. C. W. Eliot to C. M. Harwood, March 3, 1898; Blackmer, *A History of Federal and State Aid to Higher Education,* p. 19.
14. Quincy, *op. cit.,* vol. 1.

15. S. A. Eliot, *Harvard College and its Benefactors,* 1845, pp. 5-18.
16. *Ibid.*
17. *Grants of the Colony and Commonwealth of Massachusetts to Harvard College, 1636 to 1846.*

For the period before 1780, the critic concluded that the government gave only one-third as much as individuals. But in arriving at these conclusions, he omitted the funds given by the government to replace Harvard Hall, which was destroyed by fire in 1764. And he omits other items also. In her careful study Miss Foster finds that from 1636 through 1712 public gifts exceeded private by more than 50 percent. Again, whereas before 1780 the writer found that private gifts had been but one-third of public, an official estimate for 1650 to 1780 put the government grants at two-thirds of the private.

He would have strengthened his case had he included with private gifts the income on endowment. For the period from 1636 to 1712, for example, endowment accounted for 19.6 percent of income; private gifts, 24.1 percent; and government gifts, 37 percent. Hence, on the basis of the Foster estimate, government gifts exceeded private and only if endowment income were included would private contributions be larger.[18]

I am not contending that government aid was adequate or regular, or that government interference was not often troublesome. The supporters of the antigovernment position were undoubtedly justified in taking the position that the exclusion of government from control—which in turn contributed to reduced grants—was in the long run helpful to Harvard. The government moved out once private enterprise was able to assume the responsibilities.

One unfortunate aspect of government aid was its unreliability. Even in the years between 1638 and 1712 the percentage of income bestowed by the government varied greatly. In five periods within these seventy-four years, the government contribution varied from 22.7 to 52.7 percent. With exclusive reliance on property taxes, the government's capacity to help suffered greatly in inflationary periods.

Another favorable aspect of government aid was that in genuine crises, e.g., the burning of Harvard Hall, the state responded well. But in the Revolutionary War the response was not adequate, though in the troublesome years from 1752 to 1780 the government provided more help than private sources.

In the middle of the nineteenth century, criticism of Harvard had become more intense and persistent. Against these rumblings, the college had to defend itself in part by minimizing the contributions of the government and stressing the high quality of its instruction, related in large part to its substantial gifts from private sources.

The midnineteenth century was not the only period of disagreement and tension. In 1814, the college and the medical school started a campaign to get some help from the state. The outcome was favorable as the government voted $100,000 over ten years. Complaining of the generous gifts to medical education by other governments and noting that Massachusetts was losing its medical students and that Massachusetts was contributing to the financing of medical schools elsewhere by purchasing lottery tickets issued by other states, the medical faculty begged for state aid.[19]

Private and Public Aid

The table that follows summarizes the aid given by the government and from private sources. The estimates based on Eliot (rows 1,7) are overly generous in allocating gifts from individuals vis-à-vis those from the government.

A summary by a critic of S. Eliot yields private contributions four times as high as public for the years from 1636 to 1845. Should one compare Eliot's commentator's totals for the years before 1780 (row 1 minus row 7) or with official figures (row 2) or with Foster's statistics (row 3), one would infer that Eliot's case for the contribution of private aid is overstated. But for the period from 1780 to 1845 Eliot's critic's estimate is $170,000. Here the inference from comparing the public contribution from 1636 to 1845 ($170,000) and 1780 to 1845 ($170,000) is that no public help was had from 1636 to 1780.

A comparison of these results with those of a more recent observer are of some interest. The latter found

18. Foster, *op. cit.* pp. 126-127, 148
19. *Petition to General Court for Harvard College,* 1814.

Table 29-1

Estimates, gifts, public and private, 1636-1845*

		Public	Private
1.	1636–1845	$ 169,852	$ 675,395
1a.	1636–1786	216,157	?
2.	1650–1780	63,074†	90,411
3.	1636–1712‡	£ 10,927	£ 7,101 gifts
			5,747 endowment
4.	1650–1710	8,540	37,474 §.
5.	1710–1752	11,220	18,437
6.	1752–1780	48,314▲	34,501
7.	1780–1845	$ 100,000 (Bush)	$577,817
		170,000 (Eliot)	

* Also see *Grants and Appropriations In Favor of Harvard College,* 1827. Here grants are itemized.

† Eliot estimates 1650 to 1780 also as $69,851 (public) and $98,578 (private).

‡ Six years omitted.

§ 40 percent came from England.

The Eliot critic puts the figure at $30,366, for he deducts the cost of the loss of Harvard Hall.

Sources: rows 1, 7, S. A. Eliot, *Harvard College and Its Benefactors,* and G. C. Bush, *History of Higher Education in Massachusetts,* pp. 66, 67; row 1a, *Document No. 92,* 1849, House of Representatives, pp. 30-31; rows 2, 4-6, *Circulation of Information, No. 6,* 1891, Bureau of Education; Bush, *op. cit.,* Eliot, *op. cit.;* row 3, Foster, *op. cit.,* pp. 126-127 (my calculations).

---

that the legislators from 1636 to 1848 donated $550,000, and in addition about $46,000 for land grants. Private donations amounted to $1,228,000 or 2½ times as much (exclusive of 487 acres by the City of Cambridge). The public donations were more than 3 times as large as estimated by Blackmer, and the private about twice as large. [20]

Here are a few other estimates of some value. By 1869, the board of overseers estimated the gifts from the colony and commonwealth at $216,000; from individuals and societies at $2,255,000.

---

20. Blackmer, *op. cit.,* p. 92. The major items in the public gifts were $235,000, Museum of Comparative Zoology; $116,000, grants from 1626 to 1786; payments by the two bridge companies, $30,000; lotteries, $69,000; bank tax, $100,000.

Private aid had grown rapidly. Between 1860 and 1869 donations were almost 4 times as large as in the preceding 175 years. [21]

Public Gifts: Details

In scrutinizing official documents, I calculate the public grants to the college as follows:

Table 29-2.

Public grants to Harvard College, 1636-1787

	Total	Annual average	Of which building
1636–1700	£ 4,020	£ 63	–
1704–1719	5,620	351	£ 3,500
1720–1766	23,311	496	10,005
1766–1787	23,884	1,137	–

Source: A list of all grants . . . 1636 to 1846, (my calculations).

Public grants, as noted earlier, were irregular. In all, the government granted no funds in 73 of the 130 years from 1636 to 1766.

In the first 64 years, though there were some grants for general purposes, e.g., country pay, that is, assessments of products to be transferred to the college, the major outlays were for the president's pay. In the years from 1704 to 1719, the government allocated almost 40 percent of its grants to buildings and from 1720 to 1766 more than 40 percent. Beginning in 1725, the contributions toward professors' pay became of increasing importance.

It was conceded by Eliot's critic that from 1780 on the state had financed six college buildings, and the president's house; and had provided the annuity from the West Boston Bridge, $15,000 from sale of land to finance a professorship, and the ten-year grant from the State Bank Tax ($100,000). That conservatively puts the total at $170,000 from 1780 to the middle of the nineteenth century. But individuals gave the equivalent of $577,817.

---

21. *Report of the Board of Overseers of Harvard College,* 1819, pp. 32-34.

Concerned over the deficit at that time, Eliot's critic asked:

And to whom is the College to look for the supply of this deficit? Is it likely that the Commonwealth, after an interval of thirty-two years, will suddenly awaken to the interests of her people, and supply the means of receiving the best education at the lowest charge; or must the institution look with imploring earnestness to those true and generous friends who have already done so much? . . .[22]

In 1869, an overseers' committee supported this position. But this committee expressed gratitude for the government's contributions. This committee estimated total gifts at $294,772 at the time of President Kirkland's accession in 1810. But by 1869 the donations had reached $2,470,639, with the receipts since 1810 all being private gifts except $100,000. According to this report, nearly 4 times as much had been received from 1866 to 1869 as in the first 175 years. From the government the committee estimated receipts of but $216,000 out of a total of $2,470,639. [23]

Presidential and Faculty Income and Government

The trends are suggested by the payments to the president of the college. Pay does respond to some extent to the inflation, though not fully.

Professors' pay was irregular also and the subsidies varied greatly among professors, though this was partly the result of variations of endowment income of chairs. Thus Professor Wigglesworth averaged £59

Table 29-3 .

Grants to Harvard College Presidents, 1672-1780

President	Years of Presidency	Number of Grants	Average in pounds sterling for years of grants
Leonard Hoar	1672–1675	3	150
Urian Oakes	1675–1681	7	100
John Rogers	1682–1684[A]	2	100
Increase Mather[B]	1685–1701	11	50
Samuel Willard (vice president)	1701–1707	6	60
John Leverett	1708–1724	15	150[C]
Benjamin Wadsworth	1725–1737	11	354[D]
Edward Holyoke	1737–1769	32	200[E]
Samuel Locke	1770–1773	4	200
Samuel Langdon	1774–1780	6	780[F]

A. The document erroneously lists grants of £1,000, from 1682 to 1692. But Rogers was president only from 1682 to 1684, according to Morison.
B. Part-time president.
C. Plus two bonuses of £50.
D. Varied from £120 to £550.
E. Varied from 0 to £350.
F. Varied from 0 to £7,497 (in 1780, a year of great inflation).

Source: A list of all grants made to Harvard College by the Colony and State of Massachusetts from 1636 to 1846.

22. S. A. Eliot, *op. cit.,* pp. 16-17.
23. *Report of the Board of Overseers of Harvard College on* the *Condition, Needs and Prospects of the University,* 1869, pp. 33.

over thirty one years; Winthrop, £86 in fourteen years; and Monis, £21 in ten years.[24]

Critics of the government stress the value of gifts in kind by private donors. But our and their analyses do not give comprehensive results for public gifts. The land donations have indeed been disappointing in their yield. According to Eliot, the gifts of land by the government were 3,300 acres; from private sources, 3,793 acres.[25]

Perhaps the greatest criticism of the public donations, aside from their irregularity, was the contribution of the government to inflation and its failure to adjust grants to the rising price levels. The response to the inflation of the second quarter of the eighteenth century was inadequate. It was even more so in the years of the Revolutionary War. The price level rose rapidly, but grants increased slowly. [26]

On occasion, e.g., 1764, 1794, 1806, the commonwealth permitted the college to obtain funds from lotteries. Thus, in 1764, the government had no funds available for a new building which was badly needed by the college and especially since Stoughton Hall was to be taken down. [27] Lotteries are not generally included in donations by the government. But clearly a lottery made available to the college is a contribution, though not like an outright gift. The reaction of S. A. Eliot to lotteries was scarcely a generous one.

". . . The Legislature gave nothing, in fact, but a license. None of the money raised came from the State Treasury. . . . "[28]

A Historical Survey

Until the Revolutionary War, the government had provided large resources to the college though not consistently. After the Revolutionary War, the only major contribution was the $100,000 received from the tax on banks between 1814 and 1824, and of much less relative importance the 1858-1859 gift of $100,000 in relation to the provision of the Museum of Comparative Zoology.[29]

Again in 1791, the corporation listed its grievances against the commonwealth. The court had not been providing grants. And though the unappropriated capital as a result of investment in public securities, once the issue of paper money stopped, had risen to the prewar level, there was a loss involved in that this capital yielded no return whereas in prewar days the return was 6 percent. [30]

Moreover, the corporation had to advance to its officers loans which it hoped the commonwealth would take over. The loans had to be financed by the sale of private loans (bonds) by the college with an unfortunate impact on the debtors.

Between 1847 and 1849, the issue of additional help from the commonwealth received its last vigorous support. The state had accumulated a fund of $750,000 for the common schools, the interest of which was used to finance them. Once the fund reached $1 million, friends of the three major colleges proposed that a similar fund be accumulated for their benefit up to $500,000.[31] A state committee actually proposed a subsidy of $750,000.

A report of committee of the overseers was eloquent on the need of state aid when it wrote: ". . . It is apparent that the University does not grow rich by parsimony, nor feeble by extravagance!"

The state must give a "dignity, a grandeur and a celebrity to the College. . . . The State apportioned her off, some thirty years ago, with her part of the

---

24. All calculations based on *A List of all Grants . . .* cf., Quincy *op. cit., II,* pp. 27-28 for details on grants to presidents.
25. Eliot, *op. cit.,* p. 10.
26. *Ibid.*
27. *An Act for Raising by Lottery the Sum of Three Thousand and Two Hundred Pounds for Building Another Hall for the Students of Harvard College to dwell in . . . 1764.*

28. Eliot, *op. cit.,* p. 1214.
29. By 1902, however, the city of Boston had contributed about $750,000 towards the financing of the Arboretum. *Overseers Report,* May 7, 1902, p. 674.
30. President and Fellows to the Hon[ble] Senate and Hon[ble] House of Representatives of the Commonwealth of Massachusetts . . ., January, 1791.
31. Commonwealth of Massachusetts to Treasury Office, to the Hon. Samuel A. Eliot, November 22, 1847.

Bank Tax, as a rich father does his daughter on her marriage, and has left her, in the maturity of her strength, to the care and kindness of her children...." [32]

The memorialists dwelt on the need of funds and especially of the state "providing the means of an advanced education for those who, endowed with as much capacity as others for improvement, are debarred from it by deficiency of pecuniary resources only...." [33]

In the late 1840s, Samuel Eliot, Harvard's treasurer and father of President Eliot, organized a drive for additional state aid, the fruits of which would be shared by Harvard, Williams, and Amherst. Eliot hoped that allocation would not be according to numbers, for this would be costly to standards. He would leave to each college the manner in which costs would be cut for the students. He suggested three allocations: a general reduction, which he rightly considered wasteful; downward adjustments of tuition based on need; and a scholarship program.

The library also sought additional public funds. The memorialists wanted Harvard's public library to be:

a place of resort for all desirable information, in which should be congregated the literary treasures of science, literature, art, and their respective statistics and history with all the necessary illustrations and instruments.... A university aspires to impart, not merely the measure of teaching which is necessary to practical life and good citizenship, but that which is necessary to scholars; in one word, the highest form of the learned culture of the age....

For this a rich library financed partly by public funds is necessary.[34]

In the later 1840s, S. Eliot appealed for more funds. Compared to other states, the contributions of the commonwealth were held to be small indeed.

New York, for example, spent $28,000 a year on its colleges. Despite the strong support of the house committee, no appropriations were made.

Later History of Public Grants

In 1848-1849, the treasurer commented:

The period has now arrived, however, when the accumulation of wealth (which in an industrious community like that of Massachusetts increases in a much more rapid ratio than that of population) is such as to render it an object of well founded hope, that either the State, or individuals, or both, may be induced to appropriate some portion of their superfluity for an investment, in education at Harvard. [35]

As late as 1853, a committee from Harvard College asked the state to provide financial help "to set before their pupils [in common schools] the immediate object of passing by merit from them to a place in one or the other of the colleges...." The report continued with a suggestion that if a national university were to be created, Harvard would be the leading candidate. In fact the three institutions of higher learning in the commonwealth urged the state to accumulate $500,000 beyond the one million limit from the sale of lands allowed in the school fund, the interest to be divided among the three institutions of higher learning. The Harvard president pointed out that unless a college education was not expensive, it could not be had. [36]

Perhaps the most ambitious plan for state aid at this time came from President Edward Everett, who

32. *Report of Visiting Committee of Harvard College From Papers . . . During the Administration of President Sparks*, 1851, pp. 9-10, 14-15, 26-27.

33. *House Doc. No. 92, Commonwealth of Massachusetts, 1849*, pp. 1, 7-9.

34. S. A. Eliot to E. Everett, December 21, 1847 and January 31, 1849; and *Report of a Library Committee* (date and exact title not clear, probably an overseers committee).

35. *House Document No. 92, Report of the Treasurer of Harvard College*, 1848-1849, pp. 25-34, p. 2.

36. *Report of the Committee of Harvard College Appointed to Visit the University in 1852, 1853* pp. 13-14; *Report of the President of Harvard College*, 1847-1848, pp. 3-5.

had been Harvard's unhappy president in the years 1846 to 1849. He expressed concern that Harvard lacked funds to fulfill many imperative tasks, and notably, to build an adequate library. He assured the legislators that just because no one could read all 53,000 volumes did not mean the library is adequate. [37]

In 1864, the president urged an increase of means, saying: "Our nation is contented with schools . . . for the masses, and our Commonwealth is justly proud of having brought them to the highest state of efficiency. But she greatly errs in supposing that has done for her University what is really demanded. . . ." [38]

In the late nineteenth century, help for the Museum of Comparative Zoology and for the Arnold Arboretum was forthcoming. [39]

In 1917, a state constitutional amendment seemed to exclude any further gifts to Harvard or other private institutions. But the courts had held this did not apply to institutions of higher learning.

With the Great Depression and World War II, relations of the government to private institutions of higher learning once more became important, but now the issue was Federal: Relevant were World War II, the G.I. Bill, and the National Defense Education Act, with provisions for providing loans to students and aid for improving instruction. Even by the 1930s the schools of public health and of education were receiving aid from the Federal government; and during World War II, the university had received $25 million in war contracts. In the postwar era research contracts had become important, though until recent years they did not account for more than 10 percent of income. [40] By 1964-1965, contracts and grants, primarily from the Federal government, accounted for about one-third of all income. [41] The treasurer complained that though according to government principles $6,845,000 should have been paid to cover indirect expenses in 1964-1965, actually only $5,027,000 had been received.

Harvard has accepted help from the Federal government, but has been reluctant to undertake work with classified materials in peacetime. In an able statement before the Subcommittee on Reorganization of the Senate Committee on Government Operations.

Dean McGeorge Bundy in 1955 said:

we believe that a steadily growing national program of basic research, through contracts unhampered by security requirements, is not only a great reinforcement to the understanding of nature and to material well-being, but also a sheer necessity in the struggle for national survival in freedom. . . . [42]

In *Report on Harvard and the Federal Government* in 1961, based on a larger report made by Prof. Daniel Cheever, President Pusey raised numerous problems created by the large Federal grants. In 1959-1960 Harvard received more than $18 million from the government, of which $11,860,000 were for research. By 1965-1966, the university obtained $47 million from the Federal government, $41,500,000 for reimbursement of direct expenses of grants and contracts, and $5,600,000 for reimbursement of indirect expenses. In 1965-1966 the United States Government accounted for one-third of the university's income. [43]

---

37. E. Everett, *Harvard's Need for State Funds,* 1849.
38. *Report of the President of Harvard College,* 1863-1864, p. 10.
39. *Ibid.,* 1857-1858, p. 6; 1858-1859, pp. 6, 13-19; 1895-1896, p. 236; 1899-1900, p. 25; Samuel Eliot Morison, *Three Centuries of Harvard, 1636-1936,* 1937, p. 297; *Report of the Overseers' Committee on Arboretum,* May 7, 1902.
40. *Harvard Graduates Magazine,* vol. 26, pp. 67-68; Harvard University Archives, *214 Mass. 599.*
41. *Financial Report of the Board of Overseers of Harvard College,* 1964-1965, p. 10.
42. *Harvard Alumni Bulletin,* vol. 57, 1955; pp. 520-522; *Report of the President of Harvard College,* 1940-1941, pp. 292-293; 1943-1944, pp. 186-187; 1944-1945, p. 220; 1945-1946, p. 8; 1951-1952, p. 15; *Financial Summary,* 1940-1957; Harvard *Crimson,* March 19, 1958.
43. *Harvard and the Federal Government, A Report to the Faculties and Governing Boards of Harvard University, Financial Report of the Board of Overseers of Harvard College,* September, 1961, p. 5; 1965-66, p. 10.

Some Conclusions on Private vs Public Aid

In concluding his essay Samuel Eliot wrote:

The spirit of political parties is the very worst . . . that can press upon the vital energy of a literary institution; and not even Harvard College with all its resources of talent, friends, and property, will succeed as it ought to succeed and might succeed, till the preponderance of State influence in its council is so far reduced, that a mere politician shall never set his foot within her walls, not give a vote upon her laws or appointments. The great interests of education ought never to be converted into the weapons of the political arena. [44]

Along similar lines a generous friend of Harvard College, Henry Lee, said in 1885:

The marvelous growth and awakening of the college is consequent upon the transfer of the privileges and responsibility of shaping its policy from the legislature to the Alumni; and their . . . exercise of this power has inspired its friends, within and without, with new interest and confidence; and hence the continuous flow of gifts, great and small, from rich and poor, into its Treasury. [45]

There was an element of hypocrisy in the university position. In arguing against the national university in 1873, President Eliot harped upon the spirit of free enterprise in this country against:

the abject dependence on government [abroad] *. . . an accursed inheritance from the days of the divine rights of kings. . . . Let us cling to the genuine American method—universal elementary education voted by the citizens and for the higher grades permanent endowments administered by incorporated bodies of trustees. . . .*

In 1889-1890, President Eliot commented on the remarkable advances of the sciences in Germany which were so well supported by public funds.

. . . It must be confessed that the American method of diffused private endowments is, for purposes of medical research, very inferior to the government method as exhibited in Germany, being less prompt, less liberal, and paternal, and less able to effect the needed combination of resources. [46]

Despite all the troubles of the first two hundred years, Harvard is much the better for the help given by the government. Indeed, since the first quarter of the nineteenth century, the university has depended primarily on private finance. But with the growth of research and development programs of the Federal government, and these outlays in the country exceeding $15 billion, the university has been confronted with new problems, e.g., the concentration on research against teaching and the coverage of overhead costs by the government involved in expenditures that approach one-third of the budget.

In April 1968, forty-six prestigious members of the Association of American Universities urged large additional appropriations by the Federal government to cover the increased needs of billions for higher education.

---

44. *Op. cit.,* p. 18.
45. John T. Morse (ed.), *Memoirs of Colonel Henry Lee,* 1905, p. 133.

---

46. *Report of the President of Harvard College,* 1889-1890, p. 25.

30

Further Aspects of Government Aid

In the last chapter I discussed the relative contributions of public and private aid to Harvard. It remains to deal in greater detail with a breakdown of types of aid—e.g., land, buildings, faculty pay—and also to discuss further the relationship between government aid and the control of the college which stems in part from the financial aid bestowed upon Harvard by the government. In the Colonial and Provincial periods according to one authority, the government made no less than 103 distinct grants to the college.[1]

Elsewhere we discuss the gradual exclusion of the government from control of Harvard. Even as early as 1732 a committee of the house wanted to go to Harvard College and "inquire into the then present state and situation of the affairs of that Society." The board of overseers voted down this proposal. Thereafter a member of the house stated:

Now if that Society [Harvard] *derive and hold their grant from this Court and expect any assistance from them, especially when they stand in need of money, for any branch of the court to be denied or obstructed in their motives covering that College, so well founded as that vote was, in the opinion of the House, abundantly disservices them.*[2]

Powers of incorporation and settling trust matters were the major prerogatives of the commonwealth in the nineteenth century. In 1819, the commonwealth had passed legislation in furtherance of good discipline in the colleges. Innkeepers, tavernkeepers, etc., were not to "give credit to any undergraduate . . . without consent of such officer or officers of said colleges . . . ."[3]

Land Grants

Harvard received many grants of land, the income of which was to accrue to Harvard College.[4] Often the objectives of grants, and especially in Maine, were to encourage colonization and development, though at times a condition was providing ministerial help. Thus, in 1719, the court ordered for the towns of Lunenburgh and Townsend:

. . . that there be laid out and reserved for ye first settled Minister a good convenient lot, also a lot for the school and a Ministerial Lot and a lot for Harvard College, of two hundred and fifty acres each, and ye settler be obliged to build a convenient house for ye

---

1. Blackmer, *op. cit.,* p. 89.
2. *Proceedings and Collections of the Massachusetts Historical Society* vol. XI, p. 103 in *Journal of House of Representatives of Massachusetts, 1732-1734.*
3. *Laws of the Commonwealth of Massachusetts,* vol. 8, p. 260, 1818-1822; *Revised Statutes,* ch. 23, 1835.
4. See *Grants of the Colony and Commonwealth of Massachusetts to Harvard College, 1636 to 1846; Schedule of Lands and Buildings Situated in the town of Cambridge in the County of Middlesex, Commonwealth of Massachusetts holden by the President and Fellows of Harvard college, March 7, 1814.*

worship of God in each of ye said Towns, within ye term of four years.[5]

From 1762 to 1785, the commonwealth granted Harvard from $\frac{1}{64}$ to $\frac{1}{84}$ of numerous townships in Maine.[6]

Grants of land raised all kinds of problems for Harvard College, and especially where the land was far away. It was difficult to manage and even to locate at times. In 1717, a reminder was sent to the general assembly "praying that the equivalent may be allowed for one thousand acres of land granted to the College about the year 1657 in Pacatoag; the said College never having had the effect of said grant."[7]

The difficulties encountered by Harvard College in managing its land are suggested by the experience of a private grant in Rowley of two hundred acres in thirty lots. Since it was difficult to maintain and guard against trespassing, the college sought permission from the Legislature to sell their lands, and permission was granted.[8] (The government controlled the disposal of land by the college).

In one instance a Mr. Brown granted to Harvard two sixty-fourths of a township. The location was marked by a pine tree at one end and a hemlock at the other. It is not surprising that the college had difficulties in locating its land,[9] nor that eight grants of real estate given to Harvard College from 1645 to 1701 had not been availed of by 1715.[10]

Harvard had other land problems, one of the most interesting being the building of a road, by the Cambridge and Concord Turnpike, part of which would go through Harvard territory. The university objected because:

it desires seclusion and retirement, and the road will bring much trouble that way and bring Boston too near. This will lessen the number of students, favoring rival institutions: the injury caused by passage of the road over college land, which might have been avoided and the bend in the road obviated. . . .

The net result would be costly to Harvard's building program also.[11]

Buildings

In the seventeenth and eighteenth centuries, the government almost monopolized the privilege of financing Harvard's buildings, directly or through stimulating private subscriptions. The interest of the Colonial government stemmed from a genuine desire to promote higher education and an awareness of its fruits. Thus in 1730, Governor Belcher said:

. . . consider that a diffusive Blessing the College at Cambridge has been to this Country in its Learning and Religion, and how much all the Estates among you have thereby been rais'd in their Value, and that while other Plantations are obliged to send their sons abroad for Education at a great Expence, and often to the Ruin of their Morals, we reap that Advantage at Home.[12]

Government aid consisted of direct grants, of sponsoring subscriptions from the people and towns, and of receipts from lotteries. When the province, government, or state was pinched, the recourse would be to other than direct grants. Thus in the latter part of the eighteenth century a lottery financed the building of Hollis Hall and, early in the nineteenth

5. *College Books,* vol. III, p. 103; *Publications of the Colonial Society of Massachusetts,* vol. XV, pp. 280-281, 291.
6. *Treasurers' Journals,* no. 1, 1777; *Legislative Records of the Council,* vol. 57, p. 8, 1809; *Resolves of the General Court of the Commonwealth of Massachusetts,* 1828, vol. 31, p. 120.
7. *Corporation Records,* vol. VI, p. 108.
8. *Ibid,* vol. I, pp. 285-293, 295.
9. *Donation Book,* in Harvard University Archives, vol. I, pp. 84-87.
10. Foster, *op. cit.,* p. 120.
11. *Private and Special Statutes,* vol. III, pp. 181, 367, 514; Paige's *Cambridge,* pp. 179-180; *College Books,* No. 9.
12. *Massachusetts House Journal,* p. 116, quoted in *Publications of the Colonial Society of Massachusetts,* vol. 15, p. XCVIII.

century, Stoughton Hall. The preamble of the 1765 Act said:

Whereas the buildings belonging to Harvard College are greatly insufficient for lodging the students of said college ... and whereas ... it cannot be expected that any further provision for the College should be made out of the public treasury, so that no other resort is left but to private benefaction, which it is conceived will be best excited by means of a lottery ... be it enacted that a lottery be run to raise £3200. [13]

In the seventeenth century the authorities used the original grant of the government of 1636 to build the first Harvard College and the President's lodge. [14] In 1677, the college built the old Harvard College with subscriptions sponsored by the state to replace a second Harvard College. This was burned in 1764 and replaced by the state in 1766.

At the time of the burning, Harvard Hall had been occupied by the general court, which moved to Cambridge to escape a smallpox epidemic. Bernard, the governor of the commonwealth, addressed the court:

I heartily condole with you on the unfortunate accident which has happened to the College, and we have been the melancholy spectators of.... However, whether it is considered as a duty or a fresh call upon your benevolence, I shall be glad to join with you and the Council, in proper measures to retrieve this.

According to the authors of *Education, Bricks and Mortar,* the cost of Harvard Hall was £6,100. Pierce, in 1833, commented that this loss "could not be so easily borne then as ten times that amount might be at the present day." The burning of Harvard Hall did not mean merely the loss of a classroom building. This famous building was used also as chapel, library, dining hall, kitchen, and buttery. It also had housed the first physics laboratory and first lectures in *materia medica.* Benjamin Franklin, John Winthrop and later, Count Rumford were involved in its scientific work. [15]

Stoughton Hall, occupied from 1699 to 1781, cost £1020, of which all but £20 came from Lt. Gov. William Stoughton. In 1805, a second Stoughton Hall was built, which was to house Oliver Wendell Holmes, Edward Everett Hale, and the first theatricals of the Hasty Pudding Club; and which provided the Porcellian Club with its first rented quarters. Charles Bulfinch was the architect; the cost, $23,000, of which a public lottery allowed by the commonwealth provided $18,400. [16]

In 1717, the general court received a memorial from the overseers to the effect that the number of students had increased so much that there was not room enough. This gave the authorities much concern and caused them to "have uncomfortable views of mischiefs impending," since many students are "necessitated to be so much and so far from their constant inspection and ye slender authority ye college is capable of exerting in the Town." The result was Massachusetts Hall.

Massachusetts Hall is the oldest extant Harvard building. Its original construction cost of £3500 should be compared with the $175,000 cost for remodelling in 1925 and $70,000 in 1939. These figures point to the rising costs of construction over a period of two hundred years.

"Successive reconstructions have virtually gutted the building, but the brick walls, trim and end chimney remain to validate Massachusetts' claim as

13. *Acts and Resolves of the Province of Massachusetts Bay,* vol. 4, p. 834, ch. 21; *Legislative Records of the Council,* vol. 26; pp. 54, 62; Quincy, *op. cit.,* vol. II, p. 273; *Publications of the Colonial Society of Massachusetts,* vol. 55, p. 437.
14. It is not clear that the government actually built the president's house in 1644. See preceding chapter.

15. *Education, Bricks and Mortar,* published by the university, 1949, p. 69; B. Pierce, *op. cit.,* pp. 288-289, 298-299; *Legislative Records of the Council,* vol. 25, pp. 153, 190, 193-195, 314, 322; vol. 26, pp. 52, 249.
16. Quincy, *op. cit.,* p. 273; *Education, Bricks and Mortar,* p. 88.

Harvard's oldest monument." The oldest corporation in the United States, the president and fellows of Harvard College, meet in this hall.[17]

Wadsworth House, which was finished in 1726, is the second oldest Harvard building. It was the residence of nine Harvard presidents from Wadsworth (1726 to 1737) to Edward Everett (1846 to 1849), and the temporary headquarters during the Revolution of generals George Washington and Charles Lee.[18]

The third oldest building at Harvard is Holden Chapel, which was built in 1744. It is an inexpensive building, having cost only £400. It is one of the few buildings of the first two hundred years that was not built exclusively or primarily with public funds. Samuel Batchelder described it as "a little gem of a building, simple yet elegant." This was the only one ever to have been given by an English donor; "a solitary English daisy in a field of Yankee dandelions." Holden has served "as carpenter shop; fire engine house; club house; the first chemistry laboratory in the country; museum; auditorium . . . and for classrooms, [a] lecture room, public speaking classes, and choir rehersals." It served the nation in three wars and was the first home of the medical school. It functioned as a temporary seat of the Provincial House of Representatives when James Otis (AB 1743) aroused the colonists with a fiery oration.[19]

It remains to discuss only three other important buildings of the first two centuries, all financed by the government: Hollis Hall (1763), Holworthy Hall (1812), and University Hall (1815).

In honor of Harvard's great benefactor, Thomas Hollis, the court financed a new building to be called Hollis Hall. In 1763, it was necessary to allow ninety students to live outside the campus, with the result that the students were not regulated as well as they might be; hence the need for an additional dormitory. Aside from the direct cost of building, the court authorized a "further sum of five hundred pounds sterling to be paid to Royale Tyler, Esquire, towards purchasing nails, glass, and other materials in England, for the building of the new College in Cambridge, which materials the said Royale Tyler had generously offered to procure for the Province, free from any advance of profit." Among the distinguished residents of Hollis Hall were Emerson, Thoreau, Edward Everett, and President Eliot.[20]

The college built Holworthy Hall out of the proceeds of a lottery which yielded about $25,000. This was the first modern dormitory without medieval study cubicles, and the first to be lighted by gas.[21]

Finally, there is Bulfinch's gem, University Hall, which was finished in 1815 and financed out of part of the $100,000 proceeds from the bank tax which was made available to Harvard in the years from 1814 to 1824. For a century it was the center of university activities. The university entertained Presidents Monroe, Jackson, and Van Buren there, as well as the Marquis de Lafayette. The building served as a commons, a chapel, and a chemical laboratory. On the first floor there were four partitioned dining halls, one for each class.

This was the last large Harvard building to be financed by the commonwealth except for museums. In 1832, though the state Senate approved, the government refused to finance part of the cost of an addition to the library.[22]

During the Revolutionary War, troops occupied the buildings of the college. For damage done to the college by Federal troops in 1775, the court allowed

---

17. *Leverett's Diary,* quoted in *Publications of the Colonial Society of Massachusetts,* vol. 24, pp. 81-110 (esp. p. 86); *Legislative Records of the Council,* vol. 10, pp. 189, 267, 283, 350-352; vol. 11, pp. 41, 60, 85; *Donation Book,* vol. 1, p. 27; *Education, Bricks and Mortar,* pp. 78, 80.

18. *College Books,* vol. IV, pp. 96, 117; *Publications of the Colonial Society of Massachusetts,* vol. 15, pp. CXVII-CXVIII; vol. 16, pp. 508-509, 541-542; *Massachusetts House Journal,* pp. 99-100; *Education, Bricks and Mortar,* pp. 91-92.

19. *Education, Bricks and Mortar,* p. 70.

20. Quincy, *op. cit.,* vol. II, pp. 100-101; *Donation Book,* vol. I, p. 38; *Education, Bricks and Mortar,* p. 72; *Legislative Records of the Council,* vol. 24, pp. 439, 442, 625; vol. 25, p. 110.

21. *Education, Bricks and Mortar,* p. 72.

22. Documents printed by order of the Senate of the Commonwealth of Massachusetts, no. 14, 1832.

£448 7s 5d, but when this was recorded before the general court by a court order of October 29, 1781, the £448 were worth only £112 1s 10d. [23]

The college authorities petitioned for compensation.

After the evacuation of Boston by the British Army in March, 1776, the Corporation petitioned the General Court, stating, that "Immediately after the commencement of the present war in defence of American liberties, on the 19th of April, 1775, all the buildings of the College were taken possession of, and occupied as barracks, by the American army, then suddenly assembled, and have been greatly defaced and damaged ... and that they cannot doubt the Continental Congress will consider it a debt of justice to make good these losses and damages, which the seminary has thus sustained.... [24]

In general the colonial government assumed the major responsibility for buildings in the seventeenth and eighteenth centuries, and the early part of the nineteenth century. But in at least two instances, the general court had to have recourse to lotteries. In the first 150 to 200 years the overseers were especially helpful in inducing the government to be generous. Undoubtedly the declining influence of the overseers militated against continued building subsidies in the nineteenth century. The prime argument on behalf of increased space was the protection of students against harmful external influence when not residing in college dormitories. [25]

Government and Faculty Pay

The contributions of the government helped pay a substantial part of the salaries of the faculty, and for a long time the general court paid the salary of the president. But the government, with its loss of authority and with the rising contributions from private sources, gradually withdrew. The resultant unhappiness of the college is reflected in an eloquent message of Governor Bowdoin of June 2, 1786.

Among the subjects that claim your attention gentlemen, the university at Cambridge is not the least important. The encouragement of literature and the diffusion of knowledge were among the first cares of our worthy ancestors. After providing the common means of instruction they instituted Harvard College, which from that time to the present has amply answered the end of its institution. It has always been under the patronage of the General Court, who from time to time have made grants for the support of its President and professors. The last grant for that purpose was in June, 1784, for their salaries to the preceding January. With you, Gentlemen, who must be sensible of the great benefits derived to the Commonwealth from that institution, there can be little occasion for using arguments for continuing those grants.... I would recommend it to your consideration, Gentlemen, whether upon these principles it would not be proper to confirm to the College all the land grants that have been made to it as above mentioned and to secure to it one share in such townships as may henceforth be granted. [26]

In the seventeenth century the fellows, or tutors, received compensation in part from the government, and notably from the income of the ferries; from endowment funds (e.g., the Pennoyer annuity of £34 due in 1678 was to finance tutors and provide scholarships); and also to some extent out of tuition. Over the years 1693 to 1715, the college seemed to pay about one-half the salaries of tutors or fellows. During this period, the college seemed gradually to substitute a fixed sum as against a system of compensation related to some extent to the number of tutees. [27]

At first grants to professors were gratuities. By the mid-1760s, with payments made regularly, the grants

23. *Treasurers' Ledger,* 1778-1779, vol. I, p. 507.
24. Quincy, *op. cit.,* vol. II, pp. 67-68.
25. *History of Harvard College,* pp. 229, 266-271; *Report on the Rights and Duties of the President and Faculty of*

Harvard College in Relation to the Board of Overseers, 1856, pp. 39-40.
26. *Legislative Records of the Council,* vol. 27, p. 14.
27. Foster, *op. cit.,* p. 135.

became part of each professor's salary. In the Revolutionary War special additions were provided to offset the losses due to inflation. [28] Quincy claimed that the grants were barely sufficient for existence, and the college in turn repaid the grants by reductions in tuition. An attempt in 1780 to free the president from the precarious position of relying on annual grants of the court by obtaining a fixed salary failed. In July, 1786, the last grant was made. [29] In reply to a final petition of February, 1793, the commonwealth refused on the grounds that the college was rich, not on the grounds of the unfortunate state of the treasury, the usual position. [30]

Special Help

The Colonial, provincial, and later the commonwealth governments frequently expressed much interest in the financial problems of the college, though early private gifts were also helpful. The college corn (an assessment on the population by the government to help Harvard) was a source of scholarship funds. Massachusetts, Connecticut, and New Haven general courts recommended to their towns an assessment of a peck of corn or 12 pence per family. This money, £269 18s 8d in the years 1644 to 1653, helped indigent students and supported tutors. Foster estimates that frugal students might finance half their expenses out of scholarship money. In the entire Puritan period and in four periods during the years between 1650 and 1710, she estimates that from 20 to 53 percent of the students received scholarships. They often had to repay the school in services. [31]

28. Quincy, *op. cit.*, vol. II, pp. 228, 249.
29. *Ibid.*, pp. 228, 246, 249.
30. *Ibid.*, ch. 30, 31.
31. Foster, *op. cit.*, pp. 89-90, 138-140.

31

Ferry and Bridges

In 1640, the general court granted Harvard the right to income from the Charlestown Ferry, and until 1785 the college received a proportion of the ferry charges each year. This was a form of state aid, though a private ferry company leased the ferry and paid the rent to Harvard College. Rents varied from £27 to £72 in the Puritan period, with total annual revenue (according to Foster) averaging £47 from 1640 to 1712.[1]

In 1785, the incorporation of the Charles River Bridge proprietors put the ferry out of business, and Harvard was granted instead £200 each year for seventy years beginning in March 1794, the payment of which was later to be shared by the Warren Bridge, chartered in 1828.[2] The first bridge, chartered in 1792, was completed in 1796.

In response to inflationary pressure, rents per boat rose from £40 in 1715-1716 to £150 in 1749-1750. The effects of the inflation during the Revolutionary period is reflected in a rise of rents per boat of £10 (new tenor) in 1776-1777 to £150 in 1780.[3]

During the smallpox episodes and in periods when revenue suffered as a result of the river freezing, the college allowed abatements. When conflicts occurred, the college sought more revenues and urged higher charges for the consumers of the ferry service.[4]

The unhappiness of the college authorities at the failure of passenger rates and college income to respond to rising prices is revealed by two petitions of the president and fellows in 1743 and 1747.

To his Excellency William Shirley . . .
We incourage ourselves, to ask the Increase of the Fare of s^d Ferry, nor can we doubt, but that Yo^r Ex^{cy} & Hon^{rs}, will think such request most reasonable upon the following Considerations,
First, That we greatly want a considerable Addition to our annual Income; Inasmuch as the Present low State of the Money, necessitates Us to make a large Addition, to the Salaries of ye several Officers of the College, who are nevertheless able, but barely to support themselves, wch poor state of our revenue may be easily seen, by an Inspection of our Treasurers Books. Furthermore, We cannot think it improper to Add, That the present Fare of the s^d Ferry is now so low, as to satisfy all such as are acquainted with these

---

1. *Acts and Resolves of the Province of Massachusetts Bay, 1628-1641*, p. 340; Morison, *Three Centuries of Harvard, 1636-1936*, pp. 14-15; Foster, *op. cit.*, pp. 101-104, 136, 150; *Grants of the Colony and Commonwealth of Massachusetts to Harvard College, 1636 to 1846*, in Harvard University Archives.
2. *Acts and Laws of the Commonwealth of Massachusetts, 1784-1785*, pp. 135-138; 1790-1791, pp. 361, 364; 1792-1793, pp. 43-44; 1794-1795, p. 447; *Massachusetts Special Laws, 1780-1805*, vol. 2.
3. The Memorial of the Subscribers, A Committee of the Corporation of Harvard College, To the Honourable, the Senate and House of Representatives . . . January 30, 1781.
4. For details on rents, number of boats, and abatements, see *Corporation Records* vols. III-IV, various pages.

Things that it is one of the Cheapest Ferries in the whole World . . . Moreover, Yo^r Ex^{cy} & Hon^{rs} cannot be insensible That the present Fare of s^d Ferry, is not more than one Quarter part, of what it was originally; If it be answered to This, That the Country is much increas'd, & consequently the Passengers are much more numerous than They us'd to be; This We readily Grant; But then Yo^r Ex^{cy} & Hon^{rs} cannot suppose (with Us) That when the Governm^t was so kind as to give us the revenue of this Ferry, They doubtless apprehended, It would be a growing Interest. . . .

Besides it well deserved to be noted, That far the Bigger Part of Them, who cross the Ferry very often, are Markett People, who have raised the Price of what they carry over, so much, That if the Fare of the Ferry was a Penny new Ten^r yet as small a Part of their Marketting, & in most Instances, a smaller, wou'd pay their Fare now, than wou'd have done it forty years agoe. . . .[5]

As early as June 26, 1783, the president and fellows expressed concern over the possibility of a bridge over the Charles, not only on economic but also on moral grounds.

We beg leave also further to represent to Yo^r Excy & Honours, that we apprehend, that any nearer and more ready Passage, over the s^d River and especially be a Bridge, will cause Such an increase of Company & at the College, that thereby the Scholars will be in danger of being too much interrupted in their Studies, & hurt in their Morals. . . .[6]

The charter for the construction of the Charles River Bridge, given in 1785, came just at the time when Harvard had spent £300 in repairing the ferry and was beginning to receive £200 annually of rent. In compensation for the loss of ferry income the legislature first stipulated that the West Boston Bridge pay annually to Harvard College £300 for forty years;

but, in 1792, modified the terms to £200 for seventy years.[7]

According to the corporation: (act of 1785)

Shall annually pay to Harvard College or University the sum of 300 pounds, during the said term of forty years; and at the end of the . . . term, the . . . bridge shall revert . . . to Commonwealth, saving to the said College or University, a reasonable and annual compensation for the annual income of the ferry, which might have been received had not the bridge been erected.[8]

Of the Charles River Bridge it was said that "This was the first effort to erect a bridge over a broad river in the American States." With the large distance and strong current involved it was first assumed that only a floating bridge would be practical. But ultimately "a fixed bridge [was] built on 75 wooden piers. . . . About forty large bridges have been built in the United States in consequence of the erection of this structure."[9]

Festivities accompanied the opening of the bridge in June, 1796. There were at least 20,000 spectators. "The day was warm—but the lovely female forms, which filled all the windows of the houses, and the happy multitude that crowded the streets, diverted all ideas of fatigue. . . ."

Agitation soon began to undo the octopus corporation, the Charles River Bridge Company. In 1786, the par value of shares was $333.33; by 1805, $2,080. Values of many places escalated. The estate of Lieutenant Governor Phillips on Tremont Street had cost $9,500 but sold for $80,000 in 1807.[10]

The Harvard Corporation watched with concern the developing clamor for a free bridge, which might jeopardize its annuities which had been promised

---

5. *College Books*, vol. IV, pp. 255-256, 273-276, 742-743, 765-770; *Publications of the Colonial Society of Massachusetts*, vol. XVI; *Corporation Records*, vol. I, pp. 446-450.

6. *College Books*, Vol. IV, pp. 209-210; *Publications of the Colonial Society of Massachusetts*, vol. 16, p. 679.

7. *Laws of the Commonwealth of Massachusetts*, May, 1780, January 1796, pp. 182-184, 212.

8. *Ibid.*, May, 1783, February, 1789, p. 250.

9. *Historical Comment by Chairman of Boston Transit Commission*, Nov. 27, 1899; *Antique Views of Boston*, pp. 344-345.

10. *Exhibit A of Isaac Blanchard of Charlestown A Toll Gatherer.*

earlier. On January 27, 1824, the minutes of the Harvard Corporation included:

. . . the President and Treasurer [were importuned to] *attend to the College interest relating to an application for a Bridge from Charlestown to Boston, and make such Memorial and Remonstrances as they deem proper . . . upon the proposed Bridge . . . over the Charles River, near the College Wharf.*

On March 12, 1828, an act to establish the Warren Bridge Corporation was approved by the governor. The new bridge was opened late in 1828. In the first six months of 1829, tolls of the old bridge dropped to $6,500 from the $15,000 in the first six months of 1828.[11]

With the opening of the Warren Street Bridge, Harvard was to receive payments equal to one-half those made by the Charles River Bridge. The latter would receive corresponding relief.[12]

The Charles River Bridge Company began legal action when the charter was granted to its competitors. Daniel Webster and Lemuel Shaw, as counsel, filed a bill in equity declaring the bridge a nuisance and an injury to the exclusive rights of the old bridge company and asked for a preliminary injunction, which was denied.

An appeal was taken to the Supreme Court and argued before Chief Justice Marshall and other justices in 1831. Daniel Webster and Warren Dutton appeared on behalf of the Charles River Bridge. In 1834, the proprietors of the Warren Bridge Company hired Simon Greenleaf of the Harvard Law School.

Chief Justice Taney delivered the opinion of the court: "In order for the plaintiff to obtain relief, it was necessary he show," said Taney, "that the Legislature contracted not to do the Act of which the plaintiff complained. However no such agreement is in the Charter. . . ." Justice Story, also a Harvard Law Professor, dissented.[13]

In laws and Resolves 1846 to 1848 it was:

Resolved that there be . . . paid out of the Treasury of the Commonwealth to the President and Fellows of Harvard College, the sum of $666.66 per annum as and for the annuity secured to the said College [as] . . . proprietors of the Charles River Bridge . . . and to continue so long as the said annuity was, by force of the said charter, and the acts in addition thereto, to be continued.

Opposition to the Warren Bridge by the Harvard Corporation is easy to understand. To the college $666 per year was a large item, and the creation of a new company which would build a bridge that would ultimately be free of tolls would jeopardize an important source of income. Harvard College was interested in the Charles River Bridge not only as a recipient of part of the tolls but also as a proprietor of shares.

Harvard College first received annuities from the bridge company in 1786. By 1837, the college had obtained $40,393. In addition, the government provided $3,330.30 for five years when the bridge was the property of the state. Finally, for the years 1847 to 1856, the government gave $6,000, thus completing payments for the seventy years as promised.

Hence, the total receipts:[14]

$ 9,333.30   from the state
40,393.30   from the bridge companies
$49,726.60   total

An official statement summarizes the income from the ferry and bridges as follows

11. *Corporation Records*, vol. X, p. 676, November, 1810, through April, 1827.
12. *Laws of the Commonwealth of Massachusetts*, 1825-1828, pp. 851-855, especially 855.
13. *Pickering Reports*, vol. 6, p. 376, 1827-1828; vol. 7, p. 344, 1828-1829; Charles Warren, *History of the Harvard Law School*, p. 521; Harvard Law Library, *Charles River Bridge vs Warren Bridge, Agreements of Council Greenleaf; Harvard College Papers*, 2d series, vol. 6, p. 284, 1833-1835; *Corporation Records*, vol. 7, p. 376, April 12, 1827 - September 15, 1836; *Charles River Bridge vs Warren Bridge, Opinions of the Judges of the Supreme Court*, 1837, p. 16; *Peters Records*, vol. 2, p. 420; *Judge Story's Memorandum on U.S. Supreme Court Agreements*, 1831-1832, pp. 140-141.
14. *Treasurers' Journals; Treasurers' Ledgers*, both unpublished, 1785-1829 (annuities found under "Rents Unappropriated," dividends under "Interest Account"); *Report of the Treasurer of Harvard College*, 1825-1857.

The College rented this concession for £30 annually and Harvard continued to receive income from the ferry until 1785 when the first toll bridge across the Charles put the ferry out of business. The Bridge Company was forced to pay an annual fee of £200 or $666.66 to Harvard for 70 years and in 1796, when a second bridge was built, an additional $666.66 was ordered to be paid Harvard for 40 years. These payments were received regularly, with few exceptions, and the last payment called for was made in 1856, 216 years after the original concession was granted in 1640.

There are a number of inaccurracies in this account. These payments by the second bridge company were substitutes for half the payments otherwise charged to the first bridge. The gross income from the ferry and two bridges would then be:

$$\begin{array}{r} \$49,726.66 \text{ (above)} \\ \text{Ferry: } 145 \times 30\text{£*} = \underline{14,345.00} \\ \$64,071.66 \end{array}$$

In addition, over a fifty-two year period, the college received $18,852.27 in dividends from its bridge securities, of which one-half may be considered a windfall. From the ferry earnings, however, substan-tial deductions should be made. But all in all the college received around $60,000 (inclusive of half of the dividends), a tidy sum for that period. In addition, the corporation accumulated a fund of $16,240 (in 1947) from bridge receipts which had not been expended. The major part of this seems to have been returns on the investment.

According to President Quincy the college at the end of twenty years would have lost $35,401 as a result of the damage sustained by the proprietors of the estate in the Charles River Bridge. [15]

With the use of the Harvard bridge becoming free, the college, in 1835-1836, decided to write down the capital value of $11,111.11, which was the capitalized equivalent at 6 percent of the annuity of $666.66 previously paid on the Charles River Bridge but not received in the preceding ten years. Moreover, the college's two shares of stock on that bridge were written down from a book value of $2000 to $200, the latter value in 1835-1836. The West Boston Bridge Annuity also had a capital value of $11,111.11. Since the annuities were to expire in about thirty-two years from 1841-1842, the treasury estimated that a reduction, i.e., write-off of $350 per year, would be appropriate over this period of thirty-two years. [16]

---

15. Quincy, *op. cit.*, vol. II, p. 594.

16. *Report of the Treasurer of Harvard College*, 1835-1836, p. 1; 1839-1840, p. 2; 1857-1858, p. 3; *Report of the President of Harvard College*, 1827-1828, p. 47.

32

Taxation

The Harvard faculty and administration have obtained fringe benefits from time to time through special treatment by the Colonial government and the commonwealth. Tax exemption was the most important. But they were also exempt from draft into the service of the American Army during the Revolution. (In view of the Tory support at Harvard College at that time, this may well have been considered a security measure.) In 1813, college officers were exempted from jury duty, as they are today.[1]

Harvard first enjoyed exemption from taxation in its Charter of 1650. The Legislature exempted real estate of value not exceeding £500 a year and all personal property. The £500 limitation proved to be a source of conflict. It was not clear whether the limitation applied to income, value at time of acquisition or purchase, or current assessed or market value. This question became academic when the Provincial Legislature exempted from taxation "all persons who have the management and improvement of the estate of Harvard College." The issue then became whether Harvard was liable if it leased property for income rather than occupying it itself.

In 1780, when Massachusetts became a commonwealth, its constitution, in a chapter devoted specifically to the University at Cambridge, confirmed all of Harvard's ancient privileges inclusive of tax exemption. In 1753, the Province of Massachusetts Bay, confronted with numerous complaints by Harvard College that towns were levying taxes on the college, had confirmed the £500 property exemption, and the general court resolved that the original terms of exemption be included specifically in all future tax acts.

In 1808, a general law of taxation replaced the annual tax acts. The Legislature now distinguished between property used for education property and property kept as an investment. That act provided that Harvard's general tax exemption was not to be construed to prevent Cambridge from taxing houses or land belonging to the corporation "without the College grounds" except these lands improved by the president and several specified professors. An 1818 Act allowed Cambridge to tax land outside the college grounds except those properties occupied by the president, faculty, students or resident graduates, or those that were unoccupied.[2] In 1828, the Massachusetts Supreme Judicial Court interpreted the tax exemption privileges confirmed in the 1780 constitution.

---

1. *Acts and Resolves of the Province of Massachusetts Bay,* 1779-1780, vol. 5, p. 595; *Laws of the Commonwealth of Massachusetts,* 1812-1815, p. 214; *General Laws,* 1932 (taxation by the local government from 1835 to 1957 is presented in a table, with sources, in the Harvard University Archives).

2. *Hardy vs Waltham,* 7 Pickering 108; *Legislative Records of the Council,* vol. 19, p. 527; *Resolves of the General Court of the Commonwealth of Massachusetts,* various years; "Taxation of College Property," Harvard College brief for case, *Harvard College vs Assessors of Cambridge,* pp. 25, 26.

All property that was tax exempt when acquired by the terms of the charter, remains tax exempt if it is still held by the college, even if the property is not used for educational purposes.[3]

An interesting case is a piece of property left by Henry Webb to Harvard College in 1660." . . . both it [£50] and the house above mentioned may be and continue as a yearly income for the ends aforesaid forever." In the latter part of the seventeenth century this house rented for about £12. In 1961 the house was still tax exempt and was carried on the books of the treasurer at $164,604.79 as compared to £160 on February 1, 1669, or a rise of more than 300 times. This business site at 254-256 Washington Street, occupied by some saloons, is still tax exempt.[4]

In 1836, Cambridge first assessed Harvard a levy that followed an 1835 tax law, as part of the first revision of the general laws of the commonwealth. The 1835 revised statutes exempted from taxation the personal property of "all literary, benevolent, charitable, and scientific institutions" and such real estate as is actually occupied by them or their officers for the purpose for which they were incorporated. Boston's first decadal assessment was not forthcoming until 1850. The 1835 tax law, with occasional modifications, was the basis of taxation throughout the nineteenth century.[5]

Conflicts between Harvard and the towns in which it held property emerged from time to time over the meaning or purposes for which the property was developed. Massachusetts Supreme Judicial Court decisions in the second half of the nineteenth century established that real estate owned by the corporation and leased to a professor was liable for taxation; that a farm used to grow food to feed students at cost was exempt; that real estate occupied by college officers for which deductions were made from their salaries was not exempt; that buildings owned by the corporation and used to provide food at cost to students were exempt. Town officials in the years 1897 to 1910 persistently urged the state Legislature to modify tax laws so that institutions of higher learning should pay more taxes. But they had little success.[6]

In recent years, in order to improve relations, Harvard and Cambridge agreed on special taxes. Thus, in 1929, it was agreed that Harvard would pay the City of Cambridge an annual sum in lieu of the taxes which would be due if certain property were in private hands. This applied, especially when the Harvard houses were being built, to property taken off the tax rolls to be converted to Harvard property. This agreement was to hold only for twenty years and to apply to property acquired after 1928. The agreement was reviewed in 1948.[7]

In a table which has been deposited in the archives I have assembled the tax burdens of Harvard from the year 1836, when Cambridge collected $8 on an assessment of $3,300, to a total of $317,000 in 1950 and $251,600 in 1957. Cambridge and Boston accounted for the major amounts. It was not possible to estimate the tax levied by other towns, but it is clear that the amount is small.

Conflict on Taxes

In most places where universities carry on, the townspeople resent the nontaxation of universities and other nonprofit organizations. Harvard was especially suspect because of its early exemption of £500.[8]

3. *Harvard College Papers*, vol. X, August 29, 1840.

4. Foster *op. cit.*, pp. 112, 160, 181.

5. S. Hoar, "The Taxation of College Property" in *Harvard Graduates Magazine*, vol. 6, pp. 499-510, 1898.

6. *Pierce vs Cambridge*, 2 Cushing 611 (1869); *Wesleyan Academy vs Wilbraham*, 99 Mass. 599 (1868), *Williams College vs Williamstown*, 167 Mass. 505 (1896); *Harvard College vs Cambridge*, 175 Mass. 145 (1900); *Exemption from Taxation in Mass.*, pp.12-18.

7. *Harvard Graduates Magazine*, vol. 19, pp. 637-638, 1911; statement by Robert Cutler of Harvard Comptroller's Office.

8. *Report of Committee Appointed by the Corporation on November 30, 1891 . . . What Lands now Belonging to the College Are . . . Exempt from Taxation, May 31, 1892; Report of Committee on Liability of the Real Estate . . . to Treaties, Meeting of President and Fellows, May 31, 1892.*

Harvard had disagreements with numerous governments on tax issues. Boston particularly seemed to resent Harvard. In 1869, a dispute arose over an estate left by Henry Webb in 1660. Located as it was on Washington Street, this had become a valuable piece of property. The City of Boston proposed an assessment of $4,541 on this property to cover improvements made. But Harvard claimed that they were exempt from taxes, rates, etc. The City of Boston did not agree.[9] In 1874, the Committee of Legislation on Just and Equal Taxation (Massachusetts) stressed the large tax exemption of Harvard in Boston. [10]

At one time Harvard was concerned over the imposition of a transfer tax in New York State which would be costly to the college. In an attempt to persuade the government to abandon this tax on Harvard, the university revealed that Harvard in a year spent $247,500 of its own resources educating students from New York. Against costs of $600, students paid only $150. [11]

Other towns were also recalcitrant, e.g., Petersham, where Harvard had located its forest, refused to acquiesce to paying more taxes so Harvard would pay none.[12]

It was particularly with the Cambridge government that Harvard had its differences, and especially before World War I. In the 1840s the town had provided a night watch, which Harvard found most helpful in averting disturbances. But there was disagreement on the sharing of the costs. In 1914, the Cambridge mayor wanted Harvard to finance the rebuilding of Boylston Street, which he held had been damaged by heavy traffic resulting from the university construction. In 1912, the college asked permission to build a tunnel for transmitting power between the Harvard Yard and the freshman dormitories. Confronted with

some reluctance on the part of the government, the college reminded the city of the $90,000 subsidies to Cambridge students at Harvard; the financing of improvements on Broadway and Kirkland Streets by Harvard; the number of jobs created by Harvard; the Anderson Bridge given by a Harvard friend; and the 3,190 students living in Cambridge.[13]

Perhaps the most troublesome issue arose when President Lowell, just before World War I, began to take over large properties from Mt. Auburn Street to the river preparatory to building the freshman dormitories. City officials in 1907 had become disturbed by what seemed to them to be ambitious plans to take large amounts of property off the tax lists through purchase for the college's uses.

In March, 1908, Eliot tried to assure the state government. He wrote:

. . . The sole interest of Harvard University in the plans of these [Riverside] Associates is its interest in having that part of the city made more beautiful and valuable. . . the present Corporation of the University has no intention of taking out of taxation any land now taxed between Mt. Auburn Street and the River. . . .

Lowell's aggressive land buying was embarrassing, for President Eliot could not bind his successor. Jerome Greene, Eliot's secretary, defended Eliot against the charge of a conspiracy to appropriate large tracts of land. [14]

The Case Against Taxation of Institutions of Higher Learning

No one has put more vigorously and more effectively the case against taxing institutions of higher

9. President and Fellows of Harvard College and Attorney of City of Boston to Salem Judicial Court January 12, and February 7, 1870.
10. G.T. Bigelow to C.W. Eliot, March 26, 1874; C.W. Eliot to Mayor Thomas Hart of Boston, June 3, 1901.
11. F.W. Hunnewell to L.E. Sexton, March 24, 1914.
12. Various items in *A.I. Lowell Letters,* 1909, 1910.

13. *Report of Committee on Watch in Cambridge Early 1846,* January 28, 1848; W.G. Stearns, Steward, Harvard College, to President Walker, June 26, 1855; J.E. Thomas to C.F. Adams, II, February 8, 1912; Timothy I. Good, Mayor, to President and Fellows of Harvard College, September 1, 1914; *Stoughton Bell for Harvard,* about 1912. C.W. Eliot to Thomas Perkins, May 16, 1907; Jerome Greene to President Lowell, March 16, 1910.

learning than President Eliot. As early as 1874, Eliot became greatly interested in this problem. He then pointed out that Harvard was not entirely tax exempt. The college paid taxes on $600,000 of property in Boston and Cambridge.[15] To the provost of the University of Pennsylvania in 1874, he wrote a long letter in which he noted that the college pays taxes on:

. . . real estate held by a college as an investment such as land, stores, or houses leased. . . .
The State says to the public spirited benefactors: You have devoted your property forever to certain public uses, higher education, for example; we agree not to take a part of the income of that property every year for other public uses. . . . [16]

In 1899, confronted by threats of taxation, Eliot again warned against taxing institutions of higher learning. Eliot admitted however, that "the things exempted should be clearly for the use or advantage of the real beneficiaries of the trust, who are the students. . . ." [17]

But it was especially in a long essay written in 1874 and republished in 1897 that Eliot presented his most able and most comprehensive treatment of the tax issue.

The State believed upon adopting exemption from taxes that the indirect gain to its Treasury which results from the establishment of the exempted institutions is greater than the loss which the exemption involves.

Eliot insisted that the cheapest and best way to obtain certain services, e.g., higher education, "is to encourage benevolent and public-spirited people to provide them by promising not to divert to inferior public uses any part of the income of the money which these benefactors devote to this noblest public use. . . ."

Against the argument that exemption from taxes of nonprofit institutions cuts down the tax base, Eliot responded that with increased activities of non-profit institutions, actually the tax base is likely to rise.

Why did several towns compete for the Massachusetts Agricultural College and the town of Amherst finally pay $50,000 for the privilege of domiciling this institution if the tax base were to be reduced?

The resultant open spaces add to value: the university brings personal property which becomes taxable; it serves as a magnet for in-migrating families, with consequent gain in revenues; Ward I, the location of Harvard, accounts for 18 percent of the houses in Cambridge, 16 percent of the polls, and 30 percent of the taxable property; the university brings into Cambridge many consumers: fifty families of teachers, fifty unmarried faculty members, 9 thousand students, and about a hundred workers (and their families); the university collects about $150,000 in tuition; and personal property increases by $50,000 as a result of the inflow of students.

Cambridge's affluence level is not to be explained by natural conditions, for it has its fair share of bogs, salt marshes and sandy barrens. "The greater part of its surface is but a few feet above high-water mark. Nothing but the presence of the university during two hundred and forty years has made it a desirable place of residence that it is. . . ."

Eliot was especially critical of the alternatives to endowment, namely, grants by the government. Whereas the endowment method leaves the trustees untrammelled in pursing their policies, the grant method "puts them in a position of importunate suitors for the public bounty and then makes of them unscrupulous assailants of the public Treasury." [18]

On the problem of abuses of endowment, Eliot's approach would be to correct the abuses, not to destroy endowment income. On the high level of taxes and hence the pressure not to exempt institu-

15. C.W. Eliot to Professor J.H. Seelye, December 30, 1874.
16. C.W. Eliot to the Provost of the University of Pennsylvania, January 19, 1874.
17. C.W. Eliot to S. Hoar, November 8, 1899.

18. C.W. Eliot, "The Exemption from Taxation" (1874), reprinted in *American Contributions to Civilization*, 1897, pp. 299-343.

tions of higher learning of taxes, Eliot's medicine is remindful of the debates of 1967, namely, cut public expenditures.

President Pusey recently supported the Eliot position. Harvard University's total payroll of $71 million in 1965-1966 exceeded that of six leading industries in Cambridge. Harvard students spent about $15 million for clothing, services, and recreation; 1,200 landlords derive part of their income from Harvard student tenants. In a year, Harvard buys about 63,000 gallons of ice cream, 305,000 gallons of milk, 180,000 dozen eggs, 75,000 pounds of butter, more than 600 tons of meat and poultry, and almost the same quantity of vegetables. The university serves 3,250,000 meals.[19]

---

19. *New York Times,* February 5, 1967.

33

Harvard and the Government

Control of Harvard at first was by the board of overseers, representing in fact the Colonial government and the people. But in 1650 the government provided for management by what is now called the corporation—five fellows, the president, and the treasurer. The government, Colonial and state, made many attempts to modify the charter in a fundamental way. But in the long struggle the small, self-perpetuating corporation won out. The result undoubtedly has been an efficient operation, obtained increased resources and good management. The overseers have served as a watch dog and occasionally innovator over the years.

In the first two hundred years of its history, Harvard depended heavily on the general court and the state government. It is no wonder that "on the accession of every provincial governor, the corporation solicited his patronage by a formal address, invited him to the College, and received him there with great respect and ceremony." [1]

These gifts were especially important in the seventeenth and eighteenth centuries. Without them Harvard would not have survived. Rudolph, the able historian of higher education, reminds us of our great dependence on the public purse. Arguing in a more laissez-faire era against a state-supported college, President Eliot stated:

... our ancestors well understood the principle that to make a people free and self-reliant it was necessary to let them take care of themselves, even if they did not take quite so good care of themselves as some superior power might. The institutions of higher learning helped by the State [are] "engaged in a relationship of mutual obligation and responsibility with the State," and without this help Harvard would not have been born or survived. [2]

The court exercised some control over tuition charges, lightly chastised the college for extravagance, set the rents, and often controlled the use of buildings.[3]

But even as late as 1849, as is evident from the following, the state asserted its legal rights to oversee the policies of Harvard.

The General Court of the colony, by the grant of 1636, and the orders of 1637 and 1642, founded the college, and vested the powers of visitaton and government in overseers accountable to the court;

---

1. *Documents Printed by Order of the Senate of the Commonwealth of Massachusetts,* no. 158, 1849, pp. 14-15.

2. F. Rudolph, *The American College and University: A History,* 1962, pp. 13-14, 185; Henry James, *Charles W. Eliot: President of Harvard University,* 1930, vol. I, pp. 325-326.

3. *Legislative Records of the Council,* vol. 11, p. 142; vol. 13, p. 103; vol. 17, p. 45; vol. 25, p. 48; *Documents Printed by Order of the Senate of the Commonwealth of Massachusetts,* no. 158, 1849.

and, by the acts of 1650 and 1657, the court established the corporation, and vested the property and the government of the college in them, subject to the counsel and consent of the overseers.

The General Court of the colony, and of the province, from 1657 down to the establishment of the constitution of the Commonwealth in 1780, by successive acts, orders, and votes, granted several new charters—nominated the corporators—altered their number, from seven to ten, sixteen, and seventeen and back again to seven—limited the tenure of office for a part of them, to ten and to seven years, and again removed such limitation—altered the governmental powers of the college, and changed the overseers in number and character, including tenure of office, and, in one instance, in 1692, dispensed with them altogether. . . . with an inherent condition for alterations in its government, by the legislature—but in all other respects fixed, beyond control or change, without its own consent. And, under this charter, not a law can be established for the government of the college—not a vacancy can be filled in the overseers or corporation—not an officer of instruction or government can be finally elected, without the action and consent of the overseers, a majority of whom are annually chosen by the people of the Commonwealth.[4]

In 1650, a new charter appeared and in this one provision was made for government by self-perpetuating fellows: The fellows were to receive gifts, allocate resources, and dispose of assets as indicated by the donors, call meetings of the overseers "in great and difficult cases and in cases of nonagreement." The president and fellows "may meet and choose such officers and servants for the College, and make such allowances to them. . . ."[5]

Apparently the 1642 charter, which had conferred large authority on the relatively large board of overseers, had proved unworkable.

From 1650 on, the provincial government attempted on several occasions to modify the charter and notably in 1672 and 1692. But in 1707 the pro-

vincial legislature resolved "that the former Charter of the College of 1650 had not been *repealed or annulled.*" The only significant changes until 1812 were the result of providing under the new constitution for a successor to the board of overseers.[6]

At the outset the Colonial government exercised virtually complete control. The legislature exercised supreme authority in six different acts: (1) in providing a special grant; (2) in laying out an annual tax for support; (3) in designating a committee for erection of buildings; (4) in choosing the site; (5) in selecting the officer in charge and providing for his support; (6) in putting the officer on trial and appointing his successor.[7]

From the very beginning there were contests between the government and the college over control. The dispenser of funds is not likely to yield all control. But gradually, and especially in the nineteenth century, the authority of the government was reduced and, ultimately, virtually eliminated. From 1780, when the state constitution was adopted, to 1921, when Harvard was given complete control over its government, the Legislature dealt with the makeup of the board of overseers. Gradually lay influence prevailed over state and church. The years 1810, 1814, 1851, 1865, 1902 and 1921 were especially important in the movement toward Harvard and lay control. In 1851, the legislature failed in an attempt to reduce the influence of the corporation. The 1865 legislature definitely ended state representation and control.[8]

Between 1849 and 1851, the issue of the government of Harvard once more attracted much attention. Members of the Legislature in particular attacked the institution of the fellows of Harvard College. In their view, the fellows were too powerful and their term of office, far too long; and the self-perpetuation of the body especially irked members of the Legislature.

---

4. *Ibid*, pp.20-21
5. *The Charter*, 1650

6. Communication of the Corporation to the Legislature, February 27, 1812.
7. Blackmer, *op. cit.,* p. 86.
8. See especially *Laws of the Commonwealth of Massachusetts,* vol. 5, p. 200, 1809-1812; vol. 13, p. 163, 1834-1836; p. 691, 1849-1850; p. 565, 1865; p. 241, 1921.

They stressed the point that state government had never relinquished its statutory and visitorial powers, and, basing themselves on the Dartmouth College case, argued that the source of the original endowment determined control.

In reply, the defenders of the fellows expressed great confidence in their management and the achievements of the university. Moreover, in their view, a large board representing all kinds of interests and places would not be very effective. The defenders of the system were not impressed by the argument that "this increase of numbers and difference of location would bring to the Government of the College a variety of taste, knowledge and opinion, corresponding to the sentiments of the people of different sections of the Commonwealth." They also contended that the colony had renounced its rights once it turned over the college's management to trustees.[9]

The supporters of the system in vogue wrote:

Under the present constitution of the College, the Corporation, consisting of seven members with perpetual succession, is a body large enough for conservative Counsel, and not too large for prompt and responsible action. The Board of Overseers, consisting of eighty-three members, is sufficiently numerous to secure the confidence of the public, and to act in quick sympathy with all sound measures for the advancement of learning. [10]

A joint select committee of the Senate in 1851 contended that the system in vogue afforded "a model of integrity, honourable alike to the immediate parties and to the Commonwealth." Indeed, the governing body was conservative, but this was considered a desirable quality for "persons whose function it is to administer faithfully the many and large trust funds, which the hereditary love of learning, prevalent in Massachusetts, has accumulated in the

custody of the president and fellows of Harvard College. [11]

Critics wanted a change of government because in their view the college was in trouble:

...It [the college] *has lost the sympathy of the people; it is no longer the object of their affections; they regard it with but little more interest than the transatlantic university whose name it bears. ...*
While individuals are mortal and the power to change the statutes of their foundation ceases with their existence, the state, as we believe, is immortal, and rights once vested in it will continue forever. [12]

Mr. Boutwell and his supporters insisted that the state was the legal founder since its benefaction was the first; that Harvard was a public institution and therefore subject to the public will; that only the state, the founder, is permanent and hence "may regulate and govern it ... "; that in an eleemosynary institution "the law will recognize no rights but those of the founder. ... [13]

The critics failed in midnineteenth century to abrogate the Charter of 1650. Undoubtedly, had they succeeded, the university would have suffered. Control by twice as many fellows, each serving a maximum of six years would have resulted in less efficient management, and political considerations would have determined the selection of fellows.

By an Act of April 28, 1865, passed by the Legislature and agreed to by the corporation and the board of overseers, "the connections between the Commonwealth and the University was finally dissolved, and the latter became a wholly independent institution." Indeed, the Legislature reserved the

---

9. "Legislation ... to Render Harvard University more Beneficial ..." in *House Report No. 164,* April, 1850, pp. 4-5; *Minority Report,* pp. 10-14; Remarks of Samuel Hoar in *The Atlas,* May 30, 1850.
10. *House Report No. 164,* pp. 12-13.

11. *The Joint Select Committee to Whom Was Referred so much of the Address of the Governor as related to Harvard College ...,* pp. 2-3; *Documents printed by order of the Senate of the Commonwealth of Massachusetts,* no. 102, May, 1851; see also *Memorial Concerning the Recent History and the Constitutional Rights and Privileges of Harvard College, presented by the President and Fellows to the Legislature,* January 17, 1851, 3rd ed.
12. *Speeches of Mr Hoar, Mr. Eliot, Mr. Boutwell.*
13. *Speeches of Mr. Hoar ... Concerning Harvard College.*

power of repealing the original act, but this was not likely to happen.

From the early history of Harvard until 1865:

the Board of Overseers has been more or less connected with the State. . . . Men were chosen on party grounds, on sectarian grounds, and from motives of political ambition. But now, every member added to our body brings at least an earnest desire to do what he can to aid the Corporation and faculty in causing our Alma Mater to hold her rank at the head of the American literary institutions. [14]

President Eliot in his 1869 inaugural commented on the contribution of the governing boards. Without the overseers, "the President and Fellows would be a board of private trustees, self-perpetuated and self-controlled . . . the Overseers should always hold toward the Corporation an attitude of suspicious vigilance. . . . [15]

Of the corporation which Eliot considered the heart of the university, he insisted:

. . . should be small to be efficient and renewed slowly to be steady of aim; it must include sound men of finance; the actuating spirit of the Corporation must be a spirit of fidelity—fidelity to the money and various trusts reposed on them . . . a reputation for scrupulous fidelity to all trusts is the most precious possession of the Corporation. . . . [16]

---

14. *Report of the Board of Overseers of Harvard College,* 1869, pp. 60-61.

15. *Addresses at the Inauguration of Charles William Eliot,* 1869, pp. 55-57.
16. *Ibid,* pp. 57-63.

PART

5

GIFTS

34

Why Give?

Harvard's friends gave funds to Harvard for all kinds of reasons. Thus, on March 2, 1719, T. Hollis gave the college twelve casks of nails and one cask of cutting. His accompanying letter said:

I confess to bear affection towards the people of North America, those of Massachusetts and Boston, in particular, believing them to be a good and brave people . . . and the spirit of luxury now consuming us to the very marrow here at home, kept out of them! One likeliest means to that end will be, to watch well over their youth, by bestowing on them a reasonable manly education; and selecting thereto the wisest, ablest, most accomplished of men. . . . [1]

John Quincy Adams, on December 15, 1823, contributed $1,000 towards the funds for a professor of astronomy.

. . . The sum thus appropriated as my portion of the subscription was limited, not by my inclinations but by the necessary comparison of my means with other and indispensable calls upon them. I was unwilling to appear at the head of the subscription chiefly from the hope that others less restricted than I was in their power, and feeling an ardor for the accomplishments of the object equally intense, would assume their natural right of priority upon the list to which I could appear only as a more humble contributor. [2]

One of the most colorful gifts is the following:

In case my son Josiah shall dye before he arrived to the age of twenty-one years, or after he arrived to that age without issue, then upon the marriage or death (whichever shall first happen) of my Wife, I order & accordingly give & bequeath to the President & Corporation of Harvard College two thousand pounds sterling for the use and purpose of founding a Professorship of moral Philosophy, Law & Oratory & no other. [3]

All kinds of other motives account for gifts to the college. Later we discuss the donations where the college is in an unusually difficult situation—e.g., following a fire. In the early years, strong religious feelings drove many to help Harvard, which was contributing to the output of ministers. Thus, in 1640, John Newgate of Boston gave "five pounds *forever* towards the maintenance of lawfull, usefull, and good literature therein and chiefly to the furtherance of the knowledge of Jesus Christ. . ." [4]

Family loyalty also played a part. In the latter part of the nineteenth century, a widow presented Harvard with $150,000 to build Perkins Hall as a memorial to three graduates of her husband's family from 1717 to 1819. Again in 1892, a remote descendant of

---

1. Josiah Quincy, *The History of Harvard University*, 1840, vol. II, pp. 146-147; B. Peirce, *History of Harvard University*, pp. 12-13, 98-99.

2. John Quincy Adams to John Kirkland, President of Harvard University, December 15, 1823.

3. Extract of the Will of Josiah Quincy, Esq., dated February 20, 1774.

4. Peirce, *op. cit.,* p. 16 (my italics).

Thomas Hancock, the latter having in 1764 established the Hancock Professorship of Hebrew and Other Oriental Languages, gave the university $72,000 (or more) to augment the small legacy of £1,000 in 1764.[5]

In a similar vein, friends of Harvard offered help because science was advancing and Harvard might accelerate the gains:

Another proof of the fitness of the times for the plan of promoting the cultivation of science, was the readiness with which a subscription of twenty-five thousand dollars for a telescope and observatory was filled up. . . .[6]

Trends in Gifts

In its first 150 years Harvard College officials begged at home and abroad, from private interests and from the government. But the largest gifts have come in the most recent 125 years of its history. Even as late as 1834, the largest gift received by the university, that from the Gore estate, was $100,000, a large part of which was subject to the payment of annuities. Over the first 200 years the growth was surprisingly slow. In the next 123 years, however, the market value of all funds rose by more than 700 times and expenditures by about 1,000 times.

President Eliot urged gifts to the university because "it gives reasonable assurance that the benefactions will be continuously useful and will be preserved to do its work century after century. . . ." Eliot here left out of account the erosion of endowment as prices and incomes rise. He was also rather optimistic when he wrote that "no smallest gift made to Harvard University for a permanent purpose has ever been lost. . . ." [7]

In an eloquent handwritten letter for the 1919 drive Eliot, long retired, urged contributions to the

drive. He emphasized especially Harvard's contribution to the war, its greater freedom from political control, and the liberal and pioneering views of Harvard's graduates. Eliot urged giving because of a devotion to Harvard as well as to correct injustices to teachers.

Whoever studies the development of American liberty, prosperity, and stability will find that Harvard College and the University that grew out of it have been pioneers in all the educational progress which has taken place in America from the founding of the College in 1636 down to the current year. In general, the endowed institutions fostered by the state rather than the state-supported institutions have done the needed pioneering. They [private institutions] are also more likely than the state institutions to maintain active scientific and historical research and literary productiveness.[8]

Table 34-1.

Endowment and Expenditures 1840–1965, Various Years

Year	Endowment	Expenditures
1840	$ 646,235	$ 94,000
1869 Eliot's first year	2,257,989	210,511
1909 Lowell's first year	22,716,759	2,106,587
1933 Conant's first year	117,967,055	12,986,242
1964 Pusey	567,325,167	118,935,566

Sources: W. H. Claflin, Jr., "Our Endowment: Its Vital Importance to the University," in *Harvard Alumni Bulletin,* May 31, 1940, vol. 40, p. 1082; *Financial Report to the Board of Overseers of Harvard College,* 1964-1965, pp. 9-10.

President Conant observed that in the years 1912 to 1952 the gifts for current use amounted to $92

5. *Endowment Funds of Harvard University,* 1948, Harvard University, p. 207; *History of Harvard College,* pp. 18-19.
6. *Ibid.,* p. 120-127.
7. C. W. Eliot, *Educational Reform,* 1898, p. 245.

8. C. W. Eliot to Eliot Wadsworth, August 23, 1919.

million as against a rise of capital funds of $181 million.[9] Clearly, gifts other than for endowment are of great importance.

Views on Giving

J. T. Morse once noted: "Harvard College has lain in the midst of the community like a sponge upon moist ground, always thirsty and soaking up all the nourishment within reach." [10]

In presenting Soldiers Field to Harvard in 1890 Mr. Higginson said: "It is very pleasant to do you a kindness, and everyone is glad of a chance to serve the dear old College. She needs help, and thought and devotion, and gratitude from all of us, for she has given us and our land more than any one of us will give back. She will keep on giving. . . ."

On a later occasion Higginson presented the college with the Harvard Union. On this occasion, Charles Frances Adams wrote Higginson: . . . "I envy you; I would have liked to do that! That is your monument, and like a wise man, you have not waited to erect it after death. . . .Concentrate on that, and do not let anyone else touch it. . . ."

William James also wrote Higginson: " 'He will never be done with good deeds until he dies; and even then (pace Shakespeare) the memory of him ought to bring forth more and more of them in perpetuas aeternitates.' "[11]

President Lowell had said "of the needs of a university, there is, indeed, no end."[12] A year later he admitted that universities must beg, and the better their work the more begging.[13]

Perhaps the strongest argument for giving was that resources were inadequate to provide an education of quality. Thus Treasurer Samuel A. Eliot at mid-nineteenth century complained that professional schools were growing up around the college which "remains substantially in the same imperfectly supplied condition in which it has been for many years—indeed, during the whole history of its struggling life." With wealth rising more than population, Eliot expressed the hope that the state or individuals "may be induced to appropriate some portion of their superfluity for an investment, which will not indeed be returned in income or profits, but will produce a rich harvest of honor to themselves, and of blessings to posterity. . . ." [14]

On another occasion, Samuel Eliot described Harvard as:

. . . distinguished more for its struggles to live and labor, than for the abundance of its resources . . . for its practical influence upon the leading minds of the country than for the splendor of its appointments, or the dignity of its offices. . . .

Eliot denied, as many Harvard officials have ever since, that despite its great wealth ($750,000 at that time) plus grounds and buildings, that Harvard was rich. Harvard had to have adequate funds to finance the needs. Pauperism and beggary were its state.[15]

For West Point, the Congress appropriates 3 to 8 times Harvard's income from invested funds, Eliot said. Harvard's contribution is remarkable considering the relative resources and the extent and variety of education available at the two places. Enrollment was roughly equal.[16]

Despite S. Eliot's persistency, the problems are still with us. They always will be. The college needs teachers and apparatus, in fact "the external facilities of every kind for acquiring and communicating knowledge," a report to the board of overseers in 1869 tells us. Harvard's poverty, the overseers related, is the result of large investments in unproductive

9. *Report of the President of Harvard College,* 1951-1952, p. 7.

10. J. T. Morse, Jr., *Memoirs of Colonel Henry Lee,* p. 124.

11. B. Perry, *Henry Lee Higginson, The Friend of the College,* 1921, pp. 330-331, 340-341, 352-353.

12. *Report of the President of Harvard College,* 1919-1920, p. 33.

13. *Ibid.,* 1920-1921, p. 29.

14. *Ibid.,* 1848-1849.

15. A Letter to the President of Harvard College by a Member of the Corporation, Samuel A. Eliot, 1849, pp. 10-13, 26-27.

16. *Report of the Treasurer of Harvard College,* 1850-1851.

property, the care of which is costly. The library alone cost $10,000 a year to maintain. Again there are new sciences, and what we now call the explosion of knowledge.

At this point, the committee stressed the point that despite the large increase of funds, rising prices had reduced the values of endowment income: the rise of numbers requires more dormitories, class-rooms, faculty and apparatus; higher salaries are needed, which would cut down outside work, and the college needed more money for libraries. The faculty had to buy its own books or go to Boston libraries.[17]

It was during Charles Eliot's incumbency early in the twentieth century that the college put through an unparalleled drive for $2.5 million of endowment to finance a substantial rise of faculty salaries. Eliot was well aware that "Man cannot live by bread alone, Nor the joys of teaching and research"[18]

It was in the Eliot period that a band of devoted Harvard men who were especially impressed by the relationship between education and the preservation of our civilization inclusive of private enterprise, gave generously of their own wealth, and stirred up enthusiasm among others.

Henry Lee Higginson, one of the most generous of benefactors, asked "did not all that really mattered in the world depend upon enlarging the influence of Harvard before it was too late?"[19] And to his wife late in the 1860's he wrote as follows:

Your mother (Mrs. Louise Agassiz) discoursed about the poverty of the University and said that not improbably the salaries of the Professors would not be paid in full this year. Oh! if some dozen men would only put it up high and dry above want! One million dollars to start with and three million more afterward.[20]

A somewhat longer letter of March, 1886, from Higginson to a kinsman gives the flavor of this devotion to Harvard.

Dear X:

Nobody knows his duties better than yourself—therefore I presume to admonish you. I want you, as the oldest and richest member of your family and mine, to give to the College $100,000, to be used in any way which seems best to you.

My reasons are that you, a public-spirited and educated gentleman, owe it to yourself, to your country, and to the Republic. How else are we to save our country if not by education in all ways and on all sides? What can we do so useful to the human race in every aspect?

Democracy has got fast hold of the world, and will rule. Let us see that she does it more wisely and humanly than the kings and nobles have done! Our chance is now—before the country is full and the struggle for bread becomes intense and bitter.

Educate, and save ourselves and our families and our money from the mobs. . . .

We have a neighbor who gives very freely, and whom you rightly do not respect. Stand before him in all ways. I shall be sorry to see his name down for $100,000 before yours. It gives a certain power to give this money, and will give you great pleasure. Think how easily it has come. Give one fourth of your last year, and count it money potted down for quiet good. . . .[21]

Another enthusiastic and loyal Harvard man, Joseph H. Choate (class of 1852), speaking at a commencement dinner in June, 1885, had this to say:

And now, brethren, would you have your statue crowned? Would you, too, become immortal? Would you identify your names with the glory of the college? The way is open and easy. Follow exactly the example of the founder; give one equal half of all you are worth to the college, and if you wish to enjoy your own immortality, do it tomorrow, while you are

17. *Report to the Board of Overseers of Harvard College on the Condition, Needs, and Prospects of the University by a Committee of the Board of Overseers,* 1869, pp. 5, 36-37, 64-65.
18. Harvard University Archives, UAV File 136. 124.7.
19. *The American College and University: A History,* 1962, Quoted in F. Rudolph, p. 425.
20. B. Perry, *op. cit.,* 1921, vol. II, p. 327.

21. *Ibid.,* pp. 329-330.

alive. If you shrink from that, die at once and give it to them now.... [22]

Samuel Appleton in the 1850s wrote President Felton that he wanted to share with his college the excess of income available to him and his wife:

I have always taken a deep interest in our Alma Mater—having attended 35 of the 38 Commencements since I graduated... we both feel that we should be very much pleased to apply part of our surplus income of each year, for the ... [scholarship] above mentioned. [23]

Finally, here is an item on the philanthropic spirit upon which Harvard has depended. Charles Francis Adams, class of 1856, looking back fifty years early in the twentieth century wrote as follows:

... It so chances I have had to do with varied calling; but now, looking back, I find I would not have greatly cared for supreme professional success, to have been a great physician, or divine, or judge. I served in the army once; but military rank and fame now seem to me a little empty. As to politics, it is a game; art, science, literature—we know how fashions change! None of the prizes to be won in those fields now tempt me greatly; nor do I feel much regret at my failure to win them. What I now find I would really have liked is something quite different. I would like to have accumulated—and ample and frequent opportunity for so doing was offered me—one of those vast fortunes of the present day rising up into the tens and scores of millions—what is vulgarly known as "money to burn." But I do not want it for myself.... What I would now like the surplus tens of millions for would be to give them to Harvard.... [24]

But one should not assume that all Harvard alumni were of equal spirit. Even as late as 1917, the point was made that Harvard depended primarily on two hundred of its friends for meeting its deficits year after year. [25] But the president in 1901 announced that "the benefactors of the University come from a wider territory than they used to, and represent a much greater variety of racial stock, religious opinion, and professional, commercial, or industrial connection." [26]

In the Eliot period, the emphasis was on more and better professors and improved economic status for them. One of the leaders in the financial campaign, despite President Eliot's greater interest in his cash than in his advice, was Col. Henry Lee. He wanted more money for Harvard "to place her professors and other instructors on a proper footing, just to them and creditable and secure to us." [27]

The stress on the use of more money for Harvard to improve education and the support of American institutions carried over to Harvard's second large campaign, the $15-million endowment drive of 1919-1920. Its director, Eliot Wadsworth, invited attention to the steel and coal strike, and to the need of more Americanization. "... No discussion of the industrial problems which confront the country fails to bring forth the need of a better understanding between employer and employee. Many methods for bringing this about are suggested, nearly every one of which involves more education." [28]

A constant theme in seeking gifts has been the excess of cost of a Harvard education over the tuition charged. One student of the problem proposed that each graduate pay the college the difference between costs and tuition. [29] The author estimated the costs

22. E. S. Martin, *The Life of Joseph Hodges Choate,* 1920, vol. I, pp. 367-368; cf., J. H. Choate, *Education in America,* 1903, pp. 22-23.
23. N. I. Bowditch to the Corporation of Harvard College, November 27, 1854; N. I. Bowditch to President Felton, August 4, 1860.
24. Charles Francis Adams, *An Autobiography, 1835-1915,* 1916, pp. 209-210.

25. "Why Harvard Needs Money," in *Harvard Alumni Bulletin,* vol. XIX, January 18, 1917, p. 305.
26. *Report of the President of Harvard College,* 1900-1901, p. 50.
27, J. T. Morse, Jr., *op. cit.,* pp. 126, 135.
28. *Harvard Graduates Magazine,* vol. 28, 1920, pp. 459-460.
29. Harvard Endowment Fund Bulletin No. 11, 1919-1920 in the Harvard University Archives, UAV File 136. 124.5.

and tuition to graduates in the years 1870 to 1918. For a graduate of the class of 1871, the estimated debt was $1,575; for one of the class of 1918, $406.[30]

For the average alumnus the reason for giving is to provide for the increasing needs of the college. But not always.

. . . on Saturday, November 22, from two o'clock in the afternoon onwards for about two hours I shivered and wondered how much I would have to give to guarantee me a decent seat at the foot-ball game. On that day I was seated in the bend of the stadium up under the shed that runs around the top, with a cold breeze blowing down the back of my neck, leaning first against my guest on the right to crane my neck around the obstruction in front of me so that I could peek at the game, and the next moment leaning against the guy on my left trying to do the same thing. As I understand it, the class who gave the stadium are given preferred seats in that structure. How much more will I have to give to be put in that preferred class? Please consult the powers that be and advise me.

I want to make a suggestion. Please consider it seriously. It is that any man who gives $25,000 to the Endowment Fund shall be put in a preferred class for the rest of his life as far as foot-ball seats are concerned, and that he be allowed by an additional subscription of $5,000 to purchase one preferred seat to the Harvard-Yale game each year as long as he lives.[31]

For most alumni the appeal was based on nobler motives. The campaign book of the 1919 Program included the following:

The psychological aim of the campaign is to arouse the love of Harvard men for their Alma Mater, to stir them and the public with the impulse to give, based upon the needs and opportunities of Harvard for

service; to create throughout the nation an atmosphere that makes people give freely. . . .[32]

In both the 1904 and 1919 campaigns the emphasis was on endowment for teachers' salaries, the first to contend with rising competition and the improved economic status of the American people, and the second to treat the results of a serious inflation. But in the next two *large* drives, that of the middle 1920s for $10 million on behalf of chemistry, fine arts, and the business school, and the 1956 Program for Harvard College, greater emphasis was put on the plant.

In agreeing to run the campaign of the 1920s, Bishop Lawrence emphasized that "loyalty to the business traditions of my family and a conviction that this was a real missionary enterprise for the welfare of the country made me consider [the] appeal. . . ."[33] In 1955 Neil McElroy and J. F. Spang, Jr., Harvard alumni and leading businessmen, said that ". . . colleges and universities have a responsibility. . .to acquaint their students . . . with the proper meaning and advantages of this American economic order. . . ."[34] In Lawrence's view, business was "not just a mechanism for the making of money but it is a high calling for the upbuilding of civilization. Its history is full of romance, chivalry and faith." [35]

In the quest of money for chemistry, the emphasis was on chemistry as a basic science related to medicine, agriculture, industry and conservation of resources, and the contributions of chemistry to the alkali industry which gives us cheap soap and cheap gas for light. ". . . There is nothing that we touch with our hands every hour of the day, that we sit on walk on or wear, that does not have a knowledge of chemistry behind it. . . ." [36]

30. *Ibid.*
31. Harvard University Archives, UAV File 136.124.5.

32. *Ibid.,* 273.
33. W. Lawrence, *Memories of a Happy Life,* pp. 417-418.
34. *Harvard Alumni Bulletin,* 1955, p. 621.
35. W. Lawrence, *op. cit.,* pp. 778-780; Harvard University Archives, UAI 10.450.12.
36. Harvard University Archives, UAI 10.450.10, 450.14; *Harvard Alumni Bulletin,* April 10, 1924, pp. 778-780.

The Tercentenary Episode

President Conant used the tercentenary as an occasion to advance Harvard's contributions. Perhaps no president was as eloquent and brilliant as Mr. Conant in presenting the goals of Harvard. Yet the material gains were disappointing.

Undoubtedly the depression of the 1930s and the fear of New Dealism, to which Harvard had contributed so much, militated against a successful financial campaign. Writing in 1951-1952 President Conant reminded his readers of the reduction of gifts in the Great Depression, and of a reply to a question about the future of private institutions of higher learning in the 1930s, namely, "I didn't know they had a future." Conant had also been misled by the social scientists. He warned us that we appeared to be entering a static period, and our frontiers had vanished.[37]

President Conant was inclined to stress the overriding importance of the quality of faculty and students rather than finance. For Conant, the crucial issue was "what type of individual will teach in our colleges and universities in the coming years, and what will be the quality and character of the student body." Finance was indeed necessary as the letterhead of the 1936 appeal suggested: "Harvard has grown through the generosity of her sons, asking only that she might offer even more to posterity." [38]

In the view of President Conant:

The citizens of this nation are interested in education and research to an extent which has never before been equaled in this country or any other. If the institutions of higher learning, privately endowed or publicly supported, can demonstrate that they are worthy of being encouraged, I am confident they will be maintained. In the past, our own good fortune has come in no small measure as a recognition of the success of the University's undertakings. We are the beneficiaries of the skill and wisdom of those who have preceded us. . . .[39]

In developing the theme of the 1936 financial program, the emphasis was on the contributions of universities generally first and Harvard second. Universities contribute to human welfare and progress; they are stable and permanent; and their record suggests that the yield of the gifts to be had will be inspiring, lasting, and useful. Harvard's position is peculiarly strong, for its equipment is exceptional; its combination of a fine liberal arts college and first class graduate schools, highly productive; its faculty, superb; and its reputation for progressive policies, richly deserved.

For the tercentenary drive the corporation stressed the strengthening of the intellectual and spiritual life of the university and the increasing of the national scope of its usefulness. The means would be university professorships not definitely attached to any department and thirty Harvard national scholarships.[40]

Program for Harvard College

In 1956, the university announced a record $82.5 million campaign. At the 1956 commencement President Pusey said: "Ours is a very great college and a very great university, but it is not yet nor ever will be an achievement finally to be enjoyed. It is rather a process which calls for new effort and fresh advance." [41]

Proclaiming that this was the largest campaign ever undertaken on behalf of undergraduate education, the president later said:

Throughout its history Harvard has relied on the support of its alumni and friends when the occasion demanded, and it has never been disappointed. We

37. *Report of the President of Harvard College,* 1934-1935, p. 8.
38. Harvard University Archives, UAV 828.3; *Report of the President of Harvard College,* 1934-1935, pp. 6-7.
39. *Report of the President of Harvard College,* 1937-1938, pp. 28-29; Harvard University Archives, UAV 828.142, p. 63.
40. Harvard University Archives, UAV 828.142; 828.182; 828.268.
41. *Harvard Alumni Bulletin,* October 13, 1956, p. 59.

fully realize the magnitude of the task confronting us, but the generally enthusiastic response to our initial statement of need has encouraged our belief in the success of the endeavor. This is not an expansion program but a major attempt to catch up with past and present needs. It must be successful if Harvard is adequately to fulfill the demands increasingly made upon it.[42]

The sponsors of the program could point to the large rises of tuition already consummated, the failure of faculty salaries to rise *pari passu* with inflation, and the increasing real income of the working population, the overcrowding of the Harvard houses, the failure of the plant and equipment to keep up with the advances of science and the increasing enrollment, the great burdens put upon the university through rising costs of research not fully covered by the granting agency, and the attrition of endowment, a point discussed elsewhere.[43]

Again much emphasis was put upon the special involvement of business. The university hoped, according to the *Crimson,* that business would contribute as much as 25 percent of the $82.5 million.[44] The official attitude was as follows:

Corporations now are the custodians of great wealth which formerly was in the hands of individuals who gave generously to philanthropic causes. . . .
In A Program for Harvard College, business is being asked to participate in a unique all-out effort to revitalize and strengthen the backbone of the University.
Industry's stake in Harvard's role in American higher education, in the development of future leaders, and in the advancement of knowledge has been demonstrated. . . .[45]

Inclusive of libarary endowment, support of faculty salaries and new chairs, the program was to put $40 million into men and books. The remainder was for the plant and upkeep. Among the objectives were higher salaries; additional housing for students—3,971 undergraduates in 1956-1957 occupied space intended for 2,670; housing for married students—there is, of course, no real justification for a collegiate community with excellent housing for undergraduates, fair housing for single graduates, and poor housing for married graduates; new professorships to keep pace with the explosion of knowledge; increased endowment for the library; more study and classroom space for a faculty doubled in size in twenty years; more financial aid for students; a theatre and increased facilities for art; more laboratories in chemistry, and a health center for Radcliff and Harvard.[46]

Unpopular Views

Throughout Harvard history, beginning with President Dunster, the problem of raising money has been complicated by the differences of views between the college faculty and the potential donors. In the early nineteenth century, Harvard lost both students and cash as a result of the Calvinists' anti-Harvard campaign. But it was particularly in the twentieth century, when the major financial gains were made, that these conflicts might have affected the capacity of the university to raise money. No one will, however, know the material effects of these differences of view. At any rate, the 1904, 1919, 1924-1925 and 1956 campaigns were successful. Only the 1936 campaign failed of its objectives; and here the decision to seek cash unobtrusively during the Tercentenary, and the effects of the Great Depression were

42. *Ibid.,* February 16, 1957, p. 384.
43. *Financial Report to the Board of Overseers of Harvard College,* 1964-1965, pp. 10-11, ch. 44.
44. *Crimson,* October 14, 1957.
45. Program for Harvard College, *The Business Stake in Harvard College,* p. 3. Chapter 60 discusses the record recent program for the medical school; and in 1968 there is an unprecedented science program for undergraduates and numerous other programs.

46. See especially the various numbers of *A Program for Harvard College;* D. Farnsworth, "A University Health Center," in *Harvard Today,* February, 1959; *Report of the President of Harvard College,* 1953-1954, pp. 19-21; 1954-1955, p. 11; 1955-1956, pp. 6-12; Harvard *Crimson,* March 13, 1957; December 6, 1957; January 8, 1958; Boston *Daily Globe,* October 31, 1956.

relevant factors. Moreover, as the John Price Corporation suggested, Harvard could gain much by associating itself with the principle of academic freedom and the pursuit of truth.

With the outbreak of World War I, Hugo Munsterburg, a German psychology professor at Harvard, seemed in public lectures to side with Germany. A Harvard graduate, George Wiener, announced that he would leave Harvard $10 million in his will if Munsterburg were dismissed. The latter agreed to leave if Mr. Wiener would deposit $5 million to Harvard's credit. But in defense of academic freedom the corporation refused to countenance this transaction.[47]

It was especially in the troublesome early post World War I period that issues of academic freedom arose; and particularly because Harvard had launched its massive $15 million endowment campaign. One well known Harvard alumnus announced that he was very much opposed to Laski, Frankfurter, and "the damn Jews." Another famour Harvard alumnus carried on a long correspondence with President Lowell in which he attacked Laski for siding with the policemen in the Boston police strike and for holding socialistic views.

Another alumnus had this to say:

I believe that the best results would be obtained if we could see some evidence from the Intellectuals at Harvard in trying to reestablish somewhere near the old purchasing power of money. They all admit the present troubles are caused by the new conditions, and yet as far as I know they have not taken a single step in advocating publicly and with all their effort the abolishment of inflation. . . .[48]

Criticism seemed to come from extremists. Brooks Adams would not give. He wanted to know "what the bankers' control of education, or at least the higher education is likely to do." Even President Lowell did not escape criticism.[49]

Lowell was criticized on various occasions by different groups. His role in the case of Commonwealth v Sacco and Vanzetti; his opposition to Roosevelt's plan for packing the Supreme Court, and to the Child Labor Amendment; his opposition to the confirmation of Brandeis as Supreme Court Justice; his favoring the League of Nations; his opposition to forcing the social mixture of white and Negro students; his proposal to limit the increasing proportion of Jews in the student body; the intended merger of M.I.T. and Harvard; his defense of academic freedom (especially his defense of Munsterburg, Laski, and Chafee); the release of Professor Baker to Yale; the closing of the Harvard School of Forestry.

President Conant's program had to contend with alumni criticism of those who had created the New Deal. Harvard was not without responsibility, and particularly Felix Frankfurter, who had trained many of the bright young lawyers later to become Roosevelt's aides, was under attack. One alumnus wrote: "I may be very wrong-headed, but I feel, as I know a great many other Harvard graduates feel, that until Harvard rids itself of Felix Frankfurter and his crew, they will not contribute to this Fund."

A stronger statement condemned Felix Frankfurter working through the seventy-one disciples in the entourage of the administration ". . . throughout the United States the belief is prevalent that all these invidious attempts to overthrow the constitution originate at Harvard. . . ."[50]

It was particularly the 1936 fund which seemed to suffer from the charge of radicalism. There were other complications in 1936, not the least of which were the depression and economic uncertainties, the manner in which the Harvard 1936 campaign was run, some doubts about the business methods of the university, and a widely held view that Harvard had ample funds. It was even charged that the Lampoon running the flag of the Soviet Union up the Supreme Court flag pole had hurt Harvard, as did a bomb (made of peppermint candy) sent to Governor Curley.[51]

---

47. H. Yeomans, *Abbott Lawrence Lowell, 1856-1943*, pp. 315-316; M. Munsterburg, *Hugo Munsterburg*, p. 264.
48. Harvard University Archives, UAV File 136.124.5; 124.
49. H. Yeomans, *op. cit.*, pp. 346-351; Harvard University Archives, UAV 136.124.5.

50. Harvard University Archives, UAV 828.3, 828.211.
51. *Ibid.*, 136.124.5; 828.182; 828.214.

One alumnus objected to large endowment: "... they tend to materialize, i.e., despiritualize, or deintellectualize, the University's life by their over emphasis on money, organization, equipment. ..."[52]

The most frequent grumbles were related to the radicals at Harvard. In the spring of 1936 the university was getting fifteen or twenty Frankfurter letters a day. One alumnus held that there were too many bright boys already in Washington. Another considered Frankfurter not a liberal but a radical "whose purpose and philosophy was and is contrary to what had always been the accepted mode of life in this country." [53]

A typical statement of the critics who, on ideological grounds, would not help Harvard is the following:

My concern about Harvard University first centered around the Law School, which I regard as a hotbed of Socialism, Radicalism and Communism. ... I attribute much of the mess we are in at present in connection with the New Deal to the constant stream of reds and socialists of various hues, which the colleges have been turning out for the past twenty years. Harvard is one of the leaders. ...[54]

Poet David McCord, that unusual proponent of the soft sell and unique money raiser, has wisely said: "Sometimes in answering a critic of Harvard policy based on one offending action I am tempted to ask him if he will not weigh three centuries of teaching, training, and example against his split-second of displeasure." [55]

---

52. *Ibid.,* 828.5.
53. Harvard University Archives, UAV 828.211; 828.212; 828.5.
54. *Ibid.,* 828.211.
55. D. McCord, "After Thirty Years," in *Harvard Fund Council, Miscellany,* August 2, 1955; Harvard University Archives, HUD 3411.

35

Gifts

Gifts to 1845

In a book about Harvard, it was said:

In England rich men found families; in America they found universities, or they enlarge them. The family often falls away to shame; the university remains forever a noble and unsullied memorial. On its founder no stain is ever cast by the misconduct of his descendants.[1]

From the very beginning Harvard sought gifts in Massachusetts, in other provinces, and in England. The Province of Massachusetts was generous, at least until the Revolutionary War.

In the early years Harvard did not always keep tabs on its gifts, with the result that many donations were lost or applied in ways inconsistent with the wishes of the donor. Even the amount of the gift of John Harvard is not clear. Was it £800, or £700, or £400? Official records indicate only £400 were received, but the £800 total is often used.[2]

The college showed great interest in early gifts and, when the activity seemed fruitful, spent years in trying to recover a donation. Thus a Hopkins legacy of 1657 became available with the death of his wife in 1701, but it was not until 1715 that the £800 were received by Harvard and other legatees—at a cost of £60 sterling in seeking delivery.[3]

Again, there were difficulties in mobilizing the funds given by Mr. Penoyer through a bequest of 1670. In 1681 the corporation:

ordered that the Treasurer of the College be desired to cause a Letter of Attorney be drawn up to impower some one to receive what is due to the College on account of Mr. Penoyer and Mr. Dodderidge theire gifts and that they may give discharges upon the Receipt thereof:[4]

In 1638 the gifts amounted to £963 sterling inclusive of £780 sterling from John Harvard and £100 sterling from Lady Mowlson. Apparently no gifts were received until 1642 when the total obtained was £875. Included was £150 received by Messrs. Hibbons, Welles, and Peters, from "divers gentlemen and merchants of England, towards furnishing the library with books."

From 1650 to 1656, the college obtained £594 16s of lawful money inclusive of £250 from Robert Keyne of Boston and £241 from sundry gentlemen towards the repair of the college.

1. *History of Harvard College*, p. 18.
2. Quincy, *op. cit.,* vol. I, pp. 8-12, 460-462; *History of Harvard University*, p. 2.
3. *Ibid.,* pp. 101-103; see also listings in *Donation Books* and *College Books*, vol. I; Quincy, *op. cit.,* vol. I, chapters 9, 26; appendixes 1, 22-23, 25; vol. II, chapters 26, 30, 35; *Contribution to American Educational History, Federal and State Aid to Higher Education,* 1893, pp. 86-93; F.W. Blackmer, *The History of State Aid to Higher Education, Circular of Information,* 1890, pp. 30-37; S.A. Eliot, *Harvard's Benefactors,* 1849, tables 2, 3.
4. Meeting of Corporation in Boston, December 13, 1681; *College Books,* vol. I, p. 69.

By 1679 the gifts amounted to £4,580 lawful money and £1,182 sterling. In 1698, the Honorable William Stoughton gave a record gift of £1,000.

Beginning in 1712, the gifts are listed at their discount value, for the lawful money began to depreciate greatly vis-à-vis sterling. In 1712, Thomas Brattle gave £200 lawful money, but at 25 percent discount, it was listed at £150; and Henry Flynt in 1750 gave £112 10s at 90 percent discount or £11 5s in sterling.

In the years 1719 to 1722 Thomas Hollis, probably the most magnanimous of all donors to Harvard, gave £1,484 sterling for professorships and scholarships. Various Hollises gave £429 sterling from 1725 to 1733 and Mary Saltonstall, £1,000 lawful money at 68 percent discount in 1731 or £320 sterling. In addition, there were numerous gifts of silver.

Harvard received £1,045 lawful money in 1764 to rebuild Harvard Hall and £1,000 sterling from Thomas Hancock and 554 sterling from John Hancock.

Major Donations between the Revolutionary War and 1830.

Professor of Natural History, 1805	$31,333
Eliot Professorship Greek, 1814	20,000
Count Rumsford (Science Professorship) 1815	28,000
John McLean (History), 1821	25,000
James Perkins, 1823	20,000
Nathan Dane (Law School), 1823	15,000
Subscription for Theological School, 1826	36,988
C. Gore, 1826 (unrestricted)	92,000
J. Fisher, 1803	20,000

By 1845, the total of gifts amounted to $577,817. The largest gifts from 1831 to 1845 were $50,000 by John Parker, $25,000 donations for the observatory, and $21,008 for the library.

In addition, over this period of more than two hundred years, the college received 7,603 acres of land, the largest being 3,840 acres in a township of Maine by Samuel Parkman and 2,120 acres from Isaac Royall. But little of this land was in Cambridge in the vicinity of the college and the college lost much of it because of the difficulties of controlling it.[5]

Total Gifts

By 1965-1966 Harvard had accumulated investments of about $1,000 million. The return was about $28 million, a rather small return on $1,000 million. By 1968 the return exceeded $40 million. That the university pays out more than 5 percent in its investments is explained by the fact that the funds are carried at low book value, not high market values. The major part of the capital value stems from gifts first, from the capitalization of direct yield on capital invested, and also from rising prices of equities. In addition, the university has a few hundred million dollars of buildings and equipment. The Harvard houses (undergraduate colleges) alone probably could not be replaced with an investment of less than $50 million. Gifts are made of buildings and equipment, and also large sums are given for current use, the last an item of increasing importance.

Diversions

As noted earlier, the college authorities did not always receive the funds that were supposedly put at their disposal.[6] Attempts to divert the money from its intended use even attracted the colonial governments as is evident in one of the earliest gifts, that of Lady Mowlson in 1643 for £100 for help to a poor scholar:

Among the early transatlantic benefactors of Harvard College was Lady Mowlson, of whom nothing is known except that she was among the earliest of this class of benefactors, that she contributed one hundred pounds sterling for the College, and paid the amount over to Welde and Peters, the agents of the

---

5. All items from F. W. Blackmer, *op. cit.*, tables II, III.

6. See *College Books*, vol. IV, pp. 327-350; *Publications of the Colonial Society of Massachusetts*, vol. 16, pp. 832-864, for wills and testaments recorded in their exact wording; D. McCord, *In Sight of Sever*, 1963, pp. 108-125.

Colony in Great Britain. It appears, by the records of the Governors of the College, that her gift was known in this country as early as December, 1643, but that it was not at that time received. Welde and Peters settled for this amount, and for sums given also by others, with the General Court; who kept it in their treasury, and voted to allow for it to the College an annuity of about fifteen pounds per annum. Fortunately for the College, Lady Mowlson had taken a bond of Welde, that the money should not be diverted from the charitable objects to which she had devoted it. For in 1655, on a petition of the College for relief, in a state of great distress on account of the insufficiency of their buildings, the House of Deputies ordered the amount due on account of her gift to be "improved for" the repairs of those edifices. This vote the magistrates non-concurred in, "because the amount was given by the Lady Mowlson and others for scholarships, annually to be maintained there, which this Court cannot alter, and therefore desire their brethren, the Deputies, to consider of some meet way for the repairing of the College," an instance of self-control, and of the acknowledgement of restraint by principal, as honorable as it is exemplary.[7]

A similar struggle ensued over the Hopkins bequest of 1657 which provided that three-quarters would be given "to six Bachelours...of art residing at ye college...and performing such exercises in Theologic as ye corporation shall appoint them...." Apparently there were difficulties for the college in obtaining the gift, and some lack of trust of the College.[8]

J. Quincy suggested that Cotton Mather, Increase's son, unhappy that Harvard was too liberal in religious matters, tried to divert part of the Hollis bequest to Yale.[9]

---

7. *Endowment Funds of Harvard College*, p. 135.
8. *Corporation Papers*, 1712, vol. I, p. 45; *College Books*, vol. III, p. 110; *Publications of the Colonial Society of Massachusetts*, vol. XV, p. 288; *Proceedings and Collections of the Massachusetts Historical Society*, no. 1, vol. 1, pp. 161-162.

Early Issues

From the time of first receipts of funds for financing professorships, the college had to face crucial issues. In 1721, Thomas Hollis, a London merchant, made available £80 per year to finance a professorship of divinity, the first endowed chair in the university.

At this time a donor would not only provide the money but also suggest the religious views of the holder of the professorship and what he might teach.[10]

The divinity professorship raised other modern problems. Thus, the professor was to "set apart two or three hours one afternoon in the week to answer such questions of the students who shall apply to him as refer to the system of controversies of Religion . . . ." In forbidding outside work and charges to students Hollis was also precise.

On tenure, the requirement was that the commitment be for five years by the president and fellows and overseers. But he added:

he said Professor shall be at all times under the inspection of the Rev[d] the President and Fellows with the Hon[ble] and Rev[d] the Overseers for the time being to be by them displaced for any just and valuable cause. . . .

. . . the said Professor shall in all times to come be chosen by the Reverend the President and Fellows of Harvard College for the time being and shall be presented to the Honourable & Reverend Overseers of the College to be approved by them and then shall be joyntly recommended by them to me for my confirmation during my life and after my decease to such Person as I shall appoint by my last Will under my hand and Seal during the term of his life also.[11]

Even as late as 1834, the McLean Professorship reflected some of the conditions set by Hollis more

---

9. B. Wendell, *Cotton Mather*, 1926, p. 282.
10. *Endowment Funds of Harvard University*, pp. 208-209.
11. This relates to the Hollis Professorship of Mathematics and Natural Philosophy (1726).

than a century earlier: the public lectures were to be free; and should a vacancy not be filled in two years, the money would be lost to Harvard. [12]

In 1823, Nathan Dane, with a gift of $15,000, selected the professor of law and the terms of employment. The incumbent was to be Joseph Story, a member of the Supreme Court. Story proved to be an excellent teacher. Henry Ware thus described him:

... he proceeded to discourse for an hour with a fluency and eloquence that were simply marvelous. All his resources were perfectly at his command. Facts, arguments, theories, authorities, history, illustrations, everything seemed to be at his tongue's command— not superficially or crudely, but his words came from the studied results of long experience, vast learning, and an intense love of his profession. The bell announcing the expiration of the hour would stop him in the full tide of his eloquence, and if no lecture were immediately to follow, a spontaneous call of "Go on!" would often go up from the benches, where no seat was ever vacant. [13]

Meeting Conditions of Gifts

From the very beginning the college was confronted with all kinds of difficulties in performing as required by the conditions of gifts. Here are some examples of the problems confronting the university in trying to carry out the deeds of gifts.

In 1926, the university received a sum of money which by 1947 had grown to $125,699. The donor would establish a department for research in abnormal and dynamic psychology. It is scarcely possible to finance a department with an income of about $6,000. [14] Again, C. C. Stillman gave a generous sum in 1925 equal to $308,787 to finance the Charles Eliot Norton Chair of Poetry. But a condition was that the "salary of each incumbent of this chair shall

be what, at that time, is the maximum salary of a full professor at Harvard."

By 1963, the endowment had grown only to $427,000, but the president set $500,000 as the endowment for a full professorship; and now $600,000. Twenty-five years from now the fund may well yield less than half the amount required to finance the highest paid professor. [15]

A gift in 1945 of about $30,000 raises special problems.

The gift of Katharine W. Atkins.

It is my main purpose to have the income used to further the work at Soledad established by my late husband Edwin F. Atkins. However, I realize there may be opportunities to use the income of this fund to advance the general welfare of Cuba, which do not fall within the restrictions of my husband's gift and I have no objections if the income is so used from time to time. I have in mind for example research or investigations that may help to improve the health of the Cuban people; studies to improve nutrition; condition might well be furthered to good advantage. [16]

Benjamin Bussey in 1861 offered his estate in Roxbury to be used to advance agriculture. Environmental changes made nonsense of much of this grant in less than 50 years. [17]

On July 4, 1901, President Eliot enthusiastically accepted a gift from J. Pierpont Morgan to help build a new medical school. Eliot was anxious to get on with the building. He asked Morgan's advise on almost every important issue. His gratitude was so extreme that his deference to the great financier must have been embarrassing to Morgan. A few months later, when approaching the Rockefeller interests, Eliot confessed that the expansion of the medical school had to be postponed despite Morgan's promise of financing three of the five buildings needed. Financing the other two, plus operating expenses, meant

---

12. *Endowment Funds of Harvard University*, p. 63.
13. In Batchelder, *Bits of Harvard History*, pp. 216-217.
14. *Endowment Funds of Harvard University*, p. 70.

15. *Ibid.*, p. 67; *Financial Report to the Board of Overseers of Harvard College*, 1963, p. 158.
16. *Endowment Funds of Harvard University*, p. 305.
17. *Ibid.*, 388.

that $1.6 million additional had to be raised and no funds were yet in sight.[18]

One of Harvard's troublesome problems in the early years was the proper application of numerous gifts that were to be used to educate Indians. Daniel Williams' will of 1716 read: "The remainder to be paid to the College of Cambridge, New England, or such as are usually employed to manage the blessed work of converting the poor Indians there, to promote which I assign this part of my gift." It is not surprising that by the 1940s this small contribution had grown to $20,099. A similar bequest of 1691 was from Hon. Robert Boyle for the relief of poor Indian converts. But Harvard, in this and other instances, could find neither the necessary teachers nor the Indians to be taught. In 1723, the College allowed the Reverend Oliver Peabody £40 a year salary as long as he continued to preach the Gospel to the Indians. But generally the money piled up and both receipts and disbursements were spasmodic. [19]

Harvard's problems of adhering to the terms of bequests or gifts undoubtedly contributed to a view that it might be wise for donors or their agents to deal directly with the beneficiaries of a gift to Harvard. An interesting instance follows:

By ye last Will & Testament of Elder Penn (Ruling Elder of ye old church in Boston) £.10.pr An. are to be given to poor Scholars, out of ye Rents of his Farm at Pulling Point; but this money is dispos'd & order'd by ye Elders & Deacons of ye old church in Boston; so yt neither Corporation nor overseers of ye College have any thing to do in ye disposition of said £.10. pr An. [20]

Inadequacy of Endowment and Treatment

In many of the gifts given to the university the amount offered was inadequate to achieve the stated objectives. On some occasions the donor would be silent on the inadequacy of the gift in relation to the task. But generally the friend of Harvard would suggest ways of building up the endowment, as a rule by allowing the money to be invested and the income capitalized until the funds were adequate. Some interesting examples follows.

Boylston in 1771 presented Harvard with $5,000 for a professorship in rhetoric. By 1806, when John Quincy Adams was to accept the chair, the capital value had risen to $23,200. [21]

The McLean gift of 1834 of $20,552 for a professor of history provided for accumulation until "the income whereof may be sufficient for the support of such Professors. . . ." [22] By 1947 the fund had grown to $43,000 and by 1966 as a result of capital gains but primarily transfers from funds available from endowment drives had escalated to $486,000.

A rare episode is the following. A Mr. Waterhouse offered a gift of $5,000 on the condition that no use be made of it until it had accumulated to $500,000. In turning down this gift the corporation revealed that the money would not become available for at least a hundred years:

. . . it is wholly impossible to foresee the condition of the university one hundred years hence, in respect to total endowment, number of students, or best means of usefullness. No person living in 1795 could possibly have imagined the university of today. All the objects which you mention may have been provided for before that time, or some of them may have ceased to be interesting . . . . They [the Corporation] believe that the best interest on an educational endowment is procured by using immediately to train promising young men. . . . Again they feel some objection to regarding the alternate sum of $500,000, as in any strict sense your gift. . . . You indeed would have

---

18. C. W. Eliot to J. P. Morgan, July 4, 1901; C. W. Eliot to S. J. Murphy, October 25, 1901.

19. *Publications of the Colonial Society of Massachusetts,* vol. II, pp. 407, 423; *Treasurers' Journals,* 1755-1773; *Corporation Records,* vol. I, p. 153, 1723; W. Claflin, "Our Endowment," in *Harvard Alumni Bulletin,* May 31, 1940, p. 1081.

20. *College Books,* vol. III, p. 109; *Publications of the Colonial Society of Massachusetts,* vol. XV, p. 287, 1733.

21. *President Webber to Treasurer Storer,* June 9, 1806.

22. *Endowment Funds of Harvard University,* p. 65.

given the nucleus; but it would be the steady care and good judgment of the Corporation, and particularly of their treasurer, which could have multiplied the gift by one hundred. Finally, they do not consider it for the interest of the university to exhibit on its account from year to year large accumulating funds. Such funds give the impression that if not rich now, the university is going to be rich; and so far forth they check the flowing stream of benefactors. It is the fixed policy of the Corporation to spend every year, every dollar they can lay their hands on, and in the consistent effort to do this they from time to time incur considerable deficits which have to be taken out of capital. . . . [23]

Thomas Lamont, in 1925, presented the university with $101,242 to finance a professorship of chemistry. He wisely added that the president and fellows could accumulate income "if in their judgement changes in the business life of the United States or increase in the cost of living in the University community makes it desirable that the principal of the fund shall be increased."[24] But even by 1963, the fund had escalated only to $130,000. Obviously the university had to finance the major part of this professorship out of its own funds.

Perhaps the most fantastic program for building up a large fund out of small beginnings is the Jewett Fund (1937). This is worthy of full quotation. The original $10,000 did grow to $20,000 by 1963. At that rate, even if growth continued at the geometrical rate of 1937-1963, a period of almost 125 years from 1937 would be needed to provide a capital fund of $250,000.[25] These investment plans are remindful of the plans for paying off the British national debt in the eighteenth century through the accumulation of a sinking fund.

The gift of Margaret W. Jewett of $10,000 to constitute a fund which shall be known as "The Jewett

Fund" which shall be held and invested by the President and Fellows of Harvard College and the income thereof accumulated. Whenever the accumulations of income thereon shall amount to Ten Thousand Dollars ($10,000) such accumulations shall be added to and merged with the professorship endowment fund. The original fund of Ten Thousand Dollars ($10,000) shall continue to be held upon the trust to accumulate the income and to add the accumulations to the professorship endowment fund upon each occasion when such accumulations amount to Ten Thousand Dollars ($10,000) until the value of the said endowment fund shall amount to Two Hundred Fifty Thousand Dollars ($250,000). Then, if in the opinion of the said President and Fellows the income of the endowment fund is as great or greater than an amount equal to the average salary of full professors at Harvard University, the accumulation under the above provisions shall be suspended.

Richard Dana Bell in 1926 gave the Harvard Medical School $100,000, but "the principal sum of which is to be held intact for fifty (50) years. . . ." By 1963, the fund has grown to $178,000.[26]

A gain of only 78 percent in 37 years is difficult to understand. This means that the fund earned only 1½ percent a year, for 1½ percent compounded over 37 years accounts for the 75 percent gain. Since Harvard Harvard generally paid around 5 percent on book value and 3-5 percent on market value, this particular fund seems to have been treated badly. (One condition was that the capital fund was not to be used in the first 50 years.) Hence, the rise of capital value of 75 percent could measure only the accumulation of the return on the original sum.

Discretion to the University

Ordinarily only the income of a capital sum given for endowment is available. But in many instances the donor has given Harvard the discretion to use capital

23. C. W. Eliot to Professor Sylvester Waterhouse, December 3,1895 (my italics).
24. *Endowment Funds of Harvard University*, p. 72.
25. *Ibid.*, p. 58; *Financiaal Report to the Board of Overseers of Harvard College*, 1963, p. 284.
26. *Ibid.*, p. 238; *Endowment Funds of Harvard University*, pp. 250-251.

also and in many gifts or bequests has specified alternative uses of the funds donated. The latter privilege is especially helpful as the needs of society change. In numerous gifts to the medical school, for example, provision is made to divert funds to the study of other diseases once a particular disease is conquered with the help of the donor's money. To cite a specific case as early as 1739, Thomas Hutchinson gave the college £300 for the professor of divinity. But after fifteen years the corporation could decide upon alternative uses of the income.[27]

In the last generation, there has been a growing interest in allowing the beneficiary of a gift to use capital as well as income. In the Great Depression use of capital attracted much support as a road toward liquidity. Thus, in September, 1934, the General Education Board (Rockefeller) in reference to a 1926 gift of $500,000 modified the terms of the original gift to read "that this gift, whether the income only is spent or the principal as well, shall always be regarded as available for use in the broadest way so as best to promote the general purpose for which it is made." The board granted permission in ten years for related use; and:

Fifty years after the date of the gift, not only the income but the principal as well may be expended in whole or in part by those then responsible for its use, either for the specific purpose for which the gift was originally made or for any other specific purpose which in their judgment will best promote the original general purpose of the gift, with the provision, however, that such other specific purpose shall be as closely akin to the original purpose as may be found practicable at the time.[28]

It is of some interest that from 1926, when this permission to use capital was granted, to 1963 the fund had actually increased about one-half.

The Carnegie Corporation, in 1946, modified the terms of a 1937 grant of $350,000 to the dental school, and similar grants providing for capital consumption.[29]

Robert Keayne, one of the earliest benefactors of the college, in 1659 made £230 available for helping "the godliest and most hopeful of the poorer sort of Scholars." But he was not certain of the approach. Hence he wrote:

Therefore because I have but little insight in the true ordering of Scholars and other things thereto belonging in a College way, and so possibly may dispose of my gift where there is less need, and that it might do more good if it was disposed of in some other way, I am willing to refer it to the President, Trustees and Overseers that are intrusted with the care and ordering of the College, and Scholars or Students, with the things thereto belonging.[30]

In 1919, Francis E. Colburn had given the college $100,000 for research into tuberculosis. But as soon as remedies or cures were achieved, the money was to be used "for the discovery of some effectual remedy or means of cure, for some other disease, generally supposed to be incurable or known to yield with extreme difficulty to ordinary remedial measures."[31]

On numerous occasions friends of the college deprived the college of the usual discretion, either demanding special investments and segregation of funds or dictation of how the money was to be invested. For example, the bequest of Price Greenleaf (1887) required that the fund be held:

as a distinct and separate investment, apart from all other investments made and held by them, so that the amount and kind of property and estates held in trust under this will, together with the income, interest, and profit thereon may at all times clearly appear on their books of account.[32]

Under the Gray bequest, not only was the fund to be segregated but it was not to be invested "in real

27. *Donation Book*, 1739, vol. I, p. 32.
28. *Endowment Funds of Harvard University*, pp. 49-50.
29. *Ibid.*, p. 193.

30. *Ibid.*, pp. 173-174.
31. *Ibid.*, p. 255.
32. *Ibid.*, p. 393.

estate, or in stores or stock of any incorporated joint stock company."[33]

Scholarships

Harvard has received a substantial part of its endowment for scholarships. Ordinarily the stipulation has been that the aided student should be in need of funds.[34]

In one instance (1869) the issue of need was so overriding that the philanthropist requested that the applicants statement be accompanied "by a certificate of one or more municipal officers of the City or Town . . . that the facts stated in such application are true. . . ."[35]

Scholarly attainments were generally a requisite for qualification for a scholarship. But the test in these earliest years was not likely to be high grades as in the nineteenth and twentieth centuries but rather some minimum attainment.

Thomas Hollis (1722) was definite on this issue, as he was on need: "I earnestly recommend in a special manner to avoid nominating now and hereafter Dunces or Rakes as persons not fit to partake of my Bounty; or Persons reasonably judged able to maintain themselves. . . ."[36]

In Harvard's history there were numerous donors who would rule out scholarly attainments as a condition for a scholarship. These friends of the college would put such attributes as character, motivation, personality, etc. as the desired ones.

Under the terms of the Hodges Scholarship (1878) ". . . his selection was to be based on his merit depending without reference to scholarship, upon diligence and good character, though scholarship is to be no bar to the beneficence to be bestowed." Incidentally, his particular gift provided that the student sign a statement of intention to repay if able to do so.[37] A number of scholarship grants carried such provisions.

In 1912, the bequest of Grace R. Shaw ruled out choice on the basis of scholarship for a traveling fellowship. He would benefit:

. . . young men of worth, who without necessarily having attained to the highest scholarship in college, have made good use of their opportunities and give promise of success in professional or business careers. I therefore do not prescribe any formal tests, such as relative rank in scholarship, as the basis of awarding the income of this fund. . . .[38]

A 1944 scholarship was also explicit: ". . . Having in mind the numerous scholarships which are awarded primarily on the basis of academic scholastic standing, it is our desire that in the award of the William Brackett Snow III scholarship more emphasis than usual shall be placed on the character and personality of the student."[39]

In the early years, providers of scholarships often made it a condition that members of their families or their descendants should be given preference in the selection of winners. One explanation of this vogue is undoubtedly that in these years family ties encompassed a much larger part of the population than in more recent years. But in many instances, and especially in the last hundred years, with the increasing importance of new ethnic groups, the emphasis was put on scholarships for those of English background.

In 1716, the bequest of Major William Browne read: "To help support my grandchildren or their posterity when students there or if none at such college then to help maintain other poor Salem scholars . . . that may live at college. . . ."[40]

A Howard Rogers Clapp Memorial (1919) would have income paid:

. . . to a student in the college chosen as much for high character and manly qualities as for excellence in scholarship. I prefer but do not stipulate that the one so chosen shall be descended from at least two grandparents, or more remote ancestors who were natives

33. *Ibid.*, p. 350; cf., pp. 153, 269.
34. *Ibid.*, pp. 135, 173.
35. *Ibid.*, p. 143.
36. *Ibid.*, p. 123.

37. *Ibid.*, p. 122.
38. *Ibid.*, p. 153.
39. *Ibid.*, p. 155.
40. *Ibid.*, p. 92.

of the United States of America or of what is now known as Great Britain; my wish being to assist young men whose inheritance and training are derived from persons familiar with American or English institutions.[41]

The Alden Hudson Bequest of 1928 gave many alternatives with restrictive features of varying degrees.

. . . the "Alan Hudson Scholarship," the same to be available to the best-fitted and qualified applicant, in the opinion of the President and Fellows of Harvard College, from among the sons or direct descendants of the late Alan Bedford Hudson, should such apply; but failing such application of sons or direct descendants as above mentioned, then the scholarship may be awarded to any student of the name of Hudson or of the name of Baxendale, deserving and qualified; and failing such last-named applicants the said scholarship may be awarded to any deserving and qualified student from the City of Brockton, in Plymouth County, or from the Town of Bourne, in Barnstable County, in the Commonwealth of Massachusetts. This provision for said Alan Hudson Scholarship is made in memory of his great love of learning, his high ideals, and lifelong devotion to the uplift of humanity.[42]

Prizes

The Francis Bott Bequest (1904) offered a $100 prize to the writer of the best composition in "concerted vocal music." The jurors were to receive $30 each. The bequest read in part: "I suggest that the music be neither too ancient nor too modern in style. If religious, good models can be found in Mozart and Cherubini; especially in their Requiems and in the Ave verum of the former."[43]

James Bowdoin, a former governor of Massachusetts, in 1791 gave the college £400 for prizes for dissertations. By 1963, $95,071 was available. Many of the leading scholars of Harvard for the next 175 years received these prizes. I am not sure that all

conditions are now met—e.g., "to be read in public."[44]

David A. Wells' residuary bequest (of 1901) offered prizes for essays on various economic subjects. Wells ruled out essays advocating policies to which he objected on moral or economic grounds.

The Wells Prize raises a number of issues. One is how difficult it is for the university to keep in mind all the details of a bequest or gift. At times the terms are such as to exclude any possibility of conformity; at other times changed conditions make nonsense of the terms.

A second problem has been raised in other connections: inadequacy of stipends in an advancing economy. In 1900 the average per capita income was $200; in 1963, about $2,500. Hence, the Wells Prize of $500 was equal to but one-twelfth its relative value in 1963 as compared to 1900.

Unusual Gifts

Samuel Brown in 1723 was excused from doing errands during his "Freshmanship" because of physical disability. Apparently the Browns' legacy of £800 to the college and his father's offer to present "a piece of plate upon his admission of much greater value than would entitle him to the privileges and honors of a Fellow Commoner" also impressed college officials concerning the entry and treatment of the son.[45]

Paul Dudley in 1750 presented the college with a fund which would finance a series of four lectures annually. This surely must be one of the earliest gifts for a series of lectures. The income was "to be applied towards the erecting, maintaining, supporting and continuing an anniversary sermon or lectures to be held or preached at the said College. . . ."[46]

In the 1840s, businessmen became interested in the possible contribution of men of science to manufacturing. The Lawrence Scientific School was the

41. *Ibid.*, p. 96.
42. *Ibid.*, p. 124.

43. *Ibid.*, p. 179.
44. *Ibid.*, p. 180.
45. *Corporation Records*, vol. I, p. 170.
46. Paul Dudley to Ebenezer Pierpont and Samuel Winthrop, January 2, 1750.

outcome. Mr. Lawrence's gift of $50,000 in 1846-1847 to endow the scientific school was believed to have been the largest gift ever bestowed on an educational institution by a *living* person.

... in support of this project Abbott Lawrence of Boston—a great mill-owner, interested especially in the manufacture of cotton goods—came forward with generous gifts. He had learned by observation that the mills at Lowell needed great engineering works to establish their water-power securely. He observed the same thing at Lawrence later. He had come to see that men skilled in engineering and chemistry were necessary to the successful prosecution of American manufacturing in many lines.... Accordingly he founded here a Scientific School (later called by his name), built its first building, equipped therein an excellent chemical laboratory, and endowed a professorship in engineering. That was a great step toward the development of seventeenth-century Harvard College into a modern university.

But the school did not develop as Lawrence had envisaged. The appointment of Louis Agassiz as professor of zoology and geology in 1847 diverted interest from engineering, and the opening of MIT in 1862 brought unexpected competition to Harvard engineering.[47]

When Edward Austin left $433,500 to Harvard in 1899, President Eliot's comments on Federal taxation of 15 percent of the amount sounds like the 1960s.

... The bulk of the money will go to student scholarships... and yet fifteen percent of this great benefaction from a private fortune is diverted to the ordinary uses of the Government of the United States in meeting its civil and military expenses; or, in other words, $76,500 devoted by the testator forever to one of the highest permanent public uses is diverted to much lower temporary public uses. The ill-considered legis-lation which produces such inexpedient results ought to be at once repealed.[48]

Henry Lee Higginson gave $150,000 in 1899 for a Harvard Union. He wanted to increase conversation and break down isolation and social discrimination. He asked:

Is there a better or sweeter thing on earth than the free and close intimacy of young fellows, discussing everything on earth and in heaven, tossing the ball from one to another, lifting each other to a higher plane, as healthy, earnest boys will, and thus learning to know their comrades and themselves?[49]

George Baker's insistence in 1924 on giving $5 million, not $1 million for the Harvard Business School, deserves repetition. Baker had been asked for a million. Several months later Baker called on Bishop Lawrence, who thus related the episode:

... Promptly, at six, Mr. Baker appeared, alone. We sat down, passed a friendly word or two, and then he said, "Bishop, I have been thinking over the matter of the Business School. I have lost interest in your suggestion that I should give the first million. I am not going to give it or half a million either." He paused, and then told an anecdote, while I sat tight, for he evidently had something more to say. He went on, "If, however, by giving five million dollars I could have the privilege of building the whole School, I should like to do it. If it were one of several such schools or an old story, I should not care to do it, but my life has been given to business, and I should like to found the first Graduate School, and give a new start to better business standards. I want to do it alone. Do you think Harvard will let me?"[50]

Charles Eliot Norton visited his friend Thomas Carlyle on a trip to England in 1869. Through the influence of Norton and Ralph Waldo Emerson, Harvard obtained the Carlyle library. Carlyle had written Norton

---

47. C. W. Eliot, *Harvard Memories*, 1923, pp. 57-58; *Report of the President of Harvard College*, 1846-1847, pp. 7-9, 25-29; Samuel Eliot Morison, *Three Centuries of Harvard*, 1636-1936, 1937, pp. 279-280.

48. *Report of the President of Harvard College*, 1898-1899, p. 45.

49. B. Perry, *Life and Letters of Henry Lee Higginson*, II, pp. 354-355.

50. W. Lawrence, *Memories of a Happy Life*, 1926, p.420.

I suppose there never was a man who had had so much to do with books as I have, who owned so few. I never have purchased a book which I could do without, or which I did not intend to read through. But in writing about Cromwell and Friedrich I have chanced to get together some things not wholly worthless nor yet easy to find, and I've thought I should like when I die to leave these books to some institution in New England, where they might be preserved, and where they would serve as a testimony of my appreciation o' the goodness o' your people toward me and o' the many act o' kindness they have done me; and perhaps you can help me to have this rightly done. [51]

Near the end of his administration President Lowell gave the college a large sum to provide a new institution, the junior fellows. In the last thirty-five years, the success of this enterprise has been phenomenal, and notably in the quality of the students turned out.

Lowell had tried to interest the Rockefeller Foundation in a body of scholars that would function like the Trinity College, Cambridge, which had produced so many great scientists. But the foundation refused. [52]

A Boston Chinese laundryman in the midst of a campaign, entered Massachusetts Hall and presented the secretary of the corporation an unrestricted gift of $25 and six pounds of Chinese ginger wrapped up in a laundry bill. The letter follows:

Dear Sir,

Mr. Superintendent of Harvard College. In Harvard College office from Jan Quen relief twenty-five dollars to support. Sincerely yours, From: Jan Quen [53]

President Conant's national scholarship marked a great advance which added much to the quality of Harvard students. President Conant expressed his objectives as follows:

If we can but reach down through the various strata and geographical areas of this country and find the boys with talent and bring them to our various educational institutions where their talents may be trained and their character developed, we will produce, I believe, in another generation a cultural civilization the like of which this world has never seen. . . . [54]

Harvard also refused gifts. In 1878, Miss Marion Hovey would have given $10,000 to the medical school. But the medical faculty were not receptive, for a condition was the admission of female students. [55]

The corporation refused a bequest from the Whiting family in 1874-1875. [56]

One potential contribution "believing that modern feminist movement tends to take woman out of the home and put her in politics, government or business, and that this has already begun to impair the family" offered $25,000 to President Lowell to develop sound public opinion on this subject. The university did not accept the gift nor $68,000 from Dr. J. Ewing Mears who wanted to press his definitive views on eugenics.

The Corporation had just refused a bequest of the same amount by Whiting on the grounds that it was inexpedient. The original bequest stipulated that the income of the sum would be paid out as a scholarship to any descendent of Whiting who would be a student at Harvard. If there were no descendent, the interest was to be added to the principal until one should appear. The report of the committee appointed to investigate the advisability of accepting such an unusual bequest urged that it be declined, in that no provision was made for the judgment of the President

---

51. S. Norton and M. A. DeWolfe Howe, *Letters of Charles Eliot Norton*, 1913, I, pp. 336-341.
52. H. Yeomans, *op. cit.*, p. 524.
53. *Harvard Alumni Bulletin*, vol. 45, p. 116.
54. Proceedings of Tercentenary Banquet, June 9, 1936, pp. 59-60.
55. *Report of the President of Harvard College*, 1878-1879, pp. 29-32.
56. *Ibid.*, 1874-1875, pp. 14-15 and appendix II, pp. 91-93.

or Fellows, no statement of the need of the prospective beneficiary was included, no aim of general education was set or benefit was conferred to the University, and that the principal might accumulate only to remain in mortua manu, *untouchable by the University for any purpose.*[57]

No Buildings

A widely held view is that institutions of higher learning spend too much for buildings and too little for their staffs. One reason for this is that donors are more inclined to give money for buildings which in a sense are seen as monuments to the donor. The Pusey drive of the later 1950s included requests for close to $40 million for buildings and equipment. This allocation reflects largely the attitudes of donors. Certainly a strong case can be made for the medical center, additional houses, the William James Building for the Social Sciences, the Loeb Theatre, etc. Yet a case can be made out for less expenditures for physical and more for personal capital.

A few instances where donors came out against use of their gifts for the physical plant are of some interest. Thus, in offering funds for the Zoological Museum in 1859, Francis Gray ruled that "no part of said Fund shall ever be expended for real estate."

The Ira Greenleaf Bequest (1887) stipulated that "no part of such income and profit or of the principal, of said Trust Fund, shall be used or appropriated to the repair of any buildings occupied by or intended to be occupied by said Library."

In 1861, Jonathan Phillips left $20,000 to the college, but no money for erection or repair of buildings or purchasing or acquiring any title or interest in real estate. The Edgar Pierce (1929) bequest included a letter to this effect: "I do not wish it [the bequest] to be used for buildings or care of buildings."[58]

While on the subject of buildings, I comment on the Harkness gifts of about $13 million (1929-1930) which made possible the Harvard House Plan. Many would have preferred the use of this money for faculty salaries. But, as is often true, the money was not available for this purpose. President Lowell's preparedness for this gift and Yale's reluctance explain the offer of this gift by a Yale man to Harvard.

On numerous occasions, the Harvard authorities stressed the extent to which investments in lands and buildings impaired the financial strength of the universities. Thus, in 1882, Eliot estimated expenditures for purchases of land and the erection or reconstruction of buildings since September, 1869, at $2,300,000. But only $510,000 yielded income; the remainder was unproductive. The president thereupon asked for funds, especially for faculty salaries, annuities and scholarships, care of the indispensable plant, and especially unrestricted funds.[59]

Help to the Faculty

On a number of occasions friends of Harvard offered, aside from the usual gifts for financing salaries, special help to the faculty.

In 1883, a donor gave the college a substantial sum which he hoped would raise the salary of the president from $5,000 and use of a house to a maximum of $10,000.[60]

In 1942, W. M. Kendall offered the college his real estate at Sutton, Maine, as well as $25,000. "I desire that said property may be offered for occupancy, free of rent, to such members of the teaching staff. . .as may from time to time be selected.[61]

Gifts in the USA

From 1871 to 1896, gifts to institutions of higher learning amounted to $154 million.

57. H. Yeomans, *op. cit.*, p. 256.
58. *Endowment Funds of Harvard University*, pp. 50, 69, 70, 394.
59. *Ibid.*, 1881-1882, pp. 50-51.
60. *Endowment Funds of Harvard University*, pp. 24-25.
61. *Ibid.*, p. 397.

Gifts in millions of dollars

	1871-1896	1871	1896
Universities and colleges	117.4	3.43	8.34
Colleges for women	7.5	–	.61
Professional schools	22.8	.55	1.16
Schools of technology	6.5	–	1.0
Total	154.2	3.98	11.11

Source: Universities and Their Sons, 1897.

Harvard's share of the total is of some interest. In general, the college and university share has declined little in view of the growth of professional schools, women's colleges, and schools of technology.

Percent of Total Benefactors to Higher Education: Colleges and Universities, 1871-1896

1871-1896	76
1871	86
1896	75

Over roughly the same years, Harvard's endowment rose by about $10 million or 6 to 7 percent of the gifts for all institutions of higher learning in these years. The total of *gifts* would of course be much larger and may well amount to 10 to 15 percent of all gifts.

36

Gifts and Their Uses, 1636-1900

A table below gives the history of gifts to Harvard for the period 1636-1900, or the first 264 years. Here are the results:

Total gifts by individuals. For roughly equal periods, gifts by individuals were almost 3 times as great in the period 1711 to 1805 as from 1636 to 1710, and more than 10 times as large from 1806 to 1900 as from 1711 to 1805. Incidentally, the total of gifts through these first 264 years was only about 2 percent of the amount received in the twentieth century.

Gifts from England were substantial in the first two periods, equaling 13 and 10 percent of individual gifts. With the Revolutionary War these sources dried up.

The Colonial government was an important source of new money in these years: 38 percent of gifts of individuals in the first period; 78 percent in the second period; 8 percent in the third; and 16 percent for the 264 years.

In this connection, the following remarks by an outstanding historian of higher education are germane.

As such, they were clearly recognized as being engaged in a relationship of mutual obligation and responsibility with the state. Harvard was supported by the General Court from the moment of its birth; it relied on such support long past the colonial period. In 1652 and 1653 the General Court donated 2,000 acres of land to the college, and the next year it ordered a tax levy of £100 in its support. . . . Having done so, the General Court fulfilled its obligations to Harvard the next year by assigning the Charlestown Ferry rents to the college, a source of revenue that continued in one form or another for the next two hundred years. . . .

After the Civil War the colleges found new means of support among their alumni and among a crop of especially affluent millionaire benefactors; only then were they prepared to recognize what their unavailing petitions to the state legislatures had made clear to many others: the day of public support had ended, the private college had emerged. With this recognition developed a remarkable lapse of memory and the beginnings of a myth. Before long college presidents would be talking like President Eliot, as spokesman for rugged individualism, for the virtues of independence and freedom from state support. A partnership in public service, which had once been essential to the colleges and inherent in the responsibilities of government, now become insidious, or was forgotten altogether.[1]

Rudolph's criticisms of Eliot's views on public aid are justified:

Eliot felt that an "exhibition of diffused mental and moral energy has accompanied the establishment and development of a system of higher instruction in the

---

1. F. Rudolph, *op. cit.*, chapter 9, especially pp. 185-189; cf., pp. 13-14.

United States, with no inheritance of monastic endowments, and no gifts from royal or ecclesiastical personages disposing of great resources derived from the state, and with but scanty help from the public purse. . . . The endowment of the institutions of education, including libraries and museums, by private persons in the United States, is a phenomenon without precedent or parallel, and is a legitimate effect of democratic institutions. . . ." [2]

To what extent was money given without restrictions and to what extent with restrictions? Over the whole period nonrestrictive gifts were but 19 percent of the total (in recent years the unrestricted had been about 12 percent). But in the first period, i.e., 1636 to 1710, the unrestricted actually exceeded the restricted. Such faith in the managers of the university, in the sense that money is given with

Table 36-1.

Harvard Gifts, Sources, Kinds and Use 1636-1900, By Periods

	1636-1710	1711-1805	1806-1900	1636-1900
Total donations by individuals	$45,535	$133,384	$13,776,111	$13,955,030
Gifts–England	5,958	23,189	None	29,147
Percent of total	13	17.4	None	2
Government total	17,503	103,554	100,000	221,057
General fund total	23,655	24,525	2,578,522	2,626,702
Purpose specified	21,880	108,859	11,197,589	11,328,328
Present use	40,158	47,288	4,685,748	4,773,194
Permanent endowment	5,377	86,096	9,090,363	9,181,836
Amount to pious and indigent students	2,174	7,879	306,870	316,923
Professors	0	61,247	1,017,080	1,078,327
Fellowships and scholarships	3,429	2,740	806,365	812,534
Library	3,751	10,073	943,084	956,908
Gifts	30,116	82,056	6,179,209	6,291,381
Bequests	15,419	51,328*	7,596,902	7,663,649

Sources: Quincy, *op. cit.;* Barnard, "Grants and Donations to Harvard College," in *American Journal of Education,* vol. IX, Sept. 1860; *Reports of the President of Harvard College,* 1852-1900; *Reports of the Treasurer of Harvard College,* 1852-1900; J. B. Sears, compiler, *Philanthropy in American Higher Education,* 1922, pp. 23-24. (My calculations).

*Error in raw data, gifts quoted, 66 percent, bequests, 44 percent. The latter was changed to 34 percent.

2. Henry James, *Charles W. Eliot: President of Harvard   University,* vol. II, p. 274.

discretion of use to the president and fellows, did not prevail for long.

Present use or permanent endowment? Under stress, current gifts tend to become especially important, for a given sum of current gifts yields much more income in a short period than endowment money. That fact explains the unusual relationship of the years from 1636 to 1710: funds given for current use were 8 times as large as endowment funds. By the next period the relationship was greatly changed; endowment money received was close to 2 times as much as current money; and for the 264 years, twice as large. In more recent years, gifts for current use have risen to a point where they exceed new endowment.

How Much for Various Purposes? This breakdown is only of limited value, in large part because such items as gifts for the plant, equipment, and commons are omitted. In the first period scholarships, fellowships, and aid to indigent students accounted for about two-thirds of the gifts for specific purpose considered in this breakdown, and the library for about one-third. In the second period, gifts to finance professors became the dominant item, accounting for about three-quarters of the value of items listed, with the library and student aid accounting for the remainder in roughly equal amounts. In the final period, there is a roughly equal allocation among the three uses, with student aid the largest and professors next.

Gifts or Bequests? In the first and second periods, gifts exceeded bequests by substantial amounts. But in the third period, bequests moved ahead of gifts.

Some Details, Eighteenth and Nineteenth Centuries

The great benefactors in the early eighteenth century were Thomas Hollis and his family. From 1718 to 1726, Mr. Hollis gave more than £4,800 to endow two professorships and provide scholarships for ten students. In 1732-1733, the Hollis family added two more scholarships and increased the endowment for professorships with a donation of £1,050.

In the years 1712 to 1740, bequests averaged about £200 a year. In this period, of the bequests, scholarships accounted for 50 percent; endowment for professors, 25 percent; and unrestricted, 25 percent. Scholarships financed by bequests were much more important and professorial help less so than the allocations for the eighteenth century generally from *both bequests and gifts*. The era of endowed professorships had not really taken hold yet.

After the Harvard fire of 1764, alumni and friends responded with great generosity. Of special interest is the geographical origin of the £3,475 estimated as received. Great Britain, with £1,496, was the largest source, and Boston, with £1,204, next. Salem gave £114; Cambridge, £61; the New Hampshire Legislature, £300; private gifts from New Hampshire, £50; and most of the rest was received from other towns in Massachusetts, e.g., Marblehead, Gloucester, Worcester.[3]

Between 1807 and 1827, total gifts, bequests, and subscriptions came to $149,069. Bequests accounted for a little more than one-third; gifts from living donors, less than one-quarter; and subscriptions, a new approach, to about 40 percent. In this period bequests were much less important relatively than in the whole century.

Of the total sum of $149,069, professorships accounted for two-thirds; theological school and education, 18 percent; and the remainder was scattered among student aid (only 1 percent), collections (4 percent), the library (1½ percent), prizes, the medical school, the observatory, and other items. The library in particular did not profit as much from all gifts between 1807 and 1827 as from the itemized amounts in the later nineteenth century.[4]

---

3. *Donation Book,* vol. I, p. 70; Quincy, *op. cit.,* vol. II, p. 484.

4. *Donation Book*, 1776-1839, in Harvard University Archives, I, 15.420; *Endowment Funds of Harvard University*, Gifts and Bequests, A. T. Gibbs, in Harvard University Archives, I, 15.450.

Gifts, 1827 to 1857	
Gifts from living persons	$150,000
Bequests	603,000
Subscriptions	97,000
Alumni organization	9,000
Total	858,000

Unlike the first quarter of the century bequests stand out, accounting for 70 percent of the total. Both subscriptions and gifts from living persons provided much less relatively than in the first quarter of the century.

Both in this period and the first quarter (actually twenty years) of the century the total amounts received were small compared to the century total: only 1 percent of the year's total in the first quarter and 6 percent in the second quarter (actually thirty years).

The Largest Items, 1827-1857

	Thousands of Dollars	Percent
Professorships	229	27
Observatory	147	17
Library	134	16
Student aid	117	12
Museums	105	12
Appleton Chapel	50	6
Lawrence Scientific School building	27	4

In these thirty years, students and the library did not participate as much as in the century, for the limited items given for that period. The explanation is clear: the vogue for the observatory and museums was in substantial part responsible. Unrestricted gifts seem to have touched a low—2 percent. But the Gore gift of $100,000 was in fact also unrestricted, but not added to the stock fund.[5]

A milestone was the Gore Estate, valued in 1837-1838 at $100,000 and unrestricted in use. The college built its first great library out of the Gore

funds, at a cost of $73,512 or twice the original estimate.[6]

In the second quarter of the nineteenth century, the college stressed such items as the observatory, museums, chapels, etc., and not student aid or professorships. Thus the treasurer in 1845-1846 gave as the three most pressing needs: a new and larger chapel; a sufficient and permanent fund for maintenance and increase of the library; a means of procuring scientific apparatus of all descriptions, including a permanent fund in support of astronomy, natural history and the botanic gardens. The chapel, the library (Gore), and the Phillips Fund for the observatory were the responses.[7]

Increased competition and the Unitarian movement in Cambridge were also a deterrent to getting gifts. At the beginning of the Revolution, there were 9 colleges; by 1861, 250 had opened and 182 still survived. One Amherst graduate, explaining the founding of Amherst, remarked that in a commonwealth of Puritans there was much need "of a college . . . not quite so far west as Williams, and not quite so far toward Plato as Cambridge." The president of Williams often asked his students to remember people of Boston in their prayers.[8]

On occasion, members of families who were deprived of inheritances because money was given to Harvard were not very happy. Thus, S. Rumford complained that his father had provided a foundation for Harvard while he was left destitute. His father, Rumford claimed, had made an unfortunate marriage which contributed to his irritability and bad treatment of his son. The son now wrote: ". . . I cannot say that I have a particular wish to derange the donation entirely, only to receive some if not all the money during my life-time. . . ."[9]

5. *Reports of the President of Harvard College*, 1827-1857; *Reports of the Treasurer of Harvard College*, 1827-1857.

6. *Report of the Treasurer of Harvard College*, 1833-1834, p. 2; 1834-1835, pp. 1-2; 1837-1838, p. 1; 1842-1843; p. 6; *Treasurers' Ledgers*, 1838-1868, p. 28.

7. *Report of the Treasurer of Harvard College*, 1845-1846, pp. 5-10; *Report of the President of Harvard College*, 1847-1848, p. 15; 1853-1854. pp. 9-12.

8. Rudolph, *op. cit.*, p. 55.

9. S. Rumford to the President of Cambridge University, February 24, 1828.

37

Methods of Raising Money

Restraints on Begging

Throughout its history Harvard has been dependent on gifts. In the first seventy-five years or so almost half the private gifts and bequests (exclusive of real estate and annuities) came from England. Harvard's survival depended on gifts, for students could afford very little tuition in these early years. Many of the gifts came unsolicited, but many more were the result of active campaigns. An expedition to England in 1641 was instructed "but with this caution that they should not seek supply of our wants in any dishonorable way, as by begging or the like, for we were resolved to wait upon the Lord in the use of all means which were lawful and honorable."[1]

The 1641 expedition was quite successful. The beggars returned with £500. But this was only a beginning. In support of the searching for funds in England, the college produced the famous *New England First Fruits* (1643). President Dunster probably compiled Part II "In respect of the college and the proceedings of Learning therein. . ."

Others gave to the Colledge and advance of learning which was paid (some little towards the building of the Colledge per Bill, some to the President for his great laboure taken upon request of the Feoffees of the Colledge some laid out for Utensills, for the Colledge by their desires as pewter, brass, Ironware,

lynnen, some laid out in Bookes to supply their Library) and for erecting a schoole att Roxbury, besides two Schollarships of £5 per annum, apiece settled forever on the Colledge.[2]

From the early eighteenth century until Eliot's day the flow of gifts from government and private sources was helpful, in fact, indispensable, but not in large amounts. When occasion demanded, the college sought funds with zeal. In 1843, the appearance of the "magnificent apparition of the Comet of 1843" attracted attention to the heavens and offered President Quincy an opportunity to obtain funds for an observatory and equip it with the necessary apparatus, especially with an equatorial telescope, a duplicate of the one at Poulkovo near St. Petersburg. Quincy obtained the necessary funds:

. . .with small urgency, from the enlightened munificence of the capitalists and merchants of Massachusetts, chiefly of Boston, who entered into the plan with a zeal highly favorable to their intelligence and liberality. This was the crowning glory of the administration, and fitly rounded it by service of enduring value to the university and to the world.[3]

In some respects methods of raising money in the first half of the nineteenth century were similar to practices today. Thus, in 1841, the occasion was finding funds for building a room for meetings on the day

---

1. Margery Somers Foster, *"Out of Smalle Beginnings . . . ", An Economic History of Harvard College in the Puritan Period 1636-1712,* 1962, chapter VI, especially pp. 107, 114.

2. *Founding of Harvard College,* pp. 305-306.
3. E. Quincy, *Life of Josiah Quincy,* 1874, pp. 471-472.

before commencement. Charles Francis Adams was invited and a committee named.

The object of the meeting was to organize sub-divisions of the Alumni in each place upon whom shall devolve the business of exciting their companions in this business. . . .Mr. Loring [Chairman] made a remark on its extraordinary state of apathy toward the College of those who were its graduates. . . .[4]

It has been a Harvard tradition, at least since Eliot's day, that presidents do not solicit funds. President Pusey may well have broken with tradition during the program for Harvard College. He and Dean Bundy set out on a 20,000-mile financial odyssey. The president could concentrate on the $82,500,000 drive because he was fortunate in having a brilliant and effective dean of the faculty in McGeorge Bundy.

President Eliot's fixed rule was no solicitation. He liked to tell the story of one exception to this rule. He wrote Mr. Austin, the donor of Austin Hall, for a subscription to the divinity school. Austin wrote back: "I do not give a damn for the Divinity School but the President of Harvard College ought not to write a letter for less than one hundred dollars and I enclose my check for that amount."[5]

On this issue Jerome D. Greene, secretary of the Harvard Corporation under Eliot, was eloquent. In his view, the task of the president was to think constantly about ways of improving the university and to maintain high standards for both students and faculty. The Harvard community has too great a regard for the president and the university to tolerate his wasting his time in the undignified task of begging.[6]

During Eliot's forty years endowment increased from $2,400,000 to $22,700,000. Not solicitation but approval of his ideas explained this tremendous gain:

President Eliot obtained large gifts for Harvard by developing new ideas in higher education and vigorously discussing them both publicly and privately. Notable among these ideas were new theories of medical and legal education and the founding of the Graduate School of Business Administration. He was himself such an important public figure that his annual reports and innumerable speeches formed excellent publicity media. In days when the competition for philanthropic funds was nothing like what it is today, his method, sometimes assisted by Bishop Lawrence, was eminently successful.[7]

Eliot's avoidance of direct involvement does not mean that others refrained. A good example is the financing and building of Memorial Hall, a financial responsibility entrusted to Colonel Henry Lee. Funds flowed in slowly. It became necessary for the university to invest such funds until the required money was had; and there was an overt or tacit agreement that Lee would invest on behalf of the college. Lee invested in Western railroad bonds that yielded as much as 10 percent. In 1870 the college laid the cornerstone; and 1873, a depression year and hence a good year to build, was not the year to sell bonds. But the finance committee demanded the money whereupon Lee borrowed the money at 8 percent and held on to the bonds. When the note fell due Lee paid his debt and received back the securities which had risen to a record price. The college now demanded the profit. "Colonel Lee was at first irritated at the demand which seemed somewhat on the 'heads I win, tails you lose' principle; but after a little reflection he decided to make the payment."[8]

In 1892, William James, the Harvard psychologist and philosopher, wrote to his brother about another interesting episode. He tried to get some funds from the elder John Rockefeller.

. . . We have also had another scheme, at the various stages of which you, Balzac, or Howells ought to have been present, to work up for a University newly founded by the American millionaire. In this case the

4. Henry Adams and W. G. Roelker (ed.), *Extracts from Diaries of John Quincy Adams (1787) and His Son Charles Francis Adams (1825)*, 1909, pp. 13-14.
5. Harvard University Archives, UAV 828.142.
6. *Ibid.*, appendix A.
7. *Ibid.*, pp. 7-8.
8. J. T. Morse, Jr., *op. cit.*, pp. 127-129.

millionaire had announced his desire to found a pro-
fessorship of psychology applied to education. The
thing was to get it for Harvard, which he mistrusted. I
went at him tooth and nail, trying to persuade him
that Royce was the man. Letters, pour-parlers, visits
(he lives in N.Y.), finally a two-day's visit and a din-
ner for him. He is a real Balzackian figure—a regular
porker, coarse, vulgar, vain, cunning, mendacious,
etc., etc. The worse of it is that he will probably give
us nothing,—having got all the attention and flattery
from us at which he aimed,—so that we have our
labor for our pains, and the gods laugh as they say
"served them right." 9

Early Drives

A program in 1904 to raise $2,500,000 in order to increase salaries of faculty members was the major effort under President Eliot. The responsible committee was "to keep the movement as natural, spontaneous, informal and unsensational as possible." The college enlisted the aid of about twenty Harvard men who gave $50,000 each, and for the first time shifted efforts from State Street to New York.[10]

Despite the low tempo of the activites this campaign, for what in those days was a tremendous effort, was a complete success.

Harvard's great success in 1904, 1919 and 1924-1925 owed a great deal to the skill of Bishop Lawrence. The bishop seemed to believe that his acquaintanceship with many people helped him in raising money. He had confirmed at least 50,000 or 60,000.[11]

Lowell's Approach

In some respects Lowell followed the Eliot tradition. He gave to Harvard the concentration program, the House Plan, the Society of Fellows, freshmen dormitories, and the modern tutorial system. These were magnets for attracting money. But Lowell's Harvard added something: the zeal inspired by the appeals of the Red Cross and other war groups during World War I.[12]

Harvard's drive for $15 million in 1919-1920 was unprecedented. When earlier asked why the goal was $10 million (later raised) President Lowell replied "...We did not fix on $10,000,000. It is impossible for the officers of the University to say that we need so much and no more, because the field is infinite...."[13]

The campaign was unprecedented in the amounts sought, in the organization achieved, in the efforts made. A British paper, *The Spectator,* commented on the fact that in contrast to Cambridge (England) and Oxford, which needed money badly but did nothing, Harvard authorities were sturdy beggars in a good cause; "...although the Oxford commonrooms would perhaps be shocked if they saw the frank and ingenious appeals which are being circulated by these energetic Harvard Men...."[14]

In this campaign the usual slogans for help to Harvard were found: Education is America's greatest need; the alumnus owes the college the difference between costs and tuition; a gift to Harvard is a permanent (but is it?) gift "that will continue to do good as long as Harvard lives;" the non-Harvard man owes Harvard help after he gives to his own college.[15]

In this campaign, the organization was unprecedented. What was expected of Harvard men was made clear. For example, those with incomes of $5,000 or under should give 1 to 2 percent per year for five years; $25,000 to $50,000, 5 percent per year for five years, $100,000 and up, 10 percent per year for five years.

The managers stressed the need of educated men; the contributions of Harvard in war and the needs in

---

9. H. James (ed.), *The Letters of William James,* 1920, vol. I, p. 318.
10. Harvard University Archives, UAV 136.122.2; "Teachers' Endowment Fund of Harvard College," in *Harvard Graduates Magazine,* vol. XIII, no. 52, pp. 619-621, June, 1905.
11. W. Lawrence, *op. cit.,* p. 91.

12. Harvard University Archives, UAV, 828.142, pp. 8-9.
13. *Ibid.,* UAV 136.124.273.
14. "A Hint from Harvard," in *The Spectator,* vol. 123, no. 4, p. 765, October 25, 1919.
15. Harvard University Archives, UAV 136.124.5; 124.8.

peace; the inadequate pay of the faculty, with resultant losses to government and industry; the steady deficits with resultant erosion of free capital; the need of resources for research[16]

A few special features of the $15 million drive need mention. The organization was unique. For the first time the objective would be to tap the small as well as the large contributor. The managers divided their potential donors among seventy geographic areas and in addition there were classifications by college classes (inviting heavy competition), and also, in some places, by occupation. The college availed itself of the running start technique; that is, to scrutinize the twenty to thirty wealthiest men of each class with a view to finding substantial gifts at the outset.[17]

A fund of about one million dollars, devoted to research, came under the will of William F. Milton of the class of 1858. He had been just the kind of student Lowell wished to arouse. Indolent and uninterested, Milton was one boy lolling on a back bench when Professor Sophocles asked the class how a Greek came to carve lions on the gate of Mycenae. The bright boys were ready with their answers: The lions were mythological; the sculptor had traveled abroad; earlier forms of Greek animal life had been preserved in fossils; they were purely imaginary, and the like. At last the dissatisfied instructor came to Milton.
"Saw 'em in a circus," replied the bored young man.
"Mr. Milton is quite right. The Greek chieftains were in the habit of collecting animals from far and near, and undoubtedly the sculptor had seen them in some royal menagerie."
It was Dr. Walcott's suggestion that Milton's lucky shot made him a changed man. He had distinguished himself in competition with the best in this class and he liked and remembered the feeling.[18]

That the approach was not always a gentle one is indicated by the following.

I understand that Ivers Adams is back in Boston for a week or two. He is reputed to have made a large amount of money during the war. He will probably not stay beyond the Harvard-Yale game, as he follows the shooting and golf season. Someone ought to get hold of him. I think he uses the Harvard Club a good deal.

The man who spoke to me about it thinks he could well give $25,000.[19]

In 1924, a committee "to extend the national service of Harvard University" was to raise $10 million for chemistry, fine arts, and the business school. The appeal was to all Americans, but with a minimum of organization. "Since the constituency to be appealed to was a small one, and all the work would be personal, the organization was simple, almost rudimentary."[20]

Behind the campaign was the theory that a few hundred or a few thousand citizens could be found who could be persuaded of Harvard's large contribution in the past and that by giving now they could greatly increase Harvard's product.[21]

The Tercentenary Appeal

President Conant stated the issues well.[22] But the number of subscribers was disappointing: only 1,000 exclusive of the regular subscribers to the annual Harvard Fund, as compared with 17,278 for the 1919 drive.[23]

President Conant's drive during the tercentenary was not successful. Yet President Conant stood out in his years at Harvard as probably the outstanding educator in the country just as Eliot had in the years

16. *Ibid.,* UAV 136.124.273; 124.8; 124.4.
17. See *Ibid.,* 136.124.2-5, 10; 136.124.273; R. M. Saltonstall, "Harvard's New Endowment," in *Harvard Graduates Magazine,* vol. XXV, p. 313, March, 1917.
18. H. Yeomans, *op. cit.,* p. 247.
19. Harvard University Archives, UAV 136.124.5.

20. Harvard University Archives, UAI 10.450.10.
21. *Ibid.*
22. *Report of the President of Harvard College,* 1934-1935, pp.6-7.
23. Harvard University Archives, UAV 828.2.2.

1869 to 1909. Then why was the money not forthcoming? One reason clearly was the unsatisfactory economic conditions. A second was the manner of the campaign. Conant was anxious that any fund raising be incidental to the tercentenary celebration; that no large publicity campaign be undertaken; that no begging or strong pressures be exercised. An outside advisory group commented "Those alumni who showed any contagious enthusiasm were regrettably few." Again, apparently, the university professorships and national scholarships did not attract great enthusiasm.

In one respect the administration advanced beyond earlier campaigns. The authorities selected 1,000 prospects, carefully analyzed their backgrounds, and studied, rated, and assigned prospects. In fact, the university anticipated gifts of $25,000 or over from these prospects. Actually, more than half the gifts were for $25,000 or less.

It may well be that the Harvard contribution to the New Deal alienated many potential donors. Yet similar problems in 1919 did not preclude a successful campaign. One excellent statement by Henry James deserves quotation.

During the next generation what trouble there is will occur on the social science front. The whole world is changing its social and political institutions. It is going to keep on doing it and nobody can arrest the process. The result is that all discussion of political economy, sociology, constitutional law and social philosophy is likely, at almost any point and almost any moment, to get involved in issues about which people are divided and hotly divided. Are the universities, for the sake of avoiding criticism and living in an unperturbed atmosphere, to refrain from wrestling with these hot modern social and political questions? If they do, they will drift out of the main current of modern civilization. Their function of intellectual leadership will pass to the newspapers and the radio

or what not. But if they are to take part, and we hope in the long run to be helpful, then it is absolutely certain that some of their professors and some of their graduates and undergraduates will be constantly giving violent offense to one strong element in the public or another. [24]

That the soft sell was not universal even in 1936 is attested by the approach to President Roosevelt.

Nobody has yet spoken to the President so far as I know, and when it is done, you certainly need not expect any overpoweringly generous response. I do think, however, that we ought to get a thousand dollars out of him. If he gives only fifty, I hope to Heaven you publish the fact.[25]

An interesting episode: Ernst Hanfstaengl, Hitler's court musician and a Harvard graduate, had offered Harvard $1,000 which Conant refused to accept. But for the campaign, Harvard graduates were solicited abroad. To the embarrassment of the university Hitler's friend, responding to the new solicitation, now sent $10,000.[26]

The Program for Harvard College

The program for Harvard College (1956-1960) was a great success, yielding more than the $82,500,000 goal set. Good organization; heroic efforts by President Pusey, Dean Bundy, Alexander White, and many other friends of Harvard; the prosperous conditions; the diversified use of the funds to be raised and hence wider appeal; the absence of any so-called radical movement; the help of the fund raising firm of Kersting and Brown; the low costs of operation (3 percent of the "take"), the delay of widespread appeals by Harvard since the famous 1919 effort, the appeal to alumni that emphasized the availability of public funds for competitors all contributed to the success of the *Program for Harvard College*. An appeal to members of the governing board, past and

24. *Ibid.*, 828.142; for more details of the campaign, see 182.2; 211.2.2; 268.5; 272; G. P. Gardner, "The Three Hundredth Anniversary Fund," in *Harvard Alumni Bulletin*, April 10, 1936, p. 823.

25. Harvard University Archives, UAV 828.3.
26. *Ibid.*, UAV 828.214.

present, yielded $10,500,000 and served as a catalyst for the campaign.

In the late 1950s the medical school surprised most observers by raising about $50 million. Doctors were not supposed to be generous contributors. But high incomes of physicians, the prestige of the medical school, and the excellent organization for the drive with the important help of that unusual administrator Dean George Berry account for this remarkable performance. No other medical school has so far approached this achievement of Harvard.

Another interesting drive is one of equal proportions initiated in 1967 under Dean Franklin Ford for undergraduate science. I suspect that putting through a drive such as the Harvard program in the 1950s can be undertaken only once in a lifetime by the president. It is not then surprising that Dean Ford rather than President Pusey assumes the major responsibility here.

Annual Funds

As early as the first part of the twentieth century an occasional voice had been raised for annual funds and President Eliot had foreshadowed the developments.[27] This is not surprising since Yale had been seeking funds annually since the early 1890s.

In 1902-1903, the class of 1879 presented the college with an anniversary gift for its twenty-fifth reunion. President Eliot was quick to see the possibilities of exploiting the twenty-fifth annual gift, of tying it to annual giving and generally of organizing alumni for fund raising.

Some of the influential alumni during the 1919 campaign hoped that an annual fund would forestall the repetition of such a campaign as the 1919 one.

It was not until 1925 that the Harvard Fund Council came into existence, and despite the early skepticism of President Lowell.[28] The emphasis was on unrestricted gifts sorely needed by the college. "Its single purpose is to provide the University each year with money to be used to such ends as the President and Fellows may direct." By 1966 the twenty-fifth Anniversary Gift exceeded $650,000, and the Harvard College Fund reached $2,600,000. By 1969, the program called for $3,700,000 of receipts for the fund.[29]

A class agent wrote as follows:

Relatively few have been called to the peculiar office of class agent. But every College alumnus has suffered from one. A curious sort of creature he is, a kind of mosquito, probably of the genus culex (commonly pronounced "collects"), which regularly once or twice a year stings every member of his class, sucking forth draughts of silver, and occasionally of golden, blood.[30]

A class agent noted that alumni find many reasons for not giving: riots, for example. Why do faculty members consider them a joke? Yale has dealt effectively with the problem. Harvard has not. Hence, no contribution. The dissident argued that the university should find an antiriot serum. But the class agent reminded him "that after a Yale victory in the 1890s he had deprived a cop of his "helmet and billy and sat on him in the gay 90's."[31]

The Harvard fund has steadily risen in amounts and importance, for $1 million per year yield the same income as $20 million of endowment. This is especially effective because the gifts are not restrictive. The $3,300,000 goal already achieved will bring income equal to that on $66 million.[32]

27. *Report of the President of Harvard College*, 1905-1906, p. 48; 1906-1907, p. 46; 1907-1908, p. 47; see also M. Reed, "The Deficit: How to Meet It," in *Harvard Graduates Magazine*, vol. XII, pp. 532-536, 1904; Harvard University Archives, 1905, UAV 136.122.2; 124.2; 124.8; HUD 3411.226A; 237.

28. Harvard University Archives, UAV.136.124.11; Yeomans, *op. cit.*, p. 252.

29. Harvard University Archives, HUD 3411, 3411.226A; Yeomans, *op. cit.*, p. 251; "Fortieth Annual College Fund, 1965-1966," in *Harvard Alumni Bulletin*, October 21, 1968.

30. "Reveries of a Class Agent," in *Harvard Alumni Bulletin*, Vol. 40, p. 1012, June 3, 1938.

31. *Ibid.*, p. 1013.

32. *Harvard Alumni Bulletin*, October 21, 1968.

Table 37-1.

Annual contributions and contributors to
Harvard fund, various years

	1926	1929	1933	1939	1946	1958	1967
Total contributors	3,305	5,976	6,626	10,678	14,485	10,397	21,847
Total amount	$124,000	$178,000	$66,000	$107,000	$322,000	$1,336,000*	$3,004,000
Average contribution	$37.81	29.75	9.97	10.57	22.71	128.46	137.48
Percent contributors of college alumni	12.9	20.5	20.4	28.3	33.6		39.8

*Inclusive of some gifts to the Harvard College Program.

Sources: Harvard University Archives, HUD 3411, 3411.226; *Forty-first Annual Report, the Harvard College Fund, 1966-1967.*

A weakness of annual giving is that it reflects economic conditions. Thus from 1929 to 1933, the number of contributors rose by 11 percent, but the average contribution declined by about two-thirds. Even by 1939, total contributions and the average contribution were substantially below those of 1926 or 1929; but the numbers donating had greatly increased. By 1946, however, large improvements had been achieved by all criteria.

Some General Observations

Throughout its history Harvard depended heavily on gifts. Before the nineteenth century, the government contributed substantially to Harvard's needs. But once the economy began to yield large private incomes, the dependence was increasingly on private sources and particularly on the relatively affluent. It was not until Lowell's day that attempts were again made to tap the many as well as the rich. But even then the affluent contributed the largest sums.

Eliot was not inclined to beg. He would depend on the quality of the University's output as a magnet. At one point he remarked:

. . . The most effectual means of procuring new gifts is to demonstrate that all previous gifts have been used with consideration for the givers' wishes, with safety as regards the permanence of the trusts, and with discretion as regards their steady usefulness . . . .[33]

Lowell and Pusey abandoned the nonbegging image of Eliot. We have discussed the Pusey program of the 1950s. Lowell tended to minimize his abilities as a beggar.

Eliot indeed, despite his denials, was an aggressive seeker of funds when confronted with access to the Morgans', Rockefellers' and Weyerhausers'. Lowell covered more ground. He was ready when Harkness broached his college plan and thus obtained between $13 and $14 million which Yale should have had. Somehow, in the midst of the depression, Harvard received bequests of several million from the Wyeths and from Artemas Ward. The latter apparently obtained his income from penny slot machines in the New York subways. The president cultivated Higginson with great effectiveness, and sought access to any rich man who might be interested in his freshmen dormitories, the tutorial system, the House Plan, or the junior fellows. He expanded the $10 million drive of 1915 to $15 million and sought even to raise it to

33. C. W. Eliot, *University Administration,* 1908, p. 17.

$20 million. Rosenwald, the great philantropist, was not interested in higher education, but Lowell pressed him through the intermediary of Judge Mack. Lowell also greatly improved methods. He integrated programs and allowed appeals only if they were not in competition with his major objectives. If the depression had not interfered, he would probably have launched a $20 million campaign in 1931.[34]

34. See especially A. L. Lowell to Judge J. Mack, September 4, 1914 and J. P. Morgan to A. L. Lowell, June 22, 1917 in *A. L. Lowell Papers, 1914-1917*, F.s 113, 963; Memo H. S. Thompson to A. L. Lowell, June 6, 1919, *A. L. Lowell Papers*, 1917-1919, F-1981; A. L. Lowell to H. Yeomans, January 23, 1919, *A. L. Lowell Papers, 1922-1925*, F-621; H. Shattuck to A. L. Lowell, May 8, 1932 in *A. L. Lowell Papers, 1930-1933*, F-756.

38

Sources of Money

The Large Contributors

For the most part Harvard has leaned on the wealthy. This was true in the nineteenth century and earlier, when business leaders such as Gore, S. Eliot, Abbott Lawrence, and Phillips donated large sums to Harvard. And it was even more true later. One of the largest early gifts was by Governor Stoughton, the unrepentant witch hanger, who gave Harvard Stoughton Hall. Both presidents Eliot and Lowell skillfully mobilized the affluent families on behalf of Harvard. Acknowledging a gift from Mr. Thayer in 1885, Eliot remarked "it is pleasant to see the young heirs of considerable fortunes like Hemenway, George A. Nickerson, Weld and Thayer, taking to educational benefactions."[1]

Henry Higginson, the Boston financier, scouted for President Lowell. In the 1920s Baker presented the university a new $5 million plant for the business school. In 1912, Higginson reported that Baker:

....is very rich and continually is increasing his money... If you should present him something as a monument just as Stillman [infirmary] and Robinson [school of design] have monuments to them, it might attract him....

I also think that, with these men, a large thing is much more attractive than a small one[2]...

Higginson also reported on two other good prospects.

As to Henry Cabot...he may not have very much money, but his mother has a good many millions, if I can guess straight. The Cabot family can give $100,000 and not know it, and they cannot have a better chance.

As for Robert Paine, he is reported to have inherited $2,000,000. He certainly has bought a handsome house...keeps a large yacht and spends freely. Both of those fellows are great money-makers or savers, or both, and if they have any bowels, they will help you....[3]

With the help of J. P. Morgan, Jr., Lowell enlisted the support of Mrs. Sage, who gave $125,000 additional to finish a dormitory. At the same time Lowell could announce the gift to finance the Widener Library.[4]

E. H. Wells was another helpful scout. He explored the possibilities in the Philadelphia area. Edgar Scott was a likely victim. He had attended Harvard and was married into a Harvard family. Scott was rich and generous and the son of the former president of

---

1. C. W. Eliot to E. W. Hooper (tresurer), August 13, 1885.
2. H. L. Higginson to President A. Lawrence Lowell, March 25, 1912.

3. H. L. Higginson to President A. Lawrence Lowell, October 17, 1911.
4. A. Lawrence Lowell to J. P. Morgan, Junior, July 23, 1912; J. P. Morgan, Junior, to A. Lawrence Lowell, July 25, 1912.

the Pennsylvania Railroad. He wanted to send his older boy to Yale, but his wife preferred Harvard.

J. P. Morgan, Jr., was another scout for Harvard. He reported to President Lowell that Mrs. Morris Jessup "may be induced to give as much as $150,000..."[5]

August Belmont was another possible catch. John Storer reported that Belmont:

...at first emphatically said that he would not give us a cent, he said, as I left him, "I shall probably give you something before you have closed your list."...In connection with this, I would say, confidentially, he was feeling very sore and hurt because when he took his beautiful young wife to see the Harvard-Yale football game, he had been put in a seat out of the way behind the goal posts, which obstructed his view of the course....[6]

In a memorandum to himself, President Lowell noted that Charles P. Searles is supposed to have $40 to $50 million. Lowell observed that Hubbard was his counsel and his brokers were Parkinson and Burr. Lowell hoped to gain access to this wealthy man through them.[7]

Despite the thorough work of Harvard's friends, the college was not always successful. Andrew Carnegie replied cordially but said that he had decided years ago that "I should not use any of my funds to aid the large universities."[8]

On occasion the money-raising activities directed toward the wealthy was a source of embarrassment. Mr. Busch, the beer baron, had given Harvard $50,000 toward building a Germanic Museum. President Eliot wrote:

You have doubtless heard that the extreme temperance people in this country find much fault with Professor Munsterberg's article on the advantageous use of alcohol. Among their other charges against him, they say that Mr. Busch's offer to give $50,000 to the Germanic Museum is a piratical recognition of Munsterberg's recent service to the brewers.[9]

Small Contributors

On proper occasions the appeal would also be made to small contributors and particularly with the development of the Harvard annual fund drives. Among the campaigns with some emphasis on the modest philanthropist were those to build Phillips Brooks House, programs on behalf of the divinity schools, and the 1855 campaign to raise $3,000 for chimes. Here the appeals had to be to the low-income groups.[10]

Gifts for the library came from the many with modest incomes and the few with large incomes. Such well known men as Bishop Berkeley, Thomas Hollis, and Thomas Carlyle contributed to the Harvard Library. Carlyle commented as follows:

...I have now, after due considerations as to the feasibilities...decided to fulfill a fond notion that has been hovering in my mind these many years; and I do therefore hereby bequeath the books (whatever of them I could not borrow, but had to buy and gather, that is, in general whatever of them are still here) which I used in writing on Cromwell and Fredrick and which shall be accurately searched for, and parted from my other books, to the President and Fellows of Harvard College...as a poor testimony of my respect for the Alma Mater of so many of my transatlantic friends and a token of the feelings above indicated towards the Great Country of which Harvard is the chief School.[11]

5. A. L. Lowell to Right Reverend William Lawrence, D.D., February 24, 1911.
6. J. H. Storer to A. Lawrence Lowell, February 6, 1912.
7. Possible Benefactors, A.L.L., March 15, 1912, in *A. L. Lowell Papers.*
8. A. Carnegie to President Lowell, May 9, 1912.
9. C. W. Eliot to Dr. Francke, October 28, 1908.

10. *Memorandum for the Purpose of Procuring a Chime of Bells,* by F. L. Betchelder, H. M. Parker, and R. H. Dana, Jr., December A.D. 1855; *Subscription for Phillips Brooks House,* April 7, 1897; *Addresses...100th Anniversary of the Harvard Divinity School,* 1917.
11. *Harvard College,* pp. 286-290.

Faculty Contributions

Over the years the faculty has contributed much to the economic resources of the college. J. R. Lowell, a Harvard professor of literature, when he was Minister to Spain, wrote from Madrid: "I buy books mainly with a view to the college library, whither they will go when I am in Mount Auburn [Cemetery], with so much undone that I might have done."[12]

Professor Shaler, the famous geologist, was largely instrumental in obtaining for Harvard rather than MIT a gift of about $20 million for engineering from Mr. McKay.[13]

In the middle of the nineteenth century, Prof. M. Cooke was largely responsible for obtaining the resources needed to establish workable facilities in chemistry and mineralogy. At a cost to himself of $100 a year, he built a laboratory that in his opinion was the best in the land. He not only donated the necessary equipment and fixtures, but he also contributed substantial amounts of money and organized subscription drives to finance the needed buildings.

Governing Board and Similar Groups

Harvard was not averse to seeking funds from its governing boards and their agents. Members of the corporation tended to be affluent businessmen. Among the most generous supporters of the university were members of the corporation, e.g., Thomas Brattle (1693-1713), John Phillips (1812-1823), Christopher Gore (1812-1820), Alexander Agassiz (1886-1890), Nathaniel Thayer (1868-1875), Henry Lee Higginson (1893-1919). President Lowell, also a member of the corporation, was a generous donor.

Overseers seemed to come from more modest economic backgrounds. In recent years, men of wealth have more often been members of the overseers—e.g., Alexander Agassiz, F. L. Higginson George Whitney, Clarence Dillon, David Rockefeller, John Kennedy, Dwight Robinson, and Thomas Lamont.

The visiting committees of the board of overseers also contribute funds to the university. Thus, in the midst of a crises in the later 1920s and early 1930s, the directors of the Fogg Museum solicited $17,500 a year from five members of the visiting committee.

Contributions by Alumni

In an earlier chapter we discussed the annual alumni drives. The beginning of alumni promotion was in the first half of the nineteenth century. Thus, the class of 1836 announced that on graduation the class would present to the college useful works, and repeat the performance in each succeeding commencement.[14]

The class of 1802 collected $4,000 for the benefit of the college by 1852. They were not yet committed to the uses to which the money was to be put.[15]

In 1852, the alumni pronounced the need of scholarships:

The Alumni of Harvard College, assembled around the festive board of Alma Mater, in July, 1852, desirous of performing some act, which shall at once redound to the good of the college, and cement more closely the bonds, which unite classmates with each other, and classes with the university, and in the hope that their act may have the recommendation of extending the benefits of Harvard College instructions to increased numbers of meritorious youth of our country, hereby assent to and adopt the following plan for establishing a system of scholarships in the college. . . .[16]

By April, 1853, the class of 1814 announced its scholarship program under the plan of 1852.[17] By

12. *Letters of J. R. Lowell,* vol. II, p. 242, quoted in *Harvard College,* p. 200.
13. Samuel Eliot Morison, (ed.), *The Development of Harvard University, 1869-1929,* 1930, p. 321.

14. *Resolution of Class of 1836,* September 8, 1836.
15. *Report of the Class of 1802 at Brattle House,* July 21, 1952.
16. College Festival, Association of the Alumni of Harvard College, July 12, 1852.
17. S. Johnson *et als,* to the Treasurer of Harvard College, 1853.

1859, an appeal to 3,000 for help to the library yielded $10,000.

A committee of the alumni on the library circulated 3,000 copies of a report to all names in the triennial catalogue, and chose between 50 and 60 members to collect subscriptions from virtually all graduates of the nineteenth century. About $10,000 had been collected.[18]

Foundations

In the relatively recent period of Harvard history, say the last hundred years, and especially in the last twenty-five years, foundations have begun to be a substantial source of financing higher education. In the latter part of the nineteenth century, the Carnegie Foundation interested itself in a program for retirement income. When the Fogg Museum was in difficulties in 1929, the general education board contributed $500,000. The general education board contributed $500,000 in 1920 to the school of education and in 1927, $750,000 to the law school.[19]

Of special interest is a plea to the general education board by President Eliot in 1907 to help launch a graduate school of business. The president anticipated that in five years adequate resources would come from tuition and endowment. In the meanwhile, help was needed. [20]

Subscriptions Drives

Around the middle of the nineteenth century, subscription drives became an effective approach to mobilizing resources. This may have been a reflection of the increasing difficulties of tapping the affluent. But this is not clear, for many of the drives concentrated on the well-to-do.

Subscription drives were not unknown even in the seventeenth century. Thus, in 1654, twenty-six individuals gave £250 for repair of buildings, with Sir Richard Saltonstall giving £104.[21]

In the years 1645-1653 many towns contributed to the support of the college. Boston and Charlestown were especially generous (£85 and £38 respectively), but Salem gave nothing. In Charlestown each family was asked to give one peck of wheat or 12d in money. Morison tells us that these gifts maintained for at least seven years two or three teaching fellows, eight to ten scholars and exhibitioners, and two undergraduate stewards. The whole teaching staff except the president was sustained by the six thousand pecks of wheat or its equivalent in cash.

In 1669, the college was still in trouble. Portsmouth, N.H., in particular helped the college.

. . . the loud groanes of the sinking college, in its present low estate, came to our eares, the releiving of which wee account a good worke for the house of our God and needfull for the perpetuating of Knowledge, both religious and civil, among us, and our postperity after us, and therefore gratefull to yourselves, whose care and studdy is to seek the welfare of our Israell. The premisses considered, we have made a collection in our toune of sixty pounds per annum (and we hope to make it more) which sajd summe is to be pajd annually for these seven yeares ensuing, to be improoved, at the discretion of the honoured overseers of the college . . . hoping . . . that the example of ourselves . . . will provoke the rest of the country to jealousy. . . .[22]

Aggressive Fund-raising

Competition for funds even before the days of numerous colleges was strenuous indeed. A Boston minister urged Thomas Hollis to favor his church against Harvard. Mather wrote to Governor Saltonstall of Connecticut:

---

18. *Report of the Present Library Committee,* 1859, S. K. Lothrop to Reverend J. Walker, April 21, 1859.
19. *Endowment Funds of Harvard University,* pp. 217, 231, 353-354.
20. C. W. Eliot to Dr. Wallace Buttrick, December 13, 1907.

21. Quincy, *op. cit.,* vol. I, p. 164.
22. *The Founding of Harvard College,* pp. 317-318; Samuel Eliot Morison, *Harvard College in the Seventeenth Century,* 1936, pp. 376-377, 570-574.

When the servants of God meet at your Commencement, I make no doubt that they will deliberate on the interests of education and of religion, and not suffer an interview of your best men to evaporate in such a senseless, useless, noisy impertinency as it used to be with us at Cambridge. . . . [23]

Edward Hopkins in 1657 gave £500. In later years Harvard and Yale fought over this gift.

Part of this went to *deturs*, an undergraduate prize for high scholarship. Over the years among those who have received *deturs*, were Justice O. W. Holmes, Henry Thoreau, C. W. Eliot, Robert Frost, Timothy Pickering, W. E. Channing, Eduard Everett, Benjamin Peirce, Phillips Brooks, Walter B. Cannon, P. W. Bridgman, Lee Siminson, Walter Lippman, and President Conant. [24]

Aggressive searching for financial aid was a favorite occupation for President Eliot. In discussing memorial scholarships at Harvard for a Harvard man who had migrated to Iowa, Eliot wrote frankly on the great merits of Harvard.

The University of Iowa is a distinctly second class institution among state universities, and in comparison with Harvard, Yale, Columbia, and Cornell, it is a third or fourth class institution . . . private money should go to strong endowed institutions rather than to state supported institutions. Strong endowed institutions give state institutions the best possible competition and stimulation. . . . [25]

The late Dean Sperry has well stated the problem of aggressive searching by college fund-raisers. The institution is a purely American one; the cause, good, but the method, annoying.

We resent the day when in the order of nature it becomes our duty to hand over a bigger check than we think we can afford. . .in response to the high-pressured salesmanship of some classmate, who is in- *sistent that good ole '94 shall not fall behind the gift of '93 and shall set the bar a bit higher for '95. . . .* [26]

President Lowell underestimated his abilities when he wrote: "I am a very unsuccessful beggar, having neither the subtlety of the friar, nor the boldness of the highwayman." [27]

Integration of Fund Raising Programs

In 1856, the medical school faculty protested to the corporation at the competition with their $50,000 campaign of another drive to procure a medical museum and chemical laboratory. The medical school group insisted that they had priority with both the corporation and President Walker. They expressed the hope that the corporation would ask for "a temporary suspension of efforts in behalf of the more recently organized project, in favor of that to which the whole medical faculty was previously pledged. . . . [28]

President Eliot warned the librarian in 1905 that he must not approach Mr. Milton, who apparently was about to give the university a substantial gift, with a view to attracting support for the library. Apparently Mr. Lowell's priority scale differed from that of the librarian. On several other occasions the college administration requested officials not to seek funds in competition with large programs of the corporation. Thus, in 1914, President Lowell informed the law school dean that these various beggings should be done "so as not to weary people by asking them over and over again for different objects." Hence, he appointed Roger Pierce to keep in touch with all facets of begging. [29]

Rewards to the Donors

One way of inducing gifts is to show appreciation to the donor. Thus, when a likely friend of the college

23. Quincy, *op. cit.*, vol. I, pp. 226-237.
24. Based primarily on D. McCord, *In Sight of Sever; Essays from Harvard*, 1963, pp. 108-123.
25. C. W. Eliot to Thomas N. Perkins, November 3, 1908.
26. W. Bentinck-Smith, *The Harvard Book*, p. 322.

27. A. L. Lowell to Professor Richards, December 28, 1916 in *A. L. Lowell Correspondence.*
28. J. Ware, O. W. Holmes and Henry Bigelow to the President and Fellows of Harvard University, October, 1856.
29. C. W. Eliot to W. Lane, October 5, 1905; A. L. Lowell to E. R. Thayer, July 24, 1914.

asked for some bricks laid by her husband, President Lowell granted the request.

Eliot remarked:

... The most effectual means of procuring new gifts is to demonstrate that all previous gifts have been used with consideration for the givers' wishes, with safety as regards the permanence of the trusts, and with discretion as regards their steady usefulness. ...

Exploiting Special Occasions

In 1764, a fire virtually destroyed Harvard Hall inclusive of the college library. The college immediately mobilized a campaign to recover the large losses.

The guardians and governors of the college were not wanting on their part in this emergency. A Committee of Correspondence for obtaining benefactions from Great Britain, or other places, in order to restore the library and apparatus, and a Committee for procuring subscriptions for the same objects, were speedily appointed...

The committee could soon report gifts of £852 8s 6d in cash "from a great number of gentlemen in the most considerable towns in the Province .... Gifts came in large and generous amounts from distant places in Great Britain and from other provinces. . . ." 30

The year 1872 witnessed another fire that promised to be destructive of Harvard's financial position. The fire destroyed several high-priced buildings the college owned in Boston. The buildings were insured for $216,000 and were assessed at $562,000; and a sum of $300,000 was needed to rebuild them. But the college was to recover only about half the insurance, as the insurance companies were in trouble. In all, the college losses were put at $200,000 inclusive of income losses.

A plea for $50,000 went out to New York alumni. A New York paper commented:

Boston has asked no aid for herself, her poor or her merchants. But she is not too proud to ask for aid for her college; for she feels it is not a local institution, but a national one... Ought not New York and Brooklyn to be ashamed, if active measures are not promptly taken to assist Boston. ...

Within a month, an alumni committee announced that $38,700 had been collected from governing boards and the faculty of Harvard and upwards of $65,000 from Boston and its vicinity.

Of special interest were the large contributions of the faculty—and large for the level of income of that period. Among the well-known faculty donors giving $1,000 or more aside from Eliot were Gurney, Langdell and Dunbar.

Many alumni responded to the Eliot appeal, strongly supported by the newspapers in Boston and New York. A typical letter follows:

Dear Sir:

I read the appeal of President Eliot in the Advertiser this morning with an interest that need not be further executed. I have not much property and cannot afford to give much. But my father, my brothers, my sons and myself have been educated at Harvard; have received the benefits of the gifts to the college made by past generations, and like all the graduates have been furnished with what costs much more than we paid for it. I wish to do all I can, and you may put me down for a subscription of $1,000. ... 31

Harvard exploited situations other than tragedies such as the two destructive fires. The dead in the Civil

---

30. B. Peirce, *op. cit.,* pp. 288-297.

31. Statement by C. W. Eliot on the Fire of November 9, 1872, November 16, 1872; *The World,* November 24, 1872; *The Evening Mail,* November 22, 1872; *The Liberal Christian,* November 23, 30, 1872; W. G. Choate, et als, To the Alumni of Harvard College and All Others Who Have Received the Benefit of Instruction in the Various Departments of the University, December 10, 1872; *Subscription of College Officers After the Fire of 1872,* November 18, 1872.

War proved to be an occasion for building Memorial Hall which offered not only a memorial but also much needed facilities for dining and for a large theater for entertainment and meetings.[32]

32. *Final Report of the Building Committee and of the Treasurer of the Harvard Memorial Fund to the Committee* *of 50,* 1878.

39

Achievements

The campaigns of 1919 and 1956 to 1958 were more successful than that of 1904. Here, two points are especially worthy of emphasis. One is the fact that increasingly after 1900 Harvard could call on sources outside of New England. Even in the early 1900s Bishop Lawrence noted:

Colonel Henry Lee, that prince of beggars for Harvard fifty years ago, used to say that when the college needed money, she went down to State Street and got it, and that she could get it nowhere else. Up to this time Harvard alumni outside of Massachusetts had with few exceptions never taken her needs seriously . . . and yet it was clear that we must strike out somewhere, and begin to reach a wider circle. [1]

A second point is that Harvard did increasingly well despite rising competition for college endowments. Conant, indeed, was concerned that in the tercentenary period competition had greatly increased: between 1934 and 1936, he said:

. . . at least 20 leading institutions are now actively seeking, or laying definite plans to seek a total of about $125,000,000 . . . .
There is now hardly one of the major colleges or universities which is not attempting . . . to add to its endowment on a substantial scale and by the most approved methods. [2]

In relation to goals sought the campaigns of 1904, 1919, 1924 and 1956 to 1960 were successful. The college received $14 million in the 1919 program as compared to the $15,500,000 sought, with one-half of the pledges payable in the future over a period of five years. In view of the record amount received, the college authorities were more than pleased. Moreover, they had shown American higher education the way to the possibilities of large accretions of cash.

The last big general campaign, the *Program for Harvard College*, reached its goal of $82,500,000, and by the time in 1960 when the announcement of success was forthcoming, the college could also boast of an additional $5 million received as a result of earnings on investment of the gifts received inclusive of capital gains. A repetition of the 1956 to 1960 campaign is not likely for a generation, unless catastrophe strikes the nation, and in that eventuality funds would not be forthcoming. Similarly, the 1919 campaign could not be repeated for at least thirty years.

A table comparing amounts sought and received, and the trends of Harvard College enrollment and national income is of some interest. In relation to the growth of national income since 1904, the amounts received were striking in the 1919-1920, and even more so in the 1956 to 1960 campaign. In the latter the amounts received, vis-à-vis the results of the 1904 campaign, had increased 32 times and national income, an index of capacity to give, only by 12 to 13 times; the corresponding figures for 1919-1920 were rises of 460 and 208 percent respectively, and for

---

1. W. Lawrence, *op. cit.*, pp. 218-220.
2. Harvard University Archives, UAV 828.142, pp. 12-13.

Table 39-1.

Five Major Harvard Fund Drives, Amounts Sought and Received, National Income and Undergraduate Enrollment, Absolute Totals and Index (Base 1904):
Index 1904 = 100

	Amounts Sought		Amounts Received		Nat'l Income¶		Harvard College Enrollment	
	Millions	Index	Millions	Index	Billions	Index	Nos.	Index
1904	$ 2.5	100	$ 2.5	100	$ 27.0	100	1,947*	100
1919-1920	15.5	620	14.0	560	83.2	308	2,534	130
1924	10	400	10.0	400	87.7	325	2,801§	144
1936	6†	240	2.85	114	64.9	240	3,449*	176
1956-1960	82.5	3,300	82.5 ‡	3,300	367.4	1,361	4,468*	229

* Interpolated

† The amount hoped for rather than fixed. See *H. U. A.*, UAV 328.3.

‡ Exclusive of $5 million of earnings and capital gains.

¶ This figure adjusted upward before 1929 on the basis of the relative incomes in 1929 of the National Conference Industrial Board income figures and the Council of Economic Advisers income figures.

§ One of the three parts of this program is a professional school.

Sources: Historical Statistics of the U.S., 1789-1945; Economic Report of the President, 1964; Harvard University Archives, UAV 328.2; and others.

1936, an increase of 14 percent in the sums received as against a rise of income of 140 percent.

In relation to the rise of Harvard enrollment (alumni increase more rapidly) amounts received increased much more vis-à-vis 1904, with the exception of 1936. The largest relative rise emerged in 1956-1960, a rise of receipts of 25 times that of enrollment over 1904, as compared with one of 15 times for 1919-1920 and a relative rise for 1936 of only 18 percent *as much* as that in enrollment.

That since 1904 receipts increased so much more than enrollment is to be explained by such factors as the increased interest in higher education, the rising prestige of Harvard, the inflation, the rising standard of living, and the improved techniques for raising large capital sums.

Apparently 23,500 Harvard College men subscribed to the Harvard 1919-1920 drive, a number equaling 60 percent of the alumni listed in the Harvard Alumni Directory and (a guess) 70 percent of Harvard College alumni. Of this number almost 14,000 gave $100 or less, but only approximately 1,450, $1,000 or more. Despite the efforts to tap all Harvard men and make it a general appeal, the major funds came from the high-income groups. Thus, the 9,460, or more than 40 percent, who gave $500 to $1000 accounted for roughly $2 million or 14 percent of the $14 million received. But the thirteen top gifts ($100,000 and more) amounted to $1,500,000 and the 637 (3 percent of the total contributions) gifts of $5,000 or more provided more than $8 million or 58 percent of the total.[3]

---

3. *Harvard Alumni Bulletin*, vol. XXIV, no. 9, p. 186, November 24, 1921.

An allowance for delay in payments would cut the contributions. Even in October, 1923, about half the payments had not been completed. The expectation was that 8,000 subscriptions would be completed between 1924 and 1929.[4]

Discussing primarily the period from 1930 to 1950, during which endowments doubled, a Harvard treasurer noted that:

. . . perhaps the most striking fact to emerge from this study has been the dominant role of larger gifts and bequests. . . charitable giving in this country has established that nine-tenths of the money received, in the last twenty years, appears to have come from far less than one percent of the donors . . . .[5]

In the 1924 campaign, the domination of large gifts was most striking. Thus, in fine arts, four gifts accounted for $1,205,000 of the first $1,657,820 received ($2 million sought). Twelve gifts equaled $1,415,000 or 82 percent of the first $1,658,000 received. George Baker's gift of $5 million bestowed on him the honor of giving all that was asked by the business school. Results were roughly similar for chemistry[6]

Whereas the 1919 drive had attracted 23,000 donors the 1956 to 1960 program brought in 29,447 converts by July 1959, with apparently 26,000 Harvard alumni not contributing by this time.[7] The ratio of donors to graduates was not far from that achieved in the 1919 drive. The ten largest gifts yielded $22,800,000 of $67,700,000 received by the middle of 1959. The later returns were largely big gifts. Three gifts and bequests totaling $5,500,000 were received at the end. Thirteen generous donors contributed more relatively than gifts of similar size provided in 1919.

Large gifts were much more important relatively from 1956 to 1960 than in 1919-1920, and small

gifts much more important relatively in the earlier period. The importance of large gifts in the latest campaign is surprising in view of the dire predictions following the high taxes brought by World War II and the Korean War. Undoubtedly a comparison of large and small gifts in the 1919-1920 and 1956-1960 campaigns is interesting. In the earlier campaign, the top 13 donors gave $1,500,000; the middle group, who gave $100,000 or more, gave $1,500,000; and 9,460 people who gave less than $1,000 each gave a total of $2 million. In 1956 to 1959, the top 12 people gave $22,800,000; the top 102 gave $43,100,000; and the low 24,021 donors gave $3,681,000. (The latter results are based on the first $67,700,000. Of the remaining $15 million, large gifts played a disproportionate part.) [8]

A study of giving reveals that the major sources are the relatively high-income groups. The percentages of income donated does not vary too much but incomes vary greatly. One study suggests that on a national scale, of the money given in the years 1930 to 1950, nine-tenths came from less than 1 percent of the donors. If we assume that gifts of $5,000 and over and bequests of $50,000 and over are large gifts, then 90 percent of all new capital received by Harvard in this period was in large gifts. Yet in this period of all new capital received the annual take was about fifteen gifts of $5,000 and over, and six bequests of $50,000 and over.[9]

An interesting comparison is of gifts of two major drives in the 1820s and 1830s—one for a building and grounds for the theological school and one to endow a professorship of natural history—and the great drives of 1919 and 1956 to 1958. The respective yields were $19,327, $31,333, $14,000,000, $82,500,000. Here I compare the average size of gifts with per capita income in the four periods. The average donation in the four campaigns was $88, $116, $195, $524, and $2,600.

4. Calculated from Harvard University Archives, UAV 136.124.3-4; 136.124.11.
5. *Harvard Alumni Bulletin*, vol. 54, pp. 211-214. For a listing of larger gifts, 1636-1936, see Harvard University Archives, UAV 828.2.
6. Harvard University Archives, UAV 136.124.4; UAI 10.450.10.
7. But a recent estimate puts Harvard College alumni at 50,000. See *Harvard Alumni Bulletin,* October 21, 1968.
8. Calculated from Harvard University Archives, UAV 136.124.11; "A Program for Harvard College," *Newsletter No. 15*, July, 1959.
9. *Harvard Alumni Bulletin*, 1951, pp. 211-214.

**Index of Per Capita Income at Time of Drive
and of Average Gifts, 4 Drives**

	Per Capita Income	Average Gift
Theology, 1820s	100	100
Natural history, 1830s	105	168
1919 Drive	631	452
Program for Harvard College, 1956-1958	2,279	2,241

Sources: Historical Statistics of the United States 1789-1945; Economic Report of the President, 1965; Quincy, op. cit., vol. II, pp. 542-543, 550-551 (my calculations).

In view of the low per capita incomes in the early nineteenth century, the ratio of average gifts was surprisingly high for the natural history chair vis-à-vis per capita income. The ratio of average gifts to the per capita income was especially low in the 1919 drive and high in 1956 to 1958, the better result in 1956 to 1958, being explained by the prosperity, the wide appeal in terms of objectives, and the excellent organizations.

Of some interest is a comparison of the two early drives. The average gift for the natural history professor was $206 against only $88 for the theology program. No gift for the former was less than $100, but three-quarters of the gifts for the theology campaign were less than $100.

I have discussed the major campaigns. But a word should be said about another campaign. In the late 1940s, the business school sought and obtained $20 million, $5 million for endowment for research, $4 million for scholarships, $5 million for instruction, and $6 million for the plant.[10]

The campaign was most successful—compare the $20 million for a professional school with the $14 million raised for the college in 1919 when a major campaign was needed. (Prices were, however, higher in the late 1940s than in 1919-1920 and incomes were much higher. President Conant was particularly pleased by the business school drive, since he argued that the capital gifts were a vindication of the views held by those favoring endowment financing.

Some professional schools tend to have more success in raising money than others. At Harvard the business school and (recently) the medical school have been especially effective, the schools of education, divinity, and dentistry ineffective. The law school falls in between. One explanation of the varying success is the economic status of the graduates. On this score, medical school graduates might be expected to contribute much. Undoubtedly the Harvard law, medical, arts and sciences, and business schools have very high prestige. Whatever success they have may be related to their prestige.

---

10. *Harvard Alumni Bulletin*, 1951, pp. 211-214.

40

Buildings and Equipment

Trends

A chronological listing of Harvard buildings from 1637 to 1805 follows. Early buildings ordinarily had short lives:[1]

First President's House:

Peyntree House	1637-1641
First Harvard College	1642-1679

Second President's House:

Dunster's House	1645-1680
Goffe's College	1651-1660
Indian College	1655-1698
Second Harvard College	1677-1764
Third President's House	1680-1719
Stoughton College	1699-1781
Massachusetts Hall	1720

Fourth President's House:

Wadsworth House	1726
Holden Chapel	1744
Hollis Hall	1763
Third Harvard College (Hall)	1766
Stoughton Hall	1805

From 1805 to 1869, the university constructed twelve new buildings plus a number of small items costing $25,000. The total cost of these buildings was around $525,000.[2]

Another study for the period 1889 to 1914 reveals that Harvard received thirty-five new buildings at a cost of about $10 million.[3]

In May, 1814, the college listed again its land and buildings.[4] In this presentation, the college gave the boundaries of the college and the extent of its land. Apparently, the college now held more than 15 acres as against $1\frac{1}{8}$ acres in the original Harvard yard. Each building was described—e.g., "Harvard Hall, a brick building of four stories—dimensions—103 feet by 43."

In 1869, the college authorities attempted to evaluate the buildings and land available for educational purposes. The schedule, however, "must be read with understanding that it must not be exhaustive or exact, and that many of the valuations are, by necessity, merely conjectural." [5]

In contrast to the listing of 1805, the 1869 listing included only the buildings still in use for educational purposes. In the years since 1805, the value of additions amounted to $521,000 and among the important items were Holworthy, University, Gore, Appleton Chapel, and Boylston. The value put upon libraries, museums, etc. was $765,000 additional ($400,000 for the college library).

In land, values were as follows:

1. *Publications of the Colonial Society of Massachusetts*, vol. 15, p. cxxvii.
2. *Report to the Board of Overseers of Harvard College on the Condition, Needs and Prospects of the University*, 1869, p. 35.
3. A. C. Potter, *Changes at Harvard, 1889-1914*, p. 8.
4. *Schedule of lands and buildings belonging to the College*, March 7, 1814.
5. *Report of the Board of Overseers of Harvard College* on *The Conditions, Needs, and Prospects of the University*, 1869, pp. 35-36.

College yard, more than 22 acres
  at 20 cents a foot . . . .$191,664.
Delta, over 2 acres at 20 cents
  a foot . . . . 17,464.
Additional 21 acres, botanic
  gardens, observatory, divinity,
  scientific schools . . . . 78,008.

The total gold value of land and buildings was put at $1,649,826.

In the post Civil War period Harvard's physical plant expanded at a great rate. In fact generally prosperous years, e.g., the 1920s and the 1950s and 1960s witnessed larger developments. Thus, from 1870 to 1889 the university erected five large dormitories, doubled the space in the library; in 1883, added Austin Hall, the new law school, and added Sever Hall in 1880. Also in the 1870s and 1880s, aside from enlargements, the college provided additional museums and also several science buildings as well as Memorial Hall and a gymnasium.[6]

A survey late in the nineteenth century classified fixed assets as follows:[7]

I. 79 Buildings: Occupied for
  university purposes—not held
  as investments and no
  evaluation on treasurer's
  books $3,880,000
II. 10 Buildings: Investments of
  university funds but occupied
  wholly or in part for
  university purposes exclusive
  of occupation by university
  officers or employees 243,000
III. Ibid.: Occupied by university
  officers and employees 64,000

By 1910, the college estimated its endowment at $21,900,000. In addition, Harvard had $210,000 invested in some buildings and equipment. Another item, "University Houses and Lands," accounted for $586,287. Included in the last were "costs of certain lands, of certain dormitories with stores below, and of certain professors' houses, all not amounting to more than 5 percent of the value of the whole educational plant."

Buildings and equipment other than university houses and lands are not carried on the treasurer's book. The treasurer estimated land, buildings, and equipment used for instruction, research, athletics, and recreation conservatively at twelve million dollars.[8]

Low Costs

In the early nineteenth century, construction costs were much lower than today. For example, Holworthy Hall was built for $24,500 in 1813; University Hall, for $65,000 in 1819; and Gore Hall, which housed the library, for $73,512. Again, the authorities in 1817 provided the first law school building by converting a professor's house into the law school building.[9]

In July, 1825, the law professor wanted a building to house students near their library and lecture rooms. The professor and the mason estimated that with an outlay of $7,500 the school would obtain a building which would house twenty students, an office for the professor, and a library three feet square. The students would each have a room sixteen feet square. Rents would be $30 per year or $600 in all.[10]

Today, it would cost more than $7,500 capital to house one student. Indeed, the housing standards are higher today. In 1790, for example, there was no plumbing, no central heating, no lighting other than that given by candles or sperm oil lamps; for heat, the student depended on open fireplaces warmed with wood that had to be chopped and carried up.[11]

---

6. "A Historical Sketch of Harvard University," in *Four American Universities,* 1895, p. 26.
7. Harvard University Archives, UAI, 50-6, 1884-1900, pp. 1-8.
8. Comptroller to J.A.L. Blake, Statistics on Endowment, Buildings, and Equipment, August 1, 1909.
9. The Harvard Law School Association, *The Harvard Law School, 1817-1917,* pp. 4-5.
10. Steward Higginson to Financial Office, July, 1825.
11. "A Harvard Man's Budget," in *Harvard Graduates Magazine,* 1790, p. 129.

Another indication of the low cost of construction is had from an estimate in 1813 of the cost of building eight "baths of about 100 feet in length, 15 feet wide, 10 feet high." The estimated cost inclusive of seats, floors, stairs, and doors and all required materials and all work but digging was $1,250.[12]

Even in 1914 construction costs for student rooms were low. The freshmen dormitories, housing about five hundred students, cost but $1,500,000 or $3,000 per student.[13]

Inadequate Space

Inadequate space troubled the college authorities from the very beginning. The problems of housing for the president and the faculty; the shortage of rooms for students; the lack of capacity in commons to accommodate all the students; the unavailability of adequate chapel space until relatively recent years; the scarcity of lecture rooms which often led to feuds among faculty members; the shortage of space to store library books—these were problems that plagued Harvard from its earliest days. The large appropriations for the plant in the Pusey $82,500,000 drive in the late 1950s suggest that space problems still trouble the college.

A helpful episode is a statement by the corporation in 1813.[14] The corporation addressed a number of friends of the college: "There is much occasion for a considerable expenditure in providing convenient and honorable accommodations for the public purposes of the Seminary."

In commons, the corporation reminded its friends, each table carried two more students than usual, and provisions for one class had to be carried to an adjoining dormitory; and space was scarce for preparing meals.

An Official Summary

An official volume, *Education, Bricks and Mortar*, 1949, expressed the importance of buildings:

---

12. J. Moore & Co. to President Kirkland and John Lowell, July 7, 1813.

Great visions of Great men live on and serve mankind not only in their spiritual legacies, but also when these visions are expressed in physical form—buildings, books, bequests.
An obscure preacher of Charleston, Massachusetts would be unknown today had he not perpetuated the name John Harvard by the gift of his library and half his inheritance "towards the erecting of a college."

According to this study, by the late 1940s Harvard had 150 buildings owned and used for educational purposes. In the recent tenth of Harvard's history to 1947 a building increase of 63.9 percent had been achieved.[15]

This plant marks a great advance from the first building.

Goodman Peyntree's steep roofed house on Cowyard Row provided the first home for the first college in the New England Colonies.
Soon the one-and-an eighth-acre strip of property was fenced, planted in apple trees and with dignity designated the "College Yard" to distinguish it from the adjoining Cow Yards.

Then came the first Harvard College (1642-1679). The theory behind it was that of the English tradition of collegiate living, sharing not only classes but also commons, dormitories, prayers, and recreation. Here is the beginning of the House Plan idea which was put into effect in 1930.

Then followed the ill-fated Indian College, which yielded one A.B. (1665) to Caleb Cheeshahteaumuck and the first printing press in the American colonies.[16]

Building activity was still limited in the eighteenth century. Thus, in pre Revolutionary years, 1717 to 1773, the college acquired eight buildings, inclusive

---

13. Costs of Freshman Dormitories as per Contracts Estimated to Date, October 27, 1914.
14. Corporation to Samuel Eliot January 15, 1813.
15. *Education, Bricks and Mortar*, published by the university, 1949, p. 7.
16. *Ibid.*, pp. 9, 11.

of one by purchase, with a total value of £17,314. Of special interest is the fact that the government provided all but £1,100 of the £17,314 needed.[17] The only important private grant was £400 for Holden Chapel. At the time of the grant, 1743-1744, N.E. sterling was greatly depreciated and each English pound sterling was worth £4 N.E. lawful money. money.

In the listing above the third Harvard Hall (1766) is included. A costly fire had destroyed Harvard Hall on January 24, 1764, in the midst of a severe snow storm and with few students around. Members of the Legislature and the governor's council had occupied Harvard Hall in order to cope with a smallpox epidemic. Citizens of Cambridge and others barely saved Massachusetts, Stoughton, and Hollis halls and Holden Chapel. Harvard:

the most valuable of the halls, which, with the best library and philosophical apparatus in America, comprising the collections and donations of more than a century, utterly perished.... Harvard Hall soon rose from its ashes, and a library, more valuable and more richly endowed than the former, was collected within its walls.[18]

Even in the first half of the nineteenth century, building was at a modest pace when compared with more recent times. Yet there was much criticism of the pace. The reviewer of Samuel Eliot's *Sketch of Harvard College,* (1849), complained in 1849 of expenditures of $200,000 on four buildings, with three-quarters taken from the college stock funds or free money. The stock account was "only about one-half as large as it might have been but for this insane expenditure, within thirty years, upon bricks and stones,—this taste for architectural abortions...."[19]

17. Exclusive of the six-sevenths of the Cambridge Meeting House, to which Harvard had subscribed only seventh.
18. Quincy, *op. cit.,* vol. II, pp. 112-113.
19. "Eliot's Sketch of Harvard College," in *North American Review,* 1849, pp. 104-107.
20. Morison, *Three Centuries of Harvard, 1636-1936,* pp. 449-450.

Recent Trends

Morison reminds us that Lowell was the greatest builder of any Harvard president. "This building activity set in around 1911, and for twenty two years the sound of the steel-riveter, carpenter and the mason was never absent from Cambridge...."[20]

But Pusey seems to have moved ahead of Lowell. In 1962-1963, new construction amounted to $20 million and $12,700,000 were scheduled for 1963-1964. (In 1930-1931, a maximum of $10 million had been reached.) In ten years (1953 to 1963), the university had spent or committed for new construction and rehabilitation an amount in excess of $70 million. Recall that the estimate for the first 312 years was only $100 million: an annual average of $320,000 for 312 years versus an average of $7 million in the years 1953 to 1963. Of course, part of the rise is explained by rising construction costs. But President Pusey has measured the trends well. He estimates the rise of *usable space* not at (roughly) 70 percent, that is, from $100 to $170 million, but at 35 percent.

Maintenance Costs and Period of Construction

A rough indication of the importance of Harvard buildings at different times is suggested by the maintenance costs in 1947 of operating buildings constructed at different times:

Table 40-1.
Maintenance Costs, in 1947, by Periods of Construction of Buildings

Years Constructed	
18th century	$ 38,000
1st half, 19th century	80,000
2nd half, 19th century	362,000
19th century	442,000
1900-1915	709,000
1915-1948	1,878,000
Total, 1700-1948	$3,509,000

Source: Compiled and calculated from *Education, Bricks and Mortar.* (Calculations are rough, for in some instances costs were not available; in others, allocation by periods when buildings were constructed in more than one period was necessary.)

Maintenance costs for buildings constructed in the 33 years 1915 to 1948 were roughly equal to those for buildings constructed in the preceding 215 years. Maintenance costs for the nineteenth century construction were 11 times those of the eighteenth century, and for roughly the first half of the twentieth century almost 70 times the maintenance costs of the buildings of the eighteenth century.

Assessment of Physical Plant

Criticism of Harvard architecture is an old game. Many want uniformity of architecture in the yard and even the university. But a modern university needs not only dormitories as in the seventeenth century, but large libraries, laboratories, indoor athletic facilities, an engineering building, a computation laboratory, an art museum, a theater, a nuclear laboratory, an observatory, large lecture buildings, etc. It is not always easy to impose uniform architecture with such varying internal needs.

Architectural tastes change from generation to generation. The college has the choice of sticking to the Georgian of the seventeenth century, (though with the advance of education this became increasingly difficult) and not reflecting the changing values of the society, or else of giving the Harvard community and the public the buildings that reflect current tastes—e.g., combining Georgian with Richardson's Sever; with Memorial Hall and its Victorian Gothic; Littauer Center's neoclassic facade; the modern Harkness commons; and with the new Carpenter Center of Visual Arts by LeCorbusier. The Harvard yard in fact, reflecting its three hundred to four hundred years of history presents diversity above all though Georgian predominately. The attractive pre Revolutionary Georgian of Harvard, Hollis, Holden, and Massachusetts halls could not always be used in later years.

President Lowell once reminded us of the degree to which disapproval and disagreement may prevail.

It is interesting to note that University Hall, designed by Bulfinch, and now the most admired for its architectural merits of all our older buildings, did not escape severe censure when it was built. Joseph Cogswell, one of the tutors, whose bust now stands in the Faculty Room, spoke of it as the white spectre; *and a writer in the North American Review after referring to it as "the stone edifice, which insults us with its long piazza, and its wooden Ionic pilasters and the entablature which extends part way along the front," capped his criticism with the remark, "We doubt whether the world contains any other architectural abortion to be compared to this."*[21]

Anthony Trollope, in his American travels in the 1860s, was not impressed by Harvard's aesthetic contributions.

There is a handsome library attached to the College, which the young men can use; but it is not as extensive as I had expected. The University is not well off for funds by which to increase it. . . . The edifices used for the undergraduates' Chambers and for the lecture-rooms are by no means handsome. They are very ugly red-brick houses standing here and there without order. . . . It is almost astonishing that buildings so ugly should have been erected for such a purpose. These, together with the library, the museum, and the chapel, stand on a large green, which might be made pretty enough if it were kept well mown like the gardens of our Cambridge colleges; but it is much neglected. Here, again, the want of funds—the res angusta domi—*must be pleaded as an excuse.*[22]

In reply to an inquiry from Judge Ebenezer Rockwood Hoar, James Russell Lowell in 1886 commented on Harvard's architecture thus:

My dear friend, what shall I say? I know that nearly all our College buildings are hideous, that with the single exception of Boylston Hall (and a judicious effort to spoil that was made in the walleyed windows of the west wing) they are uglier as they are later in date, and that it may end, if we should ever get a man of taste on the Grand Jury, in the College

---

21. *Report of the President of Harvard College*, 1923-1924, p. 7.
22. A. Trollope, *North America*, 1851, p. 245.

319

being presented as a nuisance. If you should contrive something uglier than the President's House, for example? That would be hard, but then the Corporation are men of acknowledged ability. . . . Good taste is cheaper in the end than bad. If anybody ever leaves you any more money to build with after seeing what you made of Mr. Brooks's legacy, he must be a man of great firmness of purpose. . . .

At least spare us any more abominations, and remember that the College builds forever, or should.[23]

Eliot gave one reason for any failure. In his regime, three plans for the layout of grounds and buildings had been made by good architects. But changes in tastes, unimagined needs, and new resources made these plans obsolete.[24]

Finally, John Fiske wrote to his wife from England in 1873.

The buildings and grounds at Cambridge so far surpass what we have at Harvard, that there is no use in talking of them the same day. Anything more perfectly enchanting I have never seen; and they all acknowledge—even the Cambridge men themselves—that Oxford is still finer. So you see there's a treat yet in store for me. I don't wonder the people here are proud of the universities.

. . . I think Oxford is somewhat superior. But when one thinks of Harvard in comparison with either of them, one laughs. . . . What a monstrosity is the Memorial Hall compared to the buildings of Christ Church in Oxford! I understand it now as I couldn't when at home.[25]

But Harvard had not completely abandoned planning. Thus, President Eliot early in the twentieth century announced that the governing boards had decided that "every new site for a building and the plans for every new building should be submitted to a committee formed from among the surviving architects who had served the University professionally. . . ." Again, President Lowell in 1923 announced that building should proceed according to a definite and sensible plan which would consider beauty, function, and the future needs of the university.[26]

President Lowell's Contributions

In introducing the freshman dormitories and the House Plan, President Lowell paid much attention to the physical features of the university. His ancestor had greatly influenced him. In so far as he was not limited by the architectural heritage, e.g., the abominable Gold Coast, Lowell embraced Georgian. But he especially emphasized the moral contribution of the physical plant. In 1911-1912, he wrote that:

. . . the promotion of a better College life, physical, intellectual, and moral, has received much attention of late among men engaged in education. At Harvard we believe that a vital matter is to launch the student aright on the new freedom of college life by means of Freshman dormitories. . . .[27]

With great satisfaction, President Lowell assessed the physical and moral gains of the House Plan. He had vindicated the views of James Russell Lowell.[28]

A stranger visiting Cambridge last summer and surveying the buildings under construction might well suppose that our aims were material, our object display, and their expression bricks and mortar. But every one of the new buildings fills a long-felt want, and is designed to promote research or to strengthen the spiritual and moral force of the University. Extravagance there is none; but under the hand of the architects there are dignity and grace of a kind to impress and refine those who enter the courts, dining halls and libraries, or who pass along the banks of the

23. M. A. DeWolfe Howe, *New Letters of James Russell Lowell*, 1932, pp. 107-111.
24. James, *op. cit.*, vol. II, p. 225.
25. E. Fiske (ed.), *The Letters of John Fiske*, 1940, pp. 255, 266.
26. *Report of the President of Harvard College*, 1903-1904, pp. 8-9; 1923-1924, pp. 23-27.
27. *Report of the President of Harvard College*, 1928-1929, p. 12.
28. *Ibid.*, 1929-1930, p. 5.

river. One cannot stand in the new quadrangles at any hour of the day or evening without noting a silence and decorum not always associated with college life. The members of the Houses obviously respect them, and the architects have succeeded in giving to new structures the semblance of age.

In giving Harvard its union in 1899, H. L. Higginson reflected the views of Lowell.

. . . we will build a great house on college grounds, and vest it in the President and Fellows of the Corporation. We will call it the Harvard Union, and it shall be the meetinghouse of all Harvard men— alumni, students, teachers. It shall pay to the university a full rental for its land, and meet its own expenses, as a condition of its being, and it shall be beholden to nobody but to Harvard men and Harvard lovers. It shall have large, simple, comfortable rooms; ample space for reading, study, games, conversation; and a great hall, where all may meet and hold the freest talk in public. . . . [29]

University vs Private Dormitories

In the latter part of the nineteenth century, Harvard could accommodate only half its students in dormitories, a fact which stimulated the introduction and growth of private dormitories. The resultant Gold Coast provided luxurious suites with private bathrooms, swimming pools, locations close to the yard, and also a less democratic system of entry than in college-owned facilities. President Eliot encouraged this growth, even promising not to compete with newer college tax-free dormitories. But Eliot could not bind his successor, who was anxious to have students living in dormitories controlled by the college. Ultimately rising costs, the competition of tax-free freshmen dormitories, and the advantage of no or low capital charges for financing Harvard's dormitories, drove the private owners into selling out

to Harvard at considerable losses.

In a 1902 report of a college committee with professor (later president) Lowell as a member, the disadvantages suffered by Harvard dormitories were clarified. The college had provided no new dormitories for thirty-nine years.[30] Poor service and inadequate plumbing also received special emphasis. President Lowell was to reverse the Eliot policy in the next ten years.[31]

Through most of Harvard's history, there have been shortages of rooms and hence a motive for competitors to seek students as roomers. Even under the House Plan (1930 and later) space has not kept up with demands though in the 1930s there was some exodus from the houses and some vacancies resulted as in response to snobbish motives and the inadequacy of income, students moved into the filthy rabbit warrens. They also sought an escape from strict college parietal regulations.

In later years, Conant and Pusey also contributed to the advance of the Lowell ideas; Conant by providing living and dining quarters for graduate students, and Pusey by seeking and obtaining the vast funds required to house and dine 50 percent additional students since the building of the freshman dorms and the houses, and by providing decent housing for married graduate students.

Costs, Reproduction Value, and Maintenance

Harvard self insures its buildings. On May 1, 1957, the university's insurance covered $149,500,000 for buildings, with rates in seven different classes varying from 1.2 cents per $100 to 18 cents per $100.

For three buildings constructed in the eighteenth century, the current insured value in 1957 was 29 times the original costs; in successive periods ending with the construction period of 1916 to 1947, I estimate the 1957 insurance value at 29.1, 17.3, 7.5, 4.8 and 1.7 times the construction costs.[32]

29. Perry, *Life and Letters of Henry L. Higginson*, vol. 2, p. 355.
30. Actually the correct figure seems to be 32 years.
31. *Committee on Assignment of Rooms in College Buildings*, November 10, 1902; *History of Harvard*

University, 1896, p. 147; H. J. Coolidge to the Trustees of the Harvard Riverside Trust, November 17, 1915.
32. Wherever the information was available, I allowed for additional costs (and maintenance) after the initial construction.

Apparently the farther back we go the greater the windfall occurring to the university. To give a few examples:

Holden Chapel, constructed in 1744 at $1,300, was insured at $66,000 in 1957. Perhaps even more significant, over a period of two hundred years Holden Chapel served as:

carpenter shop; fire-engine house; club house; chemistry laboratory (probably the first in the country); museum; auditorium. . . . and for classrooms, lecture rooms, public speaking classes, and choir rehearsals. It has served in at least two other wars besides the Revolution—as a recruiting station for the S.A.T.C. in World War I and as a point of issue for naval stores in World War II, still giving service today.[33]

Hollis Hall is of special interest, for it housed Emerson, Thoreau, Edward Everett, and President Eliot. Construction costs in 1763 were $16,000. Its insurance value in 1957 was $286,800 or 18 times as much.

These large rises of value are not easy to explain. Price indexes are available only from the early nine-teenth century, and even these indexes over long periods of time are only roughly indicative of the facts. From 1800 to 1957 commodity prices rose 264 percent. This rise is obviously far below the increase of value of a number of Harvard buildings which increased in value 635 percent from the first half of the nineteenth century to 1957. The rise was actually somewhat greater than that suggested by comparing with 1800, for average prices for the years 1801 to 1850 were about 7 percent less than in 1800.

What, then, can be the explanation of these great rises of value? The answer undoubtedly lies in the marked increase of per capita incomes, and especially in those incomes relevant for construction, employments not as subject to rises of productivity as the economy generally. What is significant is that rough figures reveal a rise of per capita income of about 17 times from 1800 to 1957. This reflects inflation, but primarily rising productivity. At current high wages and costs of materials, the reproduction costs of academic buildings constructed long ago is many times as high as original construction costs.

Table 40-2.

Harvard Buildings, Percent of 1957 Values to Costs, and Maintenance Costs in Relation to Original Costs by Periods

No. of Buildings	Years	Percent of 1957 Value to Costs	Percent of Maintenance Costs to Original Costs
3	18th century	2914	84
5	1st half, 19th century	1735	38
8	2nd half, 19th century	751	18
9	1900-1915	478	8
11	1916-1947	170	3

Source: Compiled and computed from *Education Bricks and Mortars* and *Harvard University Academic Buildings, Self-Insurance Schedule*, May 1, 1957.

33. *Education, Bricks and Mortar*, p. 70.

Another interesting problem is the relationship between maintenance and original costs. As we go back to earlier times, maintenance costs tend to rise vis-à-vis original costs: 84 percent for eighteenth century buildings and only 3 percent for buildings of the years 1916 to 1947.[34] This is of course a troublesome problem. But if we should relate maintenance costs to reproduction costs, i.e., insurance values, then they do not seem out of line. Thus, in relation to reproduction costs, maintenance costs are 3 percent for the eighteenth century buildings and 3 percent for the buildings of the years 1916 to 1947.

In 1963-1964, for the country, maintenance and operation of physical plant amounted to 7.6 percent of then current fund expenditures. At Harvard in 1965-1966, the application of national figures suggests that maintenance of plant would consume $6.7 million out of $88.3 million of expenditures.[35]

Maintenance and obsolescence are old problems in Harvard's history, but especially troublesome in Eliot's days. Eliot, early in the twentieth century, would require a $50,000 endowment for a music building for maintenance and $100,000 for the building; and $13,000 for a chemistry maintenance fund and $37,000 for the building. He announced he would prefer a small building with an adequate endowment for maintenance and repairs to a larger building without endowment.[36]

Inflation

Harvard experienced many serious inflationary periods, and notably in the first half of the eighteenth century, the periods of the four major wars, and even in the peacetime period from 1896 to 1914. At such times the lapse of time from acceptance of a gift to the period of construction brought rising costs of construction. Harvard was embarrassed as prices rose and costs of construction spiraled upward. When Hollis became available in 1763, it was announced that it "cost upwards of four thousand eight hundred pounds lawful money, which exceeded the estimate and appropriation more than five hundred and thirty pounds." But the building was to yield £90 net a year.[37]

In a note to Jacob Schiff, Eliot asked permission to postpone the building of the Semitic Museum which could have been provided two years ago as planned at $52,000 and now required $65,000. Eliot's solution was to invest the money, hoping that the return on the investment would exceed the annual rise of costs, and wipe out the earlier impact of inflation.

In 1906, Eliot announced that in five years the estimated cost of five medical school buildings had risen 20 to 30 percent. Such increases in prices were the result not only of general inflationary forces but also of the lag in productivity gains in the construction industry.

The more permanent the buildings were, the more Harvard had to gain vis-à-vis her rivals, from rising costs of construction. A $10,000 building of the early eighteenth century might well cost 10 to 20 times as much to replace today.[38]

In 1911, when President Lowell was planning for a new library, the overseers estimated that $2 million would be needed for the building and a $500,000 fund for maintenance.[39]

More recently Harvard's committee on visual arts warned against expansion of the plant involving large maintenance costs.

Building repairs were not always of a routine nature. The elder Charles F. Adams noted that on July 6, 1842:

34. The large figure–84 percent for the early buildings–is related especially to the great excess of reproduction over original costs.

35. *Financial Report to the Board of Overseers of Harvard College,* 1965-1966, p. 10; *Office of Education Digest of Statistics,* 1965 ed., p. 103.

36. C. W. Eliot, *University Trustees,* p. 27; C. W. Eliot to C. H. Williams, January 18, 1906; C. W. Eliot to Professor T. Richards, September 18, 1907.

37. Quincy, *op. cit.,* vol. II, pp. 101-102.

38. C. W. Eliot to John Rockefeller, June 24, 1903; C. W. Eliot to Jacob H. Schiff, May 26, 1900.

39. Board of Overseers, Report of the Committee to Visit the Library, June 30, 1909 in *A. Lowell Letters.*

I started at my usual time this morning to attend the examination of the Sophomores in Greek, at Cambridge. Upon my arrival I found some emotion occasioned by the bursting of a shell in the spot and found it had destroyed all the windows and a great part of the plastering in the left hand entry on the second floor, making a hole down into the common room below. This is a diabolical act enough but it seems to be the character of the age to familiarize the minds even of the young with all sorts of violence, that powerful natural agents produce.[40]

Financial Problems

In financing buildings as in financing teachers, the funds made available were often inadequate. Hence, the practice of investing funds and thus increasing them prior to use. The Boylston Museum was completed in 1857 at a cost of $50,000. In 1803, Ward N. Boylston had established a *Fund for Medical Prizes*, with the stipulation that if no price were awarded in a given year, the money should be "paid to the Treasurer of Harvard College, to be placed at interest, and appropriated towards a fund for erecting a building—for an anatomical museum and Library." Unused balances from a fund for purchasing medical books were also added to the museum fund. In 1830, the fund amounted to $4,985. Interest plus the diversions noted above raised the total to $24,000 by 1857. Subscriptions provided $17,000; the Appleton Chapel Fund, $6,000; and the General Fund of the College, $10,790 additional. The cost was, however, only $50,000.[41]

One of the most difficult financial problems of Harvard was the financing of the physical plant of the medical school. Frequent changes of domicile were required. By 1906, the school had occupied five different sites, the last costing $3 million.

Gifts, notably by J. P. Morgan and John Rockefeller, financed this large new development. Rising costs early in the twentieth century forced the university to substitute brick and stone for stone alone provided in the original plan, and also to reduce the space to be made available in order to adjust the construction to the revenue available.

In some respects the financing was unusual. When the school was to be moved to Grove Street in response to an increase of the class from 50 to 150, the resources available were inadequate. Hence, the corporation advanced $13,860 for which the faculty assumed responsibility. They agreed to pay 6 percent interest and 5 percent repayment of capital per year. But the faculty found this assessment a severe burden and induced the corporation later to cut the capital amortization to 1 percent a year.

In preparation for the large expansion in the early twentieth century, the friends of the college obtained control of adequate land.

Costs in excess of planned costs are the fate of almost every building project—e.g., the President's House, Appleton Chapel, and the Baker Buildings at the Business School. A good example is the Harvard Stadium. In 1902-1903, the class of 1879 gave $100,000 for the building of a stadium. Actual construction costs amounted to $300,000. The committee on the regulation of athletic sports had contributed gate receipts to improve Soldiers Field, but once the stadium was built, the receipts were used to extinguish this large debt. In 1906-1907, the president decreed "that the Athletic Committee be instructed to apply the entire surplus of the athletic receipts over the sums needed for current athletic expenses to the extinguishment of the debt on the Stadium until that debt is rapaid. . . ."[42]

Utilities

On the whole, the college introduced modern conveniences altogether too slowly. As late as 1855, there

40. Henry Adams (1898) and W. G. Roelker (1909) (eds.) *Extracts from the Diaries of John Quincy Adams (1787) and his son, Charles Francis Adams (1825),* typed manuscript in Harvard University Archives, p. 15.

41. *Treasurer's Statement,* 1825-1857; *Endowment Funds of Harvard University,* pp. 252, 282.

42. *Report of the President of Harvard College,* 1900-1901, p. 19; 1902-1903, p. 41; 1906-1907, pp. 31, 117; *Report of the Treasurer of Harvard College,* 1903-1904, p. 23.

were no toilet facilities for women in the yard. The librarian complained to the president:

All the persons who are employed in Gore Hall [library] suffer from want of a water closet and appurtenances. The young women have no accomodations nearer their homes. The inconveniences and the injury to health will be greater when the weather is colder and the ground covered with snow. I take the liberty of asking you to lay the subject before the Corporation and hope that accommodations of the best kind may be provided as early as practicable, not only for the comfort of the workers but that literary visitors may not be obliged to wash their hands at the nose of the pump, as is now the case, or in an old rotten sink, which had served out its time in Harvard before it was moved to Gore Hall more than eighteen years ago.[43]

Incidentally, Gray's Hall (1863) was the first college hall to have water taps in the basement. Other residents in the yard had to procure their water from the yard pump or have college porters procure water for them.[44]

Competition with private dormitories forced the college in 1897-1898 to put bathrooms with hot and cold water in the yard and also to introduce steam heat in Harvard and Massachusetts halls.[45]

As late as 1878, the medical director noted that in Hollis, the water supply came from the pump in the yard or from a dirty faucet in Holworthy with its rows of water closets with old newspapers underfoot to serve as toilet paper. Neither a bathtub nor a shower was to be found in any of the dormitories.[46]

Adequate heat was a serious problem in the nineteenth century. As early as 1825, the college was considering the possibility of central heating from a furnace in the basement. Experience at a bank in Boston and a few homes in Boston was assuring. A correspondent informed President Kirkland that this kind of heating was expensive but in view of the reduced dangers of fire, the extra expense was justified.

Soon after Eliot became president, Amos Lawrence expressed the wish:

that the new dormitory may not be built like Gray's without lathes and plaster [Gray was built in 1863] which is cold as Greenland. The outside rooms cannot be warmed up to 50° by any process in cold days, not up to 40° near to the floor. . . .[47]

Generally, for heating, it was necessary to have a coal fire in the chambers or living room.

Provision of adequate light was also a troublesome problem. In 1853, a proposal was made that the college provide six lamp posts in the streets adjoining the yard: ". . . and I [the treasurer] think it would be worthwhile to go to that expense, merely as a matter of police and as a preventive of mischief in the dark. . . ."[48]

Fifty occupants of Stoughton Hall in 1859 petitioned "the faculty to take measures for the immediate introduction of gas to that building."[49] (In 1855 the corporation had provided gas light in recitation rooms and for Holworthy Hall.)[50]

As late as the 1890s, the complaint in the dental school was that the students troubled by poor lighting treated their patients badly. In winter months lighting was inadequate from 3 to 5 P.M. and generally on dark days. It was difficult to read in some rooms in the library and in the stacks, it was difficult to find books. "For want of light to find them," books were often reported out.[51]

43. J. L. Sibley to President Walker, October 21, 1859.
44. Morison, *Three Centuries of Harvard, 1636-1936,* p. 311.
45. *Report of the President of Harvard College,* 1897-1898, p. 54.
46. A. Worcester, *Reminiscencies,* chapter X, in Harvard University Archives, p. 30.
47. J. Welles to the Reverend Dr. Kirkland, January 20, 1825; A. A. Laurence to President Eliot (date not given but probably 1869 or 1870 when Thayer Hall was built).
48. *S. A. Eliot to the President, March 28, 1853.*
49. Petition in Harvard University Archives, September 1859.
50. *Report of the President of Harvard College,* 1855-1856, pp. 4-5.
51. *Librarian Report, 1891-1892,* p. 160; *Report of the President of Harvard College,* 1891-1892, p. 31; *Report of the Dental School,* 1890-1891, p. 131.

Some Conclusions

In assessing costs of education, college financial officers generally do not include costs of capital. The 1964 insurance value of Harvard's buildings was $240 million. Should we add $30 million for buildings since 1964 and $50 million, a modest allowance for land values, then the return on $320 million, say $15 million or about one-eighth of the annual budget, is not included in costs.

Apparently the university does set aside reserves to finance maintenance and repairs. The 1965-1966 charge to expenses and credit to reserves was $2,163,000; actual expenditures from reserves were $1,883,000.

Another approach is to put aside ½ of 1 percent— as suggested by President Lowell—for fifty years. At the end of that period, a sum equal to costs—on assumption of a return of 5 percent—would be had. Currently, this would require about $1,500,000. Insofar as construction costs rise—as they certainly do—this would be inadequate.[52] In fact, even if construction costs rose only 3 percent yearly—a low projection—replacement costs in fifty years would be about 4 times original costs.

We have said little about one troublesome problem, namely, the high costs of maintaining buildings. In the chapter on the library, the problem receives some attention. In general, college administrators accept buildings as gifts without adequate consideration of costs of maintenance and replacement. Indeed, in recent years there is an increasing awareness of this problem. But it still receives inadequate attention.

The periods of feverish building activities were in the 1920s, and 1950s, and the early 1960s. In the earlier period, the explanation was largely big increases in enrollment, postponement of construction during World War I, and the interest of President Lowell in housing students and the House Plan, and his unusual ability at raising money. But Lowell also mobilized funds for science buildings, a library, and museums, and contributed toward more academic facilities in the professional schools. The large building program under Pusey is also related to deficiences arising as a result of the depression and World War II and to some extent to a rise of enrollment. Both men profited from the prosperous times in the 1920s and post World War II. Pusey, like Lowell, also aggressively sought funds.

Under Lowell, attempts were made to take into account beauty, function, and the future needs of the University, and also cloistering the yard, that is, sheltering it from outside noises.

---

52. Maintenance of Freshman Dormitories, November 16, 1915, *A. L. Lowell Papers, 1914-1917,* F-213.

41

Land

Origins

Unlike the modern state university, Harvard has been most unfortunate in its land heritage. Units of the University of California begin operations with 1,000 to 2,000 acres, generally gifts of a land company or speculator. But Harvard had to be satisfied with little more than 1 acre at the outset in the 1630s. Lack of space has been a problem that has plagued Harvard from the very beginning until today, where inadequate space forces the college to expand expensively and vertically rather than economically and horizontally.

Indeed, large grants outside of Cambridge have been available. But these do not solve the Cambridge problem. Nor does a 2,000 acre grant at $27.50 an acre for a forestry school in Petersham treat the shortages in Cambridge.[1]

Current observers in the early years were not always aware of the problem.

In 1654 a eulogy appeared:

The situation of this college is very pleasant, at the end of a spacious plain, more like a bowling green, than a wilderness, near a fair navigable river... The building [is] *thought by some to be too gorgeous for a wilderness, and yet too mean in others' apprehension for a college...*[2]

In 1638, the town granted the college $2\frac{2}{3}$ acres additional on Braintree Street (Massachusetts Avenue). Between 1642 and 1654, the college derived title under deeds of Edward Goffe and in 1661 of John Betts (also on Massachusetts Avenue). The Goffe item included about 1 acre of land. The Betts property had more than 1 acre of land. In addition, in the 1630s, Eaton, the first head of the college, received $2\frac{1}{4}$ acres for the college and $2\frac{2}{3}$ and 4 acres for his personal use.[3]

Morison commented with his usual insight on the scanty land available at the beginning of the Chauncey administration (1654). Whereas Harvard owned and had in prospect only 5 to 6 acres in 1654, the government had promised the Virginia College 10,000 acres. The land for Harvard was "ridiculously inadequate; and for every enlargement the college or her benefactors have had to pay through the nose."

In 1660, the college received a gift of £20 on the condition that it be held as a stock (endowment) forever. But despite this condition, the college used this money and some additional funds to purchase badly needed land in the college yard.[4]

One reason for the *relative* scarcity of land was the concept of a college held by the founders of Harvard. They wanted a collegiate way of life, that is, students would not only recite but they would live, dine, play, discuss, study, and pray together, and in the constant

1. C. W. Eliot to J. J. Higginson, March 13, 1907.
2. W. Bentnick-Smith (ed.), *The Harvard Book*, p. 331.
3. N. I. Bowditch to the President and Fellows of Harvard College on Title of Harvard College to the Meeting House Lot, June 27, 1831. *Founding of Harvard College*, pp. 206-208; T. W. Harris to S. Eliot, November 30, 1847.
4. Morison, *Harvard College in the Seventeenth Century*, vol. I, pp. 47-48.

company of tutors. As Morison remarked, "the humblest resident tutor was accounted a more suitable teacher than the most eminent community lecturer...." To serve all these needs meant more space and more college buildings.[5]

The college even purchased lands to provide adequate and attractive grounds for burial of Harvard faculty members and administrators. In 1836, they raised $805 for this purpose and also obtained some lots free. The treasurer reported: "the space on top of Harvard Hall in Mount Auburn Cemetery containing about 5,626 feet has been surveyed and set apart for the college...."[6]

Commons and Space

Lack of space and physical plant frequently precluded adequate college commons. In 1849, for example, a crisis emerged as a result of providing commons in University Hall. The use of this important building for commons contributed to a shortage of space for class rooms and also raised other troublesome problems.

The two principal reasons for the change contemplated are (1) the annoyance, in various ways, arising from the presence of a large cooking establishment under the same roof with the chapel and recitation rooms; and (2) the great demand that now exists for the space occupied by the kitchen and eating rooms, for more important uses...

It is well known to all who have recitation or lecture rooms in University Hall that the smoke and Savor of the cooking (which runs very much in the direction of frying and broiling) find their way even to the upper story so as to be frequently offensive to those who occupy the more elevated rooms....[7]

5. *Ibid.*, p. 252.
6. *Report of the Treasurer on the Purchase of a Burial Ground* (T. W. Wood), February 11, 1836.
7. *Report of the Committee ... to Consider the Expendiency ... to Remove the College Kitchen and Commons from University Hall*, May 21, 1849.

An Alternative

Harvard might have been established where more land was available. In fact the Salem-Marblehead area in 1636 offered a 300 acre farm site for a New England college, $2\frac{1}{2}$ miles from the village center of Salem and 15 miles from Boston. Morison observed that the farm contained ample room for expansion to this day and it "is still remote from main roads such as those which now hem in the Yard and the Houses by lines of roaring motor traffic. . ."[8]

But according to Morison, the founders of Harvard preferred Newtown (Cambridge) to the desolate wilderness of Salem. Their concept prevailed of an appropriate site, derived from their Cambridge-Oxford experience. The desired site must be inland, sheltered from the fury of the ocean, must have a river and level ground for building.

Moreover, there were strong economic motives for domiciling in Cambridge. Harvard, in a sense, was one of the first, if not the first, public works project in American history. With Cambridge deserted by the magistrates and then by the residents who moved to the richer lands of Connecticut, hemmed in by Watertown and Charlestown and hence with inadequate land for grazing cattle, the college found support from the government. A college in Cambridge would give work for artisans and servants and save the town. Unless government provided additional support to the economy in the midst of a serious depopulation movement, Newton (Cambridge) would have had to be abandoned.[9]

Acquiring Land

Harvard's history has been colored by the shortage of space related to some extent to the economic expansion of the town. Lack of space encouraged speculative purchases of land in the hope of future sales to the college at profitable prices.

Spirited debates often occurred over the issue of expenditures on land. At the very outset of the Eliot

8. *Founding of Harvard College*, pp. 161-163.
9. *Ibid.*, pp. 182-188.

period, the treasurer of the college protested vehemently at Eliot's proposed policy of converting productive funds earning about 7 percent into unproductive investments in land and other assets. In fact, in the four years 1866 to 1870, the college had thus consumed $79,226 of productive funds, a very large amount at that time. The treasurer stressed especially the need of maintaining trust funds, the income of which should be allocated over the various funds. [10]   An earlier Eliot at that time (1850), treasurer of the college, proclaimed himself against a proposal to buy land near the observatory to protect it against obstruction of views and the pollution spread by industry. S. Eliot simply pronounced that funds were not available for that purpose. The undergraduates had to be protected against diversions of their funds. [11]

From the deeds on behalf of Harvard College in Middlesex County, it is not easy to estimate the amount of land given to Harvard or purchased. Before 1800, an acre might be worth as little as £5 and as much as $720; from 1800 to 1839 as little as $150 and as much as $6,000. [12]

Land deeds registered in Cambridge for the college amounted to £3943 until 1793 and $4,905 in dollars. Deeds in pounds sterling averaged about $800 and in dollars, $2,205.

President Eliot put together the best study of Harvard's land history. [13] In April, 1896, Harvard owned $82\frac{1}{3}$ acres of land in Cambridge of the 2,880 acres of the City of Cambridge ($4\frac{1}{2}$ square miles). In all, 106 known transactions were involved from 1636 to 1897: 54 separate purchases, 7 repurchases of land previously sold by the university, 8 separate devices and gifts, 25 separate sales, 4 separate sales afterwards rebought in whole or in part, 7 or more contributions, or takings by the town or city, for laying out or widening streets, and 1 taking by the city for park purposes. Of Harvard's $82\frac{364}{1000}$ acres, the city gave only $3\frac{19}{24}$ acres.

The college obtained the land constituting the college yard in 12 parcels in the years 1638 to 1835.

Between 1786 and 1816, the corporation acquired the delta on which Memorial Hall was built.

The land north of Cambridge Street and south of Everett was bought in 13 parcels between 1816 and 1819. The college sold a large part of this land and also repurchased to some extent. The purchases and sales were profitable since the repurchase price was less than the acquisition price plus compound interest.

In 1818 the land for the botanical gardens was obtained and is still held. For the observatory, the corporation bought more than 600,000 feet (about 15 acres); and sold one-half. After describing the purchases in different parts of the Harvard Square area, President Eliot concluded rather optimistically:

. . . the University now owns land enough in Cambridge to make it certain that the setting of the University buildings will be an open one for many generations to come; or, in other words, it will not be necessary that the University buildings should stand close upon the streets as houses stand in denesely built quarters of a city.

In fact, some of Harvard's buildings are now right on the noisy and bustling Massachusetts Avenue.

A rather useful compilation is the following:

The delta on which Memorial Hall stands was bought in two parcels between 1786 and 1816, one of these parcels having been procured in one of the College Yard transactions. After these purchases were made, Cambridge Street and Broadway were laid out through them. The land north of Cambridge Street and south of Everett Street was bought in thirteen parcels between 1816 and 1839. Before many years had elapsed, considerable portions of this land were sold; and there have been seven re-purchases of parts

10. N. Silsbee to the President and Fellows of Harvard College, October 23, 1870.
11. S. A. Eliot to the Corporation of Harvard College, June 1, 1850.
12. *Memo of Deeds Harvard College as Recorded in Middlesex County to January 1829.*
13. *Harvard University in its Relations to the City of Cambridge,* April, 1896.

of the parcels thus sold. In this region the President and Fellows once owned more than twice the area which they now own; but the sales made by the college were nevertheless judicious; for land within this region has been repeatedly bought back at prices less than those for which it was sold by the college with compound interest at five percent computed thereon. Of the land procured for the Botanic Garden in 1818, nearly all still remains in the possession of the college, the missing area having been taken for widening streets. Across Garden Street from the Botanic Garden more than 600,000 feet of land were bought between 1841 and 1886 for the purposes of the Observatory; but nearly one half of that area was subsequently sold. . . .

The acquisition of land by the President and Fellows has been going on gradually all through the existence of the institution, but with different degrees of activity. The first lands acquired were the western part of the College Yard and the lots near Holyoke and Dunster streets. The enlargement of the College Yard to the eastward was the next object; and then came the extensions to the north, namely, the Memorial Hall delta, the Old Gymnasium delta, and the purchases north of Kirkland Street. The observatory lands were acquired later still, while Holmes Field and Jarvis Field were not purchased till after the Civil War. [14]

In 1811, one examination revealed holdings of 15 to 16 acres. One estimate in 1848 was that "the enclosure in which are situated the greater number of the buildings, contains twenty-three or twenty-four acres, and the institutions possesses, besides, various pieces of real estate in the cities of Cambridge and Boston." By 1896, Eliot's estimate was 60 acres in Cambridge aside from the botanical gardens and land about the observatory. [15]

When a citizen of Cambridge had land to sell, he often would try to sell to the college in the hope of getting a better price.

---

14. From *Harvard University Archives* ,but exact source is not clear (apparently by C. W. Eliot).

15. E. A. Denicke to C. W. Eliot, October 16, 1896.

16. *College Books*, vol. III, pp. 264-269; vol IV, p. 457.

Land Inventories

Harvard authorities have provided a number of inventories of Harvard land. One of the earliest was by President Wadsworth. On December 31, 1733, President Wadsworth wrote:

Whereas ye Lands and Annuities belonging to Harvard College are entered in ye College Books after a broken and disjointed manner, I (Benja. Wadsworth, President Dec. 30, 1733) thought it proper to collect said entries, and that what I find further belong to them and enter them here, in a more uniform compact manner. [16]

Wadsworth checked with corporation and governmental records for both gifts and disposal of land and buildings.

Wadsworth's survey suggests especially that under the pressure of financial needs the college sold much of its land and also buildings at bargain prices. For example, the college sold 20 acres in Lexington, a gift from Cambridge, for £50. A sale of 3½ acres at Cambridge Neck had been ordered by the corporation, but Wadsworth could not find a record of sale. The college had spent £300 developing $2\frac{2}{3}$ acres given by Cambridge in 1638, but the college was never reimbursed. In 1735 the college sold 3,000 acres in Rowley for £200. The college, to show its appreciation for the Rowley gift, agreed to pay half the cost of a monument on Rowley's grave.

A more comprehensive inventory appeared in 1910: [17]

> 80 acres in Cambridge
> 63 acres in Boston
> 394 acres in Jamaica Plains—biology
> 2000 acres in Petersham—forest
> 700 acres in Squam Lake—engineering
> total = 3,237

Land was so scarce that in 1889 an engineering firm studied the problem of reclaiming swampy land. It would cost $770,000 to reclaim 43 acres. [18]

---

17. C. C. Little (Secretary) to S.A.D. Cox, September 21, 1910, in *A. L. Lowell Papers*, F 1428.

Land Values

Harvard was very much interested in land values. The price, of course, tended upward.

One of the best evaluations of property appeared in 1858. [19]

1. Graduate Hall: 12,000 ft.
   @ 50¢ a foot . . . .$ 6,000.00
2. Adjoining Graduate Hall,
   35,000 ft. @ 40¢ a foot $14,000.00
3. 8,250 ft. on Dunster Street
   @ 20¢ a foot . . . .$ 1,650.00
4. 11,952 ft. on Holyoke Street
   @ 25¢ a foot . . . .$ 2,988.00
5. 4,800 ft. of land on Holyoke
   Street north of Printing Office
   @ 25¢ a foot . . . .$ 1,200.00
6. 10,437 ft. of land, corner
   Holyoke and Harvard Streets
   @ 50¢ a foot . . . .$ 5,218.50
7. Land, easterly from observatory,
   50,000 ft. @ 8¢ a foot . . . . . .$ 4,000.00
8. Gannett Estate, on Holmes Place
   near Commons, 60,000 ft.
   @ 20¢ a foot $12,000.00
9. Land in front of Divinity Hall,
   130,000 ft. @ 10¢ a foot $13,000.00
10. Other land near Divinity Hall,
    189,837 @ 3¢ a foot . . . .$ 5,695.00
                                     —————————
                                     $65,751.50

Total Land:
    512,276 feet or 11.7 acres @ 12.8¢ per foot;
    $5,620 per acre.

This report is interesting on some other points also. Houses are carried at very low values. For example, Dana House's evaluation was but $3,000. Dana House was built around 1820 and purchased with land for $9,000 in 1835. Its value currently must be at least $200,000. [20]

When buildings are occupied for college purposes and yield no income, they carry no evaluation.

Here are a number of citations giving the price of Harvard Land. (In 1869, the board of overseers estimated the value of 22 acres in the Harvard Yard at 20 cents a foot; and over 2 acres on the Delta at 20 cents a foot. [21])

Land values continued to rise. In 1929, the college was offered a site next to Hastings Hall at $20 per foot. President Lowell considered the price too high. In 1923, an owner would sell to Harvard for $4 a foot and another in 1925, both in the general college area, at $3 per foot. [22]

In a table deposited in the archives, I listed nine pieces of property in the years 1825 to 1897, with values per foot or per acre.

This compilation invites two conclusions. First, prices rise with time. Second, prices vary at any time according to the situation, with cost of land rising as the land approaches the yard.

The College Grounds

Care of the college grounds has been a costly item and has raised many problems. One of the most difficult, never really solved, was the exclusion of outsiders. At the very beginning, Eaton set barriers to keep students from getting out.

By the early nineteenth century, Kirkland found the interior of the yard an:

18. T. W. Harris to S. Eliot, November 30, 1847; *History of Harvard College*, p. 127; H. Bigelow to President Eliot, November 14, 1870; O. W. Holmes to C. W. Eliot, January 4, 1870; C. W. Eliot and als, *Agreement with Association of Alumni Concerning Alumni Hall*, December 31, 1869; Report of H. Manley, July 7, 1889 in *Eliot Papers*.
19. Schedule of Real Estate in Cambridge Belonging to Harvard College, Representing the Entry in the Treas-

urer's Books of Houses and Lands, in Cambridge, 109.403.3, December 3, 1858.
20. *Education, Bricks and Mortar*, pp. 60-61.
21. *Report of the Board of Overseers of Harvard College on the Condition, Needs and Prospects of the University*, 1869.
22. Treasurer to A. L. Lowell, July 18, 1929 in *A. L. Lowell Papers, 1925-29*, F.13.

unkempt sheep-commons' almost treeless, provided with no regular paths, and cluttered up with a brew house, the College woodyard, and sundry privies. A neighboring nuisance was the College pigpen, where the Corporation's own porkers fought with rats for the Commons garbage; for years the hideous clamor of a pig-killing was wont to disturb recitations in University. [23]

President Everett, writing in 1847, noted that only in the United States do students have right of exit after nightfall. He also urged an enclosure as a means of improving the appearance of the grounds.

But the establishment of thoroughfares for the public, in fact, if not in law, is the evil most to be apprehended. So long as the land northeast and southeast of the College was comparatively unoccupied, there were few persons to whom it was of any convenience to pass through our grounds. Compact settlements are now growing up in both directions, and the time has already arrived when a numerous and rapidly increasing population passes habitually through the College Yard. . . . The College grounds are destitute of that air of quiet and repose so congenial with a place of education, and which produces so agreeable an impression in the English universities. Servants with parcels and dogs, noisy school boys at their sports, workmen crossing on their way to and from their place of labor, are very frequently seen within the enclosure. Vagrants, hand organists, beggars, and characters still more objectionable, are not as rare as could be wished. . . . [24]

Everett tried to deal with this problem. On advice of counsel, obstacles were placed so that entry and exit were not possible. Apparently a construction of obstacles for a day periodically and notification of the authorities of the intention to close all passageways would suffice to assure a permanent denial of trespassers.

The Harvard agent asserted that "the passages were obstructed and closed up, by fastening planks across the wooden posts, with screws, and across the stone posts with iron wires so as entirely to prevent any person from passing through the same." [25]

Somehow, the results have not been as expected as freedom of movement still prevails.

---

23. Morison, *Three Centuries of Harvard, 1636-1936*, p. 216.
24. P. R. Frothingham, *Edward Everett, Orator and Statesman*, 1925, p. 300.
25. Registry of Deeds, in *Book of Deposit*, No. 19, p. 75, March 4, 1847. S. Greenleaf to President Everett, February 5, 1847; E. Everett to B. W. Whitney and J. B. Dana, Justices of Peace, February 25, 1847.

The pursuit of knowledge in spite of difficulties is strikingly exemplified in the case of those students who board themselves.

Drawing by Nathan Hayward

*C. B., IV, May 22, 1727, pp. 547, 552.
**C. B., IV, p. 628.
***C. B., IV, December 28,1742, pp. 676, 737.

Food at Harvard College in the 17th - 18th Century. Morning bever (breakfast) consisted of a piece of bread and a mug of beer, eaten in the students' room. One graduate lived on corn meal, cooked over his fireplace.

In 1807 the bad food was referred to the senior class, who entered the Commons hall in a body, sniffed the food, and unanimously walked out.

Five Presidents, 19th Century
Quincy,   Everett,   Sparks,   Walker,   Falton

Portrait of John Thornton Kirkland, 1770-1840
President, 1810-1828
Permission Fogg Art Museum, Harvard

Portrait of Thomas Hollis, 1659-1731
Permission of Fogg Art Museum, Harvard

Dunster House

Harvard   *Stoughton*   *Massachusets*

Portrait of John Hancock, Treasurer, 1773-1777
John Singleton Copley, American, 1738-1815
Courtesy, the City of Boston
On loan at the Museum of Fine Arts, Boston

South View of the Several Halls of Harvard College.

Charles W. Eliot, President, 1869-1909

Ebenezer Storer, Treasurer, 1777-1807
The Metropolitan Museum of Art
Gift of Thomas J. Watson, 1940

PART

6

ENDOWMENTS

42

Why Endowment?

An institution of higher learning can survive on tuition fees, current gifts, and on capital for its plant. The fact is that by the early 1960s endowment income contributed only 5 percent of the income of all institutions. But for Harvard and a number of other institutions endowment income is much more important. As we shall see, its relative contribution at Harvard has fallen in the last fifty years as it has almost everywhere, but not nearly as much as in the nation. In the early 1960s endowment still accounted for almost one quarter of Harvard income and if research contracts were omitted, the contribution would rise to 30 percent. President Pusey observed that in twenty-five years the contribution of endowment had fallen from 47 percent of the cost of operating the college to 27 percent; and to provide as much relatively as fifteen years ago, a doubling of endowment would be necessary.[1]

When the treasurer issued his first report for the year 1826, endowment income accounted for 50 percent of income; in 1920 its contribution was still about half. But as noted there has been a large relative decline. In the 1920s, the ratio still was above 40 percent; in the depressed 1930s under 40 percent; and by 1950 around 25 percent.[2]

Dean McGeorge Bundy in 1957 stated the case for endowment most effectively. His major point was that in the preceding fifteen years Harvard had seriously stretched its reliance on tuition and annual gifts. It was now necessary to "find means of raising our *structure of salaries* more firmly on hard money."[3]

A statement of Harvard's views on endowment by a member of the Harvard corporation follows:

Endowment capital perpetually entrusted to the continuing care of privately-appointed custodians, has been the Rock of Gibraltar of American higher education. The private system of college and university training built on this rock has been one of our country's great contributions to history. Endowment made our education free and will keep it free . . . No university in the world has been more fortunate than Harvard in the building of a strong endowment; yet it must not be thought that Harvard has escaped the impact of the eroding influences of the last generation, the wars and depressions and uncertainties and inflation that have combined to reduce the stabilizing value of endowment capital. In 1915 it cost Harvard about $3 million to operate, and the University drew roughly half this amount from endowment income. In 1950 it cost Harvard about $30 million to operate, of which close to one-quarter came from endowment income.[4]

1. *Report of the President of Harvard College*, 1955-1956, p. 23; *A Program for Harvard College, Report from the President to the Board of Overseers*, October 8, 1956, p. 6.
2. R. Kane and D. Doten, "The Case for Endowments," in *Harvard Alumni Bulletin*, 1951, pp. 211-214.
3. McGeorge Bundy, "What Should Harvard Pay Its Faculty?," in *Harvard Today*, Spring, 1957, pp. 15-16.
4. Kane and Doten, *op. cit.*

Above all, endowment income provides opportunities to meet new contingencies and to exploit new opportunities. This function of endowment is well performed when there is the maximum freedom of use. Without these free funds, President Lowell insisted, many opportunities to find brilliant men are lost.[5]

In the Harvard tradition, President Conant also emphasized the indispensable need of more endowment. He discussed the issues fully.[6] Admitting that the inflation of the last generation had consumed the 100 percent rise of endowment, he nevertheless asked the skeptics of the value of endowment to ask where Harvard would be without its endowment. Only a runaway inflation in his view justified the doubts of those who would prefer gifts for current use to endowment.

In a similar vein, President Pusey referred to the gifts of capital which enable the university "to grow and acquire increased strength." The 20 percent of income from current gifts are appreciated, but the support goes when the current needs vanish.[7] It is the same story in every professional school.

One reason for the quest of endowment, as well as increased doubts regarding its contribution is the attrition of capital funds. Losses occur because of the inflationary process and the rising enrollment (less endowment available per student). Endowment's growing inadequacy is related to the relative decline of endowment income to the rising per capita incomes and the average cost of faculty members and employees, related in turn to inflation and rising productivity.

President Pusey pointed out that there were three colleges with endowments per student of $38,000, $40,000 and $42,700 as compared with Harvard's $30,000, and three others with $25,000 to $27,000.[8]

It is no wonder then that institutions of higher learning, heavily dependent on endowment income, relate their enrollment to the impact on endowment.

Large increases in numbers reduce the contribution of endowment per student.

The inflation problem is serious. If a $100 million endowment yields an income of $4 million, a doubling of the price level with an equal endowment reduces the real value of the income from the funds by 50 percent. Most college administrations are aware of this point. But they fail to take into account two other factors which greatly reduce the cost of inflation. One is the obvious one that institutions of higher learning increasingly protect themselves by investing in equities that respond to inflation. For example, from 1940 to 1963 consumer prices rose by 120 percent; in the same period an index of stock market prices increased by 443 percent or almost 3 times as much. If college treasurers had invested one-third of their funds in common stocks, they would have practically offset the costs of inflation. But though by the 1960s equities accounted for one-half of investments, they may well have equaled less than one-third of investments over the period 1940 to 1963.

Those disturbed by the erosive effects of inflation upon endowment leave out of account a second factor, namely the relation of inflation to income. To some extent income rises as inflation proceeds. Had prices been established from 1940 to 1963, income would have been much less and Harvard's endowment income substantially less. Inflation has not necessarily been good for Harvard, but costs have been less than is generally assumed. Under inflationary conditions, business income rises much more than prices, with beneficial effects on endowment yields.

Another factor making for inadequacy of endowment is the rise of wages and salaries, only in part the product of inflation. In fact, over modern economic history rising productivity has contributed more to rising income or rising income per employee than inflation. A $1,000 million endowment (current value) yields say $30 to $40 million today. Fifty

5. *Report of the President of Harvard College*, 1917-1918, pp. 29-30.
6. *Ibid.*, 1950-1951, pp. 23-26.
7. *Ibid.*, 1954-1955, p. 24; 1952-1953, pp. 10-11; Harvard

University Archives, UA, II, 10.73; UAV 136.124.4.
8. *A Program for Harvard College, Why Harvard Needs More Money.*

years from now, with prices rising 2 percent and productivity 3 percent, per capita incomes will rise by more than 1,000 percent. Professors' salaries, if unchanged in relation to increasing per capita income, would command only one-eleventh as much as in 1965.

Many search for more endowment because the free funds of the colleges are so small. Much of the capital, moreover, is in unproductive land and other property. In 1712, the total unrestricted income was £2,685 and even by 1773 only £10,040. Again in 1869-1870, President Eliot observed that the capital yielding income for instruction and expenses of the university and college was only $730,000. Hence, the university had to depend on tuition for two-thirds of the cost of instruction inclusive of the library. The university was suffering already from incomes insufficient to support its professorships. Eliot asked the friends of the university to consider the need for invested funds, especially unrestricted, to finance salaries, retirement allowances, scholarships, service of the library, chapel, etc.[9]

Despite this great interest in endowment, the increased reliance is on current gifts. How important these current gifts are is suggested by the following statistics provided by President Conant who compared the gifts during his twenty years against those of the preceding twenty years.[10]

Gifts, 1912-1932 and 1932-1952 in millions of dollars

	1912-1932	1932-1952
Additions to capital	84	97
Gifts for immediate use	44	48

In these years, even at a generous assumption of a 5 percent return on capital, the additional income available from new capital was $4 million and $5 million respectively as compared with $44 million

and $48 million of income from funds for immediate use. Obviously, when funds are scarce, the pressure is increasingly to depend on gifts for current use.

That current gifts exceed the income from endowment does not suggest that the attrition of endowment is not of major importance. The fact is that endowment income finances professorial salaries, scholarships, and the like. Current gifts to some extent provide funds for similar purposes, but on an annual basis. But to a considerable extent current gifts are for special uses and notably for organized research, which may to some extent be complementary to the services financed by endowment, but are largely not available for financing the services provided by endowment funds.

With expenditures relatively fixed, a college may experience embarrassing moments if dependence is excessively on gifts for short periods. The Harvard Business School offers a good example. Its short-term annual gifts varied from $259,000 to $19,000 over the years, 1929 to 1938. In the same period receipts from students were a maximum of $768,324 and a minimum of $509,119. Endowment income fluctuated between $176,084 (5.25 percent) and $129,072 (4 percent). Total income ranged from $1,171,542 to $750,748.

With such large variations of income, and especially of short-term gifts, and with expenditures on salaries, the library, and research to a substantial degree fixed, the school was bound to incur large deficits. Expenditures declined only from $822,302 to $750,348, a reduction much less than of receipts.[11]

Another example is the school of public health. Its complaint was that in 1931-1932 endowment income equaled 79 percent of the school's budget, but the 1951 budget, $4\frac{1}{2}$ times as large as that of 1931-1932, included endowment income equal to but 8 percent of the total income.[12]

Harvard's endowment and income greatly exceeded those of its competitors through most if not all of its history. In 1897, all institutions of higher learning had but $100 million in endowment. Harvard

9. *Report of the President of Harvard College,* 1881-1882, pp. 50-51; *Treasurer's Statement,* 1873-1874, p. 67.
10. *Report of the President of Harvard College,* 1951-1952, p. 7.

11. *Ibid.,* 1937-1938, pp. 229-234.
12. *Ibid.,* 1951-1952, pp. 554-555.

with about $10 million accounted for roughly 10 percent. From 1900 to the present Harvard further improved its relative position, for by now it had about 15 percent of all endowed funds.[13]

Lack of Endowment

Harvard authorities complained of the lack of endowment during most of its history. Thus, in 1731, in his address upon the occasion of the death of Thomas Hollis, Edward Wigglesworth, Hollis' Professor of Divinity, praised the benefections of Mr. Hollis and added "nor may it ever be objected in prejudice to his Memory, that he hath founded Two Professorships among us, which are called after his Name, without settling such a support of them, as is sufficient for the Eligence of the present Times."

President Everett in 1847-1848 complained of the small permanent income but nevertheless added if the "private bounty were struck out of existence, it would sink at once into the condition of an insignificant seminary."[14] Again ten years later the treasurer expressed satisfaction at the size of the endowment and the skillful investment policies; but "no provision exists for the expansion of any department."[15] This was a constant source of complaint. The president, in 1863-1864, pointed out that sufficient means did not exist "for proper care of grounds, for thorough repair of the buildings, for making necessary alterations . . . The Library cannot keep up with the serials to which it has subscribed. . . ."[15]

Time and again presidents expressed their unhappiness over the limited amount of free funds, the need of more endowment to finance the rising enrollment, and, above all, the need of free and untrammeled income.[16]

Beginning with Eliot, the major emphasis was on the need of additional endowment to finance higher salaries and increase of faculty personnel. In 1905, President Eliot obtained funds for "increasing the scale of salaries throughout Harvard College; increasing the salaries in special instances to facilitate promotions and to prevent the loss to other institutions of valued teachers." Eliot also stressed the need of more endowment to offset the decline in yield, and losses associated with imprudent investments.[17]

Under Lowell and Conant the emphasis was on the use of endowments to finance faculty salaries.[18] The problem became increasingly acute as the cost of living rose. Competition quickened, and increased funds were needed for research purposes. Again the problem of inadequate coverage of endowed chairs by endowment funds arose. In the early 1920s the law school dean complained of the fact that endowment financed less than one-tenth of the cost of most of the full professors.

In 1940-1941, Conant, influenced by current theories of stagnation, noted "that larger fortunes are rapidly disappearing . . . Income from endowment is shrinking, and the future is uncertain."[19]

In an interesting though equivocal statement the Rockefeller Foundation, upon providing a gift of endowment, said: "These [liberalizing] provisions represent an attempt to free the future from frozen funds and tired endowments in the belief that the wisdom of this generation cannot be substituted for the wisdom of the next in the solution of problems hidden from our eyes."[20]

13. C. F. Thwing, *The American College*, 1897, pp. 192-195; *Ibid*, College Administration, 1900, pp. 155-157.
14. *Ibid.*, 1847-1848, p. 5.
15. *Report of the Treasurer of Harvard College*, 1847-1848, pp. 3-4.
16. *Report of the President of Harvard College*, 1863-1864, pp. 11-15.
17. *Ibid.*, 1867-1868, pp. 4-6; *Report of the Treasurer of Harvard College*, 1867-1868, p. 4.
18. *Report of the President of Harvard College*, 1877-1878, pp. 32-41; 1878-1879, pp. 34-37; 1903-1904, p. 52;

1904-1905, pp. 11-12; "President Eliot's Report," in *The Harvard Bulletin*, vol. 1, no. 13, p. 1, Feb., 1899; also see supplement, Jan., 1902.
19. *Report of the President of Harvard College*, 1915-1916, p. 27; 1917-1918, pp. 28-39; 1923-1924, p. 185; 1924-1925, pp. 169-173; 1928-1929, pp. 125-126; 1929-1930, p. 21; 1934-1935, pp. 20-21; 1940-1941, pp. 251-252; 1945-1946, pp. 395-397; 1946-1947, p. 12; 1948-1949, p. 233; 1951-1952, p. 35.
20. *Harvard Alumni Bulletin*, vol. 40, p. 776, 1938.

By frozen funds is meant, restricted endowment. By tired endowment, the Foundation probably had in mind the lag of endowment income in relation to rising costs. The sentence also raises the question of the lack of wisdom of allocating resources through endowment in the light of rapid changes in our dynamic world.

In general, college administrations seek endowment as a means of assuring financial strength and stability for their college or university. They acknowledge that endowment may be eroded by inflation and even economic growth, and that endowment is not as useful as it might be because so much of it is restricted. Yet they are impressed by its durability. Thus, Kane relates the experience under a gift by Thomas Cotton of $156.13 in 1727, the yield to be used to help support the president. Two hundred and twenty-three years later, President Pusey still received the return on Cotton's gift, a sum of $6.57 in 1950.[21]

There is always the danger of a galloping inflation which destroys a large part of the capital funds of the university. Only a fortunate speculation by Treasurer Storer prevented this outcome during the Revolutionary War.

Yet over the years enthusiasm for endowment has prevailed. Thus, in 1903, the faculty of the medical school was seeking endowments for professional chairs.

Even President Eliot overassessed the contribution and the durability of endowments.

. . . We may be sure that our descendants of five centuries hence will have the sense to treat the endowments which we are establishing as England has treated some of her medieval endowments— reconstruct them, when they need it, without destroying them . . . . [22]

---

21. R. K. Kane and D. Doten, *op. cit.,* pp. 211-214.

22. C. W. Eliot, *The Exemption from Taxation,* p. 326.

43

Cumulation of Endowment Funds

In 1965, the Harvard funds (market value) passed the billion dollar mark. The rise is spectacular when comparison is made with £800 sterling given by John Harvard at the outset or even with the million-dollar breakthrough by 1854-1855, 218 years after the founding of Harvard. (Dartmouth, a rival, reached slightly more than $1 million in 1893).[1]

A former treasurer of Harvard expressed well the wonder of the durability of Harvard's trust funds.

Few people realize that the oldest Trust Funds in the United States are included among the many legacies and bequests that make up the Harvard Endowment. The earliest date appearing upon the records of the Treasurer is 1643, the year in which Lady Mowlson gave £100 to the Country Treasury of Massachusetts Bay Colony, the income thereof to assist indigent students at the College in Cambridge. It was not, however, until 1648 that Harvard began to receive annually £15 from this fund. As of June 30, 1939, Lady Mowlson's bequest stood upon our books at $7,160.65—the interest upon this sum of $315.08 for the year ending June 30, 1939, having been expended for scholarships. The fact that Lady Mowlson should have given money to Harvard in 1643, so soon after its founding, is of interest, but more astounding is the fact that 297 years later the fund is still in existence and functioning according to her wishes. Gentlemen,

297 years is a long time for anything to exist financially.[2]

An overseers' committee observed in 1849 that:

the grant of £400 made by the General Court in 1636, and the £779.17.2, bequeathed by John Harvard of glorious memory, have by the blessing of Providence accumulated to this princely fortune [$789,284]. The little acorn planted by the fathers of Massachusetts two centuries ago has become a gigantic oak. Young eagles are nestled in its branches . . . .[3]

The early use of the technique of building up foundations out of increased earnings as well as the control of appointments by donors is suggested by a letter from Thomas Hollis in 1721.

. . . I am mightily pleased with the character you give of the gentleman whom you have proposed to be my first Professor, and have him under my consideration. But I am thinking, whether I am yet ripe for a nomination, my adventures not being yet entered into your Treasurer's cash, and, after they are, must be placed out to improvement, to produce the designed maintenance for the one and the other purpose; so

---

1. *Treasurer's Statement,* 1854-1855, pp. 38-39; L. B. Richardson, *History of Dartmouth College,* 1932, p. 693.

2. W. H. Claflin, Jr., "Our Endowment: Its Vital Importance to the University," in *Harvard Alumni Bulletin,* May 31, 1940, p. 1081.

3. *Report of Visiting Committee Harvard University of the Board of Overseers,* January 1849, p. 13.

that, if I proceed presently to nominate, as your letter urges me to do, he must be straitened, or he must break in upon the principal, neither of which is agreeable to me at this writing.[4]

In 1685, William Browne gave the college £100 (roughly $330) for the "bringing up of poor Scholars." The son of Major William Browne in 1731 gave an additional £150 or about $500. But by 1947 the book value of the two gifts was $4,567 or more than 5 times the original fund and by 1963, $6,097. These large gains may be explained by the compound interest law but actually the gains are much smaller than might be thus explained. In a period of 50 years, for example, with an average yield of around 6 percent, the usual figure during Harvard's first 200 years, capital values if not spent would rise to 18.4 times the original investment; and 338 times for the first 100 years. No such increases are to be found over Harvard's 330 years of history for any of its funds.

Then how does one explain the large rises that occurred for many of the funds? One explanation is that the income of funds turned over to the university were not always used. Thus, the Browne Scholarship required that preference be given to ancestors of the Brownes and to residents of Salem.[5] In some years, eligible applicants did not appear and hence income was added to principal.

In 1845 an overseers' committee urged that thereafter no new professorship should be introduced unless it could carry the load without help of general funds of the college. And where already done, as soon as the chair was vacant, no further appointment should be made till the capital was adequate. A legislative committee of 1850 noted that gifts of the past for the "foundation of professorships then deemed large and sufficient, are now, by the changes in customs and requirements, small and insufficient. . . ."[6]

In discussing a gift with a prospective donor, President Eliot observed:

that in order to provide against the possibility of the income being too small for the accomplishment of your purpose in the course of generations in consequence of changes in values or in the rate of interest, the President and Fellows be authorized to have the fellowship vacant either at their discretion or for a period not exceeding . . . years in succession, the fund to be accumulated during such vacancy. . . .[7]

It was a common practice to allow a chair to be unoccupied, with a view to accumulating capital, as outlays were cut and the capital was allowed to fructify. Thus, under the McLean chair in history, the president and fellows were authorized "to add the income thereof to the principal for such length of time as may be necessary to increase said fund to a sum the income whereof may be sufficient for the support of such professor. . . ." In 1848, the administration considered favorably the practice of allowing the fund of a professorship to accumulate where the relevant instruction was not indispensable every year.

Again, the Hollis Professorship of Divinity had been vacant for forty-two years to allow funds to accumulate. In offering Bliss Perry the Smith Chair, which had been founded in 1816 and had been occupied by Ticknor, Longfellow, and J.R. Lowell, in 1905, Eliot pointed out that the chair had not been occupied since 1886.[8]

A treasury memo examined thirty-three gifts from 1719 until 1867. From 1836 to 1867, the original

4. Josiah Quincy, *The History of Harvard College,* 1840, vol. I, p. 534.
5. *Endowment Funds of Harvard University,* 1947; *Financial Report to the Board of Overseers of Harvard College,* 1962-1963; 1964-1965.
6. *Reports of the Overseers,* 1844-1847, vol. 7; *Committee on Visitation of B. O.,* January 16, 1845; House Report No. 164, April 1850; *Harvard University.*
7. Memorandum on First Travelling Fellowship in *C. Eliot Papers* (date not given).
8. Rules and Statutes of the McLean Professorship of Ancient and Modern History, (date not shown); Correspondence E. Everett and S. Eliot, October, 1848; Memo of September 19, 1856 on the Gift of Mr. Ward Nicholas Boylston; *Report of the Committee on the Bussey Institution,* February 22, 1861; G. H. Williams (editor), *The Harvard Divinity School,* p. 167; C. Eliot, *Harvard University Papers 95, Letter Book,* 1903-1906; C. Eliot to Bliss Perry, August 3, 1905.

amount of gifts remained in most instances unchanged. But gifts from earlier years showed substantial rises in most instances. From 1719 to 1835, eleven comparisons were available. The values of two rose to 3 times or more of their original value; five, from $1 \frac{1}{2}$ to 2 times; four, from 1 to $1 \frac{1}{2}$ times.[9]

The rise to 1965 of a value of 50 to 1 of an original gift is another matter. First, there were large distributions of capital gains during the post World War II years. A comparison of values of most funds in 1943 and 1963 reveals a rise of about one-third, the explanation being distributions based on realized gains from sales of securities.

The difference between the 1943 and 1965 values is not always of the order of one-third. For the Boylston Professorship of Rhetoric and Oratory the gain is no less than 10 times—from $45,000 to $497,000. The explanation of the unusually large gain is that out of the 1956-1958 endowment drive the corporation added funds to chairs established before 1900 that were yielding income much below what was necessary to finance the chair. The same procedures were applied to other chairs as well, e.g., the Fisher Professorship of Natural History, a rise from $41,000 in 1943 to $484,000 in 1965 and the McLean Professorship of Ancient and Modern History, $43,000 to $484,000.

Seven gifts received in the eighteenth century increased in value from 6 to 48 times by 1963 in relation to the original gifts. Many funds received in the nineteenth century were also much more valuable

in 1963 than at the time the donation was made. The average for eighteen endowments was a value of $5 \frac{1}{2}$ times as high in 1963 as at time of donation—the year of donation varying from 1803 to 1899. (I leave out two professorships that received special allocations by the corporation in the later 1950s.)

For the twentieth century, the average value on Harvard's books of twelve important gifts has risen to 3 times the original values. Most of these funds that escalate substantially—as high as 6 to 1 for the Knight Fund for Musical Composition—are for scholarships, fellowships, and prizes. The three professorships involved show an average rise of but 15 percent.[10]

Age has contributed substantially to Harvard's capital. The relationship between current book value and a fortiori market value to original gift values reflects some exploitation of the compound interest law. The ratio of current values to original gifts tends to be higher the older the original gift. Thus, growth in values is also related to the failure to use all income, either because many donors require Harvard to accumulate part of the income, on occasion until a given capital sum is attained, or because the college or university encounters difficulties in paying out income for purposes that meet the requirements of the donor. One will also find many instances, especially in earlier years, of careless administration of the funds and hence failure to use income. The accumulation of income invested and not paid out tends to be substantially larger on gifts for scholarships, fellowships, and prizes than for financing professorships.

9. *Memo of 1868* (no title).

10. *Endowment Funds of Harvard University*, p. 47.

44

The Decline of Endowment

Causes of Decline

Erosion of endowment goes back to the earliest days of the college. A large part of the Harvard legacy was apparently squandered by Eaton, the first head of Harvard. Treasurer Danforth included all gifts that were not restricted and unexpended balances in an account called college stock. In 1654, when Danforth became treasurer, the stock amounted to £459-£460; and by 1668, £863. In March, 1683, Danforth reported "the personal estate of the college, satisfactorily invested, amounting to £2,357. . . ." But by 1693, the college stock had sunk to £1,530. The decline was no less than £1,100, a loss associated partly with bad loans. Treasurer Nowell was unable to account for losses of £1,100 under his administration (1683 to 1686). Apparently there was some recovery by 1693.[1]

Sir Matthew Holworthy left £1,234, which were invested in twenty or more mortgages at 8 percent, to Harvard in 1678. "No Holworthy Fund was established, and the principal seems to have been gradually dissipated as the loans fell due, and money for current expenses was urgently needed. . . ."[2]

Another period in which the decline of stock was precipitous was from 1810 to 1827. Stock equaling $149,000 in 1810 had dropped to $88,000 by 1827.[3]

The reduction of the college stock was related to large outlays for capital purposes, e.g., University Hall, $65,009; Holworthy Hall, $24,500; medical college, $21,491.

In 1828 and again in 1840, the treasurer wrote down assets to their real value. The Gore legacy was removed from the stock account since it was to be used to build the Gore Library. Two shares in the Charles River Bridge, carried at $2,000, were written down to their real value of $200; and the Charles River Bridge annuity, unpaid for ten years and carried at $11,111 was discharged from the college books.[4]

Inflation and the rising scale of operations generally reduce the relative contribution of endowment. Yet according to the first Harvard Treasurer's Report (1826), with operating costs at $40,000, endowment income contributed one-half at Harvard and in roughly a hundred years later (1920), with costs up 100 times to $4 million, endowment still provided half the total income. But in the thirty-five years between 1915 and 1950 inflation and rising operations, despite an increase of endowment by $150 million, reduced endowment's share of income by one-half.[5]

In 1910, endowment of all institutions of higher learning yielded 17 percent of educational income. By 1961-1962, endowment only accounted for less

1. Quincy, *op. cit.*, vol. II, p. 232; Samuel Eliot Morison, *Harvard College in the Seventeenth Century*, 1936, vol. II, p. 388; *Founding of Harvard College*, pp. 222-223.
2. Morison, *Harvard College in the Seventeenth Century*, vol. II, p. 438.
3. Quincy, *op. cit.*, vol. II, pp. 557-558.
4. *Treasurer's Statement*, September 21, 1840.
5. Based on *Report of the Treasurer of Harvard College; Financial Report to the Board of Overseers of Harvard College*, 1965-1966.

than 4 percent of educational income. Not only has endowment income become less important but this kind of productive asset has become less significant than unproductive assets; that is, the physical plant, which is a burden on institutions of higher learning. In 1890 and 1930, endowment for all institutions was 80 percent of the value of each physical plant. By 1962, endowment was but 36 percent of the value of each physical plant.[6]

Harvard's relative dependence on endowment has fallen less than for the nation. But the trends are roughly similar. While endowment income in all United States institutions of higher learning dropped by 73 percent from 1920 to 1962, Harvard's endowment for educational and general income only dropped by 58 percent between 1920 and 1965.

Why the reduced importance of endowment? One explanation, of course, is inflation. Since the war, endowments have lost up to one-third of their total value as a result of inflation. But this does not allow for any excess of capital gains in the postwar period over losses in the 1930s. Most institutions reduced the loss due to the inflationary process by putting more of their funds into common stocks. Endowment also becomes relatively less important as per capita income at stable prices rises. Obviously, the income from $4 billion of endowment accounts for less in an economy where the per capita income has doubled than it did when the per capita income was only half as large.

Another factor that may have reduced the significance of endowment is the increase of taxes on high-income groups. Previously, many gifts to the universities came from these high-income groups. A high-income recipient ($200,000 unmarried, $400,000 married), subject to a marginal tax rate of 92 percent, (70 percent in 1965), may hesitate about making

gifts to institutions of higher learning. The reason is that he has so little left after he pays these heavy taxes. On the other hand, many contend that since a gift would cost only 8 cents for every dollar given because the tax collector would pay the other 92 cents, this stimulates giving by high-income groups. The fact is that these high-income groups have actually increased their gifts in relation to their income, although the reduction in their numbers has more than offset this advantage. Despite the large rise of tax rates since the 1920s, gifts were roughly the same percentage of income in the 1950s as in the 1920s.

Still another factor is of some relevance. Now gifts are given for endowment to a much lesser degree than in the past. Thus of private gifts, endowment received 76, 51, and 34 percent in 1919-1920, 1939-1940, and 1955-1956, respectively. At Harvard the decline was from 38 percent in 1930 to 24 percent in 1950; at MIT, from 51 to 6 percent for these two years.

A rise of enrollment only 20 percent that of the nation's colleges contributed to Harvard's relatively small decline of endowment to total income.[7] Where endowment is relatively important, administrators tend to be reluctant toward rises of enrollment.[8]

Another reason for the decline of endowment has been the abuse of endowment funds. President Eliot was aware of the erosion of endowment. In 1889, he refused to support a demand on the Boylston Fund beyond $20,000, for "to diminish principal is to restrict the continuous opportunities of a fund...."[9]

At times Eliot was too enthusiastic on past achievements. It is difficult to defend the statement

6. Department of Health, Education, and Welfare, *Digest of Educational Statistics*, 1965 ed., pp. 100, 109, 110; Department of Health, Education, and Welfare, *Financial Statistics of Institutions of Higher Education*, 1959-1960, p. 6; S. E. Harris, *Higher Education: Resources and Finance*, 1962, pp. 21, 29.

7. A similar explanation is relevant for Princeton. Endowment income declined only from 31 percent of all income in 1934 to 28 percent in 1957. But gifts rose from 6 to 18 percent. From *Princeton University Financial Reports*.

8. E. C. Budd, *Trends in Yale's Finances*, p. 2; R. A. Mestres, *The Changing Role of Endowments*, Meetings of the Eastern Association of Colleges and Universities, December 11, 1955, p. 62; S. E. Harris, "The Economics of Harvard," in *Harvard Alumni Bulletin*, February 20, 1960, pp. 383-384.

9. C. W. Eliot to Professor E. C. Pickering, May 18, 1889.

that "no smallest gift made to Harvard University for a permanent purpose has ever been lost."

Many years ago President Eliot contended " ... that the using up of unrestricted funds bearing the name of a benefactor by charging annual deficits to these funds was highly objectionable. Such a practice would in time discourage the giving of such funds. ... "[10]

In the 1930s other authorities were as pessimistic as President Eliot had been in the 1880s. In fact, Harvard's record was excellent compared to national standards.

Reeves and others have found that fewer than half the college boards investigated a generation ago had a clear record with regard to violations of trusts. Goodwin found a tendency to disregard trust provisions of endowment gifts and warned trustees to seek legal advice and pay attention to their trust obligations. Blackwell also made some interesting studies along these lines. One of the leaders in this field wrote as follows in the 1930s:

Special attention was given to the subject of endowment, about which very hazy ideas then prevailed. The nature of endowment was defined, and attention was called to many unsuitable practices then in use. Examples were given where institutions had pledged endowment funds for loans for current expenses, then had lost them because they were unable to raise the funds to pay the loans. Instances were cited where loans were made by denominational colleges on denominational properties, which tied the hands of the college trustees in enforcing collections of delinquent income and principal. ... [11]

Reduction of endowment through financing of deficits can be a serious matter. Through the years 1946 to 1957 a small liberal arts college accumulated a deficit of $620,000 largely at the expense of endowment.

Abuse of endowment should not conceal the great contribution of endowment, and especially in protecting the institution of higher learning against outside pressures. But it is also true that the availability of endowment may make the institutions too independent of current values. Adam Smith, Sir Arthur Hobhouse, and others have been critical of excessive reliance on endowment.

In the interwar period, endowment lost much of its appeal, and especially as financial pressures confronted college treasurers. Among others, J. Rosenwald, Alfred Sloan, and the general education board proposed consumption of capital as the means of improving financial conditions.[12]

From this chapter, it must be clear that inflation, rising per capita incomes, rising taxes, growing importance of current gifts and other sources of income, increases of enrollment, and mismanagement have reduced the significance of endowment income. But when endowment income is a substantial part of income and endowment gifts continue to be important, one should not write down the importance of this kind of income. For Harvard, endowment income continues to be important, though not as much as in the past.[13]

One issue of management still is troublesome. Assume either that income of an endowed chair is not used, and hence is added to the capital sum. May the corporation later use this income or is it now inviolate? Or assume capital gains. Does the university have the right to distribute them? Experience in recent years suggests that the corporation may at least distribute realized capital gains though in practice the income, not the capital, is consumed. One might argue that capital gains may also be consumed though there are difference of opinions here. Some also contend that once income, not spent, is added to

10. E. L. Hawthorne, *Fund Raising for the Small College*, 1950, p. 191; *Department of Health, Education, and Welfare, College and University Endowment Investments*, p. 4.

11. *Encyclopedia of Educational Research*, (rev. ed.) 1950, pp. 251-252.

12. S. E. Harris, *op. cit.*; pp. 445-451.

13. E. T. Stewart, Jr., "Alumni Support and Annual Giving" *The Annals*, September, 1955, p. 135 and A. P. Sloan, Jr., "Operation Expansion," *College and University Business*, April, 1956, p. 21.

endowment it cannot be consumed. Thus the treasurer to President Lowell: "I was under the impression that income so added to the principal became part of the principal and could not subsequently be reconverted into income."[14]

The Problem of Inadequate Endowment for Professorial Chairs

As prices and incomes rise, endowment income inclusive of the income from a foundation for a chair become increasingly inadequate. The problem is not only the rising cost of a professorship vis-à-vis the income available to finance it. It is also that even at the time a gift is made it is often inadequate. Samuel Eliot at midnineteenth century expressed it thus:

. . . but because the professorships which have been established in it, have been built upon insufficient foundations . . . if the Corporation were to adopt a rule to the effect that they would never again appoint a professor till the funds provided were sufficient for his support, they would take the first step to correct this evil, which has grown up entirely within the academic department. . . . [15]

A good example of the difficulties induced by inadequate endowment of chairs is given by the Hollis Divinity Chair established in 1721. The income available from the gift was £80 at that time, with £20 of income added later. By the Revolutionary War, the college authorities pointed out that the "salaries of the Hollisian Professor, which the pious Founder spoke of as an honorable support, are at this Day not worth more than three pounds sterling each year. . . . [16] Whereas in 1830 the income was about $200, the cost was $1500. But the college has maintained this chair for a hundred years and would continue to support it. A committee of 1830 would impose on the holder of the chair additional duties since the foundation paid such a small part of the costs.[17]

In 1830, the Hollis Professorship was still a source of concern. A committee of the corporation would not appoint a successor to Professor Ware to the Hollis Chair since virtually the whole cost is borne out of university general funds.[18]

In 1869 the corporation complained that with one possible exception the income from endowed chairs was inadequate. Two of the foundations did not pay a tenth part of the salary and a majority yielded less than half. The college could ask for more money not "because it has so few foundations but because it has so many inadequate foundations. . . . "[19]

14. C. F Adams to A. L. Lowell, October 21, 1910, in *A. L. Lowell Papers, 1909-1914,* F-519.
15. Letter to the President of Harvard College by Samuel A. Eliot, a Member of the Corporation, 1849, p. 35.
16. President Samuel Langdon to the Honble The Council and House of Representatives of the State of Massachusetts Bay in General Court Assembled, January 6, 1779.
17. *Report of the Committee Appointed in the Support of the Theological Department,* September 30, 1830.
18. The Committee to which was Referred the Consideration of Dr. Ware's letter. (James Walker, ch.), April 25, 1840.
19. *Report of the Board of Overseers of Harvard College on the Condition, Needs and Prospects of the University,* 1869, p. 37.

45

Endowment Drives—Objectives

Harvard's fund-raising over a period of the last hundred years rested on certain principles: the development of educational ideas, soon to be copied elsewhere, which appeal to those with a philanthropic bent, the publicization of these ideas by unusual educators and publicists like Eliot and Lowell; recourse to large drives, but only one in a generation; and the adoption by the president of a policy of not personally seeking money, but circulating new ideas and conferring with potential donors when prospects seek consultation.[1]

It does seem that over a large part of Harvard's history excessive emphasis was put on bricks against men. Even in the Puritan period, the college disbursed £5,929 for building repairs and equipment, an amount exceeding the disbursement for salaries and allowances and equal to 20 percent of total disbursements.[2]

Large expenditures for buildings are explained in part by the greater disposition to give for material things that can be seen than for funds for faculty support. Even in the Colonial period, the government was inclined to assume special responsibilities for buildings rather than for men. President Eliot weighted the need for faculty salaries and for more faculty members as heavily as it should have been. In

1904, 1919, and 1936 the objective of drives was primarily for the faculty.

But there have been periods when the case for more buildings vis-à-vis men was strong. In 1924, the business school authorities claimed they never really had a plant. "The only classrooms on which it has a first claim are two basement rooms, one of which had formerly been used as a boiler room and the other for dead storage."[3] The school was prepared to charge full costs for instruction, but sought funds for research and buildings.

In chemistry, in the early 1920s the faculty estimated that the working conditions were so deplorable that one-third of the time of teachers and students was being wasted, and crowded conditions were interfering seriously with research. There was no space even for a machine shop or a glassblowers' room. President Lowell's comment was "the less said about it the better."[4]

Harvard's House Plan has probably cost the university the equivalent of the cost of forty or fifty professorships. Many hold that the college would have been better off if the money had been used to provide more faculty members and higher salaries. Yet it is not easy to weigh the educational contributions of the House Plan, which are substantial, against those to be had from investing the money in the

1. Cf., Harvard University Archives, UAV 828, 142, p.9.
2. Margery Somers Foster, *"Out of Smalle Beginnings. . ."* — *An Economic History of Harvard College in the Puritan Period (1636-1712)*, 1962, p. 147.

3. Harvard University Archives, UAI 1o.450.10, 12.
4. *Ibid.; Report of the President of Harvard College, 1923-1924*, pp. 27-28.

faculty. Many would say the human investment would yield more. The fruits of the House Plan may well be more in the social gains and higher living standards than in pure educational values though the last, if not equal to anticipations, is substantial. But one must also take into account the fact that the alternatives were not offered to the college. At times the college, by indicating its needs, can influence the choice of objectives by donors but not in this instance.

Another interesting aspect of Harvard's gift policy relates to tax policy. Professor Yeomans, the official biographer of President Lowell, in the 1940s expressed concern lest heavy taxes would dry up the source of private charitable and philanthropic gifts.[5] But a Harvard man, Sen. H. F. Hollis (1892), introduced a bill in 1917 which would give relief to the taxpayer who gave to educational and other charitable operations. About a thousand Harvard men received a letter signed by Eliot, Lamont, Lowell, Bishop Lawrence and Charles F. Adams, which urged passage of this legislation. The tax allowances contributed much to the continued flow of gifts.[6]

The Mayor of Detroit, and affluent Ford executive, James Couzens, wrote as follows in 1919:

If all the wealthy men who have graduated from Harvard and received the benefits of a Harvard education cannot raise $10,000,000, I see no reason why others who have received no advantages, should be asked to contribute. If Harvard was a poor man's college, I would not raise the question but it is well-known that it is not.[7]

One of Harvard's problems has been that it has been reputed to be the richest institution of higher learning in the country. Hence, other institutions were inclined to be critical of, or antagonistic to Harvard's drives, and especially if Harvard's emissaries invaded the territory they considered their own. Harvard tried to contend with this problem by, for example, pointing out that Harvard's leadership would attract attention to the needs of higher education generally as it had done in 1919.[8]

The London Economist commented on this problem:

Harvard is aware that its ambitious campaign is likely to arouse some resentment elsewhere... But the main argument used by the strategists for the campaign is that Harvard, by the mere act of launching its great drive [1956] *will help all its fellow colleges by dramatizing the needs for funds to support institutions for higher education....*[9]

5. H. Yeomans, *Abbott Laurence Lowell, 1856-1943*, p. 244.
6. Harvard University Archives, UAV.135.124.7.
7. *Ibid.*, 136.124.5.
8. *Harvard Crimson*, November 1, 1956, "A Program for Harvard College," in *Now Press You On*, p. 6.
9. *The Economist*, December 17, 1957, p. 871.

46

The Issue of Restricted Endowment

Institutions of higher learning much prefer to receive gifts to be used in a manner to be determined by the administrators of the institution, but unfortunately for them donors generally have other views. Hence, gifts are not as effective as they otherwise might be. In some instances, funds have been used in a manner contrary to the deeds of the gift. This is one way of treating the problem of restricted income. But generally the college avoids this way out.

The property which is specifically given in trust for one department cannot be applied to another purpose in the same. There is a sacredness in these trusts which may not be violated, however obsolete the object of the trust may be deemed, or frivolous in the eye of modern reformers. The Indians must have the gospel preached to them according to the will of Daniel Williams. . . .[1]

Except in the seventeenth century, and to some extent in the eighteenth century, restricted gifts have been much more important than additions to the general fund. In 1777, the college fund was equally divided between restricted and unrestricted income. Over the years, the restricted gifts seemed to average about 80 percent of the total. In the 1950s unrestricted endowment income amounted only to little more than 10 percent of total endowment income.

But one estimate puts the percentage of unrestricted gifts in the years 1930 to 1950 at 30 percent.[2]

Inadequacy of Unrestricted Income

In the second quarter of the nineteenth century, time and again the authorities asked for gifts to endowment which would be unrestricted. The general fund, which was used to keep down costs of education to students, was most inadequate.

In 1841-1842, the treasurer commented on the small amount in the general funds relative to costs of undergraduate education and hence the heavy burdens on students; and on the provisions in deeds of gifts which often involved costs in excess of the money made available and often were encumbered with complicated and costly requirements. "It is believed that donors, who will give or leave their property to the *General Fund* or for the instruction of undergraduates or in the control of the Corporation, will confer a great benefit on the College".[3]

---

1. *Report of the Visiting Committee*, Harvard University, Board of Overseers, January, 1849.

2. Kane and Doten, *op. cit.*, pp. 211-214.
3. *Treasurers' Collected Papers*, 1736-1755; *Corporation Records*, vol. II, pp. 485-486, 1778; *Report of the Treasurer of Harvard College*, 1831-1832, pp. 20-31; 1837-1838, p. 1 1830; 1840-1847; *Harvard College and Early Education in Massachusetts*, sec. 21, p. 99; "Harvard's Need," in *The Harvard Bulletin*, vol. II, 20.17, p. 1, 1900; Quincy, *op. cit.*, vol. II, pp. 256, 404; *Report of the President of Harvard College*, 1828-1829; 1849-1850; 1856-1857.

In his 1860-1861 report, the treasurer complained of difficulties in paying bills: rising costs, increasing numbers of students and "especially . . . the fact that a large portion of the funds are appropriated to specific purposes" contributed to this result.[4]

Just before Eliot's incumbency, President Hill pressed the view that the wealth of the university is greatly overestimated by its friends and the public, saying " . . . she is not wealthy; partly because she has control over only a limited portion of her income. . . . " He continued that the "University received $100,000 a year as an addition to her capital of limited and conditional endowments, while she stands in pressing need of the addition to that sum of her free and untrammeled income. . . . [5]

In his inaugural address in 1869, President Eliot expressed well the issues of restricted endowment. Admitting that the corporation gratefully receives all gifts, Eliot nevertheless noted that "the interests of the University may be most effectually promoted by not restricting too narrowly the use to which a gift may be applied. . . . "

Eliot approved of gifts generally designated for books, dormitories, public buildings, scholarships, scientific collections, etc. But "experience proves that too specific and minute directions concerning the application of funds must often fail of fulfillment simply in consequence of the changing needs and habits of successive generations."[6] He consoled potential donors by assuring them that restrictions to salaries, scholarships, maintenance of laboratories or administration and services had not been found to be inconvenient.[7]

Early in 1907, President Eliot presented an eloquent and effective plea for more free money.[8] In this context it should be stressed that Harvard's system of accounting—allocating income on the basis of book, not market value—in periods of rising values reduces the cost of rigidities related to restrictive gifts. As values change, the educational contribution of older gifts declines. The college responds by giving new donors a larger share of income earned than might be suggested by the relative stakes in capital of past and current gifts.

In 1904, President Eliot had, despite his doubts about restricted money, successfully carried through a $2,500,000 campaign for endowment to finance increased salaries. This was endowment for restrictive purposes. But at least the president determined the priorities on the basis of his assessment of over-all needs.

President Lowell also complained of the restrictive nature of gifts. He wanted to rely more on the sagacity of future college administrators.[9]

A good example of the damage done by too precise definitions of use to which gifts are made is the terms of the Alford Professorship (1765). This chair was offered to the distinguished philospher, George Palmer, in the last 1880s. Palmer gladly accepted the chair, but when he read the terms of the gift he was upset. He objected to many of the provisions required of the holder of the chair.

In the great 1919-1920 drive, it was announced at first that the income from the fund would be unrestricted. In 1919, of $33,700,000 of endowment only $13,500,000 were unrestricted. But under pressure the college yielded and allowed restricted gifts. [10] Yet only 2 percent of the gifts were restrictive.

Thus, we can also explain the *Program for Harvard College* under Pusey. In the midst of large drives, the fund-seekers conceded grounds on the restrictive issue. The tendency was to offer alternatives to potential donors which combined restrictions with some freedom of choice.

The need for unrestrictive gifts was as great as ever. But the administration realized that to raise $82

---

4. *Treasurer's Statement*, 1860-1861, p. 1.

5. *Report of the President of Harvard College*, 1867-1868, pp. 4-6.

6. *Report to the Honorable and Reverend, the Overseers of Harvard University*, 1869, p. 34; *Addresses at the Inauguration of Charles William Eliot*, October 19, 1869, p. 59.

7. *Report of the President of Harvard College*, 1876-1877, pp. 6, 41; 1882-1883, p. 41.

8. *Ibid.*, 1905-1906, pp. 54-55; cf., *The Harvard Bulletin*, vol. 5, no. 12, p. 2, 1902.

9. *Ibid.*, 1911-1912, p. 24.

10. Harvard University Archives, UAV, 136.124.2, 124.10, 124.273.

million it was necessary to give donors opportunities to donate for purposes that appealed to them. Hence, a wide choice of objectives: dormitories, houses, funds for higher salaries, various chairs, office buildings, etc. At least if these were an invitation to restrictive gifts they were related to the priorities offered by the college authorities.

At other times restricted gifts continued to dominate. From 1932 to 1937 only 16 percent of the gifts were without restrictions; from 1935 to 1937 only 10 percent. [11] President Conant remarked that if the criterion of a rich university is one with large funds to spend as it wished, then Harvard is not rich. After meeting its commitments Harvard in 1935 had free income of but $50,000. "Harvard's endowment of approximately $125,000,000 has been so 'earmarked' by the donors that the authorities have little discretion as to how the income therefrom may be spent."

In still another sense the university is hampered. Each tub stands on its own bottom (though in fact there are exceptions). At Harvard, the imposition of financial responsibility on each school reduces to some extent the effective use of funds.

It is especially the Annual Harvard Fund that provides unrestricted income. In establishing the fund in 1926, the sponsor agreed that the money should be paid into the treasury "without restrictions as to its use, and with entire freedom on the part of the Corporation to use the Fund as it may determine." It was hoped that through unrestricted gifts, Harvard would be helped to "maintain her traditions through scholarships, and increase her prestige as an educational leader. . . . " In his 1935-1936 report President Conant dwelt on the great importance of the Harvard Fund just because it provided sorely needed unrestricted funds.[12] One way of increasing the usefulness of the annual funds was to divert part to current use. A million dollars put to current use yields a million dollars in that year, but if put in

endowment the income is only about $50,000. Thus, we can understand a proposal of Provost Paul Buck in 1950 to put gifts of classes out more than twenty-five years into immediate use.

In general, institutions of higher learning are undoubtedly hurt by excessive restrictions on use of money. But some arguments can be adduced against this position. First, annual giving and the rising importance of tuition, both yielding unrestricted money, reduced the damage done by giving restricted gifts for endowment. Again, to some extent, the administration may reallocate its funds to treat unwise restrictions. Then also it may well be that the pattern of spending sought by an administration through unrestricted giving is not necessarily a more deserved pattern than might be had by restricted funds.

Reducing the Damage Done by Restrictive Use of Endowment

One approach is to specify use of an endowment in broad terms if the restrictive approach is demanded by the donor. Of the Alford Professorship, Eliot remarked:

Since 1817 . . . there have been five Alford Professors whose natural gifts, education, and acquired tastes were quite different yet not one of them has found any difficulties in finding subjects in which he was interested included within the subjects permitted to the Alford Professor.[13]

To a potential donor who would finance a chair in medicine, Eliot proposed that the deed be worded in such a manner as would "permit the President and Fellows to change the subject of this Chair if a change should be for the interest of the Medical School. . . . " In this manner, the chair could be assigned to the subject which most needed it. In negotiations for a scholarship tied to a particular

---

11. *Report of the President of Harvard College*, 1936-1937, p. 29.
12. *Ibid.*, 1935-1936, p. 17.

13. C. W. Eliot to Reverend Cyrus F. Stimson, July 10, 1908.

locality, Eliot advised the insertion of the words *by preference*. Then if an acceptable candidate from the designated locality were not available, a candidate could be found elsewhere.[14]

14. C. W. Eliot to Miss Wilder, December 20, 1899; C. W. Eliot to Mrs. E. P. Miller, December 2, 1904.

47

Diversion of Endowment Funds

College and university officials can often divert funds from their intended use. Under the accounting used by Harvard until 1969 and many of the institutions in the country, more recent donors are favored in the distribution of endowment income against the earlier donors. Again, the college may not distribute the total income received from capital gifts for specific purposes, but rather divert some of the income to be used for the general purposes of the college or university. This is a practice which is not unknown in many centers of higher education.

From the very beginning, wishes of donors sometimes were not followed. William Paine gave the college £20 "which is not to be expended, but to remain as a stock to the college aforesaid forever." Despite this prohibition, the college immediately invested the £20 in land.[1]

Another example of doubtful diversion of funds is the use made of the then unprecedented E. B. Phillips bequest of $100,000 in 1849 for the use of the observatory. But somehow $8,000 of this fund found its way into the general fund of the university in the 1850s. It is not surprising then that the merchants of Boston, who showed much interest in the observatory, did not want the observatory finance tied to that of the college. Quincy observed that the merchants apparently were fearful of diversions of these gifts to the general use of the college. If the observatory funds had been isolated, then more money would have been given.[2]

It was a common practice in the nineteenth century to divert part of the return on a gift for a special purpose to the general funds of the university. President Eliot observed that "the President and Fellows had long been in the habit of allowing 5 percent on the funds belonging to the non-college departments, and appropriating to the college the rest of the income of the general investments." But the board of overseers in 1866 modified the system and distributed all income with the exception of a small payment for the management of the fund. In this manner it became possible to merge most funds, for each was to receive its share of earnings.[3] But on many occasions donors, fearful of misuse, insisted on separate investments of their gifts.

College authorities can also have recourse to more direct methods of flouting the objectives of donors. A relevant case is to abscond with college funds, as Treasurer John Hancock did during the Revolutionary War.[4] Another approach is to fail to comply with deeds of gift.

In giving the money to finance the first divinity chair early in the eighteenth century, Thomas Hollis

---

2. Josiah Quincy to Reverend President Walker, May 5, 1855; J. Quincy to President and Fellows, September 8, 1857.

3. C. W. Eliot to Overseers, p. 60; C. W. Eliot to C. F. Adams, II, July 15, 1908.

4. Quincy, *op. cit.*, pp. 508 ff.

---

1. Morison, *op. cit.*, vol. I, pp. 47-48.

stipulated "that none be refused on account of his belief and practice of adult baptism." But the overseers, with the consent of the corporation, diverted this gift to sectarian purposes and contrary to the deeds of the gift.[5]

In 1690, Increase Mather persuaded Thomas Hollis to will some money to Harvard. Because of this contribution the corporation voted the interest of this gift to Mather's grandson, scarcely a use of the funds consistent with the deed. Increase Mather's son, unhappy at Harvard's unorthodoxy, apparently tried to divert part of the Hollis bequest to Yale.[6]

In the midst of the troubles of the 1820s, the auditors proposed a number of accounting changes, inclusive of a few that suggested failure to follow the wishes of the donors and also consolidation of some accounts. A check of the treasurer's journals and ledgers reveals that these recommendations were taken seriously.[7]

In 1842, the treasurer complained of the inadequate general endowment fund. He added: ". . .It [the general and unrestricted fund of the College] has been relieved as much as possible by charging all that could be with propriety to the special funds and departments." There are obvious temptations here.[8] Again, comptroller Allen Danforth recommended in 1908 "the re-establishment of funds because the corporation has made the wrong application of money . . . ."[9]

Other studies also point to some careless applications of the wishes of donors. In 1915, Theodore

Lyman protested at the use of endowment funds for repairs of the Jefferson Physics Laboratory.[10]

Much confusion prevailed on professorships. A professorship of natural history was not filled because funds were spent elsewhere. The corporation appointed a committee to consider the problem. But the results were not reassuring.

Again, the McLean Professorship for History raised all kinds of problems. The incumbent, Prof. J. Sparks (1838 to 1849), complained bitterly of the heavy teaching burdens outside of history imposed upon him and the neglect of history.

Professor Sparks, in discussing the curtailment of the department of history, suggested that the operation reacts "unfavorably to the best interest of the college, and. . . diminishes instead of increasing a branch of study expressly intended by the foundation of the professorship to be fostered and enlarged. . . ."[11] McLean's will had provided that the income should be *exclusively and forever* [my italics] appropriated to the support of a professor of Ancient and Modern History . . . ."[12]

Some question have also been raised by J. Lowell on the Eliot Professorship of Greek. It seemed to Lowell that the use of a foundation to pay the salary of a professor already in the college really meant that the money was being used to increase the general fund of the college.

In some instances the university has appealed to the courts as a means of improving the effective use of funds. In the 1920s an appeal to the courts for permission to use the McKay engineering millions in co-operation with MIT and thus exclude unwise competition, received an adverse ruling.

Respondents Stanley and Gilbert, trustees under the deeds and will of Gordon McKay, argued that Harvard could not divest itself of its responsibilities

5. Morison, *op. cit.*, pp. 66-68.
6. K. B. Murdock, *Increase Mather,*, 1925, p. 276; B. Wendell, *Cotton Mather,* 1926, p. 282.
7. Auditors' Report on Treasurer's Account, February 1827 to August 1828, in *Report of the President of Harvard College,* 1827-1828, pp. 62-63; also see *Report of Standing Committee Appointed to Examine the Books and Accounts of the Present Treasurer,* December 18, 1828.
8. P. Cabot and L. Larrabee, "Investing Harvard Money" in *Harvard Alumni Bulletin,* May 12, 1951, p. 631.
9. *Report of Standing Committee to Examine the Books and Accounts of the Treasurer of the College,* December (?), 1828; C. W. Eliot to C. F. Adams, July 16, 1908.

10. Theodore Lyman to F. W. Hunnewell, II, October 4, 1915 in *A. L. Lowell Correspondence.*
11. J. Sparks to J. Quincy, May 7, 1843; Rules and Statutes of the McLean Professorship of Ancient and Modern History.
12. F. W. Ward, Treasurer of Harvard College, Receipt of Gift Under the Will of John McLean, October 4, 1834.

to manage the McKay millions by entering into an agreement with MIT. Their position was that McKay had ample opportunity to select MIT rather than Harvard. But he preferred Harvard.[13]

A more recent episode was the dispute over the removal of part of the Arnold Arboretum from Boston to Cambridge. In January 1953, the Harvard Corporation decided to remove the major part of the library and herbarium from the arboretum in Jamaica Plain to Cambridge. Several alumni applied to the attorney general to bring an action against the corporation for breach of trust in its function as representative of the public interest in preserving charitable trusts. But the attorney general refused to bring suit, insisting that the corporation decision did not violate the terms of the trust accepted by it in 1872.[14] On February 11, 1955, Chief Justice Stanley Qua announced in favor of the Harvard Corporation.

Diversion that is related to changing conditions that make a modified use imperative is one matter, but outright violations of trust are another. Use of Dartmouth's funds for Indians, received before the Revolution, ultimately had to be diverted for more appropriate use by the courts in the twentieth century.[15]

From what has been written in this chapter, one should not assume that the college persistently violated the deeds of gifts and bequests. In the early years, lack of administrative help and low general standards of administration contributed to the violation of trusts. With the passage of time and with increased experience and higher administrative standards, violations became much less numerous. The college has almost always been in financial difficulties. Hence, the temptation to use funds more effectively from the viewpoint of the enterprise sometimes resulted in misuse; for example, using endowment funds to pay off debts.

Yet time and again and especially in the last century, the corporation has proclaimed the sacredness of the trusts. When, for example, the college found it helpful to substitute loans for gifts, the officials carefully examined each deed and substituted loans for gifts, e.g., scholarships, only when the terms of the original gift allowed such use of the funds. Again the Hersey Professorship in the medical school raised some serious problems. The chair had been endowed before the medical school had been opened. Hence, when it began to operate, the question was raised whether the money should continue to be used for undergraduates in Cambridge or whether the funds should be transferred to Boston, to be used by the medical school. Once the school became part of the university, the medical school contended that the case for medical school control was greatly strengthened.[16]

---

13. *Commonwealth of Massachusetts, Supreme Judicial Court, President and Fellows of Harvard College vs The Attorney General et als,* pp. I-IX.
14. *Harvard Alumni Bulletin,* vol. 57, pp. 392-394, 1955.
15. *Ibid.*
16. Corporation of Harvard College, "... to Examine the Terms Upon Which the Donations for Beneficiaries are Made," February 27, 1847; *Report of Committee... Relating to the Appropriation of Funds for the Support of a Professor of Anatomy and Physics,* July 31, 1858; Dean C. Ellis to the President and Fellows, May 5, 1883.

48

Endowments: Problems of Evaluation and Growth

The Issues

When a university receives a gift to be used for endowment of a chair, scholarship, or other service, the authorities are confronted with the problem of the extent to which the new endowment is to share with the old in the income yielded by the endowment funds. The choice made raises issues of effective use of endowments, equity between old and new donors, and similar problems.[1]

Experience in the Eighteenth and Nineteenth Centuries

Once market values diverge from book values, serious problems arise. In the great inflations of the eighteenth century, the market diverged greatly from the book value. Inflation eroded the value of endowments, though the losses were reduced by tying loans by the college to a relatively stable monetary unit. During Hubbard's incumbency, in the middle of the eighteenth century, the college recognized the depreciation of the currency and the upward revaluation of the new currency by writing down the endowment in new money at a ratio of 7½ to 1.

In the 1840s the treasurer was confronted with the problem of trying to justify the diversion to the college's general fund of income on endowment. By paying out only 5 percent to the various endowment funds and earning more, the college was in fact diverting income from its original purpose. The treasurer proposed an allocation more nearly in accordance with the terms of gifts, but there is no evidence that this position was accepted in accounting practice at that time.[2]

The university seems to be committed to using book values for allocating endowment incomes. But there were many reservations to this policy. At the turn of the century, the medical school received gifts of $3 million, some of which were used for plant. But how to account for the remainder? The solution was not along current approaches:

. . . should the dividends on all the old funds be diminished because of the fact that this new gift could not earn as much as was then being earned on old investments? The advice followed by the Corporation was that it was not fair to reduce the dividends on the old funds; as in time the new millions would be treated in the same way and with a reduced rate of interest would get the same benefits as the old funds. . . .[3]

(In other words, new investments would receive a return based on their own earnings and would not share the higher returns of older investments.)

In the 1860s, the treasurer clearly raised the crucial problem of book vs market values.

---

1. For a full discussion of these problems, see S. E. Harris, *op. cit.*, ch. 32.

2. *Report of the Treasurer of Harvard College*, 1841-1842, pp. 3-4.

3. T. F. Harrington, *The Harvard Medical School*, 1905, p. 1168.

The large percentage of income arises from the fact that the invested funds of the College are much in excess of their valuation upon the books of the Treasurer. The division of all the earnings of these investments gives to funds recently placed, at their full value, upon the books, the benefit of the increase in value of the investments of earlier years, and suggests the propriety of a new valuation, or the establishment of another class of investments for future receipts.

This is the first clear statement by the Harvard authorities of a problem that was to concern them for the next hundred years. The treasurer was aware of the rise of income as the value of assets made available earlier rose, and hence the high return on the low book value. He did not see why sums recently donated should share in the *additional* returns related to rising value of assets of endowment funds given in earlier years.

Yet Treasurer Silsbee citing a corporation vote in his 1869-1870 report does not reveal that he had made a frontal attack on this problem.[4]

Treasurer Edward W. Hooper in his 1875-1876 report came to grips with the problem. The declining return on capital, reflecting also a rising price of fixed-interest assets, troubled the treasurer. He seemed concerned that the old funds could not earn as much as the customary 6 percent, and therefore he was all the more disturbed that excessive income was being credited to the new funds at the expense of the earnings of the old funds, now highly inflated in value. The corporation, however, was not prepared to revalue all funds on the books. This would raise all kinds of problems inclusive of finding adequate investments at 6 percent. But the authorities diverted some funds to the older endowments.[5]

At this time the treasurer estimated the return on the low book value at 6.75 percent and on estimated market value, 6 percent, or a little more.[6]

That the corporation may have been diverting returns on endowment funds to purposes not intended is suggested by Eliot's 1886-1887 report. A large reduction of the stock fund and the insurance and guaranty fund was made by charging to it the extension of Gore Hall, namely $89,000. But this was more than offset by additional unrestricted gifts.

In 1908, Eliot brought to the attention of the treasurer "the magnitude of the evil of allowing new gifts to drag down the annual income of old gifts. The larger the new gifts, the worse this evil is." Incidentally, Eliot also seemed to approve the distribution to participating funds of capital gains from the Webb estate in the 1870s. This was a forerunner of the large distributions in the 1950s.[7]

The Twentieth Century

It is especially in the twentieth century that the problems arising from differences in book and market value became most troublesome. In the 1920s the stock market boom tended to raise market values substantially vis-à-vis book values although at this time investment in equities were not at the scale of post World War II. It was particularly after World War II that stock market prices boomed. In 1949, the Standard and Poor's common stock index was 15.23 (1941-1943 = 10) and by 1964, 81.37, or 5 to 6 times as high. With equities accounting for at least half the investments, the market value would rise increasingly in relation to book value.

During the first sixty-three years of the twentieth century gifts for capital amounted to $391 million. But the rise of endowment was $469 million. It will be observed that endowments under Lowell and especially Pusey rose much more than capital gifts, in contrast with the experience under Conant the explanation being largely the rising value of Harvard's assets in the 1920s and in the years 1953 to 1963, and the unsatisfactory economic conditions in much of Conant's period. The gains of endowment under Lowell are overstated by several million because of a

4. *Report of the Treasurer of Harvard College*, 1869-1870, pp. 3-4.
5. *Ibid.*, 1875-1876, pp. 3-4.
6. *Ibid.*, pp. 2-3.

7. C. W. Eliot to C. F. Adams, II, July 11, 16, 1908.

writing up of values in 1930, and understated under Conant because of the reversal of the write-down by a corresponding write-up under Conant.[8]

Gifts for Capital and Harvard's Endowment: 1900 to 1965

The purpose of this section is to outline the growth of Harvard's endowment in the twentieth century and the role of private gifts for capital in that growth. It also will bring out some aspects of the financial policy of the Harvard Corporation which have had a direct bearing on the endowment.

For many reasons, Eliot's financial policies were as successful as his educational experiments, and, indeed, may have made these experiments and their success possible. In the first thirty-one years of his administration (1869 to 1900) Harvard's capital was increased from $2,387,232.77, which represented the accumulation of two and a third centuries, to $12,614,448 (the sum of Harvard's general and special investments on July 31, 1900); this figure is also equal to the "funds" of the university in the contemporary accounting practice, or what today we would call the "endowment."

In considering investments, we should distinguish investments from endowment, and also income from these two categories. For example, on June 30, 1967, endowment funds amounted to $621,800,000. But the total of investment funds was $830,500,000 (book value). Included in the larger total are such items as the balance of general investment income reserved for subsequent distribution ($103,900,000), pension reserves ($52,200,000). The endowment income availed of for 1966-1967 was $30,900,000 or about 5 percent of endowment funds. Roughly, other investments would yield about $10 million additional. Endowment income accounted for 20 percent of income in this year.

When Lowell became president in 1909 he effected the separation of the investment from endowment funds; the two figures have diverged ever

since. In the Lowell practice, the 1909 figure for the "funds" (the phrase "endowment funds" did not appear till the 1920s) is $22 million. During the twenty-four years he was president the endowment funds rose to $126 million, or an increase of $104 million. Under Lowell, gifts for capital amounted to $89 million, which is 86 percent of the change in endowment.

More than half of the discrepancy between gifts for capital and the change in endowment under Lowell is explained by a financial measure in 1930 that proved to be ill timed. Charles Francis Adams (class of 1888), who served as treasurer of the university from 1898 to 1929, had always adhered strictly to book values. Under his successor, Henry Lee Shattuck (treasurer, 1929 to 1937) the observance of this method was less strict. On June 30, 1930, in response to the rising values of the 1920s, the balances of all endowment funds participating in the general investments on June 30, 1929, were marked up 10 percent. The increases totaled $8,159,313. One-half was a paper mark-up.

During the years 1933 to 1953 (roughly the Conant administration) the endowment was broken down into three functional categories: endowment funds, annuity funds, and loan funds. We must add these categories to make meaningful comparisons with the Lowell "endowment" figures. When Lowell left office in 1933 the endowment was $126,126,369. At the end of the Conant period endowment funds totaled $215,957,867, while $2,630,776 were annuity funds, and $1,410,074, loan funds. Endowment, annuity, and loan funds had therefore increased $93,872,348 under Conant. In his twenty-year presidential tenure gifts for capital totaled almost $101 million, or 107 percent of the change in the three funds. Again, however, this percentage distorts the contribution of gifts to the change in the funds, and this time in the other direction, for the mark-up which had occurred in 1930 under Lowell was marked down in 1938 under Conant. We should therefore add the amount of the mark-up under Lowell to the recorded change in the funds under Conant in order to get a more accurate picture

---

8. A table on this period, prepared by Richard Sylla, has been deposited in the Harvard University Archives.

of the actual change. Doing this, we obtain $102 million for the actual change in endowment, annuity, and loan funds under Conant. Gifts for capital during the Conant administration then equaled 99 percent of the adjusted change in the three funds.

The mark-down of previous mark-ups occurred in 1938 and was described by William H. Claflin, Jr., Harvard's new treasurer, in his first report.[9]

Claflin and the corporation went on record as favoring the book value approach. Perhaps if the first departure from the book value approach had occurred at a more favorable time than 1930 the shift to greater use of market values would have remained permanent. Harvard picked the worst possible time to experiment with it.

Adding up what we have covered so far, we obtain the following results. From 1900 to 1953, the last year of the Conant administration, endowment, annuity, and loan funds increased by $208 million. During the same period gifts for capital amounted to $200 million or slightly more than 96 percent of the growth of the three funds.

This pattern of private capital gifts and endowment growing roughly together for the first 320 years of Harvard's history seemingly came to an end in the first ten years of the Pusey administration, which without a doubt have been the most prosperous years in Harvard history. In 1953, when Conant retired, Harvard's endowment was $216 million. Annuity and loan funds represented an additional $2,600,000 and $1,400,000, respectively. Ten years later the endowment funds had grown to $469 million, while annuity and loan funds had grown to $4,400,000 and $7,600,000 respectively. Thus, the increase in the three funds in ten years totaled $261 million. In this same decade gifts for capital amounted to $191 million, far more than in any other decade of Harvard's history, and yet only 73 percent of the increase in the three funds.

The explanation for this departure from the pattern of the past lies in the conversion of book values into market values through the mechanism of

9. *Report of the Treasurer of Harvard College,* 1937-1938, pp. 5-6.

realized capital gains. Shrewd buying and selling of securities by Harvard's treasurer, Paul Cabot, coupled with generally rising market values of investments for the economy as a whole, have brought Harvard large capital gains on its general investments. A large part of these gains have been converted into additions to the endowment and annuity funds by the corporation.

In recent years, the corporation distributed to the various accounts from the general investments and gains and loss accounts "10 percent of all said funds on the books in the years 1956, 1959, 1963 and 1965." The total amount involved in these four allocations was $144 million.

In some respects, the additions to endowment from capital gains under Pusey resemble the mark-up attempted in the 1930s. But there is an important difference. More than half of the 1930 mark-up consisted of potential appreciation as opposed to realized appreciation. No transfer of funds was involved. When in the course of the Great Depression security values fell, the unwisdom of the market value practice became apparent. In contrast, the Cabot-Pusey mark-ups consist of transfers of money Harvard actually had on hand, and not merely money Harvard might have had if it had sold some of its portfolio at opportune moments.

The $94,808,496 of capital gains added to endowment and annuity funds from 1956 to 1964 is equivalent to a little over 36 percent of the rise of endowment, annuity, and loan funds in the first ten Pusey years (the 1965 rise is additional). We saw above that gifts for capital accounted for 73 percent of the increase. This adds up under Pusey to a rise of endowment, etc. funds of over 109 percent, implying that about 9 percent of the rise in the funds has been used. Investigation has shown that this capital consumption has for the most part occurred in the years 1958 to 1963, the second five years of the Pusey administration. These have been years of great building activity and much of the construction which has taken place has been financed from funds temporarily added to investments but which were raised to finance construction. In the 1956 to 1958 drive large funds for construction were sought. As building progressed, the university used up the relevant funds that had temporarily been added to investment funds.

Capital Gifts and Endowment

Two final comments—on the relation of gifts for capital to changes in endowment funds, and on the relation of endowment to Harvard's investments—are in order. Gifts for capital have always been the major source of endowment growth, especially before the additions of capital gains in the Pusey administration. But there are other sources of change in endowment, too. Sometimes endowment income is added to the principal when all of this income is not required for the current operations of the university. Capital gains on special investments are also added to endowment year by year, unlike the gains on general investments which are held in a gain and loss account. It was from this account that the huge capital gains transfers to endowment came in recent years. Next, endowment often changes because of transfers to or from loan and life income funds, from departmental balances, and to or from the account which holds current gifts and receipts. Finally, the endowment is diminished when additions and improvements to the educational plant are charged against the principal, though here the rising endowment may well have been temporary. But until 1953 gifts for capital accounted for almost all of the growth of endowment (including annuity and loan funds), and after 1953 capital gifts, capital gains, and construction expenses similarly account for almost all of the changes. The other factors named above are marginal.

On the Harvard balance sheet endowment, annuity, and loan funds are liabilities and the general and special investments are assets. Up until the Lowell administration the sum of these investments equaled the "funds" of the university, but since then the investments have always been greater. This is because, in addition to the three funds, the investments also include other accounts carried as liabilities, such as the general investments gain-and-loss account; pension reserves for officers and employees of the university; certain other reserves for depreciation, maintenance, and replacement of buildings and equipment; and finally balances of unexpended income. These items in part explain why at the end of the financial year 1962-1963 the general and special investments were well over $100 million greater than the sum of endowment, life income, and loan funds.

One may wonder why the university in recent years has transferred capital gains to the various endowment funds, for in so doing the university authorities sacrificed unrestricted funds and increased restricted funds. In earlier years there was some disposition to divert from restricted funds by not paying out to the individual funds all the income earned. The policies since World War II reduce the effectiveness of endowment funds, but the policy is justified undoubtedly by issues of equity; the money appropriated, say, for classics, receives it appropriate share of any rise in values of the general endowment funds. By thus transferring substantial parts of capital gains to each balance the university to some extent reduces the injustices done to the sponsors of older funds by the policy of allowing new endowment funds to share on the basis of book values for older funds, a policy that favors the new gifts. By allocating part of capital gains to the existing funds, the book values of extant funds are raised and injustices to donors of the past are reduced.

The university has reduced the depreviations forced upon the "ancient" donors by adding to book values part of the capital gains. But there is still a large residue of diversions to more recent donors, justified perhaps by the difficulties of tying returns to market values and also the closer proximity of recent gifts to the current values of our society. That recent donors are still privileged is suggested by a comparison of market and book values of general investments on June 30, 1965: $967 million vs $667 million, or a 45 percent excess in market value.

As this book goes to press Harvard abandoned its long-time allocation of income on the basis of book value.

PART

7

INVESTMENTS

49

The Structure of Investments

Introduction

One of the best general statements on the appropriate structure of investments comes from President Eliot. The emphasis is on diversification, and the large changes in availability of different kinds of assets over time. Eliot also commented on uncertainities of real estate investments.[1] Elsewhere he raised questions on the wisdom of investing in manufacturing companies.

The primitive state of investments in Harvard's early years is suggested by a description of the assets transferred from Treasurer Danforth to the new treasurer on June 3, 1669.

An examination of the assets transferred by Treasurer Danforth in 1669 reveals the heavy recourse to loans to individuals and, secondarily, leasing of real estate. It is also evident at this time that the college generally agreed to repayment in provisions. Thus, From John Swan *in corn*, 32 shillings.[2]

The college also obtained income from lands given to the college, from annuities—payment of an agreed sum per year by a donor—and also from ferry revenue.

Distribution of major assets, 1712

Item	Percent
Bills, bonds and mortgages	45
Ferry (capitalized)	23
Rents and annuities	18
Cash	6
Old bills and bonds	5

In the first hundred years of Harvard history assets were relatively small and uncomplicated. When John White became treasurer in 1715, he received from William Brattle, executor of Thomas Brattle, late treasurer of the college, nearly £3,800 in personal estate and real estate yielding £280. This compares with a personal estate of £1,550 and real estate yielding £1,100 income in 1693 when Thomas Brattle had become treasurer.[3]

In 1715 the new treasurer received:[4]

> Bills of credit, £125 13s
> Bonds and mortgages, £376 7s
> 2 legacies (on the way), £168 6s 8d
> 2 annuities (Glover and Newgate)
> Annual income of £8
> Charlestown Ferry with annual
> income of £72
> Rented land and buildings
> with an annual income of £38,15 6s
> Other lands with no value given.

Even as late as 1773, John Hancock, the treasurer, received bonds and notes totaling only £15,449.14.2.

---

1. C. W. Eliot, *University Trustees*, pp. 8-9; C. W. Eliot to Milton Reed, March 13, 1894.
2. This table is deposited in the Harvard Archives.
3. Josiah Quincy, *The History of Harvard University*, 1840, vol. I, p. 411.
4. Inventory Papers 1715, Wm. Brattle, Executor of the Estate of the late Thomas Brattle, his brother to John White, unpublished.

In 1777, Treasurer John Hancock turned over to L. Hall bonds with a total value of £16,031.16.6.[5]

The college, of course, wanted to earn the largest return possible, and at least one early investment yielded 9 percent. Frequent defaults, however, reduced returns. Moreover, in 1693 the government reduced the maximum rate of interest to 6 percent. Even the great British economist, J. M. Keynes, could not have improved on the supporting argument.

Forasmuch as the abatement of interest hath always been found beneficial to the advancement of trade and improvement of lands by good husbandry; and whereas the taking of eight in the hundred for interest of money tends to the great discouragement of ingenuity and industry in the husbandry, trade, and commerce of this province, taking over 6 percent is forbidden.[6]

The Eighteenth Century

Bonds, that is, loans to private interests, were the largest element in the college portfolio in this century. The only exception was the large holding of government notes in the latter part of this period. The college had wisely gambled on the depreciation of the paper money and on the government's determination to redeem its bond at a fair price.

In 1712, bonds (private loans) accounted for almost half of the investments but in other years during this period, from 59 to 75 percent of the total. The next most important asset was the ferry income—27 percent in 1712, but only 8.3 percent by 1777 and no yield in 1807. Real estate was a substantial item—varying from 7 to 17 percent of investments in each of the years given.[7] Mortgages were of secondary importance and stock (7.1 percent) appeared for the first time in the 1807 total. Actually, in 1809, bank stocks comprised almost 71 percent of the total principal invested. In line with Harvard policy, however, this type of investment became less important and by 1819 was worth only 53 percent of the investments. In 1817 the college also received a share of the Middlesex Canal and, in 1814, shares in the Charles River Bridge.[8]

An indication of the investment policy from 1777 to 1807 is given by a table deposited in the archives.

An examination of figures in this table points to the shift from private loans payable in a depreciating currency to investments in government bonds. The shift is especially striking in the years of great inflation beginning in 1778. A large drop of Federal securities in 1785, £30,000 to £12,000, reflects a mark-down by Treasurer Storer of almost £18,000 to the low value of these securities then current. In 1792 all the Massachusetts notes outstanding as of the end of 1791 were turned in to the Continental Loan Office and Continental Loan Certificates were accepted in return. It is not surprising then that whereas *private* bonds (loans) were 81 percent of investments in 1777, by 1807 public *securities* had climbed to about 80 percent.[9]

In almost a hundred years from 1712 to 1807, the gains of investment funds were at a rather disappointing rate. Whereas general investments amounted to £4,505 in 1712, they had increased to £20,206 by 1777. By 1807, the total investment had risen to $229,525 (roughly £69,000).

In the fifty-five years from 1712 to 1777, the average rise of investments was about £240 per year

5. Inventory Papers, 1773, 1777 (unpublished).
6. Margery Somers Foster, *"Out of Smalle Beginnings . . . "–An Economic History of Harvard College in the Puritan Period (1636-1712)*, 1962, ch. VIII, esp. pp. 160-161.

7. The rents are of course capitalized at 6 percent. The lands not rented are not included in the assets. Thus, in 1777, there were numerous real estate items belonging to the college that were not rented. For example, 3 parcels in Cambridge, 32 acres in all, the Wiswell House, 1/64 of 52 townships in Maine, and 1/84 of 3 townships in Maine and 250 acres in Townsend. Against this there were 10 parcels rented with a yield in excess of £123 and a capitalized value of £2,094. See *Treasurers' Journals*, vol. I; *Corporation Records*, vol. II, pp. 405.
8. *Treasurers' Journals* and *Treasurers' Ledgers*, 1807-1819.
9. *Ibid.*, 1777-1790; Quincy, *op. cit.*, vol. II, ch. 31.

or roughly $800. Undoubtedly the explanation of this sluggish growth was partly the wars and unsettled conditions, and especially the inflation against which lenders, despite the protection offered by loans made in silver, could not adequately protect themselves.

An inventory of 1752 well suggests the nature of the problem.[10] In 1752, Treasurer Thomas Hubbard took over college property worth £23,855: bonds payable in silver, £9,443; bonds payable in old tenor, £8,891; bonds payable in lawful money, £5,521.

By 1752, a devaluation had occurred which depressed the old tenor in relation to the new at 7½ old to 1 new. These figures do not reflect this write-down. In fact, in 1721, general investments amounted to £9,545; in 1753, £6,905. By 1753, there must have been a write-down. But even allowing for this the inventory of 1752 was excessive. The decline of 28 percent seems inadequate when the currency has been devalued by 87 percent, but it is necessary to take into account the rise of assets in the years 1721 to 1753.

Perhaps the most satisfactory growth of investments occurred from 1777 to 1807, years of turmoil and slow economic growth. In these thirty years the average increase of investments was $5,500 or £1,650 per year. This satisfactory rise should be related to Harvard's successful gamble on the Federal government redeeming its bonds at a high value. The spectacular gain was from £28,000 invested in state and Federal securities in 1790 to £43,000 in 1791, a rise reflecting the improved value of government issues.

In the eighteenth century the relative contributions of interest, rent, and annuities to total endowment income did not change as much as might be expected. One might have expected relative losses in income especially affected by the inflation. But interest, for example, varied only from 57 to 63 percent of endowment income in the years 1722-1723 to 1771-1772 (based on statistics in one year for every ten-year period). A possible explanation for interest's *modest* gain as a proportion of endowment income is the rise in the proportion of bonds (private loans) in

the assets in these pre Revolutionary years, and also by measures taken to protect against inflation. (With inflation, the lender seeks compensation in higher interest.) Rents yielded 28 percent of the total in 1722-1723 to 1731-1732, and was down to 18 percent by 1762-1763 to 1771-1772. Apparently protection of rents against inflation was not as effective as for loans. The decline of the rent element is also explained partly by the relative reduction of property assets. Annuities climbed from 12 percent in the first ten years to 19 percent in the years 1762-1763 to 1771-1772. This result is rather surprising, and is explained partly by the large number of annuities provided in British sterling. As inflation proceeded in the colonies, these annuities yielded additional New England pounds.

In the years of the Revolution, however, there were drastic changes in the income contributions of different assets. In the years 1777 to 1805-1806 there were large changes in the proportion of endowment income provided by interest and rents. At this time inflation apparently affected loans much more than rents. Note the abnormally low contribution of 24 percent for interest in the Revolutionary years.

In some respects the losses of income from loans were much greater than here indicated, for endowment itself declined to the low figure of 9 percent of current income in the years 1777-1778 to 1780-1781.[11]

Table 49-1.

Sources of Endowment Income and its Share of Income by Periods

	Interest	Rents	Endowment Income, Percent of Total
1777-1780	24	76	9
1781-1792	56	36	21
1793-1805	76	17	39

11. *Treasurers' Journals; Treasurers' Ledgers; Acts and Resolves of the Province of Massachusetts Bay; Acts and Laws of the Commonwealth of Massachusetts; Resolves of the General Court of the Commonwealth of Massachusetts;* relevant years.

10. Unpublished inventory papers, 1752, in Harvard University Archives.

The Incumbency of Ebenezer Storer

A discussion of investment policy in the eighteenth century is incomplete without further comment on the incumbency of Ebenezer Storer over a period of about thirty years beginning in 1777. That Harvard remained solvent after the Revolutionary War is a tribute to that remarkable man who in the area of Harvard finance and management stands almost as high as President Eliot in the academic field. Storer carried on in the most difficult times, when war and galloping inflation eroded the income of the faculty and greatly reduced the real value of assets accumulated over the preceding 140 to 150 years. Storer's great contribution was his choice of continental and colonial securities for investment rather than paper money which steadily depreciated.[12]

Storer left a memorial which gave some indication of his contribution.[13] In this memo, Storer showed that he had contributed much to the finances of the college.

I have not mentioned this by way of boast; but only to shew in what way, and by what means the College Funds, began again to increase. I purchased these [public] *securities whenever I could, and had the satisfaction to find that the Funds not only increased to what they were before the War but greatly exceeded them. . . .*

In one instance Storer purchased 20 shares in Middlesex Canal securities. The corporation did not approve and the treasurer himself had to finance large losses over a considerable time, with unfortunate effects on his economic status.

The treasurer and his heirs complained of uncompensated services, and the losses involved in purchasing Middlesex shares. They pointed to the low pay which did not reflect the depreciation of the currency, the increasing complexity of the tasks and

Storer's large contribution to the college's strong financial position. Admitting the importance of Storer's contribution, the corporation gave £1,000 to his heirs, scarcely a generous gift in view of the extent of the contributions and the state of the family fortune.

In the Revolutionary period, the value of Harvard stock greatly declined in value.

The Nineteenth Century

In the nineteenth century investments of Harvard grew at a much more rapid rate than in the eighteenth. Thus, in the years 1810 to 1900 the average rise of investments was in excess of $100,000 per year. But the large gains came after 1860, with increase of but $14,000 average in the years 1810 to 1860, and $225,000 for 1860 to 1900.

The nineteenth century witnessed very large growth of the market for bonds in the modern sense with the result that they became a very important investment for the college: 1.25 percent in 1859-1860; 26.5 percent of the total in 1869-1870, gradually rising to 56 percent by 1900.

As bonds became increasingly important, notes, mortgages, and advances lost ground:

Percent of Investments

	Bonds	Notes and Mortgages
1859-1860	1.25	56.57
1899-1900	55.94	9.49

For Harvard, rents were a very important source of income in the nineteenth century:

	Percent
1809-1810	11.68
1899-1900	28.69
Av. 1809-10 to 1899-1900	22.40

---

12. Memorandum by Treasurer Storer, January, 1806.
13. Part of the Memorial Left by Treasurer Storer, 1807; To the President and Fellows of Harvard College by Hannah Storer . . . May 19, 1807.

One reason for the great interest in real estate was the high returns to be had. Thus in 1869-1870 yields were as follows: [14]

	Percent
Notes and mortgages	6.3
Government bonds	6.9
Real estate	9.8

Investment policies puzzle to some extent. In the second half of the nineteenth century the treasurer tended increasingly to invest in bonds, with stocks accounting for a declining percentage of investments. Yet one might have expected the reverse, for yields on bonds declined greatly and much more than those on stocks. The return on stocks was much higher by 1900 than on bonds.

What is the explanation of this perverse policy? Undoubtedly and despite the experience with inflation in the eighteenth century and in parts of the nineteenth, the college authorities still believed that investments in equities were highly risky. They seemed unaware, with the exception of Treasurer Amos Lawrence (1857-1862) that investments in

fixed interest yielding assets, e.g., bonds, mortgages, might be more risky than equities in periods of possible inflation. The penchant for investments in bonds in the second half of the nineteenth century may be supported to some extent because commodity prices tended to fall in the years 1870 to 1900, with adverse effects on profits. The higher yields of stocks suggested investments in stocks rather than bonds though the downward general price pressures discouraged investments in equities. But university investment in stocks from 1870 to 1900 would have yielded capital gains close to 1 percent a year. In addition, the average yield on stocks exceeded that on bonds.[15]

Later tables reveal the trend of investments from 1830 to later years. [16]

Notes and mortgages as a percentage of investments declined in a spectacular manner, and bonds rose correspondingly; real estate remained a substantial item throughout and especially in 1870 and later years. Stocks were significant but not substantial except in 1860.

A table deposited in the Harvard Archives gives some details on stock investments and some other assets in 1827. At this time stocks (equities) were

Table 49-2.

Yields on Bonds, Common Stocks, and Harvard Investments 1860, 1870, 1970

	Yield of Railroad Bonds	Investment in Bonds Percent All Inv.	Common Stock Yields	Percent Stocks of All Investments Harvard
1860	5.8	1.2	– –	20.4
1870	6.3	25.6	5.26	12.0
1900	3.1	56.9	4.28	8.9

14. *Report of the Treasurer of Harvard College*, 1868-1869, 1869-1870.

15. *Historical Statistics of the United States*, 1789-1945, pp. 280-281.

16. Cabot and Larrabee, "Investing Harvard Money," in *Harvard Alumni Bulletin*, May 12, 1951, p. 628.

unusually large, but rather small during most of the nineteenth century. Losses on equities tended to discourage stock purchases.

A treasurer's statement for 1840 reveals total assets yielding income at $646,235. What is especially significant is the large contribtuion of real estate compared to later periods (17 percent) and of equities, for that time, of 12 percent. Also of some interest is the early use by Harvard of a type of trust fund, for Harvard had turned over for management $60,210 (9 percent) to the Massachusetts Hospital Life Insurance Company.

Distribution of Income Yielding Assets, Harvard College, 1840

Notes and mortgages	55
Bills receivable	2
Deposits with Mass. Hospital Life Ins. Co.	9
Real estate	17
Equities	12
Annuities	2
Miscellaneous	3
	100

Source: Report of the Treasurer of Harvard College, 1840, reproduced in Quincy, op. cit., vol. II, pp. 625-627 (my calculations).

By 1842, however, the structure had changed substantially. Real estate declined to 13 percent and equities rose to 27½ percent.

Assets turned over to the Massachusetts Hospital Life Insurance rose to 11 percent.[17]

A table for 1850 to 1880, which has been deposited in the Harvard University Archives, reveals the growing interest in railroad bonds and stocks, in government bonds (notably in the 1860s with vast issues to finance the war), and in textiles, as textiles became a dominant New England manufacturing industry. Bank stocks were the earliest type to find their way into the college's portfolio.

Investments in these early years were in companies that are little known today, e.g., Boston Manufacturing Company, Pittsfield and North Adams Railroad. These companies have disappeared or moved south. It might be worth investigating when the college disposed of its heavy investments in textiles and railroads. (In the last thirty to thirty-five years the treasurer has disposed of most railroad securities.) Amos Lawrence, greatly interested in Pacific Mills, as treasurer put much Harvard money into this stock. Today one might consider this a conflict of interest.

By 1860, stocks had reached 15 percent of investments. Here the response to inflationary forces was clear. Thus, in 1861, Treasurer Amos Lawrence wrote:

To meet in some measure the steadily advancing rise of prices of expenditures, it has been deemed advisable to change the investment of a portion of the property from its form of fixed values. The amount of this property, consisting chiefly of mortgages, has been diminished to the extent of $236,619.45, and the real estate yielding income has been proportionately increased.[18]

By 1870, however, stocks had been reduced to 12 percent of investments. But the treasurers continued their interest in real estate, for by 1881 40 percent of the investment portfolio was thus invested. In that year Treasurer Hooper had acquired the corner of Washington and Summer Streets for $450,000, a site now occupied by Jordan Marsh Company.[19]

With declining rates of interest, outstanding bonds issued earlier at higher rates rose to premium prices. In purchasing bonds, the university frequently had to pay premium prices, and, therefore, as maturity dates approached, or even earlier, would write off the losses, i.e., the difference between purchase price and the redemption price. Thus, a treasury statement of 1887-1888 noted that though general investments made during the year had been chiefly in railroad

---

17. J. Quincy and J. Lowell, *Listing of Assets on September 16, 1842 on Turning Over Assets to New Treasurer.*

18. *Treasurer's Statement,* 1860-1861, pp. 3-4.
19. Cabot and Larrabee, *op. cit.,* p. 630.

bonds and temporary loans to corporations ". . . the sum of $23,536 taken from the year's income of railroad bonds has been applied as usual to repay a fair proportion of the total premiums. . . ." [20]

The Twentieth Century

This is, of course, the period of massive growth. In 1900 Harvard's general investments were still only about $10 million. By 1965, the total had risen to $677 million in book and $967 million in market value. In addition, the university in 1965 had $27 million of special investments and $30 million in other assets—e.g., money due from the government, notes receivable for student loans, accounts receivable. The rise in investments or total assets is far beyond what could be explained by rising prices or increases in enrollment. The major factors were new capital gifts, and, especially in the last generation, the rising productivity in the nation. As productivity increases, prices fall or income rises. The emphasis of late has been on the latter. In one year, 1951, for example, market value rose by 11 percent or $27 million, of which amount $7.5 million were new money and $19.5 million capital appreciation.[21]

In the last quarter of the nineteenth century, the university had profited from declining prices. Their assets and income therefore commanded increased services. But since 1900 the trend of prices has been upward. In its rather slow response to rising prices and profits, the university did not exploit the improvements in the economy by purchasing equities as much as it might have. Even as late as 1940, investments in equities were only about $40 million. Had all assets been converted into equities at that time, the $125 million would have escalated to roughly $900 million in the early 1960s. Of course no one would recommend such an extreme restructuring of investments. But a rise from one-third to two-thirds would have been possible. Then the investment assets would have risen by several hundred million dollars additional. The wisdom of such an investment policy

seems more apparent looking back rather than forward. Yet if investments in equities increased from about $4 million in 1910 to about $20 million in 1929-1930 in a period when prices of equities were rising in a spectacular manner, one might have anticipated a greater penchant for investments in common stock in the 1930s, when stock prices (1926 = 100) dropped from 190 (1929) to 150 (1930) to 49 (1932).

In the first twenty-nine years of the century, bonds and notes accounted for from 60 to 70 percent of Harvard investments. Real estate tended to become less important though the major declines, reflecting depreciation of values, occurred in the 1930s. In these years common stocks tended to become more important relatively, though in the first half of the overheated 1920s the equity portfolio declined in importance.

1930 to the Present: In Some Detail

Investment policies in the years 1930 to the present require more attention, in part because this is the period of greatest growth: from $100 million to about $1000 million.

In the years 1930 to 1940, the structure of investments experienced its largest change. The relative rise of all stocks was from 26.8 to 44.3 percent (common stocks alone showed an increase from 20.6 to 33.7 percent). These gains were at the expense of real estate especially, with a decline from 14.52 to 3.40 percent (virtually extinct by the 1950s), and notes, mortgages, etc., a reduction from 6.85 to 2.21 per cent. An apparent relative decline of bond holdings was primarily of notes.

How does one explain this revolutionary change in the portfolio? The largest shift to equities occurred in 1930. The price of bonds rose (and yield declined) and the price of common stocks declined. The index of stock prices declined from 190 to 150 from 1929 to 1930. With stock yields rising and their prices

20. *Treasurer's Statement*, 1887-1888, p. 3.

21. *Harvard Alumni Bulletin*, vol. 54, p. 62, 1951.

falling while bond prices rose, the treasurer shifted to equities.[22]

By 1932, bond yields rose (prices declined) and especially for second-class bonds. Despite a reduction of common stock prices to 49 by 1932 (190 in 1929), far beyond the drop even of risky bonds, the treasurer showed little interest in shifting further to stocks. Undoubtedly a good opportunity was missed. By the middle of the 1930s, the treasurer once more was favoring stocks. By 1937 the index of stock prices had moved up to 112. Whereas yields on less risky bonds had declined by about 2 percent or about 40 percent of 1930 yields, suggesting a rise of prices of almost two-thirds for long-term bonds since 1930, the price of stocks was low compared to the 1930 level, and the dividend yield on common stocks had risen by about 1½ percent. Hence, the yield on common stocks vis-à-vis good bonds had risen by about 2½ percent and the very high price of bonds vis-à-vis stocks encouraged a flight to equities. In general, the treasurer showed sound judgment, though looking back we might have expected a larger shift to common stocks. One serious mistake was the desertion of the real estate market. Large losses after the 1929 collapse resulted in excessive corrections. Many other institutions of higher learning did not make this mistake.

From 1940 to 1950, in view of the great improvements in the economy, the Harvard portfolio experienced relatively small changes. Harvard's ratio of common stocks was not out of line with those of Yale, Princeton, and MIT.[23] The percentage of common stocks rose by 4 percentage points and the proportion of notes (fixed returns) rose almost as much. Bonds and real estate lost ground. In this period the price index of common stocks rose by about 70 percent and the yield of bonds continued downward (and prices upward) though not at the rate of the 1930s. In fact, bond yields continuing to fall despite the vast demands of the government for funds was scarcely to be expected. In view of the large inflation

of the 1940s and a yield on common stocks from 3 to 4 percent above that for high-class bonds, it is rather surprising that the treasurer did not move into equities at a more rapid rate.

The rise of stocks held by Harvard occurred in the first half of the 1940s and tended downward in the second half. Stock prices tended to move up more in the second half of the 1940s (sometimes a deterrent to purchases) but the dividend yield was 5.59, 4.17, and 6.57 percent in 1940, 1945, and 1950 respectively. Purchases are more likely at higher yields. Bond yields continued downward, though at a slower rate than in the 1940s. Apparently the continued rise of common stock prices frightened potential investors in equities.

Another factor of importance in the 1940s was the large number of investments in government securities, a trend to be explained in part by patriotic considerations rather than market judgment. Moreover, the large rise of investments in government securities was primarily at the expense of other bonds which in the 1940s could be sold at high and profitable prices as their prices rose and yields declined.

Harvard's record seemed to have been rather spectacular in the years 1950 to 1965. The increase in value of Harvard's common stock portfolio was 473 percent. Against this the gain of a general index of common stock prices was 380 percent. In one respect the record was even better than suggested by these statistics. For the treasurer had distributed 40 percent of investment holdings by 1964-1965 which presumably reflected capital gains actually realized during this period. In addition, the corporation distributed $33,900,000 for 1966. But this comparison of stock prices and the rise in the value of Harvard's portfolio gives an exaggerated view of Harvard's investment record, for in part the rise in the percentage of investments held in equities accounts for the increased value in Harvard's common stock portfolio. In 1950, equities accounted for 38 percent of Harvard's investments or $93 million and in 1965, $533 million (market value), or 56 percent of investments.

Distributions of funds received through capital gains since World War II amounted to $144 million

22. See table deposited in the Harvard University Archives.
23. G. Putnam, Jr., "Sound Investing," in *Harvard Alumni Bulletin,* 1953, p. 628.

by 1965 ($34 million additional by 1966). Hence, the value of equities, exclusive of distribution of capital gains, should be increased by $144 million to 1965. But against this we have to deduct $165 million, a total which corrects for the rise of the percentage of equities from 38 percent in 1950 to 56 percent in 1965. Hence, a comparison of equity values in 1950 and 1965 reveals a rise of $355 million in equities, and a 380 percent rise of equity prices.[24]

This is a reasonably good record. But the calculations are rough ones. That Harvard may well purchase equities that are less risky than the general run adds to the quality of the performance.

In this period, 1950 to 1965, the price of common stocks rose by 380 percent, and that of good long-term bonds declined substantially, as revealed by a rise in yield from 1950 to 1965 from 2.62 to 4.49 percent. Moreover, the yield on common stock dropped from 6.57 to 3.00 percent. The net result of yield changes from 1950 to 1965 was about 5½ per cent in favor of bonds. Yet fixed interest assets became less attractive and equities much more attractive —the percentage of common stock to total investments rose from 38 to 56 percent. A large part of the gains of common stocks was at the expense of preferred stocks. Now Harvard clearly was trying to exploit capital gains, the annual rise of which greatly exceeded the 5½ percent loss on current yields per year in buying equities, that explains the failure to buy more bonds despite the *relative* gain on yields of 5½ percent in buying bonds. In fact, from 1950 to 1965 the average rise in the price of equities was 25 percent a year, or about 15 percent compounded. The capital gains, then, in these fifteen years were about three times as large as the rise of spread between the yields of stocks and bonds.

Response to Collapse of Stock Prices

Unlike other investors in equities, the university did not contend with the stock market collapse by selling common stock. The fact is that despite the large drop in values the university greatly increased its investments in equities. The increase in these years was from about $21 million to about $42 million, and purchases beginning with 1930 were steady. Had the university, in order to meet commitments, disposed of equities net in the 1930s, there would have been large losses. Instead, the treasurer purchased common stock at low prices which in the next twenty to thirty years were to rise greatly in price.

This does not mean that the collapse of the economy did not hurt the university. Thus, in the forty-five years from 1886 to 1931, Harvard's rate of distribution to the university from endowment income averaged about 5 percent of book value. It dropped to 4 percent in the 1930s and recovered to 4½ per cent in the early 1950s. In one year, 1932-1933, the treasury had to reduce payments to its thirty-five departments from 5.25 percent of book value to 4.8 percent.[25]

Corporate profits were down from $10 billion in 1929 to less than $3 billion in 1932. But the dividend picture was much less bleak. The reduction was large but not so serious even in 1932 if allowance is made for the fall of general prices, and hence the rise in purchasing power. We should observe, however, that Harvard did not gain as much as it might have from falling prices, for salaries were not reduced. Dividend yields on the basis of market prices increased, of course. The yield rose from 3.48 percent in 1929 to 6.69 percent in 1932 and 5.59 percent in 1940.

In so far as the treasurer purchased equities, he raised a number of problems that require some comment. First, in so far as he favored growth stocks, that is, stocks that were expected to bring small yields now to be compensated by large appreciation later, he was sacrificing present for future income. To this extent he may well be playing poor and deprive current purveyors of services, e.g., faculty members, of income to the benefit of later purveyors. Personnel at times complained of this Calvinistic policy.

Second, as values of equities rose the problem of equity among different interests in Harvard

24. The table is deposited in the Harvard University Archives.

25. *Harvard Alumni Bulletin,* vol. 39, pp. 732-734, 1932; vol. 55, p. 628, 1953.

investments troubled the treasurer. In so far as the capital values rise without accompanying distribution the constituent interests in the general investment fund do not share in these gains. The excess of market over book value is not reflected in corresponding gains for the hundreds of funds. On some occasions, however, the corporation allocated part of the capital gains (realized) among the various funds.

In addition, having been instructed by the experiences of the last generation, the corporation emphasized increasingly the importance of a guarantee fund which would assure the beneficiaries of Harvard investments a fairly stable return from year to year despite the actual fluctuations of income. As early as the 1860s the treasurer reported that:

the balance at the Commencement of the present year to the credit of the Insurance and Guarantee Fund having been unusually increased by the surplus over six percent of the dividends, it has been thought judicious to avail of so favorable opportunity to restore the stock [endowment] account to its former value which has been done to the debit of the Insurance Guarantee Fund. [26]

On June 30, 1963, this General Investment Gain and Loss Account had a balance of $28,500,000. The balance on June 30, 1965 of general investments was $51,800,000, of which $30,600,000 were authorized for 1965-1966 distribution and $21,200,000 were reserved for subsequent distribution. [27]

The relationship of market to book values needs some analysis. I consider this ratio in the years 1935 to 1963. It would be expected that as the gross national product rises, the price of common stock would also increase, and hence the ratio of market to book values would rise; and similarly with declines in the gross national product, this ratio would be expected to decline. But on the whole this correlation is not very high.

A comparison of stock prices and of market to book ratios of Harvard investments in twelve periods, generally of one year each, reveals that in every case but one a rise in the former was accompanied by one

in the latter, and declines in prices of stocks by a reduction in the market to book ratio at Harvard. One might expect that on the average, the market to book ratio would rise about one-half as much or fall one-half as much as the index of stock prices, for Harvard's investments in common stock were about one-half of total investments during this period. Actually the expected happened in only a few instances.

Here are some unexpected developments. Especially striking were those from 1950 to 1963. The price index rose by 280 percent, but the Harvard market to book ratio rose only by 11 percent. The explanation might be an unwise investment policy. But a more substantial explanation is the large number of sales of securities, with the proceeds being added to the book values of the various accounts. Hence the market to book ratio would tend to rise only modestly relative to the increase of equity prices. Another relevant factor is that equities account only for about half of the investment portfolio, and, therefore, the market to book ratio would rise less than the price of equities. Large discrepancies also occurred in 1946, 1947 and 1948.

Defaults

Defaults troubled the college throughout its history. The college was not a generous creditor. In 1786, James Richardson, who was in default of a debt to the college, wrote:

I still remain in Goal on an Execution in your favour, which I am by no means able to satisfy under my situation – I am willing to do everything that is in my power to help you to the Money (which is your Honest Due) – but whilst I remain in Confinement I cannot collect it. I would therefore be much Obliged to you, if you would Liberate me, upon my giving my security for the Debt. . . . [28]

---

26. *Treasurer's Statement,* 1862-1863, p. 2.

27. *Financial Report to the Board of Overseers of Harvard College,* 1962-1963, p. 19; 1964-1965, p. 18.
28. James Richardson to Mr. Storer, April 12, 1786; James Richardson to the President and Fellows of Harvard College, Worchester Goal, June 8, 1786.

The committee of finance examining sixty college loans valued at $179,500 in the midst of the crises of the 1820s, and raised questions concerning a number of the loans.

The implication was poor management by the treasurer. In all, the committee raised questions on nineteen items, requesting increased security, collection, or insurance. Thus, of a debtor in Concord, the committee asked that a copy of the $3,000 note "be sent to Mr. Hoar of Concord with a special request that he will at once secure as much as possible by attachment of the property, real or personal, or obtain payment or other ample security."[29]

Special Investments

There are many instances of special investments over Harvard's history; that is, investments not pooled with the general investments of the university. President Eliot nevertheless urged Harvard's friends to put their money into the general fund. His major argument was that in this manner the donor would profit from expert investment advice and from the safety resulting from diversification. Though strongly in favor of the general investment, Eliot nevertheless would gladly accept special investments. But with special investments "there is a chance of the funds being impaired or lost by a single error of judgment in making an investment. This chance may be small in any one generation but it is appreciable in centuries."[30]

Where special investments prevailed, there frequently seemed to be a disposition to be more venturesome than the college was with its general investments. For example, in 1853, the *Trustees of the Fund for Assisting Harvard College* had all investments other than $9,226.62 in bills receivable from students invested in bank stock (about $14,000). Again, a gift of $50,000 from Samuel Appleton in 1854 was wholly invested in textile companies.[31] Another donor requested that if a change in investment of his funds was under consideration, he should be consulted.[32]

It is not easy to discover whether the Harvard Corporation or the investors on behalf of special funds had the better record. From one treasurer's report, it appears that the return on $9 million of general investments was 4.27 percent, and on $2 million of special investments, 3.94 percent, a difference pointing to a better record for the Harvard managers. Returns on special investment varied greatly from fund to fund. A substantial number invested in Harvard houses and lands and most of these did poorly. Returns on investments in railroads were much higher.[33]

When one compares special investments with general investments, it is clear that the former has become much less important. Thus, whereas at the end of the nineteenth century, special investments were about two-elevenths of the total and in 1915, about one-ninth, in 1965 they had fallen to about one-fiftieth. One reason must be increasing confidence in the Harvard management.[34]

A decision of the corporation in 1873 to put $40,000 received from the sale of land at the disposal of the Massachusetts Hospital Life Insurance for investment on behalf of the college greatly disappointed Eliot. Involved was not only a diversion to special investments but other issues also. In Eliot's view, the corporation had no right to tie its hands for forty-five years, as it had done under this agreement with an early form of mutual fund; it could not bind its successors; and it was paying the insurance company for assuming Harvard's responsibilities. Allowing funds to accumulate for forty-five years at compound

29. Memorandum on Notes to be Collected as soon as may be, December 7, 1826, December 12, 1826.
30. C.W. Eliot to J.R. Putnam, September 15, 1869.
31. *Report No. 12 of the Trustees of the Fund for Assisting Students at Harvard College,* January 6, 1853; N. I. Bowditch to the Corporation of Harvard College, November 27, 1854.
32. T. Lee to President James Walker, November 15, 1856.

33. *Treasurer's Statement,* 1898-1899, pp. 3-9 (my computations).
34. *Financial Report to the Board of Overseers of Harvard College,* relevant years; Patterson, et al., *Accounting Report to F. W. Hunnewell, Comptroller of Harvard University, on Accounts of ... Harvard University,* December 10, 1915.

interest, in Eliot's view, would mislead the public and discourage gifts. All would think that Harvard was rich and would respond accordingly to pleas for financial help.

In the early years especially, but even into the nineteenth century, donors were afraid of being cheated or their funds mismanaged. Thus, the commingling of funds might well deprive some of a fair share of the income. The Harvard system of allocating income on the basis of book values in periods of rising values of equities militates against the interests of donors more the earlier the date of the gift. By insisting on special investment, the donor can be sure that his fund will gain all increases in value of investments properly allocatable to his fund.

Another source of concern of donors was that for a long period before the last hundred years of Harvard history, the treasurer paid out to the various endowment funds not what the treasurer earned, generally 6 percent or more, but rather 5 percent. The treasurer was not playing fairly with the various funds donated to the college, for the treasurer was diverting some part of the returns to the general funds. Under constant pressure, the treasurer about a hundred years ago began to allow each fund an amount determined by the earnings minus expenses of management.[35]

President Eliot was confirmed in his doubts about special investments by their use by the Bussey Trust Fund. The Bussey Institute received about one-half of its income from this trust which, as required by the will, could only be invested in stores in the best business quarters of Boston. Then came the great fire of 1872 and later loss of rentable value.[36]

If Harvard's general investment policies were not always beyond criticism, it is equally true that special funds were also mismanaged. In 1810 Samuel Dexter gave the college $5,000 for a lectureship on Biblical literature. He directed "that the President and Fellows of the University elect three gentlemen of the clergy, and two others, not of that order, to join with the Corporation in the management of the interest...." But in 1841 the corporation discovered that this investment management group had not met for twenty years.[37] The corporation and its committee had violated the provisions of the deed.

The Brattle Street Reversion

One of Harvard's most fascinating investment and default experiences was the Brattle Street reversion (David Greenough's loan). This particular episode embraced almost a century.

In February, 1818, Greenough proposed to the Harvard Corporation that he convey to them a lot of land on Brattle Street, Boston; that in return he would receive from Harvard $70,000 of 6 percent stock, build "elegant and substantial buildings" on the property, and that he and Thomas Wales would have a hundred-year lease on the buildings and that they would repay all the money ($70,000 with interest).

Wales repaid his share of the loan ($16,000) by 1833, in accordance with the original agreement. But Greenough assigned his interest in the property to Benjamin Rich and Seth Knowles, who paid some of the interest to Harvard. The college received no interest between January 1, 1824, and May, 1826. Greenough thereupon assigned to Harvard the Province House Estates, Washington Street, Governors' Alley. It is not clear whether this was in compensation for defaults or a separate transaction.

The college dispossessed Greenough from the Province Street Estates in 1828, the rents thereafter to be paid to the college. Mr. Greenough protested that he had offered the required payments and said:

35. N. Silsbee to the President and Fellows of Harvard College, October 28, 1870.

36. *Report of the President of Harvard College*, 1876-1877, pp. 33-34; *Endowment Funds of Harvard University*, p. 388; *Judge Bigelow's Report on Bussey Real Estate*, 1861 (?).

37. Endowment *Funds or Harvard University*, p. 206; *Report of the Committee Appointed on the 28th November Last, to Consider the Subject of the Trustees of the Dexter Fund, Meeting of President and Fellows of Harvard College*, January 11, 1841.

...the dispossession of me of the premises at this present time would be destructive to me as a man of credit and prudence and capacity. I earnestly request that you would take the amount due to you and restore me to that standing in society which I have ever held dear to me and it will prompt me to be a useful member of the society in the future. . . .

Interest payments seem to have been received with some regularity until 1870 and irregularly after that. The college also received payments of principal on the Greenough part of the loan from 1851 to 1869, or about $20,000 in all. We could find no later entries of principal.

According to the treasurer's report of 1901-1902, the reversion was sold for $300,000, or $296,831 after expenses. (The Brattle Street reversion was carried on the books for only $1,000 from 1815 to 1899). The college had received interest regularly on its loan in later years until 1870.

As a return only of the interest on the investment over eighty years, the Brattle Street reversion was not highly profitable. But when allowance is made for the capital gain of $283,000 or thereabouts the college received a handsome return. The college received interest fairly regularly for fifty years. A rough estimate puts annual return on this capital gain of $283,000 over eighty years on an investment of $50,000 at 2¼ percent per year compounded. If one allows for greater purchasing power of the dollar in 1900 than in 1819, the additional return beyond the regular interest associated with the capital gain may well have been around 4 percent per year compounded. [38]

In his 1902-1903 report, President Eliot described the transaction. The lease expired in June, 1919, but early in the twentieth century, the college sold the reversion for about $283,000. For an asset carried on the books at $1,000, the college had received $283,000. The corporation insisted on its legal rights. "...it is probable that the transaction was a profitable one to the descendants of Messrs. Greenough and Wales. It certainly has proved a profitable one to the President and Fellows. . . ."[39]

Real Estate Investments

Gifts of land from the Colonial government did not yield much income. President Willard, after the Revolutionary War, complained of how little was actually received. He asked for the restoration of the college lands, rights, and confirmation of rights originally granted.[40]

The financial crises of 1827 resulted in sales of land:

...the Corporation have been desirous of placing their property in a situation of producing as much income as possible — have sold some part and endeavored to sell the remaining part of such of those lands that have hitherbefore not only been without income but attended with expense and trouble. . . .[41]

The college owned numerous houses during the late eighteenth and nineteenth centuries.[42]

In the 1798 memo the treasurer listed seven houses valued from $333 to $3,033. The total value was $11,572 and rents, $1,050. This ratio of 11 to 1 of value to rents is not greatly out of line with present ratios. But the ratios varied from 5½ to 15 to 1 for different houses. If the figures are accurate,

38. *Corporation Papers, 1st series,* vol. 1, p. 185, vol. 2, pp. 147,152; vol. 3, p. 41; vol. 4, p. 3; vol. 5, pp. 73-74, 305-507; vol. 8, p. 93; vol. 9, pp. 9, 26-27; 2nd series, vol. 1-30, esp. vol. 1, July, 1826; vol. 2, pp. 63, 152, 244, 247, 249, 288-289; vol. 3, p. 41; vol. 6, p. 63.

39. *Report of the President of Harvard College,* 1902-1903, pp. 60-61; Meeting of President and Fellows of Harvard College, March 27, 1828 and March 28, 1828; N. Bowditch to F.C. Gray, June 23, 1828; *Treasurer's Statement* (on the reversion) April 1, 1828.

40 Joseph Willard, President, to the Honourable Senate and Honourable House of Representatives, "an Acct of the Bonds, Mortgages. . . also the Real Estate," 1785.

41. *Treasurer's Statement,* December 20, 1827.

42. List of Houses in Cambridge belonging to Harvard College, from No. 1 to No. 10. . . also of Estates in sundry places belonging to the College by Treasurer; *College Books;* Memorandum of June 1, 1798, Account of Houses Belonging to Harvard College.

housing investments were not very lucrative. In the years 1795-1796 to 1797-1798, repairs amounted to $4,626 and rents, $3,643.[43]

Harvard's declining interest in real estate is suggested by a comparison of income in 1915 and assets in 1965-1966. In 1915, rents from land and buildings after operating expenses amounted to $315,000, or 10 percent of the general income of $3,100,000. On June 30, 1966, assets, investment real estate, mortgages, and loans for student housing, less depreciation and amortization reserves, all together were only $9 million, or less than 1 percent of the total market value of general investments.[44]

Once the college was confronted with a serious crisis and examined its investments in land carefully, the decision was made to get rid of much of it as soon as possible.

In 1826-1827, the treasurer noted: "...The Corporation have been desirous of placing their property in a situation of producing as much income as possible; have sold some part and endeavored to sell the remaining part of such of those lands that have hithertofore not only been without income but attended with expense and trouble...."[45]

One of the peculiar aspects of Harvard investment history is the recourse to income from dormitories to pay part of the college bills. In the early years students living in the president's house contributed to the support of the president, and part of the rents from Stoughton College (seventeenth century) were available for the use of the college. In March, 1765, the Legislature voted that "the cellars and rooms of the new building (Hollis Hall) should be let at a rate to produce one hundred pounds annual rent; of which sum ten pounds should be reserved to keep it in repair, and the residue be applied to the support of tutors and the purchase of books for the library."

Later, President Eliot said:

An experience of 270 years with dormitories has demonstrated that they are not good property for the College, it having proved impossible to earn on them so good an income as the mass of the general investments the University yields. The President and Fellows have not built a dormitory with their own money since 1870-1871, and are not likely ever to build another, unless with money given for that express purpose.

Apparently the 8 percent return expected from Thayer Hall and even more from Holyoke House were not realized.[46]

In 1873-1874 one-half of the net income of Matthews Hall was available for the general purposes of the college and as late as 1924 the business school planned a return of 5 percent on its investments in dormitories. The dean hoped to finance his case gathering material from this income.[47]

At times the college administrators were optimistic about returns on college dormitories. Thus, Acting President Peabody in 1862, resting his case largely on the desire of students to live in college dormitories, proposed a new dormitory which could yield a good return. He would charge low rents on dormitories given to the university, but operate on the free market principal and charge high rents on dormitories financed by the college.[48]

Yet it is indeed difficult to build dormitories that will yield the 5 to 6 percent that Harvard investments have yielded over the years. In order to yield such income the rents have to be at a level which would frighten away students. Colleges even find it difficult

43. *Report of Committee of Corporation on Economics,* 1825.
44. Patterson, Teele and Dennis, *Accounting Report on Accounts of Burson, Year Ending June 30, 1915* and *Financial Report to the Board of Overseers of Harvard College,* 1965-1966, p. 8.
45. *Treasurer's Statement,* 1826-1827, appendix G; *Report of the President of Harvard College,* 1826-1827, p. 52.
46. "Report on New Dormitory," September 25, 1869, in *Corporation Records.*

47. Foster, *op. cit.,* pp. 79, 119; *Report of the President of Harvard College,* 1873-1874, pp. 35-37; 1905-1906, p. 51; "Official Statement of Executive Committee to Extend the National Service of Harvard University, Effort to Secure $10,000,000 to Develop the University Service," in Harvard University Archives, 1924, pp. 45-47; Quincy, *op. cit.,* vol. II, p. 102.
48. A. P. Peabody to F. B. Crowninshield, November 27, 1862.

to finance dormitories with money borrowed at 3 to 4 percent from the Federal government. As is noted elsewhere in this book, the rents charged students— say, $500 average per year—in the Harvard House Plan cover the operating expenses only, though 2 percent additional seems to be included to cover repairs, maintenance and reserves.

Harvard originally invested in homes which they in turn rented to professors. This is still done occasionally. But when returns on these investments are examined, they are generally disappointing. That the investments were not always profitable is suggested by the rents charged. In 1910, for example, 16 Quincy Street was available at $700 a year and 38 Quincy Street, $900. These were choice houses and locations. Rents today would probably be 10 times as high if the houses were available.[49]

It does not follow that the college would have been much better off if it had disposed of its real estate sooner. An excessive reaction to the losses of the 1930s, for example, was unfortunate. The college would have been much better off if it had exploited the disorganized and under-priced market of the 1930s.

49. N. Silsbee to President and Fellows of Harvard College, October 8, 1910; Treasurer's Office in *A. L. Lowell Letters,* October 26, 1910; *Report of the Committee Appointed to Consider What Disposition Should be Made of that Part of the Income of the Bussey Fund Which Belongs to the Law School,* May 31, 1862.

50

The Yield on Harvard's Investments

Early Returns

Since Harvard is the corporation with the longest investment record in the country, its investment experiences are of special interest not only to the students of Harvard's history but to all who are concerned with investments.

In 1715, the treasurer received from William Brattle, executor of Thomas Brattle, late treasurer of the college, nearly £3,800 yielding £280 (roughly 6 percent) as compared with £1,550, yielding £100, in 1693 (roughly 6½ percent).[1]

Yields on the college's capital depended on the solvency of the borrowers. As was noted earlier, defaults were not uncommon.

In 1752 the treasurer was instructed to sue as soon as possible so that the various college officers whose incomes depended upon them could be paid.

Defaults were a persistent problem for the college, especially when the college was confronted with financial crises. Thus, in the midst of the 1820s crisis, the committee of finance reported as follows:

They have examined a schedule of 60 loans submitted to them by the treasurer, amounting in the whole to $179,500 . . . . They find the several sums loaned to be well and securely invested, with the following exceptions, in relation to which they have made known their opinions . . . .

In all, thirty-six loans were listed generally with no collateral, or inadequate security. The amounts in-

volved were about one-half of the total. Obviously defaults, current or threatened, of these proportions meant a general reduction of return on investments. In general, the investment policy did not reflect high ability.[2]

An examination of the ratio of annual payments to capitalized values of endowments from the years 1715 until the Revolution reveals that the returns were frequently close to 6 percent, though throughout that period the average was less. Here is one example:

1755 Returns on Harvard Endowments

	Annual Payment			Capitalized Value		
Hollis	£17	11	8	£293	1	1
Hutchinson	2	8	0	40	0	0
Townsend	4	0	0	66	13	4
Henchman	2	0		33	6	8

In the inflationary periods a yield of 6 percent was most inadequate. With the revaluation of the currency at mideighteenth century, Treasurer Hubbard presumably reduced the value of capital assets to some extent in accordance with the value of the new

---

1. Quincy, *op. cit.*, p. 411; *History of Harvard College*, p. 13.

2. Committee of Finances, Communication to Treasurer Respecting Securities, Notes to be Collected as soon as may be, December 7, 1826; and Letter of December 12, 1826 by C. Jackson, E. Frances, N. Bowditch.

currency to the old: 7.5 of old equaled 1 of new. At this time, uncollected interest due of £3,627 8s2d was about 18 percent of Harvard's investment income.[3]

Investments in Real Estate

In Harvard's early history, real estate gifts were of much importance. Views on the profitability of dormitories have not always been in agreement, though a stronger case can be made for substantial yields when the dormitory is a gift item than if it involves investment by the college. Acting President Peabody was sanguine on the prospects of good returns in the 1850s. But a careful study in 1857 revealed that for four dormitories with all rooms rented, total receipts would be $4,000 and costs of repairs, cleaning, etc., would be $3,600, or a net revenue of $400, scarcely a substantial return on the capital involved. Moreover, it is clear that the estimates were of the roughest kind and the reliability reduced because of the joint cost problem, e.g., how much of the costs of upkeep of the yard should be charged to the four dormitories?[4]

The college purchased Brattle House in 1857. It was estimated that it would yield $3,320 of rent in a forty-week year. Food would be available for 27 cents a day or $1.89 a week. Hence, total room and board would cost but $2.50 a week for those who were anxious to economize. Brattle House had cost $47,533. The house might be had with furniture for $22,000. But it proved to have been an unprofitable investment. Holyoke Hall, it was estimated in 1870, would cost $122,000. Interest on capital at 7 to 8 percent would amount to $9,775. Rents would yield $13,000, repairs and insurance, cost $2,000; and the net income of $11,000 would exceed interest lost by more than $1,000.[5]

Pressure to Raise Returns

In the eighteenth century the college sought to raise returns on investment in all kinds of ways. The college was especially concerned over the inflation of the second quarter of the eighteenth century and its effect upon the real salaries of faculty members.

Though the college was in financial difficulties, it could be compassionate: Following a drought, 1749 to 1759, the college reduced the rent of a tenant by £60 one quarter. Again, impressed by the unusual decline in traffic on the ferry, the college remitted ten pounds old tenor to the ferrymen in the first quarter of 1750.[6]

Impact of Inflation

In the large inflation of the first half of the eighteenth century, the college was unable to protect itself as effectively as modern treasurers can. Investment opportunities were much restricted compared to those available in the twentieth century or even in the second half of the nineteenth century.

The stock was invested in three items: bills, bonds (loans), and mortgages. In 1715, the total value was £3,767, again invested in bonds primarily and a few mortgages. As prices rose the real value of stock would fall. Equities were not available. The college might protect itself by lending for short periods. Then the depreciation would be offset to some extent through higher charges on the renewal of the loan; or, as the college learned to do later, relate the loan to its equivalent in the price of a fixed amount of silver.[7]

What inflation did to the college is also suggested by the developments by 1778. The annual rents and interest appropriated by the donors to particular purposes amounted in 1777 to £692 12s 3d, of which

3. Quincy, *op. cit.,* vol. II, pp. 237-238; *Harvard College Journal,* vol. I, p. 25.
4. W. G. Stearnes to President Walker, January 21, 1857.
5. N. Silsbee to the President and Fellows of Harvard College, September 18, 1869; Memo by A. Willard on Brattle House, March 20, 1857; N. Silsbee, Chairman of

Committee, *Report on Expediency of Building Holyoke Hall,* June 10, 1870; N. Silsbee to the President and Fellows of Harvard College, 1862.
6. *College Books,* vol. IV, pp. 812-815.
7. *College Books,* vol. IV, 1693, p. 409; 1715, pp. 428-431.

£30 8s were appropriated to the professor of mathematics; £38 12s to the professor of divinity; and £80 16s to the professor of Hebrew. But the actual salaries were £92 12s, £48 18s 8d, and £60. It is quite clear that neither the investment income nor other sources of income was adequate, for since the salaries were not sufficient for their support "because of the greatly advanced prices of all the necessities of life," the corporation increased the pay of these three professors.[8] It is evident that, despite some success in tying income to the rising price level, the faculty's economic condition deteriorated. Returns of 5 to 6 percent in the 1770s scarcely reflected compensation to Harvard for inflation.

An Over-all Survey of Yields

In the eighteenth century, with the government setting a ceiling of 6 percent, yields varied from 5.38 to 5.80 percent, though yields were at times 6 percent. During much of the eighteenth century loans were made by the college requiring repayment in a given weight of silver. In this manner, the college reduced losses associated with repayments in a depreciating currency.

Nineteenth century yields remained high until after the Civil War. The maximum figure was 7.21 for 1869-1870. By 1909-1910, the yield had declined to 3.47 percent. With Harvard relying heavily on income from investments, the marked decline of yields was a serious matter, and particularly during Eliot's administration. With World War I, returns again rose, only to decline again under the impetus of the Great Depression and an economic policy directed to reducing money rates. In the 1950s, once again monetary rates rose as the Eisenhower administration introduced restrictive monetary policies, with interest rates rising by about two-thirds. In the late 1960s, yields once more are at a record level.

In general, yields decline in periods of deflation and falling prices, e.g., the latter part of the nineteenth century; and rise to some extent in periods of inflation, e.g., the first half of the twentieth century.

When the government sets a ceiling on interest rates, e.g., in the eighteenth century, yields do not rise *pari passu* with inflation.

A smart treasurer reacts to rising prices by investing heavily in assets that respond to inflation, e.g., real estate and common stocks, rather than bonds or mortgages. Thus, in 1860-1861, Treasurer Amos Lawrence responded to anticipated inflation by converting $236,619, mostly invested in mortgages, to speculative real estate.[9] In the 1920s and especially since World War II, college treasurers have responded to rising prices by investing much more heavily in common stocks.

Under Eliot the decline of returns on capital was a constant source of concern. The Boston fire in 1872 that seriously hurt the college's endowment, the business recession of the 1870s, and the deflationary trends of the fourth quarter of the nineteenth century, all were unfavorable to endowment income.

The boom after the Civil War sent returns away up. In 1874, the president commented on the unprecedented rise of yields. In the years 1867 to 1876, the average return on general investments was 7.21 percent—a maximum of 7.82 percent in 1871-1872, and a minimum of 6.50 percent in 1867-1868.

President Eliot unhappily compared 7.59 percent average return for 1870 to 1875, 4.93 percent for 1890 to 1895, and 4.73 percent by 1895-1896; and at the end of his administration the yield had fallen to 4 percent. As yields declined, the president and treasurer frequently complained, e.g., when the college in 1888-1889 had to turn in high-yielding Atchison, Topeka, and Santa Fe Railroad bonds.

A few years earlier the treasurer had raised the question of how the university could meet permanent obligations such as salaries with the yield on investments dropping from 7.44 to 5.19 percent in thirteen years.[10]

8. Corporation Meeting, January 26, 1778.

9. *Treasurer's Statement,* 1860-1861, pp. 3-4.

10. *Report of the President of Harvard College,* 1872-1873, pp. 35-38; 1873-1874, pp. 35-38; 1874-1875, pp. 30-31, 40-41; 1878-1879, pp. 34-37; 1885-1886, pp. 23-24; 1895-1896, p. 42; *Treasurer's Statement,* 1875-1876, pp. 2-3; 1879-1880, p.4; 1888-1889, p.4; 1891-1892 to 1909-1910, various issues; "President Eliot's Reports," in *The Harvard Bulletin,* February 7, 1889, p. 1.

Over the years, a return of 6 percent as against one of 3 percent makes a large difference. If the income is spent, then twice as much is available with a 6 percent return. If it is not spent, then the accumulation rises with higher rates. Thus, $1 million yielding 3 percent grows to $4,390,000 in fifty years; at 6 percent, the $1 million will escalate to $18,400,000, or more than four times as much. The compound interest law is at work.

How effective the compund interest law was, is suggested by the Lowell Fund begun in 1838 with an original subscription of $11,350. The fund advanced loans to students at 5 percent. One hundred years later, the value of the fund had risen to $485,882, and in a recent year it has cumulated to about $2 million.[11]

Varying Yields

By comparing yields over six different years, one can get some idea of the variations in yields and the reasons for changes.

Year	Reason	Percent of average yield
1809-1810	Recovery from war	6.00
1869-1870	Recovery from Civil War— shortage of capital	7.21
1899-1900	End of a period of deflation	4.35
1929-1930	War and stock market inflation	5.44
1939-1940	The Great Depression and the stock market collapse	4.80
1959-1960	War and postwar prosperity	4.90

In the first year, 1809-1810, the only yield that was far out of line with the average of 6 percent was real estate paying 9.6 percent. But at this time 71.6 percent was invested in stocks, 11.7 percent in real estate, and 16.8 percent in notes, mortgages, and advances. The crucial investments were in stocks.

The year 1869-1870, with a return of 7.21 percent on Harvard investments, profited especially from a yield of 9.8 percent from common stocks (the investments in stocks were not large). Bonds, other than government, were out of line with a yield of but 5.46 percent (the corresponding figure for other bonds for all investors was 6.4 percent).

During this period there were important switches of investments. From 1810 to 1870, investments in bonds rose from 0 to 25.6 percent; real estate, from 11.7 to 32.6 percent; and notes, mortgages, etc., from 16.8 to 29.8 percent. But investments in stocks declined from 71.6 percent to 12 percent. The large rise in bonds (especially from 1860 to 1870) reflected their increasing availability; the increase of real estate, especially in the 1860s; the inflationary prospects; the decline of stocks, despite their high yield, suggests the risks of loss. Investments in notes, mortgages, etc. actually declined steadily after 1830-1831, especially because of inflation in the 1860s and partly because of increasing availability of bonds. The high average yield for 1869-1870 (7.21 percent) is associated especially with the high return and large investments in real estate and government bonds, and secondarily with the high returns on stocks.

According to one report of the treasurer, the return on general investments in 1869-1870 was 6.7 percent and in 1868-1869, 7¼ percent. For many years, however, the university paid out not what was earned but only 5 percent. By paying only 5 percent the college was in fact treating the funds unfairly. In the sixties,[12] the system was changed in favor of the various funds.

One might expect that investments in common stocks were very profitable, but actually large losses were incurred. The decline of stock holdings from 1810 to 1870 points to the large risks involved. A good example is the $12,000 of Middlesex Canal shares received through the Gore estate. Dividends

11. *Harvard Alumni Bulletin*, vol. 41, pp. 1091-1097.

12. N. Silsbee to the President and Fellows of Harvard College, October 28, 1870.

amounted to 15 percent in the years 1835 to 1837, and then gradually dropped off to 5 percent by 1843. Liquidation began in 1844, with the college receiving in all $8,700 for the original $12,000.[13]

We now move on to 1899-1900, the culmination of a period of declining prices and returns on investment. In thirty years, the yield on Harvard investments had fallen from 7.21 to 4.35 percent. This was a serious matter during the Eliot years, as is suggested by a decline of endowment income from 60.8 percent of all income in 1869-1870 to 35.9 percent in 1899-1900. To a small extent this was made up by a rise of current gifts.

In the year 1868-1869, an inflationary year, yields tended to be high. What is more, they also varied greatly among different kinds of assets. Yields also vary greatly within the same categories. A good example is given for the year 1899-1900. Thus, special investments in land and houses varied from less than $\frac{1}{3}$ of 1 percent to as high as 9 percent for different funds. For six of nine items the yield was less than 2 percent. Even in railroad bonds, yields on seventeen issued varied from $1\frac{1}{3}$ to more than 6 percent.[14]

In 1840, sixteen real estate items produced an income of 9.2 percent, with variations from no return (awaiting capital gains?) and 2 percent to returns as high as 12 and 14 percent. Eleven other items produced only 3 percent with extremes of no return and 20 percent.[15]

By 1929-1930, a substantial recovery in yields had occurred. The overall increase was from 4.35 to 5.44 percent. The largest relative rise of yield occurred in government securities—a special accounting problem is relevant here, in notes and mortgages, and in other bonds and real estate, in that order.

In general, the rise of yield or in interest rates was related to the shortage of capital after a great war, the general inflation in the twentieth century, a trend

generally accompanied by higher interest rates—the lender demands some compensation for accepting repayment in a depreciating currency, and the prosperity reflected in higher returns on equities.

The structure of investments reflected the inflationary and prosperous trends of the period. The overall gain of yield is explained largely by the increased yield on bonds and on common stocks. The university's investment in bonds (56 to 59 percent) was relatively unchanged but in stocks rose from 9 to 27 percent. (Any capital appreciation is not reflected here.)

In this period, the university stuck to its bond issues, for their yield increased in a period of unusual demand for capital. The substantial rise of investments in stocks—especially in the 1920s—reflected the stock market boom, and a wish to share in "the high profits of the period." But the university cut its investments in real estate from 25.6 to 12.2 percent. In view of the collapse of real estate values in the 1930s, this may seem to have been smart policy but it may have been overdone if attention is paid to the high prices paid for land in the post World War II period.

Then came the Great Depression. The over-all yield dropped from 5.44 to 4.8 percent. In view of the dimensions of the depression this reduction of yield was surprisingly small, when compared with the drop from 7.21 to 4.35 percent from 1870 to 1900, years of relative prosperity compared with the 1930s. Hence, a reduction of 1 percent in yield over ten years might be compared with one of 2.86 percent in thirty years, 1870 to 1900.

Moreover, the treasurer, because of availability of reserves, was able to keep allocations of income from capital to departments relatively stable—as high as 4.8 percent at the bottom of the Great Depression.[16]

In the depressed 1930s, the structure of investments changed substantially. The percentage invested in stocks rose from 26.8 to 44.3 percent. In these ten years, the university received $42 million of capital gifts, and total investments rose by $30 million.

13. *Report of the Treasurer of Harvard College*, 1840-1841, p. 1; 1841-1842, p. 2; *Treasurers' Ledgers*, 1834-1835, p. 37; 1836-1838, pp. 67,75; 1844, p. 393; 1852, p. 16; 1853, p. 125.

14. *Treasurer's Statement*, July 31, 1899.

15. Quincy, *op. cit.*, vol. II, p. 626.

16. *Harvard Alumni Bulletin*, vol. 34, pp. 729-730, 1932.

Whereas common stocks held in 1929-1930 amounted to $21,300,000, by 1939-1940 the amount had increased to $45,100,000. Taking advantage of the low prices of equities, Harvard greatly increased its holdings of common stocks. By 1937, the price of common stocks was 40 percent below the 1929 level. The $21 million invested in 1929-1930 might well have fallen to $12 or $13 million if investments in equities were unchanged and the drop of prices of Harvard's stocks had matched that of the nation. But such decline did not occur, and in part because of purchases at bargain prices at the expense of other assets. The treasurer was already anticipating large rises in security prices. The relative investments in bonds declined to some extent. From 1929 to 1939 the price of bonds rose substantially. Such movements discourage investments in bonds.[17]

That the total yield generally declined in the 1930s is explained by defaults on bonds, and the large reduction in yield on real estate. An offset was the increased yield on common stocks and their rising importance.

From 1939 — 1940 to the middle 1960s, this country experienced unusual periods of prosperity and inflation. But unlike the first thirty years of the century, the over-all yield of Harvard's investments scarcely changed on a book value basis, and substantially dropped on the basis of market value. Thus, in 1959-1960 the return on book value was 4.91, on market, 3.65.

This was the period of great manipulation of interest rates, with rates declining greatly in the 1930s and 1940s and rising in the 1950s and 1960s.

In the years since 1939-1940, the university has greatly increased its investments in equities. By 1956-1957, common stocks were 58.7 percent (33.7 in 1939-1940) of investments on book value; and by 1964-1965, 55.1 percent on high market values. As might be expected the bond portfolio tended to become less important. The government succeeded in depressing returns on long-term bonds in the 1930s and 1940s; and despite the inflation of the 1940s, the over-all yield on high-grade corporate bonds remained roughly unchanged.

17. *Report of the Treasurer of Harvard College,* various years; *Economic Report of the President,* various years; *Historical Statistics of the United States,* 1789-1945.

PART

8

SPECIAL STUDIES

51

Productivity

Introduction

Productivity covers such problems as the following: use of personnel; conserving the time of high-priced talent; optimum allocation of resources, and their effective use; inefficiencies; discoveries; achievements by graduates; administrative advances; the quality of the product as well as the quantity of services, especially teaching and research; keeping costs down.

How productive a college or university is depends on its net product, that is, the relation of input (faculty, capital, administration, students) and the output, e.g., graduates, research. The larger the output, vis-à-vis the input the greater is the productivity of the institution. But it is well to be certain that adequate allowance is made for the input. It has been shown that Harvard students mature into very high-income graduates and in disproportionate numbers in Who's Who, etc. It is an easy generalization to explain the resultant gains as those of a Harvard education. But the high product can only in part be associated with the Harvard education.

How productive an institution of higher learning is depends upon its objectives. Undoubtedly the modern university stresses research more and more and teaching less. The responsibilities for teaching undergraduates are gradually shifting to the junior and four-year colleges. The emphasis on teaching at Harvard in 1965 is much less than in its first century when the task of the teacher was to assign readings, and devote endless hours to recitation and enforcement of parietal regulations. The teacher was part drill master, part pastor, part policeman, and part

judge. These composite responsibilities even rested on the president. The responsibility of the teacher in the first two hundred years of Harvard's history covered not one but many fields. The popular image of a teacher was that of a man available all day, presiding at the head of his class, prodding students on through their books, drilling, questioning, and examining. One college historian pointed out "that it was very satisfactory to the President and all who with him believed in all day teaching.... Everybody could see that the professor earned his salary; but when he was sitting silently in his study he was supposed to be neglecting his duty."

Misuse of Personnel

Anyone who looks back can raise questions concerning the productivity, or lack of it, of the teacher in the first two hundred years of Harvard history. But one must keep in mind the nature of the society of New England at that time. Preparation for the ministry or perhaps teaching in these early days justified an educational process different from that which is needed today. Moreover, neither the resources for research nor the opportunities to use them were available. Yet even allowing for this, one must conclude that the system was not a highly productive one.

An overseer's report of 1869 hailed the change over the preceding fifteen years, and particularly the reduced claims of disciplinary matters on the time and funds of the college. The elective system contributed much to this improvement.

. . . Henceforth, Harvard is not a school where boys are to be drilled and watched and governed, but a University where young men are invited and attracted by great opportunities and generous facilities of study. Here will, henceforth be less of the public system, and more of a scholarly esprit de corps; less constraint, and more influence. . . . And so Milton . . . bases his whole theory of education on his faith that young men ought to be drawn, not driven to knowledge . . . .[1]

A somewhat different picture of Harvard was given when it was said that the growth of the college in numbers and plant yields a high productivity evident in the influence on young minds and the college's capacity to adapt to the needs of the public.

There is nothing more striking in the character of the College, throughout its whole history, and especially in its later years of development and expansion, than the ease with which, from its organization and its unobserved influence over reflecting minds, it is enabled speedily to adapt itself to the varying and growing wants of the public. Its organization is a singular specimen of skill and good fortune combined. It is sufficiently under direct responsibility to the community, through the large and constantly changing Board of Overseers; it is sufficiently steady in its course of action, from the comparatively slow changes which take place in the Corporation. It is efficient in instruction, from securing the services of leading minds in every branch of knowledge; and it is tolerably sure of future growth, from the influence it has justly acquired in the community by its usefulness. As long as it shall retain this power of adaptation to the public wants, as long as knowledge shall be desired, freedom valued, religion and virtue

reverenced, may Harvard College continue to perform its appropriate duties, bestow and receive its appropriate honors, be cherished by the public, and live in the hearts of its alumni.[2]

Allocation of Resources

Institutions of higher learning have limited resources, and therefore should carefully determine priorities. Should money be spent on men or buildings; science or humanities; student aid directly or subsidies through tuition charges below costs; should more money go for research or for teaching? Every year the corporation has to make decisions of this kind.

In 1869, for example, a report to the board of overseers revealed that language and literature had fourteen teachers; physical sciences, nineteen; and moral sciences, five. The respective salary bills were $22,800, $18,833, and $9,283.[3]

Relief for Professors

One of the problems that plague institutions of higher learning is the relief of burdensome responsibilities for the high-priced professors who should have their time for research, creative writing, and effective teaching. Even before the Eliot period, President Hill called for the means of support for additional tutors or assistant professors, to relieve the best professors from preparing lectures and arduous teaching duties so that they would have more time for study, for teaching graduate students, and for giving undergraduates more effective instruction.[4] President Eliot dwelt further on this issue in his 1887-1888 report.[5] President Eliot raised the issue of the increase in the junior faculty in his 1904-1905 report. In his view the

1. *Report to the Honorable and Reverend, the Overseers of Harvard University on the Conditions, Needs and Prospects of the University,* 1869, pp. 66-69.

2. S. A. Eliot, *A Sketch of the History of Harvard College and of Its Present State,* 1848, pp. 127-128.

3. *Report to the Board of Overseers of Harvard College on the Condition, Needs and Prospects of the University,* 1869, p.313.

4. *Report of the President of Harvard College,* 1863-1864, p.11.

5. *Ibid.,* 1887-1888, pp. 21-22.

rise was partly due to the increase in the number of students but chiefly to the desire of the senior faculty to leave close personal relations with students to the junior faculty. The president pointed out that from 1880-1881 to 1902-1903, the number of annual instructors, assistants, and Austin Teaching Fellows had risen from 19 to 176.[6]

Some famous professors considered Eliot autocratic. In 1895-1896, however, he announced that the faculty was supreme, "but more and more it delegates work to the administrative boards, divisions, and departments and standing committees."[7] The question was whether committee work relieves or increases the burden on the faculty. This became a perennial problem. Undoubtedly the institution of committees relieves the more scholarly faculty members or those nonscholars who do not want to be bothered, from nonresearch and nonteaching responsibilities.

Inefficiences

Harvard was not free of charges of wasteful operation. An interesting episode was a statement by five members of the faculty inclusive of S. Willard in 1804. They proposed that the responsibility for many of the duties, attached to the office of the president, be concentrated in one member instead of several, with savings of outlays and with the result that "the interest of our college [would be] greatly promoted in our present melancholy and perverted state."[8]

The great George Ticknor in 1823 complained of the appalling amount of idle time of students. Counting vacations, holidays, and absences due to illness, Ticknor estimated that on the average half the four years at colleges the students escaped both instruction and discipline.[9]

At an unexpectedly early period for such careful analysis of costs, Ticknor in 1825 complained of wasteful allocation of teaching funds. The college financed three-quarters of the undergraduate instruction with one-third the sum paid for the remaining quarter. Ticknor showed that four officers with aggregate salaries of $4,300 provided 2,364 exercises annually and these he considered "as laborious, important and valuable as any given"; but eleven others whose salaries were $14,382.76, gave only 824 exercises annually, "a number less than is often given by a single professor of the first rank and ability to his classes in Europe. . . . [10]

President Quincy was not enthusiastic about increasing numbers through cuts in costs. "They bring increased care, anxiety, and labor in instruction and supervision, greater danger of noisy assemblages, more materials for the engendering of idle, dissipated, rude, and illregulated habits and manners," he said. He also thought an increase in the number of students would mean that proportionally more would have to come from the middle, southern, and western states, and this posed a threat to Harvard because the training of people from these regions was at variance with the customs and habits of New England. "In a few portions of the Union," he said, "a dagger or a bowie-knife is said to be deemed an indispensable appendage of a gentleman; and young men who carry such deadly weapons about them are apt to use them on very slight occasions.[11]

Exploitation of the Brilliant

A number of brilliant faculty members in the nineteenth century were dissatisfied with Harvard on the grounds of misuse of great abilities, or because of the demands of the college on their time and the general lack of talent in the faculty. Thus, Longfellow complained bitterly of his arduous duties, lack of free

6. *Ibid.*, 1904-1905, p. 19, table V.
7. *Ibid.*, 1895-1896, p. 35.
8. S. Willard et al., To the Corporation of Harvard College, October 5, 1804.
9. George Ticknor Papers In Harvard University Archives, 1819-1835.
10. G. Ticknor, *Remarks on Changes Proposed or Adopted in Harvard University*, Boston, 1825, pp. 8-9.
11. President Quincy's Speech to the Overseers, 1845, in Widener, Educ. 4810.311.

time to do important work, and the breach of his agreement with the corporation. Only after he resigned in 1854 after seventeen years on the faculty did he write *Hiawatha* and *The Courtship of Miles Standish*, and translate Dante's *Divine Comedy*.[12]

In 1839, Longfellow described the routine thus imposed on him;

Three days in the week I go into my classroom between seven and eight, and come out between three and four, with one hour's intermission. The other days are consumed in preparation, and in doing the usual small matters, which every man has to do; —with the usual interruptions. A few months later he wrote in his journal: "What should I be at fifty? A fat mill-horse, grinding around with blinkers on."

Henry Adams was not any happier about his Harvard experience.

The lecture room was futile enough, but the faculty-room was worse. . . . Several score of the best-educated, most agreeable, and personally the most sociable people in America united in Cambridge to make a social desert that would have starved a polar bear. The liveliest and most agreeable of men—James Russell Lowell, Francis J. Child, Louis Agassiz, his son Alexander, Gurney, John Fiske, William James and a dozen others, who would have made the joy of London or Paris—tried their best to break out and be like other men in Cambridge and Boston but society called them professors, and professors they had to be. While all these brilliant men were greedy for companionship, all were famished for want of it. Society was a faculty-meeting without business. The elements were there; but society cannot be made up of elements—people who are expected to be silent unless they have observations to make-and all the elements are bound to remain apart if required to make observations.[13]

Another unhappy member of the faculty was William James. Excessive teaching loads and routine business were too much for him, as he explained in a letter written in 1894.

I have to lecture on general "psychology" and "morbid psychology," "the philosophy of nature" and the "philosophy of Kant," thirteen lectures a week for half the year and eight for the rest. Our University moreover inflicts a monstrous amount of routine business of one, faculty meetings and committees of every sort, so that during term-time one can do no continuous reading at all—reading of books, I mean. When vacation comes, my brain is so tired that I can read nothing serious for a month. During the past month I have only read Tolstoy's two great novels. . . .[14]

Finally, the experience of Santayana is not without interest, though his complaints undoubtedly stemmed in part from some problems of maladjustment. Santayana was struck by the chaotic state of the growing university, the autocratic rule of Eliot, the wasted faculty meetings, and the second rate quality of the overworked faculty at the turn of the century.[15]

Gains in the Nineteenth Century and Later

Despite the doubts about Harvard expressed by some of its leading talent, Harvard progressed greatly in the nineteenth century. Harvard's choice of a Unitarian professor of divinity and a Unitarian president early in the nineteenth century aroused much antagonism among the Calvinists, and seriously affected Harvard's enrollment in the next twenty to thirty years. But as a keen observer, Prof. F. Rudolph, noted these elections "helped to create at Harvard an environment congenial to science, to learning and to religion if not to sectarian wrangling."[16]

12. Johnson, *Professor Longfellow of Harvard*, 1944, pp. 23-36, 69, 78-85.
13. H. Adams, *The Education of Henry Adams*, 1930, p. 307.
14. H. James (ed.), *The Letters of William James*, 1920, vol. II, pp. 44-45.
15. G. Santayana, *Persons and Places, The Middle Span*, 1945, vol. II, pp. 159-162.
16. Cf., F. Rudolph, *The American College and University: A History*, 1962, pp. 73, 134-135.

Perhaps another reason for Harvard's gains vis-à-vis its competition in the nineteenth century was its manner of government. Gradually the control by the state government was undermined. It used to be said that trustees ruled at Princeton, the president at Harvard, and the faculty at Yale.[17]

The faculty is not likely to yield the most effective management. Perhaps nothing accounts as much for the inefficiences of higher education than control by faculties. Indeed, there are reasons for this, but the fact of inefficiency cannot be denied. Even a second-rate president is likely to manage an institution much better than a first-class faculty.[18]

Harvard was especially fortunate in having a first-class scholar, administrator, and autocrat as president over a period of forty crucial years (1869 to 1909). Eliot, more than anyone, established Harvard's pre-eminent position. His great contributions were the improvement of economic status of the faculty, absolute and relative, relief from arduous tasks by the faculty through increasing use of assistants, his growing realization of the research needs of faculty, his unusual capacity to raise funds and use them effectively, and above all his choice of a faculty, and broadening of the curriculum. He improved the standards of all the schools and greatly hastened the development of first-class professional schools. Perhaps his most intriguing reform, the elective system, with much to be said for it, has been subjected to the most serious criticism. From 1876, when subject requirements for seniors were abolished, to 1894, when even for freshmen the only required courses were rhetoric and a modern language, Eliot had fundamentally changed the curriculum for the American college. Much of what he had thus created remains as the elective system in most American colleges.[19]

How effective a university is depends also on many other factors. Excessive expenditures on plant vs outlays on faculty members are relevant. The choice of students is of great importance. Use of the most effective teaching methods is important.[20] Harvard undoubtedly shares with most colleges the diseconomies of proliferation of courses, too many small courses, idle plant, etc.[21]

Economies

A few examples of economies are worth mentioning. James Russell Lowell commented on the high price of imported books and suggested remedies. In 1890-1891, the director of the Jefferson Physical Laboratory proposed means of acquiring necessary instruments and cutting their costs.[22] With the elective system, the number of courses tended to rise, and the enrollment per course to fall. A critic of the system, Dean L. Briggs, complained that the large number of small courses "precluded the use of adequate Junior faculty in helping with the large undergraduate courses."[23]

President Lowell's tutorial system received similar criticism. The president admitted that costs per student were high, but he was prepared to pay the price of expensive tutorial even for nonhonors students, because he wanted to increase the numbers of honors students.[24]

A relevant factor for estimating productivity is the number of hours of classrooms available. In 1890-1891, the president boasted of a change which yielded seven hours of lectures a day instead of six. The new hours, 9 to 1 and 1:30 to 4:30, would be compatible with the large numbers of small courses being given in later hours.[25]

17. G. W. Pierson, *Yale College, 1871-1921,* 1952, pp. 130-135, 147.

18. Cf., S. E. Harris, *Higher Education: Resources and Finance,* 1962, ch. 45.

19. *Cf.,* F. Rudolph, *op. cit.,* p. 294; T. W. Lamont, *My Boyhood in a Parsonage,* 1946, p. 166.

20. S. E. Harris, *op. cit.,* ch. 44.

21. Cf., S. E. Harris, *op. cit.,* chapters 44-52.

22. *Report Director, Jefferson Physical Laboratory,* 1890-1891, pp. 169-70.

23. *Report of the President of Harvard College,* 1901-1902, p. 103.

24. H. A. Yeomans, *Abbott Lawrence Lowell, 1856-1943,* p. 158.

25. *Report of the President of Harvard College,* 1890-1891, pp. 12-13.

Productivity depends also on the services made available beyond the usual educational ones. High costs per student stem in part from these services, ever on the increase. In so far as they improve the product, the net costs of these additional outlays are kept down. In so far as they provide services that otherwise would have to be had from some other sources, the rise of costs is specious. But it is not easy to measure the additional educational gains against additional costs.

An interesting document from Increase Mather to the founders of Yale in 1701 on how to keep expenditures down is of some interest. It is not at all clear that the gains of the imposed parsimony are as large as might be inferred.[26]

Improvements in another field are suggested, for example, by President Conant's proposals of means of improving co-operation among different departments and the need of overcoming overdepartmentalization and specialization.

. . . For perfectly obvious and understandable reasons a college curriculum tends to fall into the hands of specialists working in water-tight compartments of knowledge and instinctively holding the bulkheads tightly closed that if opened would articulate one branch of knowledge with another. . . . Any isolated branch of knowledge is of insignificant consequences by itself. . . .[27]

Discoveries

A measure of rising productivity is the series of great discoveries by faculty men. In the second quarter of the nineteenth century the new Astronomical Observatory, the first research unit at Harvard, received much attention as a scientific advance, as a financial need, and as a project of general community interest. The scientists made important astronomical discoveries with a new telescope, the same size as the largest refracting telescope in the world.[28] In 1847-1848, the university announced the first application to surgical operations by a professor of the medical school of the wonderful anaesthetic process, which, within the preceding two years had established an era in practical surgery.[29]

Professor E. Leon Chaffee contributed much to the outcome of the Battle of Britain because of his development of the radiolocator technique.[30]

In 1936, in the midst of the tercentenary celebration, it became known that Professor Pincus of Harvard had achieved a successful artificial fertilization, without involving sperm, of a rabbit egg, which was then placed in another mother.

Achievements of Graduates

In generations of Harvard output the college boasted of the great achievements of its graduates. Under President Chauncy (1654 to 1672), the graduates included chief justices of the colony, a chief justice of the Colony of New York, and successively governor of Massachusetts and of New Hampshire; and three college presidents: two at Harvard and one at Yale.[31]

College graduates shared disproportionately in the number of high-level careers. A study late in the nineteenth century revealed that of 15,138 honored in the *Appleton Encyclopedic of American Biography*, 5,322 were college men: "These 5,332 form. . .one out of each forty graduate now living; while only one out of ten thousand of the population that has not received higher education has found a place in the cyclopedic named. . . ."[32]

26. Dexter, *Increase Mather*, pp. 6,7.
27. *Report of the President of Harvard College,* 1933-1934, pp. 5-6; Harvard University Archives, UAV 828.268.5.
28. *Report of the Treasurer of Harvard College,* 1839-1840, p. 1; 1842-1843, pp. 1-2; 1844-1845, pp. 2-7; 1852-1853, p. 3; *Report of the President of Harvard College,* 1946-1947, pp. 29-31; 1847-1848, pp. 16-17; 1851-1852, p. 8.
29. *Report of the President of Harvard College,* 1847-1848, pp. 10-11.
30. *Ibid.,* 1944-1945, pp. 33-34; 1945-1946, pp. 42, 100, 224, 233.
31. *History of Harvard College,* p. 20.
32. *Higher Education in the United States: Universities and Their Sons,* 1897, pp. 7-8.

Again around the beginning of the twentieth century it was observed that about half of Congress had received a liberal education; half the speakers of Congress; twelve of the twenty-four Presidents were liberally educated. The largest contributions were made by the institutions of higher learning established before 1770 and especially by Harvard, Yale, and Princeton.[33]

Harvard was proud of its contribution to the large attainments of college graduates. Thus, of the thousand American Men of Science of special eminence, the Harvard-trained numbered seventy-nine. Of twelve branches of science, Harvard was first in five and second in three.[34]

Harvard's contributions to the Presidency, to the Court of St. James, to Yale (four presidents), and to numerous other colleges are well known. One famous teacher, Edward Tyrrel Channing, in the years 1818 to 1881 reared most of the great literary men which Harvard produced in abundance—Emerson, C. F. Adams, Hedge, A. P. Peabody, Felton, Hillard, Winthrop, Holmes, Sumner, Motley, Phillips, Bowen, Lovering, Torrey, Dana, Lowell, Thoreau, Hale, T. Hill, Child, Hall, Lane, and Norton.[35]

According to Eliot, in the late nineteenth century about 15 to 20 percent of Harvard graduates went into business. Their success pleased the president very much. In his own class of eighty-nine, fifteen had succeeded in business. He listed six very successful businessmen in his class who were known to him. Eliot argued against Carnegie and others that "it stands to reason that thorough mental training must give a man an advantage in any business which requires strong mental work." Among first-class Harvard scholars were the president of the American Bell Telephone Company and the president of the Union Trust Company. Harvard graduates included H. H. Richardson, a famous architect; George S. Morison, the well-known designer of bridges.[36]

Improved Administration

It was particularily in the Eliot and Conant regimes that measures were taken to economize on the high-priced talents and to provide an adequate administrative organization. We have already commented on one aspect of this problem, the provision of assistants to ease the burdens of professors and economize on resources.

In his early years Eliot depended for secretarial work on a succession of students who worked part-time, and until the 1890s he shared a secretary with the dean. In 1901 he appointed Jerome Greene as secretary to the president, and soon reported that Green had freed him of half his work.[37]

In 1870, President Eliot appointed a dean and a few years later he remarked that the dean now did three-quarters of the work of the president. He also appointed a dean to every department that had a faculty of its own. Twenty years later President Eliot said:

. . . every department inevitably urges on the Faculty and Corporation, in season and out of season, good reasons why it should be developed, and its appropriation for salaries and equipment increased. . . .A Departmental Administration, therefore, needs an alert supervising authority; else it will draw the University into unreasonable and untimely expenditures.[38]

In the later years of his administration, President Eliot was becoming increasingly concerned over the rising burden of administrative work for the faculty. In 1896-1897, the faculty had seventeen standing committees or one for every seven permanent members as compared to one for twelve in 1890-1891. The president in 1905-1906 boasted of reductions in committee work by enlisting nonfaculty men, consolidating committees — reducing five admission

33. *The American College in American Life*, pp. 71-77.
34. *Report of Committee to Visit the Medical and Dental Schools to the Board of Overseers*, 1910, p. 74.
35. *The American College in American Life*, pp. 146-149, 164-173.
36. C.W. Eliot to O. Ely, February 12, 1897.

37. Henry James, *Charles W. Eliot; President of Harvard University*, 1930, vol. II, pp. 133-134.
38. *Ibid.*, vol. I, p. 241; *Report of the President of Harvard College*, 1869-1870, pp. 11-13.

committees to one — and assigning secretarial help to committees.[39]

In 1889-1890 the president created a single faculty of arts and sciences, to replace the faculties of Harvard College, of Lawrence Scientific School, and of the graduate school. In this manner more effective administration was achieved.[40]

In 1905-1906, President Eliot established a board to relieve the president and fellows of handling business administration of the university. At the same time the faculty and overseers provided for economies of administrative work.[41] Nevertheless, as might be expected, the cost of administration rose greatly. In 1903, C. F. Adams pointed out that administrative costs per student had increased 43 percent in thirty-five years.[42]

It was not until 1930-1931 that the university took note of the increasing importance of employees, exclusive of faculty. At that time the Lowell administration appointed a director of personnel relations. The importance of employee relations is suggested by the fact that in 1962-1963, $25 million in wages in the university equaled the $25 million of salaries going primarily to faculty. In arts and sciences, however, salaries at $11 million exceeded wages at $6 million.[43]

The increasing complexity of the university is revealed by the 2,752 officers of instruction and administration in 1949-1950.[44]

One of President Conant's first moves was to provide for a financial vice president who was to supervise the bursar, auditor, and the newly appointed business manager, to concern himself with the financial details and to keep the president informed

of financial considerations relevant for educational policies. By obtaining this help the president sought more time and energy for treating educational problems.[45] He also appointed a financial vice president, who was to be responsible for the day to day business operations of the university,[46] and a special advisor, whose function it was to coordinate the money-raising activities.[47]

How efficient a university is depends in part upon its governing boards. Many members of these boards know little about education. Rudolph explained the presence of successful men on the boards as an endorsement of the institution; as aids in raising money and continued "their authority also enabled them to keep the colleges true to the interests and prejudices of the classes from which they were drawn."[48]

The Crisis of the Mid-1820s

It is helpful to supplement the discussion of various aspects of productivity by concentrating on a few crises periods. The crisis of the mid-1820s is a good place to begin.

This crisis stemmed in part from the failure of the commonwealth to renew a $10,000 annual subsidy available in the years 1814 to 1824.

Appointed by the corporation in 1821, a committee inquired concerning the instruction, discipline, and morals of students, seeking to know about both current practices and manners of improvement. This investigation brought some results.

A committee of the corporation in 1825 made a frontal attack on wastes and mismanagement. Above all, the committee would introduce retrenchments, with resultant reductions of costs and rising enrollment. Among the proposals were merging of some professorships and a reduction in the numbers of instructors, an increase of the work load, cuts in

39. *Report of the President of Harvard College*, 1896-1897, p. 50; 1899-1900, p. 10; 1905-1906, pp. 11-12.
40. *Ibid.,* 1889-1890, pp. 4-5.
41. *Ibid.,* 1905-1906, p. 12.
42. C. F. Adams article in *Harvard Graduates Magazine*, 1904, p.6.
43. *Report of the President of Harvard College*, 1930-1931, pp. 22-23; *Financial Report to the Board of Overseers of Harvard College*, 1962-1963, pp. 14-15.
44. *Harvard University Catalogue*, 1949-1950, p. 807.

45. *Report of the President of Harvard College*, 1933-1934, pp. 7-8.
46. *Ibid.,* 1945-1946, pp. 14-15.
47. *Ibid.,* 1946-1947, pp. 9-10.
48. Rudolph, *op. cit.,* p. 173.

salaries, and elimination of pay for extra services—a requirement that beneficiaries of aid perform services for the college, limitation of aid to the amount of income yielded by the relevant foundations, and savings in repairs. The proposed economies would, however, save only $8,000 a year—a large sum at that time, but not enough. The stress was then on teaching the ordinary undergraduate.[49]

Prof. George Ticknor implied that under his agreement with the college his salary could not be cut, but he would go along on the condition that retrenchment would prevail elsewhere and instruction be improved.[50]

Stirred up by the financial crisis, the corporation examined carefully all securities, notes, mortgages, etc. entrusted to the treasurer and all subsequent transactions, inclusive of receipts and expenditures.

A committee of the governing boards asked for a thorough check on the finances: many of these, they held to be absurdly low; they would dispose of all lands which were a liability; they would increase the teaching responsibilities of tutors, and reduce those of the proctors; they required approval by the corporation even of bills submitted by the president; and he was also to lose his secretary.[51]

The 1840s

Harvard was losing ground. According to a Harvard majority report in 1845, Yale had 394 students with

costs of government and instruction $15,201; the corresponding figures at Harvard were 254 students at a cost of $26,500. Respective unit costs were $38 and $104. The minority report, however, estimated the cost differential at $45. Yale was ahead in enrollment and offered a lower cost program. Hence, Harvard investigated the possibilities of reducing its unit costs. A majority of a committee of the overseers thought that Harvard was extravagant and that tuition should be reduced. But a minority report held that with rising electives, costs had to increase at Harvard; and also that what was relevant is not only the unit costs but also the quality of the product. Lopping off some courses or a curriculum would be like lopping off an arm. The minority also saw few possibilities of reducing the size of the faculty or increasing hours of work.

For the minority, the view was that:

a more extensive education is given at Harvard University than at any other American College . . . [that] the graduates of Harvard College are on the whole, as distinguished for their proficiency as those of any other . . . that the character of the institution, generally, as to intelligence, industry, and good morals, deserves to stand as high in the judgement of the community. . . .

But if the question be whether education be dearer at Harvard University than at other New England Colleges, due regard being had to the equivalent received, by the student in the intellectual advantages offered to him, the undergraduate is firmly convinced that the very opposite answer must be given. . . .[52]

Midnineteenth Century

At this time the university faced a new crisis. The commonwealth threatened a modification of government of the university which would have jeopardized the control of Harvard by a small governing body, the

49. C. Jackson, N. Bowditch, F. Gray, *Report of the Committee of the Corporation on Economies,* 1825.

50. G. Ticknor to the President and Fellows of Harvard College, December 30, 1826; Answers for Immediate Government, 1825.

51. C. Saunders to President Kirkland, November 19, 1828; The Committee on Textbooks. *Harvard College Report,* June 28, 1831; President to Corporation on Mathematical Department, June 21, 1832; *Report of Committee [on] Account of Dr. Webster Against the College,* March 20, 1828; C. Saunders (Steward) to E. Francis, (Treasurer), January 2, 1828; *Statement of Treasurer,* December 20, 1827; Meeting of the President and Fellows of Harvard College, December 20, 1827.

52. *Report on Diminishing the Cost of Instruction in Harvard College, Together with a Minority Report on the Same Subject,* 1845.

corporation. Harvard had to defend itself once more against the charge of incompetent management.

The reply was in part as follows:

The question does not turn so much upon what the College has been, as upon what it now is, and what have been its achievements and tendencies in recent times. If a marked and decided progress can be shown to have taken place within forty years, if it can be shown that great advances have been made in intellectual culture, pecuniary resources, the increase of the library, scientific cabinets, apparatus, and commodious buildings, in the number of students and of instructors. That the education given there is in all respects as good, to say the least, as can be obtained at any institution in America; if these can be shown, it is believed that the Legislature will be slow to yield assent to the assertions of the Committee....[53]

Replying to the charges of a Legislative committee, the Harvard authorities stressed the large increase of enrollment and faculty members since 1800; the three new important buildings, (Gore, University, and Holworthy); the increased competition, as in fifty years the number of colleges had increased from 25 to 120; a rise of library volumes from 15,000 to 57,000 (in forty years); an increase of philosophical apparatus of more than threefold.

Yale had more students but "the increase in that institution is not to be ascribed to any novelty or changes in the modes of instruction. No college has adhered more steadily to the old methods."

Above all, the Harvard Corporation stressed the rising productivity, gains evident, for example, in the improved plant and standards for admission and the higher quality of instruction.

Harvard also boasted of improved admission procedures. "Harvard has always taken the lead in this painful process, and has kept, in this respect, really in advance of the spirit of the age."

On the issue of the cost of a Harvard education, the college emphasized the high cost for both students and faculty members in the large cities. The level of tuition charges reflected conditions in the large city, not inefficiency.

Observers at midnineteenth century had been optimistic concerning the rise of productivity since the beginning of the century. In 1869, an overseers' committee was equally optimistic concerning the improvements since the early 1850s. Among the indicators of rising productivity ferreted out by this group were the elective system, the substantial rise in the faculty-student ratio, the introduction of the written examination, the increased rate of dissemination of knowledge through the intermediary of the university, the rising yield of the professional schools, the continued gains from an earlier reform, namely, tutors instructing on the basis of their specialities instead of covering the whole waterfront, and the continued profit from the rising interest of overseers.[54]

The Eliot Inaugural Address, 1869

In this brilliant address, Charles Eliot raised many questions that are relevant for the issues under discussion: First, Eliot would recognize "no real antagonism between literature and science, and consents to no such narrow alternatives as mathematics or classics, science or metaphysics. He would have them all, and at their best ...."[55] In short, the study of poetry as well as science contributes to the welfare of society. The aim of a college is "to broaden, deepen and invigorate American teaching in all branches of learning. It will be generations before the best of American institutions of education will get growth enough to bear pruning ...."

But Eliot expressed disappointment at the slow advance of language training since Luther's trumpet

53. *Memorial Concerning the Recent History and The Constitutional Rights and Privileges of Harvard College, Presented by the President and Fellows to the Legislature,* January 17, 1851, p. 6.

54. *Ibid.,* esp. pp. 6-15.
55. *Addresses at the Inauguration of Charles William Eliot as President of Harvard College,* October 19, 1869.

call or Milton's advice two centuries before on the unforgetable way to study languages. American education, in Eliot's view, was centuries behind that of the best thinkers upon education. He would import European methods of language instruction. He quoted Locke to the effect that if anyone had a facility in his mother tongue, the explanation was chance or genius, not teaching.[56]

Eliot bewailed the lack of accomplishments of high school graduates who mastered but a few pages of Greek and Latin and the bare elements of mathematics. An unintelligent system of education from primary school through college explains the fact that many college graduates "have so inadequate a conception of what is meant by scientific operation, reasoning and proof." The Revolution achieved other areas, e.g., farming should be a lesson for education. The problem is not what but how to teach.[57]

By the use of good methods he hoped to give "young men of twenty or twenty-five an accurate general knowledge of all the main subjects of human interest, besides a minute and thorough knowledge of the one subject which each may select as his principal occupation in life." Eliot would then take account of the individual traits of different minds. Division of labor is relevant here as elsewhere. A youngster of nineteen should know what his aptitudes are and whether he is "most apt at language or philosophy or natural science or mathematics." For the individual the greatest concentration and development of his faculties is needed; for the State, variety, not uniformity. For Eliot, the extension of the elective system meant giving play to natural aptitude, providing studies that students welcome and "enlarges instruction by substituting many and various lessons given to small, lively classes, for a few lessons many times repeated to different secions of a numerous class...."

Lectures, recitations and textbooks are complementary agencies in education, according to Eliot. Lectures give inspiration, guidance, and the comprehensive methodizing. Recitations alone readily degenerate into dusty repetition, and lectures alone are too often a useless expenditure of force. It is possible to economize on recitations by depending more on examinations.

Because students do not always respond to the noblest motives, Eliot considered rank least important. "Many excellent persons see great offense in any system of college rank; but why should we expect more of young men than we do of the elders?"

Finally, Eliot had sensible views on the responsibilities of the president. "... An administrative officer who undertakes to do everything himself, will do little and that little ill...." He would have in the university the divided and subordinate responsibilities which prevail in business and government. The president must discern the practical aspects of long discussions; he must seek money and seize opportunities to obtain eminent teachers and scholars; and his major and most difficult responsibility is to select young men "who have not had time and opportunity to approve themselves to the public."[58]

Keeping Costs Down

An enterprise that keeps costs down raises its productivity, for with a given input of faculty, capital, and administration, the output rises. Throughout Harvard's history, the managers of that enterprise watched its costs, and especially because reduced costs would be reflected in lower charges for the scholars. Thus, a committee of the overseers wrote in 1824:

... the Committee would respectfully suggest, whether, [when] vacancies occur, some of the professorships may not be advantageously united, so as to increase the amount of active instruction, and at the same time release some of the college funds to be appropriated towards defraying the ordinary tuition fees.[59]

---

56. *Ibid*, esp. p. 30,33.
57. *Ibid*, p. 31.

58. *Ibid*, pp. 61-63.
59. *Board of Overseers Report*, May 4, 1824, p. 10.

In 1849, another year of crises, the college seemed attracted to minute statistical studies that might measure the output of the college:

These thirty-nine Reports are the literary statistics for the year. They ought to show what is done, and what is omitted; how far, and with what time and labor, the duties of instruction are performed, and with what success; how far the driving wheels may be relied on for security and speed, to bear on the car of education with a velocity equal to the recited expectation of spectators and passengers, and of the world, to which seems to think it has opened, not indeed a royal road to learning, but a much more rapid one.[60]

Before World War I, an assistant comptroller requested of the faculty information on how time was spent on various duties of the faculty. The objective at this early date was to find out the instruction cost per undergraduate and graduate student. The answer for the government department was $217 for the former, and $790 for the latter. A current newspaper commented:

In sober truth, this news from Harvard is a very serious matter. . . .It ought to bring out from the Harvard Faculty and especially from the men of light and learning in that faculty, an impressive protest; and the most impressive form the protest could take would be that of a dignified but firm refusal to comply with the demand made upon them.[61]

A comparison of costs per student may be significant at any one time but less significant over a period of time. The point is that the plant and the faculty in 1967 are different products than in 1867. The plant is more expensive and more effective. The faculty is much better trained. In 1873, it was discovered that 40 percent of the teachers in ten selected colleges were not especially trained; in 1893, in the same colleges, only 25 percent were not so trained.[62]

By 1900, the college was also calculating costs per student. In 1901, the estimate was costs of $300 and tuition, $150.[63]

An innovator in the ambitious elective program, Eliot was also aware of the large costs involved. The president reminded the faculty that it was necessary to watch "the comparative offerings of each department and the increased offerings year by year in each department." In choosing new courses, attention should be paid to the numbers that are likely to enroll.[64]

In 1908, Eliot reminded his readers that the elective system was very expensive. A teacher who gives half his time to classes of five to fifteen students is much more expensive than the one who covers fifty to two hundred in a class. A college that does not entertain a generous elective system can get along with twenty faculty members. But Harvard, offering courses in all significant fields, had to have eighty faculty members who gave two hundred courses and offered a curriculum which would require forty years for a student to cover.

Because Eliot was responsible for an expensive elective system he studied the number of courses, student enrollment, enrollees per course, number of faculty by ranks, courses per faculty member, etc. Thus, in the early twentieth century, Eliot revealed:

Number of courses	364½
Number enrolled in these courses	14,040
Enrollees per course	39
Number of teachers	302
(66 professors; 37 assistant professors; 95 instructors; 105 assistants)	
Average courses per teacher	1.21
Average enrollees per professor	136
Average enrollees per teacher	46

Over the years one finds many instances of economical operation that reflects a great concern for

60. *Report of the Committee of Overseers as Appointed to Visit the University in 1849*, p. 5.
61. *The Evening Post*, January 7, 1913, *Instruction for Filling Instruction Schedule*, 1912; "Present Status of Cost Studies" in *A.L. Lowell Letters*, March 18, 1912.

62. C. F. Thwing, *The American College in American Life*, p. 50.
63. C.W. Eliot to R.T. Crane, September 12, 1901.
64. C.W. Eliot to Professor L.B.R. Briggs, October 26, 1902.

buying at the lowest price. Thus, in 1857, the college announced that it would not hereafter purchase from printers at a gross price. Rather, the college would negotiate with the sellers of paper and with the binder, and not allow the printer to pass on these costs plus a profit. By negotiating with sellers in this manner the college could save about 20 percent on its triennial catalogue, $1,049, by purchasing all services and materials directly from the printer and $839 by negotiating with the seller of each commodity and service.[65]

In Harvard's history the student-faculty ratio was frequently a matter of contention and especially since much emphasis was put on close relations of students and faculty members. Thus, in 1883, five faculty members were responsible for the teaching of 150 law students; in 1898, nine members taught 546 students, a rise of the student-faculty ratio from 30 to 1 to 60 to 1, a change that greatly concerned an overseers' committee.

. . . A law lecture of the old type may be well given to 500, indeed, if the acoustics of the lecture room be good enough and its size sufficient, to 5,000 as to 50 or 25; but when every student is expected to answer and encouraged to ask questions tending to insure a thorough going comprehension of every feature. . .on the subject. . .the merits of this form of teaching become illusory if more than a certain number are in attendance. . . .[66]

College authorities were aware that costs vary inversely with numbers. They noted that unit costs in commons rose as the number served declined. As enrollment declined by 150 in two consecutive months, the price of board rose twice by 17 cents a week and once by 25 cents. To achieve lower costs, more boarders were necessary.[67]

. . . the details of the President's office have by usage gradually become so numerous and burdensome that I confess I should not hesitate to decline the honorable station you proferred to me, if it involved the necessity of executing or even supervising these details. . . the mind and energy of the President should be exhausted by the perpetual recurrance and accumulation of labors of this kind. . . .[68]

The burden of attending to details had persisted despite the fact that in the 1820s, the corporation authorized the president "to be exempted from certain ministerial duties," which would now devolve on the faculty.[69]

Even as late as 1897, the president was overwhelmed by the details of the office. On an occasion when the governing boards were disposed to raise the salary of the president, Eliot demurred. The president through various funds was receiving the equivalent of $9,500 a year, or more than twice the salary of professors.

What is really needed in regard to the office of President is not a higher salary, but the distribution of some of his present functions among the Deans, and the employment of a competent assistant.[70]

Eliot's 1897 comments carried some weight, for in May 1901, the corporation received from the board of overseers a vote recommending a permanent secretary to the president.

The faculty is not always pleased with the appointment of chancellors, deans, departmental chairman, or other intermediaries between them and the

65. C. W. Eliot to Professor N. S. Shaler, August 25, 1905; *Report of the President of Harvard College,* 1900-1901, pp. 10-11; C. W. Eliot to Professor E. H. Hall, June 15, 1900; W. C. Lane, *The University During the Last Twenty Five Years,* 1906, pp. 11-12; *Report of Committee Upon the Reduction of Expenses. . .Upon the Cost of the Text Books and of Printing,* June 1, 1857.

66. *Report of the Standing Committee to Visit the Law School,* 1898, pp. 528-529.

67. H.L. Blackwell to the President and Fellows of Harvard College, April 8, 1905.

68. J. Sparks to the Corporation of Harvard College, January 15, 1844.

69. *Report of the Committee. . .Relative to Certain Reports of the Board of Overseers,* June 10, 1825.

70. C.W. Eliot to the President and Fellows of Harvard College, November 6, 1897.

president and governing boards. Thus, in 1824, a professor insisted that the new powers given to the president and heads of departments "would be degrading to the resident instructors by reducing them to the rank of mere ministerial officers, subject to the discretionary government of an individual. . . ."[71]

In the 1820s, under the leadership of Professor Ticknor, there were attempts to raise the standards of the college. Ticknor was especially critical of the recitation method universally used; and he would rank students according to their progress. Ticknor said "We are neither a University—which we call ourselves— nor a respectable high school, which we ought to be . . . ." After fifteen years, Ticknor resigned in disgust. He had not convinced the governing boards or the faculty. The college would not accept advances according to proficiency, or ranking of students.

Even the students rebelled against ranking:

We the undersigned members of the Sophomore Class without a single dissenting voice . . . petition . . . to abolish the present system of rank. . .but when we perceive its utter futility and reflect upon its injurious effects we cannot but deprecate it as hurtful in the extreme . . . .[72]

To achieve greater use of resources, the university has tried to discourage leaves by students, to reduce vacation time, and to set vacations in such a manner As to yield the most effective use of time.[73] In 1859, a committee chaired by Benjamin Peirce proposed radical changes in the calendar. The major vacation (nine weeks) would be in the summer, a period when students studied with difficulty. The major holidays would fall in vacation time and thus not interfere with the steady progress of the students.

Harvard's Quality

How productive a college is, is a function of the numbers turned out and the quality of the product. Harvard graduates fewer men than some of the large state and urban universities. But over the years, Harvard has turned out a quality product which is probably higher than that of any other institution.

However, prestigious the Harvard degree has become, it has not always satisfied Harvard men. Thus, Henry Adams had doubts about Harvard:

. . . Custom, social ties, convenience, and above all, economy, kept each generation in the track. Any other education would have required a serious effort, but no one took Harvard College seriously. All went there because their friends went there, and the college was their ideal of social self-respect.
Harvard College, as far as it educated at all was a mild and liberal school, which sent young men into the world with all they needed to make respectable citizens, and something of what they wanted to make useful ones. Leaders of men they never tried to make. . . .Four years of Harvard College, if successful resulted in an autobiographical blank, a mind on which only a water-mark had been stamped.

Later Henry Adams was more critical. But if Harvard was hurtful, it was less so than other institutions. The mind remained open.[74]

Another Adams (Class of 1888), was at least equally critical, especially of the unchanging curriculum and the obtuseness of the educators:

But in pursuing Greek and Latin we had ignored our mother tongue. We were no more competent to pass a really searching examination in English literature and English composition than in the languages and literature of Greece and Rome. We were college graduates; and yet how many of us could follow out a line of sustained, close thought, expressing ourselves in clear, concise terms. . . ?[75]

71. Quincy, *op. cit.,* vol. II, pp. 348-349.
72. *Harvard College,* pp. 216-223; Professor Ticknor to President Hall, February 4, 1863; Members of Sophmore Class to the President and Fellows of Harvard College, 1834 (?).
73. *Board of Overseers Report,* May 4, 1824.
74. W. Bentinick-Smith, *The Harvard Book,* pp. 223-224; *The Education of Henry Adams.*
75. C. F. Adams, *Three Phi Beta Kappa Addresses,* 1907, pp. 12-13.

Harvard men were not always as critical of a Harvard education as some of the Adamses were. A committee of the overseers in 1849 concluded:

It appears that, for the service required, the Academic force is large, and of course expensive; but, perhaps with a single exception not out of proportion, in numbers or cost, to the services performed. . . .[76]

Over all, President Eliot was inclined to assess both Harvard's educational standards and the Harvard student highly. In a warm exchange with Professor Barrett Wendell in 1893, Eliot wrote:

You are literally the only person whom I ever heard intimate. . .that the quality of the present Harvard undergraduate could possibly be considered lower than in 1882-83 or in 1872-73. So far as I can judge from the records, opinions of instructors, and the public behavior of the young men. . .there is not only no decline, but a distinct improvement in the general tone and manly quality of the undergraduates. . . .[77]

But Eliot at times had some reservations. Too many students considered their real work to begin in the professional schools. Everything earlier was simply enjoyment, not real preparation for life.[78]

A faculty committee of 1903 chaired by Professor Lowell revealed that students who presumably were spending six hours of study on each course were in fact giving but two to three hours to each course and the search was not for a well-planned curriculum; rather, the students sought the easy courses.[79]

Eliot's mission in the first twenty years of his administration was to convert the college into a great university.[80] President Lowell, Eliot's successor, tended to revert to the old interest in undergraduates and not only in their formal education but also in their living conditions. Hence, large sums were

devoted to acquiring high standards of room and board. The cost of a Harvard undergraduate education soared as a result, though many of the capital resources required were obtained by the president, who proved to be a much more competent beggar than he claimed to be.

Probably the most expensive item on Lowell's agenda was the tutorial system, which was introduced on a serious scale after World War I. The system was expensive in part because unlike the Oxford-Cambridge system, where virtually all the teaching resources were concentrated on tutorial work, at Harvard the tutorial was an addition to the course work, not really a substitute.

Conant assumed the presidency at the bottom of the greatest depression of American history. He had to reassess the magnitude of the resources that were to go into tutorial work. A careful survey by an excellent overseers' committee raised a number of questions about the tutorial system and proposed changes. The committee noted that Harvard was losing ground.

Harvard is still princeps, but no longer facile princeps, and the story is current that at one of America's great universities it is considered the height of academic distinction to receive an invitation from Harvard—and to decline it . . . .[81]

One conclusion drawn by the committee was that individual tutorials were wasteful for a majority of the students. Tutors estimated that 25 to 30 percent responded satisfactorily to tutorial work. Hence, the proposal of group tutorial for the average and tutorials with one or two students for the able and responsive. All sophomores would be tutored at the outset. But they would have to justify tutorial in later years by performance.

By introducing economies along these lines, it was hoped that the college could save $75,000 to $100,000 of a $300,000 tutorial budget. In addition, many small courses or small subjects might be

76. *Report of Committee of Overseers of Harvard College Appointed to Visit the University in 1849*, p. 6.
77. C. W. Eliot to Barrett Wendell, April 15, 1893.
78. C. W. Eliot to Mr. Putnam, June 10, 1889.
79. Samuel Eliot Morison (ed.) *The Development of Harvard University, 1869-1929*, 1930, pp. xlv-xlvi.
80. C. W. Eliot to Professor T. T. Goodell (date not clear).
81. *Report of Committee to Visit Harvard College*, 1934, p. 223.

dropped. Unfortunately, much progress was not made on this score, but the committee's view on tutorial economies received the support of the faculty.

Save Under Pressure

How productive the Harvard operation has been depends also on a number of miscellaneous issues. Thus, managers of the enterprise had to be economical in their disbursements. Once the college was in trouble, as in the 1820s or the 1930s, the demands for economy could not be stifled.

In 1875, the president announced that Harvard had to economize and postpone expenditures that were not absolutely necessary. The college had to save in order to build necessary dormitory space. On being asked in 1884 to reimburse a family for injuries received by a student in the college boathouse, Eliot replied that compensation could not be made, for the corporation was "bound as trustees to apply all their income to the maintenance of teaching, the support of poor students and the advancement of learning . . . ."[82]

Conserving Talent

In the seventeenth century an issue arose which has been with Harvard ever since. "Must scholars be bound to stay in the country?" asked President Dunster in 1647. The Commissioners of the Colony replied: "Yes, if they are tendered suitable employment; if such offers be refused, and they deport, they should reimburse the college for their scholarships."[83]

In so far as Harvard tolerated exports of talented men trained in Cambridge, its contribution to New England productivity was impaired; and in so far as Harvard drains bright young men from other areas,

Harvard's productivity rises more than is given by the product added by Harvard.

Mergers

Two other matters require a brief comment. Harvard's productivity could have been increased if mergers with competing institutions had been tolerated. Such issues arose in the divinity school and in the several attempts to merge with MIT. Undoubtedly a merger with MIT would have yielded a more economical operation. But inability to compromise on matters that were not of major importance and the rigidity of the law killed the MIT-Harvard mergers.[84]

Liquidation of Schools

Finally, when a college has been confronted with incessant deficits, Harvard has not hesitated to liquidate a school. Thus, the veterinary school experienced a deficit of $4,206.96 in 1899-1900 and one of $4,200 over the years. This was a signal for liquidation.[85]

Productivity and Teaching

Above all, the productivity of a university is related to the kind of teaching function that is performed. The better the quality of the teaching the greater the output vis-à-vis input. (As research in the university becomes increasingly important, the contribution of research, both absolute and relative to teaching, requires consideration.)

Undoubtedly teaching performance has greatly improved. To some extent the improvement has

---

82. C. W. Eliot to C. Lyman, July 27, 1875; C. W. Eliot to S. R. Mead, November 1884.
83. *The Founding of Harvard College*, p. 320; Samuel Eliot Morison, *Harvard College in the Seventeenth Century*, 1936, pp. 298-299.
84. See G. H. Williams (ed.), *The Harvard Divinity School*, pp. 208-209; *Commonwealth of Massachusetts, Supreme Judicial Court, President and Fellows of Harvard College vs The Attorney General...Deeds and Will of Gordon McKay.*
85. C. W. Eliot to C. Plyman, October 31, 1900 and November 12, 1900.

stemmed from the increasing attention given to teaching and the reduced efforts required to enforce discipline. The improvement became marked by the middle of the nineteenth century and especially in the Eliot period. Here the higher age of admission, the improved admission policies generally, and the impact of the elective system, which had experienced a substantial development even before Eliot, were important.

Eliot commented on the significance of the written examination. They not only help classify students on the basis of accomplishment, ". . . they constitute a valuable means of training, inasmuch as they prepare young men to meet the similar crisis which they constantly encounter in after life . . . .[86]

Under the elective system, students increasingly were encouraged to study in more advanced subjects. But especially significant was the abandonment, except in the language courses, of the recitation method of teaching, under which the student memorized the assignment and was then tested by the teacher. Under Eliot, in particular, the shift was to the lecture and quiz sections, and emphasis on the student's learning how to think and to act on his own account rather than memorize. Eliot also stressed the rising importance of written exercises since 1870 and the "laboratory method."

In laboratory work the individual student is obliged to use actively and accurately his own eye and hands, to record correctly the results of his observations, and to apprehend the general principal or law which determines the sequence of the phenomenon he observes . . . .[87]

By the end of the Eliot regime, large advances had been made in teaching techniques. The student was increasingly on his own. Under Lowell's tutorial system even more emphasis was put on what the student thought and wrote. In contrast, under Quincy (1831 to 1845), the president and members of the faculty would go over each exercise of each student, giving each student a ranking in his class.[88]

Eliot failed in an attempt to reduce costs by introducing the three-year degree. Others feared this meant a debasement of the A.B.[89]

Unfortunately, it is not easy to measure productivity in higher education as in industry—e.g., man-hour output. On the basis of costs per student, productivity seems to have declined over long periods of time. But to measure productivity, we should also allow for the change in the quality of the teaching, the nature of the changing curriculum, the contribution of the curriculum to later economic status, etc.

Miscellaneous

A university may be held to be more productive if its investment policies are highly successful. Large investments in equities since the early 1930s and especially since the early 1950s have certainly paid off. With more income, the institution of higher learning may provide more and better teaching and other services.

Harvard's record over the last hundred years seems to have been good. Its achievement in this area may well not have been as spectacular as those of Wesleyan and Rochester. Wesleyan, especially, revealed large gains. Its 1953 endowment of $18 million escalated to $161 million, or $130,000 per student. A similar per-student endowment at Harvard would raise her endowment from $1 billion, its current value, to about $2 billion. Investments in insurance companies, a book publishing firm, and in Xerox all were very remunerative for Wesleyan. The great advance of Xerox and Eastman Kodak stocks, the latter held at one time under pressure from the company, especially contributed to Rochester's gains.[90]

86. C. W. Eliot, *University Administration*, 1908, pp. 206-207.
87. C. W. Eliot, *Educational Administration*, pp. 174-175, 186-187.
88. G. Peabody, *Harvard Reminiscences*, pp. 30-31.
89. Relation of Harvard University to Schools of Secondary Education: *Second Report of Associated Harvard Clubs*, May, 1906; The Associated Harvard Clubs, *Report of the Committee on the Question of Establishing a Three Year Course for the Degree of A.B.*, May 27, 1905.
90. Especially *New Yorker*, April 1, 1967, and *Time*, May 26, 1967.

The cost of investment advice is also a matter of some importance. Manuel F. Cohen, chairman of the securities and exchange commission, wrote me that these advisory fees "traditionally have clustered around 0.50 per cent of average *net assets*, and compares these fees with the fees charged by banks and other investment advisors for investment advisory service to pension and profit-sharing plans . . . ." An official report concluded that "advisory fees paid by the larger mutual funds were substantially higher than charged for the management of other investment portfolios."[91]

It is difficult to draw conclusions on the cost of investment advice for Harvard. In 1966-1967, the university reserved $428,619, or 1 percent of *investment income* to meet management costs inclusive of investment supervision, custodial services, expenses of the gift office, accounting services, management of real estate, and miscellaneous expenses. This seems a modest charge, but the size of the account and the fact that the Harvard operation is tied to that of a very large investment trust is relevant, for that means the relevant costs are the additional ones involved in taking on Harvard's $1 billion of assets. The additional costs would be relatively small.[92]

If we could discover costs of the various services of Harvard, then it might be easier to control costs. But except for a few feeble attempts before 1914, little has been done in this area. The problems are admittedly tough. President Eliot in 1894 acknowledged that costs of graduate work per student greatly exceeded those for undergraduates. But he could not estimate costs of each; and even commingled receipts for undergraduates and graduates.[93]

At one point I had asked Dean Price of the Kennedy school about the use of faculty from various schools to teach in his school, who were not compensated by the Kennedy School of Government. He admitted that this may be true, but he listed various services given by his school to other parts of the university. It was difficult to give any precise answers.[94]

In the future, large advances in educational technology inclusive of computerization of operations may greatly reduce costs. Dean Franklin Ford is hopeful that the effects on costs will be most favorable. But it should be noted that so far the major advances have been in the production of machines by business corporations, and a failure to supplement greatly with teaching procedures by psychologists and other educators sufficiently to keep up with the output of machines.

How productive higher education will be depends to a considerable degree upon the success with which the college obtains the best students. In this connection, it is of some interest to examine the relations of acceptances of freshmen to freshmen places available. Harvard's record is easily the best among the eight ivy-league colleges. Harvard could be assured by the fact that 88 percent of those accepted would come to Harvard. Whereas acceptances by Harvard exceeded places available by only 13 percent, the corresponding figure for all eight ivy-league institutions was 60 percent.[95] Apparently Harvard could count on a very strong desire to go to Harvard by those who had applied. Next to Harvard was Yale, with about 40 percent excess in acceptances.[96]

91. Manuel F. Cohen to Seymour E. Harris, November 1, 1967; also see House Report No. 2337, *Report of the S.E.C. on the Public Policy Implications of Investment Company Growth,* 1966, pp. 114-121.

92. Letter C. W. Janke, Comptroller, Harvard University, to Seymour E. Harris, February 14, 1968.

93. C. W. Eliot Letter of January 20, 1894.

94. Dean Price to Seymour E. Harris, March 28, 1968.

95. A small excess of acceptances suggests that most offers by Harvard will be accepted by those who are acceptable to Harvard.

96. *New York Times,* April 17, 1967.

52

Growth of Harvard

Measurement of Growth

Harvard's growth until the Revolution, or even the early nineteenth century, was not spectacular when viewed from the high plateau of 1965. Yet the ascent appeared more difficult and a high achievement to those looking backward at an earlier time. Thus, an apologist for President Quincy (1829 to 1845) could boast as major gains a rise in the number of professors from twenty-one to twenty-nine, the enlargement of college property, a rise of productive funds from $451,000 to $706,000, and of students by more than 50 percent. Writing in 1923, Charles Eliot noted that the "President and Fellows between 1630 and 1810 had brought the College safely through a series of wars, paper money periods, commercial panics, the Revolution and the first twenty years of the Constitution, and were naturally proud of this record." [1]

Perhaps before we discuss growth further, we ought to clarify the meaning of the term as used here. An obvious measure of growth is the rise of enrollment. In the discussion that fellows, the emphasis is on enrollment, size of the faculty, financial resources, inclusive of endowment, and current income and expenditures. But these are only rough guides of growth. For example, it is important to consider the quality of the Harvard education as well as the quantity, i.e., enrollment. Hence, we have to take into account, for example, the faculty-student ratio and the quality of the faculty.

Thus at midnineteenth century, a committee of the State Legislature (minority) wrote:

No one can look at the position of the college twenty-five, or ten years ago, and compare it with its present position, or compare the results, which it now effects, with those of the past generation, without seeing that a change, and one vastly for the better, has been brought about in coincidence with the changes in society, and the consequent popular demand. The standard of requirements has been raised. The demands, from time to time, for instruction in particular branches, have been answered by the college, by the establishment of new departments, and the extension of old ones. The Medical and Divinity schools were successively founded as their need was felt. The law school has taken a front rank.... [2]

Seventy-four years later, when the college was acknowledging President Eliot's ninetieth birthday, the president of the board of overseers, said:

You, sir, looking back through thirty-seven years of rewarded efforts, have lived to see your influence, which transformed the little College of Harvard into a great University, gradually transcend those ample limits and help to shape a nation's destiny.... [3]

1. J. Walker, "Memoir of Josiah Quincy," in *Proceedings and Collections of the Massachusetts Historical Society,* 1866-1867; C. W. Eliot, *Harvard Memories,* 1923, p. 50.

2. *Massachusetts House Report No. 164, Minority Report,* April 1850, p. 14.
3. *The Ninetieth Birthday of Charles W. Eliot,* 1924, p. 13.

It would be helpful also to trace Harvard's growth by including the value of its land and buildings.[4] But this is not easy, in part because valuations are difficult to make, and information is available at irregular intervals.

I estimate the value of Harvard property (land and buildings) as follows: (Note the much greater increase after 1789.)

Value of Harvard Property		
Year of Acquisition	No. of Items	Value
1661–1789	23	$ 7,680
1789–1829	50	92,000

Between 1719 and 1766, Harvard obtained four buildings which were evaluated at $53,000. In 1805, the one new building was evaluated at $23,700. Between 1813 and 1869, thirteen buildings Harvard obtained cost $520,000. In 1869, more than 22 acres of college land were evaluated at 20 cents a foot, equaling a total of $191,669; more than 2 acres of delta land were evaluated at $17,424.[5]

How significant growth is depends on the trends in the economy. Among the relative variables are movements in national income, total and per capita, in prices, and also the general advance of higher education in the nation. The large gains under Eliot, Lowell, and Pusey, for example, are related to the great economic advances during their incumbencies; and the disappointing growth under Conant can be associated with the Great Depression and World War

II. Again, the trends in the eighteenth century on the whole were disappointing. Inflation and war contributed to the slow growth.

At times Harvard's slow rate of growth or decline reflected developments within the college. Thus, there was the crisis of the 1820s, and again the clash with the government and others of the midnineteenth century, disagreements related to Harvard's high costs, its reluctance to move into the vocational field, and also disagreements on religious issues. Yet, despite these unfortunate developments, Harvard advanced reasonably well in the first half of the nineteenth century.

Nongrowth

Growth has been the rule, but there also have been periods when stagnation or deterioration seemed to prevail. In periods of war or large inflations, in the crisis of the 1820s, and in the middle of the nineteenth century, the college seemed to be losing rather than advancing. Undergraduate enrollment was fifty in 1652 and only twenty-five in 1669 and 1682, and then rose to fifty-three in 1693 and fifty-four in 1712.

In 1702, petitioners addressed Gov. Joseph Dudley:

. . . whereas the said College hath by devine favour, been a rich blessing to the Western English plantations for many years, but now Languisheth . . . which bodes its dissolution, unless some speedy and effectual course be taken for the obtaining its Reestablishment. . . .[6]

Harvard frequently languished, especially in the early years. In 1641, a serious economic depression brought a crisis for the emerging college; in 1653-1654 the contributions of corn greatly declined with resultant shortages of funds for operating and for repairing the deteriorating plant; between 1657

---

4. For listing of grants of land and other property see *Grants of the Colony and Commonwealth of Massachusetts to Harvard College, 1636 to 1846*; and for failure of the college to obtain possession as a rule, see The President and Fellows of Harvard College, To the Honourable Senate and Honourable House of Representatives of General Court on accounts, January, 1787; also see J. Jackson to Corporation, March 7, 1809, on the failure of the corporation to cash in on Maine Lands given to Harvard.

5. *Report of the Board of Overseers of Harvard College on the Condition, needs, and Prospects of the University*, 1869, pp. 35-36.

6. To His Excellency Joseph Dudley, Esquire Captain, Generall and Gouvernour in Chiefe of Her Majestyes Provinces of the Massachusetts bay and New Hampshire in New England, September 26, 1702.

and 1664 it was necessary to beg for funds; in 1671, after graduation, but twenty-five students remained, scarcely enough for a viable college; and the resource problem became so serious that the court called in the governing boards, faculty, and students to find some solution; in the class of 1674, but one member graduated; and King Phillip's War (1675-1676) destroyed a large part of the wealth of the colony from which the college had to find its support. Crises in the Puritan period were numerous. But by 1732, at which time the college income — aside from restricted income — was £728, the college could boast of prosperity.[7]

Aside from the large reductions in World War I and World War II, and in the seventeenth century at intervals enrollment declined in other periods:

| | Enrollment | |
Year	Number	Reason for Decrease
1727	138	War and inflation
1747	96	
1767	177	War and inflation
1779	122	
1821	257	Financial difficulties; increased competition; religious differences
1840	236	

In this analysis I concentrate on enrollment as one important index of growth. But in some respects the number of graduates would be more significant. Thus, in the 1919 drive for a $15 million endowment, it was noted that Harvard had graduated 30,045 men and trained thousands more who took less than the full course.

Harvard also boasted of 5,500 higher degrees in the college and an output of 12,000 lawyers by 1919. By 1968, Harvard College alone had 50,000 alumni.[8]

Before the Revolution

Harvard's growth seems to have been slow and uneven in the 150 years ending with the Revolution. Slow economic development with accompanying modest gains of population, difficulties of transportation, war and inflation, and the emergence of competition all contributed to the disappointing trends.

In the middle of the seventeenth century, enrollment had reached only 50; just before the Revolutionary War the figure had climbed only to 172.

Declines occurred especially in inflationary periods. Thus, from 1778 to 1781, the total was only 124; but by 1794 to 1806, a recovery to 183 was achieved.

Compare this gain of 133 over a period of about 150 years or an average of less than 1 per year with that of more than 12,000, both college and professional schools, in the next 160 years, or a gain of 75 per year.[9]

Some rough calculations yield the following:[10]

1. Average annual rise of *endowment*, 1636 to 1909, or 273 years, $83,500
2. Average annual rise of *investments* 1909 to 1963, or 56 years (market value), $17,500,000
3. Ratio of annual rise of (2) to (1) (in the 10 years ending 1962-1963 gifts received for capital averaged $19 million and all gifts $29 million), 210 times.

On numerous occasions in earlier years one finds official announcements of the college's stock. These estimates of stock are generally much less than related investment totals of the same year or nearly the same year. It seems that the stock is really the unrestricted endowment, the income of which can be used

7. Morison, *Harvard College in the Seventeenth Century*, vol. I, pp. 253-257; 303-304; vol. II, pp. 370-372, 391, 406, 422-423; *The History of Harvard University*, p. 16.
8. "The Harvard Endowment Fund," in *Harvard and the Future*, 1919, pp. 8, 11-13; *Harvard Alumni Bulletin*, February 3, 1968.
9. *Stewards' Quarter Bill Books*.
10. *Financial Report to the Board of Overseers of Harvard College*, 1962-1963, 1964-1965.

to offset any excess of expenditures over income. A few instances follow, with the general investment of the same or proximate years. The free funds ranged from less than 40 to more than 50 percent of general investments, a level of unrestricted funds much higher than in recent years. [11]

Table 52-1.

Harvard Stock and Investments, Various Years

Year	Stock	Year	General Investments
1793	$100,000	1793	$ 180,000
1831-1832	150,000	1830-1831	399,000
1840-1841	161,000	1840-1841	515,000
1848	390,000*	1849-1850	727,000
1869	272,000	1869-1870	2,228,000

Sources: Report of the President of Harvard College, relevant years; *Harvard College and Early Education in Massachusetts,* 1848, sec. 21, p 99; Cabot and Larabee, "Investing Harvard Money," in *Harvard Alumni Bulletin,* May 12, 1951, pp. 628-629.

*Property equaled $862,000, of which $472,000 was nominally productive, but only $390,000 was really productive.

Analysis Of Growth Before The Revolution

In the uneven development of the 140 years before the Revolution growth was substantial but spasmodic, and, though significant, was at a much slower rate than in the almost 200 years after the Revolution. Enrollment moved up and down and though the trend was upward, the average enrollment from 1638 to 1652, for example, was almost as high as from 1693 to 1712.

In the first seventy-six years, the explanation of a rising budget was largely the increase of prices and a rising standard of living reflected, for example, in the improved pay of fellows and the president, as well as an increase in the number of fellows from two to three.[12] As compared to a salary of £4 per fellow in 1643, the range of pay fluctuated between £53 and £100 in the years 1693 to 1715.

A factor of some importance in the first thirty-two years of the eighteenth century was the inflation during this period. Whereas the rise of the budget and unit costs primarily reflected the improved economic situation and perhaps the restricted supplies of acceptable teachers in the seventeenth century, by the beginning of the eighteenth century inflation probably contributed more to the rising cost of education than improvements in the economic situation. An indication of the inflationary trends is given by the cost of an ounce of silver in New England pounds: 6s $10\frac{2}{7}$d in 1704, 18s in 1728, and 60s in 1749.[13] But the decline in unit costs from 1713 to 1732 is undoubtedly related to the large rise of enrollment which tended to depress costs per student.

In Harvard's first sixty to seventy years, it faced virtually no competition. But in 1701, with some help of Harvard men, Yale was founded. By the middle of the eighteenth century, Harvard had to face the competition of Columbia, Princeton, and soon of Dartmouth. Harvard was not pleased with increased competition and especially in Massachusetts. On March 8, 1762, the overseers met to consider a "charter . . . prepared [by the governor] for the establishment of a College, or Collegiate School in the County of Hampshire." Harvard spokesmen vigorously opposed the charter for the new college. The opening of a rival in the western part of the state would reduce standards and endanger Harvard's future, they thought.

. . . One College was sufficient for the Province; and, although in ancient and rich countries competition and rivalry might be useful, yet it would be very different in a young country, poor and without resources; – Harvard College was yet in its infant state, poor and meanly endowed; – founding another

---

11. The table for investments, 1652 to 1966, is deposited in the archives.
12. Margery Somers Foster, *"Out of Smalle Beginings . . ."*–

An Economic History of Harvard College in the Puritan Period (1636-1712), 1962, pp. 129-136.
13. *Ibid,* p. 43.

Table 52-2.
Income, Disbursements and Enrollment per Year
1636–1733

	Income	Disbursements	Enrollment	Disb. per Student
1. 1636-1652 £	£ 227 (1638-1652)	£ 187*	50 (1652)	£ 3.7
2. 1693-1712	577	548	54 (1712)	10.1
3. 1713-1722		1,400	47	29.8
4. 1723-1732	2,650	2,640	138	19.1

Source: Margery Somers Foster, *"Out of Smalle Beginnings. . ." – An Economic History of Harvard College in the Puritan Period (1636–1712)*, 1962.

* A general court audit revealed budgets of £175 average under Dunster in his twelve years; Samuel Eliot Morison, *Three Centuries of Harvard, 1636–1936*, 1937, p. 15.

---

would be the most effectual way to prevent its future sufficient endowment by the stream of those bounties, which would otherwise flow to it exclusively; – contests would result, not concerning the advancement of science, but for obtaining the most benefactions, or the greatest amount of public patronage; – the effect of which would be, not only to injure Harvard College, but to render both institutions inadequate to furnish such an education as Colleges ought to be able to afford. . . . [14]

The overseers at this time preserved Harvard's monopoly in Massachusetts. But Williams College's birth was postponed, not prevented.

Growth, 1772-1819

Growth in the years 1772 to 1819 was substantial despite the impact of the Revolution and one of the great inflations of modern times. The Revolution, in fact, after the first few months left New England almost untouched. [15] The same cannot be said of the galloping inflation. (There is some evidence that the Revolution was more costly to Yale than to Harvard.[16])

Harvard enrollment rose by 1.2 times; faculty by about 2 times; expenditures, 8 to 9 times; investments by 4.6 times. Investments per student declined by 5 percent; income per student rose by 3.4 times.

By comparing expenditures, income, investment, and endowment in current dollars, we tend to overestimate the gains. The index of all commodity prices (1910 to 1914 - 100) rose from 89 in 1772 to 125 in 1819, or an increase of 40 percent. Hence, the increases should be deflated by 29 percent. The adjustment would be less on capital sums which reflect prices over longer periods of time.[17]

Before commenting on the period 1819 to 1870, I should discuss the growth of Harvard during the Kirkland presidency – 1810 to 1828, an administration covered in two periods here. This was a time of unusual growth. The corporation created two new

---

14. Josiah Quincy, *The History of Harvard University,* 1840, vol. II, pp. 108-111, 468-479.

15. H. U. Faulkner, *American Political and Social History,* 5th ed., pp. 16-17.

16. B. Steiner, *History of Education in Connecticut,* 1893, pp. 120-126.

17. Prices from U. S. Census, *Historical Statistics of the United States,* 1789-1945, pp. 232-233.

schools: law and divinity; added fifteen new professorships to the ten extant in 1810 – though only eight had endowments, and some were not adequate to finance the relevant chair; substantially increased the salaries of the faculty; greatly developed and improved the appearance of the museums; and obtained the unprecedented gifts of almost $400,000.

But the president, not overly sophisticated in financial matters, had greatly overextended the operations of the university; and once the annual subsidy of the commonwealth was terminated in 1824, the college was confronted with its most serious crisis since its early years. Stunted growth, retrenchments, dismissals, increased work loads, reduced enrollment, and rationalization of operations were the aftermath of the overextension of the preceding ten years. Kirkland had to resign.

He was not supposed to be distinguished for financial abilities; but there was something in the elevation of his character and purposes, the wisdom of his designs, the benevolence of his heart, the suavity of his manners, and the contagion of his example, which commanded the resources of others, as if they had been his own . . . .[18]

Growth, 1819-1870

Enrollment rose by 1.9 times; expenditures, by 2.2 times; investments, by 6.7 times; investments per student, by 1.7 times. Income per student declined by 0.2 times.[19]

This was a period of healthy growth. The Civil War might have interrupted the advance, but not as much as might have been expected. Students did not take this war as seriously as World War I and World II, when they were subject to fairly rigid draft requirements.

In 1849, admirers wrote:

The little acorn planted by the fathers of Massachusetts two centuries ago has become a gigantic oak. Young eagles are nestled in its branches – garlands gathered of its leaves adorn the sacred temples of freedom and place.[20]

The college continued its social and intellectual life almost uninterrupted. The law school, with 27 percent of its students from the South suffered. Of 1,311 Harvard enlistments in the war, 138 lost their lives. President James Walker in his 1859-1860 report remarked on the uninterrupted harmony of the law school students in the midst of discord.[21] The Civil War, moreover, accelerated the economic advance of the country. In general, the progress from 1819 to 1860 matched that of 1860 to 1870. But one reservation is important. Prices fell from 1819 to 1860 by 16 to 32 percent depending on the index used. Hence, in these years, dollar gains were larger than the index figures suggested.

From 1860 to 1870 inflation was severe. Prices rose from 40 to 45 percent according to three indexes. Once we correct for the rise of prices – tuition at Harvard doubled – the gains of expenditures, investment per student, and income per student are largely wiped out; and the increase of investments, if adjusted by the rise of prices, is reduced from about 130 to 65 percent. But, as noted elsewhere, to adjust investments by price rises over a short period exaggerates the loss of values.

Over the whole period 1819 to 1870, a rise of enrollment of almost 2 times is especially striking, as well as a gain of investment funds of 6.7 times – from $289,000 to $2,229,000. Investment increased at an annual average rate of almost $40.000 as compared with $6,000 in the preceding forty years. The founding of the Lawrence Scientific School in 1846-1847 contributed to this result.[22]

18. *History of Harvard College*, pp. 104-109; *Majority Report of the Committee of the Board of Overseers*, 1894; Quincy, *op. cit.*, vol. II, pp. 333-335.

19. Prices from U. S. Census, *Historical Statistics of the United States, 1789-1945*, pp. 232-233.

20. *Report of Visiting Committee of Harvard College made to Overseers from Reports . . . During the Administration of President Sparks*, 1849, p. 13.

21. *Report of the President of Harvard College*, 1859-1860, p. 10; 1860-1861, p. 1; Morison, *Three Centuries of Harvard, 1636-1936*, pp. 302-304.

22. *Ibid.*, 1846-1847, pp. 7-8. 25-29.

One of the striking aspects of this period of fifty-one years was the decline in the income per student during a period of substantial price rise. Obviously Harvard was profiting from the economies of scale. With an increase of enrollment from 383 to 1,097, the authorities were able to cut costs. One evidence of this policy is suggested by an increase of faculty members from nineteen in 1826 to but twenty in 1850. Moreover, courses in these years increased only from $29\frac{2}{3}$ to $34\frac{1}{2}$. Expenditures, however, roughly roughly kept up with the rise of enrollment, though not nearly so if allowance is made for the rise of prices. This reduction of income per student prevailed even though endowment per student almost doubled.

In its 1869 report the board of overseers boasted of donations by 1869 as high as $2,470,000 as compared with $295,000 received by 1810, a doubling of enrollment and a trebling of staff in fifty-one years.

Perhaps a word should be said about the state of the university at midcentury, at which time large recoveries had been made from the Kirkland crisis. One writer noted that in the more than two hundred years of Harvard history before 1856, the enrollment had risen from twenty-four, a faculty of two or three, and one building to an enrollment of six hundred, a faculty of thirty and thirteen buildings in Cambridge alone. A visiting committee in 1849 commented:

The University is venerable for its age — renowned for its learning — and distinguished for its wealth . . . . They look upon its wealth as a fund in trust for the present and future generations — a fund devoted to the most valuable objects of public and private interest, and they believe its usefullness would increase with its means, and even to the doubling of them . . . . The Institution at Cambridge is not a College merely, but a University, — the University of the United States — competent to lead the willing pilgrim to the loftiest pinnacle of science; and its most holy recesses. . . . [23]

The Eliot Period, 1869-1870 to 1909-1910

This was Harvard's golden period. In relative terms, the gains exceeded those of Eliot's successors, though under Lowell the rise of enrollment *per decade* was greater than under Eliot, both on an absolute and a relative scale.

Eliot's great contributions are not given merely by the usual statistical surveys. James Bryce is said to have told President Eliot [in 1869] that Harvard was "no real University but only a struggling college with uncertain relations to learning and research loosely tied to a congeries of professional schools. . . ."

Another writer noted "that Harvard University, as we know it today, is practically the creation of the administration of President Eliot, the longest (forty years) since the foundation of the college . . . ." [24]

President Eliot himself produced proof of his accomplishments. The importance of the elective system received much attention. He showed the tabular view of exercises just before he came in. It is clear from this that the elective system had not advanced far before Eliot's entry as president. [25]

In analyzing eight colleges, he clarified the point that the colleges that offered more electives tended to attract more students.

Eliot showed also not only the faculty increased by nine times in his forty years, but also that enrollment had grown by less than three times. The student-teacher ratio had greatly improved, though the proportion of nonprofessional faculty members had risen from one-fourth to two-thirds. Here again the elective system was relevant.

President Eliot has also given us a unique breakdown of expenses from 1892 to 1902. Both the large percentage of expenditures for teaching salaries, namely, 45 percent of $1\frac{1}{2}$ to 2 times the relative amounts for corporation appointments for 1966-1967, and the stability in this ratio are impressive. He indeed tried to direct large resources to

---

23. *Report of the Visiting Committee of Harvard University Overseers*, January, 1849, pp. 4-5, 10-11; *History of Harvard College*, pp. 126-127.

24. *Harvard Graduates Magazine*, vol. 17, p. 376.
25. Tables have been deposited in the Harvard University Archives.

teaching. Student aid accounted for more than 10 percent, a much larger percentage than currently. The library absorbed more than 7 percent, and museums an equal percentage. Maintenance of buildings other than dormitories required 6 percent. [26]

Eliot's survey of the details of finance was also enlightening. Endowment rose by 9 times, but with reduced returns on investment, income on investments increased by less than 4 times. It may seem surprising since Eliot was a supporter of low tuition that the contribution of tuition rose in these forty years from 20 to 30 percent. The main explanation, of course, was the very large increase in enrollment. [27]

In a study of 1,000 Men of Science (1906), Eliot was quick to reveal that 237 had been educated at Harvard. Johns Hopkins was next with 171 and four other prestigious universities claimed credit from 53 to 93.

Finally, proud of his contribution to graduate studies, Eliot revealed that though Johns Hopkins led Harvard in enrollment, Harvard overtook Johns Hopkins by 1900 in degrees awarded.

A comparison on the basis of statistics uncorrected by prices understates the gains under Eliot. Wholesale prices fell almost 20 percent and an average of cost of living indexes by about 10 percent. In the Lowell, Conant, and Pusey periods prices rose, and especially under the first two. Hence, the financial improvements under Eliot should be inflated and those under Lowell, Conant, and Pusey deflated.

In the first ten years, endowment under Pusey rose by $196 million, (in addition there were $111 million of gifts for current use). The relative gains of investments were about 80 percent in this period of ten years, a remarkable rise. But in the forty years of Eliot the increase of investments was roughly 750 percent. Moreover, prices had moved upward greatly

after Eliot's day, the average price level (wholesale) being 3 times as high under Pusey as under Eliot. Prices tended to fall under Eliot and rise under Pusey. Another relevant statistic is an average gross national product per capita under Eliot and Pusey of $540 and $2,700 respectively or 5 times as great under the latter. The large endowment gains should be related to the average national per capita income under each president. [28]

In brief, the gains under Eliot were enrollment, 3 times; investments, 7.5 times; expenditures, 6.8 times; investments per student, 1.3 times; and income per student, 0.9 times.

Endowment income per student rose relatively little in comparison with the rise of endowment and that of expenditures, the explanation largely being that such large increases of enrollment cut down the gains on a per capita basis. Also relevant was the large reduction of yield on investments.

Many comparisons have been made over Eliot's first thirty-five years, which reveal gains approaching those of the forty-year incumbency. [29]

The thirty-five-year history revealed also why expenditures had increased so much. Eliot's educational reforms had resulted in a rise of half courses in the college during this period from 109 to 972; and books and pamphlets in the library, from 180,000 to more than a million. Officers of instruction increased from 58 to 549 in the university, with the major rises in the college — 34 to 318, and in medical school — 13 to 147, and dental school — 4 to 54.

The board of overseers revealed that output, e.g., number of degrees granted, had increased 4.31 times, but expenditures by 7.6 times. Each Harvard degree cost $950 in 1904 as compared with $525 in 1868, a

26. *Report of the President of Harvard College,* 1902-1903.
27. The relevant table has been deposited in the Harvard University Archives.
28. My computations from *Historical Statistics of the United States, 1789-1945; Economic Report of the President,* 1964.

29. "Harvard's Growth in 35 Years," in *The Harvard Bulletin,* vol. 6, no. 23, p. 5, 1904; *Report of a Special Committee of the Board of Overseers on the Financial Requirements of the University and the Deficit Incurred During Recent Years,* 1904, p. 4; C. F. Adams, "The Harvard Tuition Fee, Its Proposed Increase," in *The Harvard Bulletin,* 1904; R. Hofatadter, in A. M. Schlesinger, Jr. and M. White (ed.), *Paths of American Thought,* 1963, pp. 275, 284-285.

rise of 81 percent. In his report of 1890-1891, President Eliot also commented on the greater rise of expenditures than of students. He accounted for this by the extention and improvement of the plant, the large rise in the cost of laboratories and the library, which have little relation to enrollment, and the high cost per student of advanced instruction. "...the American public must enlarge its ideas of the cost of supporting a University...." [30]

A comparative study for 1900 of the twelve largest universities in the country revealed that Harvard had the largest enrollment with 4,288; the largest faculty with 496; the largest alumni body, 22,670; the largest number of books in the library with 576,900; and the highest total income of $1,376,672. Only in total gifts was it second: $710,500 against Chicago's $2,675,000. [31]

This remarkable growth in Eliot's years is all the more surprising in view of the numerous crises that had prevailed. In the 1860s, the decade preceding Eliot's great beginning, the country had experienced close to a 50 percent inflation, and tuition had risen by 100 percent in a period of six years. The inflation of the 1860s was followed by continued price rises until 1873, and then a long deflationary period in the remainder of the 1870s. Yet Eliot noted that from 1862 to 1876, the university buildings had increased from eighteen to twenty-six and their land area doubled. Despite these adverse factors, "the investments of the Corporation were kept good, the annual income was satisfactory, and the confidence of the community in the financial management of the University suffered no abatement". Later, reviewing the years 1873 to 1886, Eliot complained of the decline of returns on investments from 7.44 to 5.19 percent, and the difficulty of meeting permanent obligations such as salaries with diminishing returns on safe investments. [32]

Eliot was learning that rapid expansion was dangerous if allowances were not made for periodic or secular declines of returns on capital. He was to learn this again in the early twentieth century.

At the close of the century, an official publication summarized the economic state of the university as follows:

The University is made up of seventeen departments and a large number of museums, laboratories, and other establishments not usually reckoned as separate departments. It occupies a total area of more than 500 acres. Most of the buildings are in Cambridge and Boston. The quick capital of the University in 1898-1899 was over ten million dollars; its income sufficed for an average annual expenditure of $300 per capita of students. The value of the lands and buildings devoted to education and the advancement of learning was estimated at nearly five million dollars. The enrollment of students in all departments, including the summer school of 1898, was 4660. The officers of instruction and government number 504. [33]

After Eliot

Harvard grew at a most satisfactory rate in the Lowell, Conant, and Pusey regimes. The rate of increase of enrollment declined per year. In response to the Great Depression and increasing emphasis on standards, the annual percentage rise of enrollment declined especially in the Conant period. But even under Lowell, the university introduced restrictive measures. Of some interest here is a comparison of the percentage rise of enrollments at Harvard with that for the nation. Whereas from 1870 to 1910, the percentage rise of enrollment at Harvard was half that for the country, from 1950 to 1963, Harvard's percentage rise was only one-four hundred twentyfifth

30. *Report of the President of Harvard College*, 1890-1891, p. 35.
31. American College Statistics, in *The Harvard Bulletin* vol. III, no. 14, p. 2.
32. *Report of the President of Harvard College*, 1874-1875, pp. 30-31, 40-41; 1875-1876, p. 4; 1885-1886, pp. 23-24; *Treasurer's Statement*, 1864-1865, pp. 5-6; 1879-1880, p. 4.
33. W. G. Brown (ed.), *Official Guide to Harvard University*, 1899, Harvard Memorial Society, p. 1.

that of the nation. Such slowing down of Harvard's gains vis-à-vis those of the nation might suggest to many a great lessening of Harvard's influence. But losses in quantity were made up at least to some extent by gains of quality. This reduced rate of increase of enrollment prevailed even though the university added graduate schools of education, engineering, design, public administration, public health, and dental medicine in the post-Eliot period.

It is particularly in the rise of investment funds, endowment per student, expenditures, and income per student that Harvard's performance seemed almost incredible. On capital funds, the gains were especially large under Lowell and Pusey, and less so under Conant, who had to contend with the Great Depression, association of Harvard faculty members with the New Deal, a relationship which antagonized men of wealth, and the war and inflation. The Conant period showed a rise of endowment per student, not even equal to the inflation of the period, and hence a decline in dollars of stable purchasing power, and an increase of income per student substantially less than the rise of prices. Eliot, Lowell and Pusey revealed larger relative gains in these areas. Pusey profited both from the $82,500,000 endowment drive, and also from the unparalleled rise of stock market equities, the last reflecting the great prosperity since the end of World War II.

In assessing the gains of Harvard since 1910, one should consider that from 1910 to 1963, the gross national product had risen by almost 11 times and the wholesale prices by 159 percent. In other words, to some extent the large gains of Harvard are associated with some inflation and to the sharp growth in the economy, and hence should be deflated. Particularly under Conant, a correction for inflation reduced the nominal gains substantially, and even under Lowell and Pusey inflation was a factor.

As might be expected, in each of the four periods under consideration, budgets rose much more than enrollment. Under Eliot, with falling prices the general trend, the explanation of the increase of the budget lies primarily in the ambitious curriculum changes, the increase in the faculty-student ratio, and

the rising salary level. Under Lowell, the introduction of the expensive tutorial system and the extension of housing and commons facilities as well as some rise in prices contributed to this result.

The twenty years under Conant brought similar results. In this period price inflation was a large factor, though not as great as it might have been since salaries had responded little to the rise of prices. In all these periods the greater rise of faculty numbers than of students contributed to the rise of budgets exceeding that of the number of students. From 1900 to 1930, for example, faculty numbers in the college rose by more than twice as much as students; and from 1930 to 1963, about $4\frac{1}{2}$ times as much. The large relative increase of junior faculty members, and notably teaching assistants and (especially in the last generation) the rising importance of research contributed to this result.

A table for the years 1931 to 1951 (largely Conant years) supports the general position: the staff increased more than students; and budgets even more than the staff.[34] But this is not a universal rule.

Prospects

In the Eliot years, a deficit of less than $32,000 in two years greatly concerned the authorities. Eliot explained the deficits by the expansion of curriculum, the rising faculty-student ratio, and large outlays on buildings. He was concerned that the free funds were small. Over a period of twenty-four years (1869 to 1893), though the permanent funds had risen to $3\frac{3}{4}$ times the 1869 level, the reserves had seriously declined. The effects on future growth were obvious.

Problems in Eliot's day seem picayune compared to current ones. From 1935 to 1966, for example, the expenditures of Harvard rose between 9 and 10 times. They have been rising 20 percent a year recently. These unmet needs prevail despite the fact that Harvard in the late 1950s raised $82,500,000 in a drive, and the medical school, $58 million in the

---

34. *Report of the President of Harvard College*, 1951-1952, p. 32; the table has been deposited in the Harvard University Archives.

1960s, and total construction at about $115 million in the ten years ending 1965-1966. Looking ahead, President Pusey estimated a budget of $333 million within a decade. (On generous estimates of funds to be available, he envisages the deficit at $100 million; and hence implies the need of more Federal aid.) On top of that, the president finds that Harvard needs $160 million out of current drives for capital. In all, fourteen drives are involved inclusive of one of an omnibus character, with the science program for Harvard College ($49 million) and the school of public health ($30 million) being the largest. The undergraduate science program includes five professorships at $600,000 each ($3 million) with the largest sums (45,700,000) going for the plant and facilities. The heavy outlays for facilities is contrary to Harvard's past policies in favoring men against the plant, but apparently this is the appropriate structure of spending in the sciences. In contrast, for a Yale 10-year program which will continue to 1977, of $388 million, $241 million would be added to endowment. Faculty salaries are to rise from $22 to $50 million.

With construction costs rising rapidly and faculty salaries rising, though much less than income per employee in the country, the net effect of increasing needs and costs is a moderation of the rate of growth. At Harvard, the result is a proposed policy of stabilization of undergraduate enrollment and an increase of output of advanced degrees. Inadequacy of dormitory and house space, of laboratories and classrooms restrains large expansion of undergraduate enrollment. [35]

Pusey's estimate of roughly a doubling of the budget in ten years is far below the ten-year rise based on the 20 percent increase in a year and is a modest projection, if anything. In fact, a rise of 8 percent a year would double outlays in ten years. In view of the unusually moderate rise of prices in the 1960s, and the current inflationary pressures, even a 20 percent increase may seem to be an underestimate.

A table deposited in the archives reveals that tenure appointments in the social sciences are much less numerous than in the sciences and humanities. But costs per tenure member are highest in the social sciences. Hence, the costs will rise much more if expansion is in the social sciences than in the other two divisions.

Obviously, growth will be impeded in so far as growth is concentrated in high-cost areas, e.g., social sciences as against low cost areas, e.g., humanities. But the total effect will depend on the numbers added and the *total* costs. And relevant is also the point that variations of per tenure member outlays are large within each division.

35. *Board of Overseers Report*, January 10, 1894; *The New York Times,* November 27, 1967; Interview with Dean F. Ford in *Harvard Alumni Bulletin*, May 31, 1967; *The Program for Science in Harvard College*, November 13, 1967; Comptroller to Seymour E. Harris, June 23, 1967; *Harvard Alumni Bulletin,* February 11, 1967, October 28, 1957; Faculty of Arts and Science, *Admission to Harvard College*, 1960.

Appendix to Chapter 53.

Enrollment, Investment, Endowment Per Student, Expenditures, and Income Per Student, 1712 to 1966, Various Years

Year	Enrollment	Investments	Investments Per Student	Expenditures	Income Per Student
1712	54	£ 5,265	£ 97	£ 2,534 (1723)	£ 10 *D*
1772	172	15,809	92*C*	2,743	23.5s.
1819	383	$ 288,886	$ 754	$ 88,979	340.
1860	839	975,222 *A*	1,162	181,688 *E*	186.
1870	1,097	2,228,959	2,032	285,817 *F*	278.
1910	4,046	19,060,268	4,711	2,239,362	515.
1930	8,312	101,811,043	1,249	11,650,035	1,674.
1950	11,102	245,119,449 *B*	22,081	29,484,462	2,780.
1963	13,688	843,148,670 *B*	61,598	99,340,444	7,256.
1966	14,966	962,855,077 *B*	64,336	135,332,877	9,004.

A The Treasurer estimated total assets at $1,145,647.
B Market.
C Based on 1773 inventory.
D Average of 1693 to 1712.
E Inclusive of capital, expenditures were $423,753.
E pp. 5-7
F Capital Expenditures (investments) were $431,380 additional.

Sources: Enrollment, *Harvard University Catalogue; Stewards' Quarter Bill Books.* Endowment and Income, to 1819, *Treasurers' Journals; Treasurers' Ledgers;* later, *Report of the Treasurer of Harvard College.* Investments, 1712, 1772, capitalization of income; later years, *Report of the Treasurer of Harvard College.* Expenditures, eighteenth century, *Treasurers' Journals; Treasurers' Ledgers; Corporation Records; Stewards' Ledgers and Audited Accounts;* later *Report of the Treasurer of Harvard College.* Current income, eighteenth century, *Treasurers' Journals; Treasurers' Ledgers; Harvard College Papers; Acts and Resolves of the Province of Massachusetts Bay* (to 1780); *Acts and Laws of the Commonwealth of Massachusetts* (1780–1800); *Leg. Records of the Council;* later years, *Report of the Treasurer of Harvard College.*

53

Issues of Administration

Administrative Arrangements

How productive an operation is depends in part upon administrative arrangements. In the first serious attempt to deal with administrative problems in 1642, the general court provided for a large and unwieldy board of overseers to run the enterprise. It was soon clear that the provision made was inadequate. Hence, in 1650, the court gave to the corporation consisting of five members and the president and treasurer the major responsibilities. Three hundred and eighteen years later the structure established in 1650 essentially still remains. This is probably the oldest corporation in America. In the constitution of 1820 the commonwealth preserved the rights and authority of the corporation and the overseers.[1] Attempts have been made to prune the authority of the corporation and notably by teaching fellows in 1723 and 1822 and by the state government and the overseers in the middle of the nineteenth century. But these attempts failed.

The great issues in 1723 and 1822 revolved around the definition of a fellow. A few tutors, who were in residence, participated in the teaching and received a stipend. They held that they, and not the nonresident fellows, were eligible for appointment to the corporation. They failed to receive the support of either the corporation or the overseers.[2] It would indeed have been unfortunate if the university were to be run by members of the faculty. A serious conflict of interest would have prevailed.

. . . the resident Tutors should never be able to make a major part, because we think it contrary to the light of nature, that any should have an overruling voice in making these laws, by which themselves must be governed in their office-work for, and for which they receive salaries.

According to Eliot, the time of the corporation is devoted to the care of the property, "the determination of general policies concerning appropriations, salaries, and general expenses, and the initiation of appointments. . . . ." They seldom deal with nonfinancial problems, though in so far as any policy carries financial implications, e.g., new admission requirements, or new curriculum, the fellows and often the overseers are consulted.[3]

It is appropriate to quote from the durable 1650 Charter.

. . . the said College in Cambridge. . .shall be a Corporation, consisting of seven persons. . .and shall have

1. For the various statutes from 1642 on see especially Quincy, *op. cit.,* vol. I chapters 13, 14; *College Books,* vol. I, pp. 40-43; vol III, pp. 173-174; *Contributions to American Educational History: Federal Aid to Education* 1898, pp. 88-89.
2. On the two debates between resident fellows and nonresident see especially B. Peirce, *The History of the University* pp. 32-33, 114-119; *History of Harvard College,* pp. 44-45; G. Ticknor to President Hill, February 4, 1863; *An Historical Survey of Harvard University,* 1895, pp. 20-21.
3. Charles W. Eliot to Professor A. Chamberlain, October 21, 1907.

perpetual succession. . .they and their successors, shall and may purchase. . .and require to themselves, or take and receive upon free gift and donation any land, tenements or hereditaments. . .and sums of money whatsoever, to the use and behoof of the said President, Fellows and Scholars of the said College . . .may meet and choose such officers and servants for the college, and make such allowance to them, and them also to remove, and after death or removal, to choose. . .others. . . .

Over-all Effectiveness of Harvard's System

Over-all the Harvard system, with heavy responsibilities for a small board who reside close to the college, and with a large body (the overseers) representing the alumni and the educated population, has been most effective.

The larger body has both suggestive and veto powers. By Eliot's time, the president reminded a faculty member that the board of overseers was not inclined to propose policies, but preferred to exercise its veto power. That many decisions and especially important faculty appointments have to be approved by the overseers increases the likelihood of wise moves by the corporation. Moreover, the board of overseers over Harvard's history, though it has been a conservative influence, also has been responsible for many great advances: e.g., it germinated the elective system; introduced the financial arrangements for allocation of income on the basis of the genuine claims of each fund in the endowment total, as a substitute for distributing only 5 percent of each fund; introduced the departmental system of the faculty, and also in the early eighteenth century the division of labor among tutors, with the abandonment of the all-purpose tutor.[4]

In his history of Harvard, Quincy strongly supported the Harvard system. No better system could be devised in his view.

The Corporation consists of but a few persons; they can, therefore, assemble frequently and with facility for the transaction of business, either regular or occasional. The Board of Overseers, having a negative on the more important acts of the Corporation, is a large and popular body, a great majority of its members being such as are annually elected to places in the highest trust in the government by the people themselves. . . .

An overseers' committee in 1869 noted that the corporation being an administrative body was not inclined to initiate changes, unless evoked by enlightened public sentiment: "We, as a deliberative body, can take up, examine and discuss whatever seems to be for the advantage of the University, leaving to the Corporation to make such use of our conclusions as they may deem wise. . . ."[5]

Eliot was even more enthusiastic than Quincy over Harvard's administrative setup. In his inaugural address (October 19, 1869), Eliot said that "the real function of the Board of Overseers is to stimulate and watch the President and Fellows." The college profits from "the natural antagonism between two bodies of different constitution, powers, and privileges. . . ." In Eliot's view, the overseers "should always hold toward the Corporation an attitude of 'suspicious vigilance.' " They ought always to be pushing and prying. The overseers have been an antibody to the formidable inertia of a massive university.

Equally approving of the corporation, Eliot dwelt on its great powers, which could be wielded effectively if entrusted to a small and efficient body. Responsible for preserving the funds entrusted to the university, the corporation should include financial as well as humanistic talent. The actuating spirit of the corporation must be a "spirit of fidelity—fidelity to the many and various trusts reposed to them by the hundreds of persons who, out of their penury or their abundance, have given money. . .in the beautiful hope

4. Morison, *The Development of Harvard University*, pp. LXXIII-LXXVII.

5. *Report of the Board of Overseers on the Condition, Needs and Prospects of the University*, 1869; also see C. W. Eliot to F. W. Taussig, August 9, 1907; C. W. Eliot, *University Administration*, pp. 50-55, 58-61.

of doing some perpetual good upon this earth. . . ." According to Eliot, the corporation's powers are great, being responsible for funds, appointments, and the determination of salaries, and the corporation takes the initiative in all changes in the organic law of the university. Perhaps Eliot bestowed more authority on the corporation than it actually had by 1869.[6]

The Task of the President

An efficiently operated university also needs an able president. At Harvard, at least through its first two centuries, the president, sometimes able and sometimes not, did not allocate his energies well. The system required that he spend most of his time on disciplinary issues; on petty problems related to the plant, squables with faculty over pay and workloads, overseeing in detail all financial transactions, devotional services and the like; and begging for money. He had little time to think about important issues of education. In 1812 and again in the early 1820s, the governing boards sought to relieve the president of his "ministerial" responsibilities, and at least on paper greatly increased the presidents's authority over the faculty and generally over educational policy. There is not too much evidence that President Kirkland exploited this additional authority.[7]

Eliot was satisfied with the powers delegated to the president. The statue provided that the president was "to direct the official correspondence of the University; to acquaint himself with the state, interests and wants of the whole institution, and to exercise a general superintendence over all it concerns. . . ."[8]

Eliot was aware that the president should devote his time to the important issues: appointments of

tenure members, learning about the changing responsibilities of the university, heralding the contributions of the university, and seeking the help and cooperation of the schools. He also knew that he could be spared much by a systems of deans. He started with none and by the late 1890s had ten deans. It was also important to preside at faculty meetings. In his first year, Eliot presided at all thirty-four meetings of the corporation and seventeen of the overseers, and all forty-five faculty meetings of the college; and presided at forty-four meetings of forty-eight held at other schools. Thus, he learned about the men and problems and increased his authority.[9]

Neither Eliot nor Lowell was much concerned over the adequacy of his authority. Devoting full time to their tasks, they had a great advantage over the part-time members of the governing boards. Lowell was clear that the president should retain the initiative. "If he has the qualities he ought to possess, the members of the Board of Directors, who give only a part of their time to the concern, can hardly compete in initiative with him, and the permanent officials are essentially his subordinates, acting by, with and under him. . . ."[10]

According to the Statutes of 1826, the president was to inquire into the execution of the laws and to see that none "falls silently into disuse", and perform all such other powers and duties as the president has been accustomed to exercise and perform.[11]

President Eliot was more precise. By the end of his career, Eliot was aware of the great powers of the presidency. "He has much more power than an English head or any rector annually elected, and by usage he holds power for a long time. A good president is undubitably an effective promoter of University progress and influence, and a valuable unifying agent in a complex organization. . . ."

Among his detailed responsibilities are the provision of complete publicity on the financial condition

6. Morison, *The Development of Harvard University,* pp. LXXIII-LXXVI; C. W. Eliot, *University Administration,* pp. 4-5.
7. *Four Universities in the United States: An Historical Sketch of Harvard University,* 1895, p. 20; Quincy *op. cit.,* vol. II, pp. 333-335.
8. C. W. Eliot, *University Administration,* pp. 236-237.

9. James, *op. cit.,* vol. I, p. 243.
10. A. L. Lowell, *What a University President Has Learned,* 1938, p. 11; James, *op. cit.,* vol. II, p. 87.
11. *Statutes and Laws of the University in Cambridge in 1826,* p. 8.

of the university and its pecuniary needs; and he should make clear that the "University scrupulously respects in theory and practice the wishes of all givers, and makes the beneficent action of every endowment perpetual so far as human prudence and fidelity can go." The president should also see that the income is used correctly and frugally. A wise president must be on guard against rising outlays for materials and management as against those for direct teaching.[12]

Political Influence

If Harvard was to operate efficiently, it had to preserve its management by a small board and exclude political influence. There were many protests by Harvard that the state was excessively represented in the overseers; and it was not until 1865 that the present system of a board of overseers selected by alumni only was introduced.

S. A. Eliot wrote in 1846:

The spirit of political parties is the very worst incubus that can press upon the vital energy of a literary institution; and not even Harvard College, with all its resources. . .will succeed as it ought to succeed and might succeed, till the preponderances of state influences in its Councils is so far reduced that a mere politician shall never set his foot within her walls.[13]

In the 1850s a serious rift opened between the corporation of Harvard and the Commonwealth. Members of the Legislature sought to increase the number of fellows, the abandonment of selfperpetuation of fellows, to reduce terms to six years, and widen geographical origins. Harvard fortunately won this tussle and thus was able to continue as an efficiently run university.[14]

A special committee was appointed to investigate needed legislation "to render Harvard more beneficial to all the people of the Commonwealth." The committee was clear that the college "fails to accomplish what might reasonably be expected of it, from its early history, its great reputation, its central position, and when compared with other American institutions, its unequalled resources. . . ."[15] A major complaint of the committee was that the organization and modes of instruction remained what they had been twenty-five years before. But science and literature have become subordinate to business, a fact that the college does not recognize. ". . .It is believed that the instruction now given does not make better farmers, mechanics, or merchants. . . ." In short, the liberal arts curriculum of Harvard was a luxury in the view of the committee.[16]

The majority report of the committee sought an enlargement of the corporation, shorter terms, election by House and Senate representing all parts of the commonwealth. The committee would also reserve the right to alter the governement of the university.[17] The university fortunately won this fight.

Corporation vs Overseers

Perhaps the most spirited debate occurred at the same time. Here again the accepted way won out. The board of overseers challenged the corporation on a number of important fronts and especially on such issues as the right of the corporation to sell land, or accept donations, or invest funds without the approval of the board. Had the board won this struggle, the university could scarcely have continued to survive as an effective institution.[18] On donations, the overseers claimed that "when any one is upon a particular condition, or accompanied by a special trust, the vote of the acceptance of the Corporation is not

---

12. Especially *Charles W. Eliot: The Man and His Beliefs*, pp. 220-221; *Morison*, The Development of Harvard University, pp. LXXVI-LXXVII.

13. S. A. Eliot, *Harvard and Her Benefactors*, 1846, p. 18.

14. *House Report No. 164*, Commonwealth of Massachusetts, April 15, 1850, pp. 1-15.

15. *Ibid*, p.2.

16. *Ibid*, p.3.

17. *Ibid*, pp. 5-7.

18. *Report of the President and Fellows in Relation to the Board of Overseers*, 1856.

420

sufficient and complete until such vote is concurred in by the Overseers. . . ."

The overseers also claimed rights of confirmation of appointments, of establishement of new professorships or other offices, approval of tenure of officers, and of salaries.

In reply, the corporation wrote "if these views are correct, they [the overseers] possess substantially the whole control of the College, and have its management and interests entirely in their hands and at their will; and that the President and Fellows are nothing more than mere trustees. . . ."[19]

On the basis of the legislative acts establishing the boards and the operation under these, the corporation showed that the board of overseers was requesting powers not bestowed on them in the 1650 charter or later versions. By the 1650 charter the exercise of these powers was vested primarily in the corporation; and to that extent the grant of them to the overseers was annulled.[20]

Recent Issues

The country experienced in 1968-1969 a youthful revolution in the colleges and universities. Harvard shared in these uprisings which frequently stressed the need of a redistribution of governemental powers in higher education. Prof. Kenneth Galbraith was one of the first in the last few years to urge serious and fundamental changes in Harvard's government. Galbraith is one of the most imaginative professors on any campus. Above all, he seeks a reduction of the authority of the corporation and the inclusion in the corporation of fellows who are knowledgeable in the general area of education. Concentration of business men and lawyers in the corporation is distasteful to Galbraith, and to many others.

Over the last 320 years the government of Harvard, largely entrusted to the corporation, has been remarkably good. But Galbraith has a point. The corporation should include some members who are expert in the area of education. This does not mean that faculty members should be heavily represented in the corporation. Aside from the conflict of interests involved, large faculty representation would be costly. Student membership on the governing board does not seem a likely solution either, though their views on discipline, housing, curriculum, and the choice of faculty members sould be considered. It might be helpful to seek representation on the corporation of more young alumni.

19. *Ibid.* pp. 9-11.
20. *Ibid,* pp. 9-11.

54

Repercussions of Monetary Instability on Harvard's Economy

Scarcity of Money

Inadequate money and monetary instability plagued the New England economy in the first 150 years of its history. It should be noted that once a galloping inflation develops — as during the Revolutionary War and perhaps even in the second quarter of the eighteenth century, a genuine shortage of money prevails. Thus, if the supply of money rises by 10 times and prices by 20 times, the real value of total money falls by 50 percent. Shortage of monetary supplies retarded growth, with unfavorable effects on Harvard. The instability was also an adverse factor, for Harvard depended on tuition, interest, and rents fixed in New England pounds for a large part of its income. Unless the repayments were adjusted to the changing value of the pound or dollar, Harvard would suffer real losses.

In its earliest history, the disease was a scarcity of money no matter how defined. So scarce was the supply of money that the college had to accept "country pay," that is, such commodities as cattle and corn. The college experienced losses both because of the need of financing the transportation and storing of these items but also because of deterioration.

By the latter part of the seventeenth century the varying weights of silver coins were a cause of increasing trouble. Thus, on May 14, 1690, Harvard Treasurer Richards found that he had lost almost £4 on silver money that he had accepted. He admitted that he had received many coins lacking in weight perhaps as much as 10 to 25 percent. If he had paid the coins out he would have had to concede 6d on each of 108 pieces (legally worth 6s). To save time and trouble the treasurer sold the 108 pieces to Mr. Conry, the goldsmith.[1]

The Inflationary Problems

With primitive systems of taxation, monetary creation often had to be the main reliance of the government for paying its bills. The recourse to paper money was especially strong in periods of insecurity, e.g., King Phillip's War, the struggles with the French in the first half of the eighteenth century, and of course the Revolutionary War. The government would issue currency, with promises to redeem with tax receipts in the near future. But tax receipts were not forthcoming and hence redemption would be postponed. Even payment of interest on issues helped little for the rate of depreciation would greatly exceed that of the 4 to 6 percent interest on notes.

A large debtor class also contributed to the penchant for manufacturing money. Solid citizens tried to discourage issues, both by direct pressure on the government to contain issues, and also by requiring debtors to pay in current money an amount equal in real value of loan at time of borrowing. In March, 1780, bills of credit were circulating at one-fortieth

---

1. Foster, *op. cit.*, pp. 24-25.

of their nominal value. By May, 1781, paper money (old tenor) had sunk to $\frac{1}{500}$ of hard money.[2]

An indication of the college problems can be had from the price trends during periods of stress. Despite strong measures to increase receipts as prices rose, college income did not keep up with the inflation. Students, in particular, paid in depreciating currency.

Nevertheless, receipts rose greatly: college rents which provided £258 in 1778 yielded £16,528 in 1781; and assessments on students £1,252 and £52,048 respectively in 1781.[3] But the rise of receipts seemed to be about one-tenth the needed increase to match the inflation.

Protecting Against Inflation

With a serious inflation in the first half of the eighteenth century and especially in the second quarter, the college in making loans (purchasing bonds) or renting lands frequently tied the transactions to the weight of silver at the time of the contract. If the price of silver in New England pounds rose the debtor would have to increase payments correspondingly. Here was an early experience with adjustments of debt repayment to the changing value of the money in circulation.

An example of such contract follows.
Feb. 10, 1773.

Know All men By thefe Prefents we Elifabeth Wardfworth of Framingham Spinfter Henry Seger of said Framingham and Mofes Rice of Natick yeomen all in the County of Middlefex, in the Province of the Mafsachufets Bay &, – are Holden and stand firmly bound unto Thomas Hubbard Efq of Bofton in the County of Suffolk in the Province above said

Treafurer of Harvard Colledge and his succefsors in said office In the full and Juft Sum of one hundred pounds in Silver money at Six Shillings and eight pence p.ʳ ounce. . . .[4]

Whereas Harvard, the creditor, sought to protect itself against receipt of a depreciating currency, the government tended to seek protection for the debtor by allowing him to pay in paper currency. Thus, in 1712, an act had been processed to prevent the oppression of debtors by making old tenor legal tender.

But with rising prices, the sentiment in favor of a depreciation table that would protect the creditor increased. In 1741, the government introduced a complicated adjustment which would to some extent protect the creditor.[5]

Currency Fluctuations

Fluctuations in the value of lawful currency plagued the college. Inadequate revenue sources and, especially in war times, resultant dependence on bills of credit (paper money) greatly disturbed the economy and the college.

Another contribution to instability stemmed from variations in the cost of the British pounds in New England pounds, a matter of some importance since trade with England was substantial, and in the pre-Revolutionary period English donors provided large sums of money to Harvard which had to be exchanged for New England pounds. Any tendency for the New England pound to depreciate meant a bounty for the college, for a given amount of English pounds yielded increasing New England pounds — a favorable outcome only in so far as costs did not rise correspondingly. The rise in the value of pounds vis-à-vis the New England pound was not large until the eighteenth century though there had been a rise in English pound by 1654. In the great inflations of the eighteenth century the price of pounds rose in

2. See A. M. Davis, "The Investments of Harvard College, 1776-1790", in *Quarterly Journal of Economics,* May, 1906, pp. 406-407; J. Felt, *Historical Account of Massachusetts Currency,* 1839; A. M. Davis, *Currency and Banking in the Province of Massachusetts Bay,* 1900; C. J. Bullock, *Essays in the Monetary History of the United States,* 1900.
3. A. M. Davis, *op. cit.,* pp. 408-409.

4. Contract of Wardsworth, Seger and Rice, with Treasurer Thomas Hubbard, February 10, 1773.
5. A. M. Davis, *op. cit.,* 1960, ch. IX.

terms of New England pounds even as the price of an ounce of silver increased. The variations in the price of an ounce of silver expressed in New England pounds is given below. The price of the English pound in an ounce of silver was stabilized and hence, the cost of silver and the English pound in New England pounds rose *pari passu*. But once the famous devaluation of the New England pound of 1750 occurred, (an exchange of $7\frac{1}{2}$ old tenor for 1 of new), then the pound became relatively stabilized at £1.33 New England to £1 English; and also £1 New England to $3.33.[6]

Repercussions of Inflation and Devaluation on Harvard

At a meeting of the president and fellows of Harvard College March 28, 1750, the college declared:

The former Exhibition which have been made as in pag . . . are to be looked upon as Province Bills which have been . . . called and are now so OLD TENOUR of which there is now an End, According to Province Law and which is in Proportion to the Silver Money and Dollars now passing as 6. to 45, i.e., as $7\frac{1}{2}$ to one. And all the Summs hereafter in this book mentioned are to be taken as Silver Money in the above Proportion to s^d old Tenr.[7]

As indicated above, the Harvard treasury protected the college against the inflation much better than more recent administrations. Treasurer Hutchinson required payments in equivalent weight of silver. Should the price of silver in lawful money double, then the debtor was required to pay back twice as many bills of credit. But the college was not as effectively protected against repayment of debts, i.e., investments of the college which had not a specie

clause. Omission of such clauses was likely when the currency was stable, as it largely was in the twenty-five years preceding the Revolution.

With the Revolutionary War, local currency once more began to depreciate. The premium on gold and silver rose to 75 percent in September, 1777 and to 3,900 percent in March, 1780. An indication of the depreciation was the yield in Colonial currency of French bills of credit: December, 1778, 4 to 1; December, 1799, 24 to 1; March, 1781, 56 to 1.

In what way did the great inflations of the first half of the eighteenth century and of the years of the Revolution affect Harvard's finances? The adverse effects were treated to some extent by the requirements that debtors repay on the basis of an equivalent value in silver. The assumption here is that silver's purchasing power was stable. Indeed, this may not have necessarily been so, and prices reduced to a metallic basis tended upward in the last quarter of the eighteenth century.

That the Harvard lending techniques helped is suggested by the rise of endowment income as a percentage of total income from 37 percent between 1722 and 1732 to 52 percent between 1742 and 1752, a period during which the price of an ounce of silver rose from 19s to 40s. Had payment in New England pound bills of credit been required, the relative income from endowment would clearly have fallen. In fact, in Colonial currency, endowment yielded twice as much during a twenty-year period of substantial inflation.

But even this policy was not entirely successful, a conclusion supported by the fact that in the decade 1742 to 1752 total income and endowment income both rose only around one-half even as the price of silver doubled. Hence, despite the advanced lending techniques, the college experienced a decline in real income during this period, and this despite any increases of gifts. A fall in enrollment of about one-third may be relevant here, a loss not entirely unrelated to the price history.

As has generally been true in Harvard's history, financial developments were more satisfactory in years of relative price stability, e.g., 1752 to 1771,

---

6. Loans by Treasurer Hutchinson on behalf of Harvard were based on return of currency yielding a weight of silver equal to that which had been advanced. The assumed value of an ounce of silver is given. See table deposited in the Harvard University Archives.

7. *College Books*, vol. IV, p. 310; *Corporation Records*, vol. I, p. 497; *Publications of the Colonial Society of Massachusetts*, vol. 16, p. 816.

than in inflationary periods. Endowment income declined by about one-half and all income by about one-third in these years, but in currency units greatly enhanced in value after an 87 percent devaluation. The relative contribution of endowment dropped by one-half, a rise of enrollment of three-quarters (and hence, increased payments by students) contributing to this outcome.

During the Revolutionary War, the real value of income and endowment dropped greatly, the absolute rise being but a fraction of the increase in the price of silver, and the unsatisfactory conditions continued into the years 1781 to 1793.[8]

A good example of the adjustment to inflation is given in the transaction, quoted above, during the incumbency of Treasurer Edward Hutchinson. Not only the capital but also the interest was subject to adjustment as the price of silver in bills of credit (money) rose.

As can be seen from the August 10, 1725 entry, Hutchinson treated the actual and impending inflation through issuing bonds (loans) not for a value in money but in so many ounces of silver. As inflation became serious, upon issuing a bond, the college usually stated the obligation in weight of silver, and not only the capital sum but also interest payments ·were tied to the rising price of silver in relation to bills of credit.

A loan of £72 at 6 percent should yield £46s 6d. But in the years 1744, 1746, 1749, 1751, the charge for interest was £8 17s, £10 12s, £14 and £12 5s, the rises reflecting the reduced value of paper money per ounce of silver. A final item is payment in full of £126 5s, part of which is the original loan, and the remainder is compensation for inflation on both interest and loan.[9]

The New England pound declined in value vis-á-vis pounds sterling:

Value of Pounds Sterling in New England Pounds

1641	£ 1
1652	1.20
1654	1.33
1705-1710	1.55
1728	3.40
1749	11.00

Source: Foster, *op. cit.*, p. 43.

This depreciation of the New England pound vis-á-vis pounds sterling probably improved the economic condition of the college, for each pound sterling received in England — and in the Puritan period the British gifts and bequests were large, and substantial donations and legacies from England continued through the first half of the eighteenth century — the college would convert the pound sterling into New England pounds, reflecting the premium on British pound sterling. When the value of the pound sterling rose to equal £2 New England, a gift of £100 would yield £200 New England. If prices had increased correspondingly in Massachusetts there would have been no gains. But though prices rose, and especially in the first half of the eighteenth century, there is no evidence to suggest that prices rose nearly as much as pounds sterling.

Devaluation of assets was frequently required as a result of monetary revaluation. In 1766, the college recognized the earlier revaluation by writing down

8. For income during the eighteenth century see especially *Treasurers' Journals; Treasurers' Ledgers; Acts and Resolves of the Province of Massachusetts Bay; Acts and Laws of the Commonwealth of Massachusetts; Stewards' Quarter Bill Books.* For the price of silver and or pounds sterling and exchange ratios of old and new tenor, price of bills of finance, see Hutchinson, *Treasurers' Ledgers* and *Report of the Treasurer of Harvard College; Treasurer's Collected Papers,* 1692-1721; 1736-1755; *Corporation Records,* vol. I, pp. 399, 401, 423, 1742; *Treasurers' Journals,* 1755-1775, p. 2; *Treasurers' Journals* and *Treasurers' Ledgers,* 1778-1782; A. H. Cole, *Wholesale Commodity Prices in the United States,* 1700-1861, p. 119; D. Dewey, *Financial History of the United States,* p. 40; Foster, *op. cit.,* p. 43; Davis, *op. cit.;* Bullock, *op. cit.;* Felt, *op. cit.*

9. *Treasurers' Journals; Treasurers' Ledgers,* various issues, 1725, 1729, 1743, 1744, 1746, 1749, 1751-1753.

the value of its college buttery from £74 11s 4d to £9 8s 10d.[10] It was necessary to reduce the value of the college's stock (roughly investments) by four-fifths, a reduction less than that of the old tenor.[11]

Through most of the inflationary periods of the eighteenth century the college was aware of the losses accruing to a creditor. In April, 1729, the corporation requested the advice of the overseers on methods of avoiding the further sinking of the college stock, which lay in bonds payable in bills of public credit, that is, in loans payable in a depreciating currency. From 1731 to 1735, Hutchinson's loans were tied to ounces of silver, not to currency.

The advanced theories held then are suggested by a contract given to a minister in Ipswich in 1747: He was guaranteed an income which would buy a specified quantity of sixteen commodities, e.g., 15 bushel barrels of cider, 110 pounds of candles, 170 pounds of butter, 600 pounds of beef, and 8 gallons of Madeira wine.

In 1781, Treasurer Ebenezer Storer advanced some loans, with capital and interest payable in a silver equivalent. Andrew Bordman, the college steward, in return for the use of land in 1779, promised to pay the college annually "one Spanish mill'd Dollar, or the value thereof in Continental Currency in proportion to the difference between Silver and Paper according to the most equitable [determination]." Yet despite these precautions, the college, according to one expert, had lost the large sum of £10,000 as a result of the repayment of loans in the 1740s in highly depreciated currencies.[12] This occurred despite the fact that during a good part of the eighteenth century solid citizens sought measures to force debtors to repay on the basis of values of currency at time of borrowing.

10. *Harvard College Papers Supplement*, 1766, p. 17.
11. A. M. Davis, *op. cit.*, p. 400.
12. *Corporation Records*, vol. I, p. 243, 1729; *Treasurers' Ledgers*, 1781; Shipton, *Shipley's Harvard Graduates*, vol. IX, p. 456; C. J. Bullock, *op. cit.*, pp. 40-41; *College Books*, vol. III, p. 128, 1779; *Publications of the Colonial Society of Massachusetts*, vol. XV, p. 303.
13. A Memorial signed John Winthrop et als, November 13, 1781.

The Revolutionary War Inflation

In the Revolutionary period occurred one of the great inflations of all time up to World War I. Effects on supplies were disastrous. Governments issued forty separate emissions totaling $450 million. At the Continental Congress a devaluation at a rate of 40 to 1 was established.

New England Pounds for 1 Spanish Milled Dollar

March 1, 1778 . . . . 1.75
September 1, 1778 . . . . 4.00
March 1, 1779 . . . . .18.00
March 1, 1780 . . . . .40.00

Source: D. Dewey, *op. cit.*, p. 40

Such depreciation raised vexing problems for the college. On May 9, 1780, the corporation decreed an exchange rate of 60 to 1, that is, 60 current currency units would be accepted for 1 hard currency unit. On June 8, 1781, the corporation demanded one-quarter in silver and the remainder in paper bills of the new emission at 3 to 1, the balance for the fourth quarter to be calculated at 75 to 1 and be reduced to hard money. Harvard cleared its books of the depreciated currency at 75 to 1. On July 26, 1781, the corporation ordered the steward to receive no more paper money. The steward asked for payment in metal for wood, and urged all payments in the college in the equivalent of metals. Thus, college employees and faculty members would be protected.

At one point the students complained bitterly that the grants to the faculty were less than the assessments on students. But the reply of the corporation was that grants were made prior to assessments on students. By the time students paid, depreciation had advanced so much that assessments were much less than faculty grants.[13]

Problems for faculty members were serious indeed. Despite these attempts to adjust receipts to the depreciation, the college was unable to adjust pay of its faculty to the rising prices.

As inflation proceeded, the college steward found himself in increasing difficulties. In 1781, he commented on a rise in the price of provisions from 25 to 100 percent in one month in paper of the new emissions, and on the unwillingness of sellers to accept paper money. He now demanded hard money and would pay his help in hard money!

Foreman, 4s per day.

Second man, 72s per calendar month.

The women, 12s per week.

The steward then pointed out that the proposed pay for help was to rise less than the price of commodities.[14]

Capital Losses

As depreciation advanced, the college lost much of its capital, and despite the attempts to insert specie clauses into contracts with debtors. The college had no way of protecting itself against repayment in a depreciating currency on contracts without protective clauses.

Once new tenor money was issued, the college had to take account of the devaluation of the old money. Treasurer T. Hubbard in presenting his first account in April, 1755, "put down the capital sum at only one-fifth of the nominal sums originally given in consequence of the College funds having sunk for a number of years antecedent to 1750, by the depreciation of the paper currency."

In the post-Revolutionary years Harvard authorities estimated losses of capital at varying amounts. But that they were substantial is clear.

Losses of capital were bound to prevail as the college received payments from students and debtors in a steadily depreciating currency. The bonds available to the college amounted to £20,071 in September,

1777. But by June, 1782, there had been a loss of £8,336. [15] President Willard reported in 1787:

In 1777, after deducting the appropriated stock there remained the sum of £11,078, 3, 4 in solid specie. . . But at the present time . . . the real value falls short of appropriations £2,624, 2, 10, which makes a clear loss to the College of £13,702, 6, 2, . . . the stock if it had been left in its original state would have enabled them to have swelled to at least four times the present appearance. . . .

The president then commented also on the loss of interest.[16]

In 1786, the college had estimated the loss from depreciation as follows:

The college received £17,875 in paper. On the basis of the official scale of depreciating this amounted to £8,568 ". . . in cash. . . to no more at the highest computation than £2,570 so that it has lost the sum of £15,304,17." If used to purchase public securities, they could be had for £2,570 "so that they have clearly sunk $\frac{3}{5}$ of their capital." The college had received £17,875 in lieu of metals. The value at the official rate of depreciation was but £2,570, and hence the loss was £15,304 (£17,875 minus £2,570).

For 1787, one investigation found the investments in public securities worth only one-eighth of the consolidated value, or about one-twentieth of the cost price in the depreciated currency.[17]

The present unappropriated stock was held to be nonproductive.[18]

Even as late as 1791, the college still seemed to have lost a large part of its capital and largely because of repayment of loans in a depreciating currency, and further losses in so far as the received currency were held and depreciated further or in so far as the public securities purchased declined in value.

14. C. Garrett to the Honorable and Reverend Corporation of Harvard College, 1781.

15. In Obedience to the Orders of the Hon. House of Representatives, the Treasurer of Harvard College submits State of the Funds, 1782.

16. Joseph Willard, To the Honourable Senator and Honourable House of Representatives in General Court Assembled, January, 1787.

17. Queries from a Committee of the General Court Respecting the College. . . June 1, 1786; A. M. Davis, *op. cit.*, pp. 414-415.

18. Quincy, *op. cit.*, vol. II, pp. 236-245; Memorandum, January 1791 to the Court, cf. A. M. Davis, *op. cit.*, pp. 414-415.

Purchase of Public Securities

But the college was saved by a fortunate speculation. In 1777, the corporation voted "to invest all future funds in Continental Loan Office Certificates or in Massachusetts Treasury notes." It was considered a wise policy to "invest in the most substantial of all the shadowy forms in which the currency appeared."

Harvard's decision to invest in Continental State Loan certificates and then state notes proved a fortunate gamble. The theory behind this move was that the government would more likely protect its securities than its paper money. Once the issues of paper currency stopped it appeared that the stock (capital) of the college had been reduced by one-half or more, an outcome suggesting the limited success of the policy of forcing borrowers to pay more in proportion to price rises. Clearly, the government had not provided adequate protection to lenders. But by strict economy and purchase of public stock, the loss was made up. In 1791, the government stock was worth £30,887; by 1793, $142,900; and by 1807, $175,358.

Hamilton's funding act had saved the college, though as late as 1787 the treasurer was not sure that they had done so well.

From an inspection of the college books it will appear, that, since the paper currency stopped, the college has made great profits and a large addition to its stock, but these profits are perhaps merely imaginary *as they chiefly, if not wholly, arise from having purchased public securities at a large discount, which with the interest due on them are estimated in the books at the nominal value, and time only can discover whether these are profits or not, but if these securities are estimated at the present current value, the whole college stock would not make good the appropriations, as fully appears by the act prepared to lay before the court by their order the next session.*[19]

By 1793, Treasurer Storer could boast that the whole personal estate of Harvard amounted to over $182,000, of which $100,000 was not tied to specific objects (cf., the $55,000 estate of 1777). This unrestricted value seems very high in view of the restricted feature of most gifts and bequests. I can only explain it on the theory that the large capital gains associated with the war and early postwar investment policy were not credited to the various accounts. Harvard mobilized these gains for nonrestrictive purposes. In support of this position, I count thirty-nine gifts and legacies of a restrictive type from the founding of Harvard College to 1783 and seven of a nonrestrictive type.[20]

Later Inflations

Harvard experienced difficulties in at least three other inflationary periods, namely, during the Civil War, the steady rise of prices beginning in the 1890s and continuing through World War I, and during World War II and the Korean War. For some unaccountable reason, the large inflation in the Civil War seemed to cause no great damage, possibly because the rise of prices was only about 70 percent from 1860 to 1866—a small rise compared to that in the Revolutionary War period—or possibly because the choices of investments were adjusted to a rising price level, or possibly because prices began to fall in 1866, dropping 20 percent by 1873, and to the 1860 level by 1894.

The price increase from 1896 to 1920 was another matter. Prices more than doubled. The authorities had not yet learned to invest heavily in equities as a means of keeping up with inflationary prices. The cost of such untreated inflation was a serious deterioration in the standard of living of the faculty, a problem discussed earlier in this book. Finally, in 1919, a record endowment drive helped recapture some of the losses experienced by the faculty. In this period, not only did faculty members' salaries not respond to

19. Davis, *op. cit.,* p. 418; Memorandum. . . Storer's Three Ledgers: see Treasurer, Ledger A, p. 76, 1787.
20. Compiled from *Endowment Funds of Harvard University.*

rising prices, but the failure to adjust tuition to the rising price level and introduce an investment policy that would recoup some of the losses all made the inflation costly indeed.

The inflation from 1940 to the 1950s also hurt the university. Faculty salaries in dollars of stable purchasing power declined seriously and the losses were even greater when comparison was made with the rising real per capita income of the nation. By 1965, however, Harvard salaries were at least back to the level of pre-World War II when corrected for price rises. This was achieved by a growing tendency to invest in equities which provided an offset to inflation and the large endowment drive of the late 1950s. Again, however, the corporation had failed to adjust tuition adequately before the Pusey-Bundy period.

55

The Economics of the Curriculum

Over the first two hundred years of Harvard's history the curriculum was restricted and the costs correspondingly low. The curriculum primarily consisted of instruction in Latin and Greek, mathematics, and natural philosophy. It was not until the 1820s that the teaching of modern languages was introduced; and though at the same time the first endowed chair in history in the country was created, the teaching of history was minimal. One instructor taught history, ethics, and German in 1826—at a salary of $500.[1]

Even as late as 1856, the concentration was on the classics, with the result that most students graduated unable to use the English language.[2]

In 1827, just following the first experiments with the elective system, the number of hours of instruction was 441 to 444 hours in each of three of these fields and 324 in natural philosophy, with about one-seventh of the hours in these four fields voluntary.

At this time the professor of mathematics and natural philosophy protested the allocation of manpower. He demonstrated that taking account of preparation, discussions with students, and classroom hours, a Latin and Greek teacher was being treated much more generously than the mathematics faculty. The corporation seemed to agree, but reminded the professor of mathematics that the university was in the midst of a great financial crisis.[3]

Mathematics faculty members continued to be sensitive on this issue. In 1850, Prof. Joseph Lovering disputed a report that mathematics was the most costly instructional field. The following evidence was adduced:

Table 55-1.
Cost of Teaching in Different Departments, 1850

	Cost	Number of Students	Cost per Student
Latin	$2,645	189	$14.00
Greek	2,645	203	13.00
Modern languages	3,300	166	19.88
Mathematics and natural philosophy	4,545	281	16.17

Source: J. Lovering to President Sparks, February 5, 1850.

1. Remarks by C. W. Eliot at Meeting of Modern Language Association, December 26, 1901.
2. C. F. Adams, *Three Phi Beta Kappa Addresses.*

3. J. Farrar to the President, January 7, 1827.

The claim that mathematics teaching was more troublesome than the classics was supported by a petition of twenty-three sophomores in 1853 who would make mathematics an elective study.

... Most members of the said class, either from natural inability to acquire, or from other defects as some may call the causes of disinclination to mathematical science, have failed to reap any benefit ... supposed to proceed from the study of that department of science .... [4]

The Relevance of the Elective System

The advance of the elective system was bound to raise financial issues. Eliot, its most staunch innovator and defender, readily admitted that the elective system was very expensive compared to the cost of the restricted curriculum of Harvard's first two centuries.

That the college could accept the elective system despite its large costs is to be explained first by the uneven advance of the system—there were steps backward from 1845 to 1866 when large elements of the faculty were unsympathetic—and second, by the great economic advances of the Eliot period that made possible its financing.

It was clear that opposition was strong in the 1840s. Indeed, in 1849, an overseers' committee boasted that the course of instruction:

... includes not only those subjects which were formally deemed sufficient for a liberal education, but meets wants which are created by the prodigious enlargement of science and the arts, and adds an indefinite extent of labor under the comprehensive title of Modern Languages. [5]

An 1850 committee was very critical of the elective system: "It creates confusion and inconvenience ...." Oddly enough, at about the same time the state government attacked the college for not changing to meet the needs of an evolving society:

... Their organization and mode of instruction are, in many respects, what they were twenty-five years ago, or at any rate, are not sufficiently in accordance with the opinions of the people; while in the meantime, the business and literature of the world, the relation of man to man have undergone great changes ... while there are men who desire general learning for its own sake, there are others who seek specific learning for a specific purpose. .... [6]

This clearly was a call for electives.

Eliot's Contribution

Eliot was the creator of the modern elective system. "Any demand for instruction should be accepted," wrote Eliot, "and every kind of teaching: Recitations, lectures by the professor, individual instruction in laboratories, written exercies in great variety, observation in the field, beside study for medicine and surgery ...and the elaborate thesis ...conferences and seminars. ...." Above all, Eliot wanted students to study what interested them; what could exploit their innate abilities. The result would be greater gains from education both for the student and the teacher.

Here Eliot was in agreement with the legislators, who in 1850 protested against the excessive attention given to the old liberal arts subjects and the neglect of the more modern developments in science and subjects the study of which would help provide a livelihood. This neglect, which Eliot sensed, helped bring on the state universities with their adverse effects on the economic condition of Harvard and other institutions of higher learning.

The Costs of the Elective System

That the costs would be large, given Eliot's ambitious program for elective studies, is clear indeed. Although the elective system by 1870 had forty-five years

---

4. Petition of the Subscribers of a Large Majority of the Sophomore Class, December, 1853.

5. Report of the Committee of Overseers of Harvard College Appointed to Visit the University in 1849.

6. Commonwealth of Massachusetts, *House Report No. 164 on Harvard University*, April, 1950.

behind it, the curriculum still was largely mathematics, Greek, Latin, philosophy, and modern languages. History and chemistry were beginning to make an impression.

Expansion of the staff reflected the great advance of the elective system. From 1869 to 1909, teachers of professorial grade had increased from 45 to 194, or a rise of 331 percent. Other teachers and research fellows expanded from 14 to 416, or about 29 times. The student-professional faculty ratio dropped from 23 to 1 to 20 to 1. Allowances for the increase of the junior faculty would greatly reduce this ratio. Above all, the improvement of the student-teacher ratio is explained by the rise in the number of courses and corresponding increase in faculty.

By the early twentieth century, the number of courses had risen to 228 full courses and 192 half courses. An indication of the extent of expansion is given by the table from the president's report for 1902-1903. By this time there were thirty-three departments. The hours of instruction by the early twentieth century were about a thousand. This total should be compared with about ninety hours of instruction fifty years earlier.[7]

Eliot continued the support of the system despite vigorous criticism. He did not conceal the costs though he argued that all additions to costs should not be put on the elective system. Instruction to small groups would have expanded even without the elective system. In graduate work, which he showed to be very expensive, the elective system necessarily prevailed.[8]

Yet Eliot did not go all the way. Departments had to convince him of needs of new courses. And when a professor of paleontology offered his resignation, Eliot did not allow himself the luxury of retaining a faculty man in a field that was not widely pursued.

The subject of Paleontology has been, and probably will continue to be one which inevitably attracts only a small number of students, and is therefore, one which the University can cease to teach with comparatively little injury to the mass of its students. Such considerations would not be legitimate if the resources of the University were adequate to its expenditures . . . .[9]

By 1885 Eliot pointed out that the free-elective institution of higher learning could easily get by with twenty teachers. But at Harvard there were eighty teachers exclusive of laboratory assistants. These eighty teachers provided about 425 hours of instruction. A diligent student would need forty years to cover this curriculum.[10]

Henry Adams, discussing the Harvard of Eliot's early days, commented on the sterility of large lectures and the high costs of instruction of small groups; and especially since it was so difficult to get conversation out of his students. Henry Adams might well be considered as sympathetic with Eliot's views on education.

Even Eliot had to move slowly at times when financial problems emerged. And despite his views about electives and small but numerous classes, he had to warn his faculty to watch courses with small numbers. Even by the end of the nineteenth century the system was not complete. But it is interesting to compare the 1897-1898 salary budget with that of 1850.

The four old departments inclusive of modern languages included 10 faculty members in 1850 and salaries of a little more than $10,000. By 1897-1898 there were 52 faculty members in these departments and salaries of $96,000. These departments were still well supported at the end of the nineteenth century. But there were by 1897-1898 nineteen departments that had not been in operation in a serious way in 1850. These departments' — eight of them small — had 161 faculty members and a salary bill of almost $240,000. The college had grown greatly both in fields covered and the intensity of coverage.

7. See tables deposited in the Harvard University Archives on staff and students, 1868-1869 to 1908-1909 and also one giving courses by department, 1902-1903.

8. *C. W. Eliot, The Man and His Beliefs,* pp. 134-135, 158-159.

9. C. W. Eliot to Professor Robert T. Jackson, May 14, 1909.

10. C. W. Eliot, *Liberty in Education,* 1885, p. 126.

At this time Harvard's great philosophy team of James, Palmer, Royce, Santayana, and Munsterberg had been assembled. Their total salary was in excess of $19,000, the cost of the average Harvard faculty member in the year 1967. James and Palmer each received $5,000, the maximum Harvard salary late in the nineteenth century.

Elective System Not Alone Responsible

It would be a great mistake to concentrate on the elective system as the explanation of rising costs of the Harvard budget. Even as early as 1825 the faculty was seeking college subsidies for research; and as the demands for teaching hours increased the senior faculty sought relief through hiring of teaching and laboratory assistants. In so far as the elective system contributed to the evolution of the teaching assistant, then the incidence of rising costs is again associated with the elective system.

There are many other factors to take into account. By 1850, Professor Cooke had introduced the scientific laboratory; and as interest in science quickened—and here again in part because of the advance of the elective system—costs of higher education would rise. Associated with this source of rising expenditures was the general shortage of philosophical apparatus or teaching aids that had to be treated. A shift of emphasis from the recitation to the lecture also contributed to the rise of costs, though ordinarily lecturing is an economical manner of teaching. But in the wake of the lecture came the supplements to lectures—section meetings, quizzes, and laboratory assistants, and also greater demands on the library as the deflation of the recitation brought wider use of books that had to be provided by the library. It is well to remember that faculty salaries are only one element in costs, though much larger relatively in 1850 or 1870 than today.[11]

As prices and incomes rose, costs of instruction and other costs responded. A comparison of the rate of rise of expenditures under Eliot and Lowell would elicit the suggestion that since costs rose much more per year under Lowell than under Eliot, and since the major gains of the elective system had occurred under Eliot, other causes were also relevant.

Aside from the increase in prices and income, the gains of enrollment were important. Despite Lowell's great interest in the college, it was under Lowell that the largest advances in graduate enrollment prevailed. Lowell also departed from the Eliot objectives and spending pattern. It is well to recall the beginning of the Lowell inaugural address:

Among his other wise sayings, Aristotle remarked that man is by nature a social animal; and it is in order to develop his powers as a social animal that American Colleges exist. The object of the Undergraduate department is not to produce hermits each imprisoned in the cell of his own intellectual pursuits, but men fitted to take their places in the community and live in contact with their fellow men . . . .[12]

Here indeed was a theory of education sympathetically endorsed by Harvard's founders. But Eliot could not have cared less for this approach to education. Under Eliot, what mattered was the intellectual qualities of students and the faculty. By adopting his social theory Lowell mobilized resources for the freshmen dormitories, the House Plan, and the tutorial system. His spending pattern also diverged from the Eliot model. Lowell was, of course, committed to the elective system. But expansion was to be in other directions.

The Scientific Revolution

We have already adumbrated at Eliot's great interest in science. If science were to be taught in the face of the opposition of the traditionalists, it was necessary to impose the elective system as a technique in part for assuring adequate attention to science.

---

11. *Report of the President of Harvard College*, 1902-1903, p. 11; *Financial Report to the Board of Overseers of Harvard College*, 1965-1966.

12. Morison, *The Development of Harvard University*, p. LXXIX.

Even before Eliot's administration, concern for scientific education at Harvard had greatly increased. As early as 1838 Harvard's great mathematician, Prof. B. Peirce, revealed an interest in supporting mathematical instruction along new lines, thus enlisting the support of the student and in some ways anticipating Eliot's views.[13]

Teaching in the sciences was greatly to increase the burden of the elective system. The scientific method was costly. Moreover, the philosophic apparatus was most inadequate. For acoustics taught for one semester in 1846, for example, the "college possesses not one solitary article of apparatus for the instruction." Professor Lovering modestly asked for $500 for addational apparatus.[14]

Trends in Courses and Departments

An excessive number of courses has been a disease of higher education for many years. As courses multiply the costs of higher education escalate, not only because the number of courses rises but also because the increase tends to be more and more of small, and hence costly, courses. The tremendous expansion of courses at Harvard is explained in part by the large rise of graduate courses. These are especially expensive because they are given by the high-priced professor to a relatively small number of students. By the year 1900-1901 graduate courses accounted for 104 of 229 courses or 45 percent of the total. By 1925-1926, graduate courses were 49 percent of the total; and in 1963-1964, 47 percent, and if reading and research courses are included, 65 percent. It is no wonder that estimates of the costs of education per semester hour point to ratios of 1 to 2 to 6 for (1) freshmen and sophomores, (2) juniors and seniors, and (3) graduate students respectively.

---

13. B. Peirce to President Quincy, May 15, 1838.
14. Peirce, *Plan of a School of Practical and Theoretical Science,* February 27, 1846; J. P. Cooke to C. W. Eliot, June 27, 1871; Thwing, *op. cit.,* p. 19; J. Lovering to the President, September 26, 1846.

The number of faculty members rises more than enrollment and the major rises in courses stem from the graduate sector. In fact, undergraduate courses between 1902 and 1957 increased in numbers less than the enrollment of undergraduates.

From two tables which have been deposited in the Harvard Archives we find that even as early as 1868-1869, before Eliot's great expansion of electives, the number of courses was indeed large compared to those in the early nineteenth century, when there were four departments. By 1902-1903, the number of departments had grown to thirty-three and the number of courses had increased to 425.

Beginning with 1825-1826, I have assembled the facts on the curriculum and the faculty over a period of 140 years. Surprisingly, the relationship of faculty to numbers of courses did not change greatly. In this period the number of departments rose from eight to thirty-four. Of some significance are the areas where expansion and contraction prevailed. That expansion was large in the social sciences, which it will be recalled involve the largest cost per tenure members, and the losses large in languages inclusive of classics, where costs per tenure member are low, points to a costly restructuring of courses.

Over this period of about 140 years the relative number of courses in the sciences and philosophy did not change greatly but classics, with a decline from 39 to 3 percent, and grammer and rhetoic experienced great losses. Modern languages lost ground until 1929-1930, but with the rising needs for language instruction associated with the troublesome international situation, there was a substantial rise in the 35 years, 1930 to 1965. History became an important factor in the curriculum by 1850 and government by 1900. The other social sciences experienced large absolute and relative growth in the years since 1900. The miscellaneous group, largely humanities, e.g., music, fine arts and architecture, and the military disciplines were of some importance in the nineteenth century.

An examination of the departments offering the largest number of courses shows a trend away from the classics and mathematics to the social sciences,

Table 55-2.
Courses per Faculty Member and Number of Departments,
Arts & Sciences

	Courses per Faculty Member	Number of Departments
1825	1.6	8
1850	1.7	12
1900	1.9	25
1929	1.2	35
1963	1.5 (2.3 if Reading and Research Courses are Included)	34

Sources: *Harvard University Catalogue; Report of the President of Harvard College,* relevant years.

inclusive of history and engineering, and applied science.

In Conclusion

The penchant for the elective system stemmed from the explosion of knowledge and from the theory that the university had a responsibility to preserve knowledge in all fields, old and new. The theory of similar tastes and capacity of all students and identical programs to give the A.B. any meaning had to be abandoned for the theory of varying abilities and interest. The elective system was thought to bring great advances in the level of instruction and of knowledge; especially since students were thought to be capable of choosing among courses with judgment.[15] Eliot even argued that the explosion of knowledge and advance of instructional methods had gone so far that of the 200 courses taught late in the nineteenth century, even 20 could not have been taught at the beginning of the nineteenth century with the old methods and materials.

Lowell was critical of the elective system:

. . . .*The catalogue of 1888-1889 contained 140 courses; that of 1908-1909, 333 courses, counting towards a Bachelor's degree. With such wide choice the sporting element, materially guided by their fond widow, would cull sixteen choice flowers (mostly numbered 1) from such related subjects as Egyptoloty, Engineering, Anthropology, Fine Arts, Zoology, Social Ethics and all literature courses from Semitic to Slavic that required no knowledge of any language* . . . .[16]

One of the great obstacles to the growth of the elective system was the high cost involved. From the very beginning this objection received much attention. Even Eliot in 1875 allowd that the program could not be pushed to its logical extension so long as financial resources were not unlimited. In 1869, an overseers' committee had concluded that the substitution of 10 to 12 for 3 to 4 subjects was bound to increase costs. But in the long run, as enrollment would rise in response to the freedom given students, there would be financial gains.[17]

15. *Universities and Their Sons: History and Customs of Harvard University,* p. 148; C. W. Eliot, *Educational Reform,* 1898, pp. 65, 142-143, 224-225.

16. A. Lowell and others, *The History and Traditions of Harvard College,* 1928, p. 34.

17. *Universities and Their Sons,* p. 113; *Report of the Board of Overseers of Harvard College,* 1869, p. 66.

56

The Library

Importance

With expenditures on Harvard libraries exceeding $8 million and total university expenditures more than $150 million, the amounts spent on libraries do not seem excessive. When one considers the contribution of books, periodicals, maps, etc. to the education of students and to the contribution of knowledge, a roughly 20 to 1 ratio of all Harvard to library outlays seems like a modest one for the library. Some Washington authorities recently estimated that expenditures on computers by institutions of higher learning in a recent year equaled those on libraries and in four years would amount to twice as much. The president's advisory committee estimates annual support for computers by 1971-1972 at $414 million.[1]

Early in its history Harvard revealed an abiding interest in the library. John Harvard's library was greatly appreciated. One of the earliest tutors and fellows wrote in 1645: "You should do very well to help our College with a more compleat Library, we have very good wits among us and they grow up mightily; but we want bookes; be intreated earnestly to help us herein speedily . . . ."[2]

An overseers' committee in 1859 wrote:

. . . The earliest library in the country, coeval with the Commonwealth, and as yet hardly surpassed in size by any other in the United States, it consecrates the University to the cause of learning far beyond all other influences. It is the most valuable of her outward possessions and the immediate nutriment of her inward life . . . .[3]

Just a few years later an overseers' committee remarked that with the destruction or disuse of the library the university would die with it.[4]

One indication of the importance of the library is suggested by the value of the assets. Mr. Metcalf, the able librarian, in 1955 estimated the investment in the library at $160 million. The building plant of 12 million cubic feet was put at $25 million. Metcalf assessed the value of the 6 million books at $10 each, or $60 million. This may seem a little high, but it is justified on the grounds that rare books and manuscripts are worth more than $50 million.

In the 1950s Paul Buck, the provost and dean of the faculty under President Conant, became the director of the university library and librarian of Harvard College. He had a very good effect on the university library, for Professor Buck knew his way around the university; he could get resources for the library which would be denied to others; he shifted the emphasis from quantity to quality; and he infused into library operations a greater degree of faculty interest. This is not in any sense meant as a criticism of Keyes Metcalf, the brilliant librarian in the years

---

1. *Computers in Higher Education, Report of the President's Science Advisory Committee,* 1967, p. 51.
2. *The Founding of Harvard College,* p. 267.

3. *Report of Committee of Overseers to Visit the Library,* 1859.
4. *Special Overseers Committee on the Library,* 1864-1865.

1937 to 1955, who in fact was one of the most able librarians of all time and who contributed greatly to the growth and development of Harvard's libraries. Douglas Bryant, his successor, promises to be equally productive.

Some Aspects of Acquisitions

Librarians often tend to overbuy. Once the output escalates to very high levels, they are confronted with the problems of limited resources. They then have to become more selective, shifting their emphasis from quantity to quality. One clearly sees this shift in the 1950s at Harvard. Thus, in his 1963-1964 report Paul Buck reminded his readers that the "Library's *quality* is a major factor in determining the quality of the faculty it can recruit . . . ."[5]

But during most of Harvard's history emphasis has been on quantity. Librarian after librarian devoted endless pages to the unimportant problem of the relatively few books that had been stolen or lost.

In 1856, upon assuming the duties of librarian, complaining of the resources available—$300 per year income from the permanent funds of the library— John Sibley announced that the library "ought to contain at least one copy of every book, map and pamphlet, written or published in this country, or pertaining to America." In 1862, he reported, "I would appeal to every inhabitant of the continent to send to me everything which could be obtained, in order that every phase of mind in every section of the country . . . for the Union and against the Union . . . might be represented on our shelves . . . ."[6]

An inveterate collector, Sibley in 1863 was looking ahead at the likely size of Harvard's collection. Noting accessions of 5,000 volumes a year, rising population and education, increased manufacture of books and reading, he concluded that rather than 500,000 volumes a century hence "as they must be according to its present rate of increase, [the number] may be nearer a million." Even Sibley's projections were very low, for the actual figure a hundred years later was around 7 million.[7]

Thomas Hollis, one of the earliest benefactors of Harvard, selecting books in England in the early eighteenth century, became an agent for Harvard. It was especially the faculty that went abroad to help the college find its treasures. At times the lure of the trip and some financial gains seemed the motive. Prof. Francis Bowen in 1860 offered to act on behalf of the college in Europe. By so doing he could purchase effectively for the college, boasting that his purchase with $500 eighteen months ago "went further or procured more books through obtaining them on favorable terms, than any similar sum expended for the College Library for many years." Moreover, Bowen boasted that he had procured two-thirds of this sum through personal solicitation, as well as marshaling a campaign that brought $1,000 from classmates. Moreover, unlike some colleagues, Bowen would not ask to select the books to be ordered. One advantage of acting as a purchasing agent would be that he would not have to wait 18 months or more for a book to arrive after ordering it.[8]

C. C. Felton, professor of Greek, was authorized to purchase books for the library up to $64. But actually Felton had purchased books worth $108. He hoped the corporation would pay the unauthorized $44. ". . . If they do not consider the object of sufficient importance to justify the outlay of such a sum of course I have no objection to make, and will assume it myself . . . ."[9]

B. Pierce, the librarian, suggested to President Kirkland that Mr. Sparks, who was going to Europe, might be commissioned to buy books for the library which are not to be had in the ordinary channels of trade and "particularly such rare and curious works, as are not designed for general circulation." Moreover, he could "obtain donations (as a gentleman will

---

5. *Report of the University Librarian*, 1963-1964, p. 2.
6. Memo Harvard College Library, July 16, 1856; *Librarian's Report*, 1860; *Board of Overseers Committee on the Library*, 1862.

7. *Librarian's Report*, July, 1863.
8. Francis Bowen to the President, May 25, 1860.
9. C. C. Felton to President Walker, June 28, 1855.

beg for a public library what he would not ask for himself) . . . ."[10]

Harvard professors also contributed to a decision of Carlyle's to give his library to Harvard. He left the books used in writing some of his own works "to the alma mater of Emerson and his other transatlantic friends, as testifying 'a variety of kind feelings, obligations and regards towards New England . . . .'"[11]

Longfellow did not merely buy books for Harvard. He also accumulated them. His heirs presented Harvard with 586 volumes of American poetry, mainly presentation copies. "Who is so hard-hearted as not to be touched with pity when he reflects on the five hundred and odd letters which the unhappy recipient had to write in acknowledgement of these cruel presents . . .?"

One of the outstanding contributions to the library was by Professor Archibald Cary Coolidge who was director of the library from 1910 to 1928. His interest in the library was without limit. *Inter alia*, he provided large monetary resources; used his salary to finance increases of pay to the greatly underpaid library staff; moved hundreds of books by hand from Gore to Widener to be catalogued as the opening day of Widener approached; and took infinite interest in all kinds of details aside from his appeals for library funds from others.

In the early 1830s the president, admitting the adequacy of the library in recent years, warned that demands were rising. The library "falls short of satisfying the just claims of that body of native scholars and men of sciences who are duly rising to distinction in our country and confirming the most lasting of all honours upon the land of their birth . . . ."[12]

Harvard had its discouraging periods. In 1869, the overseers acknowledged that "until lately this library was the largest in the United States; but it has now lost that distinction, and probably will never recover it . . . ." But the committee still hoped that Harvard would be the outstanding college library in the country.[13] In 1902, a committee appointed by the corporation was rather pessimistic. The committee compared six major universities on various criteria. In buildings erected in recent years, Harvard was fourth; in capacity, tenth; in number of volumes, first; in current increases, third; in rate of rise in numbers, last.[14]

This same committee would not distinguish between dead and live books, as President Eliot at this time would. The faculty strongly opposed storage of less often used books. Above all this committee wanted service and accessibility for users of the library. They might be surpassed in the number of books; but if surpassed "in convenience of use and ready accessibility, Harvard loses one principal source of its attraction for Professors and graduate students."[15]

Growth of the Library: General Considerations

Perhaps the best index of growth available is the number of volumes in the library or libraries. Other criteria may be used, e.g., number of books circulating in a year. Harvard now has about ninety libraries, with Widener accounting for about one-third of the nearly 8 million items. The library has grown much more than anyone had anticipated. Even the increase from 41,000 to 164,000 in the thirty years from 1841 to 1871 was greater than even Sibley projected. Yet Sibley was one of the first to see the need of a research library, though he underestimated the constraints upon unlimited increases in number of items.

It is not surprising that the growth of the library accelerated under Sibley. Especially in the last hundred years growth has been phenomenal. From 1861

---

10. B. Peirce to the Rev. President Kirkland, November 15, 1827.

11. Morison, *Three Centuries of Harvard, 1636-1936*, p. 396.

12. *The Committee in Reference to the Fourth Annual Report of the President on the State of the Institution*, January 4, 1830.

13. *Report of the Board of Overseers of Harvard College on the Condition, Needs and Prospects of the University*, 1869, pp. 30-31.

14. *Report of Committee Appointed by the President and Fellows of Harvard College to Study the Future Needs of the College Library*, March 31, 1902.

15. *Ibid*, p. 6.

to 1881 the contents of the library doubled and from 1881 to 1902 doubled again. In fact, in the midst of Metcalf's regime in the 1950s, the librarian conceded that a doubling in the size of the library had been achieved at twenty-year intervals and was likely to continue to grow at a phenomenal rate. A continuation of this rate would mean that in forty years by say 2005, the Harvard libraries would hold 28 million volumes.

Sibley had predicted that Gore Hall would adequately house the Harvard library in the nineteenth century. But it proved to be inadequate even within fifteen years of its opening in the year 1841. By the end of the nineteenth century, the library held about a million items as compared with the approximate 40,000 volumes at Gore's opening.[16]

Sibley was primarily a collector. He had no acquisition policy. Moreover, his major objective seemed to be to discourage the use of the books that he collected. It is said that upon meeting the president in the yard and being asked about the state of the library, Sibley replied that the library was in good shape except that two books were out. He assured the president that he was on his way to collect them. Actually, according to Metcalf it was not until the regime of Justin Winsor (1877-1897) that an acquisition policy was forthcoming.

By early twentieth century the authorities were becoming increasingly concerned over the large output of printed material and the inability to purchase it. Doubling every twenty years could not be continued for another century. The rise from 1 to 7 million from 1900 to the 1960s was not quite a doubling every twenty years, for such rate of increase would have meant an increase to at least 8 million by 1960. Actually, even by 1965, the total was less than $7\frac{1}{2}$ million.

Even by 1955, the rate of increase was clearly declining. In that year Metcalf estimated annual acquisitions at 120,000, or 2 percent. At that rate of growth, it would require thirty-four years to double

the size of the collection. An annual growth of 120,000, which would be less than 2 percent would still give the library 15 million volumes by the year 2000.

Libraries are confronted with joint costs. They purchase or are given books. The librarian is then faced with the other costs involved in getting the book to the reader: classification, cataloguing, housing, distribution, checking, etc. These ultimately put some constraints on the collecting instinct of the librarians. The incessant cataloguing crisis throughout the nineteenth century is a measure of some of these constraints. Only in relatively recent years have librarians begun to weigh adequately the costs joint with procurement. What the librarian has to consider is not the cost of procuring a volume, say up to $10, but also the cost of these other functions which, inclusive of housing, will often exceed the costs of procurement. I am discussing marginal, not average costs here, the latter being much less. Thus in 1964-1965, other library costs, apparently largely building and maintenance charges, were almost $1 million. For 1964, Professor Buck estimated maintenance, light, and heat costs at $800,000.[17] That means about 12 cents per volume per year for housing. This does not allow for the several million spent for capital for the various libraries. But if it were not for the constraints imposed upon book collecting by the costs of complementary functions, the relative drain of library outlays would be much greater. Much depends also on the extent to which books received are free or purchased. Without a doubt gifts are too readily accepted without adequate consideration of complementary costs.[18]

Some Statistics

The tables that have been deposited in the Harvard University Archives yield some conclusions: Growth

---

16. See two tables deposited in the Harvard University Archives on the growth of the library since 1640.

17. P. Buck, *Libraries and Universities*, 1964, p. 8.
18. For material in this section see *Gifts to Library*, 1866-1867; J. L. Sibley, to the President and Fellows of Harvard College, September 24, 1877 and November 12, 1847; *Report of the University Librarian*, 1963-1964.

was irregular. For example, little progress in annual accessions was made in the first twelve years. A large rise occurred from 1764 to 1775. But this was to be explained by the concentrated effort after the fire of 1764 which destroyed Harvard's 5,000-volume library. A surprising increase in growth occurred from 1775 to 1790, a gain associated in a small degree to Harvard's receipts from the Legislature of books of Tory sympathizers.

Beginning in the period 1830 to 1848, the annual accessions tended to grow at an increasing rate. Especially notable were the increases in the period 1856 to 1868 (4,250 per year) compared to 1848 to 1856 (1,750 per year). The big gains came in the period of that dynamic librarian, Sibley. In the latter part of the nineteenth century, an acceleration of growth rate was also notable with the number of volumes doubling in the twenty years from 1880 to 1900. But it was especially in the twentieth century that the rise was phenomenal: 16,800 annual gain from 1900 to 1909 compared with 115,600 annual gain in the years 1909 to 1941.

Note that annual growth was roughly stabilized after 1909: 115,600 from 1909 to 1941, 127,700 from 1941 to 1951 and 135,700 from 1951 to 1965. This flattening of the rise reflects the measures taken to contain the increase of library expenditures by more cautious buying and economies through co-operation in acquiring as the costs of cataloguing, library buildings, service, etc. continued to soar.

It should be observed that the totals do not always include the same items. To some extent the large totals in the twentieth century reflect the consistent inclusion of pamphlets.

Some Other Economic Issues

Again and again the point has been made that as a library grows the cost per unit tends to rise. This generalization, if valid, contradicts the well-known law of economies of scale generally held to be applicable to business operations: unit costs drop as the volume increases. The rising costs also apply to the

consumers of library services. I recall well as an undergraduate about fifty years ago how easy it was to find an item in the union catalogue at Harvard and how it seems to take forever now. Obviously when seven million items are deposited in the library instead of one million, this result is almost inevitable, though some improvements in cataloguing may contain to some extent these rising costs.

A library report in 1910 commented thus on rising unit costs as the library grew:

. . . it is evidently more difficult (and expensive) in the case of a library of 500,000 volumes, as compared with a library of 50,000, to ascertain the presence or absence of a particular title before ordering, to assign a book to its correct place when received, and in recording it, to differentiate it with sufficient accuracy from other books with similar titles or authors. These elements of expense, gradually, often imperceptibly, but surely and constantly increase . . . . [19]

In his 1956-1957 report Paul Buck also commented on rising unit costs in the library:

The costs of processing materials—that is, primarily of acquiring and cataloguing them—are a major problem. Unit costs tend to rise instead of fall, as a library grows larger. Growth means that the library must deal with publications in increasingly obscure subjects and languages, that its catalogues must become increasingly complicated, and that even the relatively simple process of circulating books grows more costly. It takes longer, for example, to reshelve a book in stocks containing two million volumes than in stocks containing only a few thousand. [20]

Undoubtedly, some services, e.g., cataloguing, become more expensive as the enterprise grows.[21] But it need not follow that total real costs per unit of

19. *Librarian's Report*, 1909-1910.
20. *Report of the University Librarian*, 1956-1957, p. 35.
21. Douglas Bryant, the University Librarian, told the writer that cataloguing costs may be expected to fall with the increased effectiveness of interlibrary co-operation in cataloguing and application of computer technology.

output necessarily increase with the size of operations.

Thus, in 1966-1967, total library costs were $7,543,791. Included were approximately $1,300,000 "other library costs," and in particular $443,000 for building and maintenance charges. These unit costs need not rise as the enterprise grows. Building and maintenance charges are surely less per book for a seven-million than for a one-million-book library. Every businessman would agree.

Another relevant item is the book bill, roughly $1,200,000. Surely a library that spends a million dollars for books should obtain them at lower costs per unit than a library with 100,000 copies.[22] More economies became available to larger libraries as more use is made of computers.

Of the $7,540,000 budget, $4,500,000 are classified as salaries, casual services, and wages. It is difficult to draw any conclusions here.

One thing is certain: library salaries are low generally. Higher salaries might well increase productivity through enlistment of more talent, and output per dollar of wages would rise. Buck, aware of this problem, contributed greatly to raising the general level of library pay.

In these matters one should also distinguish the rise of real costs and that in money costs. The combination of inflation since 1940 and a relative full employment economy account for a considerable part of the rising money unit costs. For long periods Harvard libraries exploited their help: wages rose less than the cost of living and a fortiori than the pay of the average member of the labor market. With full employment and the intervention of Buck, the situation began to be corrected in the 1950s.

There is another aspect of library economics. Once a library like Widener achieves leadership as the outstanding university library in the world and one of the great five or six libraries in the world, the library becomes a magnet for increased donations. Against any rise in real units cost—if there is one—one should offset the increase of gifts as the enterprise grows.

Finally, a word about capital costs which are not generally irrelevant. Roughly, construction of Widener (1914-1915) cost $3,500,000, Lamont (1949), $2,500,000, and Houghton (1942), $600,000.[23]

I estimate capital costs per volume held: Widener, $1.50; Houghton $3; and Lamont, $18. To some extent the differences relate to the time of construction. Undoubtedly Widener would cost $18 million to build today, though a more productive job could be done. But the contrast between Lamont and Widener is striking, even allowing for the costs at time of building, and the kind of inventory in the various libraries. I find it difficult to refrain from suggesting that capital costs are much lower for the big (Widener, 2 to 3 million items) than for the small enterprise (Lamont, 142,000 items).[24]

One other aspect of the relation of size and unit costs should receive some attention, and especially because Metcalf, Buck, and Bryant have been greatly interested in technological advances, which either cut costs or improve services. Incidentally, to a considerable extent the rise of unit costs is not a genuine increase but rather a higher cost for a greater service, that is, a differentiated and better product; my point here is simply that with increased size the library can much more easily exploit the growing number of technological advances, with the result of reduced costs or (and) increased services.

Haphazard collecting may be costly. As early as 1869, a committee noted that as valuable as gifts are, "they can rarely contribute as much to the usefulness of the collection as would be done by purchases made with the view of supplying recognized deficiencies . . . ."[25]

Archibald Coolidge, the director of the library from 1910 to 1928, was aware of the need of planning:

---

22. The university librarian disagrees. Purchases are not made at lower prices than smaller libraries.

23. *Education, Bricks and Mortar.*

24. But it should be noted that the service offered by these two libraries is not identical, but in part because Lamont services people primarily.

25. *Board of Overseers, Committee to Visit the Library,* 1869.

He found the library an excellent, small collection of mingled valuable and useless material, accumulated through generations of gifts and legacies which came as they happened to come throughout the years. It was without fixed policies as to future buying or increase, lacking in any guiding principle as to that fundamental basis of all library values, cataloguing, and utterly inadequately housed . . . . The possibilities of turning out something entirely different were enormous and he put his hand to the plough and kept it there steadily, with unvarying singleness of purpose . . . .[26]

A crucial problem is the support of Harvard's ninety small libraries vs that of a large central library. Indeed, as Buck pointed out, the development of the small libraries precluded the construction of another large library. Whereas Gore held two-thirds of the total university books and pamphlets, Widener accounts for only one-third.

A small library is costly: its unit costs are likely to be high or the service poor. One cannot draw conclusions from the summary tables of the library because all costs clearly are not allocated. In 1964-1965, total expenditures allocated over the number of items in the libraries yield: Widener (2,300,000 items), 87 cents per item; Dunster (13,000 items), 44 cents per item. This does not by any means suggest that the small library is more efficient. Coolidge was not enthusiastic over the small libraries.

. . . As each departmental library grows in wealth, in strength and in pride, its professors became increasingly unwilling to consider volumes, even a few hundred feet away, as being satisfactorily situated for their purposes . . . [I had] a sharp clash with one of the most important departmental libraries because they wished to spend $500 on purchasing a rare edition of a work, of which the same edition already existed in the Widener Library . . . . You will find the demand for what is regarded as the indispensable

works of reference for each departmental library will tend to increase as time goes on . . . .[27]

There is much waste in the present system. The excessive duplication is evident to anyone who uses the union catalogue. One will sometimes find the same book catalogued in as many as seven libraries at Harvard. This does not mean that there is not a case for some special libraries yielding special service to faculty or students. Lamont provides a real service badly needed, as do the house libraries. But many of the special libraries could be dispensed with, and there is still need of improved integration among the larger special libraries, e.g., law, business, public administration, design, medicine, etc.[28]

Of course the library officials over the years have sought economical operations. At an early point duplicates became a problem. At a corporation meeting in 1682, it was "ordered that the doubl books in the Colledge Library be prized and sold, and the money improved for the buying other books that are wanting."[29]

Conserving books by rebinding was still novel as late as 1812. At that time a committee commented:

The Committee have observed with pleasure that a number of books have been economically repaired by giving new covers to the books, contributing both to their beauty and durability. They would recommend the continuance of this practice with a promptitude suited to the state of the books.[30]

One way to economize is to weed out books that are no longer needed. An overseers' committee in 1866 recommended exchanges and sales of books not

---

26. H. J. Coolidge and R. H. Lord, *Archibald Cory Coolidge*, p. 78.

27. *Ibid.,* pp. 88-89.
28. For a defense of the small libraries, see Buck, *Report of the University Librarian,* 1957-1958, p. 3; Douglas Bryant, *Report of the University Librarian,* 1960-1961, pp. 27-37.
29. W. C. Lane, *The University during the Last Twenty-Five Years,* 1906, pp. 36-37; *Report of the Committee to Visit the University Library,* 1929, pp. 386-387; *College Books,* vol. I, p. 72.
30. *Report of the Committee Appointed to Inspect the Library,* August 17, 1812.

worthy of the space and care given them. ". . . Books, superseded by more recent and more thorough works, may be positively mischievous to persons not sufficiently versed in the subject to know their relative value . . . ."[31]

But weeding out is difficult. Scarcely a book is to be found which some faculty member will not find indispensable. In recent years, however, some experimental attempts have been made at weeding out systematically. Here ruthless operations may be necessary. But few librarians would dare incur the wrath of faculty members who would strenuously object to wholesale weeding out.[32] Many would agree with Sibley that the rubbish of one generation would become the treasure of another.[33] The 1902 committee strongly objected to disposal of books or division into live and dead categories.

As early as 1948, the library officials estimated that the construction costs per volume were about $1 and current building charges for light, heat, and cleaning add 40 cents more. Then add $2.50 for the cost of acquiring and cataloguing. Here are costs of $3.90 exclusive of services for the reader and other costs.[34]

With these heavy costs per volume, the library is under great pressure to seek economies. One economy that Harvard has practiced more than most, is to put upon the consumer of library services large responsibilities for finding books. The user gets little help in perusing the catalogues, and in Widener and Lamont he is largely on his own.[35]

The librarian has also sought small economies—e.g., a rise in the fees for outsiders using the library and increased pressure for delinquents to pay the fee. Again, Harvard tends to be overly generous in the exports of its volumes to other libraries for loans as compared to its imports through loans. Thus, in 1966-1967 incoming interlibrary loans were for 1,122 volumes; outgoing, 7,259.[36]

Above all, the library in recent years has sought to reduce library costs by co-operating with other libraries through such devices as the Farmington Plan, under which a concerted effort is made to procure books on behalf of a group of research libraries, with each library assuming special responsibilities in certain fields, or through the New England Depository, which provides cheap storage space for items not greatly in demand currently; or through the Harvard-Yale, New York Public Libraries co-operating in their cataloguing activities.[37]

Losses

As books are purloined and defaced, the cost of library service soars. This type of abuse has troubled Harvard library authorities from the very beginning. Early reports of librarians devoted more space to losses and prevention than to any other subject.

In 1725, Thomas Hollis wrote to a friend: ". . . You let your books be taken at pleasure, to men's houses, and many are lost; your boyish students take them to their chambers and tear out pictures and maps to adorn their rooms . . . ."[38]

Among the library laws of 1736 were the following:

No Book shall be taken out of ye Library, or returned, without ye knowledge and presence of ye Library Keeper . . . ye name of the borrower and restorer, with ye Book itself and time of borrowing and returning; being orderly set down in ye Library Keeper's book . . . .
If any Scholar abuse, or unseasonably detain any Book borrowed by him, or injure ye Library any other way, said Scholar . . . shall pay double damages, and be debarred from borrowing till he has paid said damages . . . and has obtained leave from ye President and Tutors to borrow . . . .[39]

31. *Board of Overseers Special Committee of the Library, 1866.*
32. *Report of the University Librarian,* 1953-1954, p. 4.
33. *Ibid.,* 1964-1965, p. 3.
34. *Ibid.,* 1948, p. 7.
35. *Report of the University Librarian,* 1961-1962, p. 3.
36. *Ibid.,* 1964-1965, p. 32.

37. Cf., *Ibid.,* 1958-1959, p.5.
38. Quincy *op. cit.,* vol. I, p. 432.
39. Laws for the Library, 1736, *College Books,* vol. I, pp. 130-131. By 1847, all undergraduates had the privilege of borrowing. See *Laws and Regulations of the Public Library,* 1847.

Losses of books were a frequent theme in the reports of the librarians. In 1812, a committee found all the books but two, for which the librarian would be held accountable. Twenty years later, the librarian mentioned "the abuse of them by scribbling and drawing in them; some of the newest books are thus defaced throughout. Plates are in many instances missing, and in a greater number of cases, shamefully disfigured . . . ." A committee commenting in 1862 on the disappearance of twenty-seven volumes, wrote that "no protection has hitherto been found to secure a public library from the annoyance of petty pilferers, without a code of rules so stringent as greatly to diminish the value of books to honest readers . . . ."

To cut losses, college officials had recourse to all kinds of treatment. The most obvious one is, of course, punishment: fines, suspension, etc. Thus, a library committee of 1821 would impose penalties for overdue books, and limit accessibility of students to books.[40]

Perhaps more effective than fines is the policy of shutting off areas to students. In the seventeenth century, a British university still chained books as a means of keeping them. Harvard would not go that far.

One interesting approach presented in 1859 was longer library hours. If students had access to the library for a considerable period every day then the incentive to abscond with books would be greatly reduced. Particularly helpful would be a large extension of hours for borrowing and returning books.[41]

Perhaps the most effective measure ever taken to deal with losses was the inspection, begun in the early 1930s, of every person who leaves the library at a turnstile. ". . . our losses have fallen off to 15 percent of what they were before the barrier was set up . . . ."[42]

---

40. *Report of the Committee to Inspect the Library*, August 17, 1812; *Report of the Librarian*, 1832; *Report of the Librarian,* July 16, 1835; *Report of Board of Overseers Committee to Examine the Librarian*, 1862; *Report of the Library of the Law School*, 1862-1863; Harvard College, *p. 294.*

41. *Committee for Rendering the Public Library More Generally Useful to the Undergraduates*, 1859.

The Problem of Space

Institutions of higher learning tend to spend excessively for buildings. But this generalization does not apply to libraries. Librarians tend to buy excessively and accept gifts without adequate consideration of the accompanying costs of getting the gift into circulation. Hence, a serious lag tends to develop in the provisioning of space to hold the books.

One committee, considering the problem, supported large outlays for a building despite the universal opinion "among scholars that the purchases of books is a more important object of expenditures than the erection of buildings to contain them . . . ."[43]

The space problem had concerned presidents from the earliest years. By the latter part of the eighteenth century the problem had become increasingly serious. In 1810, the librarian insisted on the need of additional space. ". . . The books already possessed are accommodated with difficulty and their beauty, as well as that of the room, is much impaired by the necessity of crowding them together . . . ." He also complained that the books were so closely placed that the sides were injured and the tops of the back were frequently severed from the book.[44]

From 1764 to 1841, the year Gore was completed, Harvard Hall had been the only repository for the college's books. In 1838 a decision was taken to use the major part of the Gore estate to finance a new building.[45]

On the whole, Gore was a great disappointment. As early as 1856 librarian Sibley informed the president that accommodations for books were becoming inadequate. The librarian had to store several hundred volumes in the towers.[46]

By the early 1860s Sibley had launched an all-out campaign for a new building. Estimating needs at

---

42. *Report of the Committee to Visit the Library*, 1933.

43. *Board of Overseers Special Committee of Library*, 1866.

44. *The Librarian to the Visiting Committee, October 30, 1810.*

45. *Quincy op. cit.*, vol. II, pp. 430-435.

46. J. L. Sibley to President Walker, May 7, 1856.

least 5 to 10 times current ones within a century and of replacement for Gore every twenty years, Sibley would provide a new building, which might easily be enlarged.

. . . The objections to the present building, the bad light, the discomfort in winter, the entire want of private rooms for any of the officers of the library, as for strangers visiting it to make investigations, as for any of the persons employed . . . the slow but certain ruin of the books by dampness in some parts of Gore Hall—might be obviated in a new building . . . .[47]

Wolcott Gibbs, the great scientist and chairman of a committee of the council was appointed to investigate "alleged dampness, danger from badly constructed flues and want of proper and sufficient light" and reported adversely. Among other things, Gibbs revealed leaks in various parts of the building, dampness in some corners, and condensation of moisture which accounted for the dampness. Also, the flues required attention; and the verdict on light was also adverse.[48] A report of a library committee in 1869 was equally revealing.[49]

In his campaign for a new building Sibley was confronted by a worthy adversary, Charles Eliot. Sibley seemed to make some progress, for proposals were seriously considered in 1867 for raising $150,000 for a library and $150,000 for books. But Eliot became president in 1869, and he was strongly opposed to a sacrifice of Gore. In Eliot's view Gore could be improved and enlarged.

Since the 1890s, complaints of deficiencies in Gore's physical plant were increasingly frequent. In 1903, Eliot appointed a committee to consider the alternatives of a new building or an addition to Gore.

Eliot returned to the subject in 1907. He still wanted to work with Gore. He was critical of current plans that invested too much for the accommodation of readers and too little for stack space. In the meanwhile, the college might use excess capacity in the law school.[50]

In 1914-1915 Widener became available at a cost of $3,500,000. The cost was considerably higher than earlier estimates. Despite the increased capacity to house 2,500,000 volumes, it was not long before authorities again were commenting on the inadequacy of space. A visiting committee in 1933 recommended either to stop the purchase of books until a way is found to handle and care for those purchased in a suitable manner, or reserve out of the funds appropriated for purchase enough money to administer the library.[51]

Shortage of space persisted even with the availability of Widener. The problem of space had been solved temporarily at least by the growth of special libraries; by the building of new stacks; by the opening of Lamont and Houghton, by the increased care in ordering books, an improvement associated with a greater awareness of the total cost of making a book serviceable.

In 1967 a decision was made to increase underground space, which would house more than one million volumes. In the next ten years, the university library is expected to add 2,500,000 volumes, with 870,000 going to Widener, which already has fifty miles of books on its shelves. Transfers of collections to the new science library and the education library and similar special libraries will help solve the space problem. The new stacks, offices and studies under Widener will cost $5 million, a financial goal not easily reached.[52]

As the price of books rise and the number of items published each year increases, the purchases and hence the facilities for housing books are contained to some extent. The deficits in books tend to grow.

47. *Librarian's Report*, July 1863 and 1864-1865.
48. Memo (unsigned) to the Corporation, July 31, 1852; W. Gibbs for the Committee to Examine and Report upon the Library of the College, December 30, 1869.
49. Board of Overseers' Committee to Visit the Library, 1869.

50. C. W. Eliot to Mr. Billings, July 21, 1903; C. W. Eliot to C. F. Adams, October 7, 1905; C. W. Eliot to W. C. Lane, June 11, 1907; W. C. Lane, *op. cit.*, p. 37.
51. *Board of Overseers' Report of the Committee to Visit the Library*, 1911; 1910; 1933.
52. *Harvard Alumni Bulletin*, March 30, 1968.

Costs of purchases rise by 10 percent each year in response to the increasing unit prices and increase of books published. That is to say, a rise of 10 percent is required in order to maintain the rate of acquisition.[53]

Cataloguing

The Harvard librarians have generally been behind in their cataloguing. If there were no place to put a book, it was unavailable; and if it were not catalogued, it was not likely to be used. Moreover, unavailability of space would cut down on cataloguing. If books are not catalogued, the librarian does not know whether a book is or is not missing. Potential donors, moreover, as T. Hollis reminded the college in the eighteenth century, are deterred from giving if cataloguing facilities are not had, for then they do not know which books the library has. Once funds became scanty the temptation to neglect cataloguing was especially strong. Purchasing and shelving had to go on, but not so, cataloguing.[54]

Good cataloguing is an expensive matter, though much more in later than earlier years, both because the quantity has been larger in more recent times and costs per unit higher. Thus, in 1775, the college paid £12 for seventy-four days spent in cataloguing 2,027 books or roughly about 2 cents a volume. In 1907-1908, the cost of cataloguing per volume was 37 cents as compared with 78 cents for the entire cost of handling.[55]

The corporation offered ambitious plans for cataloguing. It is not clear that even by 1968 they had been implemented sufficiently.

In general, cataloguing has not kept up with procurement. Occasionally delays might save resources, for more economical systems might be exploited by waiting. But in general the lag in cataloguing contributed seriously to reduced service by the library. Though the problem is not solved, it is not nearly as serious in the twentieth century as in the eighteenth and nineteenth centuries.

Service

To assess the value of a library's contribution, one must consider the service given to the faculty, students, and public generally. Our discussion of space and cataloguing has already revealed some of the deficiencies in service.

In 1868, Ralph Emerson commented in a relevant manner on library service. Writing for a university committee he said:

The first use of a college library is to be irresistably attractive to young men. In daily experience it is not so. Young men go into them and out of it [sic] *repelled by the multitude of books which only speak to them of their ignorance—their very multitude concealing from the gazing youth the one or the few volumes which are there waiting for him with the very information and leads he wants. Would some kind scholar take pity on ... his curiosity and ... guide him to the class of works and presently to the precise author who has written as for him alone. Could not a gentleman be found to occupy a desk in Gore Hall as the Library Counselor to whom the Librarian could refer inquiries ...? We are aware that such selection would be a delicate point—easy to miss—and that it requires a man of sympathy, a lover of books and reader of books to fulfill the design ....*[56]

Emerson's message is that too many books may debase the product. The college authorities in some degree followed Emerson's wishes, but in a less understanding manner. Until the days of Eliot, the college insisted upon restricting the number of books which undergraduates might borrow and also selecting the books which he might read. From the earliest times

53. *Report of the University Librarian, 1966-1967,* pp. 6-7.
54. *Board of Overseers and Corporation Committee for Inspecting Library and Museums; Reports to Overseers, vol. I, 1761-1825; Library Report, 1909-1910.*
55. *Librarian's Report, 1909-1910,* p. 22.

56. R. W. Emerson for the Committee, October 24, 1868.

there had been such censorship on behalf of students. Even as late as 1835, a committee noted that a selected catalogue was to be made out for the use of undergraduates, "of books adapted to their studies and in the course of reading which is proper for them to pursue . . . ."

As strong a statement as any on the need of censorship of undergraduate reading appeared in 1832.

The Committee would strongly recommend that instead of an indiscriminate use of the library, by undergraduates, or their selecting such volumes, as happen to attract their notice, as they roam from alcove to alcove, often by the splendor of their binding, or the beauty of their engravings, a Selected Catalogue of about 500 volumes, adapted to their course of study, their real improvement, may be made and printed; and their use of the library confined to such . . . .[57]

Undergraduates were becoming increasingly annoyed at their exclusion . . . .[58] In 1857, they sought an undergraduate library; and a university committee urged undergraduates to gain more knowledge from reading books. This committee would open the library to all members of the university, and through proper supervision the number of lost books would drop. Moreover, library hours would be greatly extended.[59] This was a great advance over the restraints of the eighteenth century.

Thus, in the 1736 rules of the library, "No Scholar in Ye College under a Senior Sophister, may borrow a book out of ye Library." The sophister was, moreover, restricted to borrowing books that "are most proper for their reading" as determined by the faculty[60]. A similar rule was in vogue in 1667. But by 1826, all undergraduates had the borrowing privilege.[61]

Over most of Harvard's history the library hours or hours for borrowing books were brief indeed. Justin Winsor, who became librarian in 1877, revised the Sibley restrictive practices and opened the library during long hours and stressed service to students.[62]

Over the years the Harvard library has served scholars all over the world. In fact, a strong case can be made for government subsidies to the Harvard library, on the grounds that the library provides important and costly service to thousands of non-Harvard scholars every year. The college laws generally allowed scholars to use the library. Thus, an 1847 law provided "that persons, not inhabitants of Cambridge, but having a temporary residence therein, for the purpose of study, may borrow books from the library, with permission of the President . . . ."[63]

The assumption of the responsibilities for the library by Justin Winsor in 1877, who introduced the practice of reserving books for courses and began to allow direct use of the stacks, received favorable comment.[64]

A commentator in 1895 remarked that the library:

. . . is administered with a liberality and efficiency unparalleled in any college library in the world . . . . Seventeen years ago 57 percent of the students made use of it; in 1887-88 the proportion for the whole college had increased to 89 percent; for the three upper classes to 97 percent . . . in 1892-93 the number of students who made no recorded use of the library was 41 out of a total of 1,449 . . . . The advanced student who returns to Harvard after a

57. Semi-Annual Meeting: Report on the Library, January 12, 1832.
58. *Considerations in Favor of an Undergraduate Library and Reading Room*, 1857.
59. *Committee . . . Rendering the Public Library more Generally Useful to the Undergraduates*, 1859; cf. C. Folsolm to President Walker, October 29, 1859, where an exLibrarian expressed considerable doubts about giving undergraduates additional privileges.
60. *College Books*, vol. I, p. 130; Morison, *Harvard College in the Seventeenth Century*, vol. I, p. 286.
61. *Statutes and Laws of the University in Cambridge, Massachusetts*, 1826.
62. *College Books*, vol. I, p. 131; Librarian to the Committee of the . . . Overseers, for Semi-Annual Visitation of the University, May 3, 1825; *Statutes and Laws of the University in Cambridge, Massachusetts*, 1826; *Laws and Regulations of the Public Library*, 1847.
63. *Laws and Regulations of the Public Library*, 1847.
64. Justin Winsor to the President, June 11, 1884.

residence abroad finds in its open library a compensation for whatever other advantages a foreign seal of learning may offer . . . .

By the early part of the twentieth century there was a reversion to complaints. A million items were crowded into space adequate for little more than one-half; in twenty years the material doubled though space was barely adequate twenty years earlier; methods of instruction increased the pressure on the library; the undergraduates had doubled in numbers; large masses of material had been diverted to inaccessible areas; the space and location of the catalogues were subject to severe criticism; the reading room needed to be doubled to provide adequate space for potential users; "it lacks the large spaces conducive to meditative study and is barren of architectural beauty and dignity. . . ."[65]

A fascinating episode in Harvard's library history revolves around a public service involving some books and maps which Harvard had put at the disposal of the State Department in relation to the northeast boundary dispute with Canada.

In 1828, Acting President Henry Ware raised some questions concerning his legal rights to put at the disposal of the treaty commissioners Harvard's maps and books. Apparently the state government was prepared to assume responsibilities against losses and costs. Gallatin had written to the governor expressing great need of these items in the current emergency. He hoped "the Governor would lend his assistance in obtaining this from the several institutions. . . ."

The U. S. agent on the northeast boundary dispute wrote that "these books and maps are loaned and delivered upon the express condition that they shall be returned to the college, and are loaned for the purpose of being used in the discussions . . . of the question pending between the United States and Great Britain relative to our Northeastern boundary."

In May, 1843, President Quincy commented in a letter to Daniel Webster, secretary of state, on the failure of the government to return all the items loaned. (". . . the remaining thirteen books and maps which were loaned, it will be difficult if not impracticable to return. . . .") Quincy refused monetary compensation. But he hoped "that this may be regarded by yourself and those who may hereafter occupy the Department of State as an additional reason for turning towards Harvard College a portion of that bounty which occasionally overflows in the form of books and maps towards institutions of science. . . ." By 1852, most items had been returned.[66]

Financing Problems

Throughout Harvard's history the financing of the library, both for current operations and capital, has been a tough problem. By the Chauncy period (1654-1672), the library, according to Morison, had accumulated about a thousand volumes. A steady succession of librarians may be explained by inadequate resources—the first recorded pay for the librarian was £5 a year[67]—and the low status of librarians.

Library expenditures tended to rise with the increase in the student body, with the improvement of travel so that the library became increasingly available to non-Harvard users, with the newer methods of instruction which required more use of books and documents, with the advance of research with its heavy impact on library needs, and with the rising output of the printing industry.

Financial problems were especially troublesome in the middle of the nineteenth century. Undoubtedly Librarian Sibley, who had become librarian in 1856 and continued until 1877, contributed to the general concern. Sibley became a persistent beggar who was warned by the treasurer to desist, but who paid little attention to his superiors.

65. See especially *Report of the Committee to Visit the Library*, 1903, pp. 726-729.

66. H. Ware to the Corporation, October 21, 1828; Extract of a Letter from the Honorable Mr. Gallatin to the Governor, 1828; J. Quincy to the Honorable Daniel Webster, Secretary of State, May 13, 1843; J. Buchanan to Honorable John Palfrey, House of Representatives, May 4, 1848; J. Quincy to Corporation on Books and Maps Loaned in 1828, May 20, 1843; Acting Secretary of State to Jared Sparks, May 18, 1852; E. Everett to J. Sparks, December 15, 1852.

67. See especially Morison, *Harvard College in the Seventeenth Century*, vol. I, pp. 285-297.

In the twenty-five years under T. W. Harris (1831 to 1856) the library had spent $35,000 for books or $1,400 average per year. (Cf., annual outlay of $1,210,000 in 1964-1965.) In general, outlays were small, and they would have been smaller if Sibley and others had not begged. This was also the period when the practice of pressing alumni through class campaigns began to operate. Thus, in 1859, three thousand copies of a library report were circulated to alumni and then brought in about $10,000.

The library officials complained in the 1860s at the small sums available for the purchase of books— $1,400 in 1867-1868—in comparison with $16,000 spent by the Boston Public Library. The college wished for at least $10,000. Even as late as 1856, but $300 of income was to be had from permanent book funds.

With such small sums to be had, the college officials aggressively sought large permanent funds. With such small funds for purchases—and the funds were often tied to special categories and continuation of series and, hence, only a small part of available book budgets could be had to be spent freely on the basis of needs in various areas—the college looked elsewhere.

With the economic progress of the country, cash receipts grew. Thus, in the years 1924 to 1929, the library received $340,000 in capital funds and $465,000 for books. Even in 1933, the depression year, the library obtained $90,000 gifts for books inclusive of $11,000 from friends of the library.[68]

In 1864-1865 the whole income of the library was $6,182.11. Students contributed $3,540, with undergraduates providing $2,755. Expenses aside from purchase of books were $8,135.48. A milestone was the large gift of Archibald Coolidge.

An overseers' committee in 1929 reported that purchases of books were made from trust funds or by gifts made by friends of the university. The college supported the maintenance of buildings and salaries of the staff out of unrestricted funds.[69]

In 1947-1948 and 1948-1949, Provost Buck raised some fundamental questions on the financing of the college library. The library with its large capital plant was in financial difficulties, in part because of the rising level of prices and wages. The library income was not tied to tuition. If it were, with tuition rising, its financial position would be greatly improved. One result of this method of financing was that the university diverted large sums to library endowment. The major Harvard libraries were tied to the relevant faculties. Then as tuition rose the library would profit. The university transferred large sums to the faculty of arts and sciences for library use. Hence, on July 1, 1949, $18,800,000 were available, the income of which would be used for library purposes. Finally, in 1959-1960, the university greatly increased fees for outsiders' use of the library up to $50 a year, and in support pointed out that library costs at that time amounted to $200 per student in the university. (Actually, by 1965 the cost per student had risen to almost $400.)[70]

Perhaps at no time, even under Sibley, had library expenditures risen as much as in the last generation.

Note that in a period of less than thirty years expenditures rose by 7 to 8 times. (Prices had risen only by 1.2 times in these years.)

In a period of seven years, total library expenditures roughly doubled. That means a rise roughly of

68. S. A. Eliot for Committee of Library, March 28, 1846; Committee . . . Reducing and Equalizing the Charges for the Use of the Library, March 21, 1848; T. Harris to President Sparks, December 18, 1849; *Report of the Committee of the Overseers to Visit the Library*, 1850; *Librarian's Report*, 1856; J. L. Sibley on *Harvard College Library*, July 16, 1856; Library Committee, 1859; *Report of the Committee of the Board of Overseers to Examine the Libraries of the University*, 1862; *Report of Librarian*, (year not clear but probably 1860s); Board of Overseers Special Committee on Libraries, 1866; *Harvard College*, pp. 289-291; no. 79, Report of the Committee to Visit the University Library, 1929, pp. 376-370; 1933, pp. 130-133.

69. *Report of Committee to Visit the University Library*, 1929, p. 387.

70. *Report of the University Librarian*, 1947-1948, p. 3; 1948-1949, p. 4; 1959-1960, pp. 13-14; 1964-1965, p. 37; *Report of the President of Harvard College* 1965-1966, p. 1.

10 percent of expenditures per year, a rate of rise which would result in a doubling of expenditures in seven years. Hence, whereas library acquisitions were doubling in about thirty-four years, expenditures doubled in seven years.

Allocations of Library Expenditures

Harvard has tended to save on services as compared to other great libraries; that is to say, it requires the consumers to service themselves. Harvard operates on the supermarket tradition rather than on that of the grocer who serves the customer directly.

Whereas at Harvard the expenditures for services and books were relatively equal in the twentieth century, the service outlays in other libraries were 2 to 3 times as large as for books or more. This may be explained in part by the excessive outlays for books at Harvard as well as inadequate outlays for service.[71]

Much has been said about rising unit costs and declining productivity. That administrative costs rose by 133 percent from 1880 to 1908 reflects the problem of increasing complexities of library administration.[72]

For 1900 to 1908 we have a precise breakdown of costs. Total costs rose by 17 percent. The large rises were in growth and especially orders and care of shelves, and cataloguing was falling behind.

Library labor has been exploited from the early years of Harvard until recent times. Benjamin Peirce, T.W. Harris, and J.L. Sibley, librarians from 1831 to 1877, all complained of their meager pay and excessive hours. Peirce wanted adequate compensation for extra work on a nine-hundred-page alphabetical catalogue. Harris was unhappy at the pay he received for his cataloguing services and warned the corporation that his hours were impossible and though he needed an assistant badly, he wanted a rise of pay even more than an assistant. He ultimately had his pay raised to $1,500.

The attitude toward women was reflected in the absence of a water closet for female employees, and later by President Eliot, when being asked for better treatment of women, countering with a request that the productivity of women in the library be carefully considered. He expressed some doubts about their contribution. At that time (1907) women were hired only on an hourly basis.[73]

It is not surprising that the turnover of librarians was great. In a period of 210 years Harvard had sixty-six librarians, or an average tenure of $13\frac{1}{2}$ years. Even over a 300-year period the average for seventy librarians was $14\frac{1}{3}$ years. From the days of Harris, however, the situation improved. Harris, Sibley, Winsor, Lane, and Metcalf all had long tenures. In contrast, the average tenure of twenty-one presidents was 14 years.

Control of the Library

How effectively a library operates depends in no small part on its top personnel. During most of Harvard's history a librarian was in charge. By the early nineteenth century provision was generally made for an assistant librarian, and in 1866-1867 provision was made for a more formal organization. A special committee of the overseers recommended "that the control, and management of the library and the expenditures of the income, subject to the approval of the government of the college, be entrusted to a permanent body whose pursuits, tastes and knowledge make them competent for these

71. *Report of the University Librarian*, 1909-1910, p. 25; C.W. Eliot to W. Lane, December 7, 1906.
72. *Report of the University Librarian*, 1909-1910, pp. 9, 11.
73. B. Peirce to President Quincy, October 24, 1829; T. W. Harris to Mr. Sumner (law school librarian), December 18, 1833; T. W. Harris to President Quincy, July 20, 1833 and July 18, 1842; *Annual Report of Librarian*, 1835; J. L. Sibley to Honorable President Everett, June 9, 1847; Committee for Rendering Public Library More Generally Useful to the Undergraduates, 1859; J. L. Sibley to President Walker, October 21, 1859; J. L. Sibley to A. A. Lawrence, March 19, 1859; The Library Committee to the President and Fellows of Harvard College, May 16, 1860; C. W. Eliot to W. C. Lane, November 26, 1907.

purposes. . . ." This body was to become acquainted with the needs of the library, consult the faculty in different departments, direct the expenditures, and sell books that were not needed. On the basis of these recommendations the corporation and overseers provided for a permanent council of the library consisting of the president and six associates. This council would have the authority detailed above plus the hiring of all library employees except the librarian and janitor.[74]

The next big step occurred in 1910 when Archibald Coolidge was appointed director of the library. This was perhaps the beginning of faculty control of the library. The director assumed some responsibilities for libraries other than Widener. But it was especially in 1948-1949 under President Conant and Provost Buck that the faculty, increasingly responsible for financing the library, also assumed substantial control.

J. G. Cogswell (1821 to 1823), T. W. Harris (1831 to 1856), J. L. Sibley (1856 to 1877), J. Winsor (1879 to 1897), A.C. Coolidge (1910 to 1928), K. Metcalf (1937 to 1955), and P.H. Buck (1955 to 1964) stand out as great names in the Harvard library history.

Cogswell rearranged books on the basis of subject matter *regardless of donors*. He was far ahead of his time also in urging a card catalogue rather than a printed one, and he divided the library into twenty alcoves and allocated the collection under four heads. He provided both an alcove and an alphabetical catalogue.

Under Harris, who served a record twenty-five years, the library more than doubled in size. In this period, however, enrollment also doubled.

Sibley, for more than fifty years a Harvard librarian or assistant librarian, was, all things considered, a great librarian. He was indeed disposed to overaccumulate. He wanted to meet the needs of students and scholars. He would literally collect every page of manuscript or printing.

Justin Winsor was also a great librarian.

He is a born librarian. To extensive learning, a love of books, and the scholar's kindly gentle nature, he adds a common sense and enthusiasm—a rare combination—and great power to organization. "I try never to forget," he wrote, "that the prime purpose of a book is to be much read;" though it is equally true that we are under obligation to preserve books whose loss might be irrecoverable.

Under Winsor's management, the library grew at a very satisfactory rate and great advances were made in the number of days and hours the library became available.[75]

Archibald Coolidge was the first genuine director of the Harvard library. He put all his resources, physical and financial, into the library.[76]

Keyes Metcalf, who served as librarian for eighteen years before Professor Paul Buck took over, also contributed greatly to the development of the library. Metcalf showed that the library's growth was at a rate of 100 percent in twenty years, and he looked forward to a continuance of this rate. But Matcalf was confronted with serious financial problems. He helped work out new, important techniques for storing books of secondary importance and also for co-operation among the large libraries in storing and collecting books. Under pressure he had to moderate the rate of growth. He was in the forefront of the technological revolution that was beginning in the postwar period.

Paul Buck served as librarian for almost ten years after a distinguished career as provost of the university. He was able to make large contribution in part because after serving as provost he was in a peculiarly strong position to push diversion of large, but not excessive, resources to the library. He wanted the library to grow as other librarians also did, but he was aware of financial constraints that the pure collector was likely to forget. He was also aware, as Coolidge had been before him, that purchasing a book was

74. Special Committee of the Overseers . . . Have Examined the Reports on the Library, 1866; Overseers Committee to Visit the Library, 1867.

75. *Harvard College,* pp. 292-293.
76. H. J. Coolidge and R. H. Lord, *op. cit.,* pp. 74-75.

only the initial step in building a library and that the ultimate outlay per book was likely to be a multiple of the original purchase price.

Some General Considerations

Harvard libraries are a great asset but of a value difficult to measure. Much emphasis in the past has been the salary differential between the Harvard faculty and its competitiors. But Harvard's advantage in compensation in 1966-1967 was only $4,900 in relation to fifteen major competitiors: $18,700 vs $13,800. In many fields the superior quality and quantity of Harvard's libraries will hold and attract faculty members more than the pay differential. In the 1940s a study, which was based on judgements of five hundred scholars, revealed that Harvard's collections in 64 of 76 fields were among the best in the country.[77]

Harvard's pace of accumulation has steadily declined in recent years. From 1847 to 1857 the annual percentage of increase of volumes was 4.5 percent; in 1867-1877, 3.5 percent; by 1907 to 1917, 5 percent; and then an irregular decline to 2 1/4 percent for 1947 to 1954. At the 1907 to 1917 rate of accumulation the number of items in the library would rise to about 50 million in forty years (year 2007); at the 1947 to 1954 rate the increase would be only 17 million.

The need of books increases as enrollment rises. But the results are affected also by the structure of the student increase. The rises are especially great for graduate students, who require large numbers of books. Thus, from 1955 to 1965, the increase of undergraduates, graduate students, and officers was 11.6, 40.1 and 94.9 percent respectively. On the basis of the rise for these three groups from 1955 to 1965, the increase for 1965 to 1975 would be 800 undergraduates, 3,500 graduate students and 5,949 officers. The last two groups need many books.

Undoubtedly library outlays are a burden on the university, though in recent years they have not risen as much as all university outlays; and the anticipation is that though they may rise by about 200 percent in the years 1964-1965 to 1975-1976, the rate of rise would be somewhat less than that for total university outlays. These trends are in some respects puzzling. Whereas professors retire or die, and students leave after a few years, libraries hold onto their books and keep on expanding. Moreover, the pressure to buy grows with the explosion of knowledge.

Buck reminded us that the 770 million copies of books sold in 1954 were 3 times as many on a per capita basis as in 1929; and whereas in 1900 American libraries held 45 million volumes, by 1954, they housed 300 million volumes.[78]

Expenditures and needs are related not only to the number of items, but also to the cost per item. Libraries estimate the increase of costs per unit of books and periodicals at 50 percent for the years 1965 to 1976. This seems a little high when compared with the over-all index or services. But later estimates are even more pessimistic. Wages also rise greatly for libraries, particulary since wages have been rather low and employers are especially vulnerable in a period of full employment, when wages tend to rise greatly for low-paid workers. Library officials may, however, overestimate the rise of wages if they assume that they will rise as much as they did per year in the great inflationary period since 1939.[79] Per year, wages rose about one-half or one-third as much from 1947 to 1966 as in the more inflationary years 1939 to 1965.

With rising prices and wages, with large backlogs of binding and cataloguing, with the increasing level of output of printed materials, with the shortage of space, with the rising demand related to honors programs and the like, and with the large rise of faculty members and graduate and professional students who make especially large demands on the library, it is not surprising that the college authorities find their needs expensive.

77. K. Metcalf, *op. cit.,* p. 71.

78. P. H. Buck, *op. cit.,* pp. 14-15.
79. D. W. Bryant and E. E. Williams, "The Harvard Library in the 1960's," in *Harvard Library Bulletin,* January, 1967, pp. 97-98.

Financing the library has always been a troublesome problem. There has been some dependence on endowment funds, but over most of Harvard's history these have not been large. In the early years the library depended largely on gifts and neglected the complementary services that were required to make a book useful. To some extent the library depended on unrestricted funds. But many objected to financing the library out of unrestricted funds; among other, president Lowell and his treasurer.[80]

The major source of finance in 1955 was unrestricted income. In the future the library will have to depend more on gifts or on the arts and science faculty. In library finance as in other categories, too much hope seems to be placed on additional endowment. But the erosion of endowment is inevitable as prices and productivity rise. Even the endowment transfers in 1949 have by now suffered relative losses of more than 50 percent. That is, compared to per capita income in 1949 and 1967, a dollar of endowment income has lost more than 50 percent of its original value.

Anyone who examines the structure of Harvard library expenditures will be convinced that the purchase of books is not the most important expenditure. (He should allow for some allocation of salaries to books, however).

Buck has said:

...The time has come when it [the library] *must reconsider its tradition of emphasizing the need for book funds and accepting any such fund that is offered though it makes no provision for selecting or ordering the volumes it pays for, to say nothing of classifying, cataloguing, and housing them. The full implications of each gift must be faced, and it must be refused if it entails over-commitment of resources.*[81]

Library expenditures rose annually by $4\frac{1}{2}$ percent in the fifteen years from 1923-1924 to 1938-1939, and by 7.1 percent in the fifteen years from 1938-1939 to 1953-1954. At the 7.1 percent rise in the latter period, expenditures would almost double in ten years, whereas at $4\frac{1}{2}$ percent in ten years they would rise little more than one-half.

For the eleven years from 1953-1954 to 1964-1965, the rise of expenditures for the university library was from $2,100,000 to $5,730,000 or 11 percent per year compounded. For the eleven years, from 1964-1965 to 1975-1976, the projection is a rise from $5,730,000 to $14,660,000, or an increase of 10 percent per year compounded. In successive eleven year periods the increase would be 173 and 156 percent respectively.

In these same eleven-year periods the rise in the number of undergraduates would be 11.6 percent of graduate students, 40 percent; and of officers, 95 percent. Clearly, the increase of library expenditures is not by any means explained merely by the rising numbers using the library. But the change in the structure of the consumers—a greater rise for those requiring large numbers of books, periodicals and documents—is a relevant factor.

Undoubtedly, library expenditures are rising at a great rate. How the library fares will depend, more than anything else, on how university finances develop. Many are concerned over the future of higher education's finance.

The library can improve its position by charging students a fee, a technique widely used in the nineteenth century; and also by charging outside users not costs but substantially more than is charged now.

Numerous factors are at work increasing the costs of operating libraries. Prices are rising, and more than in other areas. In a recent period of thirteen years, the cost of books rose by 62 percent; and of the whole consumers' index, only 28 percent. The rate of growth of enrollment at Harvard is likely to decline, a development which should contain rises. But probably of much more importance is the large relative increase in Harvard population of those who put great strains on the library resources.

Other factors are also relevant. Competition for books and library personnel is on the increase. Many more universities are trying to build large and good

80. A. L. Lowell to C. F. Adams, November 20, 1928.
81. P. Buck, *op. cit.,* p. 85.

libraries. With the added output of books, periodicals, and documents, the pressure to purchase increases. Technological advances also induce large additional outlays. Undoubtedly to some extent, costs are reduced by these advances. But they also account for increased output of some services and to some extent instead of reduced unit costs, the net result may well be an improved product at higher cost.

Another cause of rising costs is the increasing importance of the nonbook elements in the library, e.g., microfilm, photographic departments, maps. One of the most troublesome problems confronting librarians is the preservation of materials printed in the last hundred years that are disintegrating.[82]

A few facts are to be gleaned from the volume on library statistics. In the years 1960 to 1962 library expenditures rose by 34 percent and instruction expenditures by 26 percent. But for Harvard library expenditures increased only by 20 percent.[83] Apparently other institutions of high learning were gaining on Harvard.

Again, only one institution of higher learning other than Harvard in 1961-1962 added 100,000 or more items. But thirty-two institutions of higher learning had more than 1 million volumes and only fourteen spent more than $300 per student. (Harvard's figure was $513.)[84] The average cost of a volume in the the U.S. institution of higher learning libraries was $5.78.

A Comparison of Library Items, Universities and
Liberal Arts Colleges 1961-1962

	Universities		Liberal Arts Colleges	
	Public	Private	Public	Private
Volumes — Median Unit	462,845	547,692	79,451	46,725
Expenditures Per Student	$24.	$52.	$37.	$43.
% of Total Expenditures	1.2	3.8	5.0	4.8

Source: *Library Statistics of College and Universities, 1961-1962*, Part 2, p. 12

82. For material in the last few paragraphs see especially Bryant and Faihnsod, *The Harvard University Library, 1966-1976*, 1966; E. E. Williams, *Access to Recorded Knowledge*, 1967 (mimeographed); *The Center for Research Libraries*, February 1966; Harvard College Library, *Proposed Addition*, 1967; (S. E. Harris, ed.), *Higher Education in the United States: The Economic Problems*, 1960; S. E. Harris, *op. cit.*, Office of Education, *Library Statistics of Colleges and Universities, 1961-1962*, 1962, part 2, p. 5.

83. *Report of the University Librarian*, 1959-1960; 1961-1962.

84. *Library Statistics of College and Universities, 1961-1962*, pp. 4, 6, 12, 15, 36.

57

Books

From the very beginning, the college was interested in the price of books purchased by students. It will be recalled that the price of books relative to other commodities and services was much higher in the seventeenth century than in recent times. Books are indeed a bargain now compared to their costs in the seventeenth and eighteenth centuries, both absolutely and relatively.

The first teacher of Hebrew, Judah Monis (1722 to 1760) provided a textbook on which the corporation allowed him a modest return. Early in the nineteenth century, Pres. Samuel Webber and his widow were involved in providing a book on mathematics under the supervision of the college, the corporation allowing a return to Webber and also to his widow.

The corporation in 1735 supported a printing of Monis' books.

M[r] *Monis having exhibited to y*[e] *Corporation a specimen of his Hebrew Grammar, and having also exhibited an account of y*[e] *Charges in printing, stitching & covering a thousand Copies of said Grammar, which amounts to two hundred nineteen pounds two & three pence, and y*[e] *Corporation having taken one hundred copies to dispose of as they shall see cause, and y*[e] *prime cost of y*[e] *nine hundred copies remaining, amounting to four shillings ten pence half penny each, which at one hundred & fifty per Cent. advance, makes twelve shillings two pence one farthing, therefore voted, y*t *m*[r] *Monis sell said Grammar at twelve shillings and two pence a piece, he paying to y*[e] *College Treasurer four shillings ten*

pence half penny for each Grammar, with y[e] *Jnterest thereof as he draws them out, and y*t *m*[r] *Treasurer pay to m*[r] *Monis fourteen shillings out of y*[e] *College Treasury, upon y*[e] *one farthing abated in his advance on each Book allowed in the Sale of said Grammar. And y*t *y*[e] *price of selling and paying into y*[e] *Treasury, be regulated from time to time by y*[e] *Standard of Silver money; the price of which at this day is twenty shillings per ounce.*[1]

It was especially after the crisis of the 1820s and for a generation thereafter that the university interested itself in the costs of books to students. The reasons for this were undoubtedly increased recourse to books, the high prices charged, and their great concern for the total costs of education. In 1828 the corporation appointed a committee for reducing the price of text books. By introducing purchases for cash instead of credit, the authorities hoped to depress prices. Also, they had been impressed by a modern language professor who, by importing books directly from France, effected a reduction of the price per volume from 75 to 25 cents.[2]

The Harvard Corporation assumed considerable control over the conditions of purchase of books by students. One reason for this was that the college provided much of the capital for the buying of books. Thus, in 1831, the divinity school asked the corporation to put at the disposal of the school no more than

---

1. *College Books*, vol. IV, p. 631.
2. Quincy, *op. cit.*, vol. II, pp. 560-561.

$1,500 for the purchase of manuals for the students, agreeing also to a charge being imposed on the students to finance these additional costs. The corporation approved, but warned that no further advances could be made unless tuition was increased.[3]

In 1832, the professor of rhetoric asked permission of the corporation to substitute Whateley's textbook for Blair's book in the course on rhetoric. The Whateley book "is in some respects original. . . it still makes him [the student] reflect. But the Blair book is diffuse, and Whateley's is systematic."[4]

The treasurer in 1845, to whom had been referred the problems of purchasing textbooks, proposed that the contract for all textbooks be given to a Mr. Owen. He would sell books at 10 percent less than the trade price. Indeed, one book firm was prepared to offer a price 25 percent less than the trade price but this was not considered acceptable because he would put upon the steward the responsibility of distributing the books. Owen's price would match that given by Little Brown to the law school.[5]

On occasion the faculty asked the corporation to finance purchases of books for students. Thus, Professor Greenleaf of the law school asked the corporation for twenty copies for students of Judge Story's *Conflict of Laws.*[6]

Often the faculty wanted some assurance of a market before undertaking the preparation of a book. Thus, the renowned professor of mathematics, Benjamin Peirce, wanted to prepare a textbook for college use. He requested the blessing of the corporation before he embarked on this adventure.

. . . But I cannot undertake a task that must engross so much time and is so elementary in its nature and so unworthy of one that aspires to anything higher in science, without the certainity that no circumstances will retard the publication and use of the works when prepared but their defects. Let them be submitted to the most rigid examination. If they do not satisfy it, I shall destroy them without regret. . . I dare not promise myself success when men of genius have failed and no one has yet succeeded . . . .[7]

Every effort was made to keep the price of books down. Hence, the intermediary of the college in the purchase of books. Hence, special efforts by faculty members. The renowned humanist George Ticknor related that a new French grammar priced 65 cents had been substituted for the dollar grammar of a year earlier and yet had improved paper and binding, and generally was superior to the old grammar. Copyright was kept in the control of the corporation. The thousand copies of the first year had been absorbed. So Hilliard and Brown proposed new editions of five thousand copies with a charge of but 48 cents a copy.[8]

One of the obstacles to indulging in large-scale operations and hence, to reduced prices was that increased responsiblilities were put on the administration of the college. The student would receive the book and the charge would be put on his term bill. That meant more work for the college departments. To contend with this problem, special measures were taken to assure that the use of the term bill technique for payment was limited to books approved by the faculty for college use.[9]

In seeking a reduction of prices, the college also proposed to deal with the segments of the printing industry separately, e.g., paper makers, compositors, and binders. The result would be reduced costs.[10]

As a means of keeping prices down, Harvard invited

3. *Report of Committee. . . the Votes of the Theological School. . . in Relation to Text Books in that Department,* May 19, 1831.
4. E. T. Channing to President Quincy, September 17, 1832.
5. *Report of the Treasurer [on] the Communication of the College Faculty Respecting the. . . Mode of Supplying. . . Textbooks,* May 31, 1845.
6. Professor S. Greenleaf to the President, February 24, 1834.
7. Benjamin Peirce to President Quincy, October 23, 1832.

8. George Ticknor to the President and Fellows of Harvard College, May 15, 1832.
9. C. Saunders to the President, November 19, 1830. *Report of the Committee on the Mode of Purchasing Text Books,* March 22, 1858.
10. *Report of Committee to Consider the Best Way of Providing the Students with Textbooks,* March 31, 1845; *Report of the Committee Upon the reduction of Expenses. . .Report in Part Upon the Cost of Textbooks,* June 1, 1857.

competition among booksellers. Thus, in 1831, the committee on textbooks "invited from the principal publishers in Boston and its vicinity proposals for furnishing the college with textbooks and the proposals of Messrs. Hilliard and Brown being the lowest received, the Committee have made a contract with them. . . ."[11]

Under one agreement, Hilliard and Brown would manufacture books for Harvard on certain specifications, e.g., full sheep binding. They would sell one group of books at list price without additions. Another group would be furnished "at the lowest rates at which they can with their best skill and diligence procure the same at auction. . .and shall be charged to the college at the actual cost thereof together with a commission of 12½ per cent." The contract allowed the return of books that were not wanted and payment by the college three times a year.[12]

In 1832, the college and James Brown contracted for the delivery of Latin texts by Barnes with specifications indicated. Barnes would purchase any books made obsolete by the new works. The college agreed to take fifty copies of each work printed.[13]

Competition was also severe on books that were imported from Europe. A Mr. Rich offered to procure books abroad at half the price usually set, for he would move books directly from the continent to Boston, thus avoiding the high costs of importing into London first.[14]

Control of reading assignments by the president or the corporation greatly exceeded expectations in the years 1825 to 1860. Clearly, one reason for corporate interest was that the textbook writer sought approval by the corporation and, hence, later adoption. Thus,

Prof. Charles Folsom proposed to reprint the five books of Livy at the Cambridge Press. He was "much incommoded by the gross inaccuracy of the editions printed in other parts of the country. . . ." Folsom would include more of other parts of the thirty-five volumes of Livy. But before beginning, he consulted the Latin department and a committee of the corporation. He received "a general approbation of the plan, and without any pledges, the expression of an opinion, that if it were well executed and at a suitable price, it would be adopted in the university." If the corporation approved the sheets of the volume, Folsom would expect adoption for the next freshman class. The price was to be 85 cents in good sheep binding.[15]

C. C. Felton suggested that students read an additional tragedy of Euripides. If the president and corporation approved, the cost would be only 56 cents a copy of a good edition.[16]

President Quincy in 1840 published 750 copies of his *History of Harvard University*. A few years later the enterprise was in the red by about $1,500 (inclusive of interest). In addition, Quincy had contributed $2,000 of his own funds. Pleased with the results, the corporation agreed to cancel $1,200 of the debt, and expressed the hope that an improved market would make a return of the $2,000 to Quincy possible. A price of $5 for the equivalent of 1,800 pages of usual type seemed to low to many. But an increase to $7 would have discouraged sales to teachers and ministers, who were especially likely to be interested; and besides, a wide circulation was in the interests of the college.[17]

Determined to keep prices down, in 1847 Harvard led a struggle to kill a proposed tariff on books and scientific equipment; the net effects would be higher prices of these items.[18]

11. *Report of the Committee on Textbooks*, June 23, 1831.
12. Memorandum of an Agreement Made. . . in the Year 1831 Between the President and Fellows of Harvard College and Messrs. Hilliard and Brown of Cambridge, September 1, 1831.
13. Memorandum of an Agreement Between the Committee on Textbooks and Mr. James Brown of Cambridge, August 15, 1832.
14. B. Rich to the Reverend Dr. Kirkland, July 8, 1827.
15. C. Folsom to President Quincy, August 19, 1829.

16. C. C. Felton to President Quincy, November 21, 1832.
17. Memorandum of President Quincy on the History of Harvard University, December 26, 1840; *Report of the Treasurer on Quincy's History of Harvard University*, June 5, 1845.
18. The President and Fellows of Harvard College to the Senate and House of Representatives of the United States of America February 27, 1847.

Soon after the death of Professor Sophocles in 1883, the college agreed to support the publication of 250 copies of Sophocles "Greek Lexicon, 2,204 pages."

Previous editions of 520 copies had been sold at $10 each. Proposing a new edition of the 2,204 pages of the Greek Lexicon, the publishers suggested a retail price of $7.50 "in accordance with the tendency of the times." The publishers would account to the college at the rate of $5.00 a copy, "this margin enabling us to make suitable discounts to dealers to encourage them to handle the book." These mark-ups seem rather less than current ones.[19]

This great interest in the price of books by the Harvard authorities began to wane by the Civil War.

One important reason was that books were beginning to absorb smaller relative resources. By 1967, the dean of admissions informed this writer that books and course supplies required only 2 to 3 percent of student costs, a small amount compared to costs at times in excess of 10 percent in earlier years.

Another reason for the reduced interest by the college was the declining drain of funds for textbooks, with the increasing attention paid to general literature as against textbooks. When a professor assigns readings from ten to fifty books, obviously the student can not be expected to purchase all fifty, or even ten, books.

19. John Wilson and Sons to Professor Thayer, March 4, 1884; Little, Brown and Company to Professor J. Henry Thayer, March 13, 1884.

58

Nonfaculty Wages

Faculty salaries are an important part of expenditures of Harvard. They run around 25 percent of the total currently (somewhat higher if employee benefits are included). But what is surprising is that wages are also about 25 percent of outlays. In earlier years faculty salaries were a much larger part of the total costs of higher education than they are now. Perhaps for that reason and also because of the small resources available, the university administration was not generous in its salary scales or agreeable to advances when accosted with demands for a rise of wages. At any rate, it is clear that corporation salaries, or their equivalent, were much more important relatively in the nineteenth century than in recent years.

In 1832-1833, corporation salaries were more than 3 times as high relatively as in recent years. The college outlays in 1832-1833 were $28,290, almost $60 million in 1966-1967 (arts and sciences), and $136 million for the university. It is clear that educational services are much more extended now than they were 100 to 150 years ago. The relative burden of the plant is also much greater now. This decline of importance of corporate appointments measured roughly by salaries has also been an indication of the rising importance of items other than faculty members salaries.

Persistent demands for pay increases emanated especially from the library. T. W. Harris, the librarian in the 1830s, wanted an increase in pay. How did the college expect him to get by with ten children at

Percent of Expenditures, 1832–1833 and 1966–1967

	Harvard University 1966–1967	Harvard University Arts and Science only, 1966–1967	College 1832–1833
Salaries	28*	28*	90†
Wages	28*	19*	‡
Equipment and supplies	19	14	7‡
Scholarships, etc.	9	14	3
Other	16	24	

*Included retirement payments. (Equally divided 6 per cent among salaries and wages.)

†Faculty salaries (inclusive of proctors and tutors), librarian's salary and secretarial work for corporation and treasurer.

‡Of total expenditures of $28,290 in 1832–1833, the following are included under equipment and supplies (in part, might be put under wages): Janitorial and maid service, $857.60; fuel and care of fires, $520.27; museums, philosophical and chemical departments, repairs of clocks, postage, etc. − $217.72.

Sources: Financial Report to the Board of Overseers of Harvard College, 1966-1967; Account of Income and Expenditures for the Year Ending August 31, 1833 (my calculations).

$1,000 a year? he asked.[1] "...*When you take into view the magnitude of the duty and responsibility* of the office, you will be able to render the compensation more nearly *adequate to the expense and the importance of the service situation....*" The usual arguments for higher pay was that the cost of living was high in Cambridge; that the cost was steadily rising; that workers elsewhere were being paid higher salaries; and that the working hours and responsibilities were increasing without commensurate increases in pay.[2]

Complaints did not emanate exclusively from librarians. The steward, for example, frequently sought improved economic status. At one time the steward had been subject to orders from the butler, but no longer. By 1765, he was receiving about 2½ times as high pay as the butler (£150 vs £65) He gradually assumed larger responsibilities. On one occasion, when the steward revealed the large additional burdens of his job, the corporation granted him an assistant. The bill, however, was to be paid not by the college but the law school, the point being made that the additional work stemmed from rising numbers of students at the law school.[3]

John Sibley, the fabulous librarian who served from 1856 to 1877, was one of the most determined beggars. Sibley was annoyed at his hours: "from morning commons to evening prayers in term-time." At $2.00 a day or 40 cents an hour for overtime he felt himself badly treated. At one point he asked for a rise of pay from $600 to $1,800. His hours were long, the contributions of the library to education broadly conceived in Sibley's view, at least as great as that of any department, and yet his pay at that time was equal only to that of a tutor at the beginning of his appointment. Upon recieving an offer from Connecticut, Sibley turned the letter over to the president, pointing out that the pay was higher and the cost of living less than in Cambridge. Sibley improved his position by traveling for the library and even begging for funds. But the administration discouraged such activities.[4]

Benjamin Peirce, librarian from 1826 to 1831, was also forceful and persuasive. At one point, he carefully presented a work log which showed that he had worked 11,100 hours in a year but had been paid only for 4,284 hours. This is a surprising document since 11,100 hours spread over 52 weeks gives 213 hours a week.[5]

A great deal of the agitation for higher pay was associated with the rising cost of living. Yet many of the complaints came in the 1830s and 1840s, when there was no clear upward trend in prices. Beginning in 1850, the inflationary trends became troublesome.

In this connection, it is also interesting that in 1914 the college once more was giving pay scales careful consideration. This is readily understandable since the years 1900 to 1914 were inflationary years. In 1914, the college administration classified workers, suggested pay scales, and considered fringe benefits. The authorities ruled out old age benefits. But two weeks of vacation and two weeks sick leave (half pay) were acceptable. Undoubtedly part of the problem was that wages were rising faster than prices, that is, real pay was rising. The resultant gain in real wages had an impact at Harvard. Often when the complaint was the rise of prices as the justification for higher pay at Harvard, the real catalytic agent was rising real

1. T. W. Harris, *Librarian's Fifth Annual Report,* 1836; T. W. Harris to S. A. Eliot, January 4, 1848.

2. T. Parsons to President Walker, December 21, 1852; W. G. Stearns to W. R. Andrews, Treasurer, January 23, 1856; J. L. Sibley to Hon. S. A Eliot, Treasurer..., December 20, 1845.

3. Batchelder, *Bits of Harvard History* pp. 89-90; W. G. Stearns to the President and Fellows of Harvard College, November 28, 1846; Committee on... Application of the Steward for an Increase of Compensation, December 25, 1846; *Report of the Treasurer... Respecting Salary of Janitor*, November, 1844.

4. J. L. Sibley to President Walker, November 9, 1855; March 19, 1859; to the President and Fellows of Harvard College, June 26, 1844, April 24, 1851; to President Everett, June 9, 1847; Committee...on Communication of Mr. J. L. Sibley, August 24, 1844; E. Everett, Chairman, *Report on the Compensation of the Assistant Librarian,* May 29, 1849.

5. B. Peirce to the Corporation of Harvard University, July 3, 1833.

wages on the labor market generally.[6]

An indication of pay scales and responsibilities of labor in the 1890s is given by a letter from President Eliot when he offered a trial position as superintendent of the gymnasium at $90.00 per month. The incumbent, if successful during the trial period, would work from 9 A.M. to 9 P.M. six days a week; and Eliot warned that much of the work was distasteful. Board would cost $5 to $8 a week.[7]

In more recent years the unionization of workers, or the improved levels of pay as a means of discouraging unionism, tended to bring higher wage scales. The large element of wages in Harvard's expenditure structure in the 1960s is a function both of increased services requiring more skilled and unskilled workers, and also the rising standards of pay related to the gains of productivity.

6. Memorandum of Interview with Mr. Burke, in A. L. Lowell Papers, F-150, 1914.

7. C. W. Eliot to General F. W. Lister, November 14, 1892.

PART

9

SCHOOLS

59

The Harvard Medical School

Budget

In 1783, the Harvard Medical School opened with a faculty of three professors. The Harvard Corporation assumed responsibility for the new school but provided little financial help.[1] In fact, the faculty had to depend on fees for its support and had to finance expenditures for plant and equipment out of fees or their own resources. Harvard authorities had never shown any great enthusiasm for diverting college funds to the professional schools.

It is not surprising that the first treasurer's report we discovered showed expenditures for 1823 of but $781.86 and receipts of $556.77. Much of the money, of course, did not go through regular channels. In 1834, the faculty complained of the declining enrollment and the competition of other schools that were reducing fees and competing by offering a safe curriculum. The spokesmen for the faculty expressed great concern that the decline might be cumulative.

Even on its hundredth anniversary in 1883, the school could boast of gifts and bequests of but $320,000, a rise of investment funds of $100,000, and salaries from $20,000 to $36,000, all over a period of ten or eleven years.[2]

Space was a perennial problem. In 1783, Holden Chapel in Cambridge housed the school. But to obtain patients and corpses the school moved, with the financial aid of the government, to Boston on Mason Street in 1816; to North Grove Street in 1846; to Boylston Street in 1883; and to the large plant provided by Morgan, Rockefeller, and others in the early twentieth century. In 1925, the cost of the medical school plant was estimated at $3 million and the associated hospitals at $8 million. These crises of space involved the university in concentrated begging episodes, and often in deficits. Thus, in the campaign of the early twentieth century, the president estimated that despite receipts from the sale of land and the use of some funds, the school would be confronted with expenditures annually on the new buildings of $67,416, and with additional income of $39,400, and hence an annual deficit of $28,000, a substantial sum

---

1. For details of the medical school's history, see T. F. Harrington, *The Harvard Medical School*, 1905; C. W. Eliot, *Harvard Memories*, 1923; C. W. Eliot, *Late Harvest*, 1924; C. W. Eliot, *Educational Reform*, 1898; C. W. Eliot, *University Administration*, 1908; Josiah Quincy, *The History of Harvard University*, vol. II, p. 226 et seq.; Samuel Eliot Morison (ed.), *The Development of Harvard University, 1869-1929*, 1930, pp. 556-564; Memo by J. C. Warren accepted by the Faculty of Medicine and ordered to be printed, February, 1846; S. Eliot, *The History of the University*, esp. pp. 68-71; *Four American Universities: An Historical Sketch of Harvard University*, 1895, p. 28; various reports of committees to visit the medical and dental schools; literature on the 1960s program for the medical school; miscellaneous items from the Harvard University archives.

2. T. F. Harrington, *op. cit.*, pp. 474-475; *Medical School of Harvard University; Celebration of 100th Anniversary of Founding of the Medical School of Harvard University*, 1883; J. Warren and W. Channing to President Quincy, January 22, 1834.

at that time.[3] To provide the school with three rooms in the attic in 1871, President Eliot broke a Harvard tradition: The corporation donated half of the $7,000 cost.

President Eliot's reforms, which involved much longer attendance, progressive instruction, a four-year degree, passing grades in all subjects, a college degree for admission, were bound to affect enrollment adversely, and in part would also result in higher tuition charges. The new instruction was also much more expensive. The combination of more personal instruction, emphasis on laboratories for teaching against practical work, and a larger plant were reflected in financial pressures: deficits were troublesome in the years before World War I, and there were complaints of use of endowment funds to finance repairs of buildings.[4]

In 1906, Eliot announced a need of $1,500,000 to provide endowment for fourteen professorships that were not endowed or inadequately endowed.[5] Besides, the president held that clinical medicine was underfinanced. By 1910-1911, expenditures had risen to $273,000.[6] By that time, per capita costs had risen to more than $1,000, with the major items $439 for salaries for instruction, $165 for repairs and care of buildings, inclusive of heat and light, and $165 direct expenditures for instruction.[7]

By 1965-1966, expenditures of the medical school had risen to $22,300,000, an amount higher than the preceding year by about $2 million.[8] Over a period of fifty-five years, 1910 to 1965, the rise of expenditures was 7.1 times, or an annual increase of about 4 percent. If allowance is made for price rise, the increase was 287 percent. (Prices rose by 182 percent in this period of fifty-five years). At the rate of increase of 1965-1966 over 1964-1965, expenditures would double in seven years. In this year prices were almost stable again.[9]

Student Fees

Financing of the budget requires contributions from students, current gifts, income from endowment, and government contributions, the last especially for research. Thus, in 1965-1966, government contracts and grant receipts availed of reached $15 million, or more than two-thirds of total income of the medical school.[10]

Let us concentrate on student fees at this point. One of the original faculty members of the medical school in 1818 stressed the importance of fees from private practice and some income from university funds. "These combined fees, with the Hersian salary, afforded a handsome compensation, while the Professor was not encumbered with many and heavy expenses."

From the very beginning the school relied heavily on fees. At its founding it was provided:

... that it would be expedient for the corporation as far as may be to elect into these professorships some gentlemen of public spirit and distinguished ability who would undertake the business for the present for the fees ... and should be found to undertake this, as they doubt not there will be, they flatter themselves that the utility of this Institution will soon be so obvious that it will find great encouragement among us, from gentlemen of liberal minds and easy circumstances, who are friends to the University and to the Public, and disposed to alleviate the miseries of mankind. ...

3. T. F. Harrington, *op. cit.*, pp. 1048, 1175-1176, President Eliot to Mr. Murphy (general education board), November 27, 1901; *Report of Various Committees of the Board of Overseers of Harvard College*, 1924-1925.
4. T. Lyman to F. W. Hunnewell, September 20, 1915; *Report of Overseers Committee to Visit the Medical and Dental Schools*, 1912, no. 44.
5. C. W. Eliot to Dr. Blake, October 27, 1906.
6. *Report of the Committee to Visit the Medical and Dental Schools*, 1912, no. 31; A. L. Lowell, Inter-Office Correspondence.
7. Assistant Comptroller to F. W. Hunnewell, May 24, 1912.
8. *Financial Report to the Board of Overseers of Harvard College*, 1965-1966.

9. See *Report of the Visiting Committees of the Board of Overseers*, 1965-1966; cf., *Harvard College*, 1924-1925.
10. *Financial Report to the Board of Overseers of Harvard College*, 1965-1966, p. 12.

In setting fees, the professors had to watch their competitors. In 1811, upon moving to Boston, the faculty announced:

... that the fee for attendance on the anatomical lectures has been reduced, in order that it might not exceed that established in other places. The professors avail themselves of this opportunity to remark, that in their arrangements for the medical school, they have never been guided by the hope of pecuniary compensation. On the contrary, they do not expect to receive any reward of this nature, which will compensate for the sacrifice of private practice to their official duties. ...

In 1811-1812, a spirited debate emerged over an application for a new medical school which would compete with Harvard. Harvard won this battle. But it continued to encounter competition which it would meet not only by enrolling the best of teachers in private schools but also by depressing standards.[11]

In the 1820s the faculty once more was concerned over its competition. The Berkshire School in Pittsfield could offer room, board, and washing for the modest charge of $1.75 per week and had the attraction of Professor Henry Childs as well. In five years, Harvard lost about 30 percent of its students and Berkshire gained 15 percent.[12]

A peculiar kind of competition prevailed over a good part of the nineteenth century. Professors in the Harvard Medical School would organize as private schools. For example, one school in 1834 included Dean Channing of the Harvard Medical School and five other leading Harvard Medical School staff members. In 1838, another school (Tremont Street Medical School) included Oliver Wendell Holmes on its staff. The school was located at 33 Tremont Row over Burnett's Apothecary store. These peculiar institutions could thrive because, until Eliot's days, the Harvard school operated only a few months each year.[13]

A number of physicians organized to deal with the problem of excessive competition and low charges, e.g., a fashionable doctor received but 50 cents a visit, including medicine. Out of this group the medical school was born. The fee schedule at the period of Harvard's medical school opening was as follows:

The first fees established by this medical club were half a dollar for a visit; if in consultation, a dollar; rising and visiting after eleven o'clock and previous to sun-rising, a double fee; cases in midwifery, eight dollars; capital operations in surgery, five pounds lawful money; reducing a dislocation, or setting a fractured bone, one guinea; small operations in surgery, according to circumstances; bleeding and opening abscesses, half a dollar; extracting a tooth, the same, if the person called on the doctor; if not, a fee for a visit was added. The advance on medicines found for patients, though bought of an apothecary, was enormous, often amounting to three or four hundred percent. All accounts were to be calculated and kept in hard money; and the exchange, if payment was made in paper money, according to such agreement as could be made between the parties. The profession was much benefited by these regulations.[14]

Professors depended heavily on fees from students, not only for admission to lectures, but also in payment for degrees, and contribution to repairs of buildings. Thus, in 1788, the first class graduated. The student had to pay 40 shillings for his degree if he had attained a masters' degree, £5 with a bachelor's degree and £7 for others. Each course in anatomy and surgery cost the student $26.[15] In 1810, fees for four courses cost from $15 to $25. By 1818, the school had fifty-eight students and the

11. Harrington, *op. cit.*, pp. 382-383, 496-497, 504-505; J. C. Warren and W. Channing, Committee of the Faculty to the President of Harvard University, January 22, 1834.
12. Harrington, *op. cit.*, pp. 83, 490-497, 597-598; Circular Announcing Establishment of the Medical School in Boston, June 1, 1811.
13. Harrington, *op. cit.*, pp. 496-497.
14. *Ibid.*, p.77; *Massachusetts Historical Society Proceedings, 1863-1864.*
15. Harrington, *op. cit.*, pp. 279, 289, 363, 423, 440-441.

charges varied from $10 to $20 per course. The tendency was to cut fees as competition intensified. For 1800 to 1809, the three professors were earning $807, $630, and $314 a year on the average, with fees yielding almost 40 percent and legacies about 60 percent. In the year 1847, the fee for all courses was $75, with additional payments of $3 for matriculation, $5 for dissecting, and $20 for the graduation.

In 1888, students were the major source of financing, providing $58,141; with endowment $196,000, the contribution of endowment income (about $10,000) was only one-sixth of student fees.[16] By the early twentieth century, the tuition has risen to $200 except $170 for the fourth year.[17]

The structure of income has changed greatly since the 1880s. Income from endowment had risen to more than $3 million by 1965-1966 and tuition and other student income provided only $1,500,000. Whereas student income in 1888 amounted to 6 times that of endowment income, in 1965-1966, the ratio was 2 to 1 in favor of endowment. By 1965-1966, students provided $1,800,000. Clearly, despite the rising tuition, the students' relative contribution was declining. In 1965-1966, students' fees amounted to only 30 percent of the salaries in the medical school, and less than one-quarter of the expenditures for faculty and staff members' salaries.[18]

Tuition at the medical school has been rising at a rapid rate.

Despite these large increases of tuition, student fees provided only 8 percent of the income of the medical school in 1965-1966. For the whole university, the figure was 18½ percent. The explanation of the low tuition figure of 8 percent lies in part in the high cost of a medical education. In one respect the tuition estimate greatly exaggerates its contribution.

16. Harrington, *op. cit.*, pp. 1078-1079.
17. *Report of the Committee to Visit the Medical and Dental School*, March 3, 1964.
18. *Financial Report to the Board of Overseers of Harvard College*, 1965-1966, pp. 12-15; LeClear Engineers Report to President and Fellows of Harvard College, March 1915 in *A. L. Lowell Correspondence; Dean's Report*, 1962-1963, p. 51.

Tuition Rates in Recent Years

1942–1953	$ 800.
1962–1963	1,500.
1964–1965	1,750.
1965–1966	2,000.

Source: Reports of the Dean of the Faculty of Medicine.

Against the $1,500,000 of student fees, we should put the $1,400,000 of scholarships and other student awards for 1965-1966.[19]

Endowment

The medical school did not at first rely heavily on endowment income to cover expenses. Harvard received its first important gift in 1772, eleven years before the school opened. From 1722 to 1812, six gifts amounted to more than $12,000; and the income on these paid a substantial part of the salaries of the first three professors.

Officials of the school complained of the small amount of help, if any, given by the Harvard Corporation. In 1848, the faculty noted that the government and the faculty had carried the school, not the corporation. It was not until 1899 that the corporation weakened, making available for the first time unrestricted funds for the medical school, which thus obtained $300,000. President Eliot provided a small contribution early in his administration. The corporation also gave the school a break when it allowed the school's endowment to earn the high returns on its endowment of earlier years, not the reduced income in response to smaller returns on more recent investments. Ultimately, it was held that current investments would profit from similar protection.[20]

19. *Dean's Report*, 1962-1963, p. 48; *Financial Report to the Board of Overseers of Harvard College*, 1965-1966, pp. 12-15.
20. Harrington, *op. cit.*, p. 1168; Medical Faculty to President and Fellows, September 22, 1848.

By the 1880s, the importance of endowment became increasingly clear. The case was put thus:

. . . Any institution which is essentially dependent on the number of paying students it can draw must be tempted to sacrifice its higher aims to popularity. No high standard can be reached under such circumstances, and the only way to insure the independent action of a school which aims at teaching the whole country by example is to endow its professorships, so that the very best and highest grade of instruction, and not that which is popular because it is easy and superficial, may always be given from its chairs, whether the classes be large or small. . . .[21]

In early twentieth century, a visiting committee urged the mobilization of $1,500,000 of additional endowment in order to put clinical medicine on an equal basis with laboratory teaching. At that time laboratory departments were spending 2½ times as much money as the clinical departments for current operations and 4 times as much for building maintenance.[22]

The growth of endowment was small until relatively recent years.

Estimates, endowment, various years

1812	$ 12,019*
1869	40,000
1892	273,000
1901	1,098,500
	(Before new plant)
June, 1966	75,405,522

*Sum of six gifts for endowment of professorships.

The reader should observe the large relative gains from 1869 to 1901, a period marked by the great

---

21. Medical School of Harvard University, *Celebration of 100th Anniversary of the Founding of the Medical School of Harvard University*, 1783-1883, p. 54.
22. *Report of the Committee to Visit the Medical and Dental Schools*, April, 1912, no. 31.

Eliot reforms. Apparently improving the quality of the education invited help from the moneyed groups. Whereas eighty-six years after the founding total endowment had reached only $40,000; by 1901, thirty-two years later, the endowment had climbed to more than a million dollars. But the really spectacular rises came after 1901 and especially through the $58-million drive of the early 1960s. This effort accounted for about two-thirds of Harvard's medical endowment in 1966.

Endowment now clearly plays an important part in financing the Harvard Medical School. Though Harvard depends on endowment income much more than most institutions of higher learning, the medical school relies on endowment income much more relatively than all of Harvard; 30 percent of income other than reimbursement of indirect expenses of grants and contracts for the university, and 42 percent for the medical school. There are very few universities that can match the medical school's accumulation of $75 million by 1966. The 1960s program, which yielded $58 million soon after Harvard College raised $82,500,000 in a major campaign, was unique and unparalleled for a medical school anywhere. The more striking was the success in view of the efforts made to avoid competing with the seven allied hospitals in the Boston area, the difficulties of poaching on the territory of medical centers elsewhere, and the concentration, except for the Countway Library, on financing additional staff members and higher salaries. Harvard's top ranking as a medical school, its large contribution to medical education, and its many scientific achievements all invited co-operation. What is especially striking is that inclusive of the building program of the associated hospitals the comprehensive plans called for $100 million.

Yet dependence on endowment income is not as safe as many believe. Medical schools are confronted with a problem that many others are not. They have to be located where the population is, and where land values are very high. This puts an increasing burden on their budgets. Fortunately, enrollment is largely stabilized at Harvard and hence the need of expansion is reduced. Indeed, the growth comes in new programs, especially for practicing physicians, community relations, etc.

In recent years the burden has been lightened by help from the government, and especially through research grants. As a result, the government has carried part of the teaching load, and the assessments on students and the dependence on endowment have been checked. Financial problems of the school, at least in the short run, have been aggravated by Harvard's leadership. As the length of the school year increased, examination standards and admission requirements raised, the immediate impact has been a fall in enrollment.

Gifts

Gifts were needed to cover deficits, to finance purchases of land and improvements of the plant, and to sustain endowment. By the early twentieth century, the school had received $6 million of gifts, but $3 million went into the plant, and endowment had risen to little more than $1 million.

By 1904, the medical school funds had risen to $1,087,000. Aside from a balance of $30,414, the school's funds included forty-five items. At this late date, scholarship and fellowship income from endowment amounted only to about $4,000 to $5,000. The largest gifts were five in number and accounted for $625,000 of the funds. These gifts were received from 1853 on.[23]

Because the faculty depended heavily on fees, and because the corporation was not disposed to divert college funds to the professional schools, serious disagreements arose between the faculty and the corporation. In the first quarter of the nineteenth century, the dean of the school protested at the corporation appropriating fees of the school. In response to this protest the corporation agreed to allow the medical faculty to use the fees to finance such items as minor repairs. In the financing of plant, e.g., major repairs or new buildings, the corporation insisted on financing by the faculty. Thus, when the Grove Street building was being financed in the 1840s, the school had to provide the required $40,000 out of sales of its old building and gifts for the school, and also to guarantee the uncovered $13,000, the excess of costs over available finances for the new buildings.[24] But when President Everett asked the faculty to finance the purchase of a $5,000 to $6,000 library collection, Dr. Holmes, speaking for the faculty, refused to comply. He said the faculty was impoverished and would agree only if public spirited citizens would soon relieve the faculty of this burden.[25]

Over the years, the receipt of gifts raised some interesting problems. Thus, in 1856, the school launched a campaign to raise $50,000, a large sum for that period.

William Walker in 1860 offered to the medical school real estate worth $130,000:

... for the promotion of anatomical, physiological and surgical education in Harvard College... provided that the Medical School of Harvard College can at the present time be reorganized in such a manner as to give the most efficient and best education in the above branches, by insuring to all aspirants for the office of Professors and Teachers a fair competition for the appointments to be made in the institution, for merit and merit alone according to a plan to be hereafter agreed upon between myself and the President and Fellows of Harvard College .... [26]

I find no evidence in the volume on *Endowment Funds of Harvard University* that this gift was ever made. Apparently the corporation could not accept the conditions set by Mr. Walker.

23. *Report of the Committee to Visit the Medical and Dental Schools*, 1909, no. 3; Harrington, *op. cit.*, p. 1393.
24. Dean W. Channing to the President and Fellows of Harvard University, July 23, 1827; and to the Treasurer, August 22, 1827; Harrington, *op. cit.*, p. 1393; Medical Faculty (O. W. Holmes and others) to the Corporation, March 7, 1857.
25. O. W. Holmes to President Everett, October 6, 1848.
26. William Walker to the President and Fellows of Harvard College, December 3, 1860.

George Fabyan in 1896 donated $100,000 for a chair in comparative pathology. Of interest was a condition that losses suffered in the investment of the relevant funds should be recouped by allowing income to cumulate. Another feature of this offer: the professor "shall devote his time to the duties of the Professorships, and shall not engage in private practice without the recommendations of the medical faculty, and the consent of the President and Fellows . . . ."[27]

Two great money-raising episodes were the campaign at the turn of the century to finance five new buildings, and to extend the teaching and research program, inclusive of increased use of the small section techniques of teaching as against the large lecture method. In all about $5 million were involved, a vast sum for the early twentieth century. Relative to the size of the economy the $5-million campaign in 1900 and 1901 could be as large as the $58-million campaign of the 1960s.[28]

In his proposals to Rockefeller in the early twentieth century, Eliot emphasized especially the need of space for research; "In the Department of Physiological Chemistry there is not a single room available for research. . .," and the need of small units of instruction was paramount:

. . . In preparing men for the practice of medicine, where so much depends upon the skill and training of eye and hand, and the faculty of accurate observation, the demand for laboratory training and work in small sections is greater than in almost any other kind of educational work. . . the man should be trained as an individual . . . . This system, however, requires a vastly increased space and is much more expensive. . . .[29]

Eliot also insisted that the great medical schools must be tied to great universities. They need large endowments, obtainable only if they are under conservative control of the larger universities.[30] Eliot also harped upon the larger clinical facilities available at Harvard than in the larger New York schools;[31] and on the need of research facilities for students even though 98 percent of the output would be practitioners.[32]

Clamor for gifts to strengthen endowment continued despite the success of the early twentieth century program. But note the interesting question in 1909 by a visiting committee: ". . . Are the certainties of endowment paralyzing in any degree the realization of the possibilities of individual effort, or, in other words, is the School contributing in as large a measure as might be expected to its own support and development?"[33]

Growing needs for space brought periodic crises. It seemed that in the nineteenth century every twenty years a major rebuilding program was needed. Until the second half of the nineteenth century the faculty was largely responsible for financing building programs. But thereafter this became a serious problem for the corporation.

Space crises emerged in early nineteenth century, in 1880, and after World War I.[34]

Curriculum and Fees

In the early years of the medical school, the instruction was primarily didactic lectures for a very brief period, say three to four months. The faculty spared the students much and in part because they depended to a considerable extent on private practices to

27. *Endowment Funds of Harvard University*, p. 260; *Financial Report to the Board of Overseers of Harvard College*, 1965-1966, p. 250.
28. See especially Harvard University, *Papers Concerning the Proposed New Buildings and Endowment for the Medical School*, 1900, 1901, 1902.
29. C. W. Eliot to J. D. Rockefeller, December 19, 1901, pp. 21-23.

30. *Ibid*, p. 27.
31. *Ibid*, pp. 28-29.
32. *Ibid*, p. 30.
33. *Report of the Committee to Visit the Medical and Dental Schools*, 1909, no. 8.
34. The President and Fellows of Harvard College to the Senate and the House of Representatives in General Court, 1814; Harrington, *op. cit.*, pp. 510-513, 668, 1073, 1107, 1139, 1175, 1181.

achieve a reasonable standard of living. As the curriculum gradually expanded, e.g., with the provision of a clinical professorship in 1810 in order to "enjoy one of the chief advantages which had been expected from the removal of the Medical School, a benefit which has [been] considered by medical writers, one of the most valuable means of acquiring medical knowledge. . ." and with the creation of a professorship in surgery in 1834 and greater use of laboratories, the fees paid by students increased.

Then came Eliot's great reforms. In his first annual report (1869-1870), Eliot warned:

The whole system of medical education in this country needs thorough reformation. The course of professional instruction should be a progressive one, covering three years; the winter session and the summer session should be amalgamated, and the student should give his attendance at lectures and laboratories during the whole year. . . .

By 1870, following the great Eliot reforms, the students had to pay as much as $200, a very large outlay, on fees. With the extension of instruction to three years and then to four years and with increased recourse to the laboratory, not only did the fees increase but teaching burdens also rose. By 1902, Eliot had also extended his elective system to the medical school, with the whole fourth year assigned to electives.

With the appointment of a clinical professor and increased clinical work, problems arose of the appropriate charges to students for the use of the hospital. The Massachusetts General Hospital imposed a charge of $20 for a pupil's attendance, from the first day of March until the first day of November in the year 1822.

The faculty defended compensation:

Now it is not to be presumed that any will expect physicians in full practice to leave their business and devote a considerable time to a public institution, without compensation. Every man must be paid for his labours in some way or other, and time and charge of such a public institution is not a small affair to those who would do justice to it. The idea that the

increase of reputation or of business or of benefit through the medical school are to be a sufficient compensation for the arduous duties of this place, is not well founded. . . .[35]

Eliot was largely responsible for the great reforms in the early 1870s. These changes meant much higher costs both to the school and students.

In his 1871-1872 report, Eliot dwelt on the "ignorance and general incompetency of the average graduate of American Medical Schools. . . the mistakes of an ignorant or stupid young physician or surgeon means poisoning, maiming and killing. . . ."[36]

In 1894, Eliot was still seeking higher standards.

. . . I am prepared to adopt restrictive measures on the increase of the medical school, such as rapid and decided increase in the requirements for admission. A school of 500 students of first rate quality would satisfy me better than a larger school with the present low requirements for admission.[37]

Eliot was in the forefront also in encouraging comparative and preventive medicine: ". . . In short the objects and ends of comparative study at the Medical School are all connected with preventive medicine. . . ."[38]

The block system, which was introduced for the class of 1899, also received the president's support. Students reduced the number of studies they pursued simultaneously under this system and concentrated more at the outset.[39]

In short, the expansion of the curriculum, the rising importance of clinical medicine and use of hospitals by students, the attention paid to comparative and preventive medicine, the large advances with Eliot of the elective system, the rising recourse to laboratory instruction, the block system of instruction, and the general elevation of standards, inclusive

---

35. From Warren Papers quoted in Harrington, *op. cit.*, pp. 580-581.
36. Also see H. Bigelow to C. W. Eliot, April 15, 1871.
37. C. W. Eliot to W. L. Richardson, December 27, 1894.
38. C. W. Eliot to A. Agassiz, January 1, 1907.
39. *Report of the President of Harvard College*, 1902-1903; W. C. Lane, *The University During the Last Twenty-Five Years*, 1906, p. 32.

of a three- and later four-year curriculum and higher examination standards all contributed to rising costs for the medical school and for the medical student. But if costs were high and enrollment at first was affected adversely, in the longer run enrollment and gifts also responded to the rising reputation of the Harvard Medical School.

Enrollment

Enrollment was related to such variables as fees charged, admission requirements, residence requirements, standards, etc. At the time of moving to Boston, enrollment was modest. In 1813, the school gave only thirteen diplomas, with a requirement of attendance at two winter quarters. In 1816, enrollment was 30; in 1846, 160. The school extended instruction from three to four years in 1880; and in 1900, the school introduced a B.A. requirement for entrance. Growth was substantial from 1883, the year of the new building, to 1896-1897; a rise of more than 100 percent. The four-year curriculum apparently was compatible with a large rise in enrollment as the physical capacity increased and the quality of the product became increasingly apparent.

The A.B. requirement seriously reduced enrollment. Even with the large growth of plant by 1905, enrollment had not reached earlier totals.

The Teaching Hospital Problem

Good medical instruction requires clinical experience. From the very beginning, the Harvard Medical School was confronted with a problem of inadequate clinical material. As early as 1784, the faculty sought to take over the almshouse, but was confronted with the opposition of the Boston Medical Society, which disapproved Cambridge exploiting the almshouse.

In the early nineteenth century, when the school moved to Boston in order to obtain greater clinical resources, an agreement was made with the almshouse, which then cared for 350 patients 130 of whom were paupers.

That the said Professors be permitted to visit the sick in the Alms House for the purpose expressed in their application with such number of pupils as the Overseers may think proper. . . provided that the sick in the Alms House and those in the Town who fall under the care of the Overseers shall receive from them all the necessary medical care free from expense to the Town. . . .[40]

But this was not enough. Two professors soon started a campaign which resulted in the building of the Massachusetts General Hospital by the early 1820s, an institution which gave its two major appointments to members of the Harvard Medical School.

It has appeared very desirable to a number of respectable gentlemen, that a hospital for the reception of lunatics and other sick persons should be established in this town. . . . We therefore beg leave to submit for your consideration proposals for the institution of a hospital, and to state to you some of the reasons in favor of such an establishment.[41]

Harvard's close relations with the Massachusetts General Hospital contributed greatly to the eminence of the medical school. A medical school committee in 1846 commented on the hospital:

. . . In cleanliness and comfort, and in the perfection of all those details, which are necessary for the sick and wounded, it is not excelled by any similar establishment in this country or in England. These advantages it has derived partly from the munificence of its endowment [the Committee lists 15 gifts amounting to $383,000], *and partly from having always had the benefit of the time and labour of persons distinguished by their talents and education, not less than by their benevolence. . . .*[42]

The problems were not solved, however. The school needed more beds, and control over appointments in the hospitals was by lay trustees, who paid

---

40. Harrington, *op. cit.*, pp. 277, 278, 300.
41. *Ibid*, p. 567.
42. J. C. Warren, ch. Memo, Accepted by the Faculty of Medicine, February 1846.

little attention to teaching qualifications. Moreover, appointments were rotating rather than continuous. Hence, the medical school had little authority over the important staff appointments at the hospitals and the top staff had to be limited to local choices by the trustees. Hence, for a given outlay of money the talent procured was mediocre. The medical school tried to solve this problem by providing hospitals with university resources, but this was too expensive. President Eliot complained that:

. . .it [the medical school] *is not free to call the most distinguished surgeon or obstetrician that the country contains; because it cannot offer the newcomer a hospital service. This is the reason that the conduct of a great hospital has become in some universities an indispensable function of the faculty of medicine, in spite of the fact that the conduct of a hospital is enormously expensive, and requires an administrative staff quite distinct from the medical school.*

Eliot went on to comment on the fortunate schools that have made alliances with hospitals.[43]

Some progress was made, however. By 1869, the school boasted that:

. . . the students have access, without charge, to the clinical and surgical practice of the Massachusetts General Hospital and to the new City Hospital; and also for all useful purposes, to the Marine Hospital at Chelsea, the Eye and Ear Infirmary. . . .[44]

In the early twentieth century, much progress was made. The university obtained considerable control over appointments to the hospitals. A memo from the members of the corporation of the Peter Bent Brigham Hospital of November 6, 1902, was a landmark in this development.

So far as the charitable purposes of this trust shall in our opinion permit, we hereby declare our desire to promote the objects of your medical school by seeking advice from you; and by giving careful consideration to your nomination in making appointments to

our medical staff, and by permitting access for students to the Hospital.[45]

An overseers' committee observed that "all medical and surgical research profits by continuity through long periods, and each particular research ordinarily needs the direction of a single mind, acting through a long period of time. . ." After 1912, the school boasted, it would have control of clinical appointments in several Boston hospitals: "In the future such teachers may be called from other institutions with the same freedom as is the case with all other University positions. . . ."[46]

By 1916, the university had 6,500 beds available for teaching.[47]

Some General Comments

Writing in 1898, President Eliot could look back and assess the great advances in the preceding thirty years. He recalled his differences with H. Bigelow, the professor of surgery, who in the 1860s controlled the medical school. Bigelow visited all the members of the overseers and warned them:

. . . the young President was going to wreck the Harvard Medical School; it would cease to exist in a year or two if his revolutionary reconstruction of the school were allowed! He actually proposes, said the Professor, "to have written examinations for the degree of doctor of medicine."[48]

In 1898, Eliot listed the changes: three years' residence instead of a few winter periods; a progressive curriculum instead of a nonplanned choice of lectures; greater emphasis of laboratories in place of the recourse to two meager laboratories; examinations in all nine subjects rather than the five accepted before; rising costs to the students as the standards

43. C. W. Eliot, *University Administration*, 1908, pp. 96-97.
44. *Report to the Board of Overseers of Harvard College on the Condition, Needs and Prospects of the University*, 1869, p. 12.
45. Memorandum of June 5, 1908.
46. *Report of the Committee to Visit the Medical and Dental Schools*, 1910, pp. 68-69; A. L. Lowell, Interdepartmental Correspondence, 1912, Memo.
47. A. L. Lowell, Correspondence, November 27, 1916.
48. C. W. Eliot, *Harvard Memories*, pp. 28-29; C. W. Eliot, *Late Harvest*, pp. 37-38.

improved. It required debates at the overseers for three meetings before they accepted the reforms listed above.[49]

By improving standards the cost to students greatly increased. Particularly, the increasing emphasis on individual or small group instruction tended to raise costs. Whereas costs to the student in 1869 were $350 plus room and board for a year, by 1898, the cost of the degree was $835 plus laboratory charges and the cost of board for four years (36 months vs 12 months).[50]

Increased requirements, both for admission and at the school, brought higher costs to the medical student. The school had various alternatives. It might offer increasing amounts of assistance to students. In recent years the amount of aid has increased greatly, with net costs to students—tuition minus assistance—being modest. But the crucial problem was the costs not covered by tuition and assistance. It is not easy to discover the cost of a medical school education because the school offers several joint products. But there can be little doubt that costs minus fees of students amounts to at least a few thousand dollars per student per year. The school finances this subsidy partly out of current income on government contracts, but especially out of the income on endowment. Rising costs induced the school to embark on large endowment programs.[51]

49. *Harvard Memories*, pp. 28-33.
50. C. W. Eliot, *Educational Reform*, 1898, pp. 345-347.
51. See S. E. Harris, *Economics of American Medicine*, 1964, ch. 23.

60

The Economics of the Law School

Some Brief History

The Harvard Law School opened in 1817. About twenty-five years earlier, Sir Issac Royall's will, under which a bequest had been made to Harvard for the study of law, had been probated.[1]

An advertisement appeared in the Boston Daily Advertiser of July 12, 1817:

The Government of Harvard University have lately established under the patronage of the University, a school for the instruction of students at law . . . . The students besides attending the lectures of the Royall Professor of Law and other lectures at the University . . . will have access to the College library and a complete Law School Library . . . and on having complied with the regulations of the institution, will receive the degree of bachelor of laws . . . .

On July 28, 1817, the president's official announcement appeared in the same newspaper. Tuition was to be $100, a high figure for that time.

Growth of the school was uneven. The budget was but several thousand dollars in the early years. Even as late as 1827, salaries of the two professors amounted to $2,170; and in 1828 the enrollment had fallen to four students. It was not until 1832 that the school had acquired Dane Hall under a most peculiar condition for a gift. Nathan Dane, who had provided $10,000 to finance a professorship, through unusual powers of persuasion had induced the corporation to appoint the great Supreme Court Justice Joseph Story to the Dane Chair and, even more remarkable, had induced Story to accept a $1,000 chair, though with an understanding that Story's judicial responsibilities would have priority.

With Story's accession, enrollment jumped to 32 in the first year and escalated to 150 by the late 1850s. Yet despite the large contributions of Story and professors John Ashmun and Simon Greenleaf, as late as 1834 the only serious requirement for a law degree was 18 months of residence, and as late as 1849, the library had but 4,000 volumes; the school, a hundred students; and the primary teaching tool was the text book.[2]

Ninety years after opening, income was still only $141,000.[3] In the next sixty years (to 1967) the budget had risen to an amount in excess of $4,500,000.

---

1. For histories of the Harvard Law School see especially C. Warren, *History of the Harvard Law School*, 1908; A. E. Sutherland, *The Law at Harvard: A History of Men and Ideas*, 1967; A. L. Lowell, *What a University President has Learned*, 1938, especially pp. 36-37; Annual Reports of C. W. Eliot in early 1870s; C. W. Eliot, *A Late Harvest*, especially pp. 46-49.

2. See Warren, *op. cit.*, vol. II, pp. 4-5, 349, 364-365; *Universities and Their Sons*, 1902, p. 119; Batchelder, *Bits of Harvard History*; *Report of the Committee of Overseers of Harvard College Appointed to the Law School in 1849*; *Report to the Board of Overseers of Harvard College on the Condition, Needs and Prospects of the University*, 1869, pp. 17-19.

3. Warren, *op. cit.*, p. 529.

Following Story's death in 1845, the next large development was the appointment of C. C. Langdell as Dane Professor and dean of the law school. Langdell had impressed Eliot when the latter was still an undergraduate. Langdell insisted that law was a science and persuaded Eliot of the tenability of this position; introduced the case system which swept the country; and annual examinations as a prerequisite of a college degree; and steadily raised standards, inclusive of a three-year curriculum. What especially pleased Eliot was that despite the risky raising of requirements and also of fees, the law school's financial position emerged stronger financially than in any other part of the university. Apparently, rising standards brought increased enrollment and surpluses. In fact, this financial improvement was a product of Langdell's insistence that the law school's task was not merely to produce practioners, but also teachers and researchers.

Eliot's persevering support of Langdell contributed greatly to Langdell's success in the post Civil War period, 1870 to 1895. Above all, Langdell insisted that the great teachers were not necessarily those who practiced law: they were "not those experienced in using law but those experienced in learning law."[4]

By 1906-1907, the income of the school had risen to $141,000, a great advance over the less than $10,000 in 1830, but only about 3 percent of the income of 1965-1966. Fee incomes were large in relation to faculty salaries and current outlays, a pattern that had prevailed early, and was still evident in 1906-1907. Tuition amounted to $102,000 in 1906-1907, a sum almost twice faculty salaries.[5]

At its Sesquicentennial in 1967, the school launched a program to raise $15 million, to be spent on new professorial chairs, the plant, research, and student aid. In seeking these funds, the growth of the school was revealed:

Table 60-1.

Enrollment, Faculty, and Budget, Law School, 1910, 1940, 1965

Year	Student Enrollment	Full-time Faculty	Total Operating Budget
1910	810	10	$ 147,463
1940	1,249	33	693,297
1965	1,683	62	4,656,409

In fifty-five years, enrollment had more than doubled, the full-time faculty had increased by more than 500 percent, and the budget by more than 30 times. Whereas the school's endowment was 3.29 percent of the university endowment, its portion of student enrollment was 11.37 percent. By 1966, the school was mobilizing $1,130,000 for student aid.

In a period of twenty years, the school had obtained almost $13 million in gifts for current use and $10,500,000 for endowment.[6]

This array of statistics brings out some aspects of the law school's finances. Its endowment is relatively small when compared with the rest of the university on the basis of relative enrollment totals. Again, the student-teacher ratio has greatly improved (i.e., declined) in the last fifty-five years. Finally, even if allowance were made for price rises and the increase of enrollment, the budget of the law school on a per student stable price level basis was several times as large in 1965 as in 1910.

This rise reflects the increasing general productivity of the nation yielding higher incomes at stable prices. But this is not the whole explanation. Also relevant is the more extensive product turned out by the school in recent years, e.g., more research. The budget is also inflated by another factor, namely, the large rise of student assistance. That is to say that the budget is larger in part because the school provides increasing amounts of assistance.

4. See especially C. W. Eliot, *A Late Harvest*, pp. 46-49; *Report of the President of Harvard College*, 1870-1871; 1871-1872; *A Record of the Commemoration of the 250th Anniversary of the Founding of Harvard College*, 1886.

5. Statistics from Warren, *op. cit.*, p. 529.

6. See especially *Harvard Law School*, 1817-1967; *Sesquicentennial Program for Continued Leadership*, 1967, pp. 7, 8, 9, 22-23; *A Report to the Alumni Scholarship Committee Harvard Law School*, 1966-1967; *Harvard Law School Dean's Report*, 1965-1966, p. 25.

Enrollment

The financial position of the law school has depended heavily on enrollment, for the school, from the very beginning when it imposed a tuition fee of $100, depended little on endowment; and the Harvard Corporation, notably in the period of negotiations with Dane over the financing of the Dane Building, revealed a strong opposition to diverting funds from the college to help the law school.

Even as late as 1965-1966, the law school depended heavily on fees. In that year, tuition in the university contributed $18\frac{1}{2}$ percent of all income (exclusive of direct and indirect expenses on grants and contracts the figure is adjusted upwards to 28 percent). For the law school, tuition and fees provided 56 percent of income; for education, 15 percent; for medicine, only 7 percent;[7] for arts and sciences, 27 percent (41 percent if contracts and grants are excluded); for the business school, which has always sought a tuition policy that would come near covering costs, the tuition take was 43 percent.

Law School Enrollment, Various Years

Year	Numbers
1817 (opening)	27
1828	4
1838 (September)	67
1844-45	156
1849-50	100
1858-59	126
1862-63	89
1865-66	172
1885-86	158
1894-95	413
1907-08	719
1964-65	1658
105 graduates	

Sources: C. Warren, *op. cit.; Annual Reports of the Law School Dean,* and miscellaneous sources.

The law school, at a relatively early period, attracted students from wide areas, with the administration boasting that the school was a national one. Even as early as 1843, they claimed an enrollment of 128 from 23 states, with 40 from Massachusetts. In the middle of the 1960s virtually every state and numerous foreign countries had sent students to the law school.

As standards improved, the proportion of college graduates and especially of Harvard graduates increased. (Harvard's share was 16 percent in 1870-1871 and 39 percent in 1907-1908.) The number of colleges sending students to the law school rose from 27 in 1870-1871 to 122 in 1907-1908.[8]

The impact of Eliot, Langdell, and Ames, the successive deans, is also evident in a rise of enrollment from 161 in 1880-1881 to 655 by 1900-1901.

In general the authorities, in imposing more severe standards of admissions and higher standards at the school, anticipated substantial losses of enrollment. But the results were often unexpected. In the later 1870s, for example, the school imposed an admission exam and also extended residence from two to three years. Enrollment was as follows:

Enrollment, Law School	
1875	173
1876	199
1877	196
1882	138
1886	188

Losses of enrollment were only temporary. Against the rise of standards and of costs tending to depress enrollment, higher standards, greater prestige, rising economic conditions, and increased numbers of college graduates tended to induce larger enrollments. When competition is strenuous, a college may raise standards and costs and yet experience large gains in enrollment. The improvement can then be largely at the expense of others.

---

7. *Financial Report to the Board of Overseers of Harvard College,* 1965-1966, pp. 10-13 (my calculations).

8. The relevant table is deposited in the Harvard University Archives.

Enrollment is a function of many variables. At the outset the school claimed that enrollment would not be allowed to rise to a point where close contact with students would be jeopardized. The administrators also watched the impact of increases of enrollment upon the financial condition of the school. In the productive Story-Greenleaf period, the great reputation of these teachers contributed greatly to the migration to the law school.

But the gains of tuition had to be written down as the faculty demanded additional staff members and/ or higher pay to compensate for increased enrollment. Thus, in 1839, Greenleaf wrote to the president asking for a rise of pay from $1500 to $2500, a rise he ultimately received.

... When I came into the Department the regular exercises of the Royall Professor were on 3 days only in the week, and the school contained less than one-half its present number. It has since been thought expedient by the Professors to increase the weekly exercises by nearly doubling the number, for the benefit of the students of the Institution, and the School has increased from 42 to 88, increasing the demands on my time so far as to leave me scarcely any for practise in the Courts, which is essential to supply the deficiency of salary for my current support. During the past year I have been obliged to decline professional engagements to an amount greater than the sum received from the University.

Other factors were also relevant: the great influx under the spectacular work of Story and Greenleaf, a favorable factor; the difficulties related to the high cost of living in Cambridge, the ascendancy of Unitarianism in Cambridge, and the geographical isolation of Harvard, all unfavorable. In the 1850s political events were a depressive factor and of course the Civil War cut enrollment. In the post Civil War period, rising standards and costs and the creation of numerous law schools that competed with Harvard cut down on enrollment, but this was more than offset by other factors such as the growth of the country, improved transportation, rising prestige of the school, etc.[9]

Student Aid

Enrollment depends in part on the amount of aid that is made available to students. In general, $1 of aid allocated primarily for the benefit of those who would be excluded because of the increase of tuition will finance several dollars of tuition.

The law school was slow in mobilizing funds for student aid. In 1851, the corporation on the suggestion of the law school faculty provided:

... that each Professor of the Law School may nominate to this Board a student whose pecuniary situation may require aid and who shall be employed in services useful to him and shall be compensated therefore by a remission of a part or the whole of his tuition fees until further ordered by the Corporation.

The objective of this proposal was to provide aid, but also to relieve the faculty of detailed work. Until the 1850s, whatever library service was available was provided by able and impecunious students. This could also be considered a form of aid.

In 1868-1869 the acting president wrote:

... While we doubt the expediency of extending strictly eleemosynary aid to Professional students of any class, a loan fund for law students would be an unspeakable relief and benefit; and the experience of the Professors in loans to a limited extent in cases of intense need authorizes the belief that such a fund would hardly ever incur a bad debt, so that subscriptions to it would be simply an investment, not a sacrifice.

An indication of the slow progress in obtaining student aid is suggested by the following rough summary of funds received for student aid:

---

9. Warren, *op. cit.*, pp. 4-9, 285, 369, 397, 497; *Report of the Standing Committee to Visit the Law School*, 1898, pp. 528-529; *One Hundreth Anniversary of the Harvard Law School*, 1917, pp. 308-309, 368-369.

Law School Student Aid	
1840s	$ 8,000
1850–1889	0
1900–1909	58,000
1910–1919	65,000
1920–1929	483,000
1930–1939	3,495,000
1940–1947	113,000
	4,222,000

By 1947, approximately $4,500,000 yielding about $200,000 yearly had been received. But until 1919, that is, in the first 102 years, funds for student aid had risen only to $132,000.[10]

By the 1960s the situation had greatly improved. In ten years ending 1965-1966 aid rose to $1,430,000, considerably in excess of one-half of all tuition payments. Grants had grown from $258,000 to $797,000. The average stipend had risen from $449 to $840. But average costs had increased from $2,200 to $3,900, a trend pointing to increased difficulties in paying bills on the part of students needing help. It is not surprising then that the school in its sesquicentennial sought $5 million yielding $125,000 of income in additional endowment for student aid.[11]

Increasingly, the school has improved the effectiveness of its financial programs by requiring students to mix grants with low-interest-paying loans. On the whole, the loan programs over the years have been remarkably successful. More than one-third of the students received grants and loans.

Of the $797,000 of scholarship funds made available in 1965-1966, about two-fifths went to graduate students and fellows and three-fifths to L.L.B. candidates. The major sources of scholarship funds for 1965-1966 were as follows: income of endowed law school funds, $265,000; current gifts from founda-

tions and gifts from Harvard Law School Association, Alumni Scholarship Committee, $343,000; general university scholarships, $61,000; and unrestricted funds of the law school, $100,000.[12]

On the whole, the loan program of the school supplemented by governmental programs and with modest rates of interest—2 percent while in college and 4 percent later—has been highly successful. Loans rose by 20 times in the thirty years ending 1968. Defaults have been surprisingly small, and repayments large.[13]

Financing the Law School

The school opened in 1817. In the year 1831, the treasurer first presented a separate report of the law school. At this time total expenditures were $7,673.69, certainly a modest budget even for 1831.

Major outlays were $2,500 for salaries of Professor Ashmun and Judge Story; $2,612 for books; $2,152, indebtedness. A number of miscellaneous items accounted for $238.33. Included were printing, $7.25, and fire insurance on the library which was covered for $4,000.

Major receipts came from instruction, $3,233; income for the year on Issac Royall's legacy, $397.18; and Nathan Dane's donation, $500. A large debt remained.

Law school finances flourished, especially in the period of the large contributions of Story and Greenleaf. In the years 1833 to 1838, a moderate deficit prevailed, but beginning in 1839 the law school began to show a surplus, and by 1844 the balance had risen to $23,416, the largest until 1895.

The law school's experience was unique in higher educational finance. Not only had the school financed professional pay, but large surpluses related to

10. The total is somewhat larger, for there were a few gifts, which were shared by the law school aid funds.

11. *Harvard Law School, 1817-1967: Sesquicentennial Program for Continued Leadership*, pp. 22-23; *Dean's Report*, 1965-1966, pp. 19-25.

12. *Harvard Law School; Dean's Report*, 1965-1966; *A Report to the Alumni Scholarship Committee, Harvard Law School*, 1966-1967, pp. 3-5.

13. For a more pessimistic survey see C. Mason, Bursar to F. W. Hunnewell, December 26, 1914 in *A. L. Lowell Papers, 1914-1917*, F. 319.

high fees and growing enrollment were used to finance the plant, large purchases of the library, and even to increase endowments.[14]

Professor Story was the angel. He refused to accept increases in pay, but attracted many students. An overseers' committee reporting in 1849 commented:

... But the contributions of Royall and Dane combined—important as they have been, and justly worthy of honorable mention—do not equal what has been contributed by Story. At the present moment, Story must be regarded as the largest pecuniary benefactor of the Law School, and one of the largest pecuniary benefactors of the University ....[15]

As late as 1878 the Story influence was still evident. Mr. Bemis presented the school with its fourth chair. Bemis especially noted:

the instruction which I derived from the legal department of her Schools thru ... the late Judge Story, whose memory I cherish as one of the best guides to study whom I have ever had the good fortune to meet and whose friendly stimulus to exertion I shall always gratefully remember.

In the early 1830s the law school, in need of a building, negotiated with Dane, who had financed a professorship.

On one point Dane was obdurate. The interest to be paid to the university would be obtained out of law school surpluses. On this issue the corporation as always was clear:

One of the great difficulties with which the Corporation have to contend arises from the zeal with which the friends of the respective schools press for assistance out of the general funds of the college. Now as the Corporation have in fact no, or very limited, general funds so applicable any assistance of this kind is equivalent to a tax upon the undergraduate for the support of such a school .... All these applications we are compelled to resist, and the general ground of inability and expediency, is that on which we have to depend for resisting these applications, without offending the applicants ....

The Corporation ... on the subject of a law building have been careful to do nothing which should give the friends of other schools claims which it could not answer ....

Dane replied "that it has never been my wish the Law School should be a charge on the Corporation or on public charity ...."[16]

Eliot at an early period insisted on the inadequacy of the endowment of the law school professorships relative to current salaries, and larger salaries for the future. He wanted more endowment in part because to depend more on fees was not acceptable. Pointing to the meagre $11,000 available from endowment, Eliot wrote "... some steps with regard to legal education still remain to be taken which demand a greater independence of receipts from student's fees than the School can now claim ...." He wanted a new chair in Roman law and jurisprudence which could not possibly be financed by fees.[17]

From 1845 to 1869, the law school had more serious financial problems than in the Story period. Its involvement with Brattle House, which had been purchased for student use, contributed to its problems. The adverse effects of Story's death and the Civil War also induced a deterioration of its financial position.[18]

By the 1950s, undergraduate enrollment at the law school had largely stabilized at around 1,500. Enrollment escalated especially in the 1880s, under

14. Cf., *Report of the Committee to Visit the Law School,* 1914.

15. On the last few pages, see especially S. Greenleaf, *Report on Finances, September 1, 1833 to September 1, 1847,* May 15, 1848; *The Committee of the Corporation Appointed to Consider Whether any Further Compensation and What Should be Allowed to the Professors of the Law School,* August 31, 1831; C. Warren, *op. cit.,* pp. 44-45, 92-94, 408, 445, 466-467.

16. N. Dane to President Quincy, September 13, 1831; C. Warren, *op. cit.,* pp. 472-475; A. E. Sutherland, *op. cit.,* pp. 118-121.

17. *Report of the President of Harvard College,* 1871-1872; 1872-1873; Warren, *op. cit.,* p. 434.

18. Warren, *op. cit.,* pp. 350-351.

Langdell, and since 1910, with a doubling of enrollment from 1910 to the 1960s. Rising enrollment and increases of tuition to $1,750 explain the large increase in the law school budget. But the annual current giving also became a factor of increasing importance.

The large differences were with arts and sciences and medicine. The former had about 4 times as large enrollment as law, but 12 times as much endowment. Medicine, with about one-third of the law school's enrollment, had 3 times as much endowment.

A comparison of the financial structure for the university, medicine, business, and law for 1965-1966 is of some interest. I have eliminated income from government contracts and a few other items and compared only income from endowment, gifts, and tuition.

Table 60-2.
Income from Endowment, Gifts and Tuition, 1965–1966.

	Percent from Endowment	Percent from Current Gifts	Percent from Tuition
Whole university	39	26	35
Law	19	20	60
Medicine	48	28	24
Business	10	43	47

Source: Financial Report to the Board of Overseers of Harvard College, 1965-1966.

The law school, like other branches of the university, has depended heavily on annual giving. In 1965-1966, the school received $879,000 from annual giving; and by 1965-1966, gifts for current use and receipts for special purposes availed of amounted to $1,045,000, or 20 percent of income.[19]

From the very beginning tuition charges were high at the law school. At the beginning of the Eliot regime tuition rose to $150. In the sixteen Story years ending in 1845 fees accounted for $105,000,

though salaries and other current expenses absorbed only $47,200. But the faculty expressed some concern over the school's high costs and its loss of competitive position. In the next eighty years tuition rose slowly to $250, with budgetary problems suggesting the need of higher tuition. By the 1960s, with fees rising toward $2,000, the dean boasted that tuition was lower than elsewhere in the university.[20]

It is clear that the law school stands out as the school that depends heavily on tuition income; that the medical school especially relies on endowment; that the business school obtains its resources primarily from a combination of tuition and current gifts and receives little from endowment.

Some differences prevail also in the spending patterns. For example, here is a comparison of the university, the law school, and the medical school.

The law school's outlays on salaries are large, suggesting that its resources are used especially to finance faculty salaries. It relies much less relatively on nonfaculty items, e.g., wages and equipment and supplies, and is more generous in spending for student aid. The difference between law and medicine is explained partly by the much higher costs of a medical education, evident in relatively large outlays in medicine for wages and equipment and supplies.

Even as late as 1900, the contributions to endowment were but $345,000; and by 1907, funds had climbed to $641,505. The most fruitful period occurred in the 1930s, when more than $4,500,000 were received. In all, the total exceeded $8,200,000 from 1781 to 1947.[21] The great depression brought large gifts for student aid, about 7 times the amount received for this purpose in the prosperous 1920s. In the 20 years ending June 30, 1966, the school received about $10,500,000 for endowment, or a total

---

19. *Dean's Report*, Harvard Law School, 1965-1966, p. 26; *Financial Report to the Board of Overseers of Harvard College*, 1965-1966, p. 12.

20. S. Greenleaf to President Everett, October 9, 1847; Warren, *op. cit.*, pp. 44-45, 76-77, 343, 431; *Report of the Standing Committee to Visit the Law School*, 1898, pp. 528-529; *Report of the Visiting Committee of the Board of Overseers of Harvard College*, 1927, p. 179.

21. These are rough figures and should be somewhat higher as some gifts covering more than one field had to be omitted. Wherever possible, the original gift, not the gift plus any later earnings while invested, was used.

Table 60-3.

Percent of Expenditures on Several Major Items in the 1960s

	Salaries	Wages	Retirement	Equipment and Supplies	Student Aid
University	31	25	6	20	9
Law school	30	16	6	10	15
Medical school	24	24	6	18	7

of about $19 million for 1780 to 1966, a sum that yielded an income of almost $1 million. In the last 20 years of its history, the law school received more endowment than in the first 155 years.[22]

In general, the law school has not had great success in its endowment drives. The World War I drive was a failure. In 1925-1927, the school launched a major effort to raise $5,250,000. Actually, only about half as much was had, though economic conditions were favorable. But the $2,300,000 obtained was the most successful campaign by the law school. It remains to be seen what success the 1967, $15 million campaign yields. It is well to realize that in dollar terms the source of gifts, that is, the nation's output, is now about 8 times that of the 1920s. Hence, a $15 million campaign is really equal to about $2 million in the 1920s (I assume no change in competitive position).[23]

From 1781 to 1947 the most popular use of endowment money was student aid, with about one-half of the total thus explained.

Of course the major additions to endowment have come in the last twenty years. In the twenty years ending 1965-1966, the school received $10,600,000 for endowment. But since the fund income availed of in 1965-1966 was $989,000, the endowment fund is probably of the order of $20 million. My rough calculations yield about $19 million.

Substantial contributions to endowment were infrequent. In 1829, the school received its largest

gift up to that time—$10,000, from Mr. Dane. By 1882, endowment was still very small compared to three other schools. Two campaigns, in World War I and 1927, were not successful. *Now the school seeks $15 million.*[24]

Buildings

Ordinarily buildings for institutions of higher learning are gifts and do not require special financing. As noted earlier, however, the law school's financing of buildings was unusual: the school depended heavily on its own funds and particularly student fees to pay for its physical plant.

As badly as Story wanted a new building he was fearful of the consequences of such expenditures, and notably of losses.

In the early 1830s, through the help of Dane, the school obtained a building that cost $7,000. The details of financing were rather unusual, but essentially what was involved was a $5,000 gift by Dane and a $2,000 loan. But the peculiar aspect of the transaction was that after six years the $5,000 would be transferred to the Dane Professorship Fund, thus raising the endowment of that chair to $15,000.

It was not until 1883 that Austin Hall replaced Dane Hall. In the intervening years student fees helped

22. See Harvard Law School, *Dean's Report*, 1965-1966, p. 25.

23. For some of the obstacles to the 1920s drive, see especially Sutherland, *op. cit.*, pp. 262-270.

24. *Report of the Committee to Visit the Law School*, 1914, 1927; *Committee on Disposition of Part of Income of Bussey Fund that Belongs to Law School*, March 31, 1862; Warren, *op. cit.*, pp. 350-351, 408, 429, 528-529; W. C. Loring and R. Pound to A. L. Lowell, May 2 and May 6, 1916 in *A. L. Lowell Papers, 1914-17*, F. 1080; Sutherland, *op. cit.*, p. 263.

finance some additional space. The construction cost of Austin Hall was $135,000 and was financed by a gift from Edward Austin, a Boston merchant. Langdell Hall became available in 1905 at a cost of $380,000, largely obtained from fees. The financing that was provided was largely out of law school funds.[25]

At the one hundred fiftieth anniversary of its founding, the school was seeking $6 million additional for its physical plant. At that time, with 1,683 students, the school had only seven classrooms and none with a capacity of less than 160. Smaller rooms and offices were especially needed.[26]

Faculty

In its 150 years, the Harvard Law School, the first law school in America, has been preeminent primarily because of the high quality of its faculty. In competition with the courts and private practice and later with other law schools, the school continued to gain, in part because it allowed when necessary outside work and also adhered over most of its history to a pay scale, financed out of student fees primarily, that was both competitive and generous. When occasion demanded it, the school allowed salaries in excess of the university's level.

Professor Greenleaf, one of the first stars of the school, was ready to resign in 1842 if the corporation insisted upon a residency requirement, which apparently cut down the professor's income. Residency in Boston would not be:

. . . incompatible either with official duty or with the interests of the School . . . . Indeed, all that is essential to me, is to reside in Boston and to retain my present amount of practice, which is confined to the Circuit and Supreme Judicial Courts and to causes before the Court and not before the Jury. More than this I

should not have occasion for; and less than this would not consist with the interests of the School . . . .[27]

It would of course have been impossible to interest a Justice of the U.S. Supreme Court if the university insisted upon residency. The justice asked for a guarantee that he would not lose more than $1,000 in selling his Salem house, and also that the college would provide a house in Cambridge to be leased by Story at 6 percent of the investment. Of course the corporation acceded: Story would accept only $1,000 in pay.[28] The agreement of 1845 with Story, under which he would accept residency and resign from the Supreme Court, was more generous.[29]

As enrollment rose in the law school, there was increasing pressure both to increase the size of staff and also to raise salary levels. Ultimately both an increase of staff and of pay emerged. Another approach was for the professors to seek the help of younger faculty members in cutting down on detailed work.

Professor Greenleaf in 1834 asked the corporation to appoint an instructor:

. . . the general interests of the school would be promoted by some aid in the business of daily instruction, not, however, to absolve the Professor from any active duties, which he, better than any other, can perform . . . , the aid of an intelligent instructor, to attend the exercises of the day, or to solve some minor doubt for the student would be invaluable . . . .[30]

On numerous occasions in later years there was pressure to increase the size of the staff as enrollment

25. *Education, Bricks and Mortar*, 1948, pp. 55, 76; Warren, *op. cit.*, p. 77; Lane, *op. cit.*, p. 30; *Report of the Standing Committee to Visit the Law School*, 1898, p. 528.
26. *Harvard Law School, 1817-1967, Sesquicentennial Program for Continued Leadership*, 1967, pp. 26-29.
27. S. Greenleaf to the Corporation of Harvard College, April 6, 1842.
28. S. Greenleaf to Corporation, May 19, 1829, quoted in Warren, *op. cit.*, pp. 417-419.
29. Committee Appointed by Board. . .for such addition to His [Judge Story's] Present Salary. . .to give His Whole Time and Services to the Law School, Meeting of the President and Fellows of Harvard College, at Boston, April, 1845.
30. S. Greenleaf to President Quincy, November 28, 1834.

increased. Thus, in 1898, a visiting committee of the overseers pointed out that whereas five faculty members taught 150 students in 1883, by 1898 nine faculty members (plus two instructors) were responsible for 546 students. The student-faculty ratio had risen from 30 to 1 to 61 to 1. The committee continued:

. . . A law lecture of the old type may be as well given to 500, indeed if the acoustics of the lecture room be good enough and its size sufficient, to 5,000 as to 50 or 25; but, when every student is expected to answer and encouraged to ask questions tending to insure a thorough-going comprehension of every feature of reported adjudications in the subject under consideration, the merits of this form of teaching become illusory if more than a certain number are in attendance . . . .

The view of the faculty at that time seemed to be that the numbers in a class should not greatly exceed fifty. With enrollment of 546, each class would have about 180 students; and hence, unless courses were broken up into sections, the numbers in a class would be excessive.[31]

From 1910 to 1965 there has been a steady decline in the student-faculty ratio though the improvement was slight from 1950 to 1965. Should the school obtain the six additional chairs now sought, the student-faculty ratio would decline to 25 to 1 and even a greater decline if other faculty members were added also. This does not mean that the size of classes would not be too large. Here, also crucial is the number of classes per faculty member.

At the outset salaries in the law school were low. The first professorship, the Royall, available even before the school opened, could pay only $400. John Lowell refused it, but recommended Isaac Parker, Chief Justice of Massachusetts, who accepted. In 1825-1826, Parker received $400 and Professor Stearns, $1,270. In the following year Stearns received the amounts paid by the students (about $700).[32] It will be recalled that in 1829 the Royall Professorship paid $1,500 and the Dane (to Story) on a part-time basis, $1,000, and that on a full-time basis, Story was offered $4,000 in 1845, but he died soon thereafter. By this time he was earning $10,000 a year from his writing.

Occasionally the school would call on a temporary incumbent to provide teaching services. An interesting case was that of compensation to be paid Charles Sumner, for work in the winter. The law school faculty valued Sumner highly, but he was too radical for the Harvard Corporation. Greenleaf informed President Quincy that Sumner would not name a definite sum: ". . .While he did not expect more than $200 he would not be satisfied with less than $150—I think his services deserve the latter sum, and will not be over-rewarded if the corporation should allow something beyond it. . . ."[33]

An enrollment increased in the years 1827 to 1831, the pleas for additional pay became more persuasive. In reply, a committee of the corporation proposed that the excess of student fees over the necessary contribution of fees to the $3,000 needed for the annual budget should be used to finance the library debt and raise salaries.

With rising enrollment in the 1830s to 1850s, the faculty demanded higher pay. A committee of the overseers was not greatly pleased with the movement in salaries of law school professors and those paid by competitors to the law school, notably government payments to justices.

It is clear that judges had improved their relative position. By 1898, associate judges of the Supreme Court were receiving $10,000.[34] By 1905, however, with large fees and enrollment and limited electives and hence small number of courses and faculty members, it was possible to pay salaries substantially over the university level.[35]

31. *Report of the Standing Committee to Visit the Law School*, 1898, pp. 524-529.
32. Warren, *op. cit.*, pp. 291, 365.
33. S. Greenleaf to President Quincy, August 8, 1837.

34. *Report of the Standing Committee to Visit the Law School*, 1898, pp. 530-531; *The History of the University*, p. 78.
35. O. W. Holmes to President Eliot, January 25, 1870.

The Library

One of the most valued assets of the Harvard Law School is its library. In 1964-1965, the expenditures on the library were $527,726, or about 12 percent of the law school budget. By this time the library had more than a million volumes and was accumulating at the rate of about twenty thousand yearly. The expenditures for this library, which had been accumulating for about 150 years, are surprisingly large. They compare with 4 or at most 5 percent for all Harvard University libraries. The school authorities are indeed modest when they describe the library as "an internationally outstanding collection that attempts to cover Law comprehensively." If the library should expand at the expected rate for Harvard University Libraries, the expenditures would rise to almost $1,500,000 by 1975.[36]

Expenditures on books in the year 1845-1846 to 1868-1869 were $24,807 or $1,033 per year. In view of the growth of the school the expenditures were disappointing at this time. After Story's death, the faculty showed less interest. Besides there were financial problems as well.

By 1846, a new 354-page catalogue became available. At that time a visiting committee reported that "the Law Library is not without reason judged to be the best collection of the law authorities in our Union. . . ."

In 1858, the law librarian estimated the number of books at 8,851, but the college catalogue which included textbooks and other items revealed a collection of 15,000.

The confusion was great. The visiting committee looked "upon this state of things as alarming. . . security should be the first law of such a collection. The Librarian is not a librarian in the common acceptance of the term—a keeper of books—for he exercises no supervision. . . ." The janitor, however, who runs errands for the professors, builds fires and is custodian of the library.

In the year 1846-1847, the average term bill (student payments for food and rooms and tuition primarily) averaged about $11,000 per year. Library payments in the budget accounted for about $800 or 7 to 8 percent of term bills. Currently I would estimate library outlays at about 15 percent of term bills.

Just as enrollment soared after the Civil War, so library acquisitions were especially large after the war. Thus, in 1870, the number of volumes in the library was estimated at 10,000; by 1906-1907 there were 102,826 and 11,185 pamphlets. Hence, in a period of thirty-six years the books in the library increased by 90,000 or 900 percent. In the next sixty years or so there was another rise of about 900 percent, but in numbers, 900,000. By 1889-1890 the library held only 25,000 volumes, but Dean Langdell could boast of the library:

Now it is believed to be larger (referring only to law books proper, and excluding statutes) more complete, and in a better condition, than any other law library in the United States, with the possible exception of the National Library in Washington. Its duplicates, triplicates and quadruplicates of English and American reports alone number 3,040 volumes.

For some reason the law school did not seem to experience the serious cataloguing and parking problems for books that the college library experiences. At least there seems to have been much less confusion in the law library in the nineteenth century than in the college. But by the beginning of the twentieth century the law school library began to experience problems similar to those of Gore. When Austin had been built in 1883, it was assumed that it would be adequate for fifty years. But, though by the 1890s the stack space was doubled storing 60,000 volumes, it was necessary to house 40,000 volumes elsewhere. Moreover, the library was growing at the rate of 5,000 volumes a year; and the reading room in Austin could accommodate only 240 of the 400 students.

Conclusion

Law school economics is a product of the peculiar financing and pattern of spending of the law school.

36. "The Harvard Libraries in the 1960s," in *The Harvard Library Bulletin*, January, 1967; *Report of the University Librarian*, 1964-1965, pp. 28-29.

Distinguished professors and air outstanding competitive position invited large numbers of students and made possible heavy reliance on fees. Moreover, the fees were used to finance not only current expenditures, e.g., faculty salaries and library outlays, but also capital expenditures. The unusual recourse to tuition financing was also the result of the difficulties encountered by the school in obtaining endowment funds. This failure has been the result of the inability of the law school to tap large incomes and exploit strong civic interest in law such as prevails in health problems and roads. Although the law school has about 3 times as many students seeking the L.L.B. as the medical school has students seeking the M.D.s, endowment income of the medical school is 3 times as large.

Shortages of endowment funds would have been even more costly had not large resources been obtained from current gifts and had not the resources of the law school been used disproportionately for bread and butter purposes, e.g., for faculty salaries, and less than proportionately for wages and for the plant and equipment.

Perhaps also relevant is the greater recourse to large classes in the law school. In the last generation, however, the relative contribution of endowment to income has increased to some extent and the student-faculty ratio has been reduced.

In a letter to the author, Erwin Griswold, the dean of the school, stressed the difficult financial problems of the law school for a century or more. "In all of these years, the Law School has never received a truly large gift. No one ever gives us five million dollars, or a million dollars, or even $500,000. On the whole, lawyers make good livings but do not get rich." Griswold then pointed out the large advances in mobilizing small gifts. It is largely to his credit that the comprehensive and productive student aid program, largely financed by small gifts, has developed.[37]

In a memorandum to the faculty, Dean Griswold discussed the 1967-1968 budget. That budget was 10 percent larger than the 1966-1967 budget, although enrollment was largely stabilized, the explanation being rising prices and wages, and some expansion of services. Income was to be $5,213,648 and expenses, $5,156,314.

By 1967-1968, student aid would rise to $794,000 for scholarships or 25 percent of tuition, and $600,000 in loans. The library budget shows outlays of $677,153 or more than 13 percent of the expenditures for library service—a remarkably high figure.[38]

In seeking $9 million of endowment under the $15-million program, Dean Griswold is trying to break away from the historical experience of depending excessively on tuition. Should this program be realized, then endowment income would rise by more than 40 percent as against a rise of tuition of only 17 percent.[39]

37. Erwin Griswold to Seymour Harris, June 19, 1967.
38. Memo from Dean Griswold to the Faculty, May 5, 1967.

39. Calculated from Dean's Memo to Faculty of May 5, 1967.

61

Professional Schools

Throughout this book I have discussed various economic problems raised by the professional schools. To some extent the problems are similar for all the professional schools. I did, however, devote separate chapters to two of Harvard's most distinguished professional schools, law and medicine. In the current chapter I shall discuss briefly some relevant aspects of the nine professional schools and the graduate school of arts and science, a school not unlike the other professional schools.

The first professional school was medicine, established in 1783. Then came divinity and law in 1816 and 1817. All the other schools but the science school (now extinct) and dental medicine were founded in the twentieth century. Actually, theology, medicine, law, and education were taught in Harvard College before their respective schools were opened. Troublesome problems emerged as a result. The Hersey endowment, for example, was to finance medical education, but the problem was, once the medical school had become part of the university, should the funds belong to the medical school or the college? Similar issues emerged once the divinity school began to operate.[1]

Since most of the funds were in the possession of the college, the new professional schools tried to tap this rich resource. The administrators of the college generally insisted that the college funds were a public trust, and they could not be diverted to the professional schools. That Harvard's staunchest friends were frequently hostile to the emerging professional schools, and in part because of their vocational aspects, was an additional reason for discouraging diversions of funds from the college.

As late as the 1850s, the president of Harvard was clearly hostile to the emerging professional schools though President Hill, the predecessor of President Eliot, enthusiastically supported them.[2]

Professional schools begged for financial help from the college, and were generally refused help. But at times the corporation supported diversions of funds from the law school, which the faculty considered unjust, and also appropriated funds of the medical school, which that school successfully challenged. In 1850, the law school faculty asked the corporation "not to take from the law school this fund, or any part of it . . . without giving them an opportunity to be heard on the subject. . . ."[3]

The Eliot Contribution

It was Eliot more than anyone else who was responsible for the great development of the professional schools. When he became president in 1869, the standards of admission in the professional schools

---

1. C. Ellis, Dean of Medical School to the President and Fellows of Harvard College, May 3, 1883.

2. C. W. Eliot, *Harvard Memories*, p. 24.

3. J. Parker and T. Parsons to the President and Fellows of Harvard College, July 15, 1850.

were shockingly low, and the enrollments small. Entry required only proof of good character and a high school education, and in some instances even less. Attendance rather than adequate examinations was the requirement for a degree. Eliot changed all that. He assumed the chairmanship at all faculty meetings inclusive of the professional schools. His elective system with its emphasis on broad coverage contributed to the development of the professional schools inclusive of the graduate school of arts and sciences. By 1900, he had achieved a revolution. A bachelor's degree had become a requirement for entry to most of the professional schools. Eliot's leadership also induced advances of professional standards all over the country.

Eliot was especially interested in the graduate school of arts and sciences, though he greatly raised the level in law, medicine, theology, and science also. In 1825, the great humanist Ticknor had launched a program which was presumably to introduce graduate instruction. But Ticknor failed. Moreover, Johns Hopkins preceded Harvard in its espousal of research for its faculty and in offering graduate degrees. In fact, Yale also bestowed the Ph.D. before Harvard. But Eliot gradually caught up and finally assumed a leadership which, according to the best studies, Harvard still retains.[4]

In elevating the professional schools through more demanding admission requirements, extended and improved curriculum, and higher test and degree standards, Eliot greatly burdened the budget. His raising of standards and accompanying increase of tuition both tended to cut enrollment and to raise costs. After careful consideration, however, Harvard, in order to keep costs down, decided against a requirement that the Ph.D. thesis be printed.

Eliot's greatest interest was in the graduate school. By 1873 the graduate school gave three Ph.D.s; and it was not until 1893 that the number exceeded ten. By 1900, 36; by 1914, 60; by 1940, 161; by 1967, 224 (in addition, the school of education gave 34 Ed.D.s).

By 1967, the graduate school had 3,097 students or 40 percent of the university enrollment, and the largest enrollment except for the college.

Raising standards often increased costs and reduced enrollment. But Eliot soon discovered that higher standards also attracted students. Hence, despite rising costs and standards, the trend of enrollment was upwards. Increasing income and growing attractions of education were also relevant.[5]

Science School

As early as 1838, the great mathematician Benjamin Peirce recommended the opening of an engineering school. He hoped it would bring benefits similar to those of the law school to law. "... A thorough mathematical education gives a young engineer a great command over the details of his profession...."[6]

In 1847, Abbott Lawrence gave Harvard $50,000 to launch a science school which was to train technical men who were badly needed at that time. Lawrence's insistence that the students be required to have only a free public school education, and that the professors depend partly on fees were obstacles to the development of a good school. On fees, Mr. Lawrence wrote: "... The Professors should depend to a considerable extent upon fees—it is the best guarantee to exertion ... and the permanent prosperity of the institution.[7]

The school was not a great success. The faculty tended to be isolated, and each student associated

4. See A. M. Cartter, *An Assessment of Quality in Graduate Education*, (American Council of Education), 1966, pp. 106-107.

5. See especially. Henry James, *Charles W. Eliot: President of Harvard University*, 1930, vol. I, pp. 261-301; vol. II, appendix C; *Report of the President of Harvard College*, 1873-1874, pp.. 15-16; 1890-1891, pp. 93-94; 1901-1902, pp. 169-170; Samuel Eliot Morison, *Three Centuries of Harvard, 1636-1936*, 1937, pp. 237-238; University News Office, *Enrollment, October 4, 1967*; Enrollment from 1873 to the present from Office of the Dean, Graduate School of Arts and Sciences, January 29, 1968; Morison, *The Development of Harvard University*, ch. 28.

6. B. Peirce to President Quincy, August 15, 1838; B. Peirce on School of Civil Engineers, 1840.

7. See *Report of the President of Harvard College*, 1846-1847 to 1853-1854; *Harvard University Catalogue*, 1949-1950, pp. 66-72.

with one faculty member. Attempts to get help from the more prosperous observatory or from college funds were unsuccessful.[8]

On the every tub on its own bottom principle, the observatory denied help to the school. Eliot noted in a letter to the corporation of May 19, 1863, that the debt accumulated by the school over thirteen years "has been really paid in great part out of the general fund of the college."

Poor management was costly. Thus, laboratory costs were excessive because students were not charged for breakage. In a report in the 1860s, Eliot showed the relation of charging for losses and the reduced cost of materials. Again, Lawrence was opposed to the science laboratory competing with private enterprise in selling laboratory items to students. A Rumford professor insisted that through purchases in large quantities for sales to students, the cost to the student could be reduced.

Other problems were relevant. The Rumford professor complained of his low pay and his heavy payments to the laboratory. Perhaps the greatest blow to the school was the increasing competition of M.I.T. and the Yale Scientific School. By the time Eliot took over, he was prepared to urge fundamental changes.[9]

Eliot assessed the science school in 1871. After eight years from its opening, enrollment had risen only to eighty and then tended downward. By 1871, the enrollment of thirty was disappointing. Eliot commented on the better equipment, the larger number of teachers, and a greater variety of instruction of Harvard's competitors.

Seeking aid, Eliot wrote to the family of the orig-inal donor. ". . . I have felt that the children of the founder of the school ought to know that it is dying, and why it is dying, and what may be done to save and reestablish it." He then urged a contribution of $90,000 and two professorships as the price for saving the school.[10]

A year earlier Harvard had started discussion of a possible merger of the science school and M.I.T., and a change of name. Approval by the Lawrence family was necessary. Amos Lawrence reluctantly approved. ". . . because I am an overseer and a son of the college, and because I cannot gracefully refuse; but I'm very sorry to be asked. . . ."[11]

As early as 1870, Harvard initiated negotiations with M.I.T. for collaboration. In June, 1870, President Eliot wrote to the acting president of M.I.T.:

The President and Fellows of Harvard College, being convinced that the great public interest of professional scientific education would be promoted by a union at the Institute of Technology of all the Schools of Applied Science in and near Boston, respectfully invite the Government of the Institute to consider whether some plan cannot now be devised for the accomplishment of such a union. . . .

The negotiations failed, according to Eliot, because M.I.T. wanted Harvard money to be used for applied science and did not seem to offer much in return.[12]

In 1897, the two institutions tried again without results. In 1904, a more vigorous attempt was made, undoubtedly in part because of the anticipated massive McKay gift. This particular attempt failed, apparently, because M.I.T. was not allowed to sell its land in Boston.[13]

8. *Abbott Lawrence to the President,* June 7, 1847; *Report of Committee on the Subject of Establishing a School of Science,* January 30, 1847.

9. C. W. Eliot to the President and Fellows of Harvard College, November 24, 1862; E. W. Hornsford to the Corporation of Harvard College, February 3, 1858; E. W. Hornsford to the Hon. Amos A. Lawrence, February 3, 1858; C. W. Eliot to the President and Fellows of Harvard College, May 19, 1963; Letter to the President, February 12, 1855 (sender not clear); J. Quincy to President Walker, March 7, 1855; *Report of the Committee on a Letter from Professor Hornsford,* September 25, 1858.

10. Confidential Letter from C. W. Eliot to the Children of the Founder of the School, March 23, 1871.

11. Amos A. Lawrence to President Eliot, May 7, 1870.

12. C. W. Eliot to Professor J. D. Rundle, Acting President of M.I.T., June 20, 1870; C. W. Eliot to President Rogers, February 9, 1870; Note, March 22, 1871, in *Eliot Papers,* 1871-1873.

13. *A. L. Lowell Papers, 1914-1917,* F. 160; C. W. Eliot to M. R. Copeland, August 12, 1904; C. W. Eliot to Pres. Henry Pritchett, May 16, 1904; C. W. Eliot to J. D. Greene, May 6, 1907, all in *C. W. Eliot Letter Book,* 95, 1903-1906; 96, 1906-1907.

Another attempt in 1913, in part to apply the McKay millions to the consumation of the union, also broke down. Though Harvard and M.I.T. at this time agreed, the McKay trustees dissented, arguing that McKay wanted Harvard, not M.I.T., to have his money.[14] The courts disallowed the diversion of McKay's money to M.I.T.

Over its first fifty years the science school experienced gyrations in its enrollment. Eliot boasted in 1902 that Professor Shaler was responsible for a rise of enrollment from 14 in 1886-1887 to 549 (87 special) in 1901-1902. In 1893, Eliot remarked:

One of the most interesting phenomenon in the university during the past few years has been the sudden and rapid growth of the scientific school. . . .This growth, if continued for a few years, will soon bring Harvard University to a condition resembling that of the other large universities in the United States, in which the department or departments giving degrees in pure and applied science hold an important place in comparison with the department which gives the degree of Bachelor of Arts. [15]

Instruction in the sciences continued to be a problem even after the renaissance of the late nineteenth century. Reorganization followed reorganization.[16]

Experience with the science school revealed that tying faculty salaries directly to fees impaired the effectiveness of the operation; that low standards do not necessarily bring in revenue and students; that competition of new and robust institutions with a Harvard school that was underfinanced could bring disaster to Harvard's status; that professors should not be allowed to incur large debts on behalf of a school without scrutiny by the management; that only with an improvement of standards and much

tighter administration, introduced by Eliot, could the science school grow and prosper.

The Graduate School of Business Administration

On December 13, 1907 President Eliot addressed the general education board in the hope of obtaining needed funds for establishing a business school at Harvard. The plan had been drawn up by professors in economics and government at Harvard:

. . . I join these gentlemen in believing that the new school would soon demonstrate a great capacity for public usefullness, and I have received many assurances from business men that young men who had received the training. . .would quickly make themselves highly useful in the great business organizations of the country. . . .

At the outset Eliot was enthusiastic, though there were serious financial problems. He was not clear whether the school should be independent of existing bodies, or whether it should be part of the college of arts and sciences.[17]

Progress was slow at first. Economic conditions were unstable and the idea of higher education for businessmen was not widely accepted. Yet through the help of Professor Taussig and the general education board, and the readiness of Major Higginson to guarantee the $125,000 required for a five-year trial period, the school received $125,000.[18]

Even as late as 1925, the income from endowment was only $31,000. In 1929, the school needed $150,000 for research, which could be financed by an endowment of $3 million.[19]

In part, the slow development of the school was the result of conflicts between two strong men, President Lowell and Dean Edwin Gay. The former was

14. *A. L. Lowell Papers*, 1914-1917, F-160.
15. C. W. Eliot to Professor Agassiz, January 24, 1902.
16. For details see Morison, *The Development of Harvard University*, ch. 26; *Report of the President of Harvard College*, 1921, pp. 76-77; 1928-1929, pp. 22-24; *Official Register of Harvard University*, 1967-1968.

17. C. W. Eliot to Dr. Wallace Buttrick, December 13, 1907; C. W. Eliot to Professor F. W. Taussig, August 13, 1907.
18. R. B. Perry, *Henry Lee Higginson*, pp. 374-377.
19. *Report of the Visiting Committee of the Board of Overseers of Harvard College*, 1924-1925, p. 25; *Report of the Committee to Visit the Graduate School of Business Administration*, 1929, p. 311.

annoyed at Gay's plan to raise a million dollars of endowment, in part because this drive would interfere with the president's plan for a large drive. Gay was not a very successful beggar, though he had some help from the older Thomas Lamont. [20]

In his discussions with Gay, Lowell urged upon the dean the principle of high tuition fees. He would cover costs by student fees, a principle that soon received considerable support in the school. The school has sought to cover operating expenditures with student fees. One reason for this view was the difficulty of raising endowment funds. Lowell also supported this theory in part because graduates of the school could anticipate high incomes. Indeed, there were endowment campaigns that were successful, the most striking one being the campaign in the 1920s when George Baker, upon being asked to subscribe to $1 million of a $5 million campaign, largely for the plant, replied that he would prefer to contribute the entire $5 million. But twenty years later, the dean complained at having an endowment of but $3 million as compared to one of $150 million for the university. [21]

The fact is that the school did not always rely on student fees. It sought endowment funds to cover research costs, and gifts to provide its plant. It obtained large sums as current gifts and particularly to finance the research needed to assemble cases which, unlike the law school cases, were very costly to prepare. At one time, and at an inappropriate time, 1929, the school invited 250 business leaders "to contribute $1,000 each to cover such expenses." At times, and especially when enrollment tended to decline, full-cost tuition would be so expensive that it could not be introduced. [22] In fact, in the years 1930-1931, 1934-1935, and 1937-1938, for example,

tuition was but two-thirds of total income. But this comes close to full-cost tuition.

Tuition rising with costs meant that many would be unable to enter the school. Hence, the school introduced a large loan program, with loans payable a few years after graduation plus 6 percent interest. This program was indeed helpful, but its contribution was limited. At most, the student was allowed loans equal to three-quarters of tuition: tuition was only about half of costs; and less than half of the students received loans. In 1925, the school boasted of a loan program that provided but 18 percent of total tuition payments. In 1967-1968, however, students could borrow as much as $10,000 over the two years, though a single man or a married couple without children could borrow only $7,500. [23]

Full-cost tuition raises one serious problem, namely, that with any serious drop in enrollment, large deficits are incurred. In World War I and World War II, in 1920-1921, and in the Great Depression serious declines in enrollment induced large deficits. Had large endowment funds been available and reserves accumulated, the growth of deficits would have been contained. The fact that with adverse conditions the gifts also drop further increases deficits. From 1929 to 1938, the annual volume of gifts vacillated from $19,000 to $259,000 per year; that a large part of the expenditures, e.g., faculty salaries, are fixed further induces deficits. An example of the effects of unfavorable business conditions follows: After a heroic effort in 1933, the school was able to reduce administrative expense by 25 percent; instruction and research, 12 percent; student health by 26 percent; and library outlays by 23 percent, declines not adequate to match the fall of revenue from $1,170,000 in 1930-1931 to $760,000 in 1937-1938. About one-half of expenditures could not be pruned at all. [24]

20. H. Heaton, *A Scholar in Action: Edwin F. Gay*, pp. 84-85; Lowell, *op. cit.*, pp. 40-41.
21. *Report of the President of Harvard College*, 1920-1921, pp. 129-130; 1923-1924, pp. 28-29, 119-122; 1945-1946, p. 395.
22. *Ibid.*, 1935-1936, p. 217; 1937-1938, pp. 229-231; 1945-1946, p. 395.
23. *Ibid.*, 1920-1921 through 1926-1927; 1931-1932

through 1936-1937; 1949-1950; *General Catalogue*, 1967-1968, pp. 807-808; *Report of the Visiting Committee of the Board of Overseers of Harvard College*, 1924-1925, p. 25.
24. *Ibid.*, 1937-1938; *Report of the Committee to Visit the Graduate School of Business Administration*, 1933, pp. 115-116.

The Divinity School

Harvard's divinity school, relying on the efforts of 108 men, raised $27,300 to finance a divinity school in the second decade of the nineteenth century. Laymen subscribing $5 and clergy $2 were to be annual members of the Society for Promoting Theological Education in Harvard University. The giver of a $100 subscription would be awarded lifetime membership. With these funds the school opened.

Harvard's first chair was the Hollis Divinity Chair of 1721. The amount made available was £80 per year. By the time the divinity school opened in 1816, the college had three endowed chairs in the general area of the divinity school, and these chairs were ultimately put at the disposal of the divinity school.[25] They yielded very little, however. The Hollis chair had an endowment of $32,000 as late as 1947. This was made possible by allowing the fund to grow from investments with the chair not filled—in one period, for forty years. The second chair, the Hancock, was worth only $6,000 in 1947. In the first 311 years of Harvard's history, the divinity school had accumulated only eleven chairs with $553,000 behind them in 1947, just enough to finance one chair today.

Endowed chairs clearly could not provide much support for the school. The largest endowment was for $170,000, though in support of Semitic Languages Mr. Schiff donated in all about $275,000, in part for physical plant.

Throughout its history, the divinity school has experienced financial crises. One reason was that ministers are not generally wealthy and, hence, the most obvious source of funds was not likely to be large. A second relevant factor was the declining interest in religion on the part of the American public. In 1879, in the midst of a campaign for the school, a spokesman said:

. . . If universities are to become teachers of the exact sciences only; if there be no knowledge which has edges of uncertainty; if all that is partially known is unknown; if only the facts are facts that can be weighed and measured—then, indeed, the only thing that deserves the name of knowledge is just what least deserves the respect and reverence of men. . . . [26]

Not only was the minister impoverished. The students were also impecunious. With students poor, the contribution of tuition was also small. Eliot was critical of the school for its begging and its unwillingness to help itself by raising fees. At a time when tuition in the university was $150, the charge in the divinity school was only $50, a fact that irked the president. The school was not really able to match tuition in other parts of the university. In 1967-1968, whereas tuition was $2,000 in most branches of the university, the charge was only $1,000 in the divinity school. Tuition contributes little, not only because of the inability of students to pay much, but also because enrollment, and hence total tuition, is so small.[27]

A number of attempts were made to improve the capital situation. In 1857, a large program was studied. It was hoped that two chairs might be added at a cost of $30,000 per chair (cf., the $500,000 needed now). The solution offered finally was dependence on congregations of twelve or more churches to finance a large part of the funds that were needed. The professors would accept reduced pay because they would serve their churches part-time and be freed from the requirement of full-time residence. [28]

In 1879, the corporation supported a substantial campaign with the objective of obtaining $130,000 to finance professorships. In his 1877-1878 report, Eliot showed how much better manned rival divinity schools were. Apparently, $31,000 was needed for five professorships at $4,000 each and one at $1,000,

25. *Addresses . . . 100th Anniversary of Harvard Divinity School*, 1917, pp. 9-11.

26. H. Bellows, *An Appeal of the Divinity School of Harvard University*, 1879, p. 16; *Report of the President of Harvard College*, 1844-1853.

27. James, *op. cit.*, vol. I, pp. 270-273, 379-380; *Report of the President of Harvard College*, 1895-1896, p. 141; *Harvard Register*, 1967-1968.

28. *Report of Committee of Society for Promoting Theological Education*, January 5, 1857, E. S. Gannett, Chairman.

with only $14,000 available. Additional endowment of $127,000 would finance the income gap of $7,000. This campaign which, according to Williams, yielded $140,000, was apparently successful.[29] The 1947 report of endowment funds, however, reveals only $71,677 left of the 1879 campaign for the divinity school. Was some of the capital consumed or the collections overstated? [30]

The divinity school sought help from the corporation, but the tub principle was an obstacle generally except in the 1950s when the corporation transferred $1 million to the schools. They also compensated the school for excess services given to other schools. [31]

What was espcially troublesome to the school was the small enrollment and, therefore, the high unit costs. From the very beginning, by adhering to the nonsectarian principle, the school tended to increase enrollment. In the midst of the 1870 campaign for additional endowment, Eliot reminded the country of the school's adherence to this principle:

. . . It is the practice of the principal Protestant sects to maintain theological seminaries, each for its own benefit, upon principles which hardly permit to the students the real exercise of the right of private judgement, informed, unhampered, and mature. . . .

Hence, the preference for the nonsectarian school.[32]

Another approach to reduced unit costs was to collaborate with other divinity schools. Though the Harvard School opened in 1816, in part to reduce the influence of the more orthodox Andover Theological School, nevertheless by early in the twentieth century the school was collaborating with Andover, especially, and with other schools. The objective was to reduce costs for a broadened curriculum and general-ly to share faculties and introduce other economies. The courts restrained collaboration, however.[33]

Income and Expenditures

An examination of sources of income and allocation of resources of the nine professional schools will offer an opportunity to comment briefly on a few additional professional schools, and also to relate their incomes and spending patterns to past history. [34]

The largest schools, measured by enrollment, are arts and sciences (inclusive of the graduate school of arts and sciences), business, and law; the largest on the basis of total expenditures are arts and sciences, medicine, and business. Medicine's high standing in outlays, despite its small enrollment, is explained both by its heavy research outlays and the high cost of medical education. Business achieves high standing both because of the large numbers enrolled and high per student expenditures. Though enrollment is roughly equal for law and business, the expenditures per student are almost twice as high for the latter. The business school requires a larger faculty and heavier outlays for research for cases. The management courses also add to its expenditures.

In general, costs per student are high for schools with small enrollment. Business has a large enrollment and a moderately high unit cost. Dental medicine, with its fifty-three students, reveals a very high unit cost. This school has faced difficult financial problems over most of its history. In its early years, help from the school of medicine saved this school. Over a good part of its history, the school could survive only because its faculty received no or virtually no pay. Under President Conant, the school became more of a research school rather than one turning out practioners.

---

29. *An Appeal in Behalf of the Further Endowment of the Divinity School of Harvard University*, 1879, pp. 4-11, 26-27, 30-35; G. H. Williams (ed.), *The Harvard Divinity School*, p. 147.
30. *Endowment Funds of Harvard University*, p. 206.
31. *Report of the Treasurer of Harvard College*, 1843-1844, pp. 14-15; 1844-1845, pp. 8, 18, 19; Williams, *op. cit.*, pp. 174, 213.

32. *An Appeal on Behalf of the Divinity School*, 1879, p. 23.
33. *Report of the President of Harvard College*, 1913-1914, appendix; 1921-1922, pp. 25-26; 1922-1923, p. 16; 1924-1925, pp. 24-25, 1925-1926, pp. 175-176.
34. The two relevant tables have been deposited in the Harvard University Archives.

It is of some interest that the three schools with the highest unit costs are in the medical field: a combination of small-scale operations and (related) the high cost of medical education, explained only in part by the size of operation.

With 101 students, public administration (the J. F. Kennedy School of Government) unit costs are necessarily high. In some respects the costs are higher than here indicated because the school receives gratuitously instruction from faculty members in various departments. The school also tends to keep its costs down by obtaining large financial help from the government in the form of fellowships paid by the government for study of its staff at the school. Under the management of Dean Don Price, the impact of this relatively small school has greatly increased.

In the 1930s, 1940s, and 1950s (the school was founded in 1937), the school remarkably influenced the economic policies of this country. Through activities of four or five members of its faculty, in teaching, research, writing, co-operation with Congress and the Executive, and through the influence of their students, both governmental men on leave and others—e.g., such great economists as Paul Samuelson and James Tobin—they put across the new economics. This victory of ideas increased the national income by tens of billions of dollars in the 1960s.

Education is a school with moderate enrollment and relatively low unit costs. This is a school that has had economic problems remindful of the divinity school. Its constituency—teachers—is not affluent. The school has had other problems also: the competition with Teachers' College at Columbia; and the disagreements on curriculum: how to teach or what to teach. Under the direction of Dean Keppel (1948 to 1962), the school emphasized the what rather than the how of teaching, and the school improved its position. Though education was in the Harvard curriculum under Professor Hanus from 1891 on, the school was not organized until 1920, when a fund of $2 million, given by the general education board, the corporation, and others, provided the needed financial underpinning. Within the university and especially the governing board, there was little enthusiasm for adding another professional school. Financial problems continued to plague the school. A visiting committee in the 1930s noted that the school could teach twice as many students with its current faculty.[35]

Perhaps a word should be added here about the college of arts and sciences. Cost per student has been $3,694, or eighth from highest among the ten schools. With more than nine thousand students, a smaller cost per student might be expected. But one-third of the arts and sciences enrollment is graduate students. This means that the roughly one-third in the graduate school of arts and sciences accounts for 60 percent of the expenditures by arts and sciences. Hence, the rising importance of graduate work has contributed to the increased costs per student in the graduate school. I assume that unit costs per graduate students are 3 times as great for the three thousand graduate students as for the six thousand undergraduates (the 3 to 1 ratio has often been used).

Of special interest is the John F. Kennedy School of Government, which was launched in October, 1966. Harvard renamed its graduate school of public administration the John Fitzgerald Kennedy School of Government, and created within the school an institute of politics; the Nieman Fellowship established by President Conant for journalists interested in a year's study at Harvard; and junior fellows, an innovation of President Lowell's, who had been impressed by the contributions of Trinity College, Cambridge, England. Senior Fellow Crane Brinton, in a volume published in 1959, summarized the remarkable achievements of 159 junior fellows over a period of twenty-six years. No less than 44 of the faculty members of arts and sciences in 1967-1968 of 360 tenure members had been junior fellows.[36]

---

35. See especially P. H. Hanus, *Adventuring in Education*, pp. 142-143, 215-216, 221-225; *Report of the President of Harvard College*, 1920-1921, pp. 171-174; 1950-1951, p. 500; *Report of the Committee to Visit the Graduate School of Education*, 1932, pp. 83-85; 1934, p. 199.

36. *Report of the Committee on Recruitment and Retention of Faculty*, 1968, p. 98.

Structure of Income
and Expenditures by Schools

Now let us examine the structures of income and spending of the nine schools. First, the (endowment) fund income for the whole university, in 1966-1967, was 21 percent of total income. Schools with endowment income much below 21 percent were business (9), public health (10), education (12), and medicine (14). The explanation for medicine and public health is largely the large income from the government, primarily for research, a concentration which pulls down the relative contribution of other items.[37] Business, historically, has adhered to something like full-cost tuition and therefore has managed without much endowment. Education has depended little on income from endowment, because of its large amount of Federal funds, and because its constituency is not affluent. On the high side are divinity (60), design (40), and public administration (30). In view of the difficulties confronting the divinity school in raising endowment, the 60 percent figure is surprising. Low tuition, small enrollment, and absence of government contracts explain this figure. Design's large dependence on endowment income is related to nonreceipts from government contracts, a fact that also helps explain the school's large recourse to tuition.

Gifts for current use are especially large for public administration, law, education, and divinity. Generally, this is a sign of a weak financial position though this is not a tenable position for public administration, nor probably for law.

Tuition income is $18\frac{1}{2}$ percent of total income Especially out of line are law (58), design (38), arts and sciences (27), and the 3 medical schools (8, 7, 2). Large enrollment and little recourse to government grants explains the very large contribution of tuition in the law school.

In view of the high costs of medical education, the small contribution of tuition income is unexpected.

37. *Financial Report to the Board of Overseers of Harvard College*, 1966-1967; *Report of the President of Harvard College*, 1948-1949, p. 492; 1952-1953, pp. 559-560; 1966-1967, p. 22.

Small enrollments and heavy dependence on government contracts are the major explanations. The schools with the greatest recourse (relatively) to government contracts and grants are, (in order) public health, medicine, dental medicine, and education. The others (except for arts and sciences) are much below average.

In short, business is largely dependent on tuition income and current gifts; dental medicine, on government grants and endowment income; design, on tuition and endowment income; divinity, on endowment income; education, on government grants; law, on tuition; medicine, on government grants; public

Percentage Endowment to Income Current Gift Income*	
Divinity	333
Design	267
Arts and sciences	217
Medicine	200
Public administration	170
	152
Law	95
Public health	83
Education	63
Business	22

*Government contracts and grants not included.

Source: Financial Report to the Board of Overseers of Harvard College, 1965-1966 (my calculations).

administration, on endowment income and current gifts; public health, on government. Arts and sciences relies equally on tuition and endowment income (26 percent), and 12 percent on current gifts and 35 percent on government grants.

Now, a word on the structure of expenditures. In arts and sciences, wages are relatively less and salaries more than for the university (25 and 25 percent for university vs 26 and 17 percent for arts and sciences). In general, this holds for most schools—not so for medical school. The over-all percentages apply to the entire university, inclusive of museums, libraries, laboratories, dormitories, commons, etc., where wages tend to be high. (These items that are not allocated to schools account for about $25 million of outlays or about 20 percent of all outlays.) Equipment and supply outlays are especially high for the medical and dental schools and very low for public administration (5 percent), education (7 percent), design and divinity (each 7 percent). Student aid is relatively costly, especially for law and divinity (both 15 percent), arts and sciences (13 percent); and especially low for business (despite the high tuition), medicine (6 percent), and public health (7 percent). (Medical schools have not been very successful in mobilizing funds for student aid.) The low figure for the business school is explained in part by its preference for loans over scholarships. Since loans are largely repaid, the net amount of aid is kept down by recourse to loans.

62

Radcliffe

The Radcliffe Burdens

At present, Radcliffe, a woman's college is really part of Harvard. Radcliffe shares Harvard's faculty and generally has equal access to its physical plant, with the exception of dormitories and the houses, the small residential colleges into which Harvard is divided. Not so long ago Harvard broke down one of its strongest citadels against Radcliffe's invasion and agreed to allow Radcliffe to share their valuable and unique Lamont library for undergraduates.

In his concise and very helpful history of Radcliffe, Prof. Paul Buck presented the advance from Harvard's undertaking responsibility for examining Radcliffe students in the 1870s, to its founding in 1879; to its acquisition of the privilege of issuing degrees in 1894; to Harvard's assuming responsibility for Radcliffe's instruction in the early 1940s. In 1963, Harvard bestowed its degree on Radcliffe students "when 'equivalence' had been for some time a fact."[1]

In 1942 the big move was made. President Jordan of Radcliffe and Acting President Buck of Harvard agreed, with the approval of the corporation, that Harvard would assume the responsibility for Radcliffe instruction, and Radcliffe would turn over most of its tuition money to Harvard, these funds to be used to increase the pay of the Harvard faculty.[2] Those not

teaching at Radcliffe thus received an increase of pay and those teaching at Radcliffe received higher pay in the sense that Radcliffe money received could now be had without any added teaching burdens. Some gained more than others under this arrangement.

The current arrangements seem very favorable to Radcliffe. In a recent year tuition at Harvard accounted for almost 38 percent of relevant income (excluding especially income from government grants and contracts). I assume that Radcliffe tuition income provided only 38 percent of the cost of instruction at Radcliffe. But this is on the assumption that Radcliffe operates on Harvard's level of about 12,500 students. Actually, Radcliffe in 1967 enrolled 2,583 students as against 12,413 by Harvard. Costs of instruction per student would have been much higher at an enrollment of 2,583 than at 12,413. Hence, Radcliffe would have had to provide substantially more than $2\frac{1}{2}$ times its tuition money to cover instruction. This estimate leaves out of account the important contribution of the large Harvard physical plant, built over a few hundred years, which Radcliffe students now use.

Harvard in 1967 insured its buildings for $240 million. On the assumption of a forty-year life remaining and 5 percent interest the annual cost would be $18 million. Should we include a modest $50 million for land values held by Harvard ($2 million income), the annual capital cost would exceed $20 million or almost 80 percent of tuition income of Harvard. I leave out of account the dollar value of

---

1. *Radcliffe College Catalogue for Prospective Students,* June, 1967, pp. 13-16.
2. *Report of the President of Harvard College,* 1951-1952, p. 31.

Harvard's libraries, the greatest in any university, and the contents of its numerous museums.

From all of this, I do not draw the conclusion that Radcliffe has exploited Harvard. Here it is important to distinguish marginal and average cost. Radcliffe's tuition and fees in 1966-1967 were roughly $2,200,000. Assume that Harvard gets all of this—actually, the arrangement was that it would get 88 percent. The agreement is costly to Harvard only if the union with Radcliffe increases Harvard's costs by more than $2,200,000 (or, more accurately, about $2 million) an amount equal to 1 to 2 percent of Harvard's annual expenditures.

Relevant here is a point made by President Bunting in her first report—the special instruction needed by Radcliffe students. This would increase the burden on Radcliffe.[3]

In most courses, the addition of 20 percent more students (the Radcliffe percentage) is not likely to raise costs significantly. Harvard does not hire additional professors to provide instructors for Radcliffe. More teaching fellows obviously would be needed. Undoubtedly Harvard's $25 to 30 million bill for equipment and supplies would be increased as a result of Radcliffe's interest, but surely much less than 20 percent. In this connection, we should take into account the fact that Radcliffe provides its own dormitories, some science buildings, classrooms, and even a significant part of the library service needed.

The Slow Progress Towards Coeducation

A committee appointed by the corporation in 1872 to consider coeducation expressed well the attitude of Harvard men: Their adverse decision was based "on the conviction that the great body of the friends of Harvard College are disinclined not only to the proposed change but also the agitation of the question, at least for the present."[4]

Harvard was very sensitive about not giving joint instruction for men and women. The major issue was a fear of coeducation. But economic issues were also relevant. As early as 1855, the great naturalist, Professor L. Agassiz, announced that he would open a school for ladies, with the faculty primarily his own family. Note his motives:

I have been led to this resolution, first, by the desire of introducing my children upon a career in life, which is the only one in which my circumstances and my own previous training enable me to assist them; and, secondly, by the hope of earning for myself the means of publishing the results of my scientific investigation in this country, which, from the very nature, require considerable pecuniary sacrifices.[5]

In 1847, a woman applied for entry into the Harvard Medical School. The corporation voted that they "do not deem it advisable to alter the existing regulations of the Medical School, which imply that the students are exclusively of the male sex."[6]

Of some interest is a comment by a committee of the university in 1872, the beginning of the Eliot period, on a proposal that Harvard take over the New England Female Medical College. The majority:

do not entertain objections of a broad and fundamental character to the assumption of such a trust by the University; provided, however, that the conditions on which it assumed are satisfactory to the Corporation and the Overseers,—including among these conditions the transfer to the Corporation of sufficient funds for carrying out the trust . . . . (My italics.)[7]

Even President Eliot, who in general was ahead of his time, entertained doubts about coeducation. In reply to the recommendation of the President of

---

3. *Report of the President,* Radcliffe, 1960-1961, pp. 8-9.
4. Rev. Dr. Walker on Behalf of Committee. . . Appointed to Inquire. . . into Coeducation, September 27, 1872.
5. Announcement of Proposed School by L. Agassiz, March 12, 1855.

6. W. Channing, Dean to President Everett and Vote of Corporation, July 19, 1847.
7. Committee on a Communication from the Corporation in Relation to the New England Female Medical College, September 25, 1872 (Rev. Dr. Walker, ch.).

Swarthmore that the head of his mathematics department be allowed to study at Harvard, Eliot replied:

...The presence of a woman in our lecture rooms would excite remarks, and incorrect inferences would certainly be drawn from it...from every point of view....We are in favor of higher education for young women; but opposed to their education with young men....[8]

President Eliot, who approved the use of Harvard faculty to teach competent women in the early 1870s, and particularly to improve their competence as teachers, still had reservations, as is evident from his inaugural address of October, 1869:

...Equality between the sexes, without privileges or oppression on either side, is the happy custom of American homes. While the great discussion is going on, it is the duty of the University to maintain a cautious and expectant policy. The Corporation will not receive women as students in the College proper, nor into any school whose discipline requires residence near the school. The difficulties involved in a common residence of hundreds of young men and women of immature character and marriageable age are very grave. The necessary police regulations are exceedingly burdensome...the world knows next to nothing about the natural capacities of the female sex. Only after generations of civil freedom and social equality will it be possible to obtain the data necessary for an adequate discussion of women's natural tendencies, tastes and capabilities....

By the early 1890s, Eliot's position had advanced, and with strong women colleges being found and women students accounting for as much as one-fifth of the student population, and with Mrs. Agassiz and others applying pressure gently but effectively, the agitation to increase Harvard's responsibility for its sister institution increased.

By a large majority, the Harvard faculty in 1893 voted to "assume the management of the instruction and examinations of that institution, but not its

discipline; "that if the University finds it inexpedient to assume these responsibilities the faculty will undertake the supervision as a basis for the proposed guarantee of the diploma of the annex;" that the faculty approved admitting women under suitable restrictions to selected graduate courses.[9]

On May 29, 1893, Eliot wrote Mrs. Louis Agassiz along the lines of the faculty vote. The college was to be self-governing; the president and fellows, to assume visitational powers; no instructor or examiner was to be appointed or retained without approval of the visitors; the diploma of the college (soon to be called Radcliffe) to be countersigned by the president of Harvard. Mrs Agassiz also obtained legislative approval of the proposed changes.[10]

Mrs. Agassiz and Eliot were not the only supporters of higher education for women in Cambridge. William James wrote to the president in 1891, concerning a Miss Carter who wanted to take philosophy:

...I can conscientiously say in her behalf that she is an exceptionally able woman of about 28 or 30, thoroughly well fitted for the course....Personally, I should be glad to have her request granted, quite apart from any general belief that it is an anomaly that women of serious professional aims should not have the benefits of our graduate instruction.

Opposition remained strong even after 1893-1894 agreements. Barrett Wendell, a professor of literature, was especially caustic in an article for *Atlantic Monthly* in 1899. His opposition stemmed from the temptation Radcliffe offered for moonlighting, with adverse effects on scholarly work; and the effect of having women in class upon the unfortunate tendency of professors to become increasingly obtuse

---

8. C. W. Eliot to E. H. Magill, November 12, 1879.

9. Memorandum of Informal Votes Passed by the Faculty for Transmission to the Corporation, May 9 and 16, 1893.
10. C. W. Eliot to Mrs. Louis Agassiz, May 29, 1893; C. W. Eliot to Mr. Byerly, April 18, 1894; Arthur Gilman to C. W. Eliot, November 1, 1963; A. Gilman, *The Cambridge of Eighteen Hundred Ninety-Six,* chapter IX; D. McCord, *In Sight of Sever,* 1963, pp. 175-190.

with advancing age, a tendency likely to be strengthened with women in class.[11]

The treasurer of Harvard wrote Mrs. Agassiz in April, 1893:

...If we give our degrees we must give the instruction necessary to fit women for those degrees, and that means either a duplication of our instruction, or to some extent coeducation...am quite willing to see Yale or Columbia take any risks they like, but I feel bound to protect Harvard College from what seems to me to be a risky experiment....[12]

Financial Restraints

Undoubtedly, official Harvard was fearful that giving women access to Harvard's instruction would be costly to Harvard. It may well be that Harvard's costs are increased more that what is received from Radcliffe's tuition money. But this is not clear. In most courses the rise of enrollment, say by 20 percent, will actually cut unit costs. The unit cost of lecturing to 60 instead of 50 or 120 instead of 100 will be less at the larger enrollment.

Another consideration is also relevant though its net effects are not easily measured. Radcliffe's growth under its increasing ties to Harvard and its general propinquity undoubtedly make Harvard a more attractive institution. Harvard, inclusive of Radcliffe, enlists a larger number of able students.[13] The gains here are not so much in numbers as in the average quality of Harvard students. Radcliffe's enrollment also has steadily risen as its connections with Harvard have increased.

Radcliffe's prestige is revealed also by the ratio of the number of applications to freshmen places. Its ratio of more than 8 to 1 is by far the highest of the Big Seven Women's Colleges and exceeds Harvard's ratio of 6 to 1.[14]

A table giving enrollment, fees, and salaries from 1880 to 1967 throws some light on Radcliffe's history. What is especially striking is the extent to which salaries absorbed most of the revenue. Even if in the 1890s endowment income amounted to $15,000 ($280,000 of endowment), salaries absorbed about 75 percent of income. Even by 1967, with endowment in excess of $20 million, salaries absorbed about 60 percent of all income. These figures suggest both that unit costs tend to be high with small operations, and also that with limited resources, the expenditures other than for faculty are carefully scrutinized. (Cf., Harvard arts and sciences with 30 percent of relevant expenses currently going to corporation appointments.)

The managers had to be thrifty. In 1902, Eliot remarked that "it is astonishing how much good work

Table 62-1.

Radcliffe, numbers, fees, and salaries, 1880–1967, several years

	Number of Students	Fees	Salaries
1879–1880	25	$ 3,725	$ 5,171
1889–1890	142	20,018	18,925
1894–1895	284	49,627	47,667
1966–1967	1209 (undergraduates) 2583 (all)	2,207,024	1,878,798*

*Cost of Instruction
Source: A. Gilman, *op. cit.,* p. 185

11. *Barrett Wendell and His Letters,* pp. 87-90.
12. E. W. Hooper to Mrs. Agassiz in A. Gilman, *op. cit.,* pp. 234-235.
13. President Bunting in her first Report (1960-1961, p. 5)

commented on the increased attractiveness of both Harvard and Radcliffe as the ties of the two institutions were strengthened.
14. *New York Times,* April 17, 1967.

has been done by Radcliffe College with its slender material resources. . . ."[15]

Inadequate funds plagued the Radcliffe administration. In 1881, a few years after operations began, the managers of the Harvard Annex wrote to the corporation that they recognized the fact "that the President and Fellows could not be expected to accept the trust [Radcliffe] unless a fund were put into the hands of the Treasurer sufficient to enable them to carry out their work without drawing on their resources. . . ." They were prepared to offer such funds if the women could be given the same advantages as Harvard men. The managers considered the $280,000 of endowment adequate only because of the great resource, the Harvard faculty.[16]

In 1893, President Eliot wrote:

You may assure any person to whom you apply for money for the Annex that when the society has an endowment of $250,000, in addition to its present endowment, I shall be ready to bring before the Governing Boards of Harvard University the question of acceding to a request from the society that the University take charge of the annex. . . .[17]

From 1880 to 1884, the annex raised $70,000 for endowment during a $100,000 campaign. The annex received numerous gifts in later years and notably $116,000 for a dormitory at the eightieth birthday of Mrs. Agassiz. In the 1950s, a ten-year campaign yielded $7 million in seven years as compared with a $10-million objective.

Radcliffe depends heavily on student income. As might be expected, endowment income and gifts are much less important in the Radcliffe than in the Harvard budget, a fact that partly explains the large contribution by student income.

15. *Report of the President of Harvard College,* 1901-1902, p. 41.
16. Arthur Gilman to the President and Fellows of Harvard, June 27, 1881; A. Gilman, *op. cit.,* pp. 179, 254-255.
17. C. W. Eliot to Miss Annie Barber, January 24, 1893.

PART

10

ACCOUNTING

63

Accounting Problems

Early Accounting Methods

In the seventeenth century and even the eighteenth century, accounting practices everywhere were still rather primitive, a fact that helps explain the limitations of Harvard accounting in the first hundred or even two hundred years of its life.

According to the hypothetical rules for dr and cr (of personal accounts) in the early period, a sum is to be entered in the record as "shall give," if the person involved is obliged to return at a later date an equivalent of the sum he has just received. A sum is to be entered in the record as "shall have," if the person involved is entitled to receive from me at a later date an equivalent of the sum he has just now given me.

The English practices were fixed in the seventeenth century and for the next two hundred years changes were few and unimportant. The accounts were kept upon two folios, the left for the debit and the right for the credit; account titles were definitely established as headings; and the arrangement in general was less narrative in form and more in the nature of tabulations than formerly, although each entry still carried a page reference to the contra account.

One difficulty with the Harvard accounts was that many crucial receipts and expenditures were excluded. Thus, payments by the government to cover salaries of the president and others and outlays for buildings escaped the accounting officer. Again, the steward, who was responsible for most of the financial transactions with the students, the commons, and large salary payments, reported only the net figures in his relations with the treasurer. In fact, when the net

figures tended to be high, additional payments would be imposed on the steward and his net receipts would be reduced to a small figure. Elimination of the gross receipts or disbursements for commons is not to be regretted, since room and board should be kept out of the totals for an assessment of the educational operations. But exclusion of tuition and salaries and capital items is another matter.

Not only were such items excluded, but there were many irregularities in the manner of entry of items, long delays, errors corrected many years after the relevant period, and often a bunching of items with the total or net figure alone being given. The use of a journal and ledger was common in the seventeenth century, but even in the eighteenth century, the details of transactions escaped the ledger and reference to the journal was necessary to examine numerous items. Moreover, there were often inconsistencies between entries in the journal and the ledger.

In the eighteenth century, it was not unusual for a faculty member to seek payment of a bill on behalf of the college when on a journey. Having obtained payment, the faculty member would then transfer all or part of the proceeds to his own account as payment of his salary. Another peculiar transaction was that of an individual investing in his name on behalf of the college. He would not only invest on behalf of the college, but he also would receive interest or rents on behalf of the college. Some friends of the college with accounts in Great Britain would accept a donation in pounds sterling for the college and then pay out in dollars in Cambridge. In some instances the friend would not only accept payment in London but would purchase commodities in England, export them to the United States, and sell them at a profit, thus increasing the value of the donation. All these peculiar transactions raised tough accounting problems for the treasurer and others concerned.

It is not surprising that accounting was often chaotic. An examination of the president's accounts with the college reveals that in the years 1775 to 1777 the president received earnings on investments directly as well as fees from the students. In turn, he paid the professors directly and purchased materials. The unavailability of Treasurer Hancock helps explain this unorthodoxy. On the debit side of Harvard's accounts, during President Langdon's, time were such items as rent due him from Massachusetts Hall (£15), sums due for paper purchased (£1 to £16), costs of moving furniture to Cambridge (£2 18s), cost of horse hire to go to Narragansett on college business (£2 5s 10d), for printing catalogues (£24 7s 4d), and for moving the college to Concord (£39 19s 4d). On the credit side (due to Harvard College), rent of College House (£10 3s 8d); cash or part payment from Mr. Alford's legacy (£150 12s 4d); cash from Deacon Mason for his nephew's admission to advanced standing (£24). In all, by February 1777, the payments to President Langdon amounted to £467 1s 8d, he owed the college £409 4s 3d, and, hence, the balance due the college was £57 17s 4d.

In September, 1777, the "Committee appointed to examine the President's accounts have attested that service to be right...and well vouched...." [1]

The treasurer in 1809 purchased bank stock in such quantities that he complained of an advance of $600 out of his own funds.[2]

This is one of many examples of commingling of college and personal funds.[3]

An example of careless arithmetic is revealed by John Quincy Adams.

I find upon looking over the encloſed minutes which you gave me yesterday, a ſmall mistake in the calculation which it will be neceſsary to rectify–The amount due to me from the 12th to the 30th of June, instead of $ 23 . . 20, should be $ 72 . . 46, as you will perceive by a revisal of the paper – My account therefore to 30. Sept.ʳ ſtands thus.

	Salary from
12th to 30th June	*$ 72 . . 46*
From 30 June to 30 Sept:ʳ	*348 ..*
	$420 .. 46
Received your Check for	*171 .. 20*
Balance due me –	*249 .. 26* [4]

Even as late as the nineteenth century, serious abuses prevailed. In the third quarter of the eighteenth century, the treasury had often used the phrase *President's Private Account*. The president apparently purchased supplies for the college and was reimbursed later. In the first quarter of the nineteenth century, the president, instead of receiving his salary of $2,550 at regular intervals, obtained it by drawing on the treasury and had overdrawn his account by $1,700.[5]

In some instances, and notably in relation to the donation of Thomas Hollis in the early eighteenth century, there was a requirement of a special accounting, for which Hollis paid £10 per year. He apparently was not entirely satisfied with Harvard's accounting system, or perhaps suspected possible misuse of funds. Others gave Harvard funds, but only on the condition that the funds be invested as suggested by the donor.

1. Accounts of Sam Langdon, President, April 14, 1775 to July 3, 1777.
2. J. Jackson to President Kirkland, February 24, 1809; C. Saunders to Treasurer Francis, June 25, 1828.
3. J. Jackson to Pres. Kirkland, February 24, 1809; C. Saunders to Treasurer Francis, June 25, 1828.
4. John Quincy Adams to Ebenezer Storer, Esq., November 1, 1806.
5. *Treasurers' Journals,* 1754-1777; S. E. Morison, "The Great Rebellion in Harvard College," in *Transactions,* Colonial Society of Massachusetts, 1927-1930, vol. XXVII, p. 104.

The Steward

The first steward of Harvard was Matthew Day, who ended his term in 1649. The office was occupied continuously until the term of Edward William Hooper, 1872 to 1874. In 1874, the title of the office was changed to bursar, and the first bursar was Allen Danforth, who held office to 1880. The post has continued to this day, though the bursar's responsibilities have been shifted to some extent to other officials.[6]

From almost the beginning the steward, responsible for transactions with the student and faculty and the commons, assumed large responsibilities in the financial management of the college. In parts of the seventeenth century, the steward operated on a cost-plus basis, with a minimum guarantee and some sharing with the college of any large returns. But he ultimately received a fixed salary.[7]

Early in the eighteenth century the steward's book contained individual accounts. Debits showed the amounts due the steward; credits, the collections from students. The Harvard College Account of the steward showed claims on the college (debits). Amounts due the college from the steward were credited to this account.[8]

A note from the president to the treasurer in 1715 reveals the relations among President Leverett, treasurer, the steward, and claimants on the college.[9]

Mr. Treasurer

By the vote of the corporation
1715, and April 9th 1716
Mr. Rogers was allowed as

library keeper and out of	*£ 6. . . .*
Capt. Keines Leg	*£ 5. . . .*
	£ 11-0-0

Mr. Appleton, Crocker, Rogers, Perkins &
Sewall as Scholars of the house:

*Each £4 W*ch *com*s *to*	*£ 20-0-0*
*Gote was allowed out of Mr. Penoy*rs	
Donation £8	*£ 8-0-0*
Putnam, Sewal and Green each £4	*£12-0-0*
*Oliver was allow*d *£4*	*£ 4-0-0*
	£55-0-0

*And at the same time S*r *Galpin was allowed one Quarter of £90 Sterl*g *with the Curr*t *Exch*a *out of Mr. Boyles Charity.*

*Please to pay to Mr. Andrew Bordman the Several Sums above Expr.ss'd, for the Use and acc*t *of the Respective persons to whom they are assigned; and one quarter of the allow*c *made to S*r *Galpin. I am*

*S*r

*Y*r *humble Serv*r

J. Lev

Transactions with the Steward

From time to time the corporation limited the prices to be charged by the steward, and also required the steward to share any profits with the college. When prices unexpectedly rose, the college might provide special allowances for the steward. In 1772, the butler, confronted with rising prices, was allowed to increase prices by 20 percent except for cider, price of which was annually fixed by the corporation.[10]

On September 9, 1765, the corporation ruled that the steward was to keep a careful account of all food bought for commons and to make no personal profit on it. The college allowed him a salary of £150 a year for himself and £50 to pay the cooks. He was to

6. *Harvard Quinquennial Catalogue,* 1910.
7. Cf., Margery Somers Foster, *"Out of Smalle Beginings. . ." – An Economic History of Harvard College in the Puritan Period (1636-1712),* 1962, pp. 137, 152-155.
8. *Steward's Ledger,* 1703-1731: cf., Notes from the President to the Treasurer, in 1717, 1719, 1723, in which the president promises payments for the exhibitions and suggests how much the treasurer may draw upon the steward; *Treasurers' Collected Papers,* 1692-1721; 1721-1725.
9. *Treasurers' Collected Papers,* 1692-1721 (1715).

10. *Corporation Records,* vol. I, pp. 64, 99, 109, 114, 116, 135, 171, 221, (1715 to 1723), (various years); vol. II, pp. 171, 201, 323 (years 1763, 1764, 1772).

provide at college expense breakfast, dinner, and supper for the scholars and to collect the money from them. The salary of £150 was 7½ times that of 1667. In view of the devaluation of 1750, the steward's salary did not seem to exceed greatly that in the latter part of the seventeenth century.[11] From 1754 to 1764, the steward had been allowed the whole of the amount paid by students for commons and sizings for buying food, paying the salaries of the cooks. With continued inflation, the steward's and cooks' salaries rose from £200 to £220 in 1768-1769 and £240 in 1771-1772.[12] In the 1760s it was often not clear why the steward was transferring cash to the college.

By about 1790, the steward's accounts were audited quarterly, as is attested by the following: "Memo—The Accounts at this time were examined by the Corporation and also by the Lt. Governor Adams, Hon. Thomas Russell and Williams Phillips, Esq., who made this report to the Overseers, Ye 6th 7 July, 1790."[13]

For an indication of some of the responsibilities of the butler, the corporation at a meeting of April 5, 1773, issued the following college law.

The Butler shall provide Candles for the Chapel, and fire-wood for the Library, Philosophy Chamber and private Schools, and shall take care that the Hall and Entry adjoining be swept once a day, and that the floor, tables and forms be cleased as often as the President and Tutors shall require, the expence to be paid by the Undergraduates and charged in their Quarter bills.[14]

Debts to Harvard

Attitudes toward indebtedness were interesting. On September 9, 1753, the corporation observed that despite the college law to the effect that students had to pay quarter bills within three months or get out, many neglected to pay. The corporation ordered the steward to send their bills to their parents or guardians. But in 1800 the steward was ordered to write to a student's guarantor as soon as a student's connection with the college ceased, and never allow any debts beyond six months. In 1741, the college forgave Henry Newman all his debts in consideration of his services to the college. The corporation announced in 1764 that no student was to be denied his degree because he owed the steward money. (Debts to the college were another matter.) The corporation in 1775 apprised the steward that Messrs. Sampson, Hodgson, Stinson, and Winchester should be relieved of £41 10s 7d of debt to the college since they were dead.

Capital Evaluation

In the eighteenth century, the college obtained compensation in inflationary periods for investments tied to a weight of silver. (Capital gains were made as a result.) Thus, in 1755, of £34,321 of assets, £13,430 were capital gains. Apparently, these gains were credited to the accounts of the funds which were thus invested.[15] But long before the days of heavy investments in equities and large capital gains, there were problems of how to evaluate assets that fluctuate in value.

One peculiar accounting method in the third quarter of the eighteenth century was to close out an account (an investment by the college) to Harvard College only when the interest and principal were completely paid. Hence, the Harvard College account was deprived of interest until the loan was repaid. On provincial notes, interest and capital gains and losses were merged and credited to the Harvard College account, thus, capital gains being credited to Harvard College.[16]

---

11. Foster, op. cit., p. 137; *Corporation Records,* vol. II, p. 229.
12. *Corporation Records,* vol. II, Especially p. 229, and later *Steward's Audited Accounts.*

13. *Treasurers' Journals,* vol. II, p. 186.
14. *Corporation Records,* vol. II, p. 383.
15. *Treasurers' Journals,* 1755-1775.
16. *Treasurers' Ledgers,* 1755-1773.

Valuation of Capital Assets

In May, 1791, the treasurer set at their original value college funds which had in 1750 (following a devaluation) been reduced by the corporation to below their original value. The point was made that in the great inflation of the first half of the eighteenth century and after the devaluation of 1750, the treasurer had written off 50 percent of the college stock. A stock of £10,000 would be covered at £5,000 and hence, the return (earnings of investment) would be correspondingly higher per pound of stock. But the large improvement of stock in the last quarter of the eighteenth century suggested a capital gain and lower rate of return. Apparently this rise in value was accompanied by a reduced return, for in 1805 the following appeared:

Whereas by a vote of this Corporation passed in May 1791, the appropriations were fixed at their original value and ordered to be on interest at 4 percent, being the average interest of the funded stock, and so to continue till 1801, when the deferred stock should become productive, and then to be at 5 percent:—and whereas the college funds have since increased, and it appears therefore reasonable that they should now be at the common rate of interest namely 6 percent.[17]

Distribution of Endowment Income

In October, 1891, the university introduced the account *Gains and Losses for General Investment*. As of July 31, 1909, this account had a balance of $575,499.24. It should be noted that these gains really belonged to the various endowments of the university, but the college diverted them to other uses.[18]

Relations of Departments of the University

In 1907-1908, the comptroller suggested a new method of distributing university funds. Thereafter, the professional schools were also to contribute to the overhead of the university and thus reduce the burden on the college, a reform stemming from the increased resources of the professional schools. On the basis of floor space, collections, payments made by the bursar and the number of students, the university allocates the charges for overhead.[19]

Proper Use of Endowment

From the beginning, the college distinguished restrictive from nonrestrictive endowment. There are some questions concerning the use of the latter. The college apparently did convert endowment funds into buildings, and there is evidence that in the great crisis of the 1820s endowment was consumed.

The losses suffered during the incumbency of John Hancock as treasurer from 1773 to 1777 were disturbing. Neither a journal nor a ledger is to be found for the Hancock period. Hancock, immersed in politics, did not take his responsibilities to Harvard seriously. At one point, with Hancock away for long periods, the president had to accept donations and income on behalf of the college, and in 1777, with the intervening territory occupied by the enemy, Hancock had the college records sent to him in Philadelphia, much to the annoyance of the president and fellows. In 1785, Hancock attempted to settle with the college, which sent him a bill for £1,495 14s 2d; and in 1795 his heirs agreed to pay the bill with simple interest over a period of seven years, the refusal to pay compound interest costing the college $526.[20]

17. *Corporation Records,* 1791, vol. III, pp. 377-378; 1805, vol. IV, p. 55.
18. *Report of the Treasurer of Harvard College,* 1908-1909, p. 6.
19. *Report of the President of Harvard College,* 1907-1908, pp. 49-51.
20. Samuel Eliot Morison, *Three Centuries of Harvard, 1636-1936,* 1937, pp. 153-157; Hancock Papers: Letters and Papers Relating to John Hancock and His Tenure of Office as Treasurer of Harvard College, 1754-1792; *Treasurer's Record,* a summary account by President Langdon of April, 1775, to August, 1777; *Corporation Records,* 1777; *College Papers,* 1777; Deeds and Lands Papers; *Treasurers' Journals,* 1777, vol. I; pp. 1-25, 38, 61, 79, 187; W. T. Baxter, *The House of Hancock; Business in Boston,* 1724-1775; Josiah Quincy, *The History of Harvard University,* 1840, vol. II, pp. 182-209; p. 388; Harvard College Papers Supplement, 1775-1777, p. 18.

Defaults

In the seventeenth and eighteenth centuries, large amounts were due the college and there were numerous defaults, which of course involved losses of capital. The treasury was not systematic in keeping account of these delinquencies. Thus, in the years 1721 to 1744, we could find only six instances in which a survey of outstanding debts was made. (This table has been deposited in the Harvard University archives.) It is of some interest that a period of inflation (1725 to 1743), when debtors should have been able to repay with reduced burden, the overdue debts to the college rose by about 3½ times. The Harvard practice of tying obligations to equivalent silver value helps to some extent explain this trend. The debtors did not gain as much from inflation as they might have.[21]

Irregularities under Kirkland and Davis

In the middle 1820s occurred the "great dissatisfaction." The college had experienced large rises of expenditures and serious deficits. In 1825-1826, the corporation appointed a group of five fellows to investigate the possibilities of restriction and retrenchment. Scrutiny covered seventeen years of accounts in some instances. "Some irregularities had occurred and some errors were rectified; but neither fraud nor embezzlement . . . were discovered or to be suspected. . . ." John Davis thereupon resigned as treasurer.

The accounts were in a mess. To give one example, a memo of July 17, 1827, revealed that in the years 1818 to 1822 at one point more money was received from the students for commons than was paid into commons; that Mr. Cooley, in charge of the kitchen, paid out large sums but vouchers (authority) were missing, and receipts were not to be found for payments by Cooley, and advances to Chamberlin for purchase of books were not accounted for.

An indication of the accounting and management mess under President Kirkland is given by the following by Morison:

An audit of the treasury accounts . . . a task which required six months, frequently at the rate of 12 hours a day, revealed a surprising state of affairs. Errors to the amount of $120,000 were found in Judge Davis' accounts—fortunately they largely cancelled each other. The President, instead of receiving his salary ($2,550) at regular intervals had obtained it by drawing orders at pleasure on the Steward, and had overdrawn to the amount of $1,700. He had abated at will the term-bills of students whom he deemed meritorious, without the vote of the Corporation or regard to the Charity funds, and had thus paid out over $1,000 of the College capital. Hilliard, Metcalf & Co., printers to the university, had run the corporation heavily in debt without their knowledge, and had lost or mis-laid several thousand text books which were college property. No rent had been received from the Pennoyer estate in England since 1820. Various debtors to the college had long since died, without the treasurer making any effort to collect the debts from their estates. Several thousand acres of land in Maine, granted to the college by the General Court, had had the timber cut off by trespassers, or got into the possession of squatters. Various deeds and bonds had been mislaid and a lease of the Province House estate had been left at the Suffolk registry of deeds for three years.[22]

Undoubtedly the crises induced improvements. A committee of the governing board, C. Jackson and F. C. Gray, in 1830 reported that the college kept its books in a clear and exact manner; the treasurer demanded and obtained punctuality and praised "the vigilance and skill exerted in the investment of the College property . . . offered additional evidence of the lively interest which the Treasury feels in the prosperity of the institution."[23]

---

21. *Treasury Papers,* especially *Treasurers' Journals* and *Treasurers' Ledgers.*

22. Morison, "The Great Rebellion," *op. cit.,* pp. 104-105.

23. C. Jackson, and F.C. Gray, Committee on the Treasurer's Accounts to the President and Fellows, January 20, 1830.

The treasurer following the crisis of the 1820s was now required:

. . . to present to them [the Corporation] *a statement of his expenditures each month and an annual account to be examined by the Committee, and also related vouchers. . . the treasurer was prohibited from making any payment unless sanctioned by a previous vote of the Board; without which neither the President, nor any member of the Board, had authority to loan money from the Treasury.*

A practice of distributing beneficiary funds by deducting them from term bills was no longer to be tolerated. This was a rather late date for such accounting and administration of funds to be ordered. In addition, the board requested from the treasury a general statement of receipts and expenditures, arranged under appropriate headings, and names of all faculty members, with amounts paid to each.[24]

In earlier years there were some elements of dishonesty; and at this time at least some bungling. In the early 1820s a committee of the Legislature had remarked on the complete absence of dishonesty on the part of Harvard's authorities since 1636. This statement has been repeated by C. Eliot and others. In 1851, it was said "That the financial affairs of the College as administered by the present Corporation and not less by its predecessors, from the time of the Colony to this day, afford a model of integrity. . . ."[25]

Accounting Peculiarities

In examining the journal and ledgers in the first 150 years of Harvard's history, the scholar discovers much slipshod accounting, and many inconsistencies. Thus, in the *Hutchinson Journal*, (treasurer, 1721 to 1755) one discovers that salaries are to some extent paid out by the treasurer (entry is debited to Harvard College and credited to credit bills); or the steward pays the salary and receives credit for payment in his account with the college. Obviously, a treasurer's account will not disclose the salary bill.

Other Lapses

Here are some examples of peculiar accounting in the eighteenth century. In the Hutchinson period the Hopkins legacy derived from the land at Hopkinton was not recorded except through the payments which students had to make from their grants of 2 shillings to the college for the purchase of books. Similarly, the Pennoyer legacy was recorded only once. After this, the land in England yielded rents, the proceeds often being used to buy commodities there for sale in the colonies. In the Hutchinson period, several years would often elapse before the interest and rents due were recorded on the books. Dates of interest received were often inconsistent as given by the journal and ledger. The steward, Andrew Boardman's 1721 to 1755 accounts with the treasurer were both personal and official. Thus, Boardman was lessee of a piece of land belonging to the college, and hence the balance of the account with the treasurer reflected this transaction as well as those involving students, faculty members, commons, etc. [26]

In the years of Thomas Hubbard as treasurer (1752 to 1773), Lewis Turner had repaid a bond (loan) to the college in 1757, but it was not until 1762, five years after the repayment of the bill, that the interest was recorded.[27]

Frequently it was not possible to find a ledger reference to correspond to a journal item; and there were no profit and loss statements during the Hubbard regime (1752 to 1773).

Commingling Capital and Current Accounts

Perhaps the most unsatisfactory aspect of Harvard accounting in the seventeenth and eighteenth centuries was the commingling of capital and current

---

24. Quincy, *op. cit.,* vol. II, pp. 362-369, 558-563, app. XLI.
25. Commonwealth of Massachusetts, *Senate Report,* no. 102, May 5, 1851, p. 2.

26. See *Hutchinson's Ledger,* pp. 51, 140, 195.
27. *Hubbard Ledger,* 1757, p. 44; 1762, p. 93.

accounts or, even worse, the complete neglect of capital accounts. A balance sheet with interest and annuity receipts capitalized and with entry of property acquired at cost, with corrections for depreciation and inflation, was out of the question. Well into the eighteenth century, sales and purchases of assets went unrecorded. Even as late as the Hutchinson period bad debts were carried forward year after year instead of being written off.

Modern Accounting

By the early nineteenth century, accounting practices of the college had become more modern. The methods of recording the various transactions employed by the treasurer were similar to those in use today in many respects. A journal was kept to record chronologically all the receipts and disbursements, and all the transfers among assets. These transactions were summarized in a ledger in which separate pages were maintained for each account, and from which a trial balance was drawn up each year on July 1st.

The capital accounts maintained by the treasurer consisted of special funds and a general account called the "stock account." The special funds represent donations made to the college for special purposes. The stock account represents the amount of common funds available for the general purposes of the college.

Interest and dividends received on investments were credited either to an interest account or directly to a fund. If the form in which the assets of a fund were to be held was specified by a donor, then the proceeds from those assets were credited directly to that fund. If the form in which the assets were to be held was not specified then all proceeds were credited to an interest account along with the proceeds from all other general investments. The interest account was then apportioned among the various funds according to a previously determined (apparently by the treasurer) percentage which in this period was 6 percent. Any balance remaining in the interest account was then credited to profit and loss and eventually became a part of the general funds of the college.

Current accounts include the current receipts from the funds and the current operating receipts and disbursements. When the proceeds from the investments were to be spent, the various funds were debited for the amount of the interest and, if the treasurer disbursed the money, cash was credited. However, if the interest was to be used to meet the expenses of the students, the steward's account was credited and the amount deducted from the term bills of the selected students.

All receipts by the steward were debited to the steward's account in the ledger by the treasurer and credited to the various accounts for which they were received. Similarly, all disbursements were credited to the steward and debited to the various accounts for which they were paid.

When the term bills were issued, the steward was debited for the total amount, and the various accounts, commons, rent, salaries, and other charges assessed against students were credited. When bills or salaries were paid, the treasurer issued an order to the steward directing payment, whereupon the steward's account was debited and the various accounts credited.

The steward maintained a set of books similar to the treasurer's, employing both a journal and a ledger. All receipts were credited and all payments debited to an account which he called the treasury account. Upon issue of the term bills, this account was credited and the various students debited. Upon receipt of payment, the students were credited and cash debited. Similarly, when the steward received an order to pay a bill from the treasurer, the treasury account was debited and the various accounts credited. When payment was actually made, the various accounts were debited and cash credited.

In this manner, the balance in the treasury account in the steward's ledger agreed with the balance in the steward's account in the treasurer's ledger.

At the end of the fiscal year, June 30, the treasurer closed the various accounts handled by the steward to the profit and loss account which, in turn, was closed to an account called the "stock account." Since this account was debited for any loss and credited for any gain, its balance shows the amount of the unrestricted funds belonging to the college.

After the various accounts were closed a trial balance was drawn up and recorded in the journal. On one side of the balance sheet were listed all the assets in the form in which they were held—cash, stock, bonds, real estate—and the steward's balance.[28] On the other side were listed all the funds to which the assets were accountable—legacies, funds, and the stock account. No statements of receipts and disbursements were drawn up, but they can be constructed from the treasurer's accounts.

Cost Accounting at Harvard

Cost accounting is an important weapon at the disposal of business firms. But institutions of higher learning have had little recourse to this instrument. There are many reasons why this is so. Not being a profit-seeking institution, the college is not disposed to watch costs as are private managers. It is not always easy to estimate costs, and especially since the institution of higher learning so often produces a joint product, e.g., several colleges, training of undergraduates and graduates with the same faculty, community services, research. But business firms are not so easily diverted by joint costs as are institutions of higher learning. Those who are responsible for higher education become immersed in educational objectives, and tend to neglect a relevant point, that resources are limited.

One will find little evidence of studies of costs in Harvard history. Even today, the treasurer's report reveals income and expenditures of the various departments of the university and little else. Indeed, at Harvard each department is now required to finance its own needs, though temporary help may be available from the university.

Harvard has shown interest in keeping costs down. I do not mean to imply that the business officers do not, for example, try to build in the most economical manner, and we have seen that at crucial periods the college indulged in vigorous drives to reduce disbursements. But there has been a lack of genuine cost studies. The treasurer does not tell us how much a particular program costs, e.g., the Harvard Business Management Curriculum. (Here the business school has made the most progress.) Nor do we get any idea of the costs of instruction for an undergraduate or graduate student. Occasionally we will be shown total costs and tuition payments, and it will be suggested that the student pays one-half the costs. But these are most inadequate studies—many of the costs are irrelevant and no serious attempt is made to deal with joint costs.

In an official report of 1909-1910, a promising position was taken.

Instruction in different branches of knowledge varies greatly in cost, and in some of them it is by necessity very expensive, particularly for advanced students; but that is no reason why we should not be informed precisely what it does cost. The University has been expanding so rapidly, both in the number of instructors and students and in the variety of subjects taught, that it has become increasingly difficult to survey its financial problems. The firm of Gunn, Richards and Company has, therefore, been employed to examine the accounts, suggest improvements, and enable the Comptroller to present the balances for the year at an earlier date.[29]

Another advance is the innovation in 1907-1908 under which professional schools were charged for their share of overhead expenses. The allocation was based on modern cost accounting principles.[30]

---

28. University Buildings were not valued and were not carried on the books.

29. *Report of the President of Harvard College,* 1909-1910, p. 22.
30. *Ibid.,* 1907-1908, pp. 49-51.

PART

11

CONCLUDING REMARKS

Conclusion

A Few Concluding Remarks

In view of the long summary at the outset, only a brief conclusion is needed.

From its modest beginnings in 1636, Harvard by the latter nineteenth century had attained pre-eminence in higher education. In its early years, the college depended especially on gifts and endowment income. But the contributions of the government were large in the first 150 years, and also more recently. The extension of the curriculum, the founding and expansion of professional schools, the general rise of enrollment, and the increasing unit costs associated with the rise of prices and general cost of services, not offset by equal gains in productivity, all increased expenditures. Large growth occurred especially in Harvard's last 100 years, beginning with Eliot's administration (1869 to 1909).

The problem in the 1960s had become one of finding new sources of revenue. Endowment, impaired by the rise of enrollment — endowment income per student falls as enrollment rises — and by the inflationary trends, contributed a declining share of income. Tuition income became increasingly important in the twentieth century, but the fear of excluding students from low-income homes precludes a continued rise of tuition. But as income per family rises, some upward flexibility of tuition is acceptable. Increasingly, Harvard has to rely on current gifts and the government. Harvard stresses its contributions to society and the productive revenues of the Federal government as justifying support by the Federal government.

In some respects, Harvard loses in competition with public institutions of higher learning. State tax revenues seem to respond more to current pressures than do private philanthrophy, endowment income, and tuition, upon which Harvard and other major independent institutions have to rely primarily. The public institutions definitely seem to be gaining even vis-à-vis Harvard. This is evident, for example, in the high bids for first-class faculty members by many public institutions. Tax support rises more rapidly than income on endowment.

Harvard's difficulties stem in part from frequent spells of inflation. In the eighteenth century, and notably in the Revolutionary War period, but also during the first half of that century, inflation consumed a large part of Harvard's assets. As repayments of Harvard's investments were made with a depreciating currency, Harvard's assets dropped in value. But inflation was also costly in the years 1850 to 1873 and during most of the twentieth century. Avoidance of inflation would greatly strengthen the finances of institutions of higher learning, and especially those that depend heavily on investment income.

To some extent inflation can be treated. In the eighteenth century, Harvard frequently demanded contracts in silver equivalents, which yielded repayments more nearly equal to value at time of investment, in preference to contracts in paper money. Another technique used in almost every inflationary period was to exploit the faculty. Tuition fees responded slowly to rising prices, and for this reason and because of the erosion of capital that accompanied inflation, inflation was costly to higher education's finance. With real income reduced, Harvard's defense was to stabilize salaries in current sterling or dollars, that is, pay in a depreciating currency. During the Revolutionary War, this policy was especially costly to the faculty.

Another protective device was to shift investments to assets yielding variable returns, e.g., equities. But it was not until around 1860 that the college treasurer applied this technique; and the movement in this direction for the next hundred years was generally slow.

Harvard learned another lesson. In the allocation of income from endowment, the treasurer in the last hundred years has been guided by book rather than market values. This accounting technique, when applied in inflationary periods, favors new against old investments and hence, each dollar of endowment yields more in the sense that curriculum currently valued highly, e.g., molecular biology, gets a larger share, and (say) classics gets less.

I do not mean to say that Harvard had serious economic problems only in inflationary periods. There were also troublesome deflationary episodes. At the very outset, economic stagnation almost killed the emerging college. Again, in the third decade of the nineteenth century, Harvard experienced one of its most critical periods. The source of the trouble was poor management, which allowed excessive expansion and spending, and, among other problems, also a failure to collect debts due the college. The costs of this experience were large, but as a result, university finance was put on a more secure footing.

Under Eliot, there was also trouble. Deficits, related especially to expansion of the curriculum and rapid growth, were common. Eliot supported a theory of deficit finance that is remindful of Lord Keynes. He would spend all the money he received. Aware that if enrollment declined or returns on investment were reduced that deficits would emerge, Eliot nevertheless would spend all receipts. Then the task was to beg or, in a manner not acceptable today, fire young (and even older) members of the faculty, and also to exploit the affluent members of the faculty by paying them less than a fair salary. According to Eliot, the college had thrived, that is, expanded and improved its product, not when there were surpluses, but rather when expenditures had exceeded receipts.

A source of financial trouble for Harvard throughout most of its history has been its heavy dependence on the endowed chair. A few thousand dollars provided the foundation (endowment) for a chair in the early eighteenth century, $600,000 are required today, and perhaps $6 million in fifty years. In accepting amounts that generally were inadequate to finance the services even at time of offer of the gift, the university suffered because prices and incomes rose so rapidly that within very few years after receipt of the gift the income from the foundation was likely to be inadequate to cover the expenses of the chair. Even as late as 1947 the Hollis professorship of mathematics and natural philosophy, established in 1726, had but $3,907 behind it, yielding about $200 of income. The holder of this chair receives from $25,000 to $30,000 a year. About $500,000 to $600,000 are needed today to pay the salary of the relevant professor and in fifty years perhaps $5 to $6 million. It is clear that the endowed chair, which solves financial problems for a number of years, is a technique which may well ultimately encourage excessive expansion and substantial deficits.

A comparison of relative costs in early eighteenth century and a recent year reveals some interesting facets of university finance. The teaching function, for example, measured, by the charge for tuition, has become much more costly relatively. Labor has also become much more costly. But food (commons) and books are relatively low-priced now. Housing is more expensive. A comparison of Harvard's charges for food and rooms with national trends throws some further light on Harvard's efficiency.

A problem not only for Harvard but for many service organizations is that cost per unit of service rises greatly, e.g., 10 percent a year recently in higher education, but productivity does not rise sufficiently, if at all, to match this increase of costs. Hence, the rise of prices greatly exceeds that of productivity.

The college authorities seek to improve productivity by increasing work loads, and the student-faculty ratio, and by recourse to measures such as reduction in the number of courses. A rise in the student-faculty ratio may save dollars, but may well deteriorate the product. The trend has been a reduction in the student-faculty ratio as courses have proliferated, as tutorial work has become increasingly important (with some retreat of late), and as small sections in the large courses have escalated.

The serious financial condition of Harvard, and of institutions of higher learning generally, also stems from the assumption of new responsibilities not closely tied to the purely educational function. Outlays for health, athletics, commons and dormitories, various public services—e.g., museums, libraries—all account for additional outlays. Indeed, some programs, e.g., alumni relations, attract funds to the college.

One of the striking features of Harvard's accounting is that the proportion of expenditures going to salaries is now about equal to that spent on wages. Whereas salaries used to be about twice as large relatively as wages, they are now about equal. Salaries reflect largely the teaching and other professional functions, and wages, supplementary services. In part, the change in salary-wage ratios is explained also by the lag of faculty and other professional salaries behind rising incomes in the economy, and also the tendency of workers to obtain increases in wages as their bargaining position has improved.

Harvard's position is less vulnerable because of its great success in attracting gifts, and the responsible manner in which these funds have been invested. The number of violations of trust have been surprisingly small and such treasurers as Thomas Brattle (1693 to 1713), Ebenezer Storer (1777 to 1807), Amos A. Lawrence (1857 to 1862), and Nathaniel Silsbee (1862 to 1876) have contributed much to Harvard's accumulations. Storer's wise decision to invest in loans rather than in currency may well have saved Harvard. Some questions have been raised about the management of Samuel Nowell (1683 to 1686), John Davis (1810 to 1827), and John Hancock (1773 to 1777). The last deserves criticism. Devoted to political activity in the 1770s, he ran off with the Harvard records and securities for a few years while the faculty was starved. In the end, after many years, his heirs paid the bill, but not in full.

The Harvard enterprise might have been more effective if so much were not made of the slogan, "every tub on its own bottom." Adherence to this principle simply means that the total resources of the university are not used with the maximum effectiveness. Help is denied to the school of divinity or education, for example, at the expense of more prosperous schools. Columbia has been more alert on these issues. Fortunately, the principle has not been adhered to at Harvard nearly as much as it has been proclaimed.

Harvard is so greatly concerned over its future financial position that President Pusey recently supported strongly a proposal of the American Association of Universities that the Federal government greatly increase its contribution. No wonder, since in a recent ten-year period (1953 to 1963) expenditures rose from $36 to $100 million or 178 percent. Construction outlays alone rose by $120 million. In later years the increases are even more a matter of deep concern. Costs had risen greatly, with total expenditures by 1966-1967 exceeding $150 million, and that despite careful control of enrollments.

INDEX